THE
HISTORIA REGUM BRITANNIE
OF GEOFFREY OF MONMOUTH
IV

Dissemination and Reception in the Later Middle Ages

The enormous popularity enjoyed by Geoffrey of Monmouth's History from the twelfth century onwards is a well known phenomenon, as is the work's influence on the content of literary and historical compositions in the Middle Ages and beyond. Less familiar to scholars is the material evidence for this history's success. This amounts to more than two hundred surviving manuscripts, which were catalogued by Julia Crick, some for the first time, in Volume III of this series. In Volume IV the information which the manuscripts contain both about the textual development of Geoffrey's History and about its circulation and audience is presented. Crick begins by exploring the evidence for grouping the manuscripts. External evidence such as associated texts found frequently with the *Historia* is compared with the internal evidence of textual disruption, the notorious dedications, rubrication and trial passages collated from each manuscript. This information forms the basis for an account of the chronology and geography of the circulation of the work as a whole and of its different textual types. This in turn sheds important light on the audience of the *Historia*, their tastes in reading and their status.

JULIA CRICK is a Research Fellow of Gonville and Caius College, Cambridge.

THE
HISTORIA REGUM BRITANNIE
OF GEOFFREY OF MONMOUTH

ISSN 0267–2529

I

Bern, Burgerbibliothek, MS. 568
Edited by Neil Wright

II

The First Variant Version: a critical edition
Edited by Neil Wright

III

A Summary Catalogue of the Manuscripts
Julia C. Crick

THE
HISTORIA REGUM BRITANNIE
OF GEOFFREY OF MONMOUTH

IV

Dissemination and Reception in the Later Middle Ages

Julia C. Crick

D. S. BREWER

First published 1991 by D. S. Brewer, Cambridge

D. S. Brewer is an imprint of Boydell & Brewer Ltd
PO Box 9, Woodbridge, Suffolk IP12 3DF
and of Boydell & Brewer Inc.
PO Box 41026, Rochester, NY 14604, USA

ISBN 0 85991 215 9

British Library Cataloguing-in-Publication Data
Crick, Julia C.
  The 'Historia Regum Britannie' of Geoffrey of
  Monmouth: IV. Dissemination and reception in the
  later Middle Ages. – (The 'Historia Regum
  Britannie' of Geoffrey of Monmouth)
  I. Title II. Series
  820
  ISBN 0–85991–215–9

Library of Congress Cataloging-in-Publication Data
(Revised for vol. 4)
The historia regum Britannie of Geoffrey of Monmouth.
  Vol. 1 has text in Latin; editorial matter in English.
  Vol. 4 was originally presented as the author's thesis, University
of Cambridge, 1989, under title: The reception of Geoffrey of
Monmouth's Historia regum Britanniae.
  Contents: v. 1. Bern, Burgerbibliothek, MS. 568. – v. 4.
Dissemination and reception in the later Middle Ages / Julia C. Crick.
  1. Great Britain – History – To 1066. 2. Arthurian romances –
Sources. 3. Legends – Great Britain. 4. Britons – History.
I. Wright, Neil. II. Crick, Julia C., 1963– . III. Burgerbibliothek
Bern. Manuscript. 568.
DA140.G353 1985   941.01   84–24170
ISBN 0–85991–215–9

This publication is printed on acid-free paper

Printed in Great Britain by
Woolnough Bookbinding Ltd, Irthlingborough, Northants

CONTENTS

PREFACE

This book is a corrected and only slightly revised version of my doctoral dissertation ('The Reception of Geoffrey of Monmouth's *Historia Regum Britanniae*: the Evidence of Manuscripts and Textual History', Cambridge University, 1989). Some explanation ought to be offered of why this study appears now in almost its raw state, largely untouched by the beneficial effects of hindsight and in a form designed to suit the requirements of the examiner rather than those of the general reader. There were two overriding objections to radical rewriting.

My original project was based on a survey of a largely untapped resource, the manuscripts of Geoffrey of Monmouth's *Historia*: much of my dissertation was therefore taken up with considering the results. As a major aim of publication was to make this material generally available, it seemed pointless to invest time and energy in producing a more synthetic account of what was essentially exploratory work.

The second impetus to publication is directly related. The survey was designed as an adjunct to Dr Neil Wright's editorial work on Geoffrey's *Historia*. This was carried out under the auspices of the Geoffrey of Monmouth Research Project, whose long-term aim is the completion of the first critical edition of the *Historia*. Dr Wright has already edited two versions of the text, published as volumes I and II of the *Historia regum Britannie* series, and he is working on a third. My Summary Catalogue of *Historia*-manuscripts appeared last year as volume III of the series. The present study constitutes a companion volume to the catalogue; it serves as a digest of and concordance to it and represents the first stage in processing the information generated by the survey of manuscripts, material which will feed into the associated editorial project. Indeed, the technical parts of my work have already been used for this purpose in their unpublished state by Professor M. D. Reeve, who, together with Professor D. E. Luscombe, examined my dissertation. Professor Reeve's work on the text promises to further knowledge of its development. I am most grateful to him for offering to defer publication of his findings until my dissertation has appeared in print.

I trust that the reader will recognize that large parts of the following are offered primarily for reference. Wider questions are addressed in the Introduction and in the closing chapters. Some of these have been explored further in my paper 'Geoffrey of Monmouth and Early Insular History'.

In the five years since I began working on Geoffrey's History, I have profited from the advice and assistance of more people than it is practicable to list here. Some were mentioned in the Preface to the Summary Catalogue; here I will name only those specifically involved with my doctoral project. My greatest debt is to Dr David Dumville, my research supervisor, who has masterminded the Geoffrey of Monmouth Research Project. The present study has benefited enormously from his formidable expertise and tireless criticism. Professor Christopher Brooke and Dr Neil Wright read the dissertation in final draft and suggested important improvements. Both also supplied valuable advice and information at earlier stages. I have received direction and assistance from a number of others, notably Oliver Padel. For discussion about various matters, directly or indirectly related, I must thank in addition to those already mentioned Dr Elizabeth Archibald, Dr Martha Bayless, Dr James Carley, Dr Marjorie Chibnall, Dr Sarah Foot, Dr Diana Greenway, Dr Michael Lapidge, Carin Taylor, David Thornton, Dr Elizabeth Van Houts, Dr John Watts, and particularly Mary Minty and Dr Julia Smith. I am grateful to these and others for references and guidance on a number of points.

I am glad to thank the librarians and staff of the institutions in which I have worked. I am particularly indebted to the staff of the Manuscripts Reading Room in the University Library, Cambridge, where much of the groundwork for this study was done. I have been supported in my research by a British Academy Scholarship and, since October 1988, by a Research Fellowship at Gonville and Caius College, Cambridge. I must also acknowledge the contribution of the Vinaver fund, whose grant financed the purchase of the microfilms on which much of my project, and that of Neil Wright, has depended.

Finally, I owe thanks to friends for moral support, especially Simon Clarke, Dr Anna Grabowska, Dr David Last, Dr Andrew Leech, Dr Paul Matthews and, most of all, Dr Andrew Gilbert.

J. C. Crick   July 1990
Gonville & Caius College, Cambridge

NOTE OF CONVENTIONS USED

The reader will need to bear in mind that this study is closely related to the Summary Catalogue of manuscripts of Geoffrey's History (Crick, *The Historia*, III). The numerical sigla assigned to the manuscripts in that catalogue are used in the course of the present work: they are introduced in square brackets after the first references to shelfmarks, are used subsequently in conjunction with the abbreviated shelfmarks, and constitute the sole means of reference to manuscript-witnesses in the test-collations found in Appendix II. A full list of sigla and shelfmarks precedes the text.

The following conventions have been used:

[ ] indicates supplied letters, for example where a word is suspended and the abbreviation is not absolutely clear;

< > connotes emendation or editorial interference.

LIST OF MANUSCRIPTS OF THE *HISTORIA*

s. xviii †	**1**	Aberystwyth, National Library of Wales, MS. 2005 (Panton 37, fos 63r–72v)
s. xii	**2**	Aberystwyth, National Library of Wales, MS. 11611 (*olim* Clumber 46)
s. xiii	**3** *	Aberystwyth, National Library of Wales, MS. 13052 (*olim* Phillipps 32)
s. xiii	**4**	Aberystwyth, National Library of Wales, MS. 13210 (*olim* Phillipps 26233)
s. xiii	**5** *	Aberystwyth, National Library of Wales, MS. 21552
s. xiii	**6**	Aberystwyth, National Library of Wales, MS. Llanstephan 176 (*olim* Phillipps 9162)
s. xv	**7**	Aberystwyth, National Library of Wales, MS. Llanstephan 196
s. xii/xiii	**8** *	Aberystwyth, National Library of Wales, MS. Peniarth 42
s. xiv	**9**	Aberystwyth, National Library of Wales, MS. Peniarth 43
s. xiii	**10**	Aberystwyth, National Library of Wales, MS. Porkington 17 (*olim* Ormsby-Gore Collection, MS. 17)
s. xv	**11** *	Aberystwyth, National Library of Wales, MS. Wynnstay 14
s. xii	**12**	Alençon, Bibliothèque municipale, MS. 12
s. xiii	**13**	Arras, Bibliothèque municipale, MS. 583 (871)
s. xii/xiii	**14**	Auxerre, Bibliothèque municipale, MS. 91 (85)
s. xii	**15**	Bern, Burgerbibliothek, MS. 568
s. xiii	**16**	Boulogne-sur-Mer, Bibliothèque municipale, MSS 180 + 139 + 145
s. xiii/xiv	**17**	Bruges, Bibliothèque de la Ville, MS. 428
s. xii/xiii	**18**	Bruxelles, Bibliothèque royale de Belgique, MS. 8495–8505 (3472)
s. xii	**19** *	Bruxelles, Bibliothèque royale de Belgique, MS. 8536–8543 (1489)
s. xii/xiii	**20** *	Bruxelles, Bibliothèque royale de Belgique, MS. 9871–9874
s. xiii	**21**	Bruxelles, Bibliothèque royale de Belgique, MS. II.1020 (3791) (*olim* Phillipps 11603)

† This figure refers to the date of the *Historia* in the manuscript rather than that of the manuscript as a whole.

* Indicates manuscripts which seem originally to have contained the *Historia* only.

s. xiii	22	Cambridge, Clare College, Fellows' Library, MS. 27 (N′.1.5)
s. xii	23	Cambridge, Corpus Christi College, MS. 281
s. xiii	24	Cambridge, Corpus Christi College, MS. 292
s. xiv	25	Cambridge, Corpus Christi College, MS. 414
s. xiii	26	Cambridge, Fitzwilliam Museum, MS. 302 (*olim* Phillipps 203)
s. xv	27 *	Cambridge, Fitzwilliam Museum, MS. 346
s. xii	28 *	Cambridge, Gonville & Caius College, MS. 103/55
s. xv	29	Cambridge, Gonville & Caius College, MS. 249/277
s. xii/xiii	30 *	Cambridge, Gonville & Caius College, MS. 406/627
s. xvii	31 *	Cambridge, Gonville & Caius College, MS. 450/391
s. xiv	32	Cambridge, St John's College, MS. G.16 (184)
s. xv	33	Cambridge, St John's College, MS. S.6 (254)
s. xii/xiii	34	Cambridge, Sidney Sussex College, MS. 75 (Δ.4.13)
s. xv	35	Cambridge, Trinity College, MS. R.5.34 (725)
s. xiii	36 *	Cambridge, Trinity College, MS. R.7.6 (744)
s. xiii	37 *	Cambridge, Trinity College, MS. R.7.28 (770)
s. xiv	38	Cambridge, Trinity College, MS. O.1.17 (1041)
s. xiii/xiv	39	Cambridge, Trinity College, MS. O.2.21 (1125)
s. xiv	40	Cambridge, University Library, MS. Dd.1.17 (17)
s. xiv	41 *	Cambridge, University Library, MS. Dd.4.34 (209)
s. xv	42	Cambridge, University Library, MS. Dd.6.7 (324) + Oxford, Bodl., MS. Bodley 585 (*S.C.* 2357), fos 1–47*
s. xii	43 *	Cambridge, University Library, MS. Dd.6.12 (329)
s. xiii	44	Cambridge, University Library, MS. Dd.10.31 (590)
s. xiv	45 *	Cambridge, University Library, MS. Dd.10.32 (591)
s. xv	46 *	Cambridge, University Library, MS. Ee.1.24 (913)
s. xiv	47 *	Cambridge, University Library, MS. Ff.1.25 (1158)
s. xii	48 *	Cambridge, University Library, MS. Ii.1.14 (1706)
s. xii	49	Cambridge, University Library, MS. Ii.4.4 (1801)
s. xiv	50	Cambridge, University Library, MS. Ii.4.12 (1809)
s. xv	51	Cambridge, University Library, MS. Ii.4.17 (1814)
s. xiv	52	Cambridge, University Library, MS. Kk.6.16 (2096)
s. xii/xiii	53 *	Cambridge, University Library, MS. Mm.1.34 (2295)
s. xii	54	Cambridge, University Library, MS. Mm.5.29 (2434)
s. xiii/xiv	55	Cardiff, S. Glamorgan Central Library, MS. 2.611
s. xii	56 *	Colmar, Bibliothèque municipale, MS. 448 (14)
s. xv	57	Cologny, Bibliothèque Martin Bodmer, MS. Bodmer 70
s. xiii	58 *	Dôle, Bibliothèque municipale, MSS. 348 + 349
s. xii	59	Douai, Bibliothèque municipale, MS. 880 (835)
s. xii	60	Douai, Bibliothèque municipale, MS. 882 (838)
s. xiv	61	Dublin, Trinity College, MS. 172 (B.2.7)
s. xiii	62 *	Dublin, Trinity College, MS. 493 (E.2.24)
s. xii/xiii	63	Dublin, Trinity College, MS. 494 (E.5.7)
s. xiv	64	Dublin, Trinity College, MS. 495 (E.4.30)

s. xiv	65	Dublin, Trinity College, MS. 496 (E.6.2)
s. xiv	66	Dublin, Trinity College, MS. 514 (E.5.3)
s. xiii/xiv	67	Dublin, Trinity College, MS. 515 (E.5.12)
s. xiv	68	Edinburgh, National Library of Scotland, MS. Adv. 18.4.5
s. xiii	69 *	Eton, Eton College, MS. 246 (*olim* Phillipps 25145)
s. xiii/xiv	70	Exeter, Cathedral Library, MS. 3514
s. xii	71 *	Firenze, Biblioteca Laurenziana, MS. XVII.dextr.6
s. xiv	72 *	Firenze, Biblioteca Nazionale Centrale, MS. B.R. 55 (A.4.2591)
s. xiii	73 *	Glasgow, University Library, MS. U.7.25 (331)
s. xiv	74 *	Glasgow, University Library, MS. U.7.26 (332)
s. xiii	75	Heidelberg, Universitätsbibliothek, MS. 9. 31
s. xii	76	Leiden, Bibliotheek der Rijksuniversiteit, MS. B.P.L. 20
s. xiii/xiv	77	Leiden, Bibliotheek der Rijksuniversiteit, MS. Voss. lat. F.77
s. xv	78	Leningrad, Saltykov-Shchedrin State Public Library, MS. lat. F.IV.76
s. xii	79 *	Lille, Bibliothèque municipale, MS. 533
s. xii	80	Lincoln Cathedral Library, MS. 98 (A.4.6)
s. xiii/xiv	81	London, British Library, MS. Additional 11702
s. xii	82 *	London, British Library, MS. Additional 15732
s. xii	83	London, British Library, MS. Additional 33371
s. xv	84	London, British Library, MS. Additional 35295
s. xii	85 *	London, British Library, MS. Arundel 10
s. xiii	86 *	London, British Library, MS. Arundel 237
s. xiii	87	London, British Library, MS. Arundel 319 + 409
s. xiii/xiv	88	London, British Library, MS. Arundel 326
s. xii	89 *	London, British Library, MS. Arundel 403
s. xiv/xv	90	London, British Library, MS. Cotton Cleopatra D.viii
s. xiv	91	London, British Library, MS. Cotton Galba E.xi
s. xii/xiii	92	London, British Library, MS. Cotton Nero D.viii
s. xiv	93	London, British Library, MSS Cotton Titus A.xviii + Cotton Vespasian B.x, 1–23 + Cotton Fragments XXIX, 36–39
s. xiii/xiv	94 *	London, British Library, MS. Cotton Titus A.xxv
s. xii/xiii	95	London, British Library, MS. Cotton Titus A.xxvii
s. xii	96 *	London, British Library, MS. Cotton Titus C.xvii
s. xiv	97 *	London, British Library, MS. Cotton Vespasian A.xxiii
s. xiii, xiv	98	London, British Library, MS. Cotton Vespasian E.x
s. xiii/xiv	99	London, British Library, MS. Egerton 3142 (*olim* Clumber 47)
s. xii	100	London, British Library, MS. Harley 225
s. xii	101 *	London, British Library, MS. Harley 536
s. xii/xiii	102	London, British Library, MS. Harley 3773
s. xiii	103	London, British Library, MS. Harley 4003
s. xiv	104	London, British Library, MS. Harley 4123
s. xiv/xv	105	London, British Library, MS. Harley 5115
s. xii/xiii	106 *	London, British Library, MS. Harley 6358

s. xv	147	Oxford, Bodleian Library, MS. Laud misc. 579 (*S.C.* 1496)
s. xii	148 *	Oxford, Bodleian Library, MS. Laud misc. 592 (*S.C.* 1388)
s. xiv	149 *	Oxford, Bodleian Library, MS. Laud misc. 664 (*S.C.* 1048)
s. xiii	150	Oxford, Bodleian Library, MS. Laud misc. 720 (*S.C.* 1062)
s. xiii	151 *	Oxford, Bodleian Library, MS. New College 276
s. xv	152	Oxford, Bodleian Library, MS. Oriel College 16
s. xiii	153 *	Oxford, Bodleian Library, MS. Rawlinson B.148 (*S.C.* 11519)
s. xiii	154 *	Oxford, Bodleian Library, MS. Rawlinson B.168 (*S.C.* 15441)
s. xiv	155	Oxford, Bodleian Library, MS. Rawlinson B.189 (*S.C.* 11550)
s. xii	156 *	Oxford, Bodleian Library, MS. Rawlinson C.152 (*S.C.* 12016)
s. xiii	157 *	Oxford, Bodleian Library, MS. Rawlinson D.893 (*S.C.* 13659), fos 27–28
s. xiv	158	Oxford, Bodleian Library, MS. Tanner 195 (*S.C.* 10021)
s. xvi	159	[Oxford, Bodleian Library, MS. Top.gen. c.2 (*S.C.* 3118), pp. 22–41]
s. xiii	160 *	Oxford, Christ Church, MS. 99
s. xii/xiii	161 *	Oxford, Magdalen College, MS. lat. 170
s. xii	162 *	Oxford, Magdalen College, MS. lat. 171
s. xiv	163	Paris, Bibliothèque de l'Arsenal, MS. 982 (7.H.L)
s. xiv	164	Paris, Bibliothèque nationale, MS. lat. 4126
s. xiii/xiv	165 *	Paris, Bibliothèque nationale, MS. lat. 4999A + Manchester, John Rylands University Library, MS. lat. 216
s. xii	166	Paris, Bibliothèque nationale, MS. lat. 5233
s. xii	167 *	Paris, Bibliothèque nationale, MS. lat. 5234
s. xv	168	Paris, Bibliothèque nationale, MS. lat. 5697
s. xiv	169 *	Paris, Bibliothèque nationale, MS. lat. 6039
s. xii	170 *	Paris, Bibliothèque nationale, MS. lat. 6040
s. xiii/xiv	171 *	Paris, Bibliothèque nationale, MS. lat. 6041
s. xiv	172	Paris, Bibliothèque nationale, MS. lat. 6041A
s. xii	173	Paris, Bibliothèque nationale, MS. lat. 6041B
s. xv	174 *	Paris, Bibliothèque nationale, MS. lat. 6041C
s. xii	175 *	Paris, Bibliothèque nationale, MS. lat. 6230
s. xii	176 *	Paris, Bibliothèque nationale, MS. lat. 6231
s. xv + xii	177 *	Paris, Bibliothèque nationale, MS. lat. 6232
s. xiii/xiv	178 *	Paris, Bibliothèque nationale, MS. lat. 6233
s. xii	179 *	Paris, Bibliothèque nationale, MS. lat. 6275
s. xii	180 *	Paris, Bibliothèque nationale, MS. lat. 6432
s. xiv/xv	181	Paris, Bibliothèque nationale, MS. lat. 6815
s. xiv	182	Paris, Bibliothèque nationale, MS. lat. 7531
s. xii	183	Paris, Bibliothèque nationale, MS. lat. 8501A
s. xii	184 *	Paris, Bibliothèque nationale, MS. lat. 12943
s. xv	185	Paris, Bibliothèque nationale, MS. lat. 13710
s. xiii/xiv	186	Paris, Bibliothèque nationale, MSS lat. 13935 + 5508
s. xvi	187 *	Paris, Bibliothèque nationale, MS. lat. 15073
s. xii/xiii	188	Paris, Bibliothèque nationale, MS. lat. 17569

s. xii	**189**	Paris, Bibliothèque nationale, MS. lat. 18271
s. xiv	**190** *	Paris, Bibliothèque nationale, MS. nouv. acq. lat. 1001
s. xii	**191** *	Paris, Bibliothèque Sainte-Geneviève, MS. 2113
s. xii	**192**	Philadelphia (Pa.), The Free Library, MS. E.247
s. xii/xiii	**193** *	Reims, Bibliothèque municipale, MS. 1430
s. xiii	**194**	Roma, Biblioteca Apostolica Vaticana, MS. Ottoboni lat. 1472
s. xii	**195** *	Roma, Biblioteca Apostolica Vaticana, MS. Pal. lat. 956
s. xiii	**196** *	Roma, Biblioteca Apostolica Vaticana, MS. Pal. lat. 962
s. xii	**197**	Roma, Biblioteca Apostolica Vaticana, MS. Reg. lat. 692
s. xiv/xv	**198**	Roma, Biblioteca Apostolica Vaticana, MS. Reg. lat. 825
s. xii	**199**	Roma, Biblioteca Apostolica Vaticana, MS. Vat. lat. 2005
s. xii	**200**	Rouen, Bibliothèque municipale, MS. U.74 (1177)
s. xviii	**201**	Rouen, Bibliothèque municipale, MS. 3069
s. xiv	**202**	Saint-Omer, Bibliothèque municipale, MS. 710
s. xii	**203** *	Salisbury, Cathedral Library, MS. 121
s. xv	**204**	San Marino (Cal.), Henry E. Huntington Library, MS. EL 34.C.9 (1121)
s. xiii	**205**	Sankt Gallen, Stiftsbibliothek, MS. 633
s. xv	**206** *	Sevilla, Biblioteca Colombina, MS. 7.3.19
s. xii/xiii	**207** *	Stockholm, Kungliga Biblioteket, MS. Holm. D.1311
s. xii/xiii	**208** *	Troyes, Bibliothèque municipale, MS. 273 bis
s. xiv	**209**	Troyes, Bibliothèque municipale, MS. 1531
s. xii	**210**	Ushaw, Ushaw College, MS. 6
s. xiv	**211**	Valenciennes, Bibliothèque municipale, MS. 792 (589)
s. xiv	**212**	Winchester, Cathedral Library, MS. 9
s. xvi	**213**	Würzburg, Universitätsbibliothek, MS. M.ch.f.140
s. xv	**214**	*olim* Phillipps, MS. 3117
s. xv	**215**	Roma, Biblioteca Apostolica Vaticana, MS. Ottoboni lat. 3025

INTRODUCTION

Sometimes the popularity enjoyed by histories in the Middle Ages seems almost inversely proportional to the quantity of reliable information which they impart. While a derivative work like Ranulph Higden's *Polichronicon* exists in 118 manuscripts, a prime source for historians today like Orderic Vitalis's Ecclesiastical History survives in three.[1]

This proposition is of course a caricature – the importance of Bede's History to medieval as well as modern readers is attested by widespread and numerous manuscript-witnesses – but it serves to draw attention to how the search for usable historical information conducted by generations of scholars has produced a canon of familiar texts markedly different from that favoured by, or perhaps simply available to, those seeking to know about the past in the Middle Ages.[2] It is not difficult to suggest explanations for the different collective perspectives of medieval and modern readers. One group required general historical information, the other, source material; poor access to information perhaps impeded knowledge of the best histories in the Middle Ages. Such statements, however, carry assumptions about the usage and transmission of histories in the Middle Ages which will remain speculation until the texts are examined on their own terms.[3] Paul Zumthor proposed that the first step in the reading and interpretation of medieval texts should be to investigate the text's existence as a text and the organization which promotes and justifies that existence.[4] Bernard Guenée, arguing from the position of history rather than literature, arrived at a similar conclusion. By focussing on the diffusion of medieval histories, temporarily overlooking their intrinsic value, it is possible to observe what he has called the historical culture of their readers.[5]

Geoffrey of Monmouth's unusually popular History of the Kings of Britain provides a potential subject for such a study, although no one could claim that its dubious historical content had resulted in its neglect by modern scholarship. The *Historia* was written in the 1130s, against the background of dispute over the

---

1 On the manuscripts see Chibnall, ed., *The Ecclesiastical History*, I.118–22.
2 For a list of the successful medieval texts, see Guenée, *Histoire*, pp. 250–52. On changing perceptions, see Partner, *Serious Entertainments*, pp. 2–4.
3 Paul Zumthor has remarked in the context of vernacular *gestes* that the text and the critic belong to different worlds, separated by a chronological chasm, although not an unbridgeable one: 'Le Texte médiéval'.
4 *Ibid.*, p. 7.
5 *Histoire*, p. 248.

1

succession to King Henry I, in a period of intellectual liveliness and innovation. Geoffrey traced the history of the island of Britain from its first settlement, following the fortunes of various kings of varying merit – the island was unified from the first, in Geoffrey's account – and describing their impact on the British landscape in the foundation of towns and the construction of monuments. His work was described as fabulous by later twelfth-century sceptics like William of Newburgh and Gerald of Wales,[6] but nevertheless it gained credence and was incorporated into histories at an early stage.[7] Opinion on the frivolousness or otherwise of his work is divided: Geoffrey's work can be classed as parody, fraud, or history.[8]

Geoffrey's intentions remain buried in his work and in its relationship to his sources. The reaction of the immediate audience for which it was intended is unknown. However, something of the History's wider audience and the nature of responses to it may be gauged. Previous study of its impact has concentrated on the tangible evidence of literary borrowings from it,[9] but there remains a largely unexplored, if more ambiguous, body of evidence applicable to this matter – the numerous extant manuscripts.[10] They attest when the work was copied (occasionally also where and by whom) – and sometimes who owned versions, where and when. This information, together with that of extant library lists, can be added to what is known from literary borrowings about the readership of the text.

The evidence of manuscripts contributes fundamentally to knowledge of the text in various ways; two aspects will be pursued here. First, the identification of branches of transmission as represented in groups of manuscripts will form the basis for the construction of a text-history. Secondly, using this text-historical material, some account of the work's circulation may be sought by looking at the chronological and geographical characteristics of branches of the transmission and at some of the means by which they circulated. These aims will be discussed in detail below. Before this, I propose to give some background to the work's popularity by outlining the gap in pre-Galfridian historiography, how Geoffrey made his contemporaries aware that the gap existed, and the nature of his History's success.

6 But not for entirely academic reasons: compare Crick, 'Geoffrey'.
7 For example those of Alfred of Beverley and Robert de Torigni (via Henry of Huntingdon). On their selective use of Geoffrey's material see Leckie, *The Passage of Dominion*, pp. 45–49. Compare Fletcher, *The Arthurian Material*, pp. 171–72.
8 For some recent views compare Brooke, *The Church*, pp. 95–106; Flint, 'The *Historia*'; Rosenhaus, 'Britain'.
9 Brooke, *apud* James, *Walter Map*, pp. xxxix–xliii; Keeler, 'The *Historia*'; Ullmann, 'On the Influence'.
10 On this material see the remarks of Buttenweiser, 'Popular Authors', p. 51. To my knowledge, the only such approach to the *Historia* is that of East in part of his unpublished Ph.D. dissertation, 'De Contemptu Britonum'.

British History before Geoffrey

Before Geoffrey of Monmouth, Latin Insular history effectively began with the Roman invasion led by Julius Caesar.[11] Bede started his Ecclesiastical History at this point, after a few generalized preliminary remarks about the origin of the indigenous population (from Armorica, in the case of the Britons, and from Scythia via Ireland in the case of the Picts), comments which served more as an appendix to his introductory geographical notes than as an opening to the History proper.[12] Apart from Bede, medieval enquirers into the history of the island could perhaps have turned to Gildas, whose polemical account of recent events, written in the sub-Roman period, warned the Britons of the imminent dangers threatening them as a result of their own moral degeneracy. Gildas's work was very little circulated, however, and from the twelfth century was often confused with the ninth-century Cambro-Latin *Historia Brittonum*, sometimes attributed to Gildas himself, and quite widely circulated in north-western Europe.[13] The *Historia Brittonum* provided the most detailed source for the origins of the island's population. It supplied the story of the eponymous settler of the island, Brutus, grandson of the Trojan survivor, Aeneas, and it also described the origins of the Picts and Irish.

After Bede and the author of the *Historia Brittonum*, Insular writers seem to have made little effort to delve into the British past.[14] The D, E, and F versions of the Anglo-Saxon Chronicle attest a recension which (following Bede) records the arrival of the Britons from Armorica and that of the Picts from Scythia, but none the less begins its 'narrative' with Caesar's invasion.[15] Interest in the early history of the island was not revived until the Anglo-Norman accounts.[16] James Campbell has pointed out that in the immediate post-Conquest period researches into the Anglo-Saxon past were associated with an intellectual curiosity which extended beyond national sentiment and an attempt to defend Anglo-Saxon monastic privilege and culture: non-monastic authors wrote for Norman patrons on such subjects.[17] The historiographical movement in England has been seen as part of the intellectual endeavours undertaken in this period on the common principle of 'bringing things together and sorting them out'.[18]

The view of pre-Anglo-Saxon times adopted by Anglo-Norman historians was

---

11 For a detailed discussion of Geoffrey's place in Insular historiography see Leckie, *The Passage of Dominion*.

12 On Bede's treatment of British history see Wright, 'Geoffrey of Monmouth and Bede', p. 30.

13 Edited by Faral, *La Légende*, III.4–62. A new edition is in progress: Dumville, *The Historia Brittonum*. On the Gildasian form see Dumville, 'Celtic-Latin Texts', p. 19.

14 For the parallel Continental situation see Leckie, *The Passage of Dominion*, pp. 30–37.

15 On these chronicles see Whitelock, *English Historical Documents*, pp. 109–21.

16 See Brett, 'John', pp. 101–4.

17 'Some Twelfth-century Views', pp. 133 and 142–43.

18 *Ibid.*, p. 143.

determined for the most part by that of Bede, and sometimes also by that of the author of the *Historia Brittonum*. It is clear from the stereotyped and limited nature of early twelfth-century accounts that, for this period, scarcely more than the three sources described above were available.[19] The *Chronicarum Chronica* of John of Worcester and William of Malmesbury's *Gesta Regum Anglorum* begin with the coming of the English about A.D. 450. Henry of Huntingdon less conventionally followed the account of Brutus in the *Historia Brittonum*[20] but he made no significant original contribution.[21]

The reasons for the silence in the historical record are evident; Bede used Roman sources for the period before the documentation and memories of his own time were available, but to venture back before Caesar required acquaintance with the legends of the Britons or those of their neighbours, the Irish.[22] The author of the *Historia Brittonum* claimed to have drawn on both Roman and native *traditio*. As a result, he said, he could supply the origin-legend of the Britons (from Roman tradition) and provide genealogies describing Brutus's (or Britto's) descent and family-links with other eponymous founders of European nations (from native sources).[23]

The *Historia Brittonum* was already enjoying a period of renewed interest when a new, more detailed account of this hitherto obscure corner of Insular history appeared. This Latin history purported to be a translation of an ancient book in the British language which the author, Galfridus Monemutensis, had been given by Walter, archdeacon of Oxford, a man of acknowledged culture and learning.[24]

Some context for the connection between these two men is provided by six charters (dating from 1129 to 1152) from the Oxford area: Oseney, Godstow, Thame, and St George's, a house of secular canons.[25] Five of these are issued or witnessed by Archdeacon Walter and include in their witness-lists a certain 'Gaufridus magister' or 'Gaufridus Artur'. Walter appears in his capacity as provost of St George's, a position which he held from 1115 until the suppression of the house in 1149. He died probably in 1151[26] and the sixth charter, of 1152, is witnessed by his successor, Archdeacon Robert Foliot, also with Gaufridus.[27] It is not clear why Geoffrey appears as a witness. His only official title in these

---

19 *Ibid.*, p. 138.
20 As did the Durham author of the *Libellus de Primo Aduentu Saxonum*, on which see Offler, *Medieval Historians*, p. 11.
21 Compare Leckie, *The Passage of Dominion*, p. 38.
22 *Ibid.*, pp. 29–30.
23 §§17–18: Faral, *La Légende*, III.8–9 and 15–17.
24 Called *superlative retoricus* by Henry of Huntingdon, *De Contemptu Mundi*, §4, edited by Arnold, *Henrici Archidiaconi Huntendunensis Historia*, pp. 297–320 at 302. See also Greenway, ed., *John Le Neve. Fasti*, III.35.
25 Salter, 'Geoffrey'. The second of his seven listed documents is a forgery.
26 Greenway, ed., *John Le Neve. Fasti*, III.35.
27 Thorpe, 'The Last Years', p. 664.

documents is *magister* (in 1139 and 1149), which may suggest licence to teach[28] or at least indicate that the bearer had been educated at a foreign school.[29] Two other such teachers had been recorded at the nascent university of Oxford: Theobaldus (Thibaut) of Étampes, a former *magister* of Caen, and Robert Pullen, who moved to Paris in 1139 after several years lecturing at Oxford.[30]

Geoffrey's witnessings have prompted the suggestion that he was a canon of St George's.[31] In the last two charters of the series, from 1152, Geoffrey is styled 'elect<us>' or 'episcopus' of St Asaph's (Llanelwy) in Wales; his consecration at Lambeth by Archbishop Theobald in February 1152 and his profession are recorded.[32] The consecration was noted by a contemporary, the chronicler Robert de Torigni, who added that the new bishop, Geoffrey Arthur, 'had translated the History of the kings of the Britons from "British" into Latin'. Geoffrey's elevation must have brought recognition, status, and, doubtless, income, but previous political difficulties for the Anglo-Normans in Wales were intensified in 1153 by the death of Ranulf II, earl of Chester, and probably prevented Geoffrey from occupying his see.[33] Geoffrey died in 1154 or 1155.[34]

Although, for most twelfth-century authors, writing was not a full-time occupation, it could act as a catalyst to advancement;[35] Geoffrey's literary output too has been seen as a bid for patronage.[36] Dominica Legge noted that Geoffrey's elevation to the episcopate, the summit of his career, followed the composition of his *Vita Merlini*, dedicated to Oxford's diocesan, Robert de Chesney, bishop of Lincoln.[37] Legge sought a similar explanation for the various dedications of the *Historia* to Robert, earl of Gloucester, to Robert and King Stephen, and to Robert and Waleran, count of Meulan.[38] These dedications have generally been interpreted and dated by the shifts in political allegiance precipitated by the civil war.[39] Geoffrey, Legge argued, wrote his History for Robert of Gloucester, the bastard of Henry I and patron of the arts, dedicating the Prophecies at the centre of the work to Alexander, bishop of Lincoln. When the civil war rendered both these men ineffective as patrons – Robert leaving for Normandy in 1137, and Alexander

28 Legge, 'Master Geoffrey', p. 24.
29 Compare Southern, 'From Schools to University', p. 3.
30 *Ibid.*, pp. 5–7.
31 Salter, 'Geoffrey', p. 385.
32 Richter, ed., *Canterbury Professions*, p. 47 (no. 95).
33 Lloyd, 'Geoffrey', p. 465. On the succession to the see in the 1140s, see Smith, 'The Episcopate'.
34 Brooke, *The Church*, p. 10; Wright, *The Historia*, I.x.
35 Guenée, *Histoire*, pp. 49, 51 and 61. Compare Schirmer's observation on the lack of distinction between church and court in twelfth-century England and on the importance of the court as a cultural centre: Schirmer & Broich, *Studien*, pp. 10–11.
36 Lloyd, 'Geoffrey', p. 465; Legge, 'Master Geoffrey', p. 25.
37 *Ibid.*, pp. 25–26.
38 On whom see King, 'Waleran'; Crouch, *The Beaumont Twins*, pp. 29–50, especially pp. 30–31.
39 Arguments reviewed by Wright, *The Historia*, I.xii–xvi. See also Dumville, 'An Early Text', p. 23.

being imprisoned by Stephen in 1139 – and after Oxford was besieged in 1142, Geoffrey perhaps added secondary dedications, first to Waleran of Meulan, and later to Stephen himself.[40] Legge's argument is speculative. It assumes that the single dedication to Robert preceded the two double dedications and that Geoffrey was responsible for all alterations, points which are unproven. Nevertheless, by drawing attention to the importance of the dedicatee for the author's future as well as that of his work, Legge invited further discussion of the function and thus the implications of the dedications.

The patron's role as intermediary in disseminating a work is well known. Gaimar's translation of Geoffrey's History depended on a manuscript acquired through Walter Espec from Robert of Gloucester. It has been suggested that, through Espec's interest, Arthurian material may have come to the notice of Aelred, abbot of his foundation at Rievaulx.[41] Despite the importance of the patron in a work's initial stages, its ultimate fate depended on its contents – although Guenée's statement, 'Le patron propose, mais le public dispose', has perhaps more rhetorical force than accuracy.[42]

Geoffrey's History

Geoffrey begins by remarking on the lack of written accounts of early British history despite a lively oral tradition, thus introducing Walter's ancient book. Geoffrey's 'translation' follows the dedications, and opens with a brief description of Britain – its size, countryside, rivers, cities and inhabitants. The ensuing narrative may be divided into eight sections.[43]

1. §§5–22 Brutus occupies the island of Albion

Geoffrey's History begins much where Vergil's *Aeneid* ends, with the survivors of the sack of Troy. The Trojan remnant, under Aeneas (a member of the royal house of Troy), have escaped the sack of the city and carved out a kingdom in Italy. Some years later Siluius, Aeneas's grandson, fathers an illegitimate son named Brutus. When Brutus kills his father in an accident, as soothsayers had prophesied at the time of his birth, he is expelled from Italy. After various successful military adventures in Greece and France, he settles in the remote island where he was destined to found a second Troy. He gives his name to the island, thereafter Britain, and his companions are called *Britanni*.

40 'Master Geoffrey', pp. 24–25.
41 Powicke, *The Life*, p. lxxxviii.
42 *Histoire*, p. 290.
43 Taken for convenience from *Geoffrey*, translated by Thorpe. Breaks at these points are frequently marked in manuscripts, with the exception of the fourth (at §92; it occurs more usually at §89) and the eighth (always at §177 if a division is indicated at all): below, VI.

2. §§23–53 Before the Romans came

After Brutus's death, his three sons – Locrinus, Kamber and Albanactus – divide the island between them, giving their names to the three parts of Britain: *Loegria* (England), *Kambria* (Wales) and *Albania* (Scotland). A further political unit has already been established in the West Country by Corineus, a loyal friend of Brutus, as his share in the settlement of the island. Brutus's sons and their descendants rule for some generations, founding cities and fighting campaigns until the line is broken by the suicide of Cordelia, daughter of Leir (who treated his daughters in the manner later described by Shakespeare). After a civil war, order is reestablished by Dunuallo Molmutius, son of the king of Cornwall. Dunuallo's sons, Belinus and Brennius, mount the first major offensive action ever undertaken outside Britain by its rulers. They make a joint campaign into Gaul, Germany, and Italy, eventually sacking Rome. Their descendants continue to rule in Britain for many generations.

3. §§54–91 The Coming of the Romans

Under Cassiuellaunus, brother of Lud (the founder of *Kaerlud*, London) and son of Heli, the Britons are attacked by Julius Caesar on the supposition that, although they were of the same race as the Romans, they were less skilled at fighting and could easily be forced to pay tribute. Cassiuellaunus manages to defeat Caesar in battle and the Romans are obliged to withdraw when the Gauls, seeing Caesar's vulnerability, try to rebel. Two years later, Cassiuellaunus fights off another attack from Caesar but he is betrayed by his disaffected nephew and the island becomes tributary. Then follows an account of the relations between Britain and various Roman rulers, and of constant British attempts to throw off allegiance to Rome. During this period, the island is converted to Christianity.

4. §§92–108 The House of Constantine

After the departure of Roman protection, something on which the Britons, enfeebled by attacks on their coastline, have come to rely, the ruling house of Constantine is usurped by Vortigern, chief of the *Gewissei*. This Vortigern is responsible for the settlement of the *Saxones* under Hengist and Horsa, which results in unrest and destruction. Vortigern eventually flees to Wales and attempts to ensure his own safety by building an impregnable tower. Constructional difficulties, which Vortigern's magicians are unable to explain, are solved by a strange boy, Merlin: subsidence had been caused by a pool under the foundations, in which two dragons were sleeping.

5. §§109–117 The Prophecies of Merlin

Here the author breaks in to explain that pressure from several quarters, notably from Alexander, bishop of Lincoln, obliges him to insert some prophecies by Merlin which he had already translated. This is a collection of prophecies which travelled independently from the *Historia* and which have been thought to have circulated before the appearance of the History.[44]

6. §§118–142 The House of Constantine

Aurelius, son and heir of Constantine, becomes king and kills Vortigern in his tower before defeating Hengist and the Saxons. Aurelius's reign sees the importing of a ring of stones from Ireland to Stonehenge, an operation organized by Merlin. Aurelius is poisoned by a Saxon infiltrator. He is succeeded by his brother, Uther, who likewise faces the Saxons in battle and later becomes the victim of poison.

7. §§143–178 Arthur of Britain

Uther is followed by his young son, Arthur, who had been conceived when Uther, magically disguised by Merlin, cuckolded the Duke of Cornwall. Arthur regains control of Britain by defeating the Saxons, Picts, Scots, and Irish. He then turns his attentions abroad, winning Norway and Gaul and taking his army to the Continent a second time to fight off Roman resistance. He returns victorious to Britain but is mortally wounded while defeating his treacherous nephew, Mordred, who, in Arthur's absence, has become his wife's lover and usurped the throne.

8. §§179–208 The Saxon Domination

Constantine, Arthur's cousin, becomes king and is followed by several successors. Eventually Gormund, king of the Africans, with Saxon help overthrows Keredic, an unworthy holder of the royal title. Then follows an account of St Augustine's mission to the English and the story of Cadwallo and Edwin and that of Cadualladr, romanticized versions of the narrative found in Bede's History.[45] Geoffrey's work ends with the subjugation of the degenerate Britons – reduced through plague, famine and civil discord – by the English whose newly peaceful and ordered life has brought them the crown of Loegria.

The Scale of the Historia's success

Geoffrey's History touched on many themes and the appeal of his work doubtless has complex explanations. He provided the unique connected account of this

---

44 Arguments summarized by Eckhardt, 'The *Prophetia*', pp. 169–72. No extant manuscript predates the *Historia*, however; Bernard Meehan's case for a manuscript of the 1120s fails on palaeographical grounds ('Geoffrey').

45 They may have antecedents in Welsh legend, however. On Cadualladr, see Bromwich, *Trioedd Ynys Prydein*, pp. 292–93.

period, creating history out of prehistory;[46] he illustrated, at a time when England was threatened with civil war, the effects of strong and unified kingship; and he met current popular taste for romance, toponymic legend, prophecy, and magic.[47] Whatever the reasons, the rapid, extensive, and lasting success of this work is well attested. Henry of Huntingdon's famous first encounter with it at Le Bec in Normandy took place in January 1139,[48] fewer than four years after the death of Henry I, an event which Geoffrey's work must itself postdate.[49] Thus the work was available in Normandy within a very few years, or even months, of its composition. Its popularity is witnessed by the quantity of extant manuscripts, currently numbering 215.

The significance of this figure may be gauged from Bernard Guenée's brief examination of the relative popularity of various histories in the Middle Ages, as attested by the number of surviving manuscripts.[50] The top four places in his list of seventy histories are occupied by Classical or Late Latin authors: Valerius Maximus, Orosius, Justinus, and Josephus. Their histories had potentially a longer period of circulation than a late medieval work like that of Martinus Polonus, whose success was shorter-lived but more intense. Guenée placed Geoffrey of Monmouth next after Josephus, in fifth place with 200 manuscripts. In fact, according to my figures, Geoffrey should be ranked third, topping Justinus's 207 and Josephus's 200 (although the lists of manuscripts of these last two historians may not have been so assiduously updated in recent years as has that of Geoffrey).[51] This is a commanding position. Its nearest medieval rivals are the history of Charlemagne attributed to Turpinus (174) and Bede's Ecclesiastical History (164). By comparison, a well known history which had circulated for several centuries before Geoffrey, the *Historiae Libri Decem* of Gregory of Tours, survives in about fifty manuscripts.

Circulation

Something of the geographical and chronological extent of the popularity of the *Historia* may be gauged from information about the origins, provenances, and dates of manuscript-witnesses collected in the course of a thorough text-historical investigation. Textual criteria will add precision by allowing the identification of particular groups of related manuscripts. As a result, various questions can be

---

46 Compare Leckie, *The Passage of Dominion*, pp. 41–42.
47 See also Gibson, 'History at Bec', pp. 185–86.
48 See Henry's letter to Warin, printed in *Chronicles*, edited by Howlett, IV.65–75. A new edition of the letter is being prepared by Neil Wright. See also Brooke, *The Church*, pp. 99–100.
49 Arguments concerning the *termini* for the composition of the *Historia* have been discussed by Neil Wright, *The Historia*, I.xii–xvi.
50 *Histoire*, pp. 248–58.
51 Dumville, 'The Manuscripts'; Crick, 'Manuscripts', 'The Manuscripts'.

raised: whether the work circulated in different forms in England and on the Continent or whether there was continuing cross-fertilization across the Channel, whether distinctively Continental forms are identifiable and, if so, whether their ancestors reached the Continent.[52] It is known that a manuscript was at Le Bec at an early stage, but not what proportion of Continental copies stem from manuscripts introduced in the twelfth century. Certain networks of transmission may be visible, perhaps within a particular religious order. It should be possible to use textual criteria to detect whether each acquired its copy from separate sources or whether they drew on a common source. Where several houses, of the same or different orders, in the same area are known to have owned copies, are the texts of those manuscripts related or do they suggest acquisition from separate sources?

The implications of these questions are more than textual. Antonia Gransden has pointed out how, partly because of earlier limitations of the mechanisms of circulation, political propaganda tends to be a later medieval phenomenon.[53] A study of transmission can allow exploration of notions of popularity and influence, both terms applied to this work. Foucault has attacked the assumption-laden use of the term 'influence' to describe processes operating in history: he has accused historians of creating an artificial concept, a magical medium of propagation of ideas, notions, and themes which functions as an ether and has no firmer basis in reality.[54] It may be possible to elucidate some of the processes which might underlie 'influence' by studying the transmission of texts, even in a semi-literate culture.

Another question to be considered is that of the audience of the *Historia*. Despite numerous vernacular translations into verse, it was in Latin that Geoffrey's work enjoyed major and lasting success. There was evidently a significant Latin-reading audience prepared to invest money and time in acquiring and reading a lengthy non-Classical secular history, a work moreover lacking overt moral or didactic content.[55] The contents of the *Historia* might suggest an aristocratic audience. The literary language of secular circles in the twelfth century has traditionally been regarded as the vernacular, however.[56] Indeed, Diana Tyson has suggested that it was enthusiasm in such circles for accessible adaptations of the *Historia* that created a 'great vogue for vernacular history'.[57]

A number of readers may be identified from comments on the *Historia* and summaries or extracts from it in other works. These are primarily chroniclers, both those condemning the work and those who found it convenient to draw on it,

---

52 Compare the Continental and Insular texts of Bede's History: Colgrave & Mynors, *Bede's History*, pp. xxxix–lxx, especially xli–xliv.

53 'Propaganda', p. 364.

54 Major-Poetzl, *Michel Foucault's Archaeology of Western Culture*, pp. 13–14.

55 On the importance of moral benefit to literary enjoyment see Olson, *Literature as Recreation*, especially p. 20.

56 But see Duby's remarks about numerous lay dedications of Latin works: 'The Culture', pp. 259–60.

57 'Patronage', pp. 185–86.

sometimes selectively.[58] Such evidence, unsupported, is unsatisfactory in various ways. The information which Geoffrey supplied rapidly became widely available; it is not clear how many of these chronicle-references are actually from the *Historia* or from other chronicles, Latin or vernacular.[59] Secondly, this material presents only one, obvious, facet of the *Historia*'s influence. It has been found in other contexts – used to justify the expansionism of Henry II and Edward I, in Magna Carta and the *Leges Anglorum*,[60] to glorify royal traditions and ceremonial[61] – but the problem of source arises again. These examples may not all be derived from Latin material. Again, the nature of the work's success as attested by surviving manuscripts promises to contribute significantly to any consideration of this issue.[62]

The information about the origins and provenances of manuscripts which is essential for answering these questions is unfortunately incomplete; but more general conclusions about the immediate contexts of certain volumes may be deduced from other external evidence. Information about the physical nature of a book may provide some broad indication not only of the date and perhaps region of origin but also of its context. Here the associated contents, as well as the book's appearance, may be relevant. Robin Flower noted the strange mixture of medical and religious works, scholastic poetry and Irish prose and verse found in manuscripts copied by the Irish doctor-scribes of the later Middle Ages.[63] R. W. Southern has been able to describe a post-Conquest manuscript (BL Cotton Caligula A.xv) written under Lanfranc and Anselm at Canterbury in 'a characteristic mixture of English and Latin' as 'entirely in the old tradition', with 'its miscellany of chronological data, charms, and annals'.[64]

Contents may be useful in their own right. Complex and various factors probably produced the array of texts found in one medieval volume: some works may have been associated in an exemplar, others newly added to the conglomeration as a result of practical as much as aesthetic considerations. But certain collections were carefully and deliberately chosen. Outstanding examples are the books copied in the early twelfth century under William of Malmesbury's direction. This operation, involving the collaboration of up to fourteen scribes, produced a volume of Roman history, one of military strategy, a miscellany of Anselmiana, and so forth.[65] William's organization seems to have been exceptional. Nevertheless, other volumes present intriguing combinations of texts which suggest the application of critical judgement. In one example, material

---

58 See Fletcher, *The Arthurian Material*, pp. 170–77; Keeler, *Geoffrey*.
59 For example, Geoffrey's material may have been used in conjunction with other sources; conversely, the absence of verbatim parallels does not rule out Geoffrey as a source.
60 Ullmann, 'On the Influence', pp. 258, 261–62; Liebermann, *Die Gesetze*, I.635, n. f.
61 Edward IV's household traced its origins through those of Galfridian figures: Starkey, 'The Age', p. 225.
62 Compare Guenée, 'La Culture historique', p. 261.
63 *The Irish Tradition*, pp. 132–33.
64 *St Anselm*, p. 252.
65 Described by Thomson, 'The "Scriptorium"'.

about the Crusades and the siege of Jerusalem is interspersed with texts on the fall of Troy, an apposite association which has been observed in a different context.[66] Some manuscripts bear the signs of preparation in a scriptorium – collaborating scribes copying a selected series of texts. The appearance of Geoffrey's work among a historical collection may therefore be significant.

This study is essentially a survey and is therefore exploratory. The manuscripts on which it is based are numerous and scattered; the quantity of readily assimilable information about each was very variable – some had attracted sufficient scholarly attention to gain notoriety while others were not formally catalogued.[67] Such a survey is potentially one-dimensional, giving equal weight to all manuscripts, even though some may have been little read and copied in medieval times; textual information offers a corrective, however. The survey's purpose is to observe the success of a work which has defied classification. When and where was interest in it most intense? In what milieux it was read? Factors governing its impact should also be considered: how was the text transmitted? When writing, an author was perhaps influenced by the extensiveness of circulation which he could expect for his work. More significantly, the actual effectiveness of means of transmission defined the limits of the power of the written word in the diffusion of information and ideas.

---

66 Guenée, *Histoire*, p. 276. Douai, Bibliothèque municipale, MS. 882.
67 They have now all been described: Crick, *The Historia*, III.

I

PROCEDURE

Text-history

A work of the *Historia*'s success and influence – Walter Ullmann described how it shaped a clause in Magna Carta and provided ammunition for Edward I's claims to lordship over Scotland[1] – has of course attracted a quantity of modern scholarship. Debate has largely concentrated on its dating and dedications, immediate context and genre. The present work, as part of a larger research project, is devoted to the question of text and transmission.

Despite the existence of eight editions, published between 1508 and 1929, it has remained impossible to judge which of any two manuscripts presents a text closer to what Geoffrey actually wrote.[2] The last, and best, attempts at a critical edition – by Acton Griscom and Edmond Faral – were published in 1929. These editors between them used only six of the 187 manuscripts then recorded.[3] One of these has recently been the subject of Neil Wright's authoritative semi-diplomatic edition.[4] Griscom and Faral chose their manuscripts on the grounds that they represented particular 'editions' of Geoffrey's work, a conclusion based on the supposed historical implications of the various dedications of the work.[5] The frailty of such classification has long been apparent.[6] Such dedications were vulnerable to loss or alteration independent of the text which they prefixed and so are not necessarily dependable indicators of textual types.[7]

Since 1929, the development of microfilm has facilitated much more thorough

---

1 'On the Influence'; on Scotland see also Stones & Simpson, *Edward I*, I.155–56.
2 For a discussion of the editions, see Wright, *The Historia*, I.xlvi–l. See also Brugger, 'Zu Galfrid', pp. 257–59, and Hammer, 'Remarks', pp. 522–25.
3 Aberystwyth, National Library of Wales, MS. Porkington 17 [10]; Bern, Burgerbibliothek, MS. 568 [15]; Cambridge, Trinity College, MS. O.2.21 (1125) [39]; Cambridge, University Library, MS. Ii.1.14 [48]; Leiden, Bibliotheek der Rijksuniversiteit, MS. B.P.L. 20 [76]; Paris, Bibliothèque nationale, MS. lat. 6233 [178]. Faral, *La Légende*, III.64–303; *The Historia*, edited by Griscom & Jones.
4 *The Historia*, I.
5 Faral, 'Geoffroy', pp. 18–32; Griscom & Jones, *The Historia*, pp. 31–41.
6 Hammer, 'A Commentary', p. 4, n. 3, and 'Remarks', pp. 525–29; Brugger, 'Zu Galfrid', p. 277.
7 Compare the account of rededications by Gerald of Wales given by Holzknecht, *Literary Patronage*, pp. 144–45.

textual investigation, based on a wide range of manuscripts. This work was first undertaken by Jacob Hammer, who aimed to produce a critical edition, but the project was curtailed by his death in 1953. The reasons for undertaking such an edition deserve discussion. It is widely accepted that the *Historia* is not a historical source in which errors of transmission could be seen to endanger the accuracy of factual information. Nor is the *Historia* likely to be the subject of the minute stylistic scrutiny which a Classical work might undergo, but this is partly perhaps because there is no guarantee of what Geoffrey actually wrote: the fluidity of medieval Latin complicates the process of emendation, the editions of Faral and Griscom are based on a false equation between the dedications of manuscripts and their textual groupings, and there is no account of the lively medieval transmission of the text. However, the fact of the work's influence alone makes it desirable for scholars in a variety of fields to be able to distinguish medieval additions and alterations to the text from the original. For this state to be reached, the work needs to undergo a cleaning operation which removes layers of accretion.[8] This ought also to reveal more about Geoffrey's sources and intentions. A textual investigation which seeks to identify the main branches of the text as represented in groups of extant manuscripts is an essential preliminary to a reassessment of the editorial problem. It should show how far the printed editions deviate from the mainstream of the text and therefore indicate whether a new edition is necessary.

The text-history to date

Some inroads have been made into the formidable quantity of witnesses to the text. Since Faral's and Griscom's editions, it has become clear that the *Historia* did not always circulate in the full-length version printed by its editors. Jacob Hammer, the pioneer in this field, remarked that 'It took the collation of 130 MSS to discover that there is not one text of Geoffrey of Monmouth but that there are several texts which go under the name of Geoffrey'.[9] The identification of at least two shorter versions posed the question of whether the published text should be regarded as primary and the alternative versions as abbreviations, or whether the so-called variants represent earlier versions of a subsequently expanded text. Until this question is settled it has become usual to describe the longer, commonly occurring text as the vulgate or 'version commune' and the shorter versions as variants. It should be stated at the outset that while the two main forms of variant identified to date have been analysed and textually examined, 'vulgate' remains a blanket term for the remainder (some 190 manuscripts) and has as yet little textual meaning. Some definition of this term is a major aim of this project.

8 Compare Vinaver, 'Principles', p. 157.
9 'Remarks', p. 501.

The First Variant

The First Variant was published by Jacob Hammer in 1951 from the five manuscripts known to him.[10] Three more have been added to these and the work has
now been reedited by Neil Wright.[11] The First Variant is characterized by many
additions, the liberal use of biblical and Classical quotations, a tendency to play
down rhetorical excesses and to suppress unpleasant details, and also direct
quotation of certain sources (like Bede).[12] Its independence of the vulgate has
fuelled controversy about which text has priority and about the authorship of the
Variant Version. Robert Caldwell's discovery that Wace used the First Variant in
his *Roman de Brut*, written in Geoffrey's lifetime,[13] led him to suggest that the
Variant might have preceded the vulgate.[14] Pierre Gallais refuted Caldwell's claim
of the priority of the Variant Version, suggesting that the Variant was written by
someone drawing on both the *Historia* and Wace's *Brut*.[15] Gallais insisted that
Geoffrey could not have written the Variant Version[16] and that the Variant was a
deliberate product, not a spontaneous offshoot of the manuscript-tradition.[17]
Wright has since demonstrated conclusively that the First Variant postdates the
Vulgate and predates Wace.[18]

The Second Variant

Hammer was in the process of producing an edition of the Second Variant when
he died. The following remarks are based on the only published account of his
work, that by H. D. Emanuel, who undertook to complete Hammer's work, but
died before the project's completion.[19] Unlike the First Variant, the Second is
closely related to the vulgate text. To the middle of section 3 as described above
(the conversion of Britain), there are differences in tenses, moods of verbs, and
vocabulary, but 'no examples of rearrangement of material, no appreciable
divergence in sentence-structure, no additions, no significant omissions'.[20] The

---

10 Aberystwyth, National Library of Wales, MS. 2005 [1]; Cardiff, South Glamorgan Central
    Library, MS. 2.611 [55]; Dublin, Trinity College, MS. 515 [67]; Exeter, Cathedral Library,
    MS. 3514 [70]; London, British Library, MS. Harley 6358 [106]: *Geoffrey*. For a convenient
    summary account of the manuscripts, see Frappier's critical review of Hammer's edition.
11 *The Historia*, II. The more recently discovered witnesses are: Edinburgh, National Library
    of Scotland, MS. Adv. 18.4.5 [68]; Paris, Bibliothèque de l'Arsenal, MS. 982 (7.H.L) [163];
    and a mixed text, Aberystwyth, National Library of Wales, MS. 13210 (*olim* Phillipps 26233)
    [4].
12 Hammer, *Geoffrey*, pp. 8–12; see also Wright, *The Historia*, II.liii–liv.
13 Caldwell, 'Wace's *Roman*'.
14 Caldwell, 'The Use of Sources'.
15 'La *Variant Version*', p. 30.
16 'Les deux styles sont absolument différents, inconciliables': *ibid.*, p. 3.
17 *Ibid.*
18 *The Historia*, II.lv–lxiii.
19 'Geoffrey of Monmouth's *Historia*'. Hammer's notes on the Second Variant have since been
    made available to Neil Wright.
20 *Ibid.*, pp. 105–6.

15

remainder of sections 3 and 4 (to the Prophecies of Merlin) witnesses substantial divergence, however. The Prophecies themselves are little changed. The heaviest abbreviation then occurs in the latter half of the work, where some material is omitted rather than (as previously) reexpressed in abbreviated form.

The Second Variant was known to Hammer in fifteen manuscripts,[21] to which three can now be added.[22] After extensive collation, Hammer was able to divide the Second-Variant manuscripts into three groups.[23] Groups α and γ contain extensive abbreviations, as described above. β, however, reverts to the vulgate text after the Prophecies of Merlin. Hammer appears to have based his separation of α and γ on a single reading: their independence is thus open to question.

Method

The two variants account for only twenty-six manuscripts. Of the remaining 189, six have been intensively studied by Griscom and Faral, and one of these has been the subject of Wright's semi-diplomatic edition, while a few of the remainder have been discussed by Hammer in various papers. In general, however, the area remains unmapped. The search for the textual features necessary to provide orientation is complicated by the size of the text and the number of its manuscripts. One approach is to group manuscripts according to non-textual evidence before investigating textual similarities.

This method was discussed in detail by Maurice Bévenot, when reediting St Cyprian's letters: he had needed to locate among the existing 160 manuscripts the best for collation.[24] Bévenot described the value of the distinction between *internal* evidence, the textual evidence of manuscripts – errors, agreements and disagreements with other manuscript-copies –, and *external*, 'what the manuscripts can tell us about themselves as MSS' – script, date, origin, order of contents. Theoretically, at least, complete knowledge of the date, origin, and travels of a manuscript could contribute to discovering where it was copied and when and where it became an exemplar itself, and thus its antecedents and descendants. Such information is usually imperfectly known and therefore of limited value. More fruitful could be the identification of an order of contents duplicated between two or more manuscripts. Despite the limitations of this external evi-

---

21 *Ibid.*, p. 104. Bruges, Bibliothèque de la Ville, MS. 428 [17]; Cambridge, Clare College, MS. 27 [22]; Cambridge, University Library, MSS Ff.1.25 [47] and Mm.5.29 [54]; Dublin, Trinity College, MS. 514 [66]; Lincoln, Cathedral Library, MS. 98 [80]; London, British Library, MSS Cotton Galba E.xi [91], Cotton Titus A.xxvii [95], Harley 3773 [102], Royal 4.C.xi [108], and Royal 14.C.i [114]; Oxford, Bodleian Library, MS. Bodley 977 [138], Saint-Omer, Bibliothèque municipale, MS. 710 [202]; Stockholm, Kungliga biblioteket, Holm. D.1311 [207]; Troyes, Bibliothèque municipale, MS. 1531 [209].

22 Cambridge, Trinity College, MS. R.5.34 [35]; Cambridge, University Library, MS. Ii.4.12 [50]; London, British Library, MS. Arundel 10 [85]. See Crick, 'Manuscripts', p. 162.

23 I am indebted to Neil Wright for my knowledge of these three groups and their characteristics.

24 *The Tradition*, pp. 1–2.

dence, Bévenot regarded it as 'a necessary background to the closer study of the text as an outer ring of evidence which must be worked through before we enter the inner maze of the countless variants in the MSS'.[25] The groups established using external evidence were to be tested using internal (textual) information. This task was scaled down to a realistic level by limiting the collation to thirty 'crucial' passages in the text, places where divergences between manuscripts often occurred. Thus twenty or so manuscripts were selected for full collation.

The method adopted here will in outline follow that described by Bévenot, although there will be no attempt to edit the work. The preliminary stage has taken the form of a survey of all available manuscript-witnesses. In each case, information about the book, *external* evidence, has been collected: its date and point or area of origin, contents, size, quiring, format and script as well as any indications of later history. The distinction between external and internal merges in the study of the *Historia* itself. Rubrics, book-divisions, and the quantity of text present (namely physical and other obvious lacunae) have all been recorded. Abbreviated portions of text have been noted, and passages containing readings characteristic of either of the recognized variants have been checked.

Five sections of the text have been chosen for collation: §§1–5, 100, 109–111, 179, 208. §§1–5 contain the dedications and the introductory description of Britain. They are particularly susceptible to physical loss or to alteration because of the nature of their subject-matter and their initial position. Some or all of these chapters are sometimes omitted. §§109–110 introduce the Prophecies of Merlin – Geoffrey's intervention and the dedicatory letter to Alexander of Lincoln –, and either or both could be omitted without disrupting the flow of the narrative. §208 contains the epilogue, in which Geoffrey alludes to the work of contemporary historians on related topics but claims superior knowledge on the subject in question, thanks to his 'British' source. Griscom consigned this epilogue to the apparatus of his text as it did not occur in his main manuscript, an omission repeated in just one other.[26] §§100 and 179 are less obvious targets for alteration, being embedded in the text; and so they provide something of a control for the other passages. Both have been the subject of alteration, however. §100 tells how the usurper, Vortigern, who had already employed Hengist as a mercenary leader, was so taken with Hengist's daughter that he was prepared to cede Kent to the Saxons to win possession of her. This story, taken from the *Historia Brittonum* §37, was liable to be abbreviated, whether deliberately or through eye-skip. Also it contains two phrases in English which, as Hammer noted, are translated into Latin in a few Continental manuscripts.[27] §179, after a brief note about the succession of Constantine, reports on various episcopal sees. This detail about the clergy was sometimes thought superfluous to the text and was omitted.[28]

---

25 *Ibid.*, pp. 2–3.
26 Griscom & Jones, *The Historia*, pp. 51–52 and 535–36. Cambridge, University Library, MS. Ii.1.14 (1706), and Phillipps 2324, now New Haven (Conn.), Yale University, MS. 590.
27 'Note on Geoffrey'.
28 These passages have been selected in the hope that the collation of them will uncover major

The associations suggested by each category of non-textual evidence will be discussed in turn and the resulting groups of manuscripts will be tested by comparing readings from the passages of text collated. Thus the usefulness of the various types of evidence may be compared. The identification of the textual characteristics of the groups will perhaps allow further manuscripts to be assigned to them on textual grounds alone. Finally, it is hoped that some account of the interrelation of the groups, and thus the branches of the text, will be possible.

In view of the number of manuscript-witnesses and the known textual complications, the construction of a complete hierarchical stemma will not be possible at this stage. Apart from the possibility that the author himself made annotations, many copies were in circulation during Geoffrey's lifetime. Later medieval library-catalogues show that some houses possessed more than one copy of the work. Thus texts were available for comparison against an exemplar, whether to rectify lacunose copies or just for scholarly interest. It is probable that, in Housman's words, the manuscripts will be divided into factions rather than families.[29]

It is hoped that the final stages of the process – the selection of the representatives of each group and the production of a text – will be undertaken by future editors. They lie outside the scope of one doctoral dissertation. I aim instead to apply the information from my enquiries to the question of how the work was transmitted.

In Chapters II–VII, the text-historical evidence is examined category by category to determine what patterns of association each suggests. The discussion begins with the potentially circumstantial – works which accompany the *Historia* in the surviving manuscripts – and ends with the core evidence, that of the text itself. The resulting patterns of association are assembled and the various sorts of evidence compared in Chapter VIII. The final chapters deal with the context of Geoffrey's History: the geographical and chronological extent of textual groups and the general milieu of the work – its readership and the types of literature with which it tended to become associated.

discrepancies between manuscripts. There is a danger that being susceptible to capricious alteration they may be less diagnostic for the main text than other, less prominent, sections; but experience here shows that important departures from the text are more immediately useful in grouping manuscripts than minor, but potentially less consciously made, variants.

29 Housman, *M. Annaei Lucani Belli civilis*, p. vii; quoted by Gotoff, *The Transmission*, p. 5.

II

ASSOCIATED CONTENTS

The works associated with the *Historia* constitute the outermost layer of evidence to be investigated in this survey. 'Evidence' might be thought to be too optimistic a description of items whose connection with Geoffrey's history is likely to be incidental and, on occasions, entirely fortuitous. Indeed, certain recurrent texts or patterns of texts are almost bound to emerge from an analysis of so many manuscripts, whether the sample has some known connection, like these, but also, to a limited extent, in a more random selection of literary manuscripts: some works seem to have been ubiquitous. Significant and random collocations need to be distinguished: it is inherited connections which promise to mark genealogical lines. This chapter examines the contents of *Historia*-manuscripts to see how far they can, unaided, contribute to the construction of a text-history. Spontaneous, coincidentally linked groups can be identified only tentatively at present but they will merit full discussion later.

It has been suggested (Introduction: Circulation) that this material may provide some indication of the milieu in which a particular collection was assembled and, perhaps, of how Geoffrey's History was categorized. Again, this is something of an experiment. Little is known about how texts were classed in the Middle Ages. Medieval library lists give few grounds for confidence that works outside the obvious categories of exegesis, patristics, the Classics, and so on, were grouped by any more than the most rudimentary of criteria (size, for example), although the examples cited in the previous chapter suggest that some principles of selection sometimes operated. Arguably the best means of observing the factors, conscious or random, which shaped certain collections of texts is by examining large quantities of examples. The present study provides such an opportunity. Once inherited associations have been confirmed using other criteria – especially the textual features of the *Historia* – it will be possible to turn to the necessarily heavily qualified, but possibly fruitful, evidence about how collections were made.

WORKS FOUND WITH TWO OR MORE COPIES OF THE HISTORIA

These are listed, where appropriate, under author or, failing this, under *Incipit*. Clearly defined groups of texts, such as the Alexander-literature, are listed together under a general heading and subcategories.

Ab origine mundi circa annos tria milia
Aelred of Rievaulx, *Uita Edwardi*
Alexander: *Collatio Alexandri cum Dindimo per litteras facta*
Alexander: *Epistola Alexandri ad Aristotilem* (families I, II, III+IV)
Alexander: *Epitaphium + Quicquid in humanis*
Alexander: *Epithoma*
Alexander: *Parua recapitulacio*
Alexander: *Iulius Ualerius, Gesta Alexandri*
Alexander: *Secreta secretorum*
Anglia habet in longitudine
Anglia modo dicta olim Albion dicebatur
Antenor et alii profugi
De Antichristo (Adso, Albuinus, Anselm)
Apollonius of Tyre
Ausonius, poems from *Opuscula* 7 and 13
Bede, *Historia ecclesiastica gentis Anglorum*
Chronology: *Ab Adam usque ad diluuium ann. .ii.cc.xlii.* . . .
Chronology: *In principio erat uerbum*
Chronology: *Quinquagesimo ergo quarto anno*
Commentary, Prophecy of the Eagle
Compendium de Britannie
Cosmographiae (Aethicus, pseudo-Priscian)
Credunt igitur Sarraceni
Cum animaduerterem
Cuthbert: *Epistola de obitu Bede*
Dares Phrygius
Definitiones Ciceronis
Dominus Deus uniuersorum conditor
Dudo of Saint-Quentin
Einhard
Epistolae: Emperor of Constantinople to Robert of Flanders
Epistolae: Hillin/Adrian IV
Epistolae: Patriarch of Jerusalem to bishops of the East
Epitaph of King Ceadwalla
Euolutis a mundi constitucione
Finding of the True Cross: *Post peccatum Ade*
Finding of the True Cross: *Sancta arbor*
Fulcher of Chartres, *Historia hierosolimitana*

Genealogy: *Flemish counts*
Genealogy: *Normans*
Genealogy: *Trojans*
Gerald of Wales
Gesta Normannorum ducum
Gesta Saluatoris
Godfrey of Viterbo
Guido delle Colonne
Hayton
Henry of Huntingdon (*Historia Anglorum*, letter to Henry I)
Higden, *Polichronicon*
Historia Brittonum
Historia Gothorum, Wandalorum, Sueuorum
Historia Turpini
Innocent III, *De mysteriis misse*
Jacques de Vitry, *Historia orientalis*
Libellus Bemetoli
Liber prouincialis
Mappa mundi
Marco Polo
Martinus Polonus
Meditationes
Methodius (ps.), *Reuelationes*
Mirabilia Brittonum
Nicodemus, Gospel of
Pergama flere uolo
Petrus Alphonsus
Prester John
Prima etas seculi ab Adam
Prophecies: 'Anglia transmittet . . .'
Prophecies: 'Anno cephas cocadrille'
Prophecies: 'Gallorum leuitas'
Prophecies: Gildas
Prophecies: 'Illius imperium gens . . .'
Prophecies: John of Bridlington
Prophecies: Merlin (Galfridian, Eagle of Shaftesbury)
Prophecies: Robert de Sey
Prophecies: Sibylline
Prophecies: Thomas of Canterbury
Regnum Scottorum fuit
Robert of Reims
Robert de Torigni, Chronicle
Si quis ab occidentalibus
Solinus
Status Imperii Iudaici

Superius autem excidio
Testamenta .xii. patriarcharum
Ualerius ad Rufinum
Vision of the monk of Eynsham
Uita Ade et Eue
Uita Thome
William of Malmesbury (Histories)

Ab origine mundi circa annos tria milia

This phrase constitutes the *incipit* of a brief description of how Britain was founded by Albina, daughter of a certain king of Greece. Such accounts are not uncommon in historical manuscripts of the later Middle Ages but I know of this particular version in only three manuscripts, in each of which it precedes Geoffrey's *Historia*: **London, British Library, MS. Harley 5115 [105]; Notre Dame, University Library, MS. 40 [130]; Phillipps MS. 3117 [214]**.[1] There is no further agreement between the contents of these manuscripts.

Aelred of Rievaulx, Uita Edwardi[2]

The Life of Edward the Confessor by Aelred, abbot of Rievaulx (1147–67), is found in two vulgate manuscripts: Bern, Burgerbibliothek, MS. 568 [15], and Dublin, Trinity College, MS. 172 [61]. That in MS. 15 must have been copied shortly after the work's completion in about 1162/3.[3] The other contents of these manuscripts are not related.

Alexander

A considerable number of *Historia*-manuscripts include items from the substantial and enormously popular pseudo-historical literature which collected around the figure of Alexander the Great.

---

1 Now in private hands: Dumville, 'The Manuscripts', pp. 164–65. Ward records the version in MS. 105 but does not include any further manuscripts among in his list of Albina-stories: *apud* Ward & Herbert, *Catalogue of Romances*, I.235, I.198–203.
2 Edited by Migne, *Patrologia Latina*, CXCV.737–90.
3 See discussion by Wright, *The Historia*, I.xliv.

Alexander: Collatio Alexandri cum Dindimo per litteras facta

The *Collatio* casts in the form of a correspondence between Alexander and Dindymus, king of the Brahmans, a debate about the relative merits of the *mores* of the Macedonians and Brahmans, from which the Brahmans emerge triumphant.[4] This material is found in eight *Historia*-manuscripts, Aberystwyth, National Library of Wales, MS. 11611 [2]; Cambridge, St John's College, MS. G.16 (184) [32]; Cambridge, University Library, MS. Mm.5.29 [54]; Lincoln, Cathedral Library, MS. 98 [80]; London, British Library, MS. Stowe 56 [117]; London, College of Arms, MS. Arundel 1 [118]; Paris, Bibliothèque nationale, MSS lat. 8501A [183] and lat. 17569 [188]. MSS 2, 54, 80, 117, and 188, contain the so-called *Collatio* I, the earliest of the three forms of the text.[5] It is prefaced in MS. 2 by a lengthy introduction ('Alexander imperator cum ei ... esse meliorem') which I have not been able to identify. MS. 183 contains a truncated version of the same *collatio* (ending 'criminosis apud nos').[6] The version in MS. 32 is quite different from those listed by Cary,[7] and in fact is taken from the *Pantheon* of Godfrey of Viterbo (see below).[8]

Alexander: *Epistola Alexandri ad Aristotelem*

This letter purports to have been written by Alexander to his *magister* Aristotle about his experiences in India 'among the strange and marvellous men and beasts of the Orient'.[9] Its considerable medieval popularity is attested by the many vernacular translations.[10] Nine of the sixty-seven manuscripts listed by W. Walther Boer in his edition also contain Geoffrey's History;[11] there are seven others not included by him. I follow Walther Boer's grouping into four families.

1. Family I

[12]**Leiden, Bibliotheek der Rijksuniversiteit, MS. BPL 20 [76]** (Walther Boer H)
London, British Library, MS. Cotton Nero D.viii [92] (Walther Boer Cn)

MSS 76 and 92, together with a third (not containing the *Historia*), form a subgroup of the six manuscripts which Walther Boer listed as belonging to the

---

4 Cary, *The Medieval Alexander*, pp. 13–14, 91–92, 168.
5 As printed by Kuebler, *Iuli Valeri Alexandri Polemi Res Gestae*, pp. 169–89. See Cary, *The Medieval Alexander*, p. 14.
6 Kuebler, *Iuli Valeri Alexandri Polemi Res Gestae*, p. 185, l. 14. Followed by a poem 'Nunc euuangelii textum scribendo sequutus'.
7 *The Medieval Alexander*, p. 14. (*Inc.* 'Bragmanides uidit nec eos seruire coegit. . .').
8 Ed. [Herold,] *Pantheon*, cols 267–76.
9 Ross, 'A Check-List', p. 127. On the marvels see Wright, *Geographical Lore*, pp. 274–75.
10 Cary, *The Medieval Alexander*, p. 15.
11 *Epistola Alexandri*, pp. iii–xxi. It is estimated that double the number of manuscripts is now known: Voorbij, 'Additions', p. 117.
12 Described by Walther Boer, *Epistola Alexandri*, pp. xxii–xxiii.

first family of *Epistola*-manuscripts.[13] The early portion of MS. 92 (fos 1–175) consists of two units which, despite separate sets of quire signatures, should be regarded at least as products of the same scriptorium bound together at an early point or perhaps actually conceived as a whole: both contain works related to MS. 76. The first unit includes the pseudo-Gildasian *Historia Brittonum*, which, as in MS. 76, follows Geoffrey's History and bears a distinctive set of rubrics found only in these and one other manuscript.[14] *Gesta Normannorum ducum* and the *Epistola* are found in the second unit, preceded by Dudo of Saint-Quentin's history of the Normans, separated by the epitome of the *Gesta Alexandri*, and followed by a list of Bede's works. The *Gesta Normannorum ducum* in MS. 92 belongs to Robert de Torigni's version, the so-called F-redaction, and is directly descended from MS. 76, Torigni's autograph (see below, *Gesta Normannorum ducum*). Thus Walther Boer's identification of a link between MSS 76 and 92 via the text of the *Epistola* is corroborated.

Further light is shed on the interrelation of contents by the last member of this subgroup of Walther Boer's Family I (this witness does not contain Geoffrey's *Historia*): Cambridge, Gonville & Caius College, MS. 177/210. This manuscript is in fact only part of a larger original whose remainder is now preserved as London, British Library, MS. Cotton Vitellius A.viii.[15] The combined manuscript, written at Reading in the later twelfth century,[16] is a copy of MS. 76 and derives from it a group of texts: *Gesta Normannorum ducum*, Einhard's Life of Charlemagne, *Gesta Alexandri*, *Epistola Alexandri*, and a brief history of the Frankish kings beginning 'Antenor et alii profugi'. The last item, often associated with the *Gesta*, is sufficiently uncommon to be of potential value in tracing related manuscripts.[17] The only other manuscript of the *Gesta* containing 'Antenor' and Geoffrey's *Historia* is Leiden, Bibliotheek der Rijksuniversiteit, Voss. lat. F.77 [77] which again contains Einhard's *Uita Karoli*. The *Uita Karoli* is also found in all representatives of the subgroup of Family I *Epistola*-manuscripts under discussion. Given the closeness of the connection of Einhard's Life with the

---

13 The precursor of this subgroup seems to be a Fécamp volume: Paris, Bibliothèque nationale, MS. lat. 5062 + Roma, Biblioteca Apostolica Vaticana, MS. Ottoboni 909 (fos 1–48). Avril has noted that the numerous alterations to the *Epistola* in this manuscript, both marginal and over erasure, account for the idiosyncracies of Leiden's text noted by one editor, Kuebler: Avril, 'Notes', p. 211 & references. The rubrics of BN lat. 5062 + BAV Ottoboni lat. 909 seem to be the source for those of this subgroup of the *Epistola*: 'Incipit epistola eiusdem Alexandri regis Macedonis (*or* Macedonum) ad magistrum suum Aristotelem de situ Indie'.

14 Evreux, Bibliothèque municipale, MS. 41: Dumville, 'An Early Text', p. 5 and n. 24.

15 Van Houts, *Gesta*, p. 239.

16 *Ibid.*; Hermanns & Van Houts, 'The History', p. 85.

17 Twelve manuscripts were listed by Delisle, 'Matériaux', p. 521, n. 1: Paris, Bibliothèque nationale, MSS lat. 4937, 4938, 5997, 5999, 14663; Bern, Burgerbibliothek, MS. 90; Bruxelles, Bibliothèque royale, MS. 9178; Leiden, Bibliotheek der Rijksuniversiteit, MS. BPL 20 and MS. Voss. lat. F.77. Another manuscript (Roma, BAV, MS. Christ. 946 (*sic*)) was recorded by Waitz, 'Ueber die sogenannte *Abbreviatio Gestorum regum Franciae*'. A further copy is found in Cambridge, Corpus Christi College, MS. 181.

relatives of MS. 76, a final *Historia*-Einhard manuscript may, perhaps, be a candidate for inclusion in this group: Roma, BAV, Reg. lat. 692 [197].

2. Family II + Epitaphium[18]

Cambridge, St John's College, MS. G.16 (184) [32] (Walther Boer Sj)
Cambridge, University Library, MS. Mm.5.29 [54] (Walther Boer U)
Lincoln, Cathedral Library, MS. 98 [80] (omitted by Walther Boer, but copy of U)
London, British Library, MS. Additional 33371 [83] (Not listed by Walther Boer)
London, British Library, MS. Cotton Galba E.xi [91] (Walther Boer Cg)
London, British Library, MS. Cotton Titus A.xxvii [95] (Not listed by Walther Boer)[19]
London, British Library, MS. Royal 13.A.v [110] (Walther Boer, Regi)
London, Lambeth Palace, MS. 401 [121] (Not listed by Walther Boer)
Paris, Bibliothèque nationale, MS. 8501A [183] (Not listed by Walther Boer)
Saint-Omer, Bibliothèque municipale, MS. 710 [202] (Walther Boer Aud)

Various types of *Historia*-text are accompanied by witnesses to the second family of the *Epistola Alexandri*. All the Second-Variant manuscripts containing the *Epistola* (α, β, and γ) have this form as do the five vulgate witnesses MSS 32, 83, 121, 183, and 110, in the last of which the *Historia* is considerably abbreviated.

All these Second-Variant manuscripts, together with MSS 32 and 121, include also *Epitaphium Alexandri*, which, with a short poem 'Quicquid in humanis . . .', is usually found after *Gesta Alexandri*. *Epitaphium* occurs in no other *Historia*-manuscripts and indeed is relatively rare among Alexander-texts, listed in only eleven English manuscripts.[20] Five of the seven *Epitaphium*/Family II manuscripts also include the Sibylline prophecies (*Inc.* 'Sibylle generaliter'), the exceptions being 95 and 202. Four of these five (except MS. 91) also include Dares's history. The order of these texts in the four is revealing. The contents of MS. 121 (vulgate) follow exactly the arrangement found in the Second-Variant β-witnesses 54 and 80: Dares, Sibylline prophecies, *Historia, Gesta Alexandri, Epitaphium, Epistola*. In the fourth manuscript, 32 (vulgate), these texts are split up: *Epitaphium* precedes *Historia*; the Sibylline prophecies, a history of Alexander, and the *Epistola* follow after four intermediate texts; then Dares's History is found after fifteen other texts. MS. 32 also differs from those just discussed in its form of the *Epitaphium* (the Orosian sentence 'Idem per duodecim . . . se trementem' is omitted)[21] and the absence of the *Gesta Alexandri*. MS. 91 (Second-Variant

18 Described by Walther Boer, *Epistola Alexandri*, pp. xxiv–xxvi.
19 Omitting section corresponding to Walther Boer, *Epistola Alexandri*, pp. 54, l. 5–58, l. 1.
20 By Hill, '*Epitaphia Alexandri*', pp. 96 and 99. I am aware of only one Continental copy apart from 202: Paris, Bibliothèque nationale, MS. nouv. acq. lat. 873: Hilka, 'Studien zur Alexandersage', p. 70.
21 Hill, '*Epitaphia Alexandri*', p. 100.

α-text) contains, like 32, an Alexander-history and the Sibylline prophecies with the same distinctive rubrics,[22] but 'Dares' is not present.[23] 95 lacks Dares or the Sibylline prophecies but contains the *Gesta*; 202 lacks all three having only the list of the Twelve Alexandrias which usually ends the *Gesta Alexandri*.[24] To summarize: there seem to be connections between the two β-witnesses and 121, and between 32 and 91 and perhaps 95 and 202.

The three remaining vulgate/Family-II manuscripts cannot be classified by contents. MS. 83 is fragmentary and in its present version includes no other Alexander-text. Both MSS 110 and 183 contain the *Gesta Alexandri* which, in the latter manuscript, is followed by the correspondence of Alexander and Dindymus (see above, *Collatio* I); these texts are so widespread that no significance can be attached to their presence in both manuscripts.

3. Families III + IV

Only one of the manuscripts which Walther Boer listed in each of these categories includes the *Historia*. **Paris, Bibliothèque nationale, MS. lat. 17569 [188]** belongs to Family III but two others meet Walther Boer's criteria for classification:[25] **London, British Library, MS. Stowe 56 [117]** and **College of Arms, MS. Arundel 1 [118]**. All three contain the history of Apollonius of Tyre and *Collatio* I of the Alexander-Dindymus correspondence. **Auxerre, Bibliothèque municipale, MS. 91 [14]** was the only *Historia*-manuscript assigned to Family IV by Walther Boer but another may be added according to his criteria: **Paris, Bibliothèque nationale, MS. lat. 4126 [164]**.[26] **Aberystwyth, National Library of Wales, MS. 11611 [2]** is a possible third but it witnesses a confusing mixture of readings from Families III and IV.[27]

Alexander: Epitaphium + Quicquid in humanis

Found in MSS 32, 54, 80, 91, 95, 121, 202: see above, Family II.

Alexander: Parua recapitulacio

Cambridge, University Library, MS. Mm.5.29 [54]
Lincoln, Cathedral Library, MS. 98 [80]

The *Parua Recapitulacio*, despite its title, does not summarize but supplements

---

22 'De omnibus sibillis et de nominibus earum/ipsarum et de origine et patria et actibus earum in diebus Alexandri magni'.

23 *Gesta Alexandri, Epitaphium, Epistola*, Alexander-story, Sibylline prophecies.

24 Preceded by two paragraphs on Alexander's death.

25 He lists distinctive readings: *Epistola Alexandri*, pp. xxvii–xxviii.

26 Criteria given *ibid*., pp. xxx–xxxi.

27 As for III, at 55.4 *quod*, but not those readings characteristic at 27.5 or 29.2; for IV that at 40.5 but not at 48.7.

other Alexander texts.[28] It describes Alexander's visit to Jerusalem and the power-struggles after his death.[29] The text had previously been recorded in only six manuscripts;[30] MS. 80 constitutes a seventh. All seven were written in England and the earliest, the late eleventh-century London, British Library, MS. Royal 13.A.i (which has 'a curious frontispiece in a very late Anglo-Saxon style'),[31] contains the same group of Alexander texts as 54: *Gesta*, *Epistola*, *Epitaphium*, *Collatio* I, and *Parua Recapitulacio*.[32] Something of the close connection between MSS 54 and 80 has already been seen. Besides witnessing the same versions of the *Epistola* and the Alexander-Dindymus correspondence, they include unusual texts: a Bedan chronology, 'Quinquagesimo ergo quarto anno', an account of the finding of the True Cross, beginning 'Sancta arbor' (see below), and notes on Jerusalem which appropriately follow the *Recapitulacio*. Full comparison shows that 80 follows exactly the order of contents of 54, with a few later additions at the end. Contents therefore point to the conclusion which Hammer had previously reached from the text of the *Historia* alone: that 80 is a copy of 54.[33]

Alexander: Iulius Ualerius, Gesta Alexandri

Aberystwyth, National Library of Wales, MS. 11611 [2]
Cambridge, Corpus Christi College, MS. 414 [25]
Cambridge, Trinity College, MS. O.1.17 (1041) [38]
Cambridge, University Library, MS. Mm.5.29 (2434) [54]
Leiden, Bibliotheek der Rijksuniversiteit, MS. BPL 20 [76]
Lincoln, Cathedral Library, MS. 98 [80]
London, British Library, MS. Cotton Galba E.xi [91]
London, British Library, MS. Cotton Nero D.viii [92]
London, British Library, MS. Cotton Titus A.xxvii [95]
London, British Library, MS. Royal 13.A.v [110]
London, British Library, MS. Stowe 56 [117]
London, College of Arms, MS. Arundel 1 [118]
London, Lambeth Palace, MS. 401 [121]
Paris, Bibliothèque nationale, MS. lat. 8501A [183]
Paris, Bibliothèque nationale, MSS lat. 13935 + 5508 [186]
Paris, Bibliothèque nationale, MS. lat. 17569 [188]

The *Gesta Alexandri* provided a fundamental source for Alexander's life in the Middle Ages. The text concerned here has a complex ancestry, being derived from a ninth-century (or earlier) epitome of Iulius Ualerius's fourth-century Latin

---

28 Cary, *The Medieval Alexander*, p. 70.
29 Ross, '*Parva recapitulacio*', p. 193.
30 *Ibid.*, p. 194; Hamilton, 'Quelques notes', p. 201.
31 Ross, '*Parva recapitulacio*', p. 194.
32 As does the other known recorded twelfth-century copy: BL Royal 15.C.vi. The other *Recapitulacio*-manuscripts are CUL Dd.10.24, BL Cotton Cleopatra D.v, and Harley 5054.
33 'Some Additional Manuscripts', pp. 239–40.

translation of a Greek original attributed to Callisthenes.[34] Its core position in the Alexander-literature is demonstrated by its occurrence in *Historia*-manuscripts. It appears in all the manuscripts containing the Dindymus correspondence, in thirteen of sixteen of the *Historia-Epistola* manuscripts,[35] and in six of seven of the *Epitaphium-Historia* manuscripts: the seventh manuscript, 32, has a different version of the Alexander-story ('Principium hystorie Alexandri'). Two – MSS 38 and 186 – have no Alexander texts apart from the *Gesta*. This distribution may be compared with David Ross's observations on that of Alexander-texts.[36]

Alexander: Secreta Secretorum

Secreta Secretorum claims to be the book of counsel written for Alexander by Aristotle. As such – a guide written by an exemplary king's tutor for an exemplary king – the work became a model for medieval texts on government.[37] The original Syriac seems to have been translated into Arabic, from which two Latin versions were made, one in 1125, one in about 1227 by Philip of Tripoli for a member of the de Vere family of Lincolnshire.[38] It is this second version which seems to be associated with the *Historia* as the rubric in Edinburgh, National Library of Scotland, MS. Adv. 18.4.5 [68] indicates.[39] The *Secreta* in Oxford, Christ Church, MS. 99 [160] (in a part of the manuscript physically separable from the *Historia*) begin similarly but end '. . . monarchia in septemtrione', which words conclude the final rubrics of a text of the *Secreta* in a third manuscript: Cambridge, Trinity College, MS. O.2.21 [39]. The *explicit* of this last witness agrees with that in MS. 68 but it contains only the latter part of the text (*Inc.* 'Et inter ceteras res illa est . . .'). These manuscripts share no other contents; MS. 68 is a First-Variant witness, the others are vulgate.

Alexander: Epithoma

A short text summarizing Alexander's life appears in two *Historia*-manuscripts: **London, College of Arms, MS. 1 [118]** and **Paris, Bibliothèque nationale, MS. 4126 [164]**.[40] MS. 118 it is called 'Epithoma de ortu uita et de obitu Alexandri Macedonum regis magni memorie digna (*sic*)', while in 164 the rubric is different and attributes the summary to Pompeius Trogus, whose *Historiae Philippicae* were epitomized by Justinus and contained material about Alexander.[41] The *Epithoma* follows *Gesta Alexandri* in 118, and *Epistola Alexandri* in 164. *Epistola*

34 Cary, *The Medieval Alexander*, pp. 9–10, 24–25.
35 *Not* MSS 14, 67, 117.
36 *Apud* Cary, *The Medieval Alexander*, p. 25, n. 2.
37 Cary, *The Medieval Alexander*, pp. 105–6.
38 *Ibid.*, p. 21.
39 'Incipit epistola magistri Philyppi super librum qui dicitur Secreta Secretorum'.
40 'Quoniam non est humane nature ineuitabiles casus transire . . . in perniciem mutuam armauisset.'
41 Cary, *The Medieval Alexander*, p. 17.

Alexandri is found in both manuscripts: the Family-II version is found in MS. 164 but that in 118 belongs to Family IV. The manuscripts both date from the fourteenth century and contain numerous and complex contents, none of which, however, otherwise overlap (although they contain different works associated with Joachim of Fiore).

Anglia habet in longitudine

Cambridge, University Library, MS. Mm.5.29 [54]
Lincoln, Cathedral Library, MS. 98 [80]
(London, British Library, MS. Cotton Nero D.viii [92])
London, British Library, MS. Royal 13.D.v [113]

The account of the shires and bishoprics of England beginning 'Anglia habet . . .'[42] is connected with the transmission of the version of the *Historia Brittonum* attributed to Gildas, which all four manuscripts also contain.[43] Similarities between the contents of 54 and 80 have already been observed.[44] The relationship between them and the London manuscripts is more complex: while 54 and 80 are Second-Variant witnesses, 92 and 113 contain the vulgate text. 'Anglia habet' was added *c*. 1400 to the original part of 92 (fos 1–175, which includes *Historia Brittonum*)[45] together with a number of texts not found in the other manuscripts discussed here. In MS. 113, 'Anglia habet' is only the first of a group of three texts found in identical form in 54 and 80, the others being a genealogy of the counts of Flanders (Hildricus . . . Willelmus) and a list of French kings (Clodoueus . . . Lodowicus). In 113, as in 54 and 80, this group of texts is separated from the Gildasian *Historia Brittonum* by several other works.

The text-history of the Gildasian recension of the *Historia Brittonum* clarifies the relationship. 54 and 80 belong to the same branch of the pseudo-Gildasian tradition as 113, 92 being linked with another version (see above Alexander: *Epistola Alexandri*, Family I; below, *Historia Brittonum*). At the head of the tradition represented by 54/80 stands Oxford, Bodleian Library, MS. Bodley 163 (*S.C.* 2016), fos 228–249, an early twelfth-century manuscript associated with Peterborough from which 54 and 80 derive a number of contents including a Flemish pedigree and a list of the kings of France.[46] 'Anglia habet' is not known to have entered the textual tradition before MS. 54. Therefore the Gildasian

---

42 One version printed by Hodgson Hinde from Cambridge, University Library, MS. Ff.1.27 and Arundel, Norfolk 220: *Symeonis Dunelmensis opera*, I.220–21.
43 Both texts are also found in Cambridge, University Library, MS. Ff.1.27, p. 216a/b.
44 See above, *Parua recapitulacio*.
45 See above, *Alexander: Epistola Alexandri, family I.*
46 Bodley 163 fos 1–162 constitute a separate volume, whose decoration has been compared with the decoration of the Peterborough Chronicle; fo 251, at the end of the second unit, bears a list of Peterborough books.

Historia Brittonum and lists found in 113 cannot be traced directly back to Bodley 163 but must have been transmitted through MS. 54.

As it was the Second-Variant manuscript 54 from which 113 derived these contents and not Bodley 163, the exemplar of 54, it is clear that the Galfridian component in this group of texts was at some time switched from Second-Variant to vulgate. Alternatively one might hypothesize that 'Anglia habet' had become attached, without Geoffrey's History, to some descendant of Bodley 163 and ancestor of MS. 54. Such an explanation is improbable, considering the very close relationship between MS. 54 and Bodley 163, and that Geoffrey's History occurs in the same position (before *Historia Brittonum*) in MSS 54 and 113.

Different descriptions of the shires and bishoprics of England are found in Oxford, All Souls' College, MS. 39 [133] and Exeter, Cathedral Library, MS. 3514 [70].[47]

Anglia modo dicta olim Albion dicebatur

This text, sometimes found under the title *De gigantibus*, is an account of the mythical inhabitants of Britain before the arrival of the Trojans.[48] Therefore it is not surprising to find it prefacing Geoffrey's account in **Aberystwyth, NLW, MS. Peniarth 43 [9]** and **Cambridge, Corpus Christi College, MS. 414 [25]**.[49] Contents provide no other connection between these manuscripts. *De gigantibus* follows the *Historia* at several works' distance in London, **BL, MS. Cotton Cleopatra D.viii [90]**, and **Oxford, Bodleian Library, MS. Bodley 622 (S.C. 2150) [137]**. The association between MSS 90 and 137 will be discussed later (see *Compendium*). *De gigantibus* was added to London, British Library, MSS Cotton Nero D.viii [92] and Cotton Vespasian E.x [98] in later hands, separated from the *Historia* by several works.

Antenor et alii profugi

These are the opening words of a brief history of the Frankish kings found in MSS 76 and 77: see above, *Epistola Alexandri*, Family I.

---

47 MS. 133, 111v–112r: 'Anglia habet in long. occies .c. miliare .s. a Renwaterstrece . . . Staffordsire in qua sunt .D. hyde'. MS. 70, pp. 58b–60a: 'Hec est mensura Anglie uel Britannie in longitudine .D.CCC. miliaria id est a Penpenwith . . . Staffortsyra .D. hyde unde .S. syra Anglice latine dicitur prouincia et ponitur pro uicecomitatu'.

48 See Ward & Herbert, *Catalogue of Romances*, I.198–203 (and see above, *Ab origine*). Ward notes that the version in Cotton Cleopatra D.viii [90] has *rex Grecie* where Cotton Vespasian E.x [98] and Cotton Nero D.viii [92] have *rex Hispanie*.

49 Johanek has noted other Arthurian associations of the text: 'König Artur', p. 382.

De Antichristo

The story of Antichrist and the Last Days of the world before Judgement circulated in several versions in the Middle Ages, some of which are found with copies of Geoffrey's History.

Adso

London, College of Arms, MS. Arundel 1 [118]
Saint-Omer, Bibliothèque municipale, MS. 710 [202]

Adso, who wrote in the mid-tenth century, took up the story known from other apocalyptic texts (like the Revelations attributed to Methodius) of the Last Emperor before Antichrist, who would conquer the pagans before laying down his symbols of office at Jerusalem. This emperor, *rex Romanorum* in the pseudo-Methodian version, was made *rex Francorum* by Adso, no doubt flattering his dedicatee, Gerberga, wife of one of the last Carolingians, Louis VI.[50] The presence of Adso's work in the two *Historia*-manuscripts is not immediately explicable by inheritance. Their versions of Adso's text are not identical – the prologue is omitted from 202 – and they hold no other contents in common.[51]

Albuin

Adso's account was taken up by Albuin (who died in 1031 as abbot of Tegernsee). One of Albuin's versions, dedicated to Herebert, archbishop of Cologne (999–1021), is found with Geoffrey's *Historia* in **Roma, Biblioteca Apostolica Vaticana, MS. Ottoboni 1472 [194]**.[52] There are several other versions, one prefaced by a chapter on the vices and virtues dedicated to Herebert, another to one Arnold. The second *Historia*-manuscript containing Albuin's *De Antichristo* – **Cambridge, St John's College, MS. G.16 (184) [32]** – lacks a prologue.[53]

pseudo-Anselm

A version sometimes attributed to Anselm (*Inc.* 'Scire uolentibus primo dicemus . . .') is found in two *Historia*-manuscripts: **London, British Library, MSS Arundel 326 [88] and Sloane 289 [116]**.[54] These manuscripts are otherwise known to be closely related (see below, *Chronology: In principio*).

88 and 116, then, are of seven *Historia*-manuscripts the only two containing

---

50 Brown, 'La Notion', p. 86; Verhelst, *Adso*, p. 1; McGinn, *The Visions*, p. 82.
51 Prologue beginning 'Excellentissime ac regali dignitate pollenti Deo dilectissime'; the text in 202 opens 'Omnes de antichristo scire uolentes'. Edited by Verhelst, *Adso*, pp. 22–30. See also *ibid.*, p. 16.
52 *Ibid.*, pp. 56 and 59–60.
53 *Ibid.*, p. 65; see also p. 55; text pp. 68–74.
54 *Ibid.*, pp. 161–66, also p. 157.

tracts on Antichrist in which an affiliation is clear. It seems that Geoffrey's History had an affinity with such apocalyptic literature and was readily associated with it (see also *Methodius* and *Prophecies: Sibilline*).[55]

Apollonius of Tyre

London, British Library, MS. Stowe 56 [117]
London, College of Arms, MS. Arundel 1 [118]
Paris, Bibliothèque nationale, MS. lat. 7531 [182]
Paris, Bibliothèque nationale, MS. lat. 17569 [188]

This fairytale, indebted to ancient romance, enjoyed great popularity in the Middle Ages.[56] It describes the misfortunes of Apollonius, king of Tyre, first at the hands of the tyrannical king of Antioch, then after a storm in which he believes his wife drowned; the tale is resolved happily.[57]

MSS 117 and 188, which, as has been seen above, contain the *Collatio* I version of the correspondence of Alexander and Dindymus and Family III *Epistola*-texts, are witnesses to the 'Tegernsee' recension of Apollonius.[58] MS. 118 also contains the correspondence of Dindymus but the filiation of its text of Apollonius is unknown.[59] However, like 117 and 188, it includes the *Epistola Alexandri* (Family III) as well as the correspondence between Alexander and Dindymus (*collatio* I); with 117 only it shares Dares's History.

MS. 182 belongs to the 'Stuttgart' recension, which, like the Tegernsee, represents a mixture of the A and B recension of Apollonius relying largely on the B.[60] Its contents are not related to those found in the other three manuscripts.

Ausonius

Two poems of Ausonius from *Opuscula* 7 are found in **Auxerre, Bibliothèque municipale, MS. 91 (871) [14]** and **Paris, Bibliothèque nationale, MS. 8501A [183]**. They begin 'Est et non cunctis monosillaba . . .' and 'Ter binos deciesque nouem superexit in annos . . .'. In 14, these are only the second two of four poems from *Opuscula* 7 which follow five from *Opuscula* 13. The same Ausonius collection is found in Auxerre, Bibliothèque municipale, MS. 70 (67) which also

---

55 A parallel between Merlin and Antichrist has been suggested by Paul Zumthor, *Merlin*, pp. 172–77.

56 Kortekaas, ed., *Historia Apollonii*, pp. 4–5.

57 *Ibid.*, pp. 3–4.

58 *Ibid.*, pp. 17–18.

59 *Ibid.*, p. 22.

60 *Ibid.*, p. 18. Both groups are well represented: the Tegernsee by thirteen manuscripts from the ninth century onwards, the Stuttgart by sixteen, from the twelfth century onwards: *ibid.*, pp. 17–19.

contains the works preceding the Ausonius in 14: Freculph's Universal History, a collection of chronicle extracts ostensibly taken from Eusebius, Jerome, Isidore, Bede, Prosper, and Orosius (*Inc.* 'Ab Adam usque ad diluuium anni .ii(m).cc.xlii. . . .') and a note 'De discretione temporum' (*Inc.* 'Prima etas in exordio . . .'). Auxerre 70 is dated *c.* 1200 while 14 is somewhat earlier.[61] The relationship of the two is clarified by reference to the second *Historia*-manuscript, 183. As well as the Ausonius poems, this includes the collection of chronicle extracts and a further work found in 14, but not in Auxerre 70, the 'Diffiniciones (*recte* definitiones) Ciceronis'.[62] This suggests that there is no need to posit a lost exemplar: 14 is probably the source for the other manuscripts.

Bede, Historia ecclesiastica

Cambridge, St John's College, MS. S.6 (254) [33]
(London, British Library, MS. Additional 33371 [83])[63]
Montpellier, Bibliothèque municipale, MS. 92 [126]
Oxford, Christ Church, MS. 99 [160]
Paris, Bibliothèque de l'Arsenal, MS. 982 [163]
Paris, Bibliothèque nationale, MS. lat. 5233 [166]
Paris, Bibliothèque nationale, MS. lat. 5234 [167]
Paris, Bibliothèque nationale, MS. lat. 12943 [184]
Rouen, Bibliothèque municipale, MS. U.74 [200]

According to the account by Mynors,[64] these manuscripts attest a wide variety of Bedan texts. 33 witnesses an early version of the c-form (as found in the eighth-century manuscript BL Cotton Tiberius A.xiv), whose circulation was predominantly Insular.[65] 160 also represents the c-form but a version current in the later Middle Ages, associated by Mynors with southern England in particular. This is always followed by the account of Bede's death.[66] Mynors listed MS. 200 among the few examples of the English c-text to cross the Channel.[67]

The rest of those manuscripts listed above whose filiation is known contain the m-form of the text of Bede, a version with a largely Continental distribution. The remote ancestry of all three Bibliothèque nationale manuscripts, as indeed that of

---

61 Both contain only volume I of the Freculph (from Creation to the birth of Christ); according to a study of the thirty-two manuscripts of this text, both these Auxerre witnesses (sigla Xr and Au) belong to the same (Cistercian) branch: Natunewicz, 'Freculphus of Lisieux', pp. 129–30.

62 According to rubric in 14. *Inc.* 'Nulle sunt occultiores insidie quam . . .'.

63 This manuscript is composed of fragments. It is probable on palaeographical grounds, but not certain, that the Bede was originally part of the same manuscript as Geoffrey's *Historia*: Crick, *The Historia*, III.136–37.

64 *Bede's Ecclesiastical History*, edited by Colgrave & Mynors, p. xxxix–lxx.

65 *Ibid.*, pp. xlvii–xlviii.

66 *Ibid.*, p. lviii. See below, *Cuthbert: De obitu Bede*.

67 *Ibid.*, p. lxi.

the text in France, may be traced to the Carolingian descendants of the eighth-century Moore Bede (Cambridge, University Library, MS. Kk.5.16).[68] Mynors had not examined 126 but listed it as a possible c-text;[69] there may be reason to include it in the m-group, however. It bears a rubric identical to that in 166 ('Incipit prefatio uenerabilis Bede presbiteri in historia Anglorum') (and the text of Geoffrey's *Historia* in the two manuscripts is close). The version of Bede's History in 163 may be traced back to a ninth-century copy at Nonantola and thus has been classed by Mynors as Italian. That found in 83, meanwhile, he described as German, and again ultimately descended from early copies of the Moore Bede.[70]

Abbreviated versions of Bede's History are found in association with the *Historia* in Oxford, Bodleian Library, MS. Rawlinson B.189 [155] and Notre Dame, University Library, MS. 40 [130].

Chronology: *Ab Adam usque ad diluuium ann. .ii.cc.xlii. . . .*

Found in MSS 14 and 183: see above, *Ausonius.*

Chronology: *In principio erat uerbum*

These words begin a chronology to the birth of Henry III (ending 'usque ad natiuitatem Henerici regis filii Iohannis') found in **London, British Library, MSS Arundel 326 [88]** and **Sloane 289 [116]**. Nine other items are found in a block in almost identical order, separated from the chronology by different texts. In 88, the earlier manuscript, these are *Gesta Saluatoris*, *Post peccatum Ade*, Anselm's *De Antichristo*, a text on the Finding of the Cross (*Inc.* 'Factum est cum expulsi'), three brief texts beginning 'Anna et Emeria', 'Beatus Petrus', and 'Si quis ab occidentalibus', Methodius, Sibylline prophecies. In 116, *De Antichristo* occurs at the end of this block.

Chronology: *Quinquagesimo ergo quarto anno*

This *incipit* opens a short 'Bedan' chronology found in MSS 54 and 80. This text is another of those derived from Bodley 163 (see above, *Anglia habet*).[71]

---

68 *Bede's Ecclesiastical History*, pp. lxiii–lxiv. The filiation is established by Mynors *apud* Hunter Blair, *The Moore Bede*, pp. 34–36.

69 *Ibid.*, p. lxi.

70 *Ibid.*, pp. lxix–lxx and lxv–lxvi.

71 Found also in CUL Ff.1.27 (pp. 18–19), another manuscript containing the pseudo-Gildasian *Historia Brittonum.*

Commentary on the Prophecy of the Eagle

This prophecy is frequently associated with the *Historia* (see below, Prophecy: Merlin) but commentaries are confined to three manuscripts: Cambridge, St John's College, MS. G.16 [32], Dublin, Trinity College, MS. 514 [66], and Leningrad, Saltykov-Shchedrin State Public Library, MS. F.IV.76 [78]. The commentaries in 32 and 78 are nearly identical:[72] that in 66 bears no apparent relationship to them.

Compendium de Britannie

This work (*Inc.* 'Quoniam simplicioribus') is one of a group of texts found in **London, BL, MS. Cotton Cleopatra D.viii [90]** and **Oxford, Bodleian Library, MS. Bodley 622 [137]**. In 137, *Compendium* appears on flyleaves written *c.* 1300, following an account of the foundation of Albion (*Anglia modo dicta*: see above), and followed by 'Quedam narracio de nobili rege Arthuro in sacramento altaris nunc plene credente qualiter confirmatus fuit in fide factus uere credens et quare mutauit arma sua' (*Inc.* Dominus Deus uniuersorum conditor)[73] and notes 'De episcopatibus et primo de archiepiscopatu Eboracensi', 'De archiepiscopatu Cantuarie', and 'De Normaniis (*sic*)'. The collection is copied into the body of the volume in 90 (*c.* 1400), the order being *Quedam narratio, Anglia modo dicta*, the notes on the episcopal and archiepiscopal sees, and *Compendium* (the notes on the Normans are absent). 137 might therefore be the source for these other contents and the *Historia*-text.

These works are not unique to 90 and 137 or to *Historia*-manuscripts, however. The Glastonbury manuscript, Cambridge, Trinity College, MS. R.5.33 (100ra/vb), contains *Compendium* and the notes on the bishops, archbishops and the Normans. *Quedam narracio* is found in Oxford, Bodleian Library, MS. Digby 186.[74]

Cosmographiae

Cosmographiae are found in three *Historia*-manuscripts.

Æthicus Ister

The *Cosmographia* purportedly written by Æthicus Ister is a Latin pseudo-translation (from the Greek) to be ranked with others like the Trojan history of

---

72 Translated (but not printed) by Sutton and Visser-Fuchs, 'Richard III's Books', II.354–57.

73 The story is found in the Chronicle of John of Glastonbury, §34: edited by Carley, *John*, pp. 76–78.

74 Curley, 'Fifteenth-century Glosses', p. 323.

Dares Phrygius and,[75] indeed, Geoffrey's own alleged translation. An attempt to identify its author with the eighth-century bishop of Salzburg, Vergil, has now been discredited.[76] The work begins by describing paradise, the angels, and hell, and other threes such as earth/sea/sky, and sun/moon/stars. There follows an account of the author's own journeys, and often mythical descriptions of peoples and places in various continents.[77]

Geoffrey's and Vergil's pseudo-translations are found together in Paris, Bibliothèque nationale, MS. lat. 8501A [183] and Leiden, Bibliotheek der Rijks-universiteit, MS. Voss. lat. F.77 [77]. 77 contains only an extract (concerning the Alexander story) and is separated from the *Historia* by several works, while 183 witnesses the full form of the text (which there immediately precedes Geoffrey's History).[78] Therefore the connections between the two manuscripts are slight.

pseudo-Priscian

A third manuscript, Paris, Bibliothèque nationale, MS. lat. 4126 [164], contains a different *Cosmographia* sometimes (falsely) associated with Æthicus but here attributed, equally misleadingly, to Priscian.[79]

Credunt igitur Sarraceni unum esse Deum

Material concerning Mohammed and Islam is found in four *Historia*-manuscripts but the only duplication is a text on the Moslem faith found in **Cambridge, St John's College, MS. G.16 (184) [32]** and **Cambridge, University Library, MS. Dd.1.17 [40]**.[80] The texts end differently, however, and there is no further agreement betwen the numerous and complex contents of these manuscripts.

Cum animaduerterem

These words begin an anonymous chronicle of French history to 1214,[81] found in **Dôle, Bibliothèque municipale, MSS 348–349 [58]**, **Dublin, Trinity College, MS. 493 [62]**, and **London, College of Arms, MS. Arundel 1 [118]**. Wailly noted the closeness of this text to the Saint-Denis chronicles and the early text, supposedly translated by the minstrel of Count Alfonse of Poitou, which has been

---

75 Löwe, 'Ein literarischer Widersacher', p. 904.
76 Löwe, *ibid.*; refuted by Draak, 'Virgil'.
77 Manitius, *Geschichte*, I.231–33.
78 Omitting §112 as printed by Wuttke, *Die Kosmographie*.
79 Riese, ed., *Geographici latini minores*, pp. 71–103, but the text here departs from his after p. 91, l. 4.
80 The others being London, British Library, MS. Sloane 289 [116] and Paris, Bibliothèque nationale, MS. lat. 8501A [183].
81 See Dumville, 'Celtic-Latin texts', p. 25 & n. 24.

thought to lie behind them.[82] *Cum animaduerterem* precedes Geoffrey's *Historia* immediately in MS. 62, and separated only by a brief series of annals in 58. Neither manuscript contains other items. 118, however, has numerous contents. Here *Cum animaduerterem* follows the *Historia*, but at several works' distance.[83]

Cuthbert, De obitu Bede

The account of Bede's death as printed by Charles Plummer[84] is found in two *Historia*-manuscripts: **Oxford, Christ Church, MS. 99 [160]** and **Exeter, Cathedral Library, MS. 3514 [70]**. Besides witnessing different versions of Geoffrey's text (that in 160 is vulgate, that in 70 First-Variant), these manuscripts display no other overlap between their numerous and complex contents. In 160, *De obitu* follows Bede's History; in 70, which does not contain Bede's *Historia*, *De obitu* appears within a larger text, an account of the Anglo-Saxon heptarchy.[85]

Dares Phrygius, Historia de excidio Troie

Aberystwyth, National Library of Wales, MS. 2005 (Panton 37) [1]
Aberystwyth, National Library of Wales, MS. 13210 [4]
Auxerre, Bibliothèque municipale, MS. 91 [14]
Cambridge, Corpus Christi College, MS. 414 [25]
Cambridge, St John's College, MS. G.16 (184) [32]
Cambridge, Sidney Sussex College, MS. 75 [34]
Cambridge, University Library, MS. Dd.10.31 (590) [44]
Cambridge, University Library, MS. Mm.5.29 (2434) [54]
Cardiff, South Glamorgan Central Library, MS. 2.611 [55]
Douai, Bibliothèque municipale, MS. 880 [59]
Douai, Bibliothèque municipale, MS. 882 [60]
Dublin, Trinity College, MS. 514 [66]
Dublin, Trinity College, MS. 515 [67]
Edinburgh, National Library of Scotland, MS. Adv. 18.4.5 [68]
Exeter, Cathedral Library, MS. 3514 [70]
Glasgow, University Library, MS. U.7.26 (332) [74]
Lincoln, Cathedral Library, MS. 98 [80]
London, British Library, MS. Royal 13.A.v [110]

---

82 Wailly, 'Examen', pp. 386–88.
83 118 ends '. . . per spacium .v. annorum dedit'. In 62 the text ends 'quod nisi treuga'; in 58 further annals are found after this. The text in these last two manuscripts further differs in that 62 has *capitula*-lists.
84 *Uenerabilis Baedae opera historica*, I.clx–clxiv.
85 This probably originated at Bury St Edmunds. See Dumville & Lapidge, *The Annals*, pp. li–lii.

The history of the fall of Troy attributed to the apocryphal figure, Dares the Phrygian, whose original Greek was allegedly translated by Cornelius Nepos,[86] is the single work most frequently associated with Geoffrey's *History*: the two occur together in twenty-seven manuscripts. These span all forms of the *Historia* – both families of the First Variant, α- and β-manuscripts of the Second, and vulgate copies of various sorts. The connection is logical. Geoffrey relates how Britain's population was first settled under one of the Trojan remnant, Brutus; Dares describes the circumstances which occasioned the move of Brutus's ancestors to the West. To what degree, then, is the association of these widely-circulated texts in the manuscripts inherited or spontaneous?

Analysis is hampered by the lack of progress in textual work on 'Dares' since Ferdinand Meister's edition, published in 1873. Meister provided a text but no more than a very summary mention of a few manuscripts; he ignored the later medieval textual developments. Despite the inherent problems, Neil Wright has been able to give some account of the connection between Dares-texts and the First-Variant families.[87] Only one manuscript of seven (London, BL, MS. Harley 6358 [106]), does not include Dares. The filiation of another, now lost, is irrecoverable as the manuscript is known only from a partial eighteenth-century transcript (MS. 1). Three of the remaining five manuscripts[88] include an idiosyncratic version (*expl.* 'mandauit litteris') with the rubric 'Daretis Frigii Entellii in latinum sermonem translata'.[89] Two other First-Variant manuscripts (4, 163) have a more standard form with the rubric 'Incipit epistola Cornelii ad Crispum Salustium in Troianorum hystoria que in Greco a Darete hystoriographo facta est', and ending with a list (of those killed by the Greeks) sometimes appended to the work (*expl.* 'Memnonem. Neoptholemum. Penthesileam'). This same rubric and *explicit* are found in two vulgate manuscripts: 44 and 212.[90] This rubric prefaces texts with a different *explicit* elsewhere: that in MSS 117 (vulgate), 138 and 66

---

86 Presumably the Roman historian (*c.* 99–*c.* 24 B.C.), author of Lives of Famous Men, friend of Cicero and contemporary of Sallust (84–34 B.C.).

87 *The Historia*, II.xcvi and cv.

88 67, 68, 70.

89 Wright, *The Historia*, II.xcvi. Wright gives the form *Entelli* which is found only in MS. 70. I use the spelling found in 67 and 68. Vergil mentions a Sicilian hero called Entellus: *Aeneid*, V.

90 MS. 212 adds before *facta, compilata siue.*

(both Second-Variant) ends with a longer list of the casualties (*expl*. 'Epistrophum. Scidium'),[91] while in 164 (vulgate), the lists do not appear and the text finishes 'et hucusque Daretis Frigii historia conscripta est'. Most Dares-*Historia* manuscripts, in fact, conclude with the longer form of the casualty-list ('. . . Epistropium. Scidium') but a number of different rubrics prefaces them. Three – two Second-Variant β-manuscripts (54 and 80) and a vulgate (121) – already seen to be connected (above, Alexander: *Epistola Alexandri*) – have the same rubric as 32 ('. . . hystoria . . . de Greco translata . . .'). The rubrics of three others, all vulgate, conform to some degree: '[Incipit] historia/prologus Daretis Frigii de excidio Troianorum/uastacione Troie/ bello Troiano'.[92] Two (25, 129) have no original rubric.

The shortened list of Trojan dead, as found in 164, concludes two other vulgate manuscripts: 34 and 118. There is no apparent similarity between their rubrics.

The dependence of this brief overview on superficial criteria – rubrics and *explicits* – severely limits its evidential value. However, there emerge certain patterns corroborated by other material. The 'Entellius' version is limited to association with the First Variant. The four Second-Variant manuscripts split into two groups, according to their version (α or β) of Geoffrey's text. The form of 'Dares' found in the Second-Variant β-witnesses agrees with that in a vulgate manuscript otherwise known to be associated with them.

Definitiones Ciceronis

See above, Ausonius.

Dominus Deus uniuersorum conditor

See above, *Compendium*.

Dudo of Saint-Quentin, Gesta Normannorum

The History of Geoffrey is found together with the *Gesta Normannorum* of Dudo, a fellow practitioner of the art of pseudo-history, in **Douai, Bibliothèque municipale, MS. 880 [59]** and **London, British Library, MS. Cotton Nero D.viii [92]**. These manuscripts are grouped separately in Gerda Huisman's study of the text of *Gesta Normannorum*: 92 contains dedicatory epistle, prose, and poems while 59 has some poems but lacks the dedicatory epistle.[93] There is no agreement between the other contents of these manuscripts.

91 And invert the names *Crispum Salustium* in the rubric.
92 14, 74, 189.
93 Huisman, 'Notes', pp. 123 (fig. 1), 125–26, 131.

39

Einhard, Vita Karoli Magni

This work is found in MSS 76, 77, and 197: see above, *Epistola Alexandri*, Family I.

Epistolae: Emperor of Constantinople to Robert of Flanders

This text announces itself as the letter from the Emperor Alexius Comnenus sent before the First Crusade to Robert of Flanders to request military aid; how much is invented and how much genuine is disputed.[94] It is found in two *Historia*-manuscripts – **Paris, Bibliothèque nationale, MSS lat. 13935 + 5508 [186]** and **Roma, Biblioteca Apostolica Vaticana, MS. Pal. lat. 962 [196]** – appended as usual to the romantic account of the First Crusade by Robert, monk of Reims.[95] Robert's History, an embroidered version of an eyewitness account of the Crusade used by several authors,[96] occurs in one other *Historia*-manuscript: **Roma, BAV, MS. Vat. lat. 2005 [199]**. Besides including Alexius's letter, 186 and 196 are the only *Historia*-manuscripts to contain a letter from the patriarch of Jerusalem and the bishops of the East (*Inc.* 'Ierosolimitanus patriarcha et episcopi tam Greci quam latini . . .'). The letters and Robert's History are arranged differently, however: in 186 Alexius's letter precedes Robert's History and the patriarch's letter; in 196 this order is reversed. It should also be noted that this block of texts occurs in a fifteenth-century part of 196, codicologically distinct from the thirteenth-century unit containing Geoffrey's History. 186 is fourteenth-century. Therefore there is reason to suspect that the connection is fortuitous.

Epistolae: Hillin of Trier/Hadrian IV

Three letters written in the third quarter of the twelfth century are found in **Bern, Burgerbibliothek, MS. 568 [15]** and **Roma, Biblioteca Apostolica Vaticana, MS. Ottoboni lat. 3025 [215]**.[97] They concern a dispute between Church and State. The first letter is from Emperor Frederick Barbarossa to Hillin, archbishop of Trier, the second from Hillin to Pope Adrian IV (1154–59), and the last is from Adrian to the archbishops of Trier, Mainz, and Cologne and their suffragans.[98] The letters travelled together as a group and, it has been argued, should not be taken at face value: they are a stylistic exercise in *Ars dictaminis* performed by a single author.[99]

---

94 Joranson, 'The Problem'.
95 Compare Hagenmeyer, *Die Kreuzzugsbriefe*, pp. 42–43.
96 Cahen, *La Syrie*, pp. 8–10.
97 Ed. Höing, ' "Die Trierer Stilübungen" ', pp. 318–29.
98 For details see Wright, *The Historia*, I.xxii.
99 Höing, ' "Die Trierer Stilübungen" ', p. 264.

The letters occur in the same order in both manuscripts, and in 15 are followed by four others on the same theme, mostly from the pontificate of Alexander III. In Bern the letters are located at the beginning of the manuscript (fos 1r–4r), in a unit apparently distinct from the *Historia* which now follows the letter-collection after poems and various additions.[100] In 215 the letters immediately precede Geoffrey's *History* (extracts only)[101] which is itself followed by fables of Avenus but in a different hand; together the letters and Geoffrey's History constitute a distinct portion of the manuscript, dating from the fifteenth century (the manuscript is of mixed date). The similarity of the text of the letters which the two manuscripts contain has been observed.[102]

Epistolae: Patriarch of Jerusalem to bishops of the East

This letter is a report on the progress of the First Crusade, written from the camp at Antioch in January 1098. On the two occasions on which it occurs with Geoffrey's History it is in the truncated first recension, the usual form which accompanies the History of Robert of Reims, as here.[103] See above, Epistolae: Emperor of Constantinople.

Epitaph of King Ceadwalla

Geoffrey ends his History with an account of the exiled British king, Cadualdrus, whom he equates with Bede's Ceadwalla (§202), whose death as a pilgrim in Rome marked the end of British kingship and the transition to Saxon rule. Two *Historia*-manuscripts include the epitaph of Ceadwalla which Bede quotes (*Historia ecclesiastica*, V.7). In Paris, Bibliothèque nationale, MS. lat. 6040 [170], a vulgate manuscript, the epitaph appropriately follows the *Historia*. Hammer records several special readings in this copy of the epitaph, including *splendiferumque* at line 7 and *mirificus* at line 8.[104] The other *Historia*-manuscript containing the epitaph – Dublin, Trinity College, MS. 515 [67] – conforms at these places to the readings recorded in Colgrave and Mynors' text of the Bede – *splendificumque* (*sic*) and *uiuificus*.[105] 67 differs from 170 in other ways: the epitaph is in a part of the manuscript physically separable from the *Historia*, which is a witness to the First-Variant Version, not the vulgate.

---

100   *Ibid.*, I.xxxii–xxxv.
101   §§31, 55, 111–117, 158, 8.
102   Höing, ' "Die Trierer Stilübungen" ', pp. 275–76.
103   Compare Hagenmeyer, *Die Kreuzzugsbriefe*, pp. 68–69.
104   'An Unrecorded *Epitaphium*'.
105   See also Wright, *The Historia*, II.lxxxi and n. 151.

Euolutis a mundi constitucione

These words begin another origin-story of Britain, concerning the settlement of Albion by Brutus. It is found in two *Historia*-manuscripts: **Oxford, Bodleian Library, MS. Rawlinson B.189 (S.C. 11550) [155]** and **Cambridge, University Library, MS. Dd.6.7 (324) + Oxford, Bodleian Library, MS. Bodley 585 (S.C. 2357), fos 1–48 [42]**. These manuscripts have no other texts in common but both have connections with St Albans and postdate the later fourteenth century. 155 was at Hatfield Peverel (Essex), a cell of St Albans, in the fifteenth century when an Epitome of Bede's History was added to the original *Historia*-manuscript; flyleaves at the beginning bearing *Euolutis* probably date from the same time. A note on fo 1r declares that the manuscript was at St Albans in 1537. 42 was actually written at St Albans, in the 1440s. Therefore there is a possibility that these connections will be reflected in some textual link.

Finding of the True Cross: Post peccatum Ade

One of the sources for the history of the True Cross before Christ is the thirteenth-century Latin *Legende* sometimes associated in manuscripts with the Gospel of Nicodemus.[106] This text, beginning 'Post peccatum Ade expulso eodem de paradiso...', follows the Gospel of Nicodemus in two *Historia*-manuscripts: **London, British Library, MSS Arundel 326 [88]** and **Sloane 289 [116]**. 'Post peccatum Ade' is found in another, earlier, *Historia*-manuscript, **Winchester, Cathedral Library, MS. 9 [212]**, in which it constitutes the first item in the original collection of texts (Martinus Polonus, Dares, Geoffrey of Monmouth). 212 shares no further contents with 88 and 116, and the version of 'Post peccatum Ade' which it contains diverges from the printed text in the two final chapters.[107]

Finding of the True Cross: Sancta arbor

A text describing the legend of the Cross is found in the pair of manuscripts 54 and 80. J. H. Mozley, its editor, saw it as representing the early stages of the later medieval embellishments on the story; these began in the twelfth century.[108] The full story describes the history of the holy tree from its origin as three seeds from Paradise placed in Adam's mouth after his death. The saplings performed miracles for Moses and later the grown tree was incorporated in Solomon's temple, whence it was later used for Jesus's cross. In the version beginning 'Sancta arbor', the account begins with Moses.

Mozley was apparently unaware of MS. 80. He derived his text from 54 and

---

106 Hill, 'The Fifteenth-Century Prose *Legend*', p. 204.
107 Printed by Hill, 'The Fifteenth-Century Prose *Legend*', pp. 212–22.
108 'A New Text', pp. 113–17, especially 113.

another twelfth-century witness which he regarded as the better witness: Hereford, Cathedral Library, MS. P.2.iv.

Fulcher of Chartres, Historia hierosolimitana

This twelfth-century crusading history is found in Cambridge, University Library, MS. Ii.4.4 [49] and in Douai, Bibliothèque municipale, MS. 882 [60]. While 60 contains the full text, that in 49 is truncated after Book III, s ix.[109]

Genealogy: Flemish counts

Found in MSS 54, 80, and 113: above, *Anglia habet* . . . .

Genealogy: Normans

'Anno ab incarnacione Domini .d.ccc.lxxui. Rollo . . .'

Found in MSS 22, 24, 32: see *Historia Turpini*, below.

'Normanni origine Dani .d.ccc.l.xxxui. . . .'

Thus begins a brief account of the origins of the Normans, found in **New Haven, Yale University Library, MS. 598 [129]**, and **Paris, BN, MSS lat. 13935 + 5508 [186]**. The text appears to be taken from Hugh of Saint-Victor's *Liber de tribus circumstantiis*.[110] It follows Geoffrey's History immediately in both manuscripts. Their contents do not otherwise agree.

Genealogy: Trojans

A genealogy of the Trojans beginning with Cyprius or Ciprus, ruler of Cyprus, is found in four *Historia*-manuscripts: **Cardiff, South Glamorgan Central Library, MS. 2.611 [55], Dublin, Trinity College, MS. 515 [67], Exeter, Cathedral Library, MS. 3514 [70], and Notre Dame, University Library, MS. 40 [130]**. While the first three of these are First-Variant witnesses, the last, 130, contains a vulgate text. This divergence is partly reflected in differences between

---

109 Hagenmeyer, *Fulcherii Carnotensis Historia*, p. 642.
110 Printed by Migne, *Patrologia latina*, CLXXVII.284. The whole text happens to be found in a twelfth-century manuscript to which Geoffrey's History was later added: Paris, Bibliothèque nationale, MS. 4999A + Manchester, John Rylands University Library, MS. 216 [165].

the versions of the genealogy which they contain. In 130, Ciprus is the son of Cetinus, but in the others his father is Ieuan or Yawan.[111] The text in 130, moreover, ends with Iaphet, son of Noah, and therefore seems to trace the ancestry of Cyprus, rather than that of his descendants; the three First-Variant manuscripts bring Cyprus's line down to the foundation of Britain. Both 70 and 67 end with the naming of the island (*Predae* or *Psedeyn* respectively). The text in Cardiff, however, ends '. . . a quibus tres partes Britannie nomina sortite sunt'. As for shared contents, both 70 and 130 contain the account of the Last Days attributed to Methodius (see below, *Methodius*) but in 130 this is in a physically separable part of the manuscript. Therefore the evidence is inconclusive at this stage.

Gerald of Wales

The most popular work of Gerald of Wales, *Topographia Hybernie*, is found in three *Historia*-manuscripts:
London, British Library, MS. Harley 4003 [103]
Oxford, Bodleian Library, MS. Laud misc. 720 [150]
Paris, Bibliothèque nationale, MS. lat. 4126 [164]

It probably also accompanied a fourth, now broken up, the *Historia* being now Aberystwyth, National Library of Wales, MS. 13210 [4], and the *Topographia*, Phillipps 26642.[112] Its presence in a fifth is witnessed by the contents-list in Aberystwyth, NLW, MS. Panton 37, an eighteenth-century transcript of a First-Variant manuscript [1]. The three manuscripts of the *Topographia* listed above have been classed by the work's editor as late editions: having undergone alteration or interpolation after that of the four twelfth-century recensions.[113] He does not mention Phillipps 26642.

Of Gerald's other works, *Expugnatio Hibernica* (beta-text) is found in 103[114] and is recorded as having belonged to the exemplar of 1, while *Descriptio Kambrie* (First Recension) is one of the fifteenth-century additions to London, BL, Cotton Nero D.viii [92] (for other such additions, see above, 'Anglia habet').[115]

Gesta Normannorum Ducum

A-redaction

London, British Library, MS. Cotton Nero D.viii [92]

---

111 Ieuan being the Welsh form (*ex inf.* David Dumville).
112 Strongman, 'John Parker's manuscripts', pp. 22–23. The present location of Phillipps 26642 is unknown. I know nothing of its palaeography.
113 Dimock, *apud* Brewer, *Opera*, V.xxv–xxvii; O'Meara, 'Giraldus', p. 178.
114 Bartlett, *Gerald*, p. 215.
115 *Ibid.*, p. 216.

D-redaction

Cambridge, Trinity College, MS. O.1.17 (1041) [38]
Würzburg, Universitätsbibliothek, MS. M.ch.f.140 [213]

F-redaction

Leiden, Bibliotheek der Rijksuniversiteit, MS. BPL 20 [76]
Leiden, Bibliotheek der Rijksuniversiteit, MS. Voss. lat. F.77 [77]
London, British Library, MS. Cotton Nero D.viii [92]

Gesta Normannorum ducum exists in a number of redactions, the oldest of which (C) was composed by William of Jumièges in 1070/1.[116] The D-redaction, with which two copies of Geoffrey's *Historia* travel, perhaps originated in England in the mid-twelfth century, the date being provided by the oldest witness of the redaction: Liège, Bibliothèque de l'Université, MS. 369C. This manuscript, probably written in northern England, was the exemplar for 38.[117] 213 was written in the sixteenth century and later belonged to the monastery of St James, Würzburg. Its antecedents are unknown.[118]

The F-redaction was composed by Robert de Torigni using a version by Orderic Vitalis.[119] 76, his autograph, therefore stands at the head of each of the six subgroups of the F-redaction. 77 belongs to the fourth of these, and 92 to the fifth.[120] In 92 the F-redaction is preceded by the A-redaction of the *Gesta*, which follows Dudo's History without any clear separation.[121] For the associations of the various contents of the F-redaction/*Historia* manuscripts, see above, *Epistola Alexandri*, Family I.

Gesta Saluatoris

The *Gesta Saluatoris* or Gospel of Nicodemus, among the most popular of the New Testament apocrypha in the Middle Ages, is derived from a Passion narrative composed in Greek in about 600 A.D.[122] To this was added an account of the Descent into Hell and the redemption of numerous souls, including those of Adam, Seth, John the Baptist, and the two eyewitnesses through whom the story is told: Karinus and Leucius. The most recent editor has conjectured that this section is the work of 'a highly inventive monk of the Latin West', written 'in order to document, by the official authority of the Roman Empire, the main tenets of the

116 Van Houts, *Gesta*, p. 307.
117 *Ibid.*, p. 35.
118 *Ibid.*
119 *Ibid.*, p. 307.
120 *Ibid.*, p. 43.
121 Other such Dudo-*Gesta* manuscripts listed by Huisman, 'Notes', p. 131.
122 Kim, *The Gospel*, pp. 1–2.

Christology in the Apostle's Creed'.[123] This account of the Descent commanded considerable attention in the Middle Ages, being alluded to in the Old English poem, the Dream of the Rood, for example.[124]

The first part of the text is a romanticized version of the Gospel story of the Passion, the whole supposedly preserved for posterity at Pilate's command. Christ is defended at his trial by the various figures on whom he performed miracles in the Bible, who stand up and tell their stories. The account is lent popular appeal by the naming of traditionally anonymous characters and the addition of super-natural elements.[125]

The *Gesta Saluatoris* appears in four *Historia*-manuscripts in a version close to that printed by Kim. Three have the same rubric and *incipit/explicit*:[126] **London, British Library, MSS Arundel 326 [88]** and **Sloane 289 [116]**, and **Paris, Bibliothèque nationale, MS. lat. 4999A**, part of the twelfth-century manuscript to which a copy of the *Historia* was added in the thirteenth or early fourteenth century (now Manchester, John Rylands Library, MS. 216 [165]). The fourth manuscript, **London, College of Arms, MS. Arundel 1 [118]**, has a slightly different rubric and *incipit*.[127] The separateness of 118 is confirmed by associated contents. Unlike the other three manuscripts, 118 does not include the pseudo-Methodian Revelations.

There is a fifth manuscript with a related version of the Gospel of Nicodemus: **Oxford, Christ Church, MS. 99 [160]**. This has no opening rubric and a slightly different *incipit*; it ends differently.[128] As this text occurs in a part of the manuscript which postdates and is physically distinct from that in which the *Historia* is found (although the binding shows that the two were associated before the end of the Middle Ages), it need not be considered further here.

Godfrey of Viterbo, Pantheon (extracts)

Two *Historia*-manuscripts contain material from the *Pantheon*, an encyclopaedic history, whose author served the German imperial court as chaplain and notary in the mid-twelfth century.[129] A series of paragraphs purportedly describing Roman history after Alexander's death is found in **London, British Library, MS. Cotton Galba E.xi [91]** and **Cambridge, St John's College, MS. G.16 [32]** (*Inc.* 'Post

123 *Ibid.*, p. 2.
124 Kim, *The Gospel*, pp. 6–7.
125 For example, the standards, as well as their bearers, bow their heads in veneration of Christ.
126 'In nomine Dei summi/ sancti Trinitatis incipiunt gesta saluatoris Domini nostri que inuenit Theodosius magnus imperator in Ierusalem in pretorio Poncii Pilati in codicibus publicis'. 'Factum est in anno .xix. imperii Tyberii . . . in codicibus publicis in pretorio suo'.
127 'De factis Iudeorum in Iesum que inuenit Theodosius magnus imperator . . .' etc. *Inc.* 'Factum est in anno *xiii*. . . .'
128 'Factum est in anno quinto decimo . . . quia ipsum credimus Dei filium qui cum patre . . .' etc.
129 Compare Manitius, *Geschichte*, III.392, 395–97.

mortem Alexandri in diuersis mundi partibus'), ending differently.[130] In 91, this is prefaced by seven lines 'De Gog et Magog ex scriptis Ysidori' ('Nota quod Alexander . . . at anichilatur'). 32 quotes the same material, more extensively, under similar rubrics 'De Gog et Magog' and then 'Ex scriptis Ysidori'.[131] Both manuscripts include, independently, other passages from the *Pantheon*.[132]

An analogy is provided by the story of Alexander following the Sibylline prophecies in both manuscripts with the rubric: 'Principium historie/hystorie magni Alexandri filii Philippi Macedonis/Macedoneos'. The texts which follow are broadly similar but are not the same.

It is impossible at this stage to gauge to what extent these similarities were inherited or coincidental (see also Alexander: *Epistola Alexandri*, ii). Coincidence is not improbable. The *Historia*-texts are quite unlike: 32 is vulgate and 91 Second-Variant. They extract from the *Pantheon* independently. Moreover, the selection of their contents is logical. The story of how Alexander confined Gog and Magog, an imprisonment to which they were condemned until the Last Times,[133] matches the apocalyptic tone of the Sibylline prophecies found in both manuscripts. 32 includes further eschatological material, Albuin's *De Antichristo*.

Guido delle Colonne, Historia destructionis Troie

Cambridge, University Library, MS. Dd.1.17 [40]
London, British Library, MS. Additional 35295 [84]
London, British Library, MS. Harley 4123 [104]
London, British Library, MS. Royal 15.C.xvi [115]
Paris, Bibliothèque nationale, MS. lat. 5697 [168][134]

Guido delle Colonne completed his *Historia Destructionis Troie* in 1287. Despite its claim to be based on the complementary sources of Dares Phrygius and Dictys Cretensis, it is a Latin translation of the *Roman de Troie* composed a century earlier by Benoît de Saint-Maure.[135] Benoît, who did use Dares and Dictys, recast the Trojan legend in medieval style, bringing the love stories into prominence and supplying descriptions of battle.[136] Guido's account, lent dignity by the use of Latin and a rhetorical style, omits some of Benoît's romantic excesses, allowing it to be considered historical.[137]

130 [Herold,] *Pantheon*, cols 270–73 (MS. 32).
131 *Ibid.*, cols 266–67.
132 32: 'De disputacione inter Alexandrum et regem Bragmanorum', 'Hystoria Anglorum'; [Herold,] *Pantheon*, cols 267–70 and 606–17. 91: 'Hic est finis imperii Persarum', *ibid.*, cols 262–63.
133 On which see Cary, *The Medieval Alexander*, p. 130.
134 Guido's History also forms the companion volume to Leningrad, Saltykov-Shcedrin State Public Library, MS. F.IV. 76: Sutton and Visser-Fuchs, 'Richard III's books'.
135 Meek, *Historia destructionis Troie*, p. xi.
136 *Ibid.*, p. xiii.
137 *Ibid.*, p. xv.

The works of Guido delle Colonne and Geoffrey of Monmouth – both Latin 'histories' incorporating romantic material – seem to have been considered akin: they are adjacent in all of these manuscripts except 40, Guido's work preceding Geoffrey's in all except 104. There is no clear association between these manuscripts, however. The Chronicle of Martinus Polonus, found in 40, is present in 104 in a section additional to that which contains the *Historia*.[138] 40 and 168 both contain *Historia Turpini*, but in different versions (see below, *Historia Turpini*).

Haytonus, Flos Historiarum

Cambridge, University Library, MS. Dd.1.17 [40]
London, British Library, MS. Harley 5115 [105]
Paris, Bibliothèque nationale, MS. lat. 6041A [172]

Rubrics prefacing Hayton's *Flos historiarum* declare that he, 'Chursi consanguineus regis Armenie', wrote at the command of the pope; Hayton was in fact of mixed Frankish/Armenian parentage and had come to Europe from the East in the early fourteenth century. The *Flos*, 'un vaste et précieux ouvrage sur les Mongols de son temps', was written in French for the use of Westerners.[139]

In three manuscripts, this work seems to have become associated with the *Historia* independently. 40 has very numerous and varied contents, of which only one other is found in 105 – the Book of Marco Polo. The connection with 172 would seem to be stronger – both contain *Testamenta duodecim patriarcharum* and *Historia Turpini* – but this latter text is found in a different form (see below, *Historia Turpini*).

Henry of Huntingdon

Historia Anglorum

In Geoffrey's epilogue to his History (§208), where he stakes his claim to British history, he names Henry of Huntingdon and William of Malmesbury as authorities on the separate, if related, subject of English kings. Despite Geoffrey's claim to independence, his History and Henry's were mutually indebted. Henry was the first recorded historian to have encountered the work (above, Intoduction) and he took account of it when revising his History.[140] Copies of the revisions of 1138, 1147, 1148, and 1154 are associated with manuscripts of Geoffrey's *Historia*.

The complementary nature of these two histories is evident from the earliest manuscript in which they are found together: **Ushaw College MS. 6 [210]** – a twelfth-century copy of Geoffrey's *Historia* into which Henry's *Historia Anglo-*

---

138 *Historia* dated 1349; additions made in formal late Gothic script.
139 Cahen, *La Syrie*, p. 100.
140 Greenway, 'Henry', p. 106 and p. 111 & n. 42.

rum was interpolated shortly afterwards. The original copy of Geoffrey's *Historia* was split at §178 (the coming of Augustine) and the 1138 edition of Henry's work was inserted, except for the first two books and the prologue to the third, which dealt with events before that point (see below, IV).[141]

The second *Historia*-manuscript containing Henry's History is **Rouen, Bibliothèque municipale, MS. U.74 (1177) [200]**, a manuscript of *c.* 1200 from Jumièges. This has the 1147 edition of Henry's work, the witnesses of which, Diana Greenway has argued, are derived from a copy at the nearby house of Le Bec whose text was used by Robert de Torigni (who first drew Henry's attention to Geoffrey's *Historia*).[142] The version of Geoffrey's History in 200 likewise belongs to a Norman family of manuscripts.[143]

The *Historia*-manuscript **Cambridge, St John's College, G.16 [32]**, contains a *Historia Anglorum* belonging to the third and largest group of the 1148 manuscripts, one subject to corruption and interpolation.[144]

Exeter, Cathedral Library, MS. 3514 [70] includes a copy of Henry's 1148 edition, extended to 1154 in a different hand.[145] Like 200, MS. 70 has the rubric 'Incipit prologus historie Anglorum contexte ab Henrico Huntendunensi archidiacono anno gracie .mcxxxv.' listed by Greenway in eight manuscripts of varying editions.[146] The connection between the two Histories is at some remove in 70 as the Geoffrey formed a later addition to a thirteenth-century manuscript containing Henry's work.

The final copy of the two histories, **Cambridge, University Library, MS. Dd.1.17 [40]**, is an abbreviated version of the corrupt 1148 text continued to 1154 from a further modification of Henry's History.[147] It is attributed to Marianus Scotus.

A further manuscript, Bruxelles, Bibliothèque royale, MS. 8495–8505 [18] contains part of Henry's text *De uiris illustribus* which forms Book IX, or in some classifications Book X, of his History.[148] The variety of versions of Henry's History found with that of Geoffrey suggests that the two works were placed together independently on several occasions: inherited association is not immediately perceptible in any of these manuscripts.

---

141 Levison, 'A Combined Manuscript', p. 43.
142 'Henry', pp. 109 & 112. As well as a complete version of the text, MS. 200 includes fragments from Book X (on fos 267r–278vb): Dumville, 'An Early Text', p. 6. The identification was omitted in error from Crick, *The Historia*, III.305.
143 See Dumville, 'An Early Text', especially p. 22.
144 Greenway, 'Henry', pp. 117–18.
145 *Ibid.*, p. 106.
146 *Ibid.*, p. 109.
147 Greenway, 'Henry', p. 120. See also Dumville, 'An Early Text', pp. 9–11.
148 This manuscript was not discussed by Greenway: 'Henry'.

Letter to King Henry I

This work (*Inc.* 'Cum mecum propter ea que responsione tua accepi tractarem . . .') follows Geoffrey's History in **Cambridge, University Library, MS. Dd.1.17 [40]** directly and in **BL Royal 13.D.i [111]** separated by pseudo-Turpin. They share other, more substantial texts (below, *Higden, Testamenta*).

Ranulph Higden, Polichronicon

Cambridge, Gonville & Caius College, MS. 249/277 [29]
Cambridge, University Library, MS. Dd.1.17 [40]
[London, British Library, MS. Cotton Nero D.viii [92]]
London, British Library, MS. Royal 13.D.i [111]
Oxford, Bodleian Library, MS. Oriel 16 [152]

This universal history, composed in the early fourteenth century, was widely read and circulated and became a standard work.[149] It is found with Geoffrey's History in five manuscripts, in four cases in the so-called AB 'intermediate' version.[150] The text is identical in 111 and 152, where it is divided into seven books, the last being continued to 1377 (*expl.* 'puer .uii. annorum'); the *capitula*-list extends from Abraham to Zorobabel. This continuation, known as A, is derived from St Albans material and parts of the *Chronicon* of the monk of that house, Thomas Walsingham.[151] The text and continuation in 40 is truncated at both ends but is of the same type.[152] Therefore we may look for further connections between these three manuscripts. MS. 29 contains a text similarly divided, but extended to 1376 not 1377 by the so-called (B) continuation, composed in or after the reign of Richard II.[153] The *capitula*-list begins with Abel, not Abraham. The (B) continuation is also found in the fifteenth-century copy of the Polichronicon added to 92. This does not include a *capitula*-list. It is the only *Historia*-manuscript to be accompanied by the earlier CD version of Higden's text.[154]

An example of how the *Historia* and the *Polichronicon* could be used in tandem comes from a note in a further manuscript, BL Sloane 289 [116], which reports that Geoffrey's account has been compared with Higden's and discrepancies have been observed.[155]

149 On the Polichronicon's success, see Taylor, *English Historical Literature*, pp. 97–103; Edwards, 'The Influence'; on its appeal see Gransden, *Historical Writing*, II.44–55.
150 On which see Taylor, *The Universal Chronicle*, pp. 89, 98–100.
151 *Ibid.*, pp. 122, 180–81.
152 *Ibid.*, p. 180.
153 *Ibid.*, pp. 113–14 and 178.
154 *Ibid.*, p. 97.
155 116, 2v: 'In principio istius libri notandum est quod licet in aliquibus libris pollacronicon non concordant annorum numeri in denotacione temporum quin fit excessus uel defectio m[ ]norum in uno uel in alio . . .'.

Historia Brittonum

The ninth-century pseudo-historical composition, the *Historia Brittonum*, accompanies Geoffrey's History in seven extant manuscripts, of which six contain the version attributed to Gildas. These may be grouped according to their rubrics:

Group 1

'Incipit gesta Britonum a Gilda sapiente composita'
Cambridge, University Library, MS. Mm.5.29 (2434) [54]
Lincoln, Cathedral Library, MS. 98 (A.4.6) [80]
London, British Library, MS. Royal 13.D.v [113]

Group 2

'Incipit liber Gilde sapientis de primis habitatoribus Britannie que nunc dicitur Anglia et de excidio eius'
Rouen, Bibliothèque municipale, MS. U.74 (1177) [200]

Group 3

'Incipiunt excerptiones de libro Gilde sapientis quem composuit de primis habitatoribus Brittannie que nunc Anglia dicitur et de excidio eius'
Leiden, Bibliotheek der Rijksuniversiteit, MS. BPL 20 [76]
London, British Library, MS. Cotton Nero D.viii [92]

Connections between other contents in groups 1 and 3 have already been seen (above, *Anglia habet*; *Alexander: Epistola Alexandri*, Family I). 200 stands on its own but it has been argued that its rubrics are ancestral to those of group 3.[156] The *Historia Brittonum* follows Geoffrey's History in all the manuscripts listed above in these groups.[157]

The seventh manuscript with the *Historia Brittonum*, **London, British Library, Additional MS. 11702 [81]**, contains the Vatican recension. It was written, perhaps in southern France, in the early fourteenth century,[158] and is apparently unconnected with the manuscripts discussed above which have Anglo-Norman provenances or associations and are dateable in or before the early thirteenth century.

---

156 Dumville, 'An Early Text', p. 5.
157 In 92, the connection is even closer, the *Historia Brittonum* being marked as the twelfth book of Geoffrey's *Historia*.
158 See Dumville, *The Historia Brittonum*, III.33.

Historia Gothorum, Wandalorum, Sueuorum

Histories of these peoples are found in one vulgate manuscript, Paris, BN, lat. MS. 6815 [181], and a First-Variant witness, Paris, Bibliothèque de l'Arsenal, MS. 982 [163]. Given that these manuscripts contain different *Historia*-versions and that they share no other contents, it seems that the presence of these histories here is coincidental.

Historia Turpini

Cambridge, Clare College, MS. N'.1.5 (27) [22]
Cambridge, Corpus Christi College, MS. 292 [24]
Cambridge, Corpus Christi College, MS. 414 [25]
Cambridge, St. John's College, MS. G.16 (184) [32]
Cambridge, University Library, MS. Dd.1.17 [40]
[London, British Library, MS. Harley 6358 [106]]
London, British Library, MS. Royal 13.D.i [111]
Paris, Bibliothèque nationale, MS. lat. 5697 [168]
Paris, Bibliothèque nationale, MS. lat. 6041A [172]
Paris, Bibliothèque nationale, MS. lat. 7531 [182]

The Chronicle attributed to Turpin, an eighth-century archbishop of Reims, is one part of the huge body of Charlemagne literature which includes the Chanson de Roland and later vernacular gestes. The *Historia Turpini* is a fabulous account of Charlemagne's Spanish expeditions which followed an apparition of St James at Compostela.[159]

The complex tradition of Pseudo-Turpin has been analysed in print three times in the last fifty years: by H. M. Smyser, who concentrated on manuscripts preserving an early version, by Charles Meredith-Jones using forty-nine manuscripts, and by André de Mandach, who attempted to survey the whole Charlemagne tradition.[160] All three agree in placing MS. 111 in the most archaic Turpin tradition (A).[161] Meredith-Jones and Mandach record that 40 is a direct copy of 111, Mandach adding that it belongs to a family of the archaic tradition associated with Saint-Denis and its Anglo-Norman dependencies.[162] Meredith-Jones identified two further textual groups and a final category, D, which contains those manuscripts not found in A–C. As Mandach extended and refined this classifica-

---

159 Summaries given by Ward, *apud* Ward & Herbert, *Catalogue of Romances*, I.546–60; Mandach, *Naissance*, pp. 79–81.
160 Smyser, *The Pseudo-Turpin*; *Historia Karoli*; *Naissance*.
161 Smyser, *The Pseudo-Turpin*, p. 54; Meredith-Jones, *Historia Karoli*, p. 7; Mandach, *Naissance*, p. 368.
162 Meredith-Jones, *Historia Karoli*, p. 9; Mandach, *Naissance*, p. 368, also 93–99, esp. p. 98.

tion, including three of the four *Historia*-Turpin manuscripts omitted by Meredith-Jones, I propose to follow his account.

Mandach identified 25, 168, and 172 as belonging, independently, to the version of Turpin compiled in the 1130s at Vézelay. Manuscripts of this type include a letter of authentication of the book's contents which states that it was compiled by Pope Calixtus II (formerly Guy de Bourgogne), then deposited at Compostela by a Poitevin, Aimery Picaud, and a Fleming, Gerberge. Picaud was priest of a church of St James under the overlordship of Albéric, abbot of Vézelay (on the Way of St James) (1131–38) and later cardinal-bishop of Ostia.[163] The three Geoffrey-Turpin manuscripts listed above do not fit into any of the three sub-categories of the Vézelay version identified by Mandach, but are grouped among 'les dispersés'.

Aimery's manuscript was apparently revised at Compostela in 1155–65, and material about the pilgrimage route of St James was collected together into a pilgrim's guide, with the addition of two chapters on Compostela itself.[164] 182 belongs to this stage, and was probably the exemplar for two extant copies from Pavia and Avignon.[165]

106 and 24, the remaining *Historia*-Turpin manuscripts listed by Mandach, are associated by him with the sixteenth stage of the transmission, which formed the 'lien primordial des grandes Gestes de Charlemagne du Nord-Ouest de l'Europe'.[166] Mandach identifies as the source of this version a copy made at Compostela in 1171 by Geoffrey du Breuil, historian of the court of Eleanor of Aquitaine and prior of Saint-Pierre de Vigeois, Limousin. Geoffrey's corrected version apparently reached the Plantagenet court, where it was combined with a Picaud-type text.[167] 106, copied in 1200–1216 for Rudolf de Blundeville, was a descendant of this union.[168] 24 is another early thirteenth-century descendant of the same archetype but one contaminated by a vernacular chronicle.[169]

There are two *Historia*-Turpin manuscripts not mentioned by Mandach: 22 and 32. M. R. James noted the resemblance of the Turpin text in 22 to that in 106.[170] Possible confirmation that the Clare manuscript indeed belongs to Mandach's sixteenth stage (named C) is provided by two texts which follow Turpin's chronicle in all three manuscripts; they are a genealogy of the Franks (*Inc.* 'Ex genere Priami fuit Moroueus . . .') followed by an account of the Anglo-Norman kings from their origins to approximately the thirteenth century

---

163 Mandach, *Naissance*, p. 122; Louis, 'Aimery Picaud'.
164 *Naissance*, p. 129.
165 Mandach, *ibid.*, p. 383. He attributes a date of 1373 to 182 without stating his reason. This date is improbable on palaeographical grounds and it is irreconcilable with the thirteenth-century date he gives for one of its supposed copies.
166 *Naissance*, p. 129.
167 *Ibid*, p. 130.
168 Mandach, *Naissance*, p. 385.
169 *Ibid.*, p. 387, 103–5.
170 *A Descriptive Catalogue of the Western manuscripts in the library of Clare College*, p. 44. Note also that the rubrics of the pseudo-Turpin in MS. 24 resemble those in 22.

(*Inc.* 'Anno ab incarnacione Domini .d.ccc. .lxxui. Rollo cum suis Normanniam penetrauit . . .'). Having found the same texts in 24 – the other known copy of Geoffrey's Historia and the C-Turpin –[171] and in a control C-manuscript, Paris, Bibliothèque nationale, MS. lat. 3768.4, I conclude that this is the genealogy described by Mandach as one of the additions of Geoffrey du Breuil.[172] The inclusion of the same genealogies in 32 suggests that it too is connected with the C-version of Turpin. The relationship between 22, 32, 24 and 106 does not, however, seem particularly close. In 32 and 24, the Anglo-Norman king-list ends with Edward I, while that in 106 ends with John, and in 22, with Henry III. There is a comparable variety in the texts of Geoffrey's History which they contain. 24 and 32 are vulgate witnesses while 22 has a Second-Variant text, and 106, a First-Variant. In 106, the Turpin follows the *Historia* as a discrete, and slightly later unit.

Innocent III

Innocent III's *De mysteriis misse* is found in two *Historia*-manuscripts: London, BL, MS. Cotton Titus A.xviii [93] and Oxford, Christ Church, MS. 99 [160]. 93 contains only an extract (on the opening flyleaves). The entire text is present in 160 but in a separable section of the manuscript which postdates that containing the *Historia*.

Jacques de Vitry

Cambridge, University Library, MS. Dd.1.17 [40]
London, British Library, MS. Galba E.xi [91]
London, College of Arms, MS. Arundel 1 [118]
Troyes, Bibliothèque municipale, MS. 1531 [209]

Jacques de Vitry wrote his *Historia hierosolimitana abbreuiata* after three years (1218–21) spent as bishop of Acre (1216–28) with the army of the Fifth Crusade in the East. He had begun his career in the Schools, first at Paris as a student then master, and later teaching at Liège, before becoming cardinal-bishop of Frascati (1229–40).[173] His History was planned as three books. The first describes the East – the historical background to the Crusades and a description of the area's geography, peoples, and natural history. The second narrates events in the West leading to the Crusades. Jacques never completed the third but it may have been

---

171 It should be noted, however, that the end of the Turpin in this manuscript is supplied in a sixteenth-century hand.
172 *Naissance*, pp. 131, 385. Not printed by Smyser or Meredith-Jones.
173 These details of his life from Hinnebusch, *The 'Historia occidentalis'*, pp. 3–10, and Huygens, *Lettres*, p. 1.

intended to give an account of the period between the Lateran Council and the capture of Damietta on the Fifth Crusade. The *Historia hierosolimitana* has been seen as narrow in its sources of information and in moral outlook[174] but it is a serious history, none the less.

The four *Historia*-manuscripts in which it is found contain only the first book, the *Historia orientalis*.[175] Two of these – 91 and 209 – witness the Second-Variant α-form of Geoffrey's work. The history of the emperors and popes by Martinus Polonus is also found in both, but in sections additional to the main part of the manuscript. There are no contents common to the vulgate manuscripts, 118 and 40: the presence of slightly differing Alexander-collections (with associated texts) in 118 and 91[176] seems coincidental.

Libellus Bemetoli

Cambridge, University Library, MS. Mm.5.29 [54]
Lincoln, Cathedral Library, MS. 98 [80]

This title is taken from the rubric to an epitome of the *Reuelationes* of pseudo-Methodius: 'Incipit libellus Bemetoli quem beatus Ieronimus de Greco in Latinum transtulit uel composuit'.[177] The same text and rubrics are found in Bodley 163, the source of a number of texts found in 54 (see above, *Anglia habet*).

Liber prouincialis

An account of the metropolitans and office-holders of the church beginning 'In ciuitate Romana sunt .v. ecclesie que patriarchales dicuntur . . .' and with an intermediate section 'Iuxta tradiciones ueterum' is found in six *Historia*-manuscripts.[178] It seems to have been widely circulated; it exists in multiple copies, several of those recorded by Hauréau being in German manuscripts.[179] In **London, College of Arms, MS. Arundel 1 [118]** and **Cambridge, Gonville and Caius College, MS. 249/277 [29]**, the text ends '. . . usque ad natiuitatem Christi .dcclii. annos'. In two others – Cambridge, Trinity College, MS. O.1.17 [38] and Oxford, Christ Church, MS. 99 [160] – it concludes with the archbishop of Cologne

---

174 Hinnebusch, *The 'Historia occidentalis'*, pp. 15 & 27.
175 Edited by Bongars, *Gesta Dei per Francos*, I.ii.1049–1124.
176 Respectively *Epistola* (III), *Gesta + Epitaphium*, Apollonius; *Gesta + Epitaphium*, *Epistola* (II), Sibylline prophecies.
177 It seems that *Bemetoli* is a corruption of *beati Methodii*. On the Revelations, see below, *Methodius*.
178 Compare Miraeus, *Notitia episcopatuum*, pp. 65–91. Printed from London, British Library, MS. Cotton Nero D.i by Luard, *Matthæi Parisiensis monachi sancti Albani, chronica majora*, VI.449–63.
179 *Initia*, III.119; Appendix I.270.

(ending '. . . nullum habet suffraganum'). The text is incomplete in the other manuscripts. In Dublin, Trinity College, MS. 496 [65] the beginning is lost and the remainder is difficult to make out. Some sections are comparable with the other copies but it is clear that they do not follow the same order. The text forms an addition in Dublin, Trinity College, MS. 514 [66], where it breaks off after the first verso. Except for 66, which is Second-Variant (α), all these manuscripts are vulgate. None shares any further contents.

Mappa mundi

Descriptions of the world are found in different forms in *Historia*-manuscripts. The earliest of these is **London, British Library, MS. Harley 3773 [102]**, a manuscript of *c*. 1200, perhaps from the Low Countries, in which fos 57r–74v are occupied by an account beginning 'Decriptio (*sic*) hec uniuersitati orbis comparata'. Three other *Historia*-manuscripts including world descriptions date from the fourteenth century or later. **London, British Library, MS. Harley 4123 [104]**, includes a succinct list of countries beginning 'Iste sunt partes mundi. Asia. Europa. Affrica . . .'. The version in **BL, Royal 13.D.i [111]** begins similarly, but it provides a connected description rather than a list. **London, College of Arms, MS. Arundel 1 [118]** includes a brief account in which the tripartite division of the world prefaces a list of kingdoms and provinces. This has the title 'Diuisio totius mundi'; 'Mappa mundi' is reserved for a more discursive account (fos 4r–7v).

Marco Polo

Cambridge, University Library, MS. Dd.1.17 [40]
London, British Library, MS. Harley 5115 [105]

Marco Polo's account of the East, composed at the end of the thirteenth century, achieved currency in several versions in the later Middle Ages, the most wide-spread being a Latin translation – the original was in French – made by Pipino *c*. 1320.[180] As well as a narrative of the travels of Marco himself and those of his uncle and father, the book provides historical information about the Mongol Empire and a description of the East:[181] a conventional physical geography with a largely original ethnography.[182]

In both 40 and 105, this work is followed by that of Hayton: separated from the *Historia* in 105 only by an account of the foundation of Albion (see above, *Ab origine mundi*) and by many contents in 40. There are no other connections

---

180 Ross, 'Marco Polo', p. 191.
181 *Ibid.*, pp. 187–88.
182 See Olschki, *Marco Polo's Asia*, pp. 130–32.

between the *Historia*-manuscripts in which it is found; the presence of Geoffrey in two manuscripts of Marco may well be due to chance, both being very common books.[183]

Martinus Polonus

Cambridge, University Library, MS. Dd.1.17 [40]
[London, British Library, MS. Cotton Galba E.xi [91]]
[London, British Library, MS. Harley 4123 [104]]
London, British Library, MS. Royal 13.A.v [110]
[London, British Library, MS. Royal 14.C.i [114]]
[Notre Dame, University Library, MS. 40 [130]]
Oxford, Bodleian Library, MS. Laud misc. 579 [147]
Oxford, Christ Church, MS. 99 [160]
Paris, Bibliothèque nationale, MS. lat. 6815 [181]
[Troyes, Bibliothèque municipale, MS. 1531 [209]]
Winchester, Cathedral Library, MS. 9 [212]

The chronicle of the popes and emperors completed by Martinus Polonus in the 1270s was widely circulated in the original Latin and in translation.[184] Despite his nickname, Martinus came from Opava, Czechoslovakia, whence he moved via a monastery in Prague to Italy, where he served as confessor and chaplain to Popes Clement IV and Nicholas III from 1265 until his death in 1278. The popularity of his work is attested by the numerous surviving manuscripts – 275 according to a recently published study.[185] This figure will certainly rise: Anna-Dorothea von den Brincken, the author of the study, failed to record five of the eleven manuscripts listed above.

She has established a six-part classification of the tradition. On her own admission, her criteria are superficial, being based on the layout of the papal and imperial narratives of which the chronicle is composed. She places four *Historia*-manuscripts in her class III, the best-represented category: 104 belongs to subdivision a, found especially in England, and 40, 114, and 147 to the b.[186] MS. 181 is found in class IVa.[187]

In MSS 40 and 147, the text ends '. . . sollicite prosequenda'. That in 160, not mentioned by Brincken, also ends here, suggesting that it might also be classed IIIb. The extent of the Chronicle is different in the other *Historia*-manuscripts. The version in 110 ends at 1277 while that in 212 is continued to the pontificate of John XXII (1311–34). In several manuscripts (indicated by brackets in the

---

183 Penzer, *The Most Noble and Famous Travels*, p. xxiv.
184 Molinier *et al.*, *Les Sources*, III.174. Ed. Weiland, MGH, SS, XXII.397–464.
185 Brincken, 'Studien', p. 468.
186 Brincken, pp. 483–85.
187 *Ibid.*, p. 487.

above list), the work appears in a section of the volume separable from that containing the *Historia*.

A further *Historia*-witness – Oxford, Bodleian Library, MS. Jesus College 2 [142] – is not accompanied by other works but is heavily interpolated and annotated with material mostly taken from Martinus (see below, IV: *Interpolations*).[188]

Meditationes

A series of *meditationes*, sometimes attributed to Bernard of Clairvaux, sometimes to Hugh of Saint-Victor (*Inc.* 'Multi multa sciunt'), is found in two *Historia*-manuscripts with otherwise disparate contents: **Roma, Biblioteca Apostolica Vaticana, MS. Ottoboni lat. 1472 [194]** and **Cambridge, Trinity College, MS. O.1.17 [38].** In 38 it has no title but in 194 there is the rubric: 'Incipit speculum anime . . .'. Hauréau listed many copies.[189]

Methodius

The seventh-century tract attributed to Methodius, bishop of Patara (martyred in the early fourth century), has been described as a high point in the Eastern apocalyptic tradition.[190] Originally composed in Syriac,[191] it was translated into Latin in the eighth century and was disseminated at Charlemagne's court.[192] Like the tracts on Antichrist which followed and possibly imitated it,[193] the pseudo-Methodian Revelations concern the Last Emperor. This emperor, called here *rex Romanorum*, is destined to defeat the pagan nations, but the reign of Antichrist will be heralded when the twenty-two kings (including Gog and Magog) whom Alexander confined behind the Gates of the North break through and create carnage on the Earth. The popularity of this text at the Carolingian court is not surprising, considering that it associated the *rex Romanorum* with a reign of military glory (see above, *De Antichristo*). Its original purpose, however, seems to have been to exhort the Eastern Christians in the face of the Moslem threat, the *rex* being the Byzantine emperor.[194] The work enjoyed analogous popularity in

188 Brincken has seen the inclusion of the *Liber prouincialis* in certain manuscripts of Martinus's Chronicle as a reflection of his position in the papal curia: p. 474. This seems improbable, considering how frequently this work appears in other contexts, for example with the *Historia*.

189 *Initia*, IV.110–11. A work of the same name, presumably in translation, is sometimes recorded in secular libraries. See Cavanaugh, 'A Study', pp. 331, 767.

190 McGinn, *Visions*, p. 70.

191 *Ibid.*

192 Reeves, *The Influence*, p. 300.

193 McGinn, *Visions*, p. 83.

194 *Ibid.*, p. 71.

the thirteenth century, providing 'a consolatory prophecy at the time of the Mongol invasions'.[195] Its association in *Historia*-manuscripts with other apocalyptic material shows that interest in it also stemmed from more general concerns.

An apparently full form of the text is found in six *Historia*-manuscripts: **Cambridge, MS. St John's College, G.16 [32]; Exeter, Cathedral Library, MS. 3514 [70]; London, British Library, MSS Arundel 326 [88] and Sloane 289 [116]; Notre Dame, University Library, MS. 40 [130]; Paris, Bibliothèque nationale, MS. lat. 4126 [164].**[196] In all of these except 70, the text is prefaced by an introductory paragraph 'In nomine Christi incipit liber Methodii episcopi et martiris . . .'. 70 is otherwise anomalous in being a witness to the First Variant and not the vulgate. Of the remainder, the link between 88 and 116 is well established (above, *Chronology, In principio* . . .). Some share other contents but they do not reveal any significant connections. Dares' History is found in 32, 164 and, no doubt coincidentally, in 70. The *Epistola Alexandri* is also found in the first two manuscripts but as that in 32 belongs to the second family, and that in the 164 to the fourth, it would seem that this repetition of contents is again coincidental. The Sibylline prophecies are found in 32, 88, and 116, as are tracts on Antichrist, but that in 32 is by Albuinus, while the others contain the Anselmian version.

Another *Historia*-manuscript apparently contains an epitome of pseudo-Methodius, beginning as usual (without the prefatory paragraph, however) but ending differently.[197] This is the Second-Variant **Bruges, Bibliothèque municipale, MS. 428 [17]**. A further epitome of the work, in less recognizable form, is found in two other Second-Variant witnesses (see above, *Libellus Bemetoli*).

Mirabilia Brittonum

In his History, Geoffrey regales his readers with a description of Loch Lomond's sixty streams and sixty islands topped by sixty crags and sixty eagle's nests (§149). Nearby there is a pool whose four corners are each populated by a different kind of fish, a marvel which leads Geoffrey to another: the mysterious bore of the River Severn (§150). The inclusion in the *Historia* of geographical wonders follows an established tradition in the British Isles. A lavishly illustrated pre-conquest bilingual manuscript of the Marvels of the East attests early interest there.[198] The inspiration and source of Geoffrey's account, however, is similar material incorporated in the ninth-century *Historia Brittonum*.

Five *Historia*-manuscripts include *mirabilia* found as a separate text. These

---

195 *Ibid.*, p. 72.
196 'Sciendum namque nobis est fratres karissimi quomodo in principio creauit . . . per secula seculorum. Amen'. This does not seem to correspond with the version printed by Sackur, *Sibyllinische Texte*, pp. 59–96.
197 '. . . Antichristo autem interfecto consummatio seculi et iudicium Dei appropinquabit'.
198 BL Cotton Tiberius B.v, part i.

are accompanied by a further item from the *Historia Brittonum*: a short account of the peopling of the continents by the descendants of the sons of Noah. In four of the manuscripts – **Cambridge, Sidney Sussex, MS. 75 [34], Madrid, Biblioteca nacional, MS. 6319 [125], Oxford, Bodleian Library, MS. Oriel College 16 [152]** and **Saint-Omer, BM, MS. 710 [202]** – the works are immediately preceded by Geoffrey's History. The text in 202 is quite extensive, running 'Primum miraculum est stagnum Lumonoy . . . non longe a terra'. In the other three, the *Mirabilia* follow an account of the descent of nations 'Post diluuium tribus filiis Noe . . . et repleuerunt Europiam et de his actenus' and begin 'Primum si quidem miraculum Britannie stangnum Lummonoim . . . ad paruum inuenitur' (the *explicit* is virtually illegible in 125).[199] No other shared contents are found in any of these manuscripts. The fifth *Historia*-manuscript to include separate *mirabilia* is **Dublin, Trinity College, MS. 496 [65]**. These are found at 226r–227v, the *Historia* occupying 9r–123v. Besides being separated by numerous works, they fall in different units of the manuscript. Here the *mirabilia* precede the other account. The texts are different from those described above: 'Primum miraculum est stangnum Iumonium . . . inuenitur p[ ]i lapides', 'Tres filii Noe diuiserunt orbem . . . Uenedochia id est North Wales et [Cornubia]'.[200]

Nicodemus

See above, *Gesta Saluatoris*.

Pergama flere uolo

These words begin a poem concerning the fall of Troy which sometimes goes under the grecizing title of 'Threni de excidio Troie'. Hammer, who classed the poem as doggerel, printed it from the *Historia*-manuscript **Douai, Bibliothèque municipale, MS. 880 [59]**, 13v–14v.[201] He presumed that it should be taken together with a series of verses found in this manuscript in which a certain Bernardus declares his authorship:

> Haec Bernardus ego, qui sub Domini cruce dego,
> Scriptis allego scriptaque saepe lego.[202]

'Pergama flere uolo', however, enjoyed a considerable separate circulation. Also, as Faral pointed out, there is no correspondence between the metrical scheme of 'Pergama' and the Bernardus poems, and therefore no reason *prima facie* to regard

---

199 Edited by Dumville, 'Anecdota'. Compare also Mommsen, MGH, AA, XIII.1, 213–19.
200 Edited by Dumville, *ibid*.
201 'Some Leonine Summaries', pp. 121–22. This item was omitted from the catalogue-description in ignorance: Crick, *The Historia*, III.93.
202 'Some Leonine Summaries', pp. 115 and 119–21.

59 as ancestral to these copies.[203] Faral also rejected the ascription to Hildebert found in a few manuscripts.[204] Further work on 'Pergama' has since led to the conclusion that the poem was a twelfth-century work whose material was subsequently reused in other contemporary poems on the same theme, as that by Simon Chèvre d'Or.[205]

The demise of Hammer's theory about Douai 880 lessens expectations of a close connection between those other *Historia*-manuscripts containing *Pergama*. **Douai, Bibliothèque municipale, MS. 882 [60]**, which contains other verses found in 59, provides an exception (below, III: Scribal Verses). Other *Historia*-manuscripts containing *Pergama* are **Paris, Bibliothèque nationale, MS. lat. 4126 [164]** and **London, British Library, MS. Additional 35295 [84]**, and the poem is copied on to the flyleaves of **Cambridge, St John's College, MS. G.16 (184) [32]**. Indeed, there is no immediately apparent link between these manuscripts. 164, 60, and 32 all contain Dares' History, but association with Trojan material is entirely predictable. In 164, Dares and *Pergama* are found within a group of other Trojan texts, including those of Simon Chèvre d'Or and Hildebert, and even in 84, *Pergama* occurs with the Trojan history by Guido delle Colonne. All but 84 also contain the *Epistola Alexandri* but in different forms (see above, Alexander: *Epistola Alexandri*).[206]

Petrus Alphonsus

The *Disciplina clericalis* is the second work of Petrus Alphonsus, a converted Spanish Jew, born *c*. 1050. Its evident popularity – at least fifty manuscripts are extant[207] – is easily understood. Peter used the device of the words of advice and wisdom given by a dying Arab to his son to lend coherence to a mass of stories, fables, and sayings from Arab philosophers, as well as remarks on specific disciplines like grammar and philosophy. Famous figures are invoked, like Socrates and Enoch, and subjects guaranteed to fire popular imagination are included – Alexander stories, black magic.[208]

The text occurs, apparently coincidentally, in three *Historia*-manuscripts: each represents a different version of the *Disciplina*. In **Bern, Burgerbibliothek, MS. 568 [15]**, the text follows the printed version (beginning imperfectly at the middle of Exemplum II), to the middle of Exemplum XIV '. . . quod eam intrare non permittat'. Here it diverges and comes to an end. The *Disciplina* in **Paris, Bibliothèque nationale, MS. lat. 4126 [164]** is also shorter than the printed

203 Faral, 'Le Manuscrit 511', p. 48 and 50.
204 *Ibid.*, p. 50.
205 Boutemy, 'Le Poème *Pergama flere uolo* . . .'.
206 Leningrad, Saltykov-Shcedrin State Public Library, MS. F.IV.74, a companion volume to the *Historia*, contains an extract from *Pergama*: Sutton & Visser-Fuchs, 'Richard III's Books', p. 142, and n. 28.
207 Hilka & Söderhjelm, *Die Disciplina Clericalis*, p. VIII.
208 See Manitius, *Geschichte*, III.274–76.

version. It departs from it after the middle of Exemplum XIX[209] but continues to Exemplum XXVII, apparently paraphrasing. **San Marino, Henry E. Huntington Library, MS. EL 34.C.9 (1121) [204]** offers the closest comparison with the printed edition, which it appears to follow until Exemplum XXXI, where the manuscript is mutilated.

Prester John

The fabulous account of the riches and marvels associated with the Indian priest-potentate, John, was apparently written before 1177 in Germany and was presented, according to a letter prefacing the work in the earliest manuscripts, to Emperor Frederick I.[210] The text has been seen as an idealized projection of Frederick's concept of church-state relations, designed to undermine the papal position promoted by pope Alexander III.[211] The German origins of the text strengthen the hints provided by script and later provenance of a German home for **Sankt Gallen, Stiftsbibliothek, MS. 633 [205]**, an early thirteenth-century vulgate witness.

The letter of Prester John is also found in two Second-Variant manuscripts: **London, British Library, MS. Cotton Titus A.xxvii [95]** (α) and **Saint-Omer, Bibliothèque municipale, MS. 710 [202]** (γ).[212] Both also contain the *Epistola Alexandri* (Family II) and *Epitaphium* without the other texts sometimes found with them: Dares's History and the Sibylline prophecies (see above, *Epistola Alexandri*: Family II).

Prima etas seculi ab Adam

These words begin various accounts of the Ages of the World. Different versions are found in **Dublin, Trinity College, MS. 496 [65]**, **Lincoln, Cathedral Library, MS. 98 [80]**, and **London, British Library, MS. Harley 4123 [104]**. Two other manuscripts, however, contain the same text (ending 'uerissimos .u.cxcui.'). These are London, British Library, MS. Royal 13.D.i [111] and Oxford, Bodleian Library, MS. Oriel College 16 [152], which have already been seen to agree in their particular version of Higden's Polichronicon. In both, the account of the Ages of the World immediately prefaces Higden's text, following the capitula-list.

---

209 Hilka & Söderhjelm, *Die Disciplina clericalis*, p. 30.8.
210 Hamilton, 'Prester John', p. 183. On the legend see Wright, *The Geographical Lore*, pp. 283–86.
211 Hamilton, *Prester John*, p. 186.
212 Hammer's distinction between alpha and gamma rests on a single reading.

Prophecies: 'Anglia transmittet leopardum lilia galli . . .'

This prophecy is found in Aberystwyth, National Library of Wales, MS. Llanstephan 196 [7] and Dublin, Trinity College, MS. 172 [61]. Ward records it in three other manuscripts, one of which, like MS. 61, bears the rubric 'Uersus uaticinales de Normannia de eodem sexto';[213] Walther lists a further six.[214]

Prophecies: 'Anno Cephas cocadrille . . .'

Cambridge, University Library, MS. Kk.6.16 [52]
Dublin, Trinity College, MS. 172 [61]

These manuscripts are additional to the two listed by Walther.[215] Both also contain the prophecy of Thomas of Canterbury ('Quando ego . . .').

Prophecies: Gallorum leuitas [216]

Cambridge, Gonville & Caius College, MS. 249/277 [29]
Cambridge, St John's College, MS. G. 16 [32]
Cambridge, University Library, MS. Kk.6.16 [52]
Oxford, Bodleian Library, MS. Douce 115 [140]

140 has the opening rubrics, 'Isti uersus reperiebantur in sarcophago cuiusdam sollempnis clerici in urbe Rome et per quosdam ibidem existentes Anglicos Anglie transmissi'. The first two manuscripts also include the 'Arbor fertilis' prophecy (see below, Eagle of Shaftesbury). Walther lists many copies.[217]

Prophecies: Gildas

The prophecy beginning 'Ter tria lustra tenent', sometimes attributed to Gildas, is found in the *Historia*-manuscripts Cambridge, Gonville & Caius College, MS. 249/277 [29], Dublin, Trinity College, MS. 172 [61] and Oxford, Bodleian Library, MS. Bodley 233 [135]. 29 contains a further prophecy attributed to Gildas, beginning 'Cambria Carnauan Anglie'. This is also found in the prophetic

---

213 London, BL, Cotton Claudius E.viii: see Ward, *apud* Ward & Herbert, *Catalogue of Romances*, I.317 and also I.308 and I.319.
214 Walter, *Initia*, I.52, no. 1026.
215 *Initia*, I.58, no. 1128.
216 Edited by Holder-Egger, Italienische Prophetieen', pp. 97–187.
217 *Initia*, I.353, no. 7015.

collection copied into MS. 61. (The two manuscripts also include the prophecy beginning 'Quando ego Thomas'.) See also below, *Regnum Scottorum*.

Prophecies: Illius imperium gens

This prophecy is known from several witnesses,[218] among them additions copied into the *Historia*-manuscripts **Dublin, Trinity College, MS. 172** and **Oxford, Bodleian Library, MS. Bodley 233.**

Prophecies: John of Bridlington

Aberystwyth, National Library of Wales, MS. Llanstephan 196 [7]
Cambridge, Gonville & Caius College, MS. 249/277 [29]
Cambridge, University Library, MS. Kk.6.16 [52]
Dublin, Trinity College, MS. 172 [61]
London, British Library, MS. Cotton Titus A.xxv [94]

The prophecy attributed to John of Bridlington has been described as 'a fourteenth-century political satire on contemporary events by a partisan of the Black Prince'.[219] Its usual form – poem with commentary, dedicatory epistle and three introductory sections – has been attributed to John Erghome, an Augustinian canon at York in the mid-fourteenth century.[220] Two of its three *diuisiones* deal with historical events: from Edward II's accession to the battle of Crécy (1346), then from 1344 to 1360. The third is prophecy, forecasting the future of the Black Prince, ultimately as King of France.[221]

29 and 61 also include the pseudo-Gildasian prophecy 'Cambria Carnauan ...' and this latter manuscript and 52 both have that beginning 'Anno cephas coca-drille'. All have 'Regnum Scottorum', and all but 7 'Quando ego Thomas' (see below). 7 and 29 include the prophecy of Robert de Sey.

Prophecies: Merlin

Galfridian

The prophecies of Merlin from the centre of Geoffrey's History occur as a separate item in four *Historia*-manuscripts: **Boulogne, Bibliothèque municipale, MSS 180 + 139 + 145 [16]** (vulgate), **Bruges, Bibliothèque de la Ville, MS. 428 [17]**

---

218   See Ward, *apud* Ward & Herbert, *Catalogue of Romances*, I.317; Walther, *Initia*, I.441, no. 8731.
219   Meyvaert, 'John', p. 656.
220   *Ibid.* Erghome also happened to own a copy of the *Historia* (below, IX).
221   Taylor, *The Political Prophecy*, p. 54.

(Second-Variant), and **Cambridge, Trinity College, MS. O.1.17 [38]** (vulgate) and **Oxford, Bodleian, MS. Rawlinson D.893 [157]** (vulgate). In 16, the separate copy of the Prophecies is glossed (see below, III: Commentaries). In 17 and 38, the prophecies are omitted from their normal position within the *Historia* but are appended after §208. Their prologue (§§109–110) too is absent from 17. The text is of different extent in the two manuscripts: that in 38 ends at §116.54 'et ueneratus interibit', 17 having the full text. The additional copy in MS. 16 is also truncated, this time at §116.41 'Ex quibus uulpis et lupus'.

Eagle of Shaftesbury

In the *Historia*, Geoffrey alludes to a prophecy uttered at Shaftesbury by an eagle; without further comment (or even specifying the language) he dismisses the prophecy as incredible.[222] Geoffrey's is the first reference to the existence of this prophecy although in Pliny's *Historia naturalis* an eagle was associated with one 'Seston urb<s>', which might later have been associated with *Sephtesberia*, Shaftesbury.[223] Welsh prophecies on this subject are known from later medieval manuscripts while the Latin version seems to have been popular from the thirteenth century[224] and even earlier: Gerald of Wales used it.[225]

Three versions of the Latin eagle-prophecy are found with Geoffrey's *Historia* – or rather, the same text in more or less extensive form, the fullest beginning 'Arbor fertilis', then 'Sicut rubeum draconem', to the shortest 'Mortuo leone'.[226]

1. 'Arbor fertilis'

Cambridge, Gonville & Caius College, MS. 249/277 [29]
Cambridge, St John's College, MS. G.16 [32]
Cardiff, South Glamorgan Central Library, MS. 2.611 [55]
Dublin, Trinity College, MS. 514 [66]
Leiden, Bibliotheek der Rijksuniversiteit, MS. Voss. lat. F.77 [77]
Leningrad, Saltykov-Shchedrin State Public Library, MS. lat. F.IV.76 [78]
London, British Library, MS. Royal 15.C.xvi [115]

In five of these manuscripts, the prophecy follows Geoffrey's History directly. The exceptions are 29, in which 'Arbor fertilis' is located among other prophecies,

---

222 HRB §29 'Ibi [Sephtesberia] tunc aquila locuta est dum murus edificaretur. Cuius sermones si ueros arbitrarer, sicut cetera memorie dare non diffugerem': Wright, *The Historia*, I.18.

223 Schulz, *Gottfried*, p. 463. Professor Reeve points out to me that Pliny was referring to the city of Sestos and therefore that any association with Shaftesbury is quite bogus.

224 Compare Ward & Herbert, *Catalogue of Romances*, I.292–98, 302, 312–15.

225 Scott and Martin, *Expugnatio*, pp. lxi–lxvi.

226 Printed from Leiden Voss lat. F.77 by Schulz, *Gottfried*, pp. 463–65, 464–65, and 465. The shorter versions ('Sicut rubeum' and 'Mortuo leone') were edited by J. J. Parry, *Brut y Brenhinedd*, pp. 225–26.

and 66 (Second-Variant), where the *Historia* and this prophecy are found in separate units.

The prophecy is also found as an interpolation in Oxford, Bodleian, Jesus College, 2 [142].

2. 'Sicut rubeum draconem'

Aberystwyth, National Library of Wales, MS. Llanstephan 196 [7]
Dublin, Trinity College, MS. 515 [67]
London, British Library, MS. Arundel 409 [87]
Oxford, Bodleian Library, MS. Rawlinson B.189 [155]

7 and 155 include the letter of Arthur, found in only two other copies (below, IV). Otherwise there is no agreement between the contents of these manuscripts: 7 alone includes other prophecies. 67 is a First-Variant witness.

3. 'Mortuo leone'

The prophecy beginning 'Mortuo leone iusticie surget albus rex et nobilis in Britannia . . .' is the final part of the 'Arbor fertilis' prophecy. It is found in **London, British Library, MS. Cotton Nero D.viii [92]** as a near-contemporary addition to the second of two original blocks of text and on the opening flyleaves of **Oxford, Bodleian Library, MS. Bodley 233 [135]**. That in 92 ends as normal but the version in 135 concludes 'alpes transcendet', as does at least one other copy of this work.[227]

Prophecies: Robert de Sey

The prophecy attributed to Robert de Sey ('Post factum est . . . ingemiscet') is found with the *Historia* in manuscripts containing considerable prophetic collections: **Aberystwyth, National Library of Wales, MS. Llanstephan 196 [7]** and **Cambridge, Gonville & Caius College, MS. 249/277 [29]**. The prophecy of John of Bridlington and that attributed to Thomas beginning 'Cesaris imperia' are also found in these manuscripts.

Prophecies: Sibylline

The prophecy of the Tiburtine Sibyl in the version printed by Ernst Sackur[228] seems to be descended from a lost fourth century Latin version which was reworked in the tenth or early eleventh century, perhaps in northern Italy.[229] Its

227 Ward, *apud* Ward & Herbert, *Catalogue of Romances*, I.297.
228 *Sibyllinische Texte*, pp. 177–87.
229 McGinn, *Visions*, p. 43.

origins have been traced, like those of the pseudo-Methodian Revelations, to an exhortatory prophecy of the second century B.C. which nourished a large corpus of classical oracular literature.[230] The prophecy appears to have gained force with claims that its messianic message had been fulfilled by the coming of Christ.[231] It continued to command attention and, in the twelfth century, it has been observed, gave 'wide currency to the expectation of a Last World Emperor, whether as *Carolus Redivivus* or *Rex Romanorum*'.[232] Elizabeth Brown has shown how it gave substance to Philip Augustus's otherwise dangerously threadbare claims to the legendary glory of the Capetians.[233]

The prophecies take the form of the Sibyl's interpretation of a dream of nine globes (*soles*) appearing successively in the sky. They represent nine generations, and the ninth will see widespread political disruption before the emergence of Constans, king of the Greeks, who will be the Last Emperor (see above, *De Antichristo, Methodius*) until he lays down his crown at Jerusalem, leaving divine forces to combat Antichrist.[234]

The Sibylline prophecies as printed by Sackur are found in eleven *Historia*-manuscripts: **Cambridge, St John's College, MS. G.16 [32]; Cambridge, University Library, MS. Mm.5.29 [54]; Dublin, Trinity College, MS. 514 [66]; Glasgow, University Library, MS. U.7.26 [74]; Lincoln, Cathedral Library, MS. 98 [80], London, British Library, MSS Arundel 326 [88], Cotton Galba E.xi [91], and Sloane 289 [116]; London, Lambeth Palace, MS. 401 [121]; Paris, Bibliothèque nationale, MSS 4999A + Manchester, John Rylands University Library, MS. lat. 216 [165] and 6041A [172].** They are also reported in the exemplar of the transcript NLW Panton 37 [1].

Prophecies: Thomas of Canterbury

A rare prophecy attributed to Thomas beginning 'Cesaris imperia', listed in only two manuscripts,[235] is found in three *Historia*-manuscripts: **Cambridge, Gonville & Caius College, MS. 249/277 [29], Cambridge, University Library, MS. Kk.6.16 [52], Dublin, Trinity College, MS. 172 [61].** All include the more widespread prophecy also associated with Thomas which begins 'Quando ego Thomas'. This is found in addition in Aberystwyth, NLW, MS. Llanstephan 196 [7] and London, College of Arms, MS. Arundel 1 [118].

---

230 *The Political Prophecy*, pp. 30–31.
231 *Ibid.*, p. 30.
232 Reeves, *The Influence*, p. 302; see also Southern, 'Aspects . . . 3', pp. 166–68.
233 Brown, 'La Notion', pp. 89–93.
234 Compare McGinn, *Visions*, pp. 49–50.
235 Walther, *Initia*, I.116, no. 2307.

Regnum Scottorum fuit

Aberystwyth, National Library of Wales, MS. Llanstephan 196 [7]
Cambridge, Gonville & Caius College, MS. 249/277 [29]
Cambridge, University Library, MS. Kk.6.16 [52]
Dublin, Trinity College, MS. 172 [61]
Paris, Bibliothèque nationale, MS. lat. 4126 [164]
[Also reported in Aberystwyth, NLW, MS. Panton 37 [1]]

Nineteen manuscripts of these prophetic verses, sometimes attributed to Gildas 'abbot of Glastonbury', have been counted.[236] The *Historia*-manuscripts in which it is found encompass all those containing the prophecies of Robert de Sey, John of Bridlington, and those beginning 'Anno cephas . . .' and 'Cesaris imperia'. All these manuscripts except 164 also include the prophecy of Thomas beginning 'Quando ego . . .'.

Robert of Reims

Found in 186, 196, and 199: see above, *Epistolae: Emperor of Constantinople to Robert of Flanders*.

Robert de Torigni

Leiden, Bibliotheek der Rijksuniversiteit, MS. Voss. lat. F.77 [77]
Rouen, Bibliothèque municipale, MS. U.74 (1177) [200]

These manuscripts include different extracts from Robert's Chronicle.[237] That in 77 continues Robert's version of the *Gesta Normannorum ducum* (see above, *Gesta*) while 200 includes a section covering the years 1147–57 and the continuation of Robert's work made at Le Bec. This *continuatio Beccensis* is known in five other manuscripts but the direct ancestry of the copy in 200 is unclear.[238]

'Si quis ab occidentalibus'

These words begin a description of the Holy Land (*Expl.* '. . . immolare uoluit') found in 88 and 116 (see above, *Chronology: in principio*). It is not unique to these manuscripts – being found (without the *Historia*), for example, in a collection of

---

236 I am grateful to David Dumville for supplying the list.
237 On which see Foreville, 'Robert'.
238 Delisle, *Chronique*, II.143 & 145.

crusading and Eastern material in Cambridge, Gonville & Caius College, MS. 162/83.

Solinus

The *Collectanea rerum memorabilium* of Solinus, written in the third century A.D., became one of the standard geographical works of the Middle Ages, rivalling in popularity that of Pliny, from which it derived much of its material.[239]

Paris, Bibliothèque nationale, MS. lat. 6815 [181]
Paris, Bibliothèque nationale, MS. lat. 17569 [188]

These manuscripts show no other agreement in their contents: 181 contains material predominantly about Italian history; 188 has Alexander texts.[240] Mommsen placed 181 in his third class of manuscripts: interpolated or contaminated texts.[241]

Status Imperii Iudaici

Despite its modern title, derived from the *incipit*, this work is a general survey of events in the ancient world not a specifically Jewish history.[242] Jacob Hammer and Henrietta Friedmann knew of *Status* in five manuscripts, all of which, they said, also contained the *Historia*. This is in fact true only of four: according to the catalogue of the Bibliothèque nationale, MS. lat. 5069 (Hammer and Friedmann's fourth manuscript) contains *Status* alone.[243] Two other copies of *Status* without Geoffrey's *Historia* have subsequently come to light (Bruxelles, Bibliothèque royale, MS. II.1066; Roma, Biblioteca Apostolica Vaticana, MS. Reg. lat. 629),[244] which confirms that *Status* is not merely an auxiliary to the *Historia* but an independent work.

Three of the *Status-Historia* manuscripts date from the thirteenth century and may be associated with the Low Countries. These are **Arras, Bibliothèque municipale, MS. 583 (871) [13]; Boulogne, Bibliothèque municipale, MSS 139 + 180 + 145 [16]; Bruxelles, Bibliothèque royale, MS. II.1020 [21]**, which come from houses in or near Arras and Tournai. Their contents do not otherwise overlap; two also contain works by local historians (Andrew of Marchiennes and Hermann

---

239 Wright, *The Geographical Lore*, p. 11 & n. 5; p. 44.
240 On the affinity of Solinus and Alexander material see Ross, *Alexander*, pp. 77–79. Solinus also travelled with Apollonius of Tyre, another text in this manuscript: compare Kortekaas, *Historia Apollonii*, pp. 41 & 421.
241 Mommsen, *C. Iulii Solini Collectanea*, pp. lxxxix and xli.
242 Hammer & Friedmann, '*Status imperii Iudaici*', p. 50: Boutemy, 'Note', p. 67.
243 [Mellot,] *Catalogus*, IV.37.
244 On the Bruxelles manuscript, see Boutemy, 'Une Copie nouvelle'; on Reg. lat. 629, see Pellegrin, 'Possesseurs', p. 294.

of Tournai). The fourth manuscript, **Phillipps 3117 [214]**, which contains only a fragment of *Status*, is set apart from the others by the presence of a *capitula*-list (also fragmentary) and its script, which places it as early fifteenth-century and, most probably, English. It is not linked by contents to any of the first three.

Superius autem excidio

These words begin a history of the arrival of Æneas in Italy which is found in **Cambridge, Corpus Christi College, MS. 414 [25]** and **St John's College, MS. G.16 [32]**. In 24, this text, together with the mythical account of prehistoric Britain, (see above, *Anglia modo dicta . . .*), forms an apt introduction to Geoffrey's story of the Trojan origins of the island's inhabitants. In 32, however, *Superius* occurs towards the end of a large manuscript, the *Historia* being located near the beginning. There is some overlap in contents: Turpin's History, followed by Dares, precedes *Superius* at some removes in both. They do not, however, contain the same version of the text of Turpin (see above, *Historia Turpini*); there is no obvious connection between the Dares-texts, that in 32 having a rubric, that in 25 having none.

Testamenta xii. patriarcharum

Cambridge, St John's College, MS. G.16 [32]
Cambridge, University Library, MS. Dd.1.17 [40]
London, British Library, MS. Royal 13.D.i [111]
[Oxford, Bodleian Library, MS. Rawlinson C.152 [156]]
Paris, Bibliothèque nationale, MS. 6041A [172]

The origins of the Testaments of the Twelve Patriarchs, one of the influential apocrypha to emerge in the two centuries before and after the birth of Christ, are still disputed: Greek and Hebrew versions exist but it is unclear whether the *Testamenta* are Jewish or Christian in origin.[245] The Latin version, of which seventy-seven copies have been listed,[246] was one of the translations from the Greek made by Robert Grosseteste, bishop of Lincoln (1235–53).[247]

Except for MS. 156, in which the *Testamenta* (and the History of Jacques de Vitry) are found in a late thirteenth-century manuscript now prefacing a twelfth-century copy of Geoffrey's History, all these manuscripts also contain Turpin's history. Higden's *Polichronicon* and Henry of Huntingdon's letter to Henry I are found in addition in 40 and 111.

---

245 Jonge, *The Testaments of the Twelve Patriarchs*, pp. 9–12.
246 Thomson, *The Writings of Robert Grosseteste*, pp. 43–44.
247 For others, see Callus, 'Robert Grosseteste', pp. 33–34.

Ualerius ad Rufinum

Cambridge, Corpus Christi College, MS. 414 [25]
Dublin, Trinity College, MS. 514 [66]
Dublin, Trinity College, MS. 515 [67]

The *Dissuasio Ualerii ad Ruffinum philosophum ne uxorem ducat* is one of a number of medieval tracts warning against the dangers of marriage and of women in general. Composed by Walter Map before 1183, it forms part of his *De nugis curialium*, but circulated much more extensively as a separate work: its editors estimate at least forty manuscripts in Britain and eleven in the Bibliothèque nationale in Paris.[248]

Vision of the monk of Eynsham

The account of the vision of purgatory and paradise seen in 1196 by a monk of Eynsham is found in two copies of the *Historia*. Its composition is attributed in some early manuscripts to the monk's brother, Adam, prior or sub-prior of Evesham.[249] Whatever the accuracy of this attribution, the work was probably written soon after the vision and enjoyed considerable popularity in the Middle Ages.[250] In **Dublin, Trinity College, MS. 494 [63]**, the *Uisio* follows the *Historia*. In **Heidelberg, Universitätsbibliothek, MS. 9.31 [75]**, it is separated from Geoffrey's *Historia* by one other text. The two manuscripts share no other contents.

Uita Ade et Eue

The legend of Adam and Eve describes the immediate consequences of the Fall from paradise: their failure to prevent Abel's murder despite a warning in a dream and later the powerlessness of Seth and Eve to save Adam's life after they had forfeited the right to the oil of paradise. This final part of the story forms the background to the legend of the True Cross, whose wood grew from parts of the Tree of Consolation brought back to Adam instead of the oil (see above, 'Sancta Arbor'), and one version of this legend beginning 'Post peccatum Ade' is found with the Uita Ade in both the *Historia*-manuscripts in which it occurs. These are **London, British Library, MSS Arundel 326 [88]** and **Sloane 289 [116]**.

The *Uita Ade* was edited by Wilhelm Meyer from manuscripts mainly in

---

248 Brooke *apud* James, *Walter Map*, pp. xlvii–xlviii. On the date see pp. xxiv–xxxii.
249 Salter, *Eynsham Cartulary*, II.258–59.
250 *Ibid.*, II.276.

71

Munich.[251] The version found with the *Historia*, however, belongs to the English transmission of the text as studied by J. H. Mozley.[252] 88 and 116 were attributed by him to a category of manuscripts which 'derive from a MS perhaps of the thirteenth century, by which time a number of short interpolations had been made . . . and also longer passages added from different Adam-legends . . .'.[253] Mozley identified eight manuscripts of this class, our manuscript 116 constituting a ninth being 'a close copy of Arundel 326'.[254] This observation is confirmed by the repetition in 116 of a number of contents found in 88 (see above Nicodemus, Post peccatum, *Chronology: In principio*).[255]

Uita Thome

Lives of Thomas Becket are found in two *Historia*-manuscripts. That by Edward Grim occurs in London, British Library, MS. Cotton Vespasian E.x [98].[256] Saint-Omer, BM, MS. 710 [202] contains a more complex text: a conflation of several versions made in 1199 by Elias of Evesham, with extracts from Grim's Life.[257] Both manuscripts have extensive other contents, none of which agree; they witness different forms of Geoffrey's text, the vulgate and the Second Variant.

William of Malmesbury

The full complement of William's major histories – the *Gesta pontificum*, *Gesta regum* and *Historia nouella* – is found in only one *Historia*-manuscript: London, British Library, MS. Royal 13.D.v [113]. A similar selection was assembled by the sixteenth-century compiler of Cambridge, Trinity College, MS. R.5.34 [35] but the *Gesta pontificum* and *Historia nouella* postdate the fifteenth-century copies of the *Gesta regum* and Geoffrey's *Historia* and even these may not have been associated before the whole volume was assembled. In London, British Library, MS. Royal 13.D.ii [112] and Oxford, All Souls College, MS. 35 [132], the *Gesta regum* and *Historia nouella* precede Geoffrey's *Historia*. A copy of the *Gesta regum* is found with Geoffrey's *Historia* in Philadelphia, Free Library, MS.

---

251 'Vita Adae et Evae'.
252 'The "Vita Adae" '.
253 *Ibid.*, p. 125.
254 *Ibid.*, p. 121.
255 Mozley also discussed an unnumbered manuscript in Winchester containing an abbreviated account of the legend. Winchester Cathedral 9 [212], a *Historia*-manuscript, contains the related text 'Post peccatum Ade', but it must be assumed that Mozley had another manuscript in mind.
256 Printed by Robertson, *Materials*, II.353–43.
257 The *Quadrilogus* II: Duggan, *Thomas*, p. 205 and n. 4.

E.247 [192] and another is reported to have belonged to the manuscript of which Aberystwyth, NLW, 13210 [4] was once part.[258]

Stubbs grouped MS. 35 with 132, and 112 with 113, a classification followed by Roger Mynors.[259]

Preliminary Conclusions

The evidence of shared contents permits the identification of some related manuscripts with a considerable degree of certainty; the suggested connections between others are less sure. The results may be grouped according to the nature of the evidence.

Clear, self-standing connection

This category comprises manuscripts with overlapping contents notable for their number or their rarity, or both.

1. 54 & 80

The exact equivalence between the substance and arrangement of the numerous contents of these Second-Variant manuscripts has already been observed (above, *Alexander: Parua recapitulacio*), as has the origin of some in the early twelfth-century manuscript Bodley 163 (above, *Anglia habet*). The complexity and rareness of the contents strongly suggest that the two *Historia*-manuscripts were exemplar and copy (the script of 54 being the earlier).

2. 88 & 116

These witnesses contain a number of shared texts as part of larger collections. The overlapping group occurs in nearly identical order in the later manuscript (116), but split at one point by an extra text. Given the number of shared items and the rarity of some of them, it is likely that 116 is a very close descendant, perhaps copy, of 88.

3. 90 & 137

Unusual material on the flyleaves of 137 (Geoffrey's *Historia* begins the manuscript proper) constitutes the opening items, largely in the same order, of the main part of 90 (see above, *Compendium*). The available evidence suggests that what became the shared material was first associated with the *Historia* in 137; but the distance at which 90 is removed from this process cannot be determined

---

258 Strongman, 'The Manuscripts', pp. 22–23.
259 I.lxxii–lxxiii; lxxx–lxxxiv; Mynors *apud* Potter, *The Historia novella*, pp. xxxix–xl.

without reference to textual evidence. No witnesses to intermediate stages are evident at this point, however.

Several shared works

Where several not particularly rare works are found in two or more *Historia*-manuscripts, published studies of related texts are often of value in assessing the extent of the connection. In other cases, the evidence is sometimes ambiguous.

1. 76 & 92

These manuscripts both contain the *Gesta Alexandri, Epistola Alexandri* (*Family I*), *Historia Brittonum, Gesta Normannorum ducum* (F-redaction). The connection is corroborated by the known links between the texts of the last three of these works, identified by their editors (see above, *Alexander: Epistola* Family I, *Gesta Normannorum ducum, Historia Brittonum*).

2. 40 & 111

Henry of Huntingdon's Letter to King Henry, Higden's *Polichronicon*, the *Historia Turpini*, and the *Testamenta duodecim patriarcharum* are found in these two manuscripts among numerous varied works (each contains over 250 quarto-sized folios). Both date from the later fourteenth century. Besides being unique among known *Historia*-manuscripts in their inclusion of the letter to Henry, they are connected by the nature of the texts of the *Polichronicon* and Turpin's History (see above under these headings). The later textual history of the *Testamenta* is apparently uncharted.

3. Vulgate/Second-Variant connections

Vulgate offshoots of 54/80

Blocks of some of the twenty shared works found in the Second-Variant manuscripts 54 and 80 occur in other *Historia*-manuscripts but those of the vulgate type. The connections may be described here but explanation must await further evidence.

(i) 121 (vulgate) contains, like 54 and 80 (Second-Variant), the *Gesta Alexandri, Epitaphium Alexandri, Epistola Alexandri* Family II, Dares, and the Sibylline prophecies. Groups of these texts are associated with a number of Second-Variant manuscripts (see above, *Alexander: Epistola Alexandri family II*).

(ii) 113 (vulgate) includes texts derived ultimately from Bodley 163: the pseudo-Gildasian *Historia Brittonum* and genealogies of the Counts of Flanders and Kings of France. However 113 also contains the account of the shires and bishoprics of England (*Anglia habet . . .*, see above) found in 54 and 80 but not in Bodley 163.

32 and Second-Variant manuscripts

32 holds a number of texts in common with the α-manuscript 91: extracts from

the *Pantheon* of Godfrey of Viterbo, Sibylline prophecies, the *Epistola* and *Epitaphium Alexandri*. 32 resembles a β-witness in including a copy of the *Historia Turpini* with accompanying genealogies. A similar collection is found in the vulgate manuscript, 24.

4. Collections of Prophecies

Several *Historia*-manuscripts contain a jumble of small prophetic texts, sometimes entered informally at various times on blank leaves. In five manuscripts with no other related contents there is a degree of overlap between the prophecies contained, although there is no shared pattern. The prophecies inserted in various late hands at the end of 61 (which contains mainly hagiography) form the pivot for the comparison. The equivalences are recorded here for the sake of completeness.

(i) The prophecies in 52, also added at the back of the manuscript, include five found also in 61: 'Anno Cephas cocadrille', that of John of Bridlington, the popular prophecy of Thomas beginning 'Quando ego Thomas' and the rarer 'Cesaris imperia', and 'Regnum Scottorum fuit'.

(ii) In 29 (perhaps *c.* 1464) the prophecies are found scattered among more substantial contents in the main part of the manuscript. They include, too, 'Regnum Scottorum fuit' and the prophecy of John of Bridlington and, as in 61, the pseudo-Gildasian prophecy 'Cambria Carnauan . . .' (not found in other *Historia*-manuscripts).

(iii) Two prophecies occur in both 61 and 7: 'Anglia transmittet' and that of John of Bridlington.

(iv) MS. 135 includes two prophecies found in 61: *Illius imperium gens* and *Ter tria lustra*.

Manuscripts holding three texts in common

1. 76 & 77

These Leiden manuscripts both contain the F-redaction of the *Gesta Normannorum ducum*, Einhard's *Uita Karoli*, and the brief history of the Frankish kings beginning 'Antenor et alii profugi'. 'Antenor' is not found in any other *Historia*-manuscript. 76 is thus linked with 77 through histories, chiefly relating to French and Frankish affairs, while the connection of 76 and 92 already observed is made through pseudo-historical contents.

2. 117, 118, & 188

All three contain pseudo-historical classical material: the correspondence of Alexander and Dindymus (*Collatio I* version), the *Epistola Alexandri* (Family II), and the History of Apollonius of Tyre.

3. 95 & 202

These Second-Variant manuscripts contain the letter of Prester John as well as the Alexander-texts found in a number of Second-Variant manuscripts – the *Epistola* (Family II) and the *Epitaphium*.

4. 32, 172

The Sibylline prophecies, the *Testamenta* of the patriarchs, and the *Historia Turpini* are found in these manuscripts. 32 and 172 do not agree in their particular versions of this last work, however, and so the probability of a close genealogical connection is lessened.

5. 186, 196

As seen above, these manuscripts contain three texts relating to the First Crusade: the History of Robert of Reims, the letter of the Emperor Manuel to Robert of Flanders and a letter written from the Crusade itself. They are texts, however, which probably travelled as a group, given their complementary nature; they are arranged in different order in these manuscripts.

6. 15 & 215

As seen above (*Epistolae: Hillin* . . .), the *Historia* is preceded, at some remove in 15, by three letters in identical order in these manuscripts. Therefore a direct connection is most probable.

7. 14 & 183

Two groups of poems by Ausonius are found in these manuscripts, together with a collection of chronicle-extracts and a third work 'Definitiones Ciceronis'. The evidence of a third related manuscript, not containing the *Historia*, suggests that 14 may be central in the transmission of these texts.

Fewer than three shared texts.

1. 13, 16, 21, 214

These contain the rare ancient history, *Status imperii iudaici*. This work is prefaced by a *capitula*-list only in 214, which differs from the remainder in being the only manuscript apparently of English and not Flemish origin.

2. 32, 78

These manuscripts contain the Prophecy of the Eagle in its longest form followed by a commentary. It may also be noted that extracts from the poem *Pergama* are found on the flyleaves of 32 and in the companion-volume of 78.

3. 34, (65,) 125, 152

The connection between these manuscripts requires substantiation: the *Mirabilia* could be derived easily from the *Historia Brittonum* and appear to have been well circulated. There may well be a link between MSS 34, 125, and 125: the text is positioned similarly in each.

4. 58, 62, 118

A single text connects these manuscripts: the chronicle of French history beginning *Cum animaduerterem*.

5. 129 & 186

The Norman genealogy found in these manuscripts does not seem to have been widely circulated and so may indicate a close connection between them.

6. First-Variant manuscripts

A particular link is evident between the Trojan History of Dares and the First Variant, of which six of the seven manuscripts include Dares. Three contain a version introduced by a rubric which styles Dares 'Entellius'.

7. 55 & 70

The genealogy of the Trojans which these contain is also found in a third manuscript in a different form (130). The connection between 55 and 70 is buttressed by the fact that they contain the First-Variant Version.

8. 111 & 152

These manuscripts are linked by a particular form of Higden's *Polichronicon* (prefaced by a *capitula*-list extending from Abraham to Zorobabel) divided into seven books and ending in A.D. 1377.

9. 42 & 155

Both manuscripts contain an origin-story of Britain beginning 'Euolutis a mundi constitucione' (and have associations with St Albans).

COMPOSITIONS DEPENDENT ON THE *HISTORIA*

There is a category of associated works which deserves separate consideration from the sort of material discussed above. These are the ancillary texts attached to the *Historia* which served to elucidate, expand, or summarize its contents and thus may have had limited, or no, independent circulation. Certain other items are even less separable from Geoffrey's work, perhaps having no context outside the *Historia* but being still extraneous to the text itself. These include commentaries on the Prophecies (which were also found in independently circulating *Prophetie*-manuscripts), scribal verses, and *capitula*-lists. The following begins with items which did or could have been copied apart from the *Historia* (though perhaps at the expense of sense) and moves to those bound to it whether by circumstance (like scribal notes) or contents (Prophecy-commentaries, *capitula*-lists).

Prose

Armorica siue Latauia

This phrase begins a roughly alphabetical list of glosses on some of the place-names in the *Historia*. It is found in its fuller form in two *Historia* manuscripts, London, Lambeth Palace 401 [121] (vulgate) and BL, Cotton Titus A.xxvii [95] (Second-Variant).[1] It follows the *Historia* in both: immediately in 121 and in 95 separated by a short British genealogy, paraphrasing part of the *Historia Brittonum*.[2] 121 (fourteenth-century) presents a better alphabetical arrangement of the names than 95 (*c.* 1300), in which the glosses on *Demetia*, *Deira*, *Eustria*, *Eboracum*, and *Gualenses* are placed, out of sequence, after *Picti*. There is no material difference between the texts, however. A shorter version is found in the First-Variant manuscript Aberystwyth, National Library of Wales, MS. 13210 [4] (conflated with Second-Variant), and in the vulgate Heidelberg, UB, 9.31 [75].[3] In both it follows the *Historia* directly.

---

1 Ending '. . . in signum triumphi erexit'. Edited by Dumville, 'Anecdota'.
2 Printed by Dumville, 'A Paraphrase', pp. 102–3.
3 Ending '. . . qui fluuius Loegriam secernit a Deira et Albania'. They omit the glosses on *Claudiocestria*, *Hamtonia*, *Loegria*, *Lundonia*, *Leircestria*, *Moriani*, *Ruteni*, *Turonis*, *Trinouantum*, and *Uerolamium*.

Verses

Leonine Summaries

Jacob Hammer, in an article published in 1931, drew attention to various poems found in the twelfth-century *Historia*-manuscript Douai, BM, MS. 880 [59], which included sets of Leonine verses summarizing the contents of the *Historia*.[4] Little of substance needs to be added to his remarks.

The verses are located at places where book-divisions often occur (see below, VI) – §§23, 35, 54, 73, 89, 110, 143, 163, and 177 – but only the first book is marked in the original hand. Hammer supposed that the author of these verses and, indeed, of the poems which precede the History of Dares Phrygius at the beginning of the manuscript was the Bernardus who is named in a separate poem following the *Historia*.[5] Hammer's opinion must now be modified in the light of work on one of the initial poems, the lament on Troy beginning 'Pergama flere uolo', which has been shown to have a wider circulation than Hammer imagined. It is attributed in manuscripts to various figures; there is no reason to attach particular authority to the evidence of 59 (above, II: *Pergama flere*).

The last three verses (at §§143, 163, and 177) and the final 'Bernardus' poem are found also in the copy of the *Historia* in Douai, BM, MS. 882 [60], another (perhaps rather later) twelfth-century manuscript. As Hammer noted, the inclusion of the verses coincides with a change of hand at 181r.[6] The new hand is later-looking, perhaps of the early thirteenth century. What Hammer did not record, however, is the presence of *Pergama* in 60 as well as in 59.[7] This is found in both manuscripts, after Dares's History (ending 140r) and before Geoffrey's *Historia* (beginning 143r). It occupies the first column of fo 142r, ending 'Occisos rides occubuisse uides':[8] the last twenty lines found in 59 are not present in 60 (142rb is blank).

Madog of Edeirnion

In Cardiff, South Glamorgan Central Library, MS. 2.611 [55], the *Historia*-text is prefaced by 'a glowing panegyric of the Welsh race' whose author declares himself to be *frater walensis Madocus Edeirnianensis*.[9] Hammer has accredited him with the conflation of vulgate and First Variant found in this manuscript.[10]

The poem also prefaces a purely vulgate text – the twelfth-century Cambridge,

---

4 'Some Leonine Summaries'.
5 *Ibid.*, pp. 119–20.
6 *Ibid.*, p. 117.
7 See 'Some Leonine Summaries', p. 120.
8 Line 48: *ibid.*, p. 122.
9 Hammer, *Geoffrey*, p. 18.
10 *Ibid.*

Corpus Christi College, MS. 281 [23] – but it appears on flyleaves in a humanist cursive and would seem to be an antiquarian addition.

Iohannes Beuerus

Following his work on the 'Bernardus' Leonine summaries, Hammer published another set of verses illustrating the *Historia*.[11] These are written in the lower margins of certain folios of the *Historia*-text found in Paris, BN, lat. 4126 [164] in a hand 'much later'[12] than the early fourteenth-century hand of the text. Hammer identified as the author one 'Johannes Beverus', monk of Westminster, whose Chronicle (dated *c*. 1306) R. H. Fletcher had included in his list of those containing Galfridian material.[13] Hammer also commented on the Classical, especially Ovidian, allusions in the verses.[14] Some years after this, Hammer investigated the treatment of Geoffrey's narrative in the manuscripts of Bever's Chronicle itself, printing Bever's summary of the *Historia*, Book 1, and occasional verses relating to the whole of Geoffrey's story, including some not found in MS. 164.[15] Hammer also noted that Beverus was alternatively known as John of London.[16]

Hammer's observations may be amplified in several respects. Bever's verses are to be found, albeit in rather corrupt form, in a second *Historia*-manuscript, London, BL, Cotton Cleopatra D.viii [90], where they appear, also in the margins of the *Historia*-text, in red. Comparison of these with 164 shows that Hammer failed to notice a number of Bever's verses found in the Paris manuscript written in pencil, not in ink like the others. In addition, more may be said about Bever himself.

In 90 the verses are written in the margins, mostly at the foot, in a late fourteenth-century cursive, similar to that of the main hand (using long *r*, tall-backed *t*, simple looped *e*, two-compartment *a*) but rather more compact, upright, and angular. Those in 164 are entered in a hand not unlike this, but rather later: it postdates the Gothic bookhand of the main text by perhaps 150 years.[17] I list below the verses found in 90, indicating their position in 164 and where an edition may be found. Variants are given but not alternative spellings (Hammer prints *ae* but only *e* is used in the manuscript). Verses not found in 164 are asterisked.

i. 90, 8v; 164, 135v; Hammer, 'Note on a Manuscript', p. 230 and n. 29, 'The Poetry', p. 121.

---

11 'Note on a Manuscript', pp. 230–33.
12 *Ibid.*, p. 230.
13 Hammer, 'Note on a Manuscript', p. 231; Fletcher, *The Arthurian Material*, p. 175.
14 'Note on a Manuscript', p. 234.
15 'The Poetry', pp. 121–23 and 124–31.
16 *Ibid.*, p. 119.
17 But not the bookhand of the later compilation: see Crick, *A Summary Catalogue*.

Fluxit ab Enea primum Romana[18] propago
Assimul[19] et Britones at Saxones[20] protulit Anglos.
Hec patet in lingua nostra in eoque set illa[21]
Ob in (*sic*)[22] pagana fuerat simul Anglia tota.

ii. 90, 9v; 164, 136r; Hammer, 'Note on a Manuscript', p. 231, 'The Poetry',
p. 121. Hammer also found this verse in the margin of 28 (2v).[23]

Sit mihi libertas potius maciesque famesque[24]
Quam sim seruili condicione satur.[25]

iii. 90, side margin 16v; 164, 141r (foot); Hammer, 'Note on a Manuscript',
p. 231, 'The Poetry', p. 124.

Et sic tres reges tribus addunt nomina terris
Deque suo uocitat nomine quisque suam.

* iv. 90, 19r; not in 164; Hammer, 'The Poetry', p. 124.

Set quia stare sta[tu] stabili mundana [re]cusant
Trami[te] transuerso prospera lap[sa] ruunt.

* v. 90, 20v; not in 164; Hammer, 'The Poetry', p. 125.

Cor quam femineum, mens quam generosa parenti
Grata fit ingrato, miseretur non miserenti

vi. 90, 21v; 164, 145r; Hammer, 'Note on a Manuscript', p. 231, 'The Poetry',
p. 125.

Concors uiuus erat recipit Concordia templo
Defunctum concors tempus utramque[26] tenet
Annos concordes fecit sudore quiescit
Diu[27] quam coluit cultor undeque fuere.[28]

---

18 Hammer gives *Iouiana*, but to judge from the microfilm I see no objection to the reading
Romana (with cursive long *r*) in 164 here.
19 164, *insimul*
20 *at Saxones*: 164, *Saxonia*.
21 *nostra . . . illa*: 164, *mutuoque dolore at illa*.
22 *Ob in*: 164, *Olim*.
23 As shown by a note in the College's copy of James's catalogue of the collection: *A
Descriptive Catalogue of the Manuscripts in the Library of Gonville & Caius*, I.
24 164, omits *que*.
25 164, *sator*.
26 164, *utrumque*
27 164, *Diue*.
28 *undeque fuere*: 164, *in ede sua*.

vii. 90, 24r; 164, 147r; Hammer, 'Note on a Manuscript', p. 232, 'The Poetry', p. 125.

> Proth dolor hoc[29] quod erit uos[30] mea uiscera turbant[31]
> Supernas[32] acies que mala causa mouet
> Tota tenere nequid modo uos Britannia: quondam
> Uos tenuit uenter unicus iste meus.
> Non uos materne lacrime sparsique capilli
> Nec que suxistis[33] ubera nuda mouent.

* viii. 90, 27r; not in 164; Hammer, 'The Poetry', p. 126.

> Hoc modo quis faceret, quem non cessisse pigeret
> Quin pocius raperet? Quis sic pro fratre doleret?
> Set dispendat (*sic*) ita clemens deitas Elyduro
> Sorte tripartita bis tempore regna futuro.

[Omits verse beginning 'Ut per iter . . .' 164, 149v; Hammer, 'Note on a Manuscript', p. 232.]

ix. 90, 30v; 164, 152v; Hammer, 'Note on a Manuscript', p. 232, 'The Poetry', p. 126.

> Set quoniam:[34]
> rebus in humanis non <est>[35] scincera (*sic*) uoluptas:
> Miscentur letis[36] tristia sepe iocis.

[Omits verse beginning 'Fama loquax . . .'. 164, 153r; Hammer, 'Note on a Manuscript', p. 232.]

* x. 90, 34v (with title 'Nota de prima Christianitate'); not in 164; Hammer, 'The Poetry', pp. 127 and 128.

> Lucius, in tenebris prius ydola qui coluisti,
> Es merito celebris ex quo baptisma subisti.
> Celestis medici merito curam meruisti
> Omine felici lotus baptismate Christi.

---

29 *hoc*: 164, *heu.*
30 *uos*: 164 *quid uos.*
31 164, *turbat.*
32 164, *Fraternas.*
33 164, *sugistis.*
34 *Set quoniam*: 164, omits.
35 164, *est.*
36 164: *locis.*

xi. 90, 36v; 164, 158r; Hammer, 'Note on a Manuscript', p. 233, 'The Poetry', p. 127.

> Are Martis erant.[37] Marti sacrat[38] et male Martem
> Pacat (*sic*): nam Marte mane[39] sequente cadit.

xii. 90, 41r; 164, 162v; Hammer, 'Note on a Manuscript', p. 233.

> Non bene conueniunt nec se contraria miscent
> Sit nisi[40] conflictus[41] primeque remocio forme.

xiii. 90, 44v; 164, 165r; Hammer, *ibid.*, 'The Poetry', p. 127.

> Cum mors sit certa, modus est incertus et hora
> Omnibus est una mors non mortis non[42] modus unus.

xiv. 90, 49r; 164, 169r: Hammer, 'Note on a Manuscript', p. 233 (last poem in 164 recorded there by Hammer), 'The Poetry', p. 128.

> Femina prima cibo mundum, dampnauit at ista
>   Potu confudit anglica regna suo.
> Wesseil dat letos alios, letum dedit isti.
>   Wesseil leticiam significare solet.
> Patris erat primum wesseil natique secundum
>   Mors fuit utrumque per quod uterque perit.

* xv. 90, 51v; Hammer 'The Poetry', p. 128.

> Iure stupent omnes hominem uentura referre
>   Cum sit solius scire futura Dei.

xvi. 90, 59r; 164, margin 177r (in pencil, barely legible); Hammer, 'The Poetry', pp. 128–29.

> Iure dolum sequitur dolor atque prodicionem (*sic*)
>   Cedes; felici res mala fine caret.

xvii. 90, 63r; 164, 181r (barely legible); Hammer, 'The Poetry', p. 129.

> Humanum nichil est quod non sic premia mutent
>   muneris in manibus iura fidesque latent.
> Saluat et occidit iungit disiungit amicos
>   Dat paces rumpit federa pacta noua (*sic*)

---

37 164, *arent.*
38 164, *sacrant.*
39 164, *male.*
40 Two minims with suprascript *i* in 164: could be *nisi* but Hammer transcribes *ubi. nisi* is not abbreviated in 90.
41 164, *confluctus.*
42 Intrusive; 164, omits *non.*

Iudicis excecat oculos et inebriat aures
Fit <. . . .> iuris <. . .> lex sine lege iacet.

* xviii. 90, 77r; Hammer, 'The Poetry', p. 130.

O miser, o demens, quo te tua facta (*sic*) uocarunt
Effuge dum poteris, o periture breui.
Te mors seua manet, te dira pericula mortis
Dente giganteo dilacerandus eris.

[Poems in 164 in pencil and ink, foot 192r. Not found in 90 or printed by Hammer.]

xix. 90, 83v–84r; 164, 202r (in pencil, barely legible); Hammer, 'The Poetry',
p. 131.

O Deus inuadet tociens cur femina mundum?
Feminee fidei federa nulla manent.
Femina fraus falerata, latens, fel melle linitum
Fronsque columbina caudaque uiper<e>a.
Hec (*sic*) Priamus Priamique domus Paris Hector
(84r) Achilles[43] Aiax Esconides totaque Troia perit.
Femina Sampsonem destruxerat Ypolitumque
Herculeas uires et Salamonis opes.
Mundum perdomui dominoque suo mihi seruit:
Indomitata namque[44] femina sola michi.

Differences in the selection of the verses (and perhaps in particular readings) indicate that the verses in 90 and 164 depend on some other representative(s) of the Beuerus tradition. This could be a third annotated *Historia*-manuscript with a more complete set of verses, or Bever's Chronicle itself.

Antonia Gransden has discussed evidence which associates Bever with three other historical works: the so-called Merton continuation of the St Albans *Flores historiarum*, a lamentation on the death of Edward I, and an account of the burglary of the royal treasury at Westminster in 1303.[45]

The circumstantial evidence for Bever's authorship of the 'Merton' *Flores* is corroborated by a note in one of the manuscripts of that work (quoted by Gransden), 'Cronica de edicione domini Iohannis dicti Bever' monachi Westmonasterii. De libraria monasterii Sancti Augustini Cantuariensis Distinct' T. abbatis'.[46] The abbot concerned, Gransden has suggested, was Thomas de Fyndone (1283–1310).[47] The indication which this note suggests of an association in Bever's lifetime between Westminster and St Augustine's, Canterbury,

---

43 Belongs to previous line: compare Hammer, The Poetry', p. 131.
44 Neil Wright points out to me that the metre requires a bisyllabic word with short first syllable such as *tamen* or *manet*.
45 'The Continuations', pp. 479–80.
46 *Ibid.*, p. 480, n. 41: BL Harley 641, 1r.
47 'The Continuations', p. 480, n. 41.

provides grounds for speculation about a further link between Bever and the *Historia*. Dublin, Trinity College, MS. 514 [66], a Second-Variant manuscript, contains a contents-list in an early fourteenth-century informal hand prefaced by an inscription (in the same hand) recording the gift of the book to St Augustine's by John de London (John Bever's other name).[48] The identification of the donor has previously been hindered by the ubiquity of the name Iohannes de London. The date of the inscription, however, requires that, if this *Iohannes* is not the chronicler of the same name, then he had a namesake with an interest in the *Historia* who was engaged in literary exchange with St Augustine's at the same time. Such a hypothesis seems needlessly complicated.

Commentaries on the Prophecies of Merlin (§§111–117)

The prophecies of Merlin, with their ambiguous animal symbols, invited a more focussed kind of written comment than those seen so far, whether simply a series of glosses on the text or a more formal running interpretation. The possibility that such commentaries were transmitted from exemplar to copy necessitates their discussion here.

Jacob Hammer was again the pioneer of study of the commentaries; he regarded it as a contribution to the understanding of medieval prophecy in general.[49] Directing his work away from this aim and extending it in the search for text-historical information promises little at first sight. The prophecies naturally engendered independent (potentially similar) interpretations.[50] Hammer noted in 1930 that he had come across commentaries of the Prophecies in about a dozen *Historia*-manuscripts[51] but four of the five commentaries which he printed in subsequent papers occur in single *Historia*-manuscripts only (the fifth occurs in two). The extensive independent circulation of the Prophecies presents another potential hazard in seeking text-historical results in this context: two of Hammer's five commentaries were found in a manuscript containing the Prophecies only.

Hammer edited commentaries from the vulgate Dublin, Trinity College, MS. 496 [65], Paris, BN, MSS lat. 4126 [164] and 6233 [178], the Second-Variant Lincoln, Cathedral Library, MS. 98 [80], and First-Variant Exeter, Cathedral Library, MS. 3514 [70]. MS. 164 contains a marginal commentary found also in 178, where it accompanies an interlinear gloss (the two commentaries are also found in the *Prophetia*-manuscript BL Cotton Claudius B.vii).[52] The commentary in 70 is found in the margins of the *Prophetie* within the *Historia*.[53] Hammer

---

48 The evidence for the two names is given by Hardy, *Descriptive Catalogue*, III.282, footnote, s.n. and Gransden, 'The Continuations', p. 480, n. 40.
49 'A Commentary', p. 413.
50 For example, those of John of Cornwall and Matthew Paris.
51 'A Commentary', pp. 3–4.
52 Printed by Hammer, 'A Commentary', pp. 6–18, 411–13, 413–31.
53 Edited by Hammer, 'Bref commentaire'.

reported the existence of marginal and interlinear commentaries in 80, the marginal being attached to the Prophecies within the *Historia*, and the interlinear, which he printed, belonging to a separate copy forming part of a thirteenth-century addition to the original late twelfth-century manuscript.[54] In 65, the commentary itself is separate.[55]

Hammer's findings have been extended and amplified by Caroline Eckhardt. She was unable to examine all seventy manuscripts of the *Prophetia*, still less the two hundred of the *Historia*. She was able to report on only 'a sampling'.[56] These she arranged chronologically and gave *sigla*, which I adopt here.[57] Her earliest example, X, dated 1147 x 1154, was the interlinear gloss found in 178 (and the *Prophetia*-manuscript, Cotton Claudius B.vii). The marginal commentary found in both of these and in 164, called P, was, in Eckhardt's opinion, composed in the thirteenth century. She assigned the same date to E, the commentary in 70. The last of the commentaries identified by Hammer, that in 65, remains without a *siglum*.

Eckhardt added to these L, a possibly twelfth-century commentary found within the *Historia*-text in 80; B, a thirteenth-century commentary (marginal and interlinear) in Oxford, Bodleian Library, MS. Bodley 622 [137]; and D, the fourteenth- or fifteenth-century commentary found (as a work separate from the *Historia*) in Dublin, Trinity College, MS. 514 [66].

The purposes of text-history impose a different perspective on this material. Self-standing commentaries separate from the *Historia* may be classed apart, almost as associated works. These would include those in the two Dublin manuscripts, 65 and 66. Glosses or partial commentaries within §§111–117 gain more importance than Hammer, working with a different aim, allowed: he had printed the commentary found in an addition to 80 rather than that within the *Historia*. Finally, Hammer did not deal with the interrelation of the commentaries which he printed, concentrating instead on their possible sources in the exegesis of the text offered by John of Cornwall and Alain de Lille, among others. Comparison of X and P, the commentaries in 178 and 164, indicates significant overlap.

The present survey has brought to light a further ten *Historia*-manuscripts with full or partial commentaries on the Prophecies.

F Boulogne, Bibliothèque municipale, MS. 180 + 145 + 139 [16]
G Cambridge, Gonville & Caius College, MS. 103/55 [28]
T Cambridge, Trinity College, MS. R.7.28 [37]
C London, BL, MS. Cotton Cleopatra, D.viii [90]
R London, BL, MS. Royal 13.D.ii [112]
A London, Lambeth Palace, MS. 401 [121]
M Madrid, Biblioteca nacional, MS. 6319 [125]

---

54 Edited by Hammer, 'Another Commentary'.
55 'An Unedited Commentary'.
56 Eckhardt, *The Prophetia*, pp. 10–11.
57 *Ibid.*, pp. 11–13.

O Oxford, Bodleian Library, MS. Laud misc. 664 [149]
S Paris, BN, MSS lat. 6232 [177]
Z Paris, BN, MSS lat. 5508 + 13935 [186]

There seem to be connections of varying degrees between A, B, C, L, O, R, and Z but the nature of the relationship has still to be clarified.

Scribal verses

Another possible indicator of vertical transmission (and of a more individual nature than the *Prophetie*-commentaries) is offered by the verses sometimes appended to copies of the *Historia*. As these express the scribe's sentiments and sometimes name him, they are called here 'scribal' although the adjective may well be appropriate not to the copy in hand but to some earlier and lost manuscript.

Verses following the *Historia*

i. Douai, BM, MSS 880 [59] and 882 [60], Valenciennes, BM, MS. 792 [211]

The most elaborate of these 'scribal' verses provides a seventy-line epilogue to the Trojan History of Dares and Geoffrey's History, which it follows in 59 and 60, 'Hec Bernardus ego / qui sub Domini cruce dego . . . cui Cathenesia / seruit amena'.[58] Dares is not found in 211, where this verse is separated from the *Historia* by another (below). 59 and 60 have already been to share other items: verse summaries of individual books of the *Historia* and a poem on Troy (above, Leonine summaries).

ii. (60) 211

211 has a colophon of its own which precedes the above verse,

> 'Scripsimus Arturum quem Britto putat rediturum . . .
> Ceperit huic anime sit eden uel celica tempe'.[59]

The first two lines are entered at the end of 60 (148r) in an informal hand of *c.* 1300, resembling that of the *ex libris* inscriptions elsewhere in the manuscript.

iii. Cambridge, St John's College, MS. G.16 [32], Oxford, Bodleian Library, MS. Rawlinson B.148 [153], and Manchester, John Rylands University Library, MS. lat. 216 [165]

The text of the *Historia* in 32 and 165 is followed by the lines

> Librum scribendo compleui fine iocundo
> Scribere non posco, requiescere fessus hanelo.

---

58 *Colophons*, I.251, no. 2015. Printed by Hammer, 'Some Leonine Summaries', pp. 119–20. MS. 59, 88a/b; MS. 60, 197a–198ra; MS. 211, 54va/b.

59 *Colophons*, VI.492, no. 23365.

> Hec Rogere tibi pro posse polita peregi.
> Mente manu lingua tandemque labore peracta
> Me precor indignum reputes ne semper amicum
> Promissis precio sum dignus iure peracto.[60]

153 has only the first and last lines.[61]

iv. London, BL, Stowe 56 [117] and Paris, BN, lat. 17569 [188]

The *Historia* in these manuscripts is followed by the verse

> 'Hunc primum scripsi. Socios donet Deus ipsi.'

Verses not appended directly to the *Historia*

Scribal verses are found in a number of *Historia*-manuscripts in other positions.

i. London, BL, Harley 3773 [102]

This volume is prefaced by a full page of verses which describe the *Historia* and the other contents of the manuscript (a chronicle of the see of Cologne, *Mappa mundi*). Headed 'Super hystoriam Britonum', they continue 'Actus famosos reges Britonum generosos . . . Error nox Treueris cessat uergit renouatur'. This verse and these contents are not found in any other known *Historia*-manuscript.

ii. Cambridge, UL, Mm.5.29 [54] and Lincoln Cathedral MS. 98 [80]

These manuscripts include the inscription 'Exora Cristum qui librum legeris istum / [U]t det scriptori \Ernulfo/ quicquid debetur honori'. (The name is not found in 80; it occurs as a gloss in 54.)[62] In both manuscripts this is located after the *Parua recapitulacio* and before the notes on Jerusalem and Constantinople.[63]

Capitula-lists

While *capitula*-divisions will receive discussion below among the other kinds of subdivisions of the *Historia* (VI), mention must be made here of the extensive

---

60 *Colophons*, V.259, no. 16787.

61 165 is a two-part manuscript. It is not known at what stage the part containing the *Historia* (*c.* 1300) was joined to the twelfth-century remainder; the two were detached sometime after the writing of Mellot's Bibliothèque nationale catalogue, published in 1744.

62 Attempts to identify this Ernulf have been unfruitful. Ker listed twelfth-century references to two people of that name, one associated with Rochester, who must be excluded on the grounds of date and status (he was prior then bishop, 1115–1124), and one who appears in three Gloucester manuscripts: *Medieval Libraries*, pp. 297, 265. I have examined two of the three (BL Harley 2659 and Bodleian Laud misc. 123). This *Ernulfus* appears to have been donor rather than scribe (his name appears in the genitive). The form of the inscription (the name alone, written in brown capitals on the flyleaves) is not comparable with that in MS. 54.

63 54, 157r; 80, 160rb.

lists of *capitula* which precede six *historia*-texts. These sometimes ran to several folios and provided a detailed summary of the narrative in the form of chapter-headings.

Four of the six, Second-Variant α-manuscripts, contain the list 'Descriptio quantitatis et multimode qualitatis . . . et anglice ystorie tractanda distribuit'. These are CUL Ff.1.15 [47], London, BL, MSS Cotton Galba E.xi [91] and Titus A.xxvii [95], and Troyes, BM 1531 [209]. The Second-Variant γ-manuscript, Stockholm MS. Holm. D.1311 [207] has a different list 'De qualitate et quantitate Britannie . . . quod in ipso regnum Britonum defecit'. The final example is that in the vulgate manuscript, Cambridge, St John's College, G.16 [32], 'Incipit primus liber de situ et regibus Britannie . . . de Iuor et Ini'.

Preliminary Conclusions

Some classes of dependent work would seem to have been sufficently separate from the *Historia* to have been copied by themselves into manuscripts containing different versions of Geoffrey's text. A direct genealogical explanation for the presence of *Armorica siue Latauia* seems unlikely given the variety of *Historia*-texts the manuscripts containing it are known to witness. Similarly Bever's verses were copied into the margins of MSS 90 and 164 from some third source. Commentaries on the Prophecies, from what is known of them, also seem sometimes to have been copied independently from the text itself.

Scribal verses promise more secure connections, partly because the information which they contain is less illuminating for Geoffrey's History and so they are less likely to be copied into some other manuscript already containing the *Historia*. Such verses, together with Leonine summaries, create a double bond between MSS. 59 and 60. The same scribal verses occur in MS. 211, a part of whose colophon is found in MS. 60. Scribal verses indicate further groupings: 117/188, 32/153/165, and 54/80. Finally, a particular form of *capitula*-list is found in three Second-Variant α-manuscripts.

IV

DISRUPTIONS OF THE VULGATE TEXT

The process of uncovering the original vulgate text by identifying and stripping away later forms which developed from it entails an unavoidable circularity: for it is necessary to define the term *vulgate* in order to identify the changes which it underwent. In certain cases, such as an idiosyncratic interpolation, the added material is obvious enough. Where the original reading is less clear, Neil Wright's semi-diplomatic edition of Bern, Burgerbibliothek 568 has been taken for the time being to represent the vulgate. The justice of this position cannot be assessed until all other types of evidence, especially that of test-collations, has been examined. Wright's text is, then, the fixed point against which other manuscripts are measured and interpolations, variants, and omissions identified.

INTERPOLATIONS

Passages interpolated into the *Historia* may be divided into three classes: items which amplify their immediate context in the work, those which serve as comparison rather than direct extension of the text, and finally those whose inclusion is apparently fortuitous.

Addition of material supplementing the text

Merlinus iste

A paragraph describing the mysterious birth and prophetic powers of Merlin is the best-attested substantial item interpolated into the *Historia*. It is usually found at the end of the Prophecies of Merlin. It runs 'Merlinus iste inter Britones sapientissimus fuit . . . an malos spiritus futura propalare consueuit' and was printed by Jacob Hammer from Lincoln Cathedral MS. 98 [80].[1] Hammer noted that it is found in five other *Historia*-manuscripts: CUL, MS. Mm.5.29 [54]; Dublin, Trinity College, MS. 514 [66]; London, BL, MS. Royal 14.C.i [114];

---

1 'Some Additional Manuscripts', p. 239.

Oxford, Bodleian Library, MS. Laud misc. 664 [149]; Ushaw College, MS. 6 [210]. Three may be added to his list. They are Aberystwyth, NLW, MS. 21552 [5] (in which it is found in the margin), CUL MS. Ii.4.12 [50][2] and Alençon, BM, MS. 12 [12], a manuscript recently added to the total of *Historia*-witnesses.[3] *Merlinus iste* has also been identified in one manuscript not containing the *Historia*: Tokyo, Prof. T. Takamiya, MS. 62 (*olim* Bradfer-Lawrence 2).[4] In all except 66 the interpolation is found after §117. This is the case even in 5, where the entry is marginal but clearly linked to the beginning of §118 by a *signe de renvoi*. In 66, the passage precedes the Prophecies, following the Prologue (§§109–110). This manuscript is also anomalous in being the only Second-Variant α-witness among the none manuscripts.

The most obvious division of the remaining eight is between the four vulgate and the four Second-Variant β-manuscripts 50, 54, 80, and 114. These last four represent all but one of the known manuscripts of the β-subgroup. As the remaining manuscript, Cambridge, Clare College, MS. 27 [22], lacks the end of the Prophecies after §116.62 (the text resumes at §156), it is quite possible that all members of the group originally included *Merlinus iste* after §117.

Two of the four vulgate manuscripts, 12 and 210, (both twelfth-century) originally contained only the second half of the *Historia* (see below, OMIS-SIONS). This suggests a connection with the β-manuscripts, which revert to vulgate in the latter half of the text. The two remaining vulgate manuscripts containing the *Merlinus iste* interpolation date from the thirteenth and fourteenth centuries.

Paris, BN, lat. 6232 [177]

Another passage about Merlin is found at the beginning of the Prophecies in MS. 177. This runs along the outer margin of the text of §§110–112 (58v).

> Merlinus iste filius fuit Mathioc que fuer[a]t filia regis [u]alliarum.[5] Sed si quis pater eius exst<it>erit [?n]escitur plures tamen [a]sse<n>ciunt ipsum ex incubo spiritum progenitum esse. Non quia hoc pro uero sciant [sed] quia dicuntur calo (*sic*) demones inter lunam et terram habitare qui cum mulieribus coire solebant. Unde incubi demones appellantur. Sed quicquid si de patre non est dubium ipsum habuisse spiritum prophetie cum ea que hactenus dixerit manifestum est euenire. Si quis autem querit quo spiritu prophetauit sciat (*sic*) quia si bonum spiritum habuit potuit futiua (*sic*) predicere. Etiam si malum [h]abuerit potuit predicere futura. Testantibus scripturis que etiam malos prophetura ostendunt ut Caypham pontificem et Baalaam prophetam et sibillam preser[t]im cum he due insule Britannia uidelicet et Hibernia naturaliter prophetas habuit.

---

2 Both previously identified by David Dumville.
3 Crick, 'Manuscripts', pp. 159–60.
4 *Ex inf.* D. N. Dumville. Described by Giles, 'A Handlist', p. 87.
5 See Appendix at end of chapter.

Bruxelles, BR, 9871–9874 [20]

A third interpolation concerning Merlin is found in the middle of §143 in this manuscript. After the words 'diademate insignuit (*sic*)' and the rubric 'Prophetia Merlini de Arturo', there is a passage describing a dialogue between Arthur and Merlin concerning the date of Arthur's death (140r/v).

Ego Merlinus, rogatus ab Arturo prima luce militie sue ut quantum in hac uita duraturus esset super terram insinuarem, obieci: Quantum uixisti?

At ille: Quere a matercula mea que et dies et annos dinumerauit.

Ego autem, cum presentem eius nutricem uiderem, allocuta ea dixi: Numquid nosti (*sic*) quantum alumpnus tuus uixerit?

At illa: Qui sexto idus Aprilis militis nomen induit. Si Iulium uixerit kalendas Augusti .xviii. annorum rex coronabitur. Sic quidem pater eius et ego numerauimus.

Ego autem hiis auditis satisfaciens rogationi et non roganti dixi ad Arturum: Dies tui numerant tempora mundi. Exitus uero uite tue erit dubius. Uera loquor. Hec ultima de me studio apti habeant in quibus quanto quis magis studuerit tanto minus sapiens sibi uidebitur.

Arthur's Letter

Another interpolation consists of a fictitious document inserted in the text presumably to lend vividness to the narrative. This is the letter of Arthur placed, in Oxford, Bodleian Library, MS. Bodley 233 [135], the earliest manuscript in which it is found (*saec.* xiv[1]), after the account of the Battle of Camlann, in which Mordred was killed and Arthur fatally wounded (§178). The interpolation is entitled here (and in the three other manuscripts in which it occurs) 'Littere quas misit Arturus inuictus rex Britannie Hugoni capillano (*sic*) de Branno super Sequanam cum palefrido'. In Aberystwyth, NLW, MS. Llanstephan 196 [7] (fifteenth-century) and Oxford, Bodleian, MS. Rawlinson B.189 [155] (late fourteenth-century), Arthur's letter precedes the *Historia*, in MS. 7 following the rubric 'Incipit tractatio historie Bruti'. In Würzburg, UB, M.ch.f.140 [213] (sixteenth-century) the text runs on after §208 without a break.[6]

Littere quas misit Arturus inuictus rex Britannie Hugoni cappellano de Branno super Secanam cum palefrido anno Domini .m.c.lvii.[7]

---

6 In 7 and 155 the *Historia* is followed by the Merlin prophecy beginning 'Sicut rubeum draconem' (see above, II: Prophecies: Merlin).

7 The date not found in MSS 7 or 155. It is tempting to speculate that this text has something to do with the struggle of the Bretons against the Angevins in the 1150s and 1160s. Peter Johanek has recently argued that Stephen of Rouen's composition, *Draco Normannicus*, which drew heavily on Arthurian, and Galfridian, material, marked the subjection of Brittany to Henry II in 1167: 'König Arthur', pp. 383–88. Tensions were already beginning to build up by 1157, the date of our text: Chédeville and Tonnerre, *La Bretagne féodale*, pp. 84–88. Thirty years afterwards the son of Geoffrey of Anjou and Constance of Brittany was named Arthur: see Hillion, 'La Bretagne', p. 113. I hope to discuss this matter fully elsewhere.

Arturus Dei gratia utriusque Britannie rex desideratissimus .H. uenerabili capellano salutem et expectationis tante fructuosam retribucionem. Occulta cordis desideria .uii. nocte mensis septimi septem Dei famuli nobis sepcies reuelauerunt. Quiescant ergo intima suspiria. Appropinquat enim manifestacionis nostre gloria. Affectus cotidiani maturos inuenient effectus. Si[nu]s uniuerse matris nequaquam tibi aperietur quo usque tetrathas (*sic*) occidentis et aquilonis regulos ante fortitudinem manus nostre corruisse uidebis Adhuc modicum et ecce moriganis (*sic*) optatos expetens amplexus ignem frigescere stupebit. Recurret ad consuetum antique artis auxilium et societatis fastidium renouacione doloris euincere temptabit. Uerum tamen medulle nichil mouebuntur quoniam lapide celitus inmisso purpurei riuuli cessabit inundatio. Tunc duo mondi (*sic*) climata imperio nostro pariter munientur. Terraque a Ioue (*sic*) ad Isium (*sic*) libere tibi pro dignitate tue promocionis famulabitur.

BL MSS Arundel 319 + 409 [87]

This manuscript, now bound in two parts, contains eight lines interpolated into the Prophecies of Merlin (MS. 319, 73r, beginning at line 17).

Dolor conuertetur in gaudium cum matris in utero patrem filii trucidabunt. Orientis priuilegio gaudebit occidens et terrarum tam princeps quam primates ?ueri uestigia martiris adorabunt. Ex delicto geniti delinquunt in genitorem et precedens delictum fit causa sequencium delictorum. In ?uirum sanguinis sanguis inst[ ]get (*sic*) et disparabilis fiet afflictio donec Albania peregrinantis fleuit penitenciam. Quinti quadriga uoluetur in quartum et bis binario sublato, bina superstes regna calcabit.

The Seaxburh phrase

The account of the landing of a Saxon army in Northumbria which signalled the end of British power (§204) sometimes names the queen of that region, Seaxburh.[8] After 'Quod cum ipsis indicatum fuisset', where the vulgate reads 'Nefandus populus iste', there is the variant 'Quedam nobilissima regina Sexburgis nomine que uidua fuerat'. §204 is absent, whether by physical loss or deliberate truncation of the text, from forty-three manuscripts, although in some the end has been supplied in later hands (and contains the vulgate chapter §204). Forty-two of the *Historia*-manuscripts in which the relevant part of §204 is found include the note about Seaxburh.

Aberystwyth,
NLW, MSS
  21552 [5]
  Llanstephan 176 [6]
  Peniarth 42 [8]
  Peniarth 43 [9]

---

[8] I am grateful to Neil Wright for suggesting at the beginning of the survey that this phrase might be valuable as a text-historical indicator.

Alençon, BM, MS. 12 [12]
Cambridge,
    Clare College, MS. 27 [22]
    Corpus Christi College, MS. 292 [24]
    Gonville & Caius College, MS. 103/55 [28]
    St John's College, MS. S.6 [33]
    Trinity College, MS. O.1.17 [38]
    University Library, MSS
      Dd.4.34 [41]
      Dd.6.7 [42]
      Ii.4.12 [50]
      Kk.6.16 [52]
      Mm.5.29 [54]
Dublin, Trinity College, MS. 495 [64]
Firenze, Biblioteca Nazionale, MS. B.R. 55 [72]
Lincoln, Cathedral Library, MS. 98 [80]
London, BL, MSS
    Add. 35295 [84]
    Arundel 319 + 409 [87]
    Cotton Titus A.xviii [93]
    Cotton Titus A.xxvii [95]
    Cotton Vespasian E.x [98]
    Egerton 3142 [99]
    Harley 225 [100]
    Royal 13.A.iii [109]
    Royal 13.D.v [113]
    Royal 14.C.i [114]
    Royal 15.C.xvi [115]
  College of Arms, MS. Arundel 1 [118]
  Lambeth Palace, MSS
      454a [122]
      503 [124]
Olomouc, Archive, MS. 411 [131]
Oxford, All Souls' College, MS. 35 [132]
  Bodleian Library, MSS
    Add A.61 [134]
    Douce 115 [140]
    Laud misc. 720 [150]
  Christ Church, MS. 99 [160]
  Magdalen College, MS. lat. 170 [161]
Paris, BN, MS. lat. 6233 [178]
Ushaw College, MS. 6 [210]
Winchester, Cathedral Library, MS. 9 [212]

One group among these is clearly distinguishable: seven of the eight manuscripts in which the *Merlinus iste* passage is found after §117 of the *Historia* also include the phrase about Seaxburh. These are the Second-Variant β-manuscripts 50, 54, 80, and 114 and the vulgates 5 (in which the *Merlinus* passage is marginal), 12, and 210.[9] The only other Variant witness listed above is 22, which also belongs to the β-subgroup. As the end of the Prophecies is lacunose it is probable that the absence of the *Merlinus* passage from this alone of β-manuscripts is due to accidental loss rather than deliberate omission.

Addition of relevant comparative material

Eusebius-Jerome Chronicle

Four *Historia*-manuscripts include after §5 the entry from the Eusebius-Jerome Chronicle for 1157 B.C., which records the flight of Æneas:[10]

> Anno ante incarnationem Domini .m.c.lvii. et ante condicionem Rome .ccc.l.xxxvi. et ab origine mundi .iii(m).cccc.xlix. annis peractis Eneas cum Ascanio filio diffugiens Italiam nauigio adiuit.[11]

The four are: Cambridge, St John's College, G.16 [32], Glasgow, UL, 331 [73], London, BL, Cotton Vespasian E.x [98], and Oxford, Bodleian, MS. Rawlinson B.148 [153].

The text of the interpolation is also found in a form nearly identical to this in BL Add. 35295 [84] (in the margin of 137v)[12] in a hand resembling one found in another part of the same manuscript.

Oxford, Bodleian Library, MS. Jesus College 2 [142]

The text of the *Historia* in this fifteenth-century paper manuscript is heavily interpolated and annotated with comparative chronicle material, mostly concerning Roman and Old Testament history. This is found within §§6, 33, 52, 64, 79, and 100, and after §§74 and 78. There is also an addition of a different sort at the end of the Prophecies.

The first interruption of Geoffrey's text, on 1r, is headed 'Nota ut habent in cronicis Martini'. The interpolation which follows (ending on 2r) is the historical introduction to the chronicle of popes and emperors by Martinus Polonus, a work often associated with Geoffrey's text (above, II) and which provides an account of the Trojan remnant parallel to Geoffrey's own.[13] Besides annotations

---

9 The vulgate Oxford, Bodleian, Laud misc. 664 [149] is the only manuscript including *Merlinus iste* after §117 but not the Seaxburh phrase.

10 The source of the text was identified by D. N. Dumville, who was aware of the presence of the interpolation in these manuscripts.

11 The main clause 'Eneas ... adiuit' is a summary version of the first sentence of §5.

12 *Ex inf.* D. N. Dumville. For *diffugiens Italiam* it reads *Troiam deserens*.

13 Edited by Weiland, MGH SS XXII.398 (l. 49)–399 (l. 20).

elsewhere, the lower margins of fos 17v–33r are filled with running text, taken mostly from the same source.[14] The interpolations in §§64 (47v–48r) and 75 (55r) may also be traced to Martinus.[15] I have not been able to identify the sources of the other historical interpolations (mostly concerning Israelite history).

The addition at the end of the Prophecies is of a different kind: the beginning of the Prophecy of the Eagle of Shaftesbury, mentioned by Geoffrey himself and which follows the *Historia* in a number of manuscripts (above, II: *Prophecies*).[16]

Mirabilia

As well as the *Mirabilia* found in *Historia*-manuscripts appended to the text or occurring as separate works, two related witnesses contain such material as an interpolation after §5. These are London, BL, MSS Arundel 326 [88] and Sloane 289 [116].[17] The interpolated passage (found respectively on 63v–64r and 120v–121r) runs 'Quoddam namque stagnum . . . et qualiter Troianos trans tot equora ista longe positis regnis in Britanniam adduxerit'.[18]

Henry of Huntingdon, *Historia Anglorum*

Ushaw College MS. 6 [210] has been mentioned briefly above in connection with *Merlinus iste*. It contains a larger and more unusual interpolation, however, that of a nearly complete text of Henry's *Historia Anglorum*, to which Wilhelm Levison first drew attention in 1943.[19] He described how, not long after it was copied, Geoffrey's *Historia* had been divided at §178 'quia omnes fere duces' (as proved by a hiatus in the quire signatures), and part of the text after the hiatus recopied (from §178 'qui in ambis partibus' to the end of §187), and Henry's History, minus the first two books and the prologue to the third, substituted. Thus Geoffrey's account was supplemented by Henry's version of events from the Augustinian mission.[20] The text of the *Historia Anglorum* is an early witness to the edition of 1138.[21] Levison, regarding the *Historia* as a single production, failed to notice a further complication in the manuscript's make-up, namely that the reviser was also responsible for the presence of §§1–109, as Dumville has shown.[22] Two other volumes seem also to have been constituted in two distinct parts, §1–109 and §§110–208 (below, OMISSIONS).

---

14 *Ibid.*, XXII.399 (l. 25)–403 (l. 41).
15 *Ibid.*, XXII.408 (ll. 12–26); 448 (ll. 1–10).
16 Found on 145r/v: 'Arbor fertilis a proprio trunco decisa . . . in hac tribulacione remedium'. Edited by Schulz, *Gottfried*, pp. 463–64.
17 Whose contents have already shown to be closely connected (above, II: Chronology: *In principio*).
18 Printed by Dumville, 'Anecdota'.
19 'A Combined Manuscript'.
20 *Ibid.*, p. 43.
21 Greenway, 'Henry', p. 108.
22 'The Origin', pp. 316–17.

Uera Historia de morte Arturi

This work is interpolated in its entirety between §§178 and 179 of the First-Variant manuscript Paris, Bibliothèque de l'Arsenal, MS. 982 [163].[23]

Apparently accidental interpolation

BL Arundel 10 [85]

This Second-Variant manuscript contains an incongruous interpolation on heretics before §6 (3rb/va). This takes the form of a lemma from Augustine's *Enarrationes in psalmos*, 10.5,[24] with accompanying gloss.[25]

> **Imperatorum constitutionem frustra obicitis[26] catholici cum in uestris castris priuati fustes ignesque sic seuiant.**
> Constituerunt romani imperatores ut donatiste heretici omni suarum rerum possessione priuarentur et insuper nisi resipiscerent multis ac uariis cruciatibus torquerentur. Hec lex scripta reperitur in libro quem maiorem codicem iuris periti uocant. Hanc constitucionem ipsi heretici catholicis obiciebant, dicentes eos non scientia disputandi non fidei ueritate confidere. sed terrore huius legis disputando aduersarios deterrere. Hoc frustra et insipienter agebant. Nam et ipsi in suis conuenticulis fustibus et ignibus catholicos torquendos esse instituerunt. conuenticula hereticorum castra uocat. quia in ipsis more militantium contra catholicos heretici seuiebant. Priuati fustes id est a priuatis hominibus instituti; priuati enim dicuntur qui publicis non sint dignitatibus implicati.

The origin of the gloss has proved elusive. The passage was copied at the same time of the text of the *Historia*, in the late twelfth century, and therefore it antedates a number of authors who commented on Augustine's *Enarrationes*.

BL Egerton 3142 [99]

This *Historia*-text contains an apparently accidental interpolation which was cancelled in red by the scribe/rubricator. After the end of the Prophecies (§117),

---

23 Wright, *The Historia*, II.xc. Edited by Lapidge, 'An Edition', pp. 79–83.
24 Ed. Dekkers and Fraipont, *Sancti Aurelii Augustini Enarrationes*, p. 78, lines 48–50. I owe the identification of the text to Professor M. D. Reeve.
25 An explanation for this and the similar position of the interpolations of chronicle and *mirabilia* material might be sought in the separability of the opening chapters from the main text; rubrics and book-divisions show this sometimes to have been considered to begin at §5 or §6, below, VI. If the opening chapters were written on a separate leaf (see below, OMISSIONS: entire passages), then the blank space perhaps left at the end of the introductory chapters could have been used for notes, which might later be incorporated into the text.
26 Dekkers and Fraipont print *obicientem* but record *obicitis* in their apparatus.

the scribe copied, mid-page, a letter of Pope Innocent III to Master Aimon, canon of Poitiers, dated 18 October, 1208.[27]

SECTIONS DIFFERING SUBSTANTIALLY FROM THE VULGATE TEXT

Recognized variants (including Pudibundus Brito)

The two variants identified by Jacob Hammer – the First and Second – remain the most divergent form of the text still recognizable as Geoffrey's *Historia*. Their salient features have already been described (above, I). Outright abridgements and paraphrases will not be considered here.

Mention has also been made in print of a third variant. This was the name given by David Dumville to manuscripts bearing a revised form of the prologue and dedicatory epistle to the Prophecies which excludes the name of the dedicatee, Alexander, bishop of Lincoln:[28] its author, in conventionally modest vein, describes himself as *pudibundus Brito*. Edmond Faral had used one such manuscript in his edition – Paris, BN, lat. 6233 [178], which also lacks the opening dedication(s). Faral regarded the absence of both dedications as authorial and duly fitted it into his scheme of four 'editions' of the text (later revised to three), a classification based on the supposed historical contexts of each of the dedications.[29] 178 was his sole representative of the last of these editions. He viewed it as a final revision made by Geoffrey in search of patronage after the deaths of his main dedicatees, Robert of Gloucester and Alexander of Lincoln, in 1147/8.[30] Hammer expressed justifiable scepticism about the realities of Faral's classification. Having found §§1–5 to be absent from a manuscript textually dissimilar to 178, Hammer concentrated his attention on the possible textual significance of the revision of §§109–110, ignoring the opening chapters. Thus he was able to pair MS. 178 with Oxford, Bodleian, MS. Rawlinson C.152 [156], which does bear the initial dedication.[31] Dumville, using the same criterion, increased the list of so-called 'third-variant' manuscripts to nine.[32] The present total stands at 15 (the items additional to Dumville's list are asterisked).

Aberystwyth, NLW, MS. Peniarth 43 [9]

* Cambridge, Gonville & Caius College, MS. 450/391 [31]

27 Identified by Wright, *The British Museum Catalogue of Additions to the manuscripts 1936–1945*, I.334. Potthast, *Regesta*, I.304, no. 3519.
28 'The Manuscripts', p. 128. Printed by Faral, 'Geoffroy', pp. 31–32; *La Légende*, II.24–26. For the usual contents of this prologue, see below, OMISSIONS.
29 'Geoffroy', pp. 18–32; 'L'*Historia*'.
30 'Geoffroy', p. 30.
31 'A Commentary', p. 4, n. 3.
32 'The Manuscripts', p. 128.

Cambridge, UL, MSS
>Dd.4.34 [41]
>Dd.6.7 [42]
>Dd.10.31 [44]

London, BL, MSS
>Cotton Titus A.xviii [93]
>Royal 13.D.v [113]

London, College of Arms, MS. Arundel 1 [118]
* Oxford, All Souls' College, MS. 35 [132]
* Oxford, Bodleian Library, MSS
>Douce 115 [140]
>* Jones 48 [143]
>* Laud misc. 720 [150]
>Rawlinson C.152 [156]

Paris, BN, lat. 6233 [178]
* Winchester, Cathedral Library, MS. 9 [212]

Despite Hammer's surmises about the accidental nature of the absence of §§1–5 from 178, Faral's precarious categorization (although not his deductions about it) finds some support here, ironically enough. 9 and 143 omit §§1–4, while 41, 132, and 140 originally began at §6, exactly like 178.[33] 31 is acephalous and so could have been another example of a manuscript from which the dedication is omitted.

The phrase about Seaxburh is present in all representatives of this group, except those lacking the closing chapters (31, 44, 143, and 156).

Other variant sections

§5

Two manuscripts contain a form of §5 which includes material sufficiently foreign to the text to be considered here rather than with the test-collations (VII). These are London, British Library, MSS Arundel 326 [88] and Sloane 289 [116].[34] Besides minor variants (to be discussed later) and two short additions within the chapter, its ending departs totally from the usual text.

The first interpolation occurs near the beginning of the chapter, after '.cc. uero in latum', to which is added 'et in circuitu tria milia milium et sexcenta'. Later, after 'ciuitatibus olim decorata erat', is the addition 'Preter castella innumera que et ipsa muris et turribus portis ac seris erant instructa firmissime'. This last interpolation is taken from Bede's Ecclesiastical History, I.i, or perhaps Henry of Huntingdon, who quotes it verbatim in his *Historia Anglorum* (I, §3). The normal text is truncated at 'iuxta Christianam tradicionem prestant. Postremo', and the

---

[33] On the construction of MS. 132, see below, *Merlinus uero incipiens*.
[34] Compare above, II: Chronology, *In principio*; IV: *Mirabilia*.

new ending substituted: 'quibusdam admiranda est mirabilibus que tamen et si solis audientibus ficta uideantur illis tamen qui ea intuentur uera esse manifestum est'.

OMISSIONS

Omissions from the text can have various causes: the editing out of certain passages not evidently germane to the text, omission of sections (presumably inessential) in the body of the text simply for the sake of brevity, or accidental loss whether caused by scribal error or by the copying of a physically imperfect exemplar. While the first may have happened independently on several occasions, the second two circumstances are likely to be more direct pointers to a line of transmission.

Entire passages readily separable from the text

The Opening Chapters

Interpolations between §§5 and 6 have already been seen to illustrate the separability of the opening chapters, as will be discussed more fully below (V).[35] This division is explained by subject-matter. Geoffrey began his work by advertising the necessity for the writing down of the history of the British kings (§1). In §2 he explains how he obtained his source (*librum uetustissimum*) from Walter, archdeacon of Oxford. The succeeding chapters contain the dedications of the work. That to Robert of Gloucester is usually found in §3 – §4 (which provides the secondary dedication) being omitted. In the double dedication to Robert and Waleran of Meulan, the primary dedication to Robert in §3 is retained and the secondary found in §4. The order is reversed in the Stephen-Robert dedication found in Bern 568 [15], in which the king's name takes precedence. §5 contains a geographical description of the island along classical lines.

§§1–4

One of the eight witnesses in which the text begins at §5, BL Royal 13.A.v [110], has a unique abbreviation of §§5–8. Five others are First-Variant: Dublin, Trinity College, MS. 515 [67], Aberystwyth, NLW, MSS Panton 37 [1] and 13210 [4], London, BL, MS. Harley 6538 [106], Paris, Bibliothèque de l'Arsenal, MS. 982

---

35 Compare, for instance, the rubrics at §1 'Incipit prologus Gaufridi Monemutensis in historia regum Britannie', and §5 'Explicit prologus. Incipit historia'. There are numerous similar examples.

[163].[36] The final manuscripts beginning at §5 are Aberystwyth, NLW, Peniarth 43 [9] and Oxford, Bodleian, Jones 48 [143], which both include the *Merlinus uero incipiens* version of §118 (see below) and the *pudibundus Brito* passage (above, Recognized Variants).

§§1–5

Various types of text may begin at §6. The two relatives of the only known manuscript dedicated to Stephen and Robert of Gloucester begin thus (see below, V): London, BL, MS. Arundel 237 [86] and Rouen, BM, MS. U.74 [200]. The explanation for the absence of §§1–5 perhaps lies in the location of these chapters in their relative, Bern, Burgerbibliothek, MS. 568 [15], on a separate bifolium prefacing the text.[37] A similar case in which the opening chapters were separated from their context is provided by the Second-Variant BL Royal 4.C.xi [108]: §§1–3 and 5 are written on the folio facing the end of §208, the main text having begun at §6.

Four witnesses beginning at §6 contain the revised version of §§109–110, as mentioned above. These are CUL Dd.4.34 [41], Oxford, All Souls' College 35 [132] and Bodleian Douce 115 [140], and Faral's chosen manuscript, BN, lat. 6233 [178]. Two other vulgate copies begin likewise: Eton College 246 [69] and Jesus College 2 [142]. They have no other contents.

The abridgements in BL Arundel 220 and BN lat. 11107 also begin at §6.[38]

§5 omitted

The description of Britain (after the opening chapters) is omitted from only one manuscript: Cambridge, St John's College, MS. S.6 [33].

§§1–109 or 110–208

Two manuscripts seem originally to have begun at the introductory epistle to the Prophecies. 210 began here but the text (§§110–208) was later expanded and interpolated (above, II: *Historia Anglorum*). The *Historia*-text in 12 forms an addition at the end of a somewhat earlier manuscript, and consists of *Merlinus iste* followed by §§118–208, a unique arrangement. MS. 210 also contains *Merlinus iste*.

In two manuscripts – Cambridge, Corpus Christi College, MS. 281 [23], and Lambeth Palace, MS. 454b [123], both twelfth-century –, there is a marked difference between the script and layout of §§1–109 and 110–208, which

---

36 As 1 is an eighteenth-century transcript containing extracts from a First-Variant manuscript, there is room for doubt on this point; but it begins with §§5 and 6. While §§1–4 were originally lacking from 4, they were entered in a margin of the manuscript (10v) in an Early Modern hand.

37 Dumville, 'An Early Text', pp. 15, 17, and 21.

38 On which see Crick, *A Summary Catalogue*, Appendix V.

constitute physically distinct units. In MS. 123, §§1–109 are written in the earlier hand. In MS. 23, the relative age of the two units is more difficult to determine. They are physically distinct.[39]

Other manuscripts show some disruption or change at the Prophecies, their introduction, or before. In Paris, Sainte-Geneviève, MS. 2113 [191], a twelfth-century manuscript, §109 begins in a new, slightly later-looking hand at the foot of the last leaf of a quire. This new scribe completed the copying of the text.[40] In three other manuscripts, hands change at less well-marked points: in §105 in Arras, BM, 598 [13], between §§101 and 108 in Cambridge, Trinity College, MS. R.5.34 [35], and at §116.51 in Cambridge, University Library, MS. Dd.6.12 [43]. In addition, in Glasgow, UL, 332 [74] there are changes of hand at the Prophecies and at §118, both of which begin on fresh quires.

The Prologue to the Prophecies

At §109 the author interrupts the narrative to include the prophecies delivered by Merlin to Vortigern in order to explain the mysterious repeated subsidence of the tower which the king is having built. Geoffrey tells how, when he got to this point in the story, he was beset by requests from various sources and so impelled to include a translation of the Prophecies (§109). This he dedicates to Alexander, bishop of Lincoln, in a flowery epistle (§110).

Only §109 omitted

This omission is to be noted in a single manuscript, the Second-Variant Oxford, Bodleian, MS. Bodley 977 [138]. The last phrase of §108 ('tantam in eo . . . esse in illo') is also absent.

§110

This is lacking in its entirety from three manuscripts. Two are the Second-Variant γ-manuscripts, Saint-Omer, BM, 710 [202] and Bruges, BM, 428 [17]. The third is Aberystwyth, NLW, Peniarth 42 [8] (vulgate). §110 is absent except for the first clause 'Coegit me . . . dilectio' from Manchester, John Rylands, lat. 216 [165] and London, BL, Cotton Vespasian E.x [98]. 98 has the interpolated chronicle entry after §5 found in MS. 32 and elsewhere (above, Eusebius-Jerome).

§§109–110

The prologue to the Prophecies is omitted from several First-Variant manuscripts. These are NLW 13210 [4], BL Harley 6358 [106], and Arsenal 982 [163]; the

---

39 §110 begins at 30r on a fresh quire; §§1–109 are found on the preceding three complete quires and the first five leaves of a fourth gathering (the final three have been excised).
40 Michael Reeve has discussed MS. 194 in a forthcoming paper.

chapters are marginal additions in a fourth, Exeter 3514 [70]. Ten vulgate witnesses omit these chapters: Arras, BM, 583 [13], Bruxelles, BR, 9871–9874 [20], Cambridge, Sidney Sussex College, 75 [34], BL, MSS Arundel 326 [88], Harley 5115 [105], Royal 13.D.i [111], and Sloane 289 [116], Lambeth Palace 454b [123], Bodleian, Additional A.61 [134] and Phillipps 3117 [214].

The Prophecies themselves (§§111–117)

In two manuscripts the Prophecies (§§111–117) are missing from their usual position within the *Historia* and are found instead after §208. In Bruges, BM, MS. 428 [17] this results in the loss of their prologue as the text of the *Historia* jumps from §§108 to 118. §§109–110 are in their usual position in Cambridge, Trinity College, MS. O.1.17 [38], despite the displacement of the Prophecies. Dublin, Trinity College, 494 [63], may have been arranged similarly but as its text of the *Historia* is now truncated at §204, there is no indication of whether the Prophecies followed.

The prophecies were omitted entirely from Oxford, All Souls' College, 35 [132], a manuscript containing the *pudibundus Brito* version of §§109–110, although the absent chapters were later supplied on an extra leaf inserted into the text, the additions being marked by *signes de renvoi*. The original omission occasioned some rewriting (see below, *Merlinus uero incipiens*).

The omission of text within the body of the Historia

This classification has different implications from the above in that sections within the text, being less prominent, were less subject to capricious omissions, scribal error excepted. The boundaries between the classes are blurred, however, as certain passages were extraneous to the narrative and might have invited editorial exclusion. Several cases have come to light in the course of checking the extent of the text in each manuscript. The following omissions therefore mostly occur across chapter-divisions or take the form of obvious truncation of chapters. They can represent only a sample of a more widespread phenomenon whose traces are embedded within the text and whose extent only full collation can identify.

§§5–8

BL Royal 13.A.v [110] lacks the initial dedicatory material, beginning instead with the description of Britain at §5. Several passages are absent from this and the following three chapters, the end of §7 and §8 being replaced by a short linking phrase.

§5 is reduced to its opening and closing sections, the text from 'Omni etenim genere' to 'Christianam tradicionem prestant. Postremo' being omitted. The last sentence of §6 is absent and the text ends at 'sagitte interfecit'. A phrase is missing from the opening of §7 'indignantibus parentibus . . . Exulatus ergo' and the chapter is truncated in the middle after 'in captionem teneri preceperat'. Geoffrey's text resumes at the letter to Pandrasus in §8 'Pandraso regi Grecorum', the end of §7 and the beginning of §8 being summarized: 'Brutus in Gretiam ueniens factus est dux eorum statimque cum suo exercitu nemora et colles occupauit. Deinde literas suas regi in hec uerba direxit'.

§§25–26

In Cambridge, Trinity College, MS. R.7.28 [37] text is lost between the end of §25 and beginning of §26. This is unique among *Historia*-manuscripts. §25 ends 'alia lingua Sabrina uocatur'; then, after the linking phrase 'Regnauitque cum [ ]ace et diligencia .xl. annis', §26 begins 'Quo defuncto discordia'.

§§42–43

In four manuscripts there is a leap from §42 'ipsos deditioni coegerunt' to §43 'et petentes Romam et tota'. The explanation would seem to lie in eye-skip between 'deditioni (coegerunt)' and the phrase which occurs at the end of the omitted material, 'deditioni (compulsissent)'. This omission is found in NLW Peniarth 43 [9], Bodleian Jones 48 [143] (compare above, §§1–4), and also in BL Cotton Titus A.xviii [93] and BN lat. 4126 [164]. 9, 93, and 143 bear the *pudibundus Brito* prologue to the Prophecies.

§§83–84

In six manuscripts, the text of §83 is truncated at 'acquieuit ei Octauius' and that of §84 begins 'Ut igitur transfretauit', the join being effected by a summarizing phrase. This results in the loss of the description of the ravaging of Southumbria by Conan Meriadocus, the narrative being moved on directly to the invasion of Gaul.

In Bruxelles, BR, 9871–9874 [20], Montpellier, BM, 92 [126], and Paris, BN, lat. 5233 [166] §83 ends 'adquieuit ei Octauius', followed by the link 'Igitur post acceptum regnum Britannie affectauit Maximianus sibi Gallias subiugare'. §83 ends a phrase later in the other three manuscripts and is followed by a shortened form of the same linking phrase 'quin affectaret Gallias subiugare'. This is found in Paris, BN, MSS lat. 6041B [173] and 6230 [175], and Oxford, Bodleian, MS. New College 276 [151]. The six manuscripts contain other abbreviated sections (§§173–174, 179, and 184), which are discussed below.

The linking phrase is present as an interpolation without the accompanying abbreviations in Oxford, All Souls' College, MS. 39 [133]. After the words 'militem Britannie collegit' in §84 follows the sentence 'Non sufficiebat ei regnum Britannie quin affectaret Gallias subiugare'.

§150

§150 is truncated after the first sentence 'His itaque gestis . . . numero adesse' in BL MSS Arundel 326 [88] and Sloane 289 [116], thus losing a description of two miraculous pools, one in Scotland, one in Wales. As Geoffrey derived much of this material from the *mirabilia* of the *Historia Brittonum*, it is noteworthy that material of a similar kind and origin is interpolated after §5 in both manuscripts (above, INTERPOLATIONS). They also lack text from §§177 and 179.

§§171–173

San Marino, Huntington Library, MS. EL 34.C.9 [204] contains a text from which material in these chapters has been omitted deliberately, whether the editing was original to this manuscript or inherited from an exemplar. This results in the loss of details about the battle of Saussy. §171 is truncated, ending 'et Kaius dapifer letaliter uulneratus'. The following chapter is entirely absent except for one reworked sentence, the text resuming in the middle of §173, 'Hoelus uero et Galwagnus quibus meliores'. The link, from §172, runs 'In parte namque Romanorum exceptis innumerabilibus aliis rex Hispanie rex Babilonis cum pluribus ualentibus senatoribus cor[ruer]unt'. Other edited passages in this manuscript are found in §§179, 181, 186, 200, and 202.

§§173–174

The six manuscripts omitting part of §§83–84 – 20, 126, 151, 166, 173, and 175 – contain a similar abbreviation in §§173–174: the contiguous ends of these chapters are truncated and a linking phrase supplied. As a result, the account of the rallying of the Romans at the battle of Saussy is omitted. §173 is ended at 'Romani subito recuperantes', §174 beginning 'audita[41] strage suorum', and the link supplied is 'imperatori subueniunt. Hoelumque et Galganum[42] usque ad aciem Arturi expellunt;[43] Arturus'.[44]

§177

The first part of §177 is lacking in a number of manuscripts, in which the chapter begins 'Ut igitur infamia'. The absent section contains Geoffrey's only reference outside §§1–5 and 109–110 to his dedicatee, who is unnamed here but appealed to as *consul auguste*. Chambers, arguing for the priority of the single dedication, attached some importance to the wording of this appeal, unaware that it was absent from any manuscripts.[45]

---

41 *uisa*, 126.
42 *Galgamum*, 20, 166, 175.
43 *repellunt*, 126.
44 20 adds *autem*; 126 adds *uero*.
45 *Arthur of Britain*, p. 43. The address was in the singular and Robert of Gloucester was the most appropriate candidate for the title *consul*. See below, V.

Some of the manuscripts with this abbreviation have other revisions. CUL Dd.1.17 [40] and BL Royal 13.D.i [111][46] also contain an abbreviation of §179. BL MSS Arundel 326 [88] and Sloane 289 [116] lack sections of text in §179 as well and in §150. Oxford, All Souls' College, 39 [133], mentioned above in connection with §84, lacks the opening phrase of §104 'Quod cum ... esset'. The other manuscripts in which §177 begins 'Ut igitur' are Dublin, Trinity College, MS. 172 [61] and Firenze, B.R. 55 [72], both of which omit the last phrase of §178 'Anima ... quiescat'.

§179

§179 provides an example of a passage in the main part of the text susceptible to change because of its subject-matter. The chapter begins after the coronation of Constantine but then moves on to a digression concerning the state of episcopal sees at that time. This passage is treated identically in CUL Dd.1.17 [40] and BL Royal 13.D.i [111], where the centre of §179 is lacking (the text jumps from 'Urbis Legionum episcopus Dauid' to 'Et pro eo ponitur'). BL MSS Arundel 326 [88] and Sloane 289 [116] omit two sections: 'et .N. Gloecestrensis ... erigitur' and 'infra abbatiam ... sepultus est'. Another abbreviated form of this chapter is found in six manuscripts which, as seen above, contain other such abbreviations: 20, 126, 151, 166, 173, 175. Here the text moves directly from 'religiosissimus antistes' to the final sentence 'et pro eo ponitur'.

Two unique omissions are to be noted. The chapter ends at 'eas obtinere ceperunt' in San Marino EL 34.C.9 [204] (see above, §§171–173). Oxford, Bodleian, Rawlinson, C.152 [156] lacks only one sentence here, 'Dum ibi ... sepultus est'.

§181

The chapter ends at 'nisi foret ciuilis belli amator' in MS. 204. The omitted passage describes the crimes perpetrated by Aurelius Conanus in his bid for the crown.

§184

The group of six related manuscripts (20, 126, 151, 166, 173, 175) contains a further abbreviation: §184 is truncated after the opening sentence, ending 'gentem patrie subiugauit'. Thus they omit the narrative of the invasion by the Saxons with African help and the adventures in Britain of Gormund, king of the Africans. 20 is an exception here, as the whole text is deliberately truncated at §180 'que lingua Anglorum Stragen uocatur' (see below, The End of the Text).

---

46 Related by contents and rubrics (II, VI).

§185

In §185 Geoffrey interrupts his account of a disastrous civil war to deliver a general exhortation to unity. This is omitted from the Second-Variant manuscripts CUL Ff.1.25 [47], TCD 515 [66], BL MSS Arundel 10 [85], Cotton Galba E.xi [91] and Titus A.xxvii [95], and Harley 3773 [102], Bodley 977 [138], Saint-Omer BM 710 [202] and Troyes BM 1531 [209]. 202 is the only γ-manuscript in this list: most are α-texts or of unknown affiliation. The text has reverted to vulgate in the β-manuscripts by this point and there is no trace of a hiatus here.

§186

The last sentence, which contains a reference to another projected work of Geoffrey's, his translation of the Book of Exile (describing the flight of the Britons from the Saxons), is not present in MS. 204.

§200

MS. 204 also lacks Geoffrey's account of a revolt conducted against King Oswi by his son and nephew. Instead, §200, in which this is found, is truncated after the brief opening section (after 'sibi submisit').

§202

A digression concerning Cadualladr's mother, found at the end of this chapter, is absent from MS. 204. The text here is truncated after 'discidium inter Britones ortum est'.

The End of the Text

One particular sort of omission merits treatment separate from the others since it has on one occasion been used as the basis for a major editorial judgement. This is the absence of the final chapters without physical explanation.

Acton Griscom noted that the text in a twelfth-century manuscript, CUL Ii.1.14 [48], ends mid-folio at §207 'qui primus inter eos diadema portauit'; this is followed by the word 'Explicit' written in capitals by the scribe. So, he presumed, the consequent absence of Geoffrey's allusions to his fellow historians, William of Malmesbury, Henry of Huntingdon, and Caradog of Llancarfan (and to the degeneracy of the Welsh), was deliberate.[47] Not only did Griscom consider it 'hardly probable that a scribe would have omitted so important a concluding paragraph' but he regarded the presence of such an epilogue as chronologically indicative: 'we may safely surmise that Geoffrey first published the *Historia* without any reference to other historians, and that, not until his published work

---

[47] *apud* Griscom & Jones, *The Historia*, p. 33 and plate VII.

was challenged, did he add in a later edition a renewed statement about his sources'.[48]

Griscom had already concluded that the presence of the double dedication (to Waleran of Meulan as well as Robert of Gloucester) in 48 'affords the strongest evidence, as we shall see below, that the manuscript represents the first version or edition of Geoffrey's work'.[49] The absence of the epilogue provided him with a means of distinguishing 48 from other double-dedication manuscripts as 'the inference was clear that all the six manuscripts which did contain this additional paragraph were later, even though four were of the twelfth century'.[50] Furthermore, Griscom used this feature as a measure for other kinds of *Historia*-texts. His pronouncement that Bern, Burgerbibliothek, MS. 568 [15] 'must be classed as a later and probably the second edition' of the text was made on the basis that it included the end of §207 and all §208.[51]

As with his treatment of the dedications (below, V), Griscom allowed historical inferences drawn from the wording of the text to influence, if not determine, his editorial stance. His arguments concerning the primary state of the truncated text have never been justified textually. They failed on purely logical grounds to convince Brugger, who reviewed both editions of 1929. Brugger observed that the epilogue could be original as it balanced the prologue. There was no reason, moreover, to regard its omission as impossible, as Griscom had done: a copyist or reviser might have regarded it as arrogant or irrelevant.[52]

Brugger noted another point. Griscom had reported that 'Out of scores of complete manuscripts' he had encountered only one other truncated text like 48, the twelfth-century Phillipps 2324, now New Haven, Yale University, MS. 590 [128].[53] He had never seen it but believed it to bear the single dedication. He omitted, however, to discuss any implications which this observation might have on his theory of the priority of the shorter text within the double dedication. They did not escape Brugger.[54] He used the apparent discrepancy between the dedications to attack Griscom's arguments for the 'original' status of 48 and to launch his own case for the priority of the single dedication. Faral corroborated Brugger's criticisms by noting that 48 was by no means textually superior to other manuscripts containing the same dedication.[55]

Griscom's argument is reprieved on this count, however: 128 in fact contains the double dedication. 128 ends, but without a rubric, just as 48 does and again the loss has no physical explanation: the remainder of the page is blank. As it is possible (but not certain) on palaeographical grounds that 128 antedates 48, the

48 'The Date', p. 137.
49 *The Historia*, p. 32.
50 *Ibid.*, p. 33.
51 *Ibid.*, p. 52.
52 'Zu Galfrid', pp. 266–67.
53 *The Historia*, p. 51 and n. 2.
54 'Zu Galfrid', p. 268.
55 'L'*Historia*', pp. 485, 488–96, 498–99.

ending may not have been so final as Griscom found the rubric in 48 to suggest: physical loss suffered by an ancestor of these manuscripts or deliberate truncation on scribal whim remain possibilities. Brugger had reasoned as much without knowledge of the manuscripts.[56] There is therefore no prima facie reason to regard the ending of 48 and 128 as representing Geoffrey's original.

Griscom might have placed less weight on the truncation of MS. 48 had he been aware of other, different, examples of the same process. All three result in the loss of some of the narrative as well. The text in BL Additional 11702 [81] (c. 1300) extends only to the end of §179, the description of the state of the British church immediately after Arthur's death. The verso following this is blank. Bruxelles, BR, 9871–9874 [20] ends a chapter beyond this, after §180 'que lingua Anglorum Stragen uocatur', and the death of Arthur's successor, Constantine. This is followed by the rubric in the scribe's hand: 'Explicit historia regum Britannie'. The truncation occurs even earlier in the final example, Reims, BM, 1430 [193]. This does not appear to be premeditated: the text breaks off in the middle of the reign of Uther (§140 'In hostes conducerent') but in the first column of a verso, leaving the second blank. In this case, physical loss in the exemplar may be the explanation.[57] There is no reason to presume that such a process did not cause the three other known truncations, this stage being hidden in exemplars no longer extant.

Other omissions

Parts of §§65 and 75 in Oxford, Bodleian, MS. Jesus College 2 [142] have been displaced by the comparative chronological material heavily interpolated into this text of the *Historia*.[58]

Omissions resulting from physical loss

Peculiar absences of sections of text which cannot be explained as deliberate omissions must be accounted for by scribal error or an imperfect exemplar. Only two such manuscripts have come to light. Unfortunately it has not been possible to identify any of the surviving fragmentary manuscripts as the source of either. There is a leap, mid-page, in BN lat. 6041 [171] between §§200 'et Ioduualdum fratris sui' and §205 'purificati ab Alano'. BL Additional 11702 [81], itself subject to physical dislocation (which has not caused any losses), lacks the text between the end of §21 'in presentem diem dicitur' and §24 'Duxit atque Locrinus'. This

---

56 'Zu Galfrid', p. 269.
57 I have not encountered any candidate for identification as exemplar.
58 There are also signs of blank spaces left by the scribe of Boulogne BM 180 + 139 + 145 [16]. That in §62 between 'Proinde' and 'Non eram igitur' (22ra) was filled by an Early Modern annotator. A blank may also have been left and then filled in by the scribe in §151 after perhaps 'suorum miserandas' and '-biliores solito iterum', as the usual regular spacing of the words breaks down here.

is a cleaner break – an initial was often marked here in §24 – and so perhaps physical loss is not the cause. The omission is unlikely to be deliberate, however, as the first part of the story of Locrinus and Corineus is lost. Eye-skip between the large initials beginning these sections (that at §22 being also a *D*) seems a possible explanation.

Dislocated Texts

The use of a complete but disorderly exemplar could also result in a nonsensical copy. Quires may have remained unbound for long periods, precipitating losses and rearrangement. Errors could also occur in the binding process at any stage in the book's history. I know of only one *Historia*-manuscript which testifies to the disarray of a medieval exemplar. This is the early fourteenth-century Paris, BN, MSS lat. 13935 + 5508 [186], in which §§10–20 are located in the middle of §29 with no explanation provided by the quiring of the extant book.

The physical separation of the prefatory chapters and the prophecies could explain the location of §§1–3 and 5 *after* the text in BL Royal 4.C.xi [108] and of §§111–117 after the text in Cambridge, Trinity College, O.1.17 [38], and Bruges, BM, 428 [17]. There is no necessity to suppose such an explanation, however.[59]

Merlinus uero incipiens (§118)

Aberystwyth, NLW, Peniarth 43 [9] and Oxford, Bodleian, Jones 48 [143] witness a rearrangement of the narrative of Merlin and Vortigern. The episode in which Merlin tells Vortigern the nature of his death usually follows the Prophecies. Here it is found instead immediately before §111, after the introduction to the Prophecies. The opening phrase of §118, 'Cum igitur hec et alia prophetasset Merlinus . . .', becomes 'Merlinus uero incipiens coram rege Uortigerno prophetare . . .'. Then follows the text of §118 as normal and the first sentence of §119 ('. . . Aurelius Ambrosius'), to which is added the final phrase 'cum germano suo decem milibus militum comitatus'. The Prophecies then begin as usual. They are truncated before the antepenultimate sentence however ('. . . prorumpent Pliades') and the text moves directly to §119 'Rumore itaque . . .', the phrase which would usually follow the now-displaced section of text. An initial marking the start of a new block of text is often found in *Historia*-manuscripts at this point.

59 The following manuscripts have themselves been subject to physical disruption, although at what stage is unknown. Cambridge, Corpus Christi College, MS. 292 [24] (§§94–96); Dublin, Trinity College, MS. 494 [63] (§§190–195); London, BL, MSS Add. 11702 [81] (§§25–29); Harley 3773 [102] (fragments not arranged consecutively); Oxford, Bodleian MS. Add. A.61 [134] (§§58–90); Oxford, Magdalen College, MS. lat. 170 [161] (§§167–170); Paris, BN, lat. MSS 5234 [167] (§§124–128, 143–147); 6040 [170] (§§60–87); 13710 [185] (§§155, 159–160).

An explanation for the rearrangement may be sought in the thirteenth-century manuscript, Oxford, All Souls', MS. 35 [132]. Here the text of the *Historia* originally lacked Prophecies and opening dedications (beginning instead at §6). The usual dedication of the Prophecies to Alexander of Lincoln in §110 was absent; instead, §§109–110 took the *pudibundus Brito* form (which omits reference to the dedicatee), which prefaced the version of §118 described above beginning 'Merlinus uero incipiens'. The added final phrase is not present; the text continues directly without loss from the end of the first sentence of §119. This arrangement resembles that of 9 and 143, which also lack the opening dedications (including §5, the description of Britain, however) and have the *pudibundus Brito* form of §§109–110.

132 underwent considerable modification not long after completion; the additions are in a hand close in style and date to the original. §§1–3 and §5, bearing the nameless and not the usual single dedication (below, V), were added on the verso of a leaf facing the *Historia*. The prophecies with their normal dedication were inserted at the same time on two new leaves; the non-vulgate sections of the original (*pudibundus Brito* and opening phrase of §118) were crossed through and the added vulgate text signalled by *signes de renvoi* (from §109 'non alter in clero' to §118 'prophetasset Merlinus').

Although the subsequent introduction of the Prophecies into a manuscript from which they were originally absent would explain the dislocation of the 'Merlinus uero incipiens' passage in 9 and 143 – before and not after the Prophecies – the revision of 132 does not provide a model. This process resulted not only in the elimination of the *pudibundus Brito* version of §§109–110 but the restoration to vulgate of the text of §§118–119. It would seem necessary to look for a model for 9 and 143 in some precursor of 132 or in that manuscript in its original state with the addition of §§5 and 111–117 from some other copy.

Preliminary Conclusions

It is evident that certain texts underwent several forms of revision. The *pudibundus Brito* manuscripts contain the interpolation about Seaxburh. Some of them are also acephalous and, in three of these, the material in §118 is displaced (*Merlinus uero incipiens*). Two manuscripts (9 and 143) with all four of the disruptions just described have also a hiatus in the text between §§42 and 43. This last feature is found in a less unusual *pudibundus Brito* manuscript (93). The passage beginning 'Merlinus iste . . .' has connections with manuscripts experiencing some textual change at the Prophecies. MSS 88 and 116 offer an extreme example of multiple disruption: the addition of Bedan material in §5, the interpolation of *Mirabilia* before §6, and the omission of parts of §§150, 177, and 170, and all of §§109–110. There are several examples of repeated abbreviation: MSS 20, 126, 151, 166, 173, and 175 have undergone revision in §§83–84, 173–174, 179, and 183–184. Similarly several chapters towards the end of the text were revised in MS. 204.

Other manuscripts have only one major departure from the vulgate: the interpolation of Arthur's letter, or a Eusebius-Jerome passage, or the truncation of the text without physical loss.

Appendix: Mathioc

(see above, INTERPOLATIONS, BN lat. MS. 6232)

From a personal communication from Oliver Padel, May 1989: '*Mathioc*. This is to be connected with the Welsh name *Meidwc* which appears as that of the father or mother of Myrddin in a poem, probably of the twelfth century, found in the Red Book of Hergest, a manuscript of the late fourteenth century: "myrdin yw vy enw amheidwc", "Myrddin is my name, son of Meidwc": Evans, *The Poetry*, p. 5a, lines 7–8. However, the form *Mathioc* ought not to be Welsh, as it stands, for the **i** in the second syllable should have caused affection of the preceding **a**, giving an expected form **Meithioc*: Jackson, *Language and History*, p. 582. The latter form is sufficiently close to that of the Red Book *Meidwc* (where **d** could stand for either [d] or [ð]) for the two names to be considered identical. The Welsh name is not found elsewhere, as far as can be ascertained, and Manon Jenkins tells me that it has hitherto presented a problem for Welsh scholars studying the legend of Merlin.

It is strange that the form in BN lat. 6232 fails to show vowel-affection, a sound-change which occurred in Welsh in about the seventh century: Jackson, *Language and History*, pp. 616–17. One can hardly suggest that the scribe had access to a written source so early as not to show the sound-change, and the matter remains a puzzle.'

V

DEDICATIONS

The scarcity of dependable information about both Geoffrey's life and the composition of the *Historia* (see above, Introduction) has caused a considerable amount of attention to be focussed on the various dedications of the work. The most commonly occurring dedication is that to Robert, earl of Gloucester, bastard son of Henry I and patron of William of Malmesbury. The others are less expected: jointly to King Stephen and Robert, political opponents for the greater part of the Anarchy which began roughly at the time of the appearance of the *Historia*; jointly, too, to Robert and to Waleran of Meulan, a Norman noble whose only connection with Robert can have been in juxtaposition with Stephen, whom Waleran supported until 1141.[1] The incongruity of these combinations has invited discussion of their historical context. The datings produced have been extended to apply to the texts which follow each dedication, a leap in reasoning which formed an essential prelude to the editorial decisions behind both editions of 1929. Although this controversy is long dead, its implications for the former study of the text justify a brief description of it here.[2]

The debate was opened by an article published in 1858 by Frederick Madden advertising the existence of a manuscript dedicated not to Robert alone as were all printed texts (and the majority of manuscripts), but to Stephen as well.[3] This was Bern, Burgerbibliothek, MS. 568 [15]. The circumstances of Stephen's succession and the Anarchy would have rendered such a combination of dedicatees highly offensive to both parties if made at any time outside the years 1136–38, when the two men were seemingly on amicable terms.[4] This thesis effectively rebutted claims made by Thomas Wright two years earlier that the *Historia* had not appeared until after 1147, when he supposed that Alexander, bishop of Lincoln, referred to in the past tense in §110, had died.[5]

Ensuing comments on the dedications largely concentrated on their value for the dating of the text. In 1883, Harry Ward had argued that the description of

---

1 On the fashion for double dedications in the early twelfth century, see Guenée, 'L'Histoire entre l'éloquence et la science', p. 261.
2 Compare Neil Wright's account of the debate and its implications on dating the text: *The Historia*, I.xii–xvi.
3 'The Historia Britonum', pp. 300–1.
4 *Ibid.*, p. 310. Compare Crouch, 'Robert', pp. 232–33.
5 See Madden, 'The Historia Britonum', p. 304 and references. Alexander in fact died in February 1148: Greenway, *John Le Neve. Fasti*, III.2.

Geoffrey's History made by Henry of Huntingdon in his *Epistola ad Warinum* differed from the known *Historia*-texts to such a degree that it must represent an early and more primitive edition.[6] He envisaged that the *Historia* appeared only shortly before Alfred of Beverley paraphrased it in 1149; Ward explained away the purportedly earlier Bern dedication as 'a rough sketch accidentally preserved'.[7] In 1900, W. L. Jones, in the course of revising Ward's account, connected 15 with the idea of a first edition. Henry of Huntingdon's description was not irreconcilable with the known copies of the *Historia*; 15, with its 'early' dedication and 'less polished' latinity could represent such 'an earlier edition of the work'.[8] Fletcher, the following year, expressed scepticism, reporting that Jones had since modified his opinion about the extent of the variants in 15 and noting that they could be scribal.[9]

The arguments about dedications and editions took new shape after 1927, when Griscom reported his discovery of a third dedication.[10] This was the Robert-Waleran dedication, which he had found in seven manuscripts. The union of political opponents which it involved again gave rise to speculation about the date of the dedication. 1136 seemed the only time when both men could have been in England and, through their allegiance to Stephen, not in open political disagreement.[11] Faral seems to have encountered the Robert-Waleran dedication independently. His conclusions about it were different, however, as he imagined that the period of amity between the two men must date from after the battle of Lincoln in 1141, when Waleran abandoned Stephen's cause.[12] This surmise is inaccurate both as to the nature of Waleran's relationship with Robert in 1141 and as to the date of his return to France[13] and Faral later jettisoned it, won over by Griscom's literary arguments about the priority of the Robert-Waleran over the Stephen-Robert dedications.[14]

Griscom, like W. L. Jones, was tempted to draw inferences about the whole of the text from the dedications. He doubted that the single dedication 'actually represents the first edition', as the double dedication was a more credible candidate. The two parts of the dedication were well balanced; the omission of the epilogue from his Cambridge manuscript, 48, suggested its proximity to the author; the blatant division of a previously familiar single dedication would have been distinctly unflattering to the original recipient; the majority of manuscripts bear the single dedication 'and these appear to represent a more carefully written or polished version'; finally, the wording of §4 suggested the priority of the double

---

6   *Catalogue of Romances*, I.209–13.
7   *Ibid.*, I.212, 213.
8   'Geoffrey', pp. 64–67.
9   'Two Notes', p. 464.
10 'The Date', pp. 130–32.
11 *Ibid.*, p. 140. Crouch would extend this period to 1137 as well: 'Robert', p. 230, and also p. 231.
12 'Geoffroy', pp. 29–30.
13 Compare Crouch, *The Beaumont Twins*, pp. 49–51.
14 Faral, 'L'*Historia*', especially p. 482; Griscom, 'The Date', pp. 150–54.

dedication.[15] This conclusion determined Griscom's editorial policy: he took a manuscript of the Robert-Waleran type and collated against it the Stephen-Robert manuscript and a single-dedication text.

A similar principle guided Faral's choice of manuscripts. He had identified three 'texts' on the basis of dedications, which he arranged chronologically.[16] In the introductory volume to his edition, he dated to early 1136 the Robert and Robert-Waleran dedications which together constituted his first class (a and b); the second 'text', the Stephen-Robert dedication, was assigned to April 1136. The last category, represented by a single manuscript lacking dedications to the prophecies and the whole text, he dated to about 1148, after the deaths of Geoffrey's main dedicatees (Robert, earl of Gloucester, and Alexander, bishop of Lincoln).[17] But in Faral's actual edition, the single dedication was relegated to third position, after the dedication to Stephen and Robert.[18] This adjustment did not alter the structure of his edition, however, which was based on a manuscript dedicated to Robert and Waleran (Cambridge, Trinity College, MS. O.2.21 [39]) with variants taken from 15 (Stephen-Robert dedication), a single-dedication witness (Leiden, UB, BPL 20 [76]), and the text lacking dedications (Paris, BN, lat. 6233 [178]).[19] A further twist to the argument came with Chambers's literary analysis of the relationship of the dedications to the text, which led him to conclude that the single dedication was the original.[20]

The progress of the debate demonstrates the essential malleability of the evidence on which it was based, whether historical or literary: Griscom was able to argue for the priority of the Robert-Waleran dedication using inferences similar in kind to those employed by Chambers, who reached opposite conclusions. Underlying the arguments was the assumption that the dedications prefaced distinct and datable editions. Faral had already produced evidence which brought into question the supposed textual coherence of the Robert-Waleran group, although this was not his purpose. In his attempt to demonstrate the textual superiority of the Robert-Waleran manuscript which he had used (39) over Griscom's (48), he had noted that 48 showed agreement with 15 (Faral's type II) against his Robert-Waleran representative.[21] This, however, failed to alert him to the possibility that the dedications might not be datable prefaces to separate editions, a deduction made long before by Fletcher.[22]

Doubts about the inseparability of dedication and edition were voiced soon after the publication of the two editions of 1929. Brugger was utterly sceptical, even suggesting that the incongruous Stephen-Robert dedication might have been

---

15 'The Date', pp. 154–55.
16 *La Légende*, II.10–26.
17 *Ibid.*, II.26–28.
18 *Ibid.*, III.64–65.
19 *Ibid.*
20 *Arthur of Britain*, pp. 43–44.
21 'L'*Historia*', p. 505.
22 'Two Notes', pp. 463–64.

the work of some French scribe ignorant of political realities in England.[23] This challenges assumptions about the function of the dedication: how much post-authorial tampering can be expected? To what extent are dedications separable from the following text? Brugger argued that the dedications might have been lost in the course of transmission rather than by deliberate authorial omission (as Faral had imagined).[24] Text-historical analysis should clarify the situation.

The most informed discussion of the textual implications of the dedications came from Jacob Hammer, whose knowledge of the textual problems of the *Historia* was unrivalled.[25] He considered the four-fold grouping useful but limited: 'It does not take the text into consideration, since out of 170 MSS only six have been examined'.[26] Such a textual examination has uncovered considerable complications, as Hammer reported from his investigation of the Robert-Waleran group (to which he added an eighth manuscript).[27] The other groups also presented difficulties. Hammer identified a manuscript textually close to 15 but which lacked the opening dedicatory chapters.[28] The single-dedication manuscripts were far from homogeneous; among them were witnesses to what Hammer described as a different recension.[29] That text has since been recognized as sufficiently different from the vulgate to be classed as a variant – the Second. Hammer also expressed doubt about Faral's fourth class, a single manuscript lacking the opening dedicatory chapters and the dedications at the prophecies (see below, *No dedication*).[30] He advertised an absence of dedication of a different kind: where the dedicatees' names have been omitted by a slight change of phrasing. He listed eight forms of these, found in 'a rather large group of MSS', none of which he named.[31]

Suspending historical, literary, and even textual questions for the present – the evidence of trial collations will be examined later –, what do the dedications add to the text-historical evidence examined so far? The following is arranged according to the number of *Historia*-manuscripts bearing each sort of dedication.

Stephen-Robert (1 witness)

15, the manuscript publicized by Madden, remains the sole witness to this dedication. Two close relatives of this manuscript have now been identified, however (one by Hammer, one by Dumville),[32] both of which lack the opening chapters.

---

23 'Zu Galfrid', pp. 273–75.
24 *Ibid.*, p. 276.
25 He claimed to have collated over 130 manuscripts: 'Remarks', p. 501.
26 *Ibid.*, p. 525.
27 *Ibid.*
28 *Ibid.*, pp. 525–26.
29 *Ibid.*, pp. 526–28.
30 *Ibid.*, p. 528.
31 *Ibid.*, pp. 529–30.
32 Hammer, 'Remarks', p. 525; Dumville, 'An Early Text', pp. 16–17.

Robert-Waleran (9 witnesses)

Griscom's total of seven manuscripts bearing this dedication, increased to eight by Hammer,[33] has grown again with the discovery that the manuscript known to Griscom as Phillipps 2324 (now New Haven, Yale University, MS. 590 [129]) is dedicated to Waleran as well as Robert.

The manuscripts are

Cambridge,
>Trinity College, MS. O.2.21 (1125) [39]
>UL, MSS
>>Ii.1.14 [48]
>>Ii.4.4 [49]

London, BL, MS. Lansdowne 732 [107]
New Haven, Yale University Library, MS. 590 (*olim* Phillipps 2324) [128]
Oxford, Bodleian Library, MSS
>>>Add. A.61 [134]
>>>Bodley 514 [136]

Paris, BN, MS. lat. 6040 [170]
Roma, BAV, MS. Vat. lat. 2005 [199]

No dedication (16 + 27 witnesses)

Although Faral's Group IV (manuscripts lacking dedications to the Prophecies as well as the whole work) has been swelled from a single manuscript to four or possibly six (see above, IV: Recognized Variants), Hammer's caution about the class still holds: he was prepared to accept it 'only on the basis of the abbreviated version of the epistle to Bishop Alexander'.[34] This revision has already been discussed and has no further relevance at this point.[35] One may note, however, that the variety of texts witnessed by the sixteen manuscripts lacking the dedicatory opening chapters confirms Brugger's suspicions about the possibility of the independent loss of those sections.[36]

There is ample evidence for a different category of manuscripts without dedications, as Hammer first pointed out.[37] These are the witnesses following the usual single dedication format of §§1–3, 5–208, but in which the name of the dedicatee is absent from §3, occasioning some rewriting. This chapter usually

---

[33] London, BL, MS. Lansdowne 732 [107]: *ibid.*, p. 525.

[34] *Ibid.*, p. 528.

[35] Above, IV. The four (or six) manuscripts resembling Faral's BN lat. 6233 (178) lacking both sets of dedications must be viewed as a subgroup of the *pudibundus Brito* manuscripts.

[36] The acephalous manuscripts are the First-Variant 1, 4, 67, 106, 163; the relatives of Bern (15) 86, 200; *pudibundus Brito* manuscripts 9, 41, 132, 140, 143, 178; and three other vulgate manuscripts, 69, 110, 142.

[37] 'Remarks', pp. 529–30.

begins with Geoffrey's appeal 'Opusculo igitur meo, Roberte, dux Claudiocestrie, faueas, ut sic te doctore, te monitore corrigatur quod non ex Gaufridi Monemutensis fonticulo censeatur exortum . . .'; in the revised version, the opening phrase is adjusted.[38] Hammer recorded eight different ways in which this was done.[39] I add a ninth (viia). The versions are listed below according to Hammer's headings, together with the manuscripts (twenty-seven in all) in which I have found them.

i. + vi. [40] Opus igitur Deo (or Deo igitur) meo corrigatur

Aberystwyth, NLW, MS. 11611 [2]
Cambridge, Trinity College, MS. R.7.6 [36] (type vi)
Dôle, BM, MSS 348+349 [58]
Paris, BN, MS. lat. 6231 [176]
Sankt Gallen, Stiftsbibliothek, MS. 633 [205]

ii. Opusculum igitur in eo corrigatur[41]

Montpellier, BM, MS. 378 [127]
Troyes, BM, MS. 273 bis [208]

iii. Opusculo igitur meo corrigatur

Cambridge, UL, MS. Mm.1.34 [53]
Madrid, Biblioteca nacional, MS. 6319 [125]
Oxford,
    All Souls' College, MS. 35 [132]
    Bodleian Library, MS. New College, 276 [151]
Paris, BN, MSS
    lat. 5697 [168]
    lat. 6230 [175]
Roma, BAV, MS. Pal. lat. 962 [196]

iv. Opus igitur meum per te corrigatur

Bruxelles, BR, MS. 8536–8543 [19]

---

38 Neil Wright has since demonstrated that the whole class of manuscripts developed from a single faulty exemplar (in a Cambridge seminar, May 1989). On the same occasion he suggested alterations to my revised version of Hammer's categories, which is presented below.

39 'Remarks', p. 529.

40 Hammer's sixth category is identical to the first except that *igitur* is replaced by *sibi*. The only manuscript in which such a dedication is found is Cambridge, Trinity College, MS. R.7.6 [36]. It seems likely that the variation is explained by the use in this thirteenth-century manuscript of the abbreviation $\tilde{g}$ for *igitur*, which looks very like $\tilde{s}$ for *sibi*.

41 Hammer's omission of *corrigatur* in his list here seems accidental.

v. Opus igitur in eo corrigatur

Bruxelles, BR, MS. 9871–9874 [20]
Montpellier, BM, MS. 92 [126]
Paris, BN, MSS

lat. MS. 5233 [166]
lat. MS. 6041B [173]
lat. 7531 [182]

vi. Opus Deo sibi meo corrigatur

See above, i.

vii. Opus deest igitur in eo corrigatur

Paris, BN, MSS

lat. 6041 [171]
lat. 12943 [184]

vii A (not listed by Hammer). Opus de eo igitur in eo corrigatur

London, British Library, MS. Add. 11702 [81]
Paris, Bibliothèque nationale, MS. lat. 8501A [183]

viii. Si autem in hoc libello corrigendum est aliquid a te corrigatur

Aberystwyth, NLW, MS. 13052 [3]
Auxerre, BM, MS. 91 [14]
Paris, BN, MS. 18271 [189]

Robert of Gloucester

Some fifty-three manuscripts have been mentioned so far: ten bearing double dedications, sixteen omitting the introductory chapters, and twenty-seven witnessing the nameless dedication. Apart from twenty-one acephalous manuscripts, the remainder are dedicated to Robert alone. As Hammer's discovery of the Second Variant demonstrated, the texts witnessed by the single-dedication manuscripts lack the uniformity apparently expected by Griscom and Faral, each of whom represented this 'edition' by a single manuscript.[42] Two witnesses of the

---

42 Faral used Leiden, UB, BPL 20, a manuscript from Le Bec, Normandy, once alleged to have been the copy seen there by Henry of Huntingdon in 1139. It was certainly there by the 1150s: Dumville, 'An Early Text', pp. 2–4. Griscom's manuscript was less venerable. His belief that the double dedications represented 'the first and second recensions of Geoffrey's

First Variant, a text which departs markedly from the vulgate, bear the single dedication, for example: Cardiff, South Glamorgan Central Library, MS. 2.611 [55], and Exeter, Cathedral Library, MS. 3514 [70]. The evidence examined in the preceding chapters suggests further diversification.

Preliminary Conclusions

According to present evidence, the *Historia* bore four different dedications. These may be arranged in descending order of frequency: the dedication to Robert of Gloucester, the nameless dedication, that to Robert of Gloucester and Waleran of Meulan, and finally that to King Stephen and Robert of Gloucester.

work' led him to use a single-dedication manuscript (the late thirteenth-century Harlech 17, now NLW Porkington 17) only as a contrast, to demonstrate 'the later and more stereotyped form which the *Historia* assumed': *The Historia*, p. 34.

VI

RUBRICS AND BOOK-DIVISIONS

The sheer size of sample provided by *Historia*-manuscripts (215) allows general trends of scribal practice to be observed and discussed with an unusual degree of certainty. Rubrics are a case in point. Viewed in isolation, individual rubrics impart a limited amount of information. When there is enough information to distinguish the idiosyncratic from the ordinary, however, the potential for drawing conclusions about them increases markedly. Rubrics are not strictly speaking part of the text but particularly open to interpretation by scribes. However, if they were treated by scribes as authoritative and accurately transferred from exemplar to copy, they may indicate lines of textual transmission. Alternatively, scribes may have exercised their imaginations and concocted new or more elaborate rubrics.

Rubrication can be of various sorts. Apart from colophons, which have already been mentioned (III), rubrics can function as a title; they can summarize the narrative or comment on it; they generally direct the reader. Book-divisions are also a form of rubrication and will be dealt with at the end of this chapter.

The wording of rubrics reflects the range of medieval terminology used to describe the *Historia*. This is relevant to the continuing debate over the work's genre and may also assist the identification of further copies in the lists of medieval libraries.

RUBRICS

The overwhelming majority of *Historia*-manuscripts are rubricated. Of the 214 manuscripts surveyed, only thirty-nine lack rubrics; twelve of these are fragmentary and so may originally have had them. Rubrics were added before the fourteenth century in three of the remaining twenty-seven.[1] In four of the balance of twenty-four, the initials, which were often entered at the same time as the rubrics, were never completed.[2] The progeny of such manuscripts would have

---

1 Bern, Burgerbibliothek, 568 [15]; Bruxelles, BR, 8536–8543 [19]; London, BL, Lansdowne 732 [107].
2 NLW Wynnstay 14 [11], Fitzwilliam Museum 346 [27], Lambeth Palace 454a [122], Roma BAV Reg. lat. 692 [197]. There is a fifth, Bodleian Tanner 195 [158], a fourteenth-century

entered a textual tradition, unrubricated, mid-stream, perhaps causing rubrics to be supplied from another copy, or resulting in a tradition, however short, of unrubricated manuscripts. Thus the remaining twenty unrubricated manuscripts are of some interest: is their unrubricated state inherited? Did copies of the *Historia* have rubrics from the earliest time or is there any basis for regarding them as scribal additions, much as Griscom considered book-divisions?[3] Discussion must be suspended temporarily until textual evidence can be brought to bear on the subject.

The classification of manuscripts by their rubrics is by no means straightforward. Some similarities are perhaps superficial: some rubrics, simple ones especially, would have been obvious; certain phrases in the text itself could influence or shape certain sorts of rubrics. Then there is the problem of assessing the degree of variation possible within a group of related rubrics – where does similarity end? Using keywords and phrases, some attempt has been made here to identify clusters of rubrics.

Groups of related rubrics found attached to the prologue, Prophecies, and conclusion (beginning with the most clearly identifiable), will form the main subject of this chapter, but some of the unique rubrics will also be discussed. I shall attempt to deal with all relevant comparisons: silence on a particular point may be taken to indicate the *absence* of further rubrics or of comparable material.

Test-cases – the Variant Versions

First, I intend to use the rubrics of manuscripts of well established categories of *Historia*-text to investigate the degree of association which might be expected between text and rubrics.

The First Variant

Neil Wright's recent work on the First Variant has identified one subgroup of three and one of two manuscripts, as well as a witness with affiliation to both subgroups and two outliers.[4] All members of the group of three – Dublin, TC, 515 [67], Edinburgh Adv. 18.4.5 [68], and Exeter Cathedral 3514 [70] – have the opening rubric (at §5 in the case of 67, which lacks §§1–4) 'Incipit historia Britonum a Galfrido Arturo Monemutensi de britannica lingua in Latinum translata'. This is also found in NLW Panton 37 [1] (which, like 67, lacks §§1–4), whose text is intermediate between the two subgroups.[5] Main rubrics are thereafter absent from

manuscript whose initials are unfiligreed, perhaps deliberately or possibly because the decoration (and therefore rubrication) was never completed.
3   *The Historia*, pp. 26–30. See also below, VI.
4   *The Historia*, II.xciii–cxvi.
5   *Ibid.*, II.cx–cxi.

68 and 67 has only 'Explicit' after §208. 70 has in addition at §6 'Explicit descripcio Britannie insule'.

The opening rubric in Arsenal 982 [163] (which lacks §§1–4) reads 'Incipit hystoria Britonum ab antiquis Britonibus tracta'. That in NLW 13210 [4], which Wright has shown to have descended from the same hyparchetype, is also found at §5 and agrees with this rubric as far as *antiquis* but ends *libris Britonum*. The equivalence between the rubrics of the two manuscripts is exact at §6 'Incipit narratio' and at §111 'Incipit liber .uii. de propheciis Merlini', but after §208 4 has 'Explicit hystoria Brittonum correcta et abbreuiata' while 163 has 'Explicit hystoria Britonum a Galfrido Arthuro de Britannico in Latinum translata est. Deo gracias'. This last rubric compares with that in 1 but that manuscript has *magistro* before *Galfrido* and *Monemutensi* for *Arthuro* and lacks *de Britannico* and *est*.[6]

Cardiff 2.611 [55] and BL Harley 6358 [106] have apparently quite independent rubrics. 55, according to Wright's stemma a distant relation of the 67/68/70 subgroup,[7] has at §1 'Historia Britonum', at §110 'Epistola G. Monumutensis episcopo Lincoll. directa', and after §208 'Explicit tractatus'.

Those in 106, a manuscript which Wright has regarded as textually closest to 4, begin (§5) 'Incipit prologus in hystoriam Britonum', then at §6 'Explicit prologus. Incipit hystorie Britonum liber primus. De Enea, Ascan[ ]', at §111 'Prophetia Merlini incipit', and §118 'Explicit prophetia Merlini'.

Thus the filiations of rubrics within the First Variant generally reflect Wright's stemma; the exception is the connection established by Wright between 4 and 106, which is not evident from the rubrics.

The Second Variant

Although Hammer never brought his work on the Second Variant to the point of publication, his extensive collations allowed him to assign the manuscripts to three subgroups, α, β, and γ.

The only original rubric found in the manuscript which Hammer used as his base text, BL Royal 4.C.xi [108], is at §1 'Incipit historia Brittonum'. This bears scant relation to the rubrics found in all manuscripts of his α-subgroup:

§1 Incipit prologus Gaufridi Monemutensis in sequentem historiam
§5 Descripcio Britannice insule
§109 Prefacio hystorici et epistola de interpretatione propheciarum Merlini
§111 Incipiunt prophecie Merlini ex mistica pugna draconum.

These manuscripts are CUL Ff.1.25 [47], TCD 514 [66] (but at §111 it lacks *Incipiunt*), BL Cotton Galba E.xi [91], BL Cotton Titus A.xxvii [95] (no rubric at

---

6 The use of Geoffrey's title *magister* in rubrics is of some interest. He never refers to himself thus in the *Historia*, but he is given the title in charter-attestations: on these see Salter, 'Geoffrey'. The same title is found apparently independently in the rubrics of Roma, BAV, Ottoboni lat. 1472 [194] (see below). For an analogous reference to Geoffrey, using forms found outside the *Historia*, see below, *Prologus/editio*.
7 See Wright, *The Historia*, II.cxiii.

§1, has *Incipit* before that at §5), Oxford Bodley 977 [138] (no rubric at §5), and Troyes BM 1531 [209] (but at §5, *ca. .i.* not *britannice insule*). Final rubrics are found in all but 91, 95, and 209: *Explicit historia/hystoria Britonum* (*Hic* before *explicit* in 138). Occasional additional rubrics are also found. 95 and 138 have at §6 'De origine Britonum qualiterque Brutus iuxta presagium patrem ac matrem peremit et in Grecia Troianarum reliquiarum dux effectus sit'. 66 and 138 have at §118 'Explicit Merlinus'.[8] A set of rubrics comparable to those of the α-subgroup is found in one vulgate manuscript, London, College of Arms, MS. Arundel 1 [118]. This has at §1 'Incipit prologus Gaufredi Monemutensis in sequente hystoria' (found in no other vulgate manuscript), §5 'Descripcio Britannie insule', §208 'Explicit'.

Hammer's β-subgroup was known to him in four manuscripts. The two later witnesses, Cambridge, Clare College, MS. 27 [22] and BL Royal 14.C.i [114] have no rubrics. CUL Mm.5.29 [54] (and its copy, Lincoln Cathedral 98 [80]) agrees with the α-form of rubrics at §§1, 5 (not found in 80) and 208: there are no rubrics at the Prophecies. Both manuscripts have in addition at §6 'Explicit descriptio Britannie insule. Incipit hystoria'.

The justification for separating subgroup γ from α was far from cogently set out by Hammer. Nevertheless, the rubrics of none of the three γ-witnesses which he identified coincide with the clearly defined set of the α-group. Saint-Omer, BM, 710 [202] has an opening rubric only: 'Incipit prologus Gaufridi Monemutensis in libro de nominibus regum Britonum qui uocatur hystoria Bruti'. The rubrics in Stockholm Holm.D.1311 [207] are also unlike any of the Second-Variant type.[9] The third of Hammer's γ-manuscripts, Bruges, BM, 428 [17], lacks rubrics.

Three further Second-Variant witnesses have recently been discovered.[10] One, Cambridge, UL, Ii.4.12 [50] (fourteenth-century), seems to belong to the β-group. This, like the other late witnesses of this subgroup, has no rubrics. The filiation of the other newly discovered Second-Variant manuscripts is undetermined. BL Arundel 10 [85] has only the final rubric 'Explicit historia Britonum' (found in some members of the α-group), which also constitutes the sole rubric in the fragmentary witness (known to Hammer), BL Harley 3773 [102]. The only rubrics in the third manuscript, Cambridge, Trinity College, R.5.34 [35] (fifteenth-century), – 'Historia Galfridi Monemutensis' at §1 – cannot be compared with those of any known Second-Variant witness.

The findings from the α- and even from the β-subgroups show that a considerable degree of overlap may in some cases be displayed within a group of related manuscripts.

---

8 MS. 138 alone has at §110 'Incipit edicio Galfridi Monemutensis de dictis Merlini'.

9 §1 'Incipit prefacio Gaufridi Monemutensis in hystoriam Brittonum'; §5 'Explicit prefacio. Incipit liber primus hystorie Brittonum'; §110 'Incipit prefatio Gaufridi Monemutensis in prophetiam Ambrosii Merlini'; §111 'Explicit prologus. Incipit prophetia Ambrosii Merlini'.

10 Crick, 'Manuscripts', p. 162.

Groups of rubrics

Within the vulgate, several distinctive sets of rubrics link groups of manuscripts.

The Leiden group

Incipit prologus Gaufridi Monimutensis ad Rodbertum comitem Claudioces-trie in hystoriam de regibus Maioris Brittannie que nunc Anglia dicitur quam hystoriam idem Gaufridus nuper transtulit de Brittannico in Latinum

The above rubrics from the mid-twelfth-century manuscript Leiden, UB, BPL 20 [76], from Le Bec, Normandy, are among the most elaborate *Historia*-rubrics to have gained any currency and, moreover, are the only ones to have received any consideration in print.

David Dumville drew attention to the phrase 'Britanni<a> que nunc Anglia dicitur', also found in the rubric to the *Historia Brittonum* which follows Geoffrey's History in this manuscript.[11] This second rubric is apparently a reworking of a more primitive version which prefaces a text of the *Historia Brittonum* ancestral to that of 76 known from a manuscript from Le Bec's Benedictine neighbour, Jumièges (Rouen, BM, U.74 [200]).[12] Dumville has suggested that the process of elaboration of both text and rubrics of the *Historia Brittonum* attested by 76 provides an analogy for the development of the rubrics, and perhaps also the text, of the copy of Geoffrey's History in the same manuscript.

The Leiden rubrics of Geoffrey's *Historia* are also unusual for the form of his name in the opening rubric, 'Gaufrid<us> Monimutensis', rather than the common *Monumetensis* or similar forms.[13]

The other major rubrics in MS. 76 are as follows:

§5 Explicit prologus. Incipit liber primus
§110 Incipit prologus de prophetiis Merlini
§111 Explicit prologus. Incipiunt prophetie
After §208 Explicit liber decimus historie de regibus Britonum quam nuper transtulit Gaufridus Monemutensis

These are not reproduced *verbatim* and in full in any other manuscript. Those at §§1 and 5 are found in nearly identical form in Paris, BN, lat. 6815 [181] but there are no rubrics at §111 and after §208. London, BL, Cotton Nero D.viii [92] follows all the Leiden rubrics except the last, which is slightly expanded: 'Explicit liber historie de regibus Britonum quem nuper *de Britannico in Latinum* transtulit Gaufridus Monemutensis'. Firenze, Bibliotheca Laurenziana XVII dext. 6 [71], is likewise identical to MS. 76 except for the final rubric (written in an informal

---

11 Dumville, 'An Early Text', pp. 5–6.
12 One of two acephalous relatives of the Stephen-Robert manuscript, Bern 568 [15]: see above, V.
13 I am grateful to Oliver Padel for pointing out to me that the form *Monemutensis* is nevertheless preferable to *Monumetensis*.

hand), which reads correctly *undecimus* for *decimus*.[14] BL Cotton Vespasian A.xxiii [97] follows the rubrics in 71 exactly except for the modified opening rubric, 'Incipit prologus [lacks Gaufridi . . . Claudiocestrie] in historiam de regibus Maioris Britannie que nunc Anglia dicitur [lacks quam . . . Latinum]', and final rubric (truncated after *regibus Britonum*).

Another modified form of the opening rubric is found in Leiden, UB, Voss. lat. F. 77 [77]: 'Incipit prologus Gaufridi Monemitensis (*sic*) in librum de gestis regum Maioris Britannie que nunc Anglia dicitur ad Robertum comitem Glocestrie [lacks quam . . . latinum]'. The rubrics of this manuscript agree with those of 76 only at §5. At §109 we read **Incipit prologus in librum septimum qui continet prophetias Ambrosii Merlini**, at §110 **Incipit prologus ad Alexandrim** (sic) **Linlinensem** (sic) **episcopum**, and at §111 **Incipit liber septimus qui continet prophetias Ambrosii Merlini**;[15] there is no final rubric. This group is repeated almost exactly in Sainte-Geneviève 2113 [191] except for the absence of a rubric at §5.

One of the phrases found in the Leiden rubrics occurs *verbatim* in the rubrics of BAV Ottoboni lat. 1472 [194], 'Incipit liber magistri Gaufridi Monemutensis quem *transtulit de Britannico in Latinum* de regibus britannicis'. The apparent connection is perhaps misleading as there is a common source, Geoffrey's own phrase found (in the infinitive) in §110.

Prologus/editio Gaufridi Arturi Monemutensis de gestis

A second group of rubrics clusters around a less easily identifiable core, which may be represented as **Prologus/editio Gaufridi Arturi Monemutensis de gestis**. This witnesses an interesting combination of names: Geoffrey's self-styled *Monemutensis* together with the by-name, Arthur, by which he is distinguished in charter-attestations.[16]

1. Prologus . . .

Beginning again with the most elaborate form of the rubrics, we find the following in the thirteenth-century manuscript, Cambridge, Fitzwilliam Museum, 302 [26]:

§1 Hic incipit prologus Galfridi Arturi Monemutensis de gestis regum Brittannie insule

§5 Explicit prologus. Hic incipit descriptio Britannie insule

After **§208 Explicit liber de historiis regum Brittannie insule.**

A fifteenth-century manuscript, CUL Ii.4.17 [51], offers the closest parallel to these, but reading at §1 *Britonum in Anglia* for *regum Britannie insule*, adding to

---

14 This rubric was erroneously reported in the catalogue. Read *Britanniæ* for *Britanniam*: Crick, *The Historia*, III.118.

15 In the catalogue-entry §§109 and 110 should be reversed: Crick, *The Historia*, III.126.

16 See Padel, 'Geoffrey', pp. 1–4. The phrase is found in the First Variant as well: Wright, *The Historia*, II.liii.

that at §5 *que nunc Anglia uocatur*[17] and lacking *insule* at §208. At §110 (there is a lacuna here in 26), 51 has 'Incipit prologus de prophetia Merlini'.

A related and better attested set of rubrics centres on an inverted form of this opening rubric: **Gaufridi Arturi Monemutensis de gestis Britonum prologus incipit**. This form is found in London, BL, MSS Royal 13.D.ii [112] (late twelfth-century) and Harley 4003 [103] (late thirteenth-century, reading *Galfridi* and *Monutensis*), whose other main rubrics are:

at §5 **Britannie insule descriptio** (112, reads *Birtannie*)

§109 **Incipit prologus in prophecias Merlini** (103, for *in . . . prophecias*, reads *de . . . prophethiis*)

§111 **Explicit prologus. Incipiunt prophecie** (103, om. *Explicit prologus*; after *incipiunt, hic*; for *prophecie, prophethie Merlini*)

§118 **Expliciunt prophetie Merlini. Sequitur liber .uiii. unde supra** (103, after *Merlini, Incipit liber uii*)

§208 no rubric in 112 (103, *Explicit liber*).

Aberystwyth, NLW, 21552 [5] has the same opening rubric with the spelling *Galfridi* but a longer form of the rubric at §5 'Explicet (*sic*) prologus. Britanie insule descriptio incipit'. The final rubric in MS. 112 runs 'Deo gracias. Explicit iste liber Deo gloria qui incepit et compleuit. Amen'. These rubrics may be compared with those following a less elaborate opening rubric, lacking *Arturi*, found in three manuscripts – London, BL, Cotton Cleopatra D.viii [90], Oxford Bodleian MS. Bodley 622 [137], and Magdalen College lat. 171 [162] (90 and 162 omit *incipit* also). At §5, 137 agrees with the version in 103; 90 adds *Incipit* after *descriptio*; 162 adds *Incipit*, as do 5, 26, and 51. 137 conforms exactly with 112 at §§109 and 111, as does 90 at §109, but at §111 MS. 90 resembles 103, adding *Merlini*. At §118, 90 agrees with 112 but omits *Merlini*; 137 follows 5. Final rubrics are uninformative, 90 and 137 having simply *explicit*, and 162 (like 112) none at all.

A further permutation of the opening rubric examined above is found in Lambeth Palace 401 [121] and Paris, BN, lat. 13710 [185]: **Galfridi Arturi Monemutensis (de gestis) Britonum liber. Incipit prologus**. The only other rubric in 121 is at §5 'Incipit Britannie insule descriptio'. After §1, 185 has no other rubrics except the final one which includes the word *liber* (as do those in 103 and 5): 'Explicit hic liber qui nuncupatur Brutus'.

Another candidate for inclusion under this heading is Paris, BN, lat. 5234 [167]. The opening rubric includes no mention of Geoffrey but the other elements are found in that of 121 and 185: 'Incipit prologus in libro de gestis Britonum'. The later rubrics are also comparable: at §5 'Descriptio brittannice insule', §110 'Incipit prologus prophetie Merlini', §111 'Explicit. Incipit prophetia Merlini'. One component is found in the final rubric of CUL Ee.1.24 [46] – 'Explicit liber de gestis Britonum' – but the comparison is not corroborated by the only other rubric, at §1 'Historia Britonum'. Cambridge, St John's College S.6 [33] offers a more promising comparison, despite the absence from its opening rubric of

---

17 Compare the Leiden group 'Britannia que nunc Anglia dicitur'.

references to *prologus* or Geoffrey: 'Incipit liber de gestis Britonum primus. Capitulum primum'. Its rubric at §109 is as 112, with the addition after *prologus* of *Gaufridi Monemutensis*; at §118 the rubric resembles that in 5 but the words after *sequitur* have been replaced by *capitulum .ii.*. The final rubric is not equivalent to others in this group: 'Explicit cronica de gestis Britonum'.

2. Editio

These rubrics are hardly separable from those just discussed. In one manuscript, Oxford, Bodleian, Laud 664 [149], both keywords are used: 'Incipit edicio Galfridi Mo\ne/mutensis de gestis Britonum. Prologus'.[18] However, this rubric and that at §5, 'Descriptio Britannie', differ from the *Prologus* type in ways witnessed by most '*editio*' rubrics: the spelling *Galfridi* for *Gaufridi* at §1 (the most unstable feature) and the omission of *incipit* at §5. A further characteristic is the reference to the Prophecies in the singular (rather than the plural as in the main representatives of the *Prologus* group).[19]

One group of manuscripts with the *editio* rubric exhibits a degree of coherence. Lambeth Palace, MS. 379 [120] and Salisbury Cathedral 121 [203] (both twelfth-century) have

at §1 Incipit edicio Galfridi Arturi Monemutensis de gestis Britonum
§5 Descriptio insule
§6 Narratio hystorie
§110 Prologus
§111 Hic incipit prophetia Ambrosii Merlini

and 120 has after §208, *Explicit Brut[]*. The rubrics at §§1 and 5 are found in nearly identical form in CUL Dd.6.12 [43], a twelfth-century manuscript containing no other original rubrics. Dublin, Trinity College, MS. 494 [63] (*c.* 1200, or later) agrees at §§1 (but *Gaufredi Monumetensis*, not *Galfridi Monemutensis*) and 110 but has at §5 'Laus Britannie'.

There are several outliers, whose relationship with this group is not yet clear. BL MSS Arundel 319 + 409 [87] has the 120/203 form of the opening rubric, omitting *Arturi* (see *Prologus*, above), but at §5 'De situ Britannie et eius pulcritudine' and at §111 'Incipit prophecia Merlini'. A shorter form of the opening rubric, 'Incipit edicio Gaufridi Arturi Monsmutenensis' (*sic*), is found in Glasgow, UL, 332 [74], which contains no other original rubrics. The opening rubric in Oxford, Bodleian, MS. Rawlinson C.152 [156], also demonstrates affinities with those mentioned above: 'Gaufridi Mon\u/tensis de gestis Britonum secundum Caratonum editio'. I have not found the phrase *secundum Caratonum* elsewhere. The other rubrics in 156 are not comparable, however.[20]

---

18 Compare 103, *Monutensis* (see also Oxford, Bodleian, MS. Rawlinson C.152 [156], *Mon\u/tensis*).

19 149 has at §111 'Liber .uii. de prophetia Merlini' (not found in any others of these manuscripts but implied by the rubrics of 5).

20 §5 'Explicit prefac[ ]. Liber incipit primus', §111 'Prophetie Merlini Britonis' (final chapters lost).

In one case the *editio* form, which usually introduces the text, is found in the final rubric: 'Explicit edicio Gaufridi Monumetensis de gestis Britonum'. Unfortunately the manuscript in which it occurs, Bruxelles, BR, 8495–8505 [18], contains only a fragment of the *Historia* (§§204–208).

3. Translatio

Geoffrey's double name is found in the rubrics of one more *Historia*-manuscript: Notre Dame 40 [130] has at §1 'Translacio Gaufridi Arciri (*sic*) Monemutensis de gestis Britonum'.

Cambridge, St John's G.16 [32] and relatives

The above cases have been described and even defined by their opening rubrics. The rubrics in 32, however, are made noteworthy by those after the prologue at §5: 'Incipit primus liber de situ et regibus Britannie et qui prius eam inhabitauerunt'. This is found in three other manuscripts: Glasgow, UL, 331 [73], BL, Cotton Vespasian E.x [98], and Bodleian, Rawlinson B.148 [153]. The other main rubrics in 32 are as follows:

§1 Incipit prologus
§108 Uerba Merlini/De uerbis Merlini
§109 Uerba auctoris
§111 Incipiunt uaticinia Merlini coram Uortegirno edita.

153 has no contemporary opening rubric; 73 and 98 both have 'Prologus'. 98 has all the other rubrics listed above; 153 has those at §§108 and 111 only (no rubric at §109). The Prophecies and surrounding chapters are lacking from 73.

The same unusual rubrics at §§108 and 109 are found in a further witness: Manchester, John Rylands University Library, MS. lat. 216 (+ BN lat. 4999A) [165]. Here the *Historia* is acephalous (hence no comparable rubrics at §5) but there is no such explanation for the absence of the rubric at §111. There is some disruption here, however, as most of §110 was deliberately omitted (after 'nobilitatis tue dilectio'); the same omission occurs in 98 but in no other *Historia*-manuscript known to me (see above, IV).

Incipit prologus Gaufridi Monemutensis in hystoriis/historia regum Britannie

Of manuscripts bearing this heading, Bruxelles, Bibliothèque royale, MS. 9871–9874 [20] contains a fairly representative set of rubrics. It has at §5 'Explicit prologus. Incipit hystoria', and after the *Historia* 'Explicit historia regum Britannie'.[21] Such rubrics as there are in Paris, BN, lat. 6041B [173], at §1 and 5, agree with these. Montpellier, BM, 92 [126] agrees with the rubrics of 20 at §1 and also

---

21 It ends at §180, however. There is a further rubric, at §143. None of the manuscripts with the *hystoriis* form, like 20, has rubrics at the Prophecies themselves (§§109, 111, 118).

after §208 but here they continue '. . . translata a Gaufrido Monemutensi'; 126 has at §5 'Incipit liber historiarum regum Britannie'. London, BL, Additional 33371 [83], a fragmentary manuscript, has the same opening rubric but the only other rubric to survive is that in the margin by §106 'Historia Mellini'. The same spelling – *Mellini* for *Merlini* – is found at §111 in BN lat. 5233 [166], the only manuscript with the *historia* not *hystoriis* form of the initial rubric. It has no further rubrics. The manuscripts just mentioned include four of five witnesses to Hammer's fifth type of nameless dedication. The dedicatory section is lost from 83.

The form 'historia regum Britannie', used by Geoffrey himself (§1), is found in the final rubrics of two further manuscripts. It constitutes the only rubric in Roma, BAV, Pal. lat. 962 [196] (here *regum* is a correction from *regnum*) (type-iii nameless dedication). Cambridge, UL, Mm.1.34 [53] (also type-iii) bears both the *regum* form after §208 and at §5 the rubric found in 20 and 173. Its other rubrics are not equivalent, however: at §1 'Incipit prologus historie Britonum', after §8 'Historia Britonum', and in the margin by §111 'Uaticinium Merlini'. Roma, BAV, Vat. lat. 2005 [199] has at §1 'Incipit historia regum Britannie' but as there are no other rubrics nothing can be said about its relationship to the manuscripts discussed above. 199 is conspicuous, however, in being the only one not to bear the nameless dedication: its dedication is to Robert and Waleran.

Incipit in historiam Britannorum prefacio Gaufridi Monomutensis

This distinctive opening rubric is found in three manuscripts while a fourth contains an apparent elaboration.

One of the three, Aberystwyth, NLW, 13052 [3], has in addition at §5 'Explicit prefacio. Incipit historia', §118 'Explicit prophetia Merlini', and after §208 'Explicit histori (*sic*) Britannorum'. The rubrics in Paris, BN, lat. 18271 [189] agree with these at §§1 and 5 but there are none at the Prophecies and only 'explicit' after §208. Both these manuscripts bear the type-viii nameless dedication. Auxerre, BM, 91 [14] (type-viii nameless dedication) agrees with 3 at §§1 and 208, having simply 'Explicit' at §118; the only other rubric is at §111 'Incipit prophetia Merlini'. Paris, BN, lat. 12943 [184] resembles MS. 3 in its rubrics at §§5 and 118, and has the rubric at §111 found in MS. 14, but those at §1 and after §208 are more elaborate: 'Incipit prefacio magistri Gaufridi Monemutensis in historia Britonum', and 'Explicit historia de primordio Britannie Maioris que nunc Anglia uocatur' (this last phrase echoing again the Leiden rubrics).

Paris, BN, lat. 6041 [171] may also have rubrics related to this group: at §1 'Incipit in historia Britonum prefacio Gaufridi Monemitensis', and at §111 the rubrics found in MS. 14. Like MS. 184 it bears the seventh type of nameless dedication. One of the problems of this potential group is that the rubrics are ordinary and obvious; the case for a connection is strengthened, however, by their appearing only in nameless-dedication manuscripts. Paris, BN, lat. 5697 [168] (type iii), for example, is comparable in its central rubrics – at §5 and §111 it has those found in 184 and others – but at §1 'Incipit hystoria Britonum'. The mention of *prefacio* at §5 increases the possibility of some connection with the manuscripts discussed above.

Other prologus and prefatio rubrics

The components of the last two sets of rubrics discussed are quite ordinary and obvious but, arranged in a particular order, may signal some connection between manuscripts. When the components remain ordinary but are further simplified, what is the result?

1. [Prologus] historia Britannorum/Britonum

Two manuscripts bear rubrics comparable with those seen above under *Incipit prologus Galfridi Monemutensis in hystoriis/historia regum*. These are Troyes, BM, 273 bis [208] and Montpellier, BM, 378 [127], the sole representatives of Hammer's type-ii nameless dedication. Their only rubrics are at §1 'Prologus Galfridi in istoria Britannorum' (208: adds *Incipit*, reads *Galeridi, historia*), and at §5 'Finit prologus. Incipit istoria Britannorum' (208: *Explicit, historia*). (This last rubric, in the form found in 208, is the only rubric found in the single-dedication manuscript Douai, BM, 880 [59].) Two further manuscripts have a similar form, but with the variant *Britonum* for *Britannorum*.[22] 'Prologus Galfridi in hystoria Britonum' (§1) is the only rubric in Cambridge, Sidney Sussex College, 75 [34]. The opening rubric in Cambridge, Trinity College, R.7.28 [37] is almost identical (but the whole is prefaced with *Incipit*), the only other rubric being the final *Finit historia Britonum*.[23]

Before dealing with the more succinct forms of the rubric, relatively full versions found in two manuscripts deserve mention. The basic structure of the rubrics under discussion is obscured by Galfridian material in CUL Dd.6.7 [42]:[24] §1 'Incipit prologus Gaufridi Monemutensis ad Robertum comitem Glaudioces-trie in historia Britonum', after §208 'Explicit historia Britonum a Galfrido Monemutensi de Britanico in Latinum translata'. Other rubrics are at §5 'Commendacio insule' (apparently unique) and the more standard 'Incipit prologus in prophecias Merlini' at §109 and at §111 'Incipit prophetia Merlini'. The rubrics in Cambridge, Trinity College, O.1.17 [38] are ordinary but do not fit the *Prologus. . . . historia regum Britannie* category examined above or the *Prologus in historia Britonum* group to be discussed below. They are, at §1 'Incipit prologus Galfridi Monemutensis in historiam Britonum', at §6 'Incipit historia', after §109 'Explicit', at §111 'Incipit prophetia Merlini'. This divergence from the other manuscripts accords with its dedication: not the nameless form but to Robert and Waleran.

---

22 *Britannorum* is by far the rarer form (found in the *prefacio* manuscripts just examined). A further example is provided by the opening rubric of Aberystwyth, NLW, 11611 [2] 'Incipit hystoria Britannorum' (the only other rubric is a final 'Explicit').

23 Both 34 and 37 are dedicated to Robert of Gloucester.

24 A *pudibundus Brito* manuscript.

131

Some copies begin with the entirely predictable 'Incipit prologus in hystoria Britonum'. The other rubrics of these manuscripts are generally ordinary as well and lack a clear pattern. Some measure for comparison is offered by the rubrics in Oxford, Bodleian, Laud misc. 720 [150],[25] which has after the opening rubric as given above (but note the spelling, *historia Brittonum*) at §5 'Explicit prologus. Incipit hystoria Brittonum', at §109 'Incipit prologus de prophetia Merlini', and at §111 'Incipit prophetia Merlini'. CUL Ii.4.4 [49][26] lacks an opening rubric but has rubrics at §§5 and 111 similar to those in 150. Paris, BN, lat. 6231 [176] (fragmentary) has the rubrics at §§1 and 5 (and no others). BL Cotton Titus C.xvii [96] has that at §1 only. Another manuscript with this opening rubric, BL Arundel 326 [88], displays in its other rubrics independence from the type seen in 150: at §5 'Explicit prologus. Descripcio insule Maioris Britannie', §109 'Incipit indissolubilis prophetie Merlini liber de hystoriis Britonum' (unique), §118 'Explicit prophecia Merlini'.[27] A slightly different form of this opening rubric is found in Cambridge, Trinity College, R.7.6 [36] (nameless-dedication, vi): 'Incipit *prologus hystorie* Brithonum et Anglorum'. The other rubrics are at §5 'Descripcio Britannie', §6 'Incipit hystoria', §111 'Prophecie Merlini', §208 'Explicit Brutus de uita regum Anglie'.

Two manuscripts have a similar opening rubric but the adjectival form is found in place of the genitive plural *Britonum* or *Brittanorum*. Bruxelles, BR, II.1020 [21] has at §1 'Prologus in hystoria brittanica', §110 'Prologus in prophetia Merlini', §111 'Incipit prophetia Merlini. Liber vii'. The only rubrics in Sankt Gallen 633 [205] bear little resemblance to these: §1 'Incipit prologus in Britannicam hystoriam', §5 'Textus hystorie'.[28]

Some vulgate *historia*-texts (as well as the Second-Variant BL Royal 4.C.xi [108]; see above) are introduced merely by 'Incipit hystoria Britonum'. This constitutes the only original rubric in BN lat. 4126 [164] and Firenze, Biblioteca nazionale centrale, MS. B.R. 55 [72]. Winchester Cathedral 9 [212] is perhaps another example but the third word of the rubric is illegible. NLW 11611 [2] has the *Britannorum* form and also a final 'Explicit'.

Apart from indicating a connection between 127 and 208, these findings are inconclusive. There is, however, common ground of a rudimentary nature between most of these rubrics in that they describe the History (at §5) as *historia* and the Prophecies (at §111) as *prophetia*. 88 and 36 provide exceptions.

Prefatio

Outside the fairly well defined *prefatio* group discussed above, rubrics describing the early chapters of the *Historia* as a preface display even less conformity than

---

25 *pudibundus Brito.*
26 Dedicated to Robert and Waleran.
27 The rubrics in BL Sloane 289 [116], shown by contents to be closely related to 88, are only a shadow of these. §1 'Prologus', §5 'Explicit prologus', §118 (as Arundel), §208 'Explicit'.
28 21 is dedicated to Robert while 205 bears the nameless dedication.

the *prologus* types. We have already seen that the rubrics of a Second-Variant witness, Stockholm Holm. D.1311 [207], contain this element (above, n. 9); the set found in 207 cannot be paralleled by that in any vulgate manuscript, however. New Haven, Yale 598 [129] has the same opening rubric as 207, but different rubrics at the prophecies (its final rubric is illegible on microfilm).[29] Cambridge, Corpus Christi College, 281 [23] has at §1 'Incipit prefatio in libro Brittonum', §5 'Explicit prefatio. Incipit liber'.

Explicit prologus. Incipit prophetia eiusdem

The above, a rubric found at §111 (where the Prophecies of Merlin begin), is perhaps an unlikely signpost to a group of related manuscripts, especially in the temporary absence of other types of corroborating evidence. The rubric is found, however, in a number of manuscripts and in some is not a free-standing heading, there being no preceding rubric to provide the antecedent of *eiusdem*. It would seem, therefore, that inheritance must play some part here.

In two manuscripts *eiusdem* is unexplained: the only other rubric in Paris, BN, lat. 6041C [174] is the final 'Explicit hystoria Britonum a tempore Bruti usque ad tempus Cadualadri scripta'; Reims, BM, 1430 [193] has none. In BN lat. 6041A [172], the only explanation of the *eiusdem* rubric is provided by preceding rubrics entered in smaller script in the margin: 'Incipit prologus de Merlino' at §109 and '.vi. .vii. incipit' at §111. (There is also a final rubric, 'Explicit iste liber scriptus feliciter'.)

The other witnesses bearing the *eiusdem* rubric have at §110 'Incipit prologus de prophetia Merlini'. Four lack an opening rubric. Lille, BM, 533 [79] and Bodleian, Rawlinson B.189 [155] have no rubrics other than those at §§110 and 111. BN nouv. acq. lat. 1001 [190] has only 'Explicit', while BN lat. 6039 [169] has 'Explicit Britannicus magistri Ualterii partinens. Finito libro sit laus et gloria Cristo'. Only one manuscript with these rubrics at §§110 and 111, Oxford, Bodleian, Bodley 233 [135], has an opening rubric (but no final rubric): 'Incipit liber qui uocatur Brutus per Galfridum Monemutensem a Britannico in Latinum translatus. Prologus'.[30]

Pairs of rubrics

Certain sets of rubrics are found in two manuscripts but cannot at present be assigned to a wider group.

---

[29] §109 'Prologus Gaufridi in prophetiam Merlini', §110 'Epistola [. . .]' (illegible), §111 'Prophetia Merlini de regibus Britonum'.
[30] 135, like 155, contains the interpolation Arthur's letter (above, IV: INTERPOLATIONS).

Lambeth Palace 454b [123] and Bodleian, Fairfax 28 [141]

There is no rubrication in these twelfth-century manuscripts at the main points of the text; but they contain a substantial series of rubrics mostly at chapter-divisions within the narrative, some being placed marginally and some incorporated into the body of the written page. These begin at 'Genuit' in §27: 'Ciuitas Eboraci conditur a rege Ebrauco et rex Dauid regnat in Iudea. Siluius uero Latinus in Italia et Gad et Nathan et Asaph prophetant in Israel'. The rubrics of these manuscripts are almost identical until §103, but MS. 141 includes at §§69 and 93 rubrics not found in MS. 123. No rubrics are found in MS. 123 after §103 but they continue in MS. 141 at §§132, 135, 142 and 143 (below, Appendix: Synchronisms).

BL Harley 5115 [105] and Phillipps 3117 [214]

These manuscripts[31] have the unique opening rubric: 'Incipit historia regum Britannie Maioris secundum Galfridum Monemutensem'. Both have simply 'Explicit' after §208. 214 has rubrics at §§118 and 124; there are none here in 105.

All Souls', 35 [132] and BN lat. 7531 [182]

132 originally contained only §§6–109 and 118–208 of the *Historia*. §§1–5 and 111–117 were supplied, however, shortly after the volume was completed (above, IV: *Merlinus uero incipiens*), and it was at this stage that the rubrics relating to those in 182 were added: §1 'Incipit liber de gestis Anglorum ante aduentum Christi a Gauterio editus', and §5 'De insula (132, *insulis*) Britannie'. 182 has also a final rubric but there is nothing in 132. The added opening chapters of 132 bear the nameless dedication, as does 182.

Gonville & Caius College, 450/391 [31] and BL Royal 13.D.v [113]

These manuscripts are connected by rubrics at §§109 and 111 alone: 'Prologus Galfridi in uaticinationes Merlini'; 'Incipiunt uaticinia Merlini Ambrosii'.[32] 113 has distinctive rubrics at §5 and after §208 – §5 'De aduentu Enee in Italiam et natiuitate Bruti'; §208 'Explicit hystoria Britonum. Et de ambagibus Merlini' – but comparison is prevented by physical loss at both ends of 31. The rubric at §5 is, however, found in a further witness: Dublin, Trinity College, MS. 496 [65]. The other rubrics of this last manuscript are quite unlike those just discussed.[33]

---

31 Which share an unusual item of contents (above, II: *Ab origine mundi*).

32 The expression *uaticinia Merlini* is found at §111 in a number of manuscripts (BL Royal 15.C.xvi [115], Oxford, Bodleian, Lat. misc. e.42 [146], BN lat. MSS 6232 [177] and 13710 [185]) but in only one other is Merlin called *Ambrosius*. Oxford, Bodleian, Jesus College 2 [142] has here 'Explicit prologus. Incipiunt uaticinia Ambrosii Merlini qui floruit circa annum Domini .cccc.xxx. in tempore Uortigerni regis Britannie'.

33 At §110 'Prologus de profeciis Merlini', §111 'Incipiunt prophecie Merlini', §118 'Expliciunt propheti[ ]', after §208 'Explicit. Explicit hic Bruti de gestis iste libellus cuius uirtuti

CUL Dd.1.17 [40] and BL Royal 13.D.i [111]

These manuscripts are only weakly connected by rubrics owing to the lacunose state of 40. Both have the final rubric 'Ualete. Explicit hystoria de gestis Britonum'. §111, where an elaborate rubric is found in 111,[34] is physically absent from 40.

BN lat. 6232 [177] and BAV Reg. lat. 825 [198]

The comparison of the rubrics of these manuscripts rests on elaborate descriptions of the text at §1 and after §208; the headings at the prophecies display no overlap.[35] This situation is explained by the physical state of 177. Its initial and final rubrics belong to sections added in the fifteenth century to create a complete text out of a twelfth-century core. (198 was written c. 1400.)

MS. 198 has at §1 'Incipit hystoria regum Britonum a tempore Bruti eorum primi regis usque ad Cadualladrum ultimum inclusiue etc.', which may be compared with *Historia* §2 '. . . (librum uetustissimum) qui a Bruto primo rege Britonum usque ad Cadualadrum . . .'. MS. 177 has here 'Incipit Brutus siue hystoria regum Britannie Maioris a Bruto ipsius primo rege usque ad Cadualladrum ultimum ipsius regem'. This, like the rubric in 198 and unlike the *Historia*, refers to Cadualadrus as *ultimus*, the last king. The final rubrics of the two manuscripts repeat this idea and add a further element not found in this context in the *Historia*: *inclusiue*. MS. 198 has 'Explicit hystoria Bruti primi Britonum regis necnon aliorum regum sequencium usque ad Cadualladrum inclusiue ultimum regem Britannie Maioris etc.'. MS. 177 reads 'Explicit historia regum Britannie Ma[] a Bruto ipsius primo rege usque ad Cadualadrum regem ultimum ipsius inclusiue. Deo gratia'.

A similar rubric is found in Dublin, Trinity College, MS. 493 [62] (later thirteenth-century) but this seems to be derived directly from the *Historia*: (§1) 'Incipit prephacio Galfridi Monumetensis ad Robertum comitem Claudiocestrie de hystoria Britonum a tempore Bruti primo rege Britonum usque ad tempus Cadawaladri filii Cadewallonis'. The final rubric is also Galfridian.[36]

---

congaudeat anglica tellus'. 65 and 113 have some connection, however: 65 was probably written at Wymondham, a cell of St Albans, the house where 113 spent at least part of the Middle Ages.

34 'Explicit historia usque adhuc et incipit prophetia Ambrosii Merlini quam dixit ex precepto Uortigerni regis Britonum'.

35 177: §109 'Incipiunt uaticinia Merlini secundum eundem Galfridum Bonemutensem (*sic*). Liber uii', §111 'Incipiunt uatticinia Merlini'. 198: §109 'Incipit prologus de propheciis Merlini', §111 'Explicit prologus. Incipit prophecia'.

36 'Explicit liber Bruti quem Galfridus Monemutensis transtulit de britannico sermone in Latinum'.

Colmar, BM, 448 [56] and Dôle, BM, 348+349 [58]

The rubrics in 58 are sufficiently unusual to be included among the idiosyncratic rubrics listed below except that one of the rarest finds a parallel in another manuscript, 56.

58 has at §1 'Incipit hystori[ ] de origine Brittonum translata a Gaufrido Monumetensi de brittanica lingua in Latinum', at §5 'Explicit praefa[ ]', §6 'Textus hystorie incipit', §109 'Reuelatio hystoriografi de Merlino', §110 'Reuelatio hystoriografi de eodem', §111 'Incipiunt prophetie Merlini'. Although the opening rubric is plainly Galfridian (*Historia*, §110), I have not found it in this form in any other manuscript.[37] The naming of the main part of the work *textus historie* (at §6) is paralleled in Sankt Gallen 633 [205] (but at §5). The most unusual rubrics are those at the Prophecies, which find some equivalent in 56 which has at §109 'Relatio historiagrafi (*sic*) de Merlino'. The other rubrics in 56 (which is acephalous) are at §110 'Prefatio', §111 'Incipiunt prophetie Merlini' and after §208 'Explicit liber'.[38]

BL Stowe 56 [117] and BN lat. 17569 [188]

The rubrics of these manuscripts are modest but identical: at §1 'Prologus sequentis operis', and at §5 'Incipit britannice hystorie liber primys' (188, *.i.* for *primys*). A scribal colophon takes the place of a final rubric (see above, III). The opening rubric 'Prologus sequentis operis' is found in only one other manuscript, Arras, BM, 583 [13], which contains no other rubrics.

NLW, Peniarth 43 [9] and CUL, Dd.4.34 [41]

The rubrics of these manuscripts, uniquely among those examined, include the component *historia gentis Britannie*. 41 has only the final rubric 'Explicit liber hystorie gentis Britonum'; 9 has here 'Explicit historia gentis Britonum'. The other rubrics in 9 are at §6 (where the text begins) '.i. liber historie gentis Britonum', and at §111 'Incipiunt prophetie Merlini'. §§1–4 are absent from 9 and 1–5 from MS. 41.

Oxford, Bodleian, Jones 48 [143], which also lacks §§1–4, bears only one rubric, at §111, which reproduces exactly that found in MS. 9.

Idiosyncratic rubrics

Certain manuscripts have rubrics which defy association with others. I list these below.

---

37 On this phrase see above, Leiden group. Compare also the opening rubric of the First-Variant subgroup 67/68/70 (above).

38 58 and 205 bear the type-i nameless dedication; 56 is acephalous.

Aberystwyth, NLW, MS. Llanstephan 196 [7] (*saec.* xv or later)

§1 Incipit tractatio historie Bruti
§5 De insula Britannie
§6 De fuga Enee post bellum Troie
§110 Prologus de prophetia Merlini
§118 Hic finitur prophetia Merlini
§208 Explicit tractacio historie Bruti cum prophetia Merlini

Aberystwyth, NLW, MS. Porkington 17 [10] (*saec.* xiii ?[2])

§1 Incipit liber Bruti
§5 De Brittania
§109 Item de Merlino
§110 De Alexandro Lincolinensi episcopo
§111 De prophecia Merlini q. dicit
§208 Explicit liber Bruti

Cambridge, Gonville & Caius College, MS. 103/55 [28] (*saec.* xii)

§1 Domino Rodberto comiti
§18 Qualiter Brutus cum Pictauensibus pugnauit[39]

Cambridge, Trinity College, MS. O.2.21 [39] (*saec.* xiii/xiv)

§1 Incipit prologus super librum hystoriarum regum Britannie
§5 Descripcio insule
§208 Ualete

Cambridge, UL, MS. Dd.10.32 [45] (*saec.* xiv ?[2])

§1 Hic incipit liber Britonum qui uocatur Brrutus (*sic*) de gestis Ang[ ]
§21 Hic applicuit Brutus in terram Britannie uocatam modo Angliam

London, BL, MS. Add. 35295 [84] (*c.* 1422)

§1 Incipit historia Britonum et quomodo Brutus primus rex Brutannie uenit in istam insulam cum gente sua post Troiam destructam fraude Attenor<is> et Enee qui Eneas postmodum Turno rege ab ipso deuicto regnauit in Italiam Lauinia ducta ab eo filia regis Litinorum (*sic*) de qua filium Siluuium genuit ut patet in sequenti historia
§5 De Britannia insula
§111 Incipit prophetia Merlini liber .uii.

---

39 Occasional rubrics are found elsewhere.

§208 Explicit historia libri Britonum que in octo libris continetur[40]

London, BL, MS. Egerton 3142 [99] (*saec.* xiii/xiv)

§1 Incipit liber de gestis Bruti editus a magistro Waltero Oxif. archidiacono
§5 De mensura Britanie Maioris que nunc dicitur Anglia secundum longitudinem insule et latitud[inem]
§109 De prophetia Merlini et eius actibus
§110 Hic rogauit Lincoliensis episcopus de translacione prophecie .M.
§111 De bello draconum et de significatione belli per Merlinum
§208 Explicit liber Bruti et de gestis Britanorum usque ad tempus et aduentum Anglorum

Oxford, Bodleian Library, MS. Jesus College 2 [142] (*saec.* xv)

§6 Incipit historia Britonum
§110 Incipit prohemium siue littera transmissa[41] domino Alexandro Lincoln. episcopo in prophetias Ambrosii Merlini
§111 Explicit prologus. Incipiunt uaticinia Ambrosii Merlini qui floruit circa annum Domini .cccc.xxx. in tempore Uortigerni regis Britannie
§208 Explicit historia Britonum

Oxford, Christ Church, MS. lat. 99 [160] (*saec.* xiii [2])

§1 Incipit prologus in gestis Bruti et ceterorum regum Britannie

Paris, BN, MS. lat. 8501A [183] (*saec.* xii *med./2*)

§1 Incipit liber in regum historiis qui Britanniam ante incarnationem Christi inhabitauerunt et postea successerunt
§5 Explicit prologus. Incipit liber metas Britannie et quicquid in ea fertile siue delectabile inuenitur describens. Capitulum .i.
§208 Explicit

Rouen, Bibliothèque municipale, MS. U.74 (1177) [200] (*saec.* xii *ex.*)

§1 Incipit historia Anglorum edita a Gaufrido Monemutensi iussu Alexandri Linconiensis episcopi[42]

---

40 Occasional rubrics are found elsewhere.
41 Not *tranmissa*, as reported in the catalogue: Crick, *The Historia*, III.230.
42 As David Dumville has pointed out, the mention here of Alexander of Lincoln as patron reflects the absence from the manuscript of the usual opening dedicatory chapters and consequent reliance of the dedication on §§109–110: 'An Early Text', p. 15.

Würzburg, Universitätsbibliothek, MS. M.ch.f.140 [213] (*saec.* **xvi**)

§1 Incipit prologus in historia de regibus et gente Brittonum
§5 De situ et quantitate Britt[annie]
§110 Prophecia Merlini. Prologus
§111 Incipit prophecia Merlini

Other rubrics

Certain copies of the *Historia* have only one rubric. These are listed here partly
for the sake of completeness, and partly in case it should become possible to
explain this sparseness of rubrics by inheritance when other evidence is available
for comparison.

Opening rubrics

Five manuscripts contain only opening rubrics: Arras 583 [13], Cambridge Sidney
Sussex 75 [34], Cambridge Trinity R.5.34 [35], Oxford Christ Church 99 [160],
Rouen U.74 [200]. There are no agreements between their wording.

Rubrics at the Prophecies

Rubrics are found only at the beginning of the Prophecies in Bern 568 [15]
(added), Boulogne 180+145+130 [16], Cambridge Corpus Christi 414 [25], Douai
882 [60], Dublin TC 172 [61], BL Harley 225 [100], Bodleian Bodley 514 [136]
and Jones 48 [143], San Marino EL 34.C.9 [204]. There is no significant
agreement over their form.

Explicit hystoria Britonum (after §208)

NLW Llanstephan 176 [6], Cologny-Genève Bodmer 70 [57], Heidelberg, UB,
9.31 [75], Bodleian Oriel College 16 [152].

Explicit (usually after §208)

CUL Ii.1.14 [48] (mid-§207: text originally truncated), London, Lambeth Palace,
MS. 188 [119], Bodleian MSS Douce 115 [140], New College 276 [151], and
Rawlinson D.893 [157] (fragmentary), BN lat. 6230 [175].

Colophons

Three manuscripts have no rubrics except for a final colophon, or rubric and
colophon combined. The first type is attested by Paris, BN, lat. 15073 [187] 'Deo
gratias et sic est finis huius libri'. London, BL, Harley 4123 [104] provides an
example of the second, 'Explicit hystoria de gestis regum Britannie quam Bruti

appellamus quam scripsit Albertus filius Iohannis presbiter de Dyst . . .', as does Dublin, Trinity College, MS. 495 [64] (acephalous), 'Et hec dicta sufficiunt per Dominum nostrum Iesum Christum. Explicit Brutus'.

Terminology

Opening and closing rubrics provide descriptions of the *Historia* of varying elaborateness, the simplest being perhaps *liber* or *liber Brittonum*.[43] I summarize below the kinds of title indicated by rubrics and discuss those not previously encountered.

[Historia/gesta] [Britonum/Britannorum]
Historia [regum Britannie/ de regibus Britannie]
[Liber/historia] de [historia/gestis] Britonum (or Anglorum)[44]

Others not based on historia/gesta

(i) *Cronica*. The *Historia* is so described in three late manuscripts whose rubrics display no other connection. The final rubric in the fifteenth-century manuscript Cambridge, St John's S.6 [33] reads 'Explicit cronica de gestis Britonum'. Olomouc 411 [131] has after §208 'Explicit cronica regum Britannie' (the only other rubric being at §111 'Hic incipiunt prophetie Merlini'). The rubrics added at the ends of the *Historia* in Paris, BN, lat. 4126 [164], when the original part of that manuscript was incorporated into the present larger compilation *c.* 1400, are at §1 'Cronica Galfridi Monumetensis' and after §208 'Explicit cronica Galfridi Monumetensis in hystoriam Britonum'.

(ii) *Tractatus*. The rubrics of only one manuscript use this word to describe the *Historia*: Cardiff 2.611 [55] has after §208 'Explicit tractatus'. There is also the apparently unrelated *tractatio* found in the initial and final rubrics of NLW Llanstephan 196 [7].[45]

(iii) *Brutus*. Although the various Bruts (of which Geoffrey's History was the ultimate progenitor) were mainly vernacular chronicles, rubrics show that the *Historia* itself was sometimes entitled *liber Bruti, historia Bruti*, or simply *Brutus*. The earliest instance known to me dates from the second half of the twelfth century: Lambeth Palace 379 [120] has after §208 in the hand of the original rubricator, 'Explicit Brut[ ]'. Other examples may be listed in roughly chronologi-

---

43 Compare the final rubrics of 56, 103, 109.
44 Other mentions of *Angli*: 36, 45, 51, 107 (added rubric), 182, 200.
45 §1 'Incipit tractatio historie Bruti', §208 'Explicit tractatio historie Bruti cum prophetia Merlini'.

cal order. References to *Historia Bruti* are excluded here as their implication is somewhat different.[46]

saec. xiii [1]: Cambridge, Trinity College, MS. R.7.6 [36]: §208 'Explicit Brutus de uita regum Anglie'

saec. xiii: Oxford, Bodleian, MS. Add. A.61 [134]: §1 'Incipit Brutus Anglie. Prologus'

saec. xiii [2]: London, BL, MS. Cotton Vespasian E.x [98]: §1 'Incipit Brutus' (at foot of page facing start of text)

saec. xiii [2]: Aberystwyth, NLW, MS. Porkington 17 [10]: §1, §208 'Incipit/Explicit liber Bruti'

saec. xiii [2/ex.]: Dublin, Trinity College, MS. 493 [62]: §208 'Explicit liber Bruti quem Galfridus Monemutensis transtulit de Britannico sermone in Latinum'

saec. xiii [ex.]: London, BL, MS. Lansdowne 732 [107] (added rubric): §1 'Hic incipit liber Bruti de gestis Anglorum'

saec. xiii/xiv: London, BL, MS. Egerton 3142 [99]: §208 'Explicit liber Bruti et de gestis Britanorum usque ad tempus et aduentum Anglorum'

saec. xiii/xiv: Oxford, Bodleian, MS. Fairfax 28 [141] (added): §1 'Liber Bruti et continet quater .xx. et .x. folia et .cc. et .v. capitula', §208 'Explicit liber Bruti'

saec. xiv [1]: London, BL, MS. Cotton Titus A.xviii [93]: §208 'Explicit historia Britonum que dicitur Brutus'

saec. xiv [1]: Oxford, Bodleian Library, MS. Bodley 233 [135]: §1 'Incipit liber qui uocatur Brutus per Galfridum Monemutensem a Britannico in Latinum translatus. Prologus'

1349 London, BL, MS. Harley 4123 [104]: §208 'Explicit hystoria de gestis regum Britannie quam Bruti appellamus quam scripsit Albertus filius Iohannis Alberti presbiter de Dyst . . .'

saec. xiv (after [1/4]): Dublin, Trinity College, MS. 495 [64]: §208 'Et hec dicta sufficiunt per Dominum nostrum Iesum Christum. Explicit Brutus'

saec. xiv [2]: Cambridge, UL, MS. Dd.10.32 [45]: 'Hic incipit liber Britonum qui uocatur Brrutus (*sic*) de gestis Ang[ ]'

saec. xiv/xv London, BL, MS. Royal 15.C.xvi [115]: §208 'Explicit liber qui uocatur Brutus'

c. 1464 Cambridge, Gonville & Caius College, MS. 249/277 [29]: §1 'Brutus sed est Galfridus Monemutensis de gestis Anglorum', 'Primus liber Bruti'.

saec. xv [2] Paris, BN, MS. lat. 13710 [185]: §208 'Explicit hic liber qui nuncupatur Brutus'.

---

[46] Found, for example, in CUL Kk.6.16 [52], BAV Reg. lat. 825 [198], Saint-Omer, BM, 710 [202].

Other rubrics

A few manuscripts have yet to be mentioned. Their rubrics are not sufficiently complete or distinctive to allow them to be assigned at present to groups or listed among the unique rubrics.

Cambridge, UL, MS. Kk.6.16 [52]

After §117 'Explicit prophecia Merlini', §208 'Explicit historia Bruti. Script. Wigorn. anno Domini .m.ccc. uicesimo septimo. Amen'.

London, BL, MS. Cotton Titus A.xviii [93]

§109 'Uerba magistri', §111 'Hic incipiunt prophetie Merlini', §208 'Explicit historia Britonum que dicitur Brutus'.

Oxford, All Souls' College, MS. 39 [133]

§1 'Incipiunt historie regum Britannie que nunc dicuntur (*sic*) Angli[ ]', §111 'Incipit de Merlino'.

Oxford, Magdalen College, MS. lat. 170 [161]

§111 'Prophetia Merlini', §78 'De natiuitate Helene regine', §88 'Undecim milia uirginum'.

Paris, BN, MS. lat. 6233 [178]

After §117 'Explicit', §208 'Explicit'.

Paris, BN, MS. lat. 6275 [179] (fragmentary)

§194 'Dolendum' 'Responsio Salomonis regis ad Caduallonem'.

Preliminary Conclusions

Apart from a few manuscripts with particularly distinctive or non-Galfridian rubrics, it is the pattern of the rubrics which is often the determining factor in classification. Even obvious terms used to describe the introduction to the work, the main text, and the prophecies can provide a framework for comparison. The incomplete state of some sets of rubrics, whether because never copied or because of physical losses, hampers the examination of rubrics, however. Without a pattern, only particularly distinctive phrases carry much significance. Therefore the full extent of inheritance, borrowing, or scribal inventiveness is not visible at this stage, but may become so with the addition of other forms of evidence.

The evidence of rubrics has produced more immediate results by confirming classifications of manuscripts already discussed. The case of the nameless-dedication manuscripts is particularly striking. Apart from clusters of manuscripts linked by rubrics (132 + 182, 58 + 205), it is possible to assign whole sets of rubrics to this group. This has demonstrated some degree of coherence between manuscripts bearing certain forms of the dedication (type v, for example) but indicated a degree of interrelation between others (types i, vii, and viii). The rubrics of Robert-Waleran manuscripts demonstrate no coherence, but neither any strong affinity with others bearing different dedications. The small 'family' represented by 15, the Stephen-Robert manuscript, seems to have had no original inherited rubrics: the opening rubric found in one, 200, reflects the state of that particular manuscript.

Within the single dedication, groups centred on 76 and 32 demonstrate marked coherence in their rubrics. Smaller groups have emerged: 9/41/143, 56/58/205, 31/113, 40/111, 105/214, 123/141, 117/188, 132/182, and 177/198. Those in 118 resemble rubrics found in Second-Variant manuscripts. It has yet to be established whether this diversity was caused by the need to supply rubrics in the copies of an unrubricated exemplar, or whether there is an underlying textual divergence as well.

Finally, it is clear that Geoffrey's History travelled under a number of titles, *Historia* and *Gesta* especially, but occasionally others, such as *Cronica* and *Brutus*.

BOOK-DIVISIONS

Though perhaps unpromising as a type of evidence, book-divisions constitute an adjunct to rubrication which, as seen above, can confirm or point to lines of transmission. Book-divisions are in effect rubrics, being added as part of the same operation. Some of the difficulties inherent but invisible in the evidence of other rubrics are quite clear here: an occurrence mentioned above, the omission or partial copying of a series, is absolutely obvious when a sequence of numbers is involved. There are problems particular to the evidence of book-divisions, however. When intermediate divisions (in a sequence of books in an exemplar) had been omitted during copying, what then happened when the imperfect sequence was itself copied? Was the imperfect sequence reproduced exactly, were the positionings of divisions maintained but silently renumbered, or were the missing books marked at seemingly appropriate places? Doubtless the response of scribes to such situations varied, but this potentially hidden complication demands a more circumspect approach to grouping book-divisions: simple classification by numbers of books present can be misleading.

The possibility of imperfect sequences was not addressed directly in the only published discussion of the *Historia*'s book-divisions, that by Acton Griscom in the introduction to his edition of 1929. Griscom sought to investigate the manuscript-evidence for the divisions into nine or twelve books found in the early printed editions and for Thomas Tanner's theory of division successively into four, eight, then twelve books.[47] The results, he found, failed to authenticate any of these arrangements. Only four twelfth-century manuscripts were divided into nine, and one of these, as Griscom said, only because Books VIII, IX, and XII of the later printed editions were not rubricated. Furthermore he noted that 'no single known XII century MS is divided into twelve books, so we may feel that there is certain proof that this division also was not original with Geoffrey'.[48] However, only a few pages below, Griscom described a group of seven twelfth-century and four later manuscripts which show consistent division into eleven marked at the same places as the modern division into twelve, only omitting the final book (at §190). He dismissed these without discussion, as 'from internal evidence they give no proof of being copies of the earliest form', whatever he might have meant by that.[49] He also discussed various four-book divisions but discarded them as too late to have been original to Geoffrey. His classification is too confused to be of value, however. Griscom included Cambridge, St John's, G.16 [32], which has four extant divisions, but he failed to register the implication from the preceding *capitula*-list and indeed from the extant book-marking (VI at §143) that seven books were intended.

The motivation for Griscom's interest in book-divisions, presumably his concern to justify their appearance in an edition (despite his conclusions, he followed the traditional twelve-book arrangement), perhaps provides some excuse for his method of investigating them. However, by taking as his yardstick Early Modern ideas of how the work should be divided and by being unrealistically reliant on number rather than position, he was over-dismissive of the medieval evidence: as book-divisions were not found in 115 of his 184 manuscripts (27 of 48 twelfth-century witnesses) he reasoned that division into books, therefore, seems not to have formed any 'part of Geoffrey's original composition'.[50]

Griscom's observation that undivided texts outnumber those with book-divisions still stands, despite the discovery of new manuscripts: 131 of the present total of 215 lack books (but sixteen of the 131 are fragmentary). A further five originally lacked them, although divisions were marked later.[51] The weight of

---

47 Griscom & Jones, *The Historia*, pp. 26–27.
48 *Ibid*. The only twelve-book manuscript is in fact fifteenth-century, CUL Dd.6.7 [42]: II §23, III §54, IV §73, V §89, VI §98, VIII §118, IX §143, X §163, XI §177, XII §188.
49 *Ibid*., pp. 28–30 (p. 30).
50 *Ibid*., p. 27.
51 Six more are divided into *capitula* rather than books. It has not yet been possible to examine three manuscripts of the 215.

Griscom's conclusions, however, would hardly seem to be supported by his summary and inconsistent discussion. I propose here to undertake a more comprehensive investigation, whose initial organizing principle is not simply the number of books but the connection between book-divisions and other rubrics. Therefore I begin by discussing each group already established on the basis of rubrics, before moving on to other observations.

The First Variant

The division between the two subgroups identified by Wright and maintained by rubrics is also partly evident in book-divisions. Of the 67/68/70 subgroup, the related NLW Panton 37 [1], and the more distantly related Cardiff 2.611 [55], only MS. 70 has book-divisions marked. These are I at §6, II §23, III §35, IV §54, V §73, and VII at §143.[52] The connection between Arsenal 982 [163] and NLW 13210 [4] seen in other rubrics is reinforced: their divisions follow those in 70 to V, then VI is at §90, VII §111, VIII §118, IX §143, X §163 (not found in 163), XI §177. Harley 6358 [106], a relative of 163 whose rubrics have been seen to display independence from it and 4, follows these markings for Books III–V and VII–XI, but II is at §22 and VI at §98.

The Second Variant

In this case the evidence of book-divisions tends to confirm that of rubrics. Hammer's chosen base manuscript for edition, BL Royal 4.C.xi [108], has no original divisions but all members of the α-group have a distinctive arrangement:[53] CUL Ff.1.25 [47], TCD 514 [66], BL MSS Cotton Galba E.xi [91] and Cotton Titus A.xxvii [95], Bodley 977 [138], and Troyes BM 1531 [209] have at §54 II, §98 III, §143 IV.[54] This particular division into four, spanning the whole text, is unique to the α-version of the Second Variant.[55]

None of the β-manuscripts, including CUL Ii.4.12 [50], has book-divisions. The γ-manuscripts display the same independence from the α in this area as in other rubrics. Saint-Omer 710 [202] has II at §23 and III at §35, points where divisions were often made. Stockholm Holm. D.1311 [207] has the same with, in addition, I marked at §5; other divisions were added, c. 1400, at §54 IV, §73 V, §89 VI, §143 VIII, and §163 IX. Bruges 428 [17], the last of Hammer's γ-manuscripts, has only I at §6. The remaining new witnesses and Harley 3773 [102] have no book-divisions.

---

52 Capitals are found in MS. 67 at §§5, 6, 54, 90, 98, 111, 116 'Tres fontes', 118, 143, and 163 and in MS. 68 at §§5, 6, 35, 54, 90, 111, 118, 143, 161, 177.

53 Divisions added in 108 at §23 II, §35 III, §54 IV.

54 MSS 47, 91, 95, and 209 have *capitula*-lists. The book-divisions in 91 begin II §54 (19ra) and III §98 (30vb), not as printed in the catalogue: Crick, *The Historia*, III.147.

55 Compare, however, the rubrics of Notre Dame 40 [130] (I §6, II §54), and Rawlinson C.152 [156] (I §5, 2 §54, III §109).

The Leiden group

The connection already established by rubrics between a number of manuscripts of which Leiden BPL 20 [76] is an early and notable representative is further reinforced by the evidence of book-divisions. Griscom apparently unknowingly identified some of its members when he listed the twelfth-century manuscripts with eleven books but he passed over them without comment. 76, BL MSS Cotton Nero D.viii [92] and Vespasian A.xxiii [97], and Firenze XVII. dext. 6 [71] all have eleven books (although V is not marked in MS. 71), the last beginning at §177 with the seventh occurring at §109, the others being I at §5, II §23, III §35, IV §54, V §73, VI §89, VIII §118, IX §143, X §163, XI §177.[56] The divisions present in BN lat. 6815 [181] agree with these but III–VII are not marked and VIII–XI are indicated only by the final rubric of the previous book. The book-divisions in Leiden Voss. lat. F.77 [77] and Sainte-Geneviève 2113 [191] are related, like their other rubrics, to 76 but in modified form: they too have eleven divisions made at the same places (V–VI are not marked in MS. 77, nor is X in 191) except that VII begins at §111 and not 109.[57]

Prologus/editio Gaufridi Arturi Monemutensis de gestis

These manuscripts are divided like those of the Leiden group but whereas the Leiden-type series began at §5, the first book here is consistently marked at §6. The manuscripts will be discussed in the order in which they were treated before.

1. Prologus

Fitzwilliam 302 [26] has eleven books with the last at §177: I §6, II §23, III §35, IV §54, V §73, VI §89, VII §111, VIII §118, IX §143, X §163, XI §177. Apart from I and VII, these agree with the Leiden divisions. CUL Ii.4.17 [51] is divided similarly but there is no rubric at §163, §177 being marked X. The book-divisions in Royal 13.D.ii [112] are identical to those in 26 (except that it omits III and VII). Harley 4003 [103], like 51, has ten books but after VI the numbering diverges from that in 51 as the leap in the sequence occurs at the Prophecies and not at §163: VII is marked at §118, and therefore VIII at §143, IX at §163 and X at §177. VII is found at §118 in NLW 21552 [5] as well (I–VI, too, are in the same places) but thereafter in that manuscript there are no further divisions. Cotton Cleopatra D.viii [90], Bodley 622 [137], and Magdalen lat. 171 [162] all have the eleven-

---

56 The start of XI is marked in 76, despite the erroneous *decimus* in the final rubric (§177 should be added in the catalogue-entry, after XI: Crick, *The Historia*, III.125). It should be noted that a twelfth book is marked in MS 92 but this begins after §208 and comprises the *Historia Brittonum*.

57 In MS. 191 Book VI ends with §108; §109 is marked as the beginning of the Prologue to Book VII, which itself begins at §111. (In the catalogue, §109 is erroneously reported as the *start* of Book VII: Crick, *The Historia*, III.296.) The arrangement in MS. 77 is similar.

book division found in 26, but VII is not marked.[58] This pattern is reproduced exactly (VII is again omitted) in a further manuscript, Bruxelles, BR, 8536–8543 [19]. Here the divisions are additional. The manuscript does not bear the *prologus/editio* rubric.

Lambeth 401 [121] and BN lat. 13710 [185] (which include a distinctive version of the rubric stated above) have book-divisions comparable with those of other members of this group. 121 has eleven books with the last at §177, but Books V–IX are not marked. 185 has major capitals at the points where the eleven books begin but there is no formal rubrication.

Of the manuscripts mentioned as possibly belonging to this group, only BN lat. 5234 [167] has book-divisions comparable with those discussed above, but Books II–VI only are marked. CUL Ee.1.24 [46] has no book-divisions while those in St John's S.6 [33] are anomalous after I (at §6): II is at §27, III §43, IV §64, V §98, VI §111, VII §127, VIII §143, IX §175. Books II–IV and IX are positioned unlike the divisions in any other manuscript.

2. Editio

Laud misc. 664 [149], whose opening rubric contains both *editio* and *prologus* elements, is divided into ten books, arranged like those in 103 (but the fourth is not marked).[59] The other manuscripts grouped before under this heading display weaker affinities with the *prologus* type. Lambeth Palace 379 [120] and Salisbury Cathedral 121 [203], witnesses with nearly identical rubrics, have no original book-divisions.[60] CUL Dd.6.12 [43], whose opening rubrics are the same as those in 120 and 203, has Books II–V marked according to the eleven-book pattern (II at §23, III at §35, IV at §54, V at §73 (comparable with MSS. 26 and 103).

The manuscripts classed as possibly belonging to this group display even less coherence. Books II–IX and XI are marked in BL Arundel 326 [88] as in 26 except for the positioning of VII at §119 and VIII at §135. Glasgow, UL, 332 [74] has peculiar divisions – V at §111, VI at §118 then VII at §143.[61] V and VI are found in these places within a more complete sequence of divisions in two other manuscripts, Sidney Sussex 75 [34] and Oriel 16 [152].[62] Rawlinson C.152 [156] is the only manuscript of those listed under the *prologus/editio* heading in which I begins at §5, the other divisions occurring at §54 (II), §109 (III). Notre Dame 40 [130], which bears the *translacio* form of the rubric, happens to be the only

---

58 X should be added before §163 in the catalogue-description of MS. 137: Crick, *The Historia*, III.224.

59 A comparable arrangement is found in two other manuscripts. Laud misc. 579 [147] is divided likewise, with Book I beginning at §5 not 6. BL Additional 35295 [84] has II–VI as 76, then VII at §111, VIII at §143.

60 Post-medieval markings were added, however, in 203.

61 In the catalogue-entry for MS. 74 Book VI is marked twice. The second VI should read VII: Crick, *The Historia*, III.121.

62 II §23 (34 and 152); 34 has in addition III §35, IV §89, VII §163. 152 has no opening rubric; 34 has 'Prologus Galfridi in hystoria Britonum'.

other vulgate manuscript in which II is marked at §54; it has no further divisions apart from I at §6.

Cambridge, St John's G.16 [32] and relatives

The unusual nature of some of the rubrics of this group is matched by the independence of their book-divisions from the types seen so far. 32, taken for convenience as a point of comparison, has at §5 I, §35 II, §111 ?III (not rubricated but indicated by the *capitula*-series), §143 VI, §187 VII. The positioning of Book II at §35 is otherwise found only in Glasgow 331 [73], Rawlinson B.148 [153], and Manchester 216 [165], all previously identified as being related to 32, and in the rubrics added in Rouen U.74 [200]. The marking at II is the only division in 153. 165 has in addition III at §89, IV §111, V §118, and VI at §143 (this last like 32). The added rubrics in 200, not a member of this group, are identical except for the placing of IV at §110. 73 has at §5 I, §54 III, §89 V. These are comparable with the divisions in a manuscript with apparently unrelated rubrics, CUL Dd.6.7 [42]: II §23, III §54 (the only other manuscript with this marking), IV §73, V §89, then VI §98 (a unique division), VIII–XI as in the Leiden eleven-book arrangement and XII at §188.

The only manuscript in which the similarity to 32 evident in rubrics is not matched by its book-divisions is 98, which has less unusual divisions: I at §5, III §35, VI §89, VII §118, VIII §143.

Incipit prologus Gaufridi Monemutensis in hystoriis/historia regum Britannie

None of the manuscripts discussed as main representatives of this type of rubric – Bruxelles, BR, 9871–9874 [20], London, BL, Additional 33371 [83], Montpellier, BM, 92 [126], Paris, BN, lat. 5233 [166] and 6041B [173] – is divided. Nor does any of the manuscripts with rubrics peripheral to these have book-divisions, but BAV Vat. lat. 2005 [199] has *capitula* (see below).

Incipit in historiam Britannorum. Prefacio Gaufridi Monomutensis

Book-divisions are found in none of the three main witnesses to this rubric (NLW 13052 [3], Dôle BM 348+349 [58], BN lat. 12943 [184]) nor in the possible additions to the group, BN MSS lat. 5697 [168] and 6041 [171].

Possible groups based on prologus or prefatio rubrics

Book-divisions do a little to clarify the associations suggested by the miscellaneous *prologus* rubrics. Neither Troyes BM 273 bis [208] nor Montpellier BM 378 [127], whose rubrics are nearly identical, has book-divisions, but Douai BM 880 [59], with which their rubrics at §5 were compared, has III–VI as in the eleven-book arrangement, then VII at §110 and VIII at §143. Sidney Sussex 75

[34] has seven peculiarly-spaced books having some connection with the eleven-book type, but whose distribution, as seen above, bears some relation to that of an *editio* manuscript, Glasgow, UL, 332 [74]. Despite having an opening rubric identical to that in 34, Cambridge, Trinity College, O.1.17 [38] has no books. CUL Dd.6.7 [42], whose rubrics were seen to be an embroidered form of the *prologus* idea, has an incomplete and slightly idiosyncratic version of the eleven-book arrangement with Book XII occuring at §188 (see above, Cambridge, St John's G.16).

Some *prologus* manuscripts have no divisions. These include most of those grouped around Laud misc. 720 [150] and all three bearing only the opening rubric 'Incipit historia Britonum': Cambridge, Trinity College, O.1.17 [38]; Bodleian, Laud misc. 720 [150]; CUL Ii.4.4 [49]; BN lat. 6231 [176]; BL Cotton Titus C.xvii [96]; Cambridge, Trinity College, R.7.6 [36]; Sankt Gallen 633 [205]; BN lat. 4126 [164]; Firenze B.R. 55 [72]; Winchester Cathedral 9 [212]. The remainder of the manuscripts discussed, BL Arundel 326 [88] and Bruxelles II.1020 [21], contain (as does 42) incomplete versions of the eleven-book division (see below, *Divisions following the eleven-book pattern*).[63]

Prefatio

The impression, gained from other rubrics, of disparity between the three manuscripts listed in this category is not dispelled by their book-divisions. Cambridge, Corpus Christi College 281 [23] has none while Stockholm Holm. D.1311 [207] and Yale 598 [129] have different modifications of the eleven-book sequence (207 has nine books and 129, eleven, only four of which are marked): see above, *Second Variant*, and below, *Divisions following the eleven-book pattern*.

Explicit prologus. Incipit prophetia eiusdem

The manuscripts with these rubrics at §111 and without the corresponding explanation at §110 have no formally marked book-divisions. These are BN MSS lat. 6041C [174] and 6041A [172] (which, at §110, has Book VII marked in the margin), and Reims BM 1430 [193]. Of the witnesses with the rubric at §110 'Incipit prologus de prophetia Merlini' as well as that at §111, all have some book-divisions (but Lille BM 533 [79] has Book XI only). Four remaining copies with both rubrics have some form of the eleven-book scheme. Bodley 233 [135] has II–VI in the usual places with VII at §110, VIII §143, IX §163 and X §177. VII begins at §110 in only one other manuscript, Würzburg, UB, M.ch.f.140 [213], whose other divisions are as in MS. 135, with the unusually-placed variation of IX at §165 and X at §179.[64] 155 has a less complete version of the sequence found

---

63 BL Sloane 289 [116], which contents and, to a lesser extent, rubrics suggest is related to 88, has major capitals at the places marked in 88 but in addition markings at §§5, 6, and 118.

64 213, like 135, and like Rawlinson B.189 [155] (one of the four manuscripts under discussion here), has the interpolated 'Arthur's letter' (above, IV). The final manuscript containing Arthur's letter, NLW Llanstephan 176 [7], has divisions II–VI as usual but VII at §143.

in 135: II §23, V §73, VI §89, VIII §143. The book-divisions in the other *prophetia eiusdem* manuscripts are comparable. BN lat. 1001 [190] has II–VI as above, then major capitals at §§118, 143, 163 and 177. Books IV and VI occur in the standard places in BN lat. 6039 [169], with VII at §111, IX at §143, X §163 and XI §177.

1. Manuscripts paired by rubrics

Four of the eight pairs of manuscripts identified on the basis of related rubrics lack book-divisions.[65] Three further pairs are mixed, with one manuscript only containing books.

Harley 5115 [105] lacks books but Phillipps 3117 [214] has the unique marking II at §118. The discrepancy between the divided BN lat. 6232 [177] and the undivided BAV Reg. lat. 825 [198], whose other rubrics are related, is explained by the fact that the book-divisions occur in the original part of the manuscript while the related rubrics are located in the sections added at either end to complete the text. CUL Dd.4.34 [41] and NLW Peniarth 43 [9] were also seen to have similar rubrics but 41 lacks books while 9 has at §6 I, §23 II, §35 III, §54 IV, §72 V, §89 VI and §143 'ultimus'. This division is matched exactly (including 'ultimus' but with no marking for IV) in a third manuscript, Bodleian, Jones 48 [143], which like 9 lacks §§1–4. (41 lacks §5 as well.)[66] Book-divisions are found in both paired manuscripts on two occasions. BL Stowe 56 [117] has eleven books from §5 to §177, just like Leiden Voss. lat. F.77 [77] (with VII at §111, not §109); VIII and X are absent. BN lat. 17569 [188], the manuscript linked to 117 by other rubrics, has similar divisions (lacking IV as well as VIII) but there is no marking at §163 with the consequent marking X at §177. Lambeth 454b [123] and Fairfax 28 [141], which contain elaborate and unusual rubrics, both have only one book-division, III marked at §35.

Divisions following the eleven-book pattern

The divisions found in manuscripts of the Leiden and *prologus* groups are substantially the same, the placing of I and VII being the main variable factors. The common arrangement, seen repeatedly in the above discussion, is II at §23, III §35, IV §54, V §73, VI §89, then usually VIII §118, IX §143, X §163, XI §177; VII occurs at §109 or 111. Parts of this sequence are found in a number of manuscripts. The apparent ubiquity of the divisions and their incorporation into at least two different series of books makes it impossible to do more than list them

---

65 All Souls' 35 [132] + BN lat. 7531 [182], BL Royal 13.D.v [113] + Gonville & Caius 450/391 [31]; CUL Dd.1.17 [40] + BL Royal 13.D.i [111]; Dôle BM 348+349 [58] + Colmar BM 448 [56].

66 The divisions found in the First-Variant manuscript Exeter 3514 [70] are the same: I–IV and VII only are marked. In Boulogne 180 [16], which has the eleven-book placings of II–VII and XI, VII is also found, marked in words, at §143 quite illogically (IX would be more appropriate in view of the other divisions).

here. With further evidence it may emerge that inheritance, not mere chance, lies behind the recurrence of the same imperfect sequence.

II only

Found in CUL Dd.10.32 [45]; Oxford, Bodleian Douce 115 [140].

III only

Gonville & Caius College, 406/627 [30], Lambeth Palace 454b [123], Bodleian Fairfax 28 [141].

VII only

Paris, BN lat. 6041A [172] (marked in the margin).

XI only

Lille BM 533 [79].

II–IV

Added in BL Royal 4.C.xi [108] (see above, *Second Variant*).

II–V

Cambridge, Corpus Christi College, 414 [25].

II–VII

NLW Llanstephan 176 [7].

III, V, VI, XI

New Haven, Yale University, 598 [129].

I–VII, IX

Bruxelles, BR II.1020 [21]: VII is located at §111 (as Leiden Voss. lat. F.77 [77]).

II–VI, VIII, X, XI

Gonville & Caius College, 249/277 [29].

III–VII, VIII, IX

BL Additional 15732 [82].

Capitula

Another form of division of the text needs to be considered here: *capitula*-markings. Several manuscripts have both *capitula*-divisions and books, the text in some of these being prefaced by a *capitula*-list (see above, III). The contents of the *capitula* subdividing the four-book scheme are described in three Second-Variant α-manuscripts by the list 'Descriptio quantitatis et multimode qualitatis . . . et anglice ystorie tractanda distribuit'. These are CUL Ff.1.25 [47], BL MSS Cotton Galba E.xi [91] and Titus A.xxvii [95], and Troyes BM 1531 [209]. In these the *capitula*-series restarts at every book (§§54, 98, 143).

A nine-book division is indicated by the *capitula*-list in the Second-Variant (γ) Stockholm, Holm D.1311 [207] (early thirteenth-century): 'De qualitate et quantitate Britannie . . . quod in ipso regnum Britonum defecit'. Books IV–IX and the *capitula* were marked in the text *c*. 1400. Only one vulgate manuscript includes a *capitula*-list, Cambridge, St John's College, G.16 [32] ('Incipit primus liber de situ et regibus Britannie . . . de Iuor et Ini').

Certain vulgate manuscripts divided into *capitula* contain books as well. The nine books in Cambridge, St John's College, S. 6 [33] are subdivided into *capitula*, as are the twelve *partes* of CUL Dd.6.7 [42]. There are also indications of subdivision of large units in a fragment containing §§193–195. Oxford, Bodleian, Lat. misc. b.17 [145] (twelfth-century) has at §194 .xiii., and §195 .xiiii.. These low values indicate that there must have been several sequences of *capitula*-numbers, presumably restarting at book-divisions.

The remaining manuscripts with *capitula*-divisions lack books and so have a continuous sequence of numbering. A twelfth-century division into 200 chapters is found in BAV Vat. lat. 2005 [199]. BL Cotton Titus A.xviii [93] has a similar division and this is reproduced in its copy, Rouen, BM, 3069 [201]. Three manuscripts have imperfect *capitula*-sequences. That in TCD 493 [62] stops at §110 (*capitulum* 116). In BN lat. 8501A [183], each division indicated by an initial is numbered serially up to §20 'Armauerunt' (.xv.). This numbering does not correspond with that in Vat. lat. 2005 [199]. San Marino, Henry E. Huntington Library, MS. EL 34.C.9 [204] has only a small section divided into *capitula*: the manuscript is acephalous (beginning §67) and the sequence stops just before the Prophecies (§106 'Peragratis ergo', .lxi.). In BL Sloane 289 [116] divisions are made as for books at §§6, 23, 35, 54, and so forth, but these are labelled *capitula*.

Preliminary Conclusions

This examination reveals several consistently parallel series of text, rubrics, and book-divisions. All Second-Variant α-manuscripts have a particular four-book arrangement. The Leiden group manuscripts are divided into eleven, the distinction between the 76 type and the 77 type being detectable here (in the placing of VII) as well as in rubrics. Manuscripts bearing the *prologus Gaufridi Arturi*

Monemutensis rubric, and to a lesser extent the *editio* version of the same, have some version of the eleven-book scheme seen in Leiden but it is distinct from this in the location of I (at §6 not 5), and of VII (not at §109). Another type of division is found in the group centring on MS. 32. These manuscripts contain a more diverse set of books but all but one agree on the unique placing of II at §35. This marking is found in one manuscript outside the group but it was an addition, most probably copied from a member of the group.

Even where rubrics do not provide marked patterns, their evidence does little to undermine conclusions reached about groups from other criteria. None of the nameless-dedication manuscripts contains any form of division. The three representatives of the Bern type have no original book-divisions (those in 200 are added). The manuscripts of the Waleran-Robert dedication similarly seem to have lacked divisions, the marking of the first book in 134 being the single exception. The possibility remains that, as with rubrics, when an exemplar lacked book-divisions, the deficiency could be supplied from other copies of the work or the scribe's imagination.

The overriding impression gained from the evidence is that where book-divisions exist, the eleven-book type in various forms predominates. The only major departures from this pattern are found in the Second Variant and in the group around MS. 32. Simple permutations of the eleven-book division, including a frequent and easily explained variant, ten, are the standard. While these divisions are sufficiently consistent to permit hope that they may be associated with a particular branch of the text, it would be premature to speculate whether they originated with Geoffrey. That must wait until we can gauge the proximity to the author of the text(s) to which they are attached.

Appendix: Synchronisms and Annotations in Lambeth 454b [123] and Fairfax 28 [141]

I list below passages found in the margins or in majuscules in the text of these manuscripts. Until §69 the manuscripts are in agreement: the text is taken from MS. 123 with variants from MS. 141. After §69 I list the rubrics in the order in which they occur in the text. Rubrics found only in one manuscript are asterisked.

§27 (after *dolorosum*)
Ciuitas Eboraci conditur a rege Ebrauco et rex Dauid regnat in Iudea. Siluuius et Latinus in Italia et Gad et Nathan et Asaph prophetant in Israel. Conditur etiam ciuitas Aldclud uersus Albaniam id est Scotiam et Castellum Puellarum extruitur.

§28
Urbs Karleil a rege Leil conditur et rex Salomon templum Domini edificat et regina Sabam uenit ad eum.

§30
Aggeus et Amos et Ieu et Ioel et Azarias hoc tempore prophetabant.

§31 (at foot of page)
Hoc tempore orauit Helyas ut non plueret super terram.

§33
Ysaias et Osee prophetant et Roma conditur.

§44
Roma capta est.

§53 'Succedente quoque' (in margin)
Hic uocatur Trinouantum Lundonia.

§54
Iste[67] Iulio Cesare, quomodo primo in Britanniam uenit.

§56
Hic applicuit Iulius in Britanniam.

§57
Iulius a Cassibelliano uincitur.

§60
Iterum Iulius petit Britanniam.

§61 'Cesar igitur'
Hic Cesar a Britonibus secundo uincitur.

§62 (in margin)
Lucanus de laude Britonum.

§63 'Erat Uectigal' (in margin)
Uectigal Britannie.

§64 (in margin)
Christus natus est.

§65 'Aderat secum' (in margin)
De Claudio Cesare

§68 (in margin)
De Petro apostolo.

* §69 'Quo audito' MS. 141 only (in margin)
Uespasianus mittitur a Claudio in Britanniam.

§69
Quomodo Iuuenalis facit mentionem de rege Aruirago Britannie.

§70
De Mario rege.

§78 (margin)
De Helena et Constantino filio eius.

§79 'His igitur et aliis'
Constantinus Romam sibi subiugauit.

---

67 MS. 141, *De.*

* §83 MS. 141 only (in margin)

Maximianus efficitur rex Britonum et Conanus Meridic. nepos regis Octauii rebellat.

§84 (MS. 141 in margin)

Maximianus et Conanus reconciliatur.

§88

De .xi. mil. uirginum.

* §93 'Dederunt etiam ei' MS. 141 only (in margin)

Constantinus pater Uther in Brit<annia>m applicuit et rex efficitur.

* §94 MS. 123 only

Constantinus interficitur.

* §94 'Constantinus occiditur' MS. 141 only (margin)

De Uortegirno.

§97

Uortegirnus rex factus est.

§98

Horsus applicuit cum fratre suo Hengisto in Britanniam.

§100 'In tempore illo' (margin)

De Germano Altisiodorensi episcopo.

* §101 'Qui adquiescens' MS. 141 only (margin)

Uortimer rex factus est.

§103

Uortimer moritur.

[no further rubrics in MS. 123]

* §103 MS. 141 only (margin)

Prodicio Hengisti in Britones.

* §132 'Quibus donis' MS. 141 only (margin)

Eopa Saxo mortem Aurelii Ambrosii sub mercedis pactione promittit Pascentio.

* §135 MS. 141 only (margin)

Utherpendragon pater Arturi fratri suo Ambrosio succedit in regnum.

* §142 'Fontem namque' MS. 141 only (margin)

Rex Uther haustu aque ueneno permix<te> defungitur.

* §143 MS. 141 only

Arturus rex efficitur per manum sancti Dubricii Urbis Legionum episcopi.

The rubrics in both found at the beginning of the work serve to draw attention to synchronisms mentioned in the accompanying text. Certain marginal rubrics in Cambridge, Corpus Christi College, MS. 281 [23] have a similar function. Rubrics equivalent to those in MSS 123 and 141 are found at §27 'In hoc tempore renabat (*sic*) Dauid rex in Iudea', §28 'In hoc tempore reg[ ] Salomon' and at §30 'In hoc tempore prophet[ ] Helyas propheta'. Certain rubrics in MS. 23 concern synchronisms passed over in MSS 123 and 141: at §22 'In hoc tempore regnauit

Hely sacerdos in Iudea', §25 'In hoc tempore Samuel propheta regnabat in Iudea', and §26 'In hoc tempore regnabat Saul in Iudea'.

Synchronisms are also distinguished in the text of MS. 23. At §32/33, where MSS 141 and 123 have a rubric, the equivalent passage in the text 'Tunc Ysayas et Osea . . . Romulo' is written in majuscules in 23. Attention is drawn to exactly the same passage in another manuscript, London, BL, Cotton Cleopatra D.viii [90], where it is underlined in red and labelled 'Incidentia'.[68] Certain passages earlier in the text are marked similarly in 90. On closer inspection, it emerges that these areas in the text correspond exactly with the synchronisms marked out by rubrics in MS. 23: at §§25 ('Tunc Samuel propheta . . . poeta habebatur'), §26 'Tunc Saul . . . Lacedemonia'), §27 ('Et tunc Dauid . . . in Italia'), §28 ('Tunc Salomon cepit . . . sapientiam Salomonis'), and §30 ('Tunc Helias orauit . . . menses sex'). These same sections, with the addition of one at §22 ('Regnabat tunc in Iudea Hely'), are marked out in three manuscripts by the label *Incidentia* found in the margin. The synchronisms at §§22, 25–28, 30, and 32 are so distinguished in 9 and 143.[69] All these passages, with the exception of those in §§28 and 30, are marked also in 112.

90 and 23 display a further correspondence beyond this marking of the synchronisms: the distinguishing in §64 of the record of Christ's birth, 'In diebus illis . . . obligatur'. This phrase is found in majuscules in 23 and is underlined and labelled as before in 90. It is also marked in 112. A further (twelfth-century) manuscript, BL Cotton Titus C.xvii [96], exhibits the same feature; here the passage has been filled in by a hand different from that of the main text. 96 has two other such passages. At §68 a passage noting Peter's foundation of the church at Antioch and the composition of the Gospel of Mark, 'Eodem tempore Petrus . . . scripserat', is written in red Romanesque majuscules as is the description of martyrdoms in Roman Britain in §77, 'Inter ceteros utriusque . . . conuolauerunt'. The passages in §§64 and 68 are also marked in 123 and 141 but by rubrics: at §64 'Christus natus est' and §68 'De Petro apostolo'. The passage at §68 is marked within the text in 90 (underlined and labelled *Incidentia*), and that at §77 in 23. 96 has none of the rubrics found in the other manuscripts, however. A further passage, not found in the others, is marked in 90: §100 'In tempore illo . . . Britonibus predicarent'.[70] It should be mentioned here that the note of Christ's birth in §64 is distinguished in a further manuscript. In Oxford, Christ Church, MS. 99 [160] (13r), the phrase is written in a square area set into the ruled space (top right-hand corner) and separated from the rest of the text by a blank border.

The practice of distinguishing on the page synchronisms of particular importance is not confined to *Historia*-manuscripts. J. K. Fotheringham, who edited the Eusebius-Jerome chronicle, recorded in his apparatus the use of red ink or Uncial script or Rustic Capitals to highlight events of particular importance.[71] Molly

---

68 *Incidentia* also found in Oxford, Bodleian, Jones 48 [143].
69 Manuscripts related by rubrics and other forms of evidence.
70 Compare the marginal rubric here in 123 and 141: 'In tempore illo'.
71 *The Bodleian Manuscript*, pp. 32–33; *Eusebii Chronici*, p. 144.

Miller, unaware that such passages were marked out in *Historia*-manuscripts too, noted one such entry as a possible source for Geoffrey: 'Tunc Ysaias et Osee prophetabant apud Hebraeos Osee Amos Esaias Ionas'.[72] It is interesting that Geoffrey's version of this same passage is marked out in the text in MSS 9, 23 and 90, and by a rubric in 123 and 141.

The special treatment of these synchronisms in *Historia*-manuscripts suggests interesting possibilities. Given that MSS 23, 96, 123, 141, and possibly 112 date from the twelfth century, it is possible that we are simply observing a twelfth-century scribal fashion: the distinguishing of parallel chronological passages on the page. However, an examination of various historical manuscripts dating from this period has not yielded much to support this assertion. It may be that all these manuscripts belong to one branch of the text, descended from some progenitor whose scribe took particular care over synchronistic passages; but we need to bear in mind the variety of passages and treatments evident in the *Historia*-manuscripts described above. A final possibility is that the notion of marking out synchronisms was derived from one of Geoffrey's sources. If this was indeed the case, then there is reason to hope that such attention to synchronisms might be found in manuscripts not far removed from the author himself.

---

72 'Geoffrey's Early Royal Synchronisms', p. 386.

VII

TEST-COLLATIONS

The evidence assembled so far has suggested possible routes into the textual history from the outside, and some from the inside. To these can be added the evidence of the text itself.

Of the nine chapters collated from each manuscript (ten, where §4 is present), complete apparatus of the variant readings of four have been drawn up. These are §§1, 2, 100, and 208 (presented in Appendix II). The most obvious peculiarities of the dedication-bearing chapters (3, 4, 109, and 110) have received some attention above (IV, V) and some account has been given of abbreviation and rewriting of §§5 (the account of Britain) and 179 (the description of the state of the British church). The subject-matter of §§1, 2, and 100 would seem not to have invited editorial intervention to the same extent.

The test-collations of §§1, 2, 100, and 208 will first be examined in isolation from the rest of the evidence: the resulting patterns constitute the final layer in the accumulated picture of the textual tradition. It should be noted that, while the preceding chapters have been directed towards presenting the external evidence as comprehensively as possible, the results offered here cannot claim to represent the whole of the textual tradition. Apart from the hazards of attempting to identify related manuscripts on the basis of small and scattered samplings of text – even the evidence assembled here is enough to show that witnesses could be composed of at least two types of text – there is also the strong possibility that other patterns of association would have been thrown up had another set of collated passages been selected. The results presented here should therefore be taken as an illustration of the process, not a comprehensive exposition of it. The following deals first with groups of manuscripts suggested by the evidence resulting from test-collation and then with affiliated pairs of manuscripts which cannot yet be placed within a wider context.

It must be noted that the most striking collocations of manuscripts will be those that diverge from the mainstream of the vulgate tradition, whether as a result of error or deliberate revision. As before (IV), the Bern manuscript (15) is being taken as the measure against which the manuscripts are compared.

Groups of manuscripts

Where the emerging groups are so well represented as to make it impracticable to cite them by numerical sigla, some title has been devised, often from a reading particularly characteristic of the group. In the following, an asterisk is used to signal readings regarded as especially symptomatic.

1. The *Nimirum quod* group (§1, nn. 7–9)

The appended collation of the opening chapter indicates several well attested points of divergence from the text found in the Bern manuscript, for example at nn. 7, 8, 32, 35 and 39. Those at nn. 8, 32, and 35 are particularly significant as they are unlikely to have resulted independently from mechanical error. Thirty-one manuscripts agree at all five points against the printed text (Bern): MSS 2, 3, 14, 19, 20, 36, 53, 58, 81, 83, 105, 125, 126, 127, 132, 151, 154, 166, 168, 171, 173, 175, 176, 182, 183, 184, 189, 196, 205, 208, 214.[1] Many of these witnesses share elsewhere readings contrary to the Bern text, sometimes among a variety of other witnesses but often in near-isolation. Broad agreements against Bern are evident in §§1 and 100.[2] Agreements against Bern may also be found in §§2 and 208 but, like certain other readings in §§1 and 100, they are limited to a small number of these manuscripts.[3]

The prominent place which members of this group occupy in the apparatus indicates their frequent distance from the Bern text, the readings offered by the group often constituting apparently valid, although inferior, alternatives rather than straightforward mechanical errors. The structure of the first chapter, a single sentence, is reshaped by the omission of *contuli*, the main verb (n. 8), and *cum*, the conjunction which governs the final clause (n. 32). For this to make sense, the sentence has to be linked with the beginning of §2 and *optulit* taken as the main verb of the whole. This has the merit of compressing into the same sentence the balancing phrases *Cum mecum multa et de multis sepius animo reuoluens* and *Talia michi et de talibus multociens cogitanti*, but this would seem to be out-weighed by clumsinesses introduced by the loss of the main verb earlier on.[4] It

---

1 It will be seen that the acephalous witnesses 56 and 75 are further relatives.
2 §1, n. 7 *nimirum*, n. 8 omission of *contuli*, n. 32 omission of *cum*, n. 35 the rephrasing *digna eternitatis laude*, n. 39 *predicentur* or *predicerentur*; §100, n. 5 *conduxeruntque*, n. 14 inversion of word order, n. 23 addition of *et* after *ut*, n. 27 inversion of word order, n. 40 *uero* for *ergo*, n. 42 *refertus* or *repletus* for *refectus*, n. 69 word order, n. 77 and 84 omission of several phrases, sometimes substitution of *Qui dixit* or *Qui ait*, nn. 175 and 178 word order, n. 203 addition of *in* before *eadem*.
3 For example §2, n. 11 *id est peregrinus* / *exosticis*; n. 14 *Britonici/Britonei sermonis librum*, n. 40 *tantum stilo*, n. 43 *contemptus*, n. 54 *magis exponendis uerbis* / *magis in componendis uerbis*; §208, n. 2 omission of *eorum*, or *illorum*, n. 17 *scribendo(s)* for *scribendi*, n. 52 omission of *de*; §1 n. 38 *quasi inscripta iocunde*.
4 For example, the function of *quod* (n. 9).

159

may be that various alterations resulted from an attempt to remedy some deficiency in the text (perhaps the loss or miscopying of *contuli*).

The divergence from the Bern text displayed by the witnesses to the group is persistent and extensive. Most of these witnesses in fact contain one of the more radical revisions undergone by texts of the *Historia* while remaining recognizably Galfridian – the removal of the names of the dedicatees in §3. The exceptions are three bearing the dedications to Robert of Gloucester (105, 154, 214), which will receive further consideration below. Comparison of readings in §100 indicates further manuscripts to be associated with this so-called 'nameless-dedication' group but not identified above since they lack the opening dedicatory chapters. These are MSS 56 and 75. They, together with MS. 83 (in which the opening sentence of §3 is physically lacunose), may tentatively be added to the list of twenty-seven nameless-dedication manuscripts (they bear more resemblance to these than to the three single-dedication relatives), giving a total of thirty.

Certain erroneous readings unique to this group are found in only limited numbers of its members (above, n. 3); these may be separated into subgroups.

i.   MSS 56, 58, 205

These witnesses agree frequently and are often idiosyncratic.[5] MSS 58 and 205 bear the first type of nameless dedication (see above, V); 56 is acephalous.

ii.   MSS 20, 83, 126, (151,) 166, 173, (175)

These witnesses share unique errors, although these are not found in all of them:[6] MSS 20, 83, 126, and 166 agree particularly.[7] Occasionally this subgroup (excepting 151 and 175) agrees against most of the nameless-dedication texts.[8] But its members follow the majority of these (and almost the entire manuscript tradition) in §100 in including the phrase *quos . . . posuerat* after *propter paganos* and not after *affecerat* (nn. 252, 262) as is the case in eight nameless-dedication witnesses.[9] In this respect this subgroup resembles the previous one, with which some of its representatives sometimes agree.[10]

As with the first subgroup, these manuscripts mostly bear one particular form of nameless dedication: type v, in this case. The exceptions are the acephalous

---

5   For example, §1, n. 4; §100, nn. 10 (*Ronuen*), 47, 58, 59, *226, *227, *232, 247.

6   But note §100, n. *77 *Qui ait*.

7   §2, n. 4 *Uualterius* (not 126), n. 11 *exosticis* (not 83), n. 40 *tantum stilo*, n. 54 *magis in co(m)ponendis uerbis*; §100, n. 3 omission of *uero nuntii*, n. 10 *uocabulo Norguen*, n. 60 translation of English into Latin (20, 166 only), n. 138 *in eum*, n. 142 omission of *in corde suo*, n. *230 *Kartirgen/ Rartirgen*, n. 277 word-order.

8   §1, n. 26 *quam pluribus*, n. 39 *predicarentur*.

9   MSS 3, 14, 81, 168, 171, 183, 184, 189.

10 See §100, nn. 243, 239.

MS. 83 and two manuscripts which resemble this subgroup but often disagree with its readings, the type-iii manuscripts, 151 and 175.[11]

iii.   MSS 3, 14, 81, 168, 171, 183, 184, 189

This subgroup has already become apparent from the unique placing of *quos . . . posuerat* after *affecerat* in §100. The connection is reinforced by errors attested by various of them.[12]

These comprise all witnesses to types vii (MSS 171, 184), viia (MSS 81, 183) and viii (MSS 3, 14, 189) of the nameless dedication; one manuscript bears the third type (MS. 168).

iv.   MSS 36, 53, 127, 196, 208

These manuscripts are distinguished at §100, n. 77, where they read *Qui dixit* (found otherwise only in MSS 75 and 56, 58, and 205); members of the second subgroup identified above have *Qui ait* while those of the third omit the phrase completely. This suggested connection between the first and fourth subgroups is corroborated by other evidence from test-collation.[13] Some of these readings are also found in two members of the second subgroup, 151 and 173.[14]

They bear the first (36), second (127, 208), and third (53 and 196) types of nameless dedication.

v.   The remainder

MSS 2, 19, 75, 125, 132, 176, and 182 are the remaining nameless-dedication manuscripts; their filiation is less clear-cut than that of the others. 125 and 182 may be compared with certain single-dedication manuscripts (below).

vi.   MSS 105, 154, 214 (125, 182, 180, 130)

105, 154, and 214 are the single-dedication manuscripts found above to bear readings generally characteristic of the nameless-dedication type. In §1 their readings are nearly identical (but MS. 154 diverges at n. 33). These three witnesses show less agreement with the nameless-dedication group in §2 but here there are no points at which all the nameless-dedication manuscripts diverge as a group from the printed text. MSS 105 and 214 are especially close, sharing a number of errors.[15] At §100 all three show agreement, often witnessing rare or

---

11 Note that 151 and 175, together with 173, have at §100 n. 10 the reading *Ronguen*. The type-v manuscripts 20, 83, 126, and 166 have a corrupt form of this, *Norguen*.

12 §100, n. 10 *Rowen*, n. 42 *refertus* for *refectus*, n. 50 *dein* for *deinde*, n. 68 *Deinde* for *Denique*, n. 77 omission of *Qui . . . dixit*, n. 125 *Uoltegirnus/Woltegirnus*, n. 199 *ea*; §208, n. 2 omission of *eorum*, n. 24 omission of *Willelmo*; n. 55 *edictum*.

13 §100, (n. 5 *conduxert.que*,) n. 58 *hing*, n. 59 *Wesseil/Wessal*, n. 77 *Qui dixit* (with 56, 58, 205), n. 104 *ab illa*, n. 134 omission of *eam*.

14 §100, nn. (5,) 58, 59, 104.

15 §2, nn. 11, 21 *Cawala(n)drum*, 35.

unique readings,[16] but again, there is a marked resemblance between 105 and 214.[17]

At least one reading in §100 suggests a link between MSS 105/214 and 154 and the nameless-dedication manuscript, 125. At n. 95, MS. 125 has *ac* before *iussit*, an addition incorporated into the text of these three manuscripts only. Similarly, at n. 130, *est* is written but cancelled in MS. 125 before *intrante Sathan*; *est* is included (uncancelled) in only three other manuscripts – 105, 154, 214. Where MS. 125 displays independence from the majority of nameless-dedication manuscripts, 105, 154, and 214 follow.

At n. 103 all four read *adamauit* for *potauit*, a reading found in only one other nameless-dedication manuscript, 182. It is noteworthy that at n. 130 this same manuscript resembles those under discussion (adding *et* rather than *est* before *intrante*) and agrees at nn. 52, 103, 123, and 170. MS. 182 bears the fifth type of nameless dedication and 125, the third.

Two other manuscripts occasionally witness predominantly nameless-dedication readings.[18] MS. 180 (acephalous and fragmentary) agrees with the readings of 105, 154, and 214 in various places[19] and sometimes shares with 125 and 154 spellings not found in MSS 105/214,[20] and several errors with 125 only.[21] Extensive comparison is prevented by the absence from MS. 180 of the opening chapters. Weaker agreements may be found in MS. 130 (single-dedication), which is the only manuscript apart from 125 to include in the margin the section characteristically lacking from nameless-dedication manuscripts (at n. 84).[22] MS. 130 has none of the nameless-dedication characteristics in §1, however, which may suggest that an original nameless dedication was discarded from the front of the text and replaced by the dedication to Robert.

The nameless-dedication group, therefore, demonstrates considerable solidarity; the first and fourth subgroups appear to be especially closely related.

2. The *Tres filios* group (§100, n. 224)

A deliberate but obvious addition to the text in §100 is made in twenty-two manuscripts: the number of Vortigern's sons is specified (unnecessarily).[23] The likelihood that this addition, once made, was inherited prompts investigation of

---

16 §100, n. 85 *quid*, n. *95 *ac iussit*, n. 103 *adamauit*, n. *130 addition of *est*, n. 189 addition of *regi*. Cf. also nn. 23, 27, 40, 52, 123, 170.

17 n. 6 *x. naues et octo*, n. 10 *nomine Ronwen/Rouwen*, n. 59 *Washail*, nn. 89, 94, 124 *Drinkhail*, n. 91 *igitur*, n. 116 *Washail*, n. 190 omission of *Uortegirno*, n. 195 *Goroganno*, n. 200 *dominabatur*, n. 228 word-order, n. 247 *fuit*.

18 For example, reversed word-order at §100, n. 27.

19 §100, nn. 23, 32, 40, 52, 85, 103.

20 §100, n. 58 (*ching*), n. 124 (*Drinchail*).

21 §100, nn. 59 *Wosseil*, 116, 245.

22 §100, nn. 27, *103, 124, 170, *195.

23 §100, n. 224. MSS 8, 10, 28, 30, 32, 39, 45, 49, 61, 88, 98, 100, 109, 116, 119, 123, 133, 134, 141, 142, 153, 165.

the witnesses of this reading for filiation, whether ultimately homogeneous (suggesting that the addition was made only once) or in several groupings (implying that the addition was made on several separate occasions).

Seventeen of the twenty-two (not MSS 49, 88, 116, 119, 133) read *Intrauit* for *Intrauerat* (n. 137) and eighteen (not 49, 88, 116, 133) alter the word-order at n. 160. As MSS 49, 88, 116 and 133 witness neither reading, and considering that they are only linked to the others by an easily made addition, they will be discarded. The remaining manuscripts agree, often on unusual readings, at a significant number of places in §100.[24]

§2 is absent from three of the eighteen manuscripts still under consideration, being physically lacking from MSS 119 and 165, and being omitted from MS. 142. Eleven of the remaining fifteen omit *multociens* from the first phrase[25] and others of the fifteen agree on certain forms.[26] All these, with one exception, follow Bern, unlike many witnesses to the vulgate manuscript-tradition, reading at §1 (n. 35) *digna eternitatis laude*, not *digna eternitate laudis*; the exception is MS. 153, which shows signs of alteration at this point.

There is a possible addition to the group, MS. 73. Although this does not have the interpolation concerning Vortigern's sons, it agrees with other members of the group at thirteen of the seventeen places in §100 at which agreement has been noted.[27]

Particular connections between certain members of this disparate group may be observed. Four subcategories result.

i. MSS 32, 73, 98, 153, 165

Among the core manuscripts in the *Tres filios* group are five previously identified as relatives, of which the pivotal manuscript is MS. 32 (Cambridge, St John's College, MS. G.16). The collations do not suggest particular idiosyncrasy, rather a tendency for the group to agree, especially on erroneous readings not found in others of the manuscripts under discussion,[28] or in only a small number of them.[29]

---

24 §100, n. 6 *xviii. naues* (8, 10, 28, 30, 32, 39, 45, 49, 61, 98, 100, 119, 123, 134, 141, 142, 153, 165); n. 21 (8, 10, 28, 30, 32, 39, 45, 98, 100, 109, 119, 123, 134, 141, 153, 165); n. 40 with Bern (8, 10, 28, 30, 32, 39, 45, 61, 98, 100, 109, 119, 123, 134, 141, 142, 153, 165); n. 76 (30, 32, 39, 45, 98, 119, 123, 141, 153, 165); n. 85 (8, 28, 30, 32, 39, 98, 100, 109, 119, 123, 141, 142, 165); n. 104 (8, 10, 28, 30, 32, 45, 61, 98, 100, 109, 119, 123, 134, 141, 142, 153, 165); n. 106 with Bern (8, 10, 30, 32, 39, 61, 98, 119, 123, 141, 142, 153, 165); n. 158 (39, 45, 61, 98, 109, 119, 123, 141, 142, 153, 165); n. 180 (32, 61, 98, 153); n. 239 *Altisiodorensis* (28, 30, 45, 61, 119, 123, 141, 165); also n. 10 *Ronuen* (8, 28, 30, 39, 45, 61, 119, 123, 141), *Ronwen*, 32, 88, 98, 153.

25 §2, n. 2 (MSS 8, 10, 30, 32, 45, 98, 100, 109, 123, 141, 153).

26 §2, n. 22 *Cadwallonis* (MSS 10, 28, 30, 32, 39, 98, 100, 123, 141, 153); n. 28 *pulcris* (MSS 10, 30, 32, 45, 100, 109, 123, 141).

27 §100 nn. 6, 10 (*Ronwen*), 21, 40, 76, 85, 104, 106, 137, 160, 239; §2, nn. 2, 22.

28 §1 n. 12 *De eis Gillas* (MSS 73, 98, 153); §100 nn. 79 (MSS 73, 153), 230 *Katigern* (MSS 32, 73, 98, 153).

29 §100 nn. 76 (with MSS 30, 39, 45, 119, 123, 141), 123 (32, 73, 119, 123, 153), 180 (MSS

ii. MSS 100, 134, (28)

MSS 100 and 134 agree in §100, sometimes in uncommon errors,[30] on more than half these occasions with MS. 28 as well.[31] 100 and 134 also agree against Bern at §208.[32] They are quite unlike one another in the opening chapters, however, where MS. 134 does not share readings found in the majority of the manuscripts under discussion and does not agree with MS. 100 where it departs from the Bern text. Comparison with the remainder of the opening chapters provides clarification. MS. 134 bears the double dedication to Robert of Gloucester and Waleran of Meulan, while MS. 100 and all but one of the other *Tres filios* witnesses, MS. 39, are single-dedication.[33]

iii. MSS 119, 142

The agreement between MSS 119 and 142 is idiosyncratic, with three rare or unique errors in §100.[34] Neither manuscript contains the opening chapters, 119 beginning imperfectly in §84, and 142 omitting §§1–5. MS. 142 is heavily interpolated (above, IV) and departs markedly and uniquely from the Bern text in places (for example, §100, nn. 266–69, 271).

It would seem that both manuscripts should be regarded as well down the *Tres filios* tradition.

iv. MSS 123, 141

Unique orthographical errors signal a final pair of related manuscripts. MSS 123 and 141 read *Drinckeil* at §100 n. 124 and *loculento* at §1 n. 14. They also have the spelling *Catigern* at §100 n. 230, which is found besides in MSS 8, 30, and 61.[35]

Smaller Groups

A number of manuscripts deviate from the mainstream of the tradition in various ways but cannot yet be assigned to a larger group.

32, 98, 153, with MS. 61), 214 *(in) inimiciam (sic)* (MSS 73; 32, 165, with 123, 133), 255 (8, 32, 98, 134, 153); §208 nn. 11 *Lambarbanensi/Lamcarbanensi/Lanicarbanensi* (165, 153, 32, 119, 141), n. 25 *Malmesbiriensi* (45, 142, 153, 165).
30 §100, nn. 50, 100, *(Wesheil)* 116, 213, 219, 229, *(Catigernus)* 230, 276, 282; unique errors, 7, 218, 238.
31 §100, nn. *50, 116 (with 10, 28, 32, 100, 133, 153), 229, 230, *282 (with 10, 133).
32 §208, n. 28 *(Huntendunensi)*, 40 (compare n. 18).
33 There is no notable equivalence between 39 and 134. 39 tends to depart from the text of Bern further than MS. 134. There is some weak similarity between 134 and 128, another double-dedication manuscript, in the opening chapters: §1, n. 26; §2, n. 60.
34 nn. *41, 48, 230 *(Gaugernus)*.
35 Rubrics also indicate a connection between MSS 123 and 141 (VI, Appendix).

MSS 38, 131; 99, 122

38 and 131 share a number of erroneous readings,[36] some of which indicate deliberate minor revision.[37] 99 and 122 have a less idiosyncratic set of readings some of which are, nevertheless, unique.[38] There is indisputable common ground between the two pairs of manuscripts, seen in shared error in §§100 and 208.[39] This is not reflected, however, in the opening chapter, where MSS 38 and 131 resemble St John's G.16 [32] and its relatives.[40]

MSS 72, 133; 89, 160

MSS 72 and 133 bear signs of minor emendation or inaccuracy throughout the chapters collated. At §1 n. 31, for example, they read *recepissent* for *repperissem*, which makes some sort of sense in the context but is clearly inferior to the original reading; it perhaps arose from a scribal attempt to rectify a corrupt reading, or a failure to recognize *repperissem*. They witness almost unique readings elsewhere[41] and display broader agreement.[42]

Two other witnesses resemble these closely, although they depart less far from the mainstream of the vulgate tradition. MS. 160 agrees with several of the rarer[43] and some of the better attested readings identified above.[44] As MS. 89 is acephalous and lacunose, comparison rests on §100. Agreement here in error is significant,[45] especially of 89 with 160[46] and of 89 and 160 together with 72 or 133.[47]

MSS 172, 174, 197, 198

Another group is signalled by the alteration of a phrase in §100: 'Omnibus unum consilium fuit' becomes 'Omnibus uisum est consilium' (n. 175). The shift from *unum* to *uisum* did not necessarily result from deliberate interference; it may, perhaps, have originated accidentally, the *n* being read as *si* (in some Gothic bookhands *s* scarcely rises above neighbouring minim letters), thus necessitating

---

36 §2, nn. 2, 28, 38; §100 nn. 75, 138, 199, 220; §208 nn. *39, *46. §2 nn. 2 and 28 and §100 n. 75 are found in the same form in *Tres filios* manuscripts.

37 §100 n. 52 *ad regem* for *regi*, n. 151 *uellet* for *desiderabat*, n. 202 and 206 *puella regi* for *rex . . . pagane*.

38 §2 nn. 1, *45; §100 nn. *9, 10 (*Ronwein*), 199, *262; §208, n. *51.

39 §100, n. 6 *ducem et octo naues*, n. 104 *Ab illa*, n. 122 word-order, n. 222 (not 122), n. 279 omission (not 131). See also §100 nn. 23, 100, 106, (170,) (174,) 178, 180, 203, 222, 230 *Cartigern/Kartigern*, 231 *Paschen*; §208 nn. 11 *Lancarbrenensis/Lancabrenissis*, 66.

40 For example, §2 nn. 2, 28.

41 §1 nn. 5, 6; §2 nn. 3, 4; §100 nn. *10 *Ronwenn(i)am*, 59 *Wusheil*, 70, 89, 188.

42 §100 nn. 5, 32, 106, 181, 239, 252, 282; §208 n. 40.

43 §1 nn. 5, 6; §2 n. 4; §100 n. 59 *Wsheil*, 70, 181, cf. n. 188.

44 §100 nn. 5, 106, 252.

45 §100, nn. 59 (*Wusheil*), 70, 106, 181, 188.

46 §100, n. 10 (*Rowenne*), 15, 66, 96, 137, 153, 180, 219.

47 With 72, §100, nn. 44, 75; with 133, n. 170.

the alteration of *fuit* to *est*.[48] Whatever its origin, the phrase points to a well differentiated group of four single-dedication manuscripts[49] with a particular correspondence between MSS 174 and 198.[50]

MSS 5, 84, 124

An addition to §1, apparently made deliberately, distinguishes these manuscripts. *eos dixisse* is inserted into the phrase *nichil de regibus* to clarify the sense (n. 17). These words are added in a different hand in MS. 5;[51] in MSS 84 and 124 the addition is incorporated into the text. The respective dates of the manuscripts (thirteenth-, fourteenth-, and fifteenth-century) permit consideration of the possibility that the explanatory amplification was first made in MS. 5, then copied and transmitted. A second alteration made in MS. 5, in §2, is similarly copied in MSS 84 and 124 but in no other manuscript.[52]

The three manuscripts display other agreement in §1[53] especially between 84 and 124.[54] MS. 124 differs from 5 and 84 at one place, departing from the Bern reading.[55]

At §100, the distance between MSS 5 and 84/124 is greater. MS. 5 differs from Bern in certain well attested ways,[56] not always followed by MSS 84 and 124,[57] while 84 and 124 have a number of readings not found in 5, some of them rare.[58] MS. 84 departs from the printed text in several places where 124 does not.[59]

The same trends are further evident in §208. There is considerable overlap between 84 and 124,[60] although 84 departs further (and sometimes idiosyncratically) from the text of Bern.[61] 5 shows only the vaguest agreement with 84 and 124.[62]

The lack of striking similarity between the versions of §§100 and 208 found in MSS 5 and 84/124 may suggest that the readings in §§1 and 2 entered in MS. 5 and found also in MSS 84/124 did not originate in 5 but were taken from a fourth manuscript. This was not the direct exemplar of 5 but must have been ancestral to that of 84/124.

Another witness containing the interpolation *eos dixisse*, MS. 115, agrees with

48 The nameless-dedication MS. 175 reads *uisum omnibus consilium fuit*.
49 In §100, nn. 69, 71, 91, 115, *156; §1, nn. 35, 39; §208, n. 28.
50 See §100, nn. 224–225, 264.
51 Already associated with others by its distinctive rubrics (above, VI: *Prologus/editio*).
52 §2, n. 11 *exorcistis*.
53 §1, nn. 22, 39.
54 §1, nn. 12, 24.
55 §1, n. 35 *digna eternita[] laude*.
56 For example at §100, nn. 10 (*Ronwen*), 106, 178, 203, 252.
57 For example, §100, nn. 10 (MS. 124 only,) 68, 174.
58 §100, nn. 11, (40,) *104, *123, 179, 234.
59 §100, nn. 15, 55, 121, 170.
60 §208, n. 18.
61 §208, nn. 19, 26.
62 §208, nn. 40, 45.

certain readings found in 84 and 124 in §§1 and 208.[63] MS. 6 also shows agreement with 84, 115, and 124[64] sometimes agreeing only with 115.[65]

MSS 26, 27, 51

The existence of a link between these manuscripts becomes apparent from the description of Walter, archdeacon of Oxford, in §2 (nn. 8, 12). Usually he is 'uir *in oratoria arte* atque *in exoticis historiis* eruditus'. In four manuscripts, however, *eruditus* is found after *arte*. The balance of the sentence is restored in MS. 10 by the addition of *usus* after *historiis*, but the clumsiness is uncorrected in MSS 26, 27, and 51. The three, and sometimes all four, agree elsewhere in this chapter and §1[66] but in other collated sections particular agreement is confined to MSS 26 and 51.[67]

MSS 76, 92, 97

These manuscripts have a few unique errors[68] and some uncommon readings[69] and generally fall within a band of well-attested readings found in the vulgate tradition.[70]

MSS 156, 161, 212

These three all omit the description of Walter of Oxford (§2, nn. 7–12), as do MSS 111 and 177. A particular connection between certain of the five is suggested by an omission from §1 (n. 24) found in MSS 156, 161, and 212 (and two other manuscripts besides), and a unique error in the same chapter found in 156 and 212.[71] In §100, the agreement between the three is less idiosyncratic but nevertheless close.[72] There is no notable overlap at §208 (which is, in any case, absent

---

63 §1 nn. 12, 22, (n. 35 compare MS. 124,) 39; §208 n. 18. But 115 shows only vague similarity with other members of the group in §100: not nn. 11, 104, 123, 179, 234 but with MSS 5 and 124 at n. 10 (*uocabulo Ronwen*), and with MSS 5, 84, 124 at nn. 106, 178, 252.

64 §1 n. 12, 35 (not 84), 39; §100 nn. 11 (not 115), 23 (not 124), 59/116 *Weshail* (with 84), 69 (not 124), 106, 178, 203 (not 115); §208 n. 18.

65 §100 nn. 43, 66, 126.

66 §1 nn. 17, 35; §2 nn. 11 (MSS 26, 51), 14, 22, 33, 38 (26, 51).

67 §100 n. 3, 43, 134; §208, n. 7.

68 §100 n. 56; §2 n. 53 (76, 97 only).

69 §1 n. 2; §100 nn. 230, 264; (§208 n. 28).

70 §100 nn. 5, 6, 10 (*Ronwen*; 92 *Ronuuen*), 23, 40 (76, 97 only), 59/116 (*Wasseil*), 69, 174, 178, 203, 252, 284; §208 n. 45 (*Walterus*).

71 §1, n. 6.

72 §100 nn. 5, 10 (MSS 156, 212), 40 (MSS 156, 212), 44 (MSS 156, 161), 75 (MSS 156, 161), 76 (MSS 156, 212), 106 (MSS 161, 212), 112 (MSS 156, 161), 170, 206 (MSS 156, 212), 214 (MSS 156, 212), 218, 230 (MSS 156, 161), 252, etc.

from MS. 156).[73] The collation of §100 suggests a particular connection between MSS 156 and 212.

Second Variant

MSS 17, 22, 35, 47, 50, 54, 66, 80, 85, 91, 95, 102, 108, 114, 138, 202, 207, 209

Readings of Second-Variant manuscripts have been included in the collations of §§1, 2, and 208 but not §100, where they would confuse the apparatus as they diverge more radically from the vulgate.

There are few readings (in the chapters collated) witnessed by all Second-Variant manuscripts.[74] Members of the β-subgroup often diverge from those of the α and γ.[75] The α demonstrates some cohesion[76] but in these chapters the γ-manuscripts do not depart from the α.[77]

MSS 35 and 66 share a number of innovations in §§ 1 and 2[78] and display more general agreement.[79] The truncation of MS. 35 hampers further comparison here.

Pairs of manuscripts

The following associations can be observed from the test-collations assembled but on this evidence alone it is not possible to determine any wider filiation.

MSS 7, 155

These manuscripts have several errors in §2 and §100 unique to themselves.[80] MS. 155 sometimes departs further from the Bern text than 7.[81]

MSS 9, 143

Both these manuscripts omit the opening chapters, beginning at §5. MS. 143 lacks the final chapters and so comparison here rests on §100.

---

73 §208, nn. 40, 45.
74 §1 n. 35 with Bern (except MS 138), n. 39 (predicentur).
75 §1 n. 24 (50, 114); §2 n. 13 (22, 50, 114); §208 nn. 28 Huntendoniensi (22, 50, 54, 80, 114), 25 Malberiensi (22, 54, 80), 63 (22, 50, 114).
76 [§1 n. 38 (47, 209);] §2 n. 50 illirassem (35, 47, 66, 91, 138).
77 §208 nn. 8 successeret (17, 66, 85, 95, 108, 202, 207, 209), 10 Caradoco (66, 95, 202), 11 Lencarbanensi/Loncarbanensi (17, 85, 95/ 47, 66, 202, 207, 209), 28 Huntendunensi (17, 47, 66, 85, 95, 108, 207, 209), n. 48 (17, 66, 95, 108, 138, 207, 209).
78 §1 nn. 9, 22; §2 nn. 3, 33.
79 §1 n. 39; §2 nn. 4, 50.
80 §2 n. 41; §100 nn. 113, 114, 173, 213 [223 (with MSS 129 and 135 only)]. They show broad agreement in §1 and elsewhere: §1 nn. 35, 39; §2 n. 11 (exorticis/exortitis); §100 nn. 5, 6, 23, 40, 69, 106, 178, 203, 252; §208 nn. 40, 45.
81 §2 nn. 38, 55.

9 and 143 share unique errors – *eius* for *regis* at n. 157 and *Laured* for *Lauerd* (n. 57) – and have other rare variants.[82] There is widespread agreement between them.[83]

MSS 23, 96

A connection between these manuscripts is signalled by a single innovation in §100 (n. 186).[84] MSS 23 and 96 share other unusual readings (§100 nn. 253, 280) and consistently agree in §§1–2 (where they remain very close to Bern) and 100.[85] Agreement is less marked in §208. The fact that MS. 23 is constructed of two units of text (§§1–109, 110–208) distinct in quiring and script would seem to provide an explanation for the lack of evidence in §208: the part of the text of 23 closest to 96 belongs to its rather later first half.

MSS 40, 111

The lacunose state of MS. 40 permits comparison with 111 only in §208, a chapter where the witnesses generally lack idiosyncratic readings. The connection between 40 and 111 is quite clear, however. They suffer several omissions (nn. 11, 15–17) and additions (n. 25 *Salesburiensi*, n. 66 *ualete*). The first sentence does not read 'Reges . . . Karadoco . . . in materia scribendi permitto' as usual but 'Reges . . . Karadoco . . . scribere permitto', which creates the ungrammatical 'reges scribere'.[86]

MSS 48, 128

These manuscripts tend to remain unusually close to the Bern text, especially in the opening chapters.[87] A connection between them is indicated by the unique and apparently deliberate innovation *annotauit* for *parauit* at the end of §100 (n. 290). There are several other unusual readings in this chapter and elsewhere,[88] besides agreement on better attested readings.[89] 128 is sometimes further from the Bern text than 48, however.[90]

---

82 §100, nn. 49, 50.
83 §100, nn. 5, 6, 23, 76, 100, 106, 183, 203, 214, 239, 252.
84 The addition of *sibi* in the phrase 'Pro ea prouinciam Cantie (sibi) ab illo'.
85 §1 nn. 35, 39; §100 nn. 3, 23, 40, 44, 59 (*Washeil*), 75, 100, 137, 203, 214, 230, 231; also §208 nn. 40, 45.
86 40 and 111 also share better attested readings: §208, nn. 2, 40, 45.
87 For example, §1 n. 39; §2 n. 11 (and §100 n. 5).
88 nn. 149, 171, 173, 188; §2 n. 60.
89 §100 nn. 23, 170.
90 §100 nn. 79, 236.

MSS 59, 60

A striking idiosyncrasy in §100 suggests a connection between these manuscripts: they name Vortigern's second and third sons not *Katigernus* and *Paschent* but *Iabin* and *Goman* (nn. 230, 231). They show unique agreement in minor errors at two other points in this chapter (nn. 52 and 64) besides displaying a more general resemblance here and elsewhere.[91] MS. 60 is sometimes idiosyncratic, however; in it the English expressions in §100 are translated into Latin.[92] Compare MSS 117, 188 below.

MSS 63, 203

These single-dedication manuscripts resemble Bern particularly closely (especially MS. 203).[93] They display widespread agreement in §100.[94] As they contain readings diverging so little from Bern, it is difficult to confirm a connection from the collations. Comparison with another chapter, §179, serves to reinforce the connection, however.[95]

MSS 78, 206

These manuscripts contain unique errors and spellings.[96]

MSS 88, 116

These manuscripts have a series of unique (or almost unique) and erroneous readings, some of which result from deliberate intervention in the text.[97] 88 and 116 also witness a more common set of errors, some of which suggest alliance with the *Tres filios* group described above.[98] MS. 88 lacks the final chapters.

---

91 §100 nn. 5, 6, 23, 68, 106, 178, 180, 203; §1 nn. 7, 35, 39; §2 n. 11; §208 nn. 11, 25, 40, 45, 46.

92 For example §100 nn. 60, 89, 116, 124.

93 But with occasional rare readings (§1 nn. 3, 6). Both readings are also found in the First-Variant MS. 70 (Exeter, Cathedral Library, MS. 3514).

94 nn. 23, 40, 59, 75, 214, 252.

95 Both read *Menia* for *Meneuia* and omit *est* before *Pro*.

96 §100 nn. 42, 59 (*Uuashail/Uuashan*), 65; §208 nn. 8, 11 (*Lanc' albanensi/Lanc' banensi*), 57, ?also n. 19 (conjectural emendation of faulty reading). They also witness several rare readings: §100 nn. 87, 138; §208 nn. 26, 53.

97 §1 nn. 6, 12; §2 nn. 1, 45, 50; §100 nn. 66, 75, 101, 122, 147, 181–182, 201, 223, 225, 288, 290.

98 §1 n. 26; §2 n. 28, §100 nn. 3, 6, 40, 106, 170, 224, 229, 230, 282. Note that they share contents with MS. 32: Sibylline prophecies, pseudo-Methodian *Reuelationes*.

MSS 104, 194

These manuscripts testify to a number of unique minor revisions.[99] There are other agreements between them[100] but also some points of divergence.[101]

MSS 107, 136

There are signs that the text of these manuscripts has been revised: at §100 nn. 202 and 206 'Nupsit . . . rex . . . pagane' becomes 'Nupsit . . . regi . . . pagana'. They have other unique agreements in error;[102] but they also often agree with the Bern text where many manuscripts depart from it, especially in the opening chapters.[103]

MSS 110, 199

As MS. 110 begins with §5 and lacks §208, comparison again rests on §100. Here 110 and 199 have two unique agreements, of word-order at n. 56 and the reading (at n. 103) *potauit et adamauit* (compare above, 105, 154, 214, etc.).[104] There remain many point of divergence between them.[105] The two unique readings must either be regarded as coincidences or it must be accepted that these witnesses are distantly related.

MSS 117, 188 (13, 167)

Although there is little in the collation of §§1 and 2 to suggest a special link between these manuscripts,[106] §100 yields several rare, even unique, shared errors, inversions of word order, or revisions.[107]

Several manuscripts with no external resemblance to MSS 117 and 188 agree with them significantly. MSS 13 and 167 display frequent agreement,[108] each

---

99 §100 n. 135 *patri* for *a patre*, n. 290 *preparauit* for *parauit*. Besides unusual readings and word-order: §2 nn. 17, 33; §100 nn. 55, 60, 166; §208 n. 22. N.B. also §100 n. 30 *iuit/fuit* for *uenit*.

100 §1 n. 35, §2 n. 11 (*ex(h)orticis*); §100 n. 40; §208 n. 40.

101 §100 nn. 234, 282.

102 §100 nn. 87, 243. Besides rare readings – §100 nn. 10 (*Renwen*), 116 (*Washeil*), 196 – and agreements on details, as at §2, n. 4 (*Galterus*), n. 21 (*Caduallanum*), n. 38 (*phalerata*). There are also general similarities: §100 nn. 23, 58, 59 (*Washeil*), 214, 282.

103 §1 nn. 35, 39; §2 nn. 4, 5; §100 nn. 40, 203; §208 nn. 25, 40.

104 There are other more common points of agreement (nn. 27, 69, 178, 203, 252).

105 §100 nn. 75, 76, 96, 106, 126, 129, 138, 156, 167, 170, 175, 180, 195, 201, 202, 218, 229, 230 231, 243, 264.

106 But note §1 nn. 7, 35; §2 nn. 11, 46.

107 nn. 175, 240, 291; *21, *48, *58, *151. There are other extensive agreements here and in §208: §100 nn. 6, 10 (*Ronuuen*), 23, 40, 69, 106, 121, 132, 178, 203, 231, 240, 252; §208 nn. 25, 33, 40, 46.

108 §1 n. 35, §2 n. 46; §100 nn. 10, 23, 40, 69, 106, 175, 178, 203, 230 (*Karcartigernus/ Kartartigernus*), cf. 240, 252, 287, *291

sometimes independently agreeing with 117/188.[109] MSS 59/60, described above, also resemble 117/188,[110] particularly MS. 59.[111]

MSS 129, 186

Repeated correspondence (against Bern) is evident between the readings of these manuscripts in §100; MS. 186 is acephalous and so further comparison is limited. At least two variants in §100 confined to these manuscripts suggest deliberate revision: *tempore* for *die* at n. 105 and *dederunt* for *fuit* at n. 174. There are other unique errors, possibly slips.[112] It should be noted that MS. 129 lacks a section of text found in MS. 186 ('Generauerat . . . Paschent', §100, nn. 222–31).

Preliminary Conclusions

Preliminary analysis of this substantial but relatively restricted body of textual evidence – in the form of test-collations of §§1, 2, 100, and 208 – indicates connections between 106 of 189 vulgate manuscripts. Thirty-five belong to the nameless-dedication (*Nimirum quod*) group, nineteen belong to the *Tres filios* group, and a further twenty-four are accounted for by seven smaller groups. Fourteen pairs of manuscripts have also been identified. More sophisticated analysis of these results and further collation is an essential next step in Galfridian textual research; the results achieved with this small sample are promising but are open to qualification or even to being overturned by further work.

---

109 MS. 13, compare §100 nn. 21, 58; MS. 167, §1 n. 7, §2 n. 11.
110 §1 nn. 7, 35; §2 n. 11; §100 nn. 23, 106, 178, 203; §208 nn. 25, 40.
111 §2 n. 46, §100 nn. 69, 121, 132.
112 §100, nn. 52, 56, 171; and more common agreements (nn. 71, 126).

VIII

TOWARDS A TEXTUAL HISTORY

Test-collations may provide the most authoritative means of establishing the links which will later fit together into a text-history, but they do not displace the value of external evidence. The readings most useful for the present purpose are the most idiosyncratic ones – those arising from peculiar error or deliberate revision and whose repeated occurrence in manuscripts is therefore unlikely to be fortuitous; such readings, however, represent deviations from the main goal of text-historical analysis, the core of the text-history. External evidence draws more on the commonplace and so tends not to fragment in the same way.

The connections suggested by external evidence but not immediately obvious from the chapters collated (and so not already discussed in VII) can now be assessed using textual information. The results of the findings of Chapters II–VII are presented in what follows. I proceed according to the numerical sequence of the sigla. Each group of manuscripts is discussed under the heading of the first manuscript contained in the group. Other members of that group do not appear independently in the list, unless they show conflicting affiliations which associate them with more than one group.

MS. 1: First Variant

MSS 1, 4, 55, 67, 68, 70, 106, 163
The characteristics of these manuscripts have been amply described by Wright.[1] The following summarizes the external features which link them.

Wright's subgroup 67/68/70 contains a particular form of the history of Dares Phrygius and shares an opening rubric (also found in MS. 1); 70 alone is divided into books. Book-divisions are also found in MSS 4, 106, and 163, those in 4 and 163 agreeing particularly as do their rubrics.

MSS 67, 70 and 55 contain a Trojan genealogy (compare below, MS. 130).

---

[1] *The Historia*, II.

MS. 2: The Nameless-dedication group

MSS 2, 3, 14, 19, 20, 36, 53, 56, 58, 75, 81, 83, (105,) 125, 126, 127, (130,) 132, 151, (154,) 166, 168, 171, 173, 175, 176, (180,) 182, 183, 184, 189, 196, 205, 208, (214)[2]

None of the nameless-dedication manuscripts is divided into books (although two single-dedication relatives are, see below); none contains the phrase about Seaxburh. MSS 3, 36, 53, 151, 171, 175, and 176 lack other contents.

Five subgroups are apparent from the test-collations. Certain manuscripts from different subgroups have common features, however. MSS 132 and 182 bear a set of unusual rubrics. MSS 83, 166, 184 and possibly 126 contain the m-text of Bede's Ecclesiastical History. MSS 2 and 183 contain Alexander-texts: *Gesta*, *Collatio*, and *Epistola Alexandri*. MS. 2 witnesses the fourth family of this last text, as does MS. 14, while 189 witnesses the second. In MSS 20 and 81 the text ends prematurely, without physical loss, but at different points in the text (above, IV, Omissions: The end of the text).

The five subgroups identified in the previous chapter will be taken not in strict numerical sequence but in the order in which they were discussed before.

1. MSS 56, 58, 205

MSS 58 and 205 bear the type-i dedication; 56 is acephalous. 56 and 58 have the rubric 'Incipiunt prophetie Merlini' at §111 and, at §109, the unique 'Re[ue]latio historiografi de eodem/Merlino'. 'Textus hystorie incipit', found in MS. 58 at §6, resembles 'Textus hystorie' in MS. 205 at §5.

2. MSS 20, 83, 126, (151,) 166, 173, 175

§§83–84, 173–174, and 184 are abbreviated in all these manuscripts (above, IV) except for the lacunose MS. 83 from which these sections are lacking. 20, 126, 166, and 173 bear the type-v nameless dedication. 83 is acephalous. 151 and 175 have the third type, whose only material difference from type-v is in reading *opusculo* not *opus*. The following rubrics are found in whole or in part in all these type-v manuscripts and 83: §1 'Incipit prologus Gaufridi Monemutensis in hystoriis/historia regum Britannie', §5 'Explicit prologus. Incipit hystoria', after §208 'Explicit historia regum Britannie'. Bede's *Historia ecclesiastica* is found in MSS 83, 126, and 166. MS. 20 contains a unique interpolation concerning Merlin in §143.

2 The bracketted manuscripts are single-dedication relatives of the nameless-dedication type.

3.   MSS 3, 14, 81, 168, 171, 183, 184, 189

This group encompasses manuscripts bearing types vii, viia, and viii of the nameless dedication and one type-iii manuscript (168). MSS 3, 14, 189 (type viii) have 'Incipit in historia Britannorum prefacio Gaufridi Monomutensis', a rubric echoed in the type-vii manuscripts (171, 184) and MS. 168. Poems of Ausonius, a series of chronicle-extracts, and a pseudo-Classical work are found in MSS 14 and 183. 14 and 189 contain the History of Dares Phrygius.

4.   MSS 36, 53, 127, 196, 208

This group is more diffuse, containing manuscripts bearing types i, ii, iii, and v of the nameless dedication. The type-ii witnesses, 127 and 208, have clearly related rubrics. Those in 53 and 196 (type-iii) have been compared with those of the second subgroup, a connection mirrored in the test-collations.[3]

5.   Single-dedication relatives

MSS 105, (125, 130,) 154, (180, 182,) 214

MSS 130 and 214 (both single-dedication) are divided into books, unlike the nameless-dedication proper. MSS 105 and 214 have a distinctive opening rubric 'Incipit historia regum Britannie Maioris secundum Galfridum Monemutensem'; 125, 154, and 180 lack rubrics. MSS 105 and 214 omit §§109–110. 105, 130, and 214 include the account of the foundation of Britain beginning 'Ab origine mundi. . .'.

MS. 4

This manuscript, which witnesses a conflation of First- and Second-Variant texts,[4] contains *Armorica siue Latauia*, a dependent text found in similar form in the nameless-dedication (but acephalous) manuscript, 75 (above, III). A shorter version of *Armorica* is found in a Second-Variant and a single-dedication manuscript (95, 121); their relationship is not clarified by test-collations but MS. 121 contains other texts usually associated with the Second Variant (Alexander texts, above, II).

---

3   At §100, n. 77, where many nameless-dedication manuscripts omit the phrase found in Bern, the second group reads *Qui ait*; the five representatives of the fourth subgroup, like those of the first, have *Qui dixit*.

4   See Wright, *The Historia*, II.lxxvii–lxxix.

MS. 5

MSS 5, (6,) 84, (115,) 124

Test-collations indicated a link between these manuscripts. 6 and 115 sometimes agree together against the others. All five contain the interpolation about Seaxburh in §204. 5, 6, and 84 are divided into books.

On MS. 5, see also below MS. 12, MS. 26.

MS. 7: 117/188 type

MSS 7, 13, 16, 21, 59, 60, 79, 117, 135, 155, 167, 169, 172, 174, 188, 190, 197, 198, 211, 213

This group took shape during the discussion of test-collations (VII). When other forms of evidence are presented for comparison, five subgroups can be identified.

1. MSS 7, 135, 155, 213

All these manuscripts contain the letter of Arthur. 7, 135, and 155 contain the Prophecy of the Eagle (in 135 beginning 'Mortuo leone', and in 7 and 155 'Sicut rubeum draconem'). 135 and 213 uniquely begin Book VII at §110. Test-collations indicated a particular connection between 7 and 155. They also demonstrate common features between the four,[5] but also certain idiosyncrasies.[6]

2. MSS 13, 16, 21

These manuscripts contain the rare text, *Status imperii iudaici*, found in only one other *Historia*-manuscript, 214 (above, Nameless dedication). The affiliation of MS. 13 with 117/188, 167, and others has already been suggested (above, VII: 117, 188). 16 and 21 agree extensively with this general pattern of readings[7] but show particular agreement with each other.[8] One of these readings – the erroneous *tantum* for *tam subitum* at §100 n. 36 – points to further relatives: 190, 211, and also 60, which has already been seen to be related to 59 and 117/188 (above, VII).[9]

---

5 §1 nn. 35, 39; §2 n. 11 *exorticis/exortitis*; §100 nn. 5, 6, 23, 40, 69, 106, 178, 203, 252; §208 nn. 40 and 45. Note also §§100 nn. 10 *Ronwein* (155, 213), 223 (7, 135, 155).

6 MS. 135: §1 n. 33. MS. 213: §1 nn. 6, 26; §2 nn. 30, 40; §100 nn. 170, 175.

7 §1 nn. 35, 39; §100 nn. 5, 6, 10, 23, 69, 75, 170, 178, 203, 214, 287.

8 §2 n. 11; §100 nn. 36, 230 (*Castigern(us)*), 231.

9 These all agree at §1 nn. 35, 39; §2 n. 11; §100 nn. 5, 10 (*Ronuuen*, 13, 16, 21, 190), 23, 36, 69 (not 21, 60), 75 (with Bern), 106, 170 (not 190), 178, 203, 214 (not 60), 287 (not 21, 60). See also §100 nn. 230 *Castigernus/Castigern* (16, 211, 21), 231 (16, 21, 211).

3. MSS 59, 60, (211)

Test-collations, the presence of the poem *Pergama flere uolo*, Leonine summaries of the *Historia*, and scribal verses link 59 and 60; the same scribal verses occur in 211. The first two lines of a colophon found in MS. 211 are also present in 60.[10]

4. MSS 117, 188

MSS 117 and 188, which test-collations show to be related, contain identical rubrics, a unique scribal verse, and various texts: the *Epistola Alexandri* (Family III), the correspondence of Alexander and Dindymus, the *Gesta Alexandri*, and the History of Apollonius of Tyre (Tegernsee recension).

5. MSS 172, 174, 197, 198

The filiation of this group is apparent from test-collations. The rubrics of 172 and 174 are related.

6. The whole group

Book-divisions are found in all except the textually distinctive subgroup 172, 174, 197, and 198 (although 172 has one marginal note of a book-division). MSS 135 and 213 are divided into ten, with VII placed in a unique position, at §110; 169 and 190 are comparably divided. 172 and 174 have the rubric 'Explicit prologus. Incipit prophetia eiusdem'[11] as do MSS 79, 135, 155, 169, 190. MSS 7 and 155 have already been compared and found to agree generally (above), a broad similarity shared by MSS 79, 169, and especially 190.[12] The rubrics of MS. 13 resemble those of 117 and 188 (above, VI).

These readings conform to the pattern found in 59, 60, the *Status* manuscripts and 117/188. These and those just mentioned, like the nameless-dedication manuscripts, are distinguished in §1, where they read *digna eternitatis laude* for *digna eternitate laudis*. 59/60, 117/188 and 16/21 read at §2 n. 11 *exorticis* for *exoticis*. This latter reading is also found in 7/135/155/213 as well as in MS. 197; 172, 174, and 198 have a further corrupted form *exorticiis*.

Exorticis is found at §2 n. 11 in a total of nineteen manuscripts; all but four have *eternitatis laude* in §1. 7, 16, 21, 59, 60, 117, 135, 167, 188, 190, 197, 211, and 213 have been discussed. Others with this double correspondence are 11, 104, 199. (104 and 199 were discussed in the previous chapter, the first in connection with MS. 194 and the second with 110.) Further use of MS. 11 is hampered by

---

10 211 shows some agreement with 60 (above), for example, §100 nn. 5, 23, 106; §208 n. 40.
11 174 adds *Merlini*, after *eiusdem*.
12 §1 nn. 35, 39; §2 n. 11 (7, 16, 21, 59, 60, 135, 190, 213); §100 nn. 5, 23, 69, 106 (not 79, 169), 178, 203; §208 nn. 40 (not 169), 45 (not 169).

the loss of §100 from this manuscript. The remaining witnesses show only limited agreement with the pattern already established.[13]

Dares is found in 59, 60, and 117, and (various) crusading chronicles in 60 and 117.

MS. 8: Tres filios group

MSS 8, 10, 28, 30, 32, 39, 45, 61, 73, 98, 100, 109, 119, 123, 134, 141, 142, 153, 165

This category absorbs the group of manuscripts associated with St John's G.16 (32 + MSS 73, 98, 153, 165), whose relationship has repeatedly been apparent. In MSS 32, 153, and 165, the *Historia* is followed by a scribal verse; MSS 32, 73, 98, and 153 contain an interpolation after §5. It is possible that all these manuscripts originally included both features. 73 and 98 have not retained their original closing chapters[14] and so once may have included the scribal verse; and 165 is acephalous and so may originally have contained the interpolation.[15] The group's rubrics and book-divisions are distinctive.[16] §110 is truncated in MSS 98 and 165.[17] None of these manuscripts contains the Seaxburh phrase except 98, whose closing chapters are not original.

Test-collations have established the coherence of the group as a whole. The St John's subgroup has distinctive rubrics, but no other rubrics may be identified as typical of the wider group – rather the reverse. Four members contain only very simple rubrics: at the Prophecies only (61, 100) or after §208 (109, 119). Several sets of idiosyncratic rubrics identified (above, VI) happen to be found in manuscripts of this type: 28, 39, 45, 142, and 123/141. Those in 123 and 141 comment on synchronisms within the text, a feature which suggests some link with 90 and 112, in which synchronisms within the text are marked (see below, MS. 26). The group also includes a high proportion of manuscripts bearing *Brutus* rubrics (10, 45, 98, 134, 141), although these differ in format. This situation may be compared with the distribution of book-divisions. Apart from 32 and its relatives (except for 98), which are divided in a unique manner, only MSS 30, 45, 123, 134, and 141 are divided and each contains only a single marking (Book II or III). The overall capriciousness evident in rubrics and book-divisions may suggest that the text originally travelled without rubrication.

123 and 134 omit §§109–110. Test-collations suggest particular proximity between 123 and 141, 100 and 134, 119 and 142. 100 and 134, together with 8

---

13 §100 n. 23 (104, not 199), 40 (not 104, 199), 69 (both), 106 (both), 178 (both).

14 73 is truncated physically in the middle of §200 (but continued in a Secretary hand to §202); in 98, a break is apparent in §174, where the quiring alters from sixteens to twelves and a new, rather later-looking hand begins.

15 The text begins in §17.

16 §1 'Incipit prologus', §108 'Uerba Merlini'/'De uerbis Merlini', §109 'Uerba auctoris', §111 'Incipiunt uaticinia Merlini coram Uortegirno edita'.

17 The whole of §110 is lacking from MS. 8, a member of the wider *Tres filios* group.

and 28, stand out from other manuscripts in the wider group in that they include the Seaxburh phrase, even though §204 is present in all in their original state. MS. 134 is also anomalous in that it, like MS. 39, bears the Robert-Waleran dedication.

MS. 9: Pudibundus Brito

MSS 9, 31, 41, 42, 44, 93, 113, 118, 132, 140, 143, 150, 156, 178, 212

Repeated agreement between 9 and 143 – two manuscripts bearing the reworked, nameless, introduction to Merlin's prophecies – has already been observed in the discussion of disruptions, rubrics (in which they resemble MS. 41), book-divisions, and test-collations. 9 and 143 omit §§1–4; §§42–43 are compressed, as in a third *pudibundus Brito* manuscript, 93; the text around the prophecies is displaced (*Merlinus uero incipiens*) as in 132, another *pudibundus Brito* manuscript.[18]

The wider group of *pudibundus Brito* manuscripts appears almost to monopolize certain readings in the test-collations, especially in §100.[19] Other readings are witnessed by a high proportion of the fourteen *pudibundus Brito* manuscripts, in §100[20] and elsewhere.[21]

This group lacks easily identifiable general characteristics, except that the Seaxburh phrase is present in all its members except those which have lost the closing chapters (31, 44, 143, 156). There is no sign of a widely transmitted set of rubrics or book-divisions: most manuscripts are undivided except 9 (seven books), 42 (twelve parts), 140 (two books), 143 (seven), 156 (three), and despite two sets of unusual rubrics (9/41/143, 31/113), there is nothing which can be identified as typical. Certain manuscripts, besides 9 and 143, display a close

---

18 §§1–3 and 5 were added to MS. 132 in nameless-dedication form together with the vulgate version of §§109–110 and the Prophecies. §100, as part of the original text, is available for comparison. It shows only limited agreement with 9/143 (compare above, VII): §100 nn. 5, 23, 40, 76, 100, 252 but not 106, 183, 203, 214, 239.

19 n. *50 *inde* (31, 93, 113, 132, 140, 150, 178; om., 9, 143), n. 206 (41, 44, 93, 118, 132, 140, 156, 178, 212), n. 218 om. *suorum* (9, 31, 41, 42, 44, 93, 113, 118, 132, 140, 150, 156, 178, 212).

20 §100 n. 23 (9, 31, 41, 44, 93, 113, 118, 132, 140, 143, 150, 156, 178, 212), n. 44 (31, 41, 44, 113, 118, 132, 156, 178), n. 75 (31, 44, 93, 113, 132, 140, 156), n. 76 (9, 31, 41, 42, 44, 93, 113, 132, 140, 143, 150, 156, 178, 212), n. 92 *Uortigernus* (31, 41, 42, 113, 132, 140, 212), n. 100 (9, 31, 41, 42, 93, 113, 118, 132, 140, 143, 150, 178), n. 106 with Bern (9, 41, 42, 44, 93, 113, 118, 140, 143, 150, 156, 178), n. 123 *Respondit* (44, 93, 118, 140), n. 124 *Drinkheil* (9, 140, 143, 150, 212), n. 125 *Uortigirnus* (44, 118, 140, 143, 178, 212), n. 138 *namque* (9, 42, 150), n. 170 *faceret* (31, 41, 42, 44, 93, 113, 118, 132, 140, 143, 150, 156, 178, 212), n. 190 *Uortigirno* (44, 118, 143, 178), n. 203 with Bern (9, 31, 41, 42, 44, 93, 113, 140, 143, 150, 156, 178, 212), n. 286 *tractu* (31, 113, 156).

21 §208 n. 2 *illorum* (118, 178), n. 28 *Hontendonensi* (9, 113, 118, 140, 150, 178), n. 46 *Oxenfordensis* (9, 140, 150, 178); §1 n. 35 with Bern (all representatives in which the chapter is present: 42, 93, 113, 118, 150, 156, 212) – note that MSS 9, 31, 41, 44, 140, 143, 178 are acephalous; MS. 132 also lacks original opening chapters.

affinity with each other. Six manuscripts omit the opening chapters (9, 41, 132, 140, 143, 178). Test-collations demonstrate particular proximity between MSS 156 and 212.

In MSS 113 and 132, the *Historia* is accompanied by William of Malmesbury's *Gesta regum* and *Historia nouella*. The ubiquitous History of Dares Phrygius is found in 44, 118 and 212. Jacques de Vitry's *Historia orientalis* precedes the *Historia* in 118 and, as a separable item, in 156. The presence of different texts concerning St Wilfrid in 93 and 212 (alone among *Historia*-manuscripts) seems coincidental. MSS. 31, 156, and 178 lack original associated contents.

MS. 11

Compare above, MS. 7 (117/188).

MS. 12: Merlinus iste

MSS (5,) 12, 50, 54, 66, 80, 114, 149, 210

This passage about Merlin is found in five Second-Variant and four vulgate manuscripts. MS. 66 is fully Variant (α; omitting §185, for example) and is otherwise anomalous among the nine in that *Merlinus iste* is found before and not after the Prophecies. The remaining four Variant manuscripts belong to the β-subgroup (whose only other member – 22 – is lacunose here). As already mentioned (above, IV), the characteristic reversion of the β-manuscripts to vulgate after the Prophecies suggests an immediate association with MSS 12 and 210, which originally contained only the second half of the text.

The test-collations are of only limited assistance here as comparison must rest on the generally featureless §208. There are some equivalences, however.[22] One significant feature is the presence of the Seaxburh interpolation in all these manuscripts except 66 and 149; 22, 50, 54, 80 are, with MS. 95, the only Second-Variant manuscripts to include it. *Merlinus iste* was added in the margins of MS. 5, which, like 149, has *Prologus/editio* rubrics (below, MS. 26).

MS. 15: The Bern Group (Stephen-Robert Dedication)

MSS 15, 86, 200, ?215

The connections of the acephalous manuscripts 86 and 200 (they lack §§1–5) with MS. 15 are well known.[23] The survey has not indicated any further members of this immediate group except for 215, which contains certain letters relating to

---

22 n. 7 *Gualliis* 50, 66, 114, 210; n. 63 5, 50, 114.
23 The evidence is summarized by Wright, *The Historia*, I.li.

a dispute between Church and State found also in 15. Comparison is limited as 215 contains only extracts but these agree closely with the printed text (of MS. 15).

The members of the group apparently did not originally bear rubrics or book-divisions.

MS. 17: Second Variant

MSS 17, 22, 35, 47, 50, 54, 66, 80, 85, 91, 95, 102, 108, 114, 138, 202, 207, 209

1. The α-subgroup (MSS 47, 85, 91, 95, 209)

All omit §185 (as do the unfiliated witnesses 66, 102, 138, and the γ-manuscript, 202), have distinctive rubrics and are divided into four books. This study suggests that the newly-identified witness, 85, is an α-manuscript. MSS 47, 91, 95 contain a *capitula*-list. Certain Alexander-texts (*Gesta*, *Epistola* Family II, *Epitaphium*) and the History of Dares Phrygius have a particular association with this subgroup. The history of Jacques de Vitry is found in MSS 91 and 209.

2. The β-subgroup (MSS 22, 50, 54, 80, 114)

MS. 50 is an addition to Hammer's list. The vulgate part of the β-text includes the Seaxburh interpolation.[24] All physically intact manuscripts contain the *Merlinus iste* interpolation after §117. None is divided into books. Rubrics are found only in 54 and 80, which a scribal verse and a series of miscellaneous contents show to be closely related.

3. The γ-subgroup (MSS 17, 202, 207)

These manuscripts differ from both groups in details but demonstrate little internal coherence, except that MSS 17 and 202 omit §110. The γ-manuscript, 202, like the α, 95, contains the *Epistola* and *Epitaphium Alexandri*, and the letter of Prester John. 207, like certain α-manuscripts, contains a *capitula*-list, but it is of a different type.

Of the remaining unclassified manuscripts, test-collations suggest particular agreement between MSS 35 and 66.

---

[24] Another link with vulgate manuscripts is suggested by the gloss found in the Prophecies in MS. 80; this resembles other texts found solely in vulgate manuscripts.

MS. 23

This manuscript is associated with 96 by synchronistic rubrics and test-collations (above, VI, VII). Both lack book-divisions. The reader's attention is drawn to synchronisms by various means in the *Prologus/Editio* manuscripts 90 and 112, and the *Tres filios* witnesses 123, 141. 123, like 23, appears originally to have contained only one half of the text (the division falling between §§109 and 110).

The poem by Madog of Edeirnion found in MS. 55 forms an Antiquarian addition to MS. 23.

MS. 24

24, like MSS 22 (Second-Variant), 32, and 106 (First-Variant), contains the *Historia Turpini* and genealogies of kings of France and of England, texts apparently associated with one branch of the Turpin tradition. The English royal genealogies end in 24 as in 32 with Edward I but the two manuscripts display no affinity in test-collations.

MS. 25

No evidence has emerged to suggest any filiation for this manuscript but it, like MS. 32, contains the Histories attributed to Dares and Turpin and a text concerning the itinerary and arrival in Italy of Æneas, which begins 'Superius autem excidio . . .'.

MS. 26: Prologus/editio Gaufridi Arturi Monemutensis de gestis

MSS (5,) 26, 51, 90, 103, 112, 137, 162; 149; 43, 63, 120, 203 (18, 74, 87, 154)

The identification of a connection between these manuscripts has rested largely on rubrics and book-divisions (a ten- or eleven-book arrangement beginning at §6, with VII at §111 or 118). Particular connections have emerged between some. Rubrics, book-divisions and test-collations indicate that MSS 26 and 51 (*Prologus*) are closely related. The test-collations of 63 and 203 (*Editio*) show significant agreement; these two manuscripts, unlike the rest of the group, lack book-divisions (although they were added in MS. 203). MSS 90 and 137 are connected by a series of unusual contents. Their text, while not marked by any peculiarity, displays consistent agreement.[25] 112, which, like 90 and 137, contains

---

25 See §100 nn. 5, 10, 21, 59 (*Wassail*), 76, 96, 106, 170, 174, 203, 230 (*Katigen*), 231, 264.

glosses on the Prophecies, is another relative.[26] The rubrics of the three are particularly close. The Prophecies in 149 are also glossed. Other manuscripts with 'Prologus' rubrics display some similarity with these.[27]

As for more general features, none of these manuscripts except 5 and the only peripherally related 87, contain the interpolation about Seaxburh. All follow Bern at §100, n. 35, in reading *digna eternitatis laude*.

MSS 5, 43, 120, 162, and 203 lack other contents (though a text was added to the end of 43 in the fifteenth century). The *Merlinus iste* chapter is found in 5 and 149 (above, 12).

MS. 27

Test-collations indicate a superficial resemblance between this manuscript and MSS 26 and 51 (VII: 26, 27, 51; above, MS. 26).

MS. 28

See above, MS. 8. 28 contains verses of Iohannes Beuerus, also found in MSS. 90 (*Prologus/Editio*) and 164.

MS. 29

This manuscript shares certain prophecies with 61 but there is no other indication of a connection. The prophecies are additional in MS. 61.

MS. 32

See above, MS. 8. This is the only vulgate manuscript which contains a *capitula*-list: the others are Second-Variant.

MS. 32 shares different blocks of contents with MSS 25 (see above), 78 (Eagle-prophecy and commentary), 91 (Godfrey of Viterbo, Sibylline prophecies, and Alexander-texts), and 172 (*Historia Turpini*, Sibylline prophecies, and *Testamenta*). Each block appears in every case to have been derived independently.

---

[26] It agrees at all the readings noted above, except for §100 nn. 21, 76, and 96.
[27] Notably MSS 5 (at 5, 10, 23, 40, 106, 174, 203, 230, 231), 26/51 (at 5, 10, 40, 106, 170, 203), 103 (at 5, 10, 23, 40, 106, 203, 231), 149 (at 5, 10, 59, 106).

MS. 33

This manuscript uniquely lacks §5 (the description of Britain) after the dedicatory chapters.

MS. 34

34 (74, 147,) 152

The connection between 34 and 152 which the presence of *Mirabilia Britannie* suggests is corroborated by test-collations. They witness rare readings[28] besides others more widely represented, sometimes remaining unusually close to the Bern text.[29] Book-divisions also suggest a connection between them. Certain of their rarer readings are found in another manuscript, 147, and there are more general agreements.[30] The other manuscripts containing the *Mirabilia* – 65 and 125 – witness none of the rare readings and only a scattering of the very common ones.[31] MS. 125 is a nameless-dedication manuscript some of whose relatives have already been identified (above, MS. 2: Nameless dedication).

Book-divisions suggest a possible relative of 34/152, MS. 74 (which bears *Editio* rubrics), but test-collations indicate only general agreement.[32]

MS. 37

The rubrics of this manuscript '[Prologus] . . . historia Britannorum/Britonum' preface two related nameless-dedication manuscripts (127, 208), a *pudibundus Brito* (42), two others with previously determined different filiations (34 and 38) and a third single-dedication manuscript, 37, which only vaguely resembles any of these. 37 has none of the rare readings of MSS 34/152/147 and of the thirteen general readings noted agrees only at §100 nn. 170, 178, 203 and §208 n. 40.

37 lacks text between §§25 and 26; there is no physical explanation.

---

28 §1 n. 21; §2 n. 58 *immorari/immorare*; §100 nn. *6 *octo et decem naues*, 66 *tantam eius speciem*, 180 *peteretur*, 183 *prouintia*; §208 n. 17.
29 §1 n. 35 (with Bern); §2 n. 22 *Cadwallonis*; §100 n. 23 (with Bern), 40 (with Bern), 59 (*Washeil*), 106 (with Bern), 170 (with Bern), 178, 203, 214, 231 *Paschen*; §208 nn. 7 *Gualliis*, 40 (+ 65, 125).
30 For example, §2 n. 59; §100 nn. 66, 180, 183. See also §2 n. 22; §100 nn. 23, 40, 106, 178, 203, 214; §208 n. 40.
31 §100 nn. 23 (125), 106 (125), 178 (125), 203 (65, 125), 214 (125); §208 n. 7 (65).
32 For example at §100, nn. 40, 59, 170, 214, but not nn. 23, 106, 178, 203, 231.

MS. 38

38, 131; 99, 122

Test-collations have indicated a connection between these manuscripts. None has book-divisions; all four contain the interpolation about Seaxburh in §204.

MS. 39: Robert-Waleran dedication

39, 48, 49, 107, 128, 134, 136, 170, 199

Test-collations have indicated particular closeness between 48/128 (whose text ends in §207) and 107/136. Three are associated textually with manuscripts bearing other forms of dedication: MSS 39 and 134 have affinities with the predominantly single-dedication *Tres filios* group, though not in their opening chapters; MS. 199 has been compared above (VII) with MS. 110, which begins at §5. Furthermore, the rubrics of MS. 199 resemble those of certain nameless-dedication manuscripts. 134 is anomalous in being the only representative of the group to include the passage about Seaxburh and to display evidence for book-divisions (but only one, in fact).

Some agreement across the nine (often with Bern) may be observed[33] but 39 and especially 134, and 199 tend to be more independent of Bern, often agreeing together.[34]

None of the nine shares associated works with any of the others; MSS 48, 107, 128, 134, 136, and 170 lack other original contents.

MS. 40

40, 111

40 and 111 share several associated contents, have related rubrics and lack text from §§177 and 179 (above, II, IV, VI). Their test-collations also show significant agreement.

---

[33] §1 nn. 35 (not 199), 39 (not 199); §100 nn. 5 *conduxerantque* (48, 49, 107, 128), 10 (*Renwein* 48, 128, 170; *Renwen* 49, 107, 136), 23 (not 134, 199), 40, 58 *Ching* (107, 136, 199 only), 106 with Bern (not 134, 199), 170 with Bern (39, 49, 107, 134, 136, 170 only), 203 with Bern (not 39, 134, 199), 214 with Bern (not 107, 134, 136), 282 (107, 136 only).

[34] §100 nn. 23, 106, 178, 203, 234. For other examples of rededication without thorough textual revision see Holzknecht, *Literary Patronage*, pp. 142, 144–45; also Gaiffier d'Hestroy, 'L'Hagiographe', pp. 160–61.

MS. 42

See above, MS. 9 (*pudibundus Brito*). Like 155, a manuscript of the 117/188 type, 42 contains *Euolutis a mundi constitucione*. The connection of both manuscripts with St Albans may explain the association of a rare work with two otherwise dissimilar *Historia*-texts.

MS. 46

No evidence has emerged which suggests any filiation for this manuscript.

MS. 52

52 includes certain prophecies found in MS. 61, but there seems to be little connection between the *Historia*-texts which they contain; the fact that the prophecies form an addition in MS. 61 is possibly a factor here (compare above, 29).

MS. 57

No evidence has emerged which suggests any filiation for this manuscript.

MS. 61

See above, MS. 8. This manuscript has added prophecies, of which some are found in MS. 29 and others in MS. 52.

MS. 62

This manuscript, like 58 and 118, contains the chronicle beginning 'Cum anim-aduerterem'. It bears no further relation to them, 118 being a *pudibundus Brito* manuscript, and 58, a nameless-dedication.

MS. 64

Acephalous. No evidence has emerged which suggests any filiation for this manuscript.

MS. 65

This manuscript bears at §5 an unusual rubric found also in the *pudibundus Brito* manuscripts 31 and 113 although the connection is not corroborated in the test-collations. 65, like MSS 34, 125, and 152, contains *mirabilia* (see above, MS. 34).

MS. 69

This manuscript lacks §§1–5. There is nothing to associate it with any of the groups to which other manuscripts beginning at §6 belong (Bern, *pudibundus Brito*, *Tres filios*).

MS. 71

71, 181
See below, 76. MS. 181 contains material about Florence, the medieval home of MS. 71.[35]

MS. 72

72, 89, 133, 160
This group is apparent from test-collations. Its members lack book-divisions; they have no rubrics in common. The beginning of §177 is absent from MSS 72 and 133. MS 133 contains as an interpolation a phrase used in the revision of §§83–84 found in the nameless-dedication manuscripts 20, 126, 151, 166, 173, 175 (above, MS. 2).

MS. 76: The Leiden group

76/92/97, 77/191
The text of the *Historia* confirms a connection between MSS 76 and 92 previously established on the basis of the text of the *Historia Brittonum*. Associated contents indicate a link between MSS 76 and 77 (F-redaction of the *Gesta Normannorum ducum*, Einhard, 'Antenor'), and MSS 76 and 92 (F-redaction of the *Gesta Normannorum ducum*, *Gesta* and *Epistola Alexandri*, *Historia Britto-*

---

35 Michael Reeve has pointed out to me that 181 and 71 are copy and exemplar: in 181 the *Historia* breaks off at the point (in §203) at which 71 is damaged.

num). Rubrics, book-divisions, and test-collations suggest that while 76 and 92 are immediate relatives (as is MS. 97), 77 is less close: while MS. 77 does not share any of the unusual readings found in MS. 76 and its immediate relatives (above, VII: 76, 92, 97), it agrees in all general characteristics.[36] Rubrics and book-divisions show that MS. 191 is connected to both 77 and 76.[37] They indicate that MSS 71 and 181, whose rubrics resemble those of the other Leiden relatives, display only very general agreement with them,[38] although they often agree with each other.[39]

MS. 78

78, 206

These manuscripts are associated by test-collations only; 78, unlike 206, has rubrics, book-divisions, and other contents.

MS. 82

No evidence has emerged which suggests any filiation for this manuscript.

MS. 87

This contains *Editio* rubrics but its text bears little textual relation to that of other manuscripts with similar rubrics.

MS. 88

88, 116

Complex contents, the interpolation of *mirabilia* and Bedan material, and omissions (from §§150, the opening of 177, the middle of 179, besides all of 109–110) indicate the close correspondence between these manuscripts. Their text bears similarities to the *Tres filios* type.

---

36 Compare §100 nn. 23, 40, 59, 69, 174, 178, 203, 252.
37 With 76/92/97 at §100 n. 230; with MS. 77 §208 n. 46; with Leiden type in general §100 nn. 5, 6, 23, 40, 69, 116, 174, 178, 203, 252 and §208 n. 45.
38 For example, at §100 nn. 5, 6, 23, 40, 69 (181 only), 252, 284; not at §1 n. 2, §100 nn. 230, 264, and §208 n. 28.
39 §100 nn. 44, 75, 123, 230.

MS. 94

Fragmentary. No evidence has emerged which suggests any filiation for this manuscript.

MS. 101

Fragmentary. No evidence has emerged which suggests any filiation for this manuscript.

MS. 104

Test-collations suggest some similarity between MSS 104 and 194 although the connection is not evident from features external to the text. Compare also above, MS. 7: 117/188.

MS. 110

The text in this manuscript begins at §5; §§5–8 are abbreviated. The test-collation of §100 (MS. 110 lacks §208) suggests some agreement with MS. 199 (above, VII).

MS. 111

See above, MS. 40. This manuscript, like 152, contains a particular version of Higden's *Polichronicon*, preceded by a *capitula*-list. There is no sign of any other connection between the two.

MS. 113

A collection of pseudo-Classical texts signals a link between the vulgate manuscripts 113 and 121 and the Second Variant. The nature of the connection remains obscure; 113 and 121 bear little resemblance to each other (for MS. 113 see above, MS. 9: *pudibundus Brito*).[40]

---

[40] MS. 121 has none of the distinctive *pudibundus Brito* readings and agrees with only a fraction of their more widely attested characteristic readings: §1, n. 35; §100 nn. 23, 106; §208 n. 28.

MS. 118

118, a *pudibundus Brito* manuscript, contains three works found also in MSS 117 and 188. Test-collations indicate only very broad agreement between them.[41]

MS. 121

121 contains a group of contents found commonly in Second-Variant manuscripts (above, MS. 113), and also *Armorica siue Latauia* (above, MS. 4). Glosses found in the Prophecies resemble those found in certain manuscripts with *pudibundus Brito* rubrics (above, MS. 26).

MS. 129

129, 186
    These manuscripts, which test-collations indicate are related, contain a genealogy of the Normans (*Inc*. 'Normanni origine Dani .dccclxxxui. . . .').

MS. 130

This manuscript is related to a subgroup of the nameless dedication (above, MS. 2). It also contains a Trojan genealogy, a text also found in three First-Variant manuscripts (above, MS. 1).

MS. 139

Fragmentary. No evidence has emerged which suggests any filiation for this manuscript.

MS. 144

Fragmentary. No evidence has emerged which suggests any filiation for this manuscript.

---

[41] §100 nn. 5, 10, 23, 203, 252; §208 n. 40. Not §1 n. 35.

MS. 145

Fragmentary. No evidence has emerged which suggests any filiation for this manuscript.

MS. 146

Fragmentary. No evidence has emerged which suggests any filiation for this manuscript.

MS. 148

Fragmentary. No evidence has emerged which suggests any filiation for this manuscript.

MS. 157

Fragmentary. No evidence has emerged which suggests any filiation for this manuscript.

MS. 158

Acephalous. No evidence has emerged which suggests any filiation for this manuscript.

MS. 159

John Leland's précis of a manuscript-witness; no evidence has emerged which suggests its filiation.

MS. 161

Test-collations suggest links between MS. 161 and the *pudibundus Brito* manuscripts 156 and 212.

MS. 164

Three forms of evidence connect this manuscript with others, but in no case is there any corroborating evidence, particularly textual.

164, like MS. 90 (a manuscript with *Prologus/Editio* rubrics), contains verses of Iohannes Beuerus, but there is little evidence of textual filiation.[42] This is not unexpected: in both cases the verses are written in a hand different from that of the text (see above, III). One of the verses occurs in the margin of MS. 28, which shows different filiation again (see above, *Tres filios*).

The presence of a certain commentary on the Prophecies in the margins of 164 and 178 suggests the possibility of an inherited connection but collation lends this little support: MS. 164 has none of the rare readings associated with 178 and its *pudibundus Brito* relatives and it witnesses only a fraction of the common ones.[43]

MS. 164 lacks text in §§42–43, as do three other manuscripts (9, 93, 143), all of them with the *pudibundus Brito* version of §§109–110.

MS. 177

The rubrics found in later repairs to the original text of 177 resemble those in MS. 198. 177 agrees with a number of the readings found in 198 and its relatives (VII: 172, 174, 197, 198)[44] but only in the repaired sections: the opening and final chapters.

MS. 179

Acephalous. No evidence has emerged which suggests any filiation for this manuscript.

MS. 185

No evidence which suggests any filiation for this manuscript has emerged from the survey.

---

42 For example, they disagree in §100 nn. 21, 76, 96, 170, 174, 203, 230, 231, 264.
43 §100 nn. 23, 100, 203.
44 §1 nn. 35, 39; §2 n. 3, 55; §208 n. 28.

MS. 186

See above, MS. 129. The presence in 186 of a group of texts about the First Crusade suggests a link with 196; this is not borne out by test-collations. The prophecies in MS. 186 are glossed.

MS. 187

No evidence has emerged which suggests any filiation for this manuscript.

MS. 192

Lacunose. No evidence has emerged which suggests any filiation for this manuscript.

MS. 193

This manuscript is truncated at §140.

MS. 194

See above, MS. 104.
    The resemblance of the rubrics of MS. 194 to those of the Leiden group is demonstrably not directly inherited.[45]

MS. 195

Acephalous. No evidence has emerged which suggests any filiation for this manuscript.

MS. 200

See above, MS. 15. The book-divisions of this manuscript are comparable with those of the St John's group (above, MS. 8, and VI).

[45] 194 displays only very general agreement with the Leiden manuscripts: §100 nn. 5, 23, 59, 178, 203, 252.

MS. 201

This is a transcript of MS. 93.

MS. 204

This manuscript contains several abbreviated passages of a kind not found in any other witness.

MS. 214

This manuscript belongs to the single-dedication subgroup of the nameless dedication (above, MS. 2) but contains *Status*, a text otherwise found only in members of the 117/188 group (above, MS. 7).

Conclusions

These results vindicate the method employed in that many of the associations which emerged from the test-collations had already been suggested by various forms of external evidence. The potentially fragile evidence of rubrics and book-divisions in particular is borne out; it seems that scribes tended to be conservative and to rely on what they found in exemplars. Book-divisions generally reinforce the groupings suggested by rubrics. Some rubrics, however, are potentially too polygenetic to prove useful in classification.[46] The particular contribution of the test-collations is to allow the the amalgamation of certain of the smaller groups already established. The areas of text collated are too small to provide more information; when the manuscripts are lacunose or lack external criteria such as associated contents or rubrics, it has often not been possible to determine their filiation. There are several instances of manuscripts whose evident external similarities are not reflected in their text. MSS 42 and 155 contain a rare origin-story of Britain; here the connection would seem to be the association of both with St Albans. *Armorica siue Latauia* is found in a First-Variant, a Second-Variant, a nameless-dedication, and a single-dedication manuscript. No explanation is readily apparent in this case. Contents closely connected with the transmission of the Second-Variant β-manuscripts, 54 and 80, are found in the *pudibundus Brito* text, 113, while the *Tres filios* manuscript, 32, contains works

46 The ordinary and obvious rubric 'Incipit prologus in hystoria Britonum' prefaces a variety of manuscripts, including a representative of the *pudibundus* group (150), the double and nameless dedications (49, 36), and MS. 96, of undetermined filiation. The same is true of the rubric 'Incipit historia Britonum', MS. 212 belonging to the *pudibundus Brito* group while MS. 72 has been seen to resemble 133.

found in certain α-witnesses of the Second Variant. The commentary on the Prophecies found within the Second-Variant manuscript, 80, would seem to be related to others found within vulgate manuscripts, a number of which are also of *Tres filios* type (90, 137, etc.). The rubrics of 71 and 181 are strikingly similar to those of the Leiden group but there is little textual resemblance. 200, a member of the generally unrubricated Bern group (represented by MS. 15), is divided into books following the pattern otherwise confined to the St John's group (represented by MS. 32).

Such cross-connections between groups can have more than one explanation. The distribution of *Armorica* and the commentaries suggests that material supplementing the text was sometimes considered sufficiently valuable to have been copied from one manuscript of the *Historia* into another. A genealogical connection may also underlie some of the similarities, however: the broader affiliation of certain groups has emerged only from test-collations and more will become apparent after further collation. One example which is already visible is that of the double-dedication types. It has been observed (above, VII) that the Robert-Waleran group adheres closely to the readings found in the Bern manuscript. This may be illustrated by a single example. In §1 n. 35 the witnesses are split. The nameless-dedication, 117/188, and Leiden groups diverge from the double-dedication (Bern) reading, together with certain smaller groupings. The groups which differ here from Bern and the other double-dedication manuscripts display similarity elsewhere, particularly in the case of Leiden and the nameless-dedication manuscripts.[47] It is interesting that these same groups are particularly to be associated with the transmission of the *Historia* on the Continent (see below, IX).

---

[47] For example, §100, nn. 23, 40, 178.

IX

CIRCULATION AND READERSHIP

In the introduction to this study two aims were proposed – to identify branches of transmission and to give some account of the circulation of the *Historia*. Detailed discussion has allowed filiation for more than half the vulgate manuscripts to be suggested. We can now consider what patterns of diffusion they indicate.

It has already been said that by studying the diffusion of a work, it may be possible to observe something of the 'historical culture' of its readers (Introduction) and, furthermore, that Geoffrey's *Historia*, a pseudo-history in historical clothing which enjoyed spectacular success, offers a promising subject. Manuscript-evidence is relevant to questions both of readership and transmission. By including all available material which witnesses the use of the *Historia*, it is possible to avoid the selectivity inherent in examining purely literary evidence for readership.[1] Moreover, without manuscript-evidence, there is virtually no indication of how the work was disseminated: we have only Gaimar's description of how the *Historia*-text he used was obtained via Walter Espec from Robert of Gloucester.[2] The present method provides a new source of information – textual filiation.

Our problems lie in the distorting effect of manuscript-survival. Books tend to be preserved in the most stable institutions: Abelard's works, for example, despite their scholastic origin and use, are extant almost exclusively in manuscripts from French religious houses.[3] Medieval book-lists partly offset this distorting effect but their survival is similarly capricious. The vulnerability of such evidence does not negate it, but it limits the breadth of the conclusions which can be drawn from it.

The material presented here can point to only a sample of the work's audience. The evidence of textual filiation will be described first, then discussed in the context of all known provenances.

---

1 Compare Edwards's method of assessing the readership of Higden: 'The Influence', p. 115.
2 Caldwell, 'Wace's *Roman*', p. 682.
3 Luscombe, *The School*, pp. 64–65.

Circulation

Where practicable, the circulation areas of the following groups have been plotted. The resulting maps may be found in Appendix III.

The First Variant

The First Variant has not received much attention here having recently been the subject of Neil Wright's full study.[4] Little can be added to the remarks of its editors and others. Jacob Hammer suggested that a Welsh redactor was responsible for the versions found in four manuscripts (55; 67, 70, and 106) and noted Welsh marginalia in one of them (67).[5] Three (55, 67, 70) contain a genealogy from the Trojans to the foundation of Britain which begins with Cyprus, son of *Ieuan*, and certainly has Welsh connections. These associations are reinforced by the identification of Whitland, West Glamorgan, as the house where Geoffrey's History and other texts were added to 70.[6] The only other religious house with which the First Variant may be associated happens also to belong to the same order: MS. 4, a mixed First- and Second-Variant text, was written by a *laicus* of Robertsbridge, Sussex. It is interesting in view of the perceived moralising tendency of the First Variant[7] that it should be associated with the Cistercians, whose libraries, in the early thirteenth century at least, have been described as narrower than those of other orders.[8]

Two manuscripts have Continental connections. Hammer reported that 55 may have been written on the Franco-German border, perhaps near Metz.[9] 163, dating from the later fourteenth century, was in the possession of the Jean le Bègue who, in 1411 and 1413, compiled inventories of the French royal library at the Louvre.[10] This manuscript may well have been copied on the Continent: the *Historia* is accompanied by the chronicle of Spain (to 1243) by Ximenes and a copy of Bede's History ultimately derived from an Italian archetype.

Apart from one late twelfth-century witness (106), extant copies of the First Variant belong to the later thirteenth and early fourteenth centuries. (There is no indication of the date of the exemplar from which MS. 1 was transcribed.)[11] This chronological distribution demonstrates the limitations of such information: we know that the First Variant was completed before Geoffrey's death in 1154 but

---

4 *The Historia*, II.
5 *Geoffrey*, pp. 18–19 and p. 6.
6 Beverley Smith, 'The "Chronica de Wallia" '.
7 See Morris, 'Uther and Igerne', p. 76.
8 Cheney, 'English Cistercian Libraries', p. 344.
9 *Geoffrey*, p. 8.
10 Hallaire, 'Quelques manuscrits', pp. 291–92.
11 It contains the Articles of Munster of 1310 but it is impossible to gauge how this part of the manuscript related to the rest.

the earliest manuscript dates from a generation or more after this and the bulk of the manuscripts from at least a century afterwards.[12]

The Second Variant

1. The β-group

The Second Variant has also remained peripheral in this study but, nevertheless, certain patterns within this group have been clarified, notably the cohesion between manuscripts of the β-subgroup. The distribution-area of this subgroup is correspondingly well defined. David Dumville has deduced from the text of the *Historia Brittonum* that MSS 54 and 80 originated in midland England.[13] This assertion receives support from other manuscripts in the subgroup. M. R. James noted references to East Anglian dependencies of St Albans on the flyleaves of 22[14] and the connection has since been reinforced by the identification of a marginal drawing within the manuscript as the work of the St Albans school of Matthew Paris.[15] 22, dating from the third quarter of the thirteenth century, may therefore be localized to the Eastern Midlands.

The two remaining β-manuscripts happen to be provenanced. Both were at Norwich Cathedral by the second quarter of the fourteenth century and both bear the names of monks (Roger[us] de Bliclingge, 50, and Galfrid[us] de Smalbergh, 114). They contain texts newly, or relatively newly, composed in East Anglia. 50 includes the *Summa* of Richard Wetherset, chancellor of the University of Cambridge in the mid-thirteenth century. The *Historia* in 114 constitutes the first book of three of the History written at Norwich in the 1290s by Bartholemew Cotton. This text was one manifestation of an awakening interest in history evident at Norwich at this time, in the aftermath of a fire which, in 1272, had destroyed many books and records.[16] Cotton drew on many sources, including the Chronicle of John of Wallingford, a monk of St Albans who retired to Wymondham,[17] one of the houses mentioned on the flyleaves of MS. 22. So it is possible to envisage the lines of communication between St Albans and Norwich by which the β-text travelled.

2. The α and γ groups

The survey has provided some, limited, clarification of the alpha and gamma categories of the Second Variant. It is clear from rubrics, book-divisions, and test-collations that the α-manuscripts cohere in a way in which the γ do not. The

---

12 Caldwell, 'Wace's *Roman*', pp. 675 and 682.
13 *Ex inf.* D. N. Dumville.
14 *A Descriptive Catalogue of the Western Manuscripts in the Library of Clare College*, p. 44.
15 Morgan, 'Matthew Paris', p. 90, n. 22, and p. 92.
16 Dodwell, 'History', pp. 40 and 42.
17 *Ibid.*, p. 46, but note that John's chronicle is not 'an abridgement of the work of Matthrew Paris', *ibid.*: see Vaughan, *The Chronicle*, pp. x–xii.

γ appear to be on the periphery without displaying any clear characteristics to link them as a group.

Manuscript-evidence throws some interesting light on this. Our only provenanced α-manuscripts – 66, 91, 95 – were all at Canterbury in the later Middle Ages, the only *Historia*-manuscripts known to be from there: 66 and 91 were at St Augustine's and 95 belonged to the Franciscan house. The provenanced γ-manuscripts are from Flanders. 202 (*saec.* xiv [1]) seems to have been written and to have remained near Saint-Bertin. 17 was recorded at the Cistercian abbey of Les Dunes in the 1640s.[18] 85, a manuscript not attributed to any subgroup, has an Early Modern provenance of Cambrai.

The appearance of clusters of manuscripts in these two areas is reminiscent of another, earlier diffusion of British pseudo-historical information (including *Mirabilia Britannie*). In the 1120s, Lambert of Saint-Omer used material about Britain in his *Liber floridus*; his source has been traced to a recension of the *Historia Brittonum* localizable to Kent, and particularly Canterbury.[19] There are two striking coincidences here. First, 95 is one of the Canterbury witnesses of this recension of the *Historia Brittonum*. Secondly, the Saint-Bertin manuscript, 202, includes *Mirabilia Brittonum*, the only identifiably Continental *Historia*-manuscript to do so. It also includes a text of Canterbury interest – a Life of Becket.[20]

The Double Dedications

1. Stephen-Robert

The early history of the Stephen-Robert manuscript, 15, and its relatives 86 and 200, has been discussed in detail by David Dumville.[21] They date between the late twelfth and mid-thirteenth centuries and two, 15 and 200, were apparently written at the Benedictine abbeys of Fécamp and Jumièges in Normandy.

2. Robert-Waleran

This better-represented form of double dedication does not signal an immediately definable textual type. Manuscripts bearing it sometimes agree, often resembling the text of Bern, but, in the chapters collated, have generally tended to remain featureless. Their relationship will only be clarified by fuller collation; but test-collations are sufficient to show that the dedication could be detached and grafted on to a different textual type. The manuscripts may none the less be discussed together, as witnesses to an unusual formula (much as interpolations were discussed above, IV), if not to a readily recognizable textual type.

None of the nine witnesses postdates the thirteenth century; the earliest may

18 Isaac, *Les Livres*, p. 285.
19 The Harleian recension: Dumville, 'The *Liber floridus*', p. 106.
20 On which see above, II. MSS 95 and 202 are two of the three *Historia*-manuscripts which include the letter of Prester John.
21 'An Early Text', especially pp. 16–18.

have been written in the third quarter of the twelfth. There are two provenanced manuscripts, from the northern English Cistercian houses Roche (128) and Jervaulx (136). Three others were certainly in England in the Middle Ages, having annotations in English hands or, in the case of MS. 134, a note of ownership. This belonged to a friar, *Guillelmus de Buria*, according to a fifteenth-century note.[22]

The Nameless Dedication

All but three of the thirty manuscripts bearing or presumed to have borne the nameless dedication belong to the twelfth or thirteenth centuries.[23] None has an Insular provenance. Six come from Continental Cistercian houses, three from Benedictine, two were in private hands abroad, and four have Continental associations. The only subgroup containing indisputably English manuscripts is that with vulgate connections.

1. 56, 58, 205

Fifteenth-century evidence places 56 in the Augustinian house of Marbach, near Basel, and 205 at Sankt Gallen (Benedictine), in the neighbouring diocese of Konstanz. Script and contents suggest that the manuscripts could well have been copied in that region.[24]

2. 20, 83, 126, (151,) 166, (173,) 175

MS. 126 has been associated with the Cistercian abbey of Pontigny (diocese of Auxerre) and 151 with Belle-Perche, a house of the same order in the county of Toulouse (diocese of Montauban).

3. 3, 14, 81, 168, 171, 183, 184, 189

183 and 184 both date from the second half of the twelfth century and originate from northern Benedictine houses: Saint-Vincent, Metz (Upper Lorraine), and Saint-Germain-des-Prés. 14 comes from a Cistercian house not far from Pontigny, Vauluisant (diocese of Sens). Three others – 3, 171, and 189 – have Continental associations.[25]

4. 36, 53, 127, 196, 208

Only one of these is provenanced: in the fifteenth century 208 was at Clairvaux (diocese of Sens), another Champenois Cistercian house.

---

22 Ker notes one dom Willelmus Bury, associated with the abbey of Bury St Edmunds *c.* 1435, but his epithet *monachus* and the different name-form impedes identification with the owner of MS. 134: *Medieval Libraries*, p. 233.

23 The exceptions being MSS 171 (*saec.* xiii/xiv), 182 (*saec.* xiv), and 168 (*saec.* xv).

24 See above, II: Prester John.

25 MSS 3 and 189 are written in Continental script; 171 contains a note in French.

5. 2, 19, 75, 132, 176

Three of these unclassified manuscripts are provenanced. 19 was given to the Belgian Cistercian house of St Bernardts opt Scheldt by one *magister Martinus de Lyra* according to a late thirteenth-century inscription. 75 belonged to the Cistercians of Salem (diocese of Konstanz). The margins of the first part of 132 contain letters written by W. de Bernham, a Scot who studied at Oxford and Paris in the mid-thirteenth century and later belonged to a 'circle of influential civil-servant ecclesiastics'.[26] The editors of the letters argue that they were composed in Britain rather than France[27] although there is no indication of where they were copied. The manuscript bears a sixteenth-century *ex libris* of St Martin's, Leuven.

6. 125, 182 + 105, 154, 214 (130, 180)

The connections of the single-dedication members of this group are exclusively with England. 105, like 130 and 214, contains an account of the foundation of Britain. It also bears fifteenth-century Latin annotations concerning the property of a Robert Grey, and a sixteenth-century English note. 214 is written in English script and has an eighteenth-century English provenance. 130 contains a chronicle in English and bears the *ex libris* of Valentine Leigh (dated 1560). 154 was in the hands of Thomas Hearne in the eighteenth century.

As for their nameless-dedication relatives, the Protogothic script of 125 is quite possibly English. The manuscript bears the Early Modern signature of one Thomas Norton. 182, which has been compared with these other manuscripts, has a different history. It is written in an early fourteenth-century cursive script which resembles that found in scholastic manuscripts. It was in the library of the counts of Milan by 1426.[28]

117/188 type

This group of eighteen manuscripts is overwhelmingly Continental, to judge from available evidence. Most date from the later twelfth, thirteenth, and fourteenth centuries, with four outliers from between *c.* 1400 and the sixteenth century.

1. 13, 16, 21, 59, 60, 117, 167, 188, 190, 211

These manuscripts are all from Flanders or northern France. Five come from Benedictine abbeys in a small area. 21 seems to have originated at Tournai (Saint-Martin), which was also the Early Modern home of MS. 190; 60 was at

---

26 Ker & Pantin, 'Letters', II.473. The nameless-dedication part of this manuscript and the opening section bearing the letters (containing histories by William of Malmesbury) are additions made 'in the hand of a professional scribe of the first half of the thirteenth century' (*ibid.*, II.472) to an original *pudibundus Brito* text. Ker & Pantin identified the hand of the added dedication as that of notes on the kings of France on 14r: *ibid.*

27 *Ibid.*, II.473.

28 Pellegrin, *La Bibliothèque*, pp. 155–56.

Marchiennes soon after it was written; 13 and 59 are provenanced on Early Modern evidence to Arras (Saint-Vaast) and Anchin. 13 almost certainly originated in the area: it contains the *Status imperii Iudaici*, a text largely confined to Flemish manucripts.[29] This work is also found in 16, which is again associated on Early Modern evidence with Arras: the Augustinian house of Mont-Saint-Eloi. The Flemish associations of *Status* are confirmed by the presence in 16 of a locally produced work, the *Historia succincta* of Andreas Syluius, house-historian of the neighbouring houses of Anchin and Marchiennes.[30]

One member of the subgroup has an early Cistercian provenance: 188 was at Chaalis (diocese of Senlis) by the late twelfth century. Two others have Premonstratensian contexts. A fifteenth-century note suggests Saint-Jean, Amiens, as the home of the twelfth-century MS. 167. 211 is located on Early Modern evidence at Vicoigne (diocese of Arras). This manuscript shares scribal verses with two manuscripts from the same diocese, 59 and 60.

2. 172, 174, 197, 198

Three of these date from the fourteenth century or later. None is provenanced. The script of 172 has been identified as Italian;[31] that of 197 also appears to be Continental. 198 contains a letter attributed to Henry of Hessen, which may suggest that it had Continental antecedents.

3. 7, 79, 135, 155, 213

The only manuscripts with British connections found in the 117/188 type belong to this subgroup. 7 and 135 contain prophecies relating to Britain and seem to have been written in Insular hands. 155, which, like them, contains the apocryphal letter of Arthur, is securely provenanced, having belonged to Hatfield Peverel, the dependency of St Albans, and later to St Albans itself. 213, the final witness to Arthur's letter, is a sixteenth-century manuscript containing material relating to the see of Würzburg and was owned, soon after copying, by an abbot of Spanheim. 79, identified as a manuscript on the periphery of this group, belonged, in Early Modern times, to the Cistercian house of Loos, Flanders.

Tres filios

Seventeen manuscripts of this type have been identified, none with Continental associations. The only securely provenanced manuscript is 32, which was sent to Thomas Austell, treasurer of Exeter Cathedral (1492–1515), with instructions to circulate it among the cathedral clergy.[32] Several others have British, or specifically English, contents or script.

---

29 See above, II: *Status*.
30 Werner, 'Andreas'.
31 France, 'Note', p. 414.
32 Letter of R. A. B. Mynors to the librarian of St John's College, Cambridge, 10.12.1950.

Their dates extend from the second half of the twelfth century to the fifteenth.

Pudibundus Brito

No members of this group show signs of Continental origin or provenance. 132 is a possible exception. It was in Leuven in the sixteenth century but would seem to have been in Britain even after the original text had been revised to nameless-dedication (above, Nameless dedication and IV, OMISSIONS: Prophecies).

Five of the seventeen were housed in Benedictine libraries. Two come from St Albans – 42 and 113 –, two from Durham – 93 and 150 –,[33] and one, 212, belonged to a canon of Southwell Cathedral. There is a sixth provenanced manuscript: 143 was owned by William de Dalton, abbot of the Cistercian house of Furness, Cumbria (1412–23).[34]

Witnesses of this type mostly date from the thirteenth to fifteenth centuries. There is one mid-twelfth-century witness, 156, and a seventeenth-century transcript, 31.[35]

Prologus/editio

This group has fifteen members ranging in date from the middle of the twelfth to the fifteenth centuries. They come from a variety of provenances but circulation again seems to have been restricted to the British Isles. The contents of 137 suggest some connection with Glastonbury. 74 was at the Brigettine abbey of Syon, Isleworth, in the early sixteenth century. 112 bears a late medieval *ex libris* of the Cistercian abbey of Margam, Glamorgan. Part of MS. 120 comes from Lanthony *secunda*, Gloucestershire (Augustinian),or possibly its Irish cell, Duleek, and 162 has been associated with the Benedictine priory at Tynemouth.[36] Another northern provenance is suggested by a document dated 1295 and issued in the name of Alexander de Pundsoneby, rector of the church of Kyrkam, Whithorn (? Kirkcolm, Stranraer), copied into MS. 87.[37]

Smaller groups of manuscripts

Those whose wider filiation has not been determined.

---

33 But the association of MS. 150 with Durham is Early Modern.
34 Hunt *et al.*, *A Summary Catalogue*, III.42.
35 Note that MS. 156, by far the earliest witness to the *pudibundus Brito* passage, bears the unique opening rubric (99r), 'Gaufridi Mon\u/tensis de gestis Britonum secundum Caratonum editio'.
36 Watson, *Medieval Libraries*, p. 66.
37 Described by Ward, *apud* Ward & Herbert, *Catalogue of Romances*, I.233. On *Kyrkhun* compare Johnston, *Place-names*, p. 228.

1. 38, 131; 99, 122

99 and 122 are datable *c*. 1300; 38 and 131 are fourteenth- and fifteenth-century. 122 and 131 contain no other contents and are unprovenanced. Chronicle-entries in MS. 99 show that it was written at the Benedictine abbey of St Benet's Hulme, Norfolk, and later belonged to the Augustinian canons of Hickling in the same county. 38 in the fifteenth century was at the Cistercian house of Whalley, Lancs.

2. 72, 133, 89, 160

These range in date from the later twelfth to the fourteenth centuries. The presence of Peter Langtoft's chronicle of the wars of Edward I in 133 (*saec*. xiv[1]) would suggest a northern English provenance.[38] 72 was listed in the fifteenth-century catalogue of the convent of S. Maria, Florence;[39] it bears the sixteenth-century inscription 'Abbatie florentine . . .'.

3. 5, 84, 124

These are all apparently English manuscripts. 84 was part of a collection made *c*. 1422 by John Strecche, a canon of Brooke, Rutland.[40] 124 (fourteenth-century) was owned in the fifteenth century by a chantry priest from St Anne's, Shaftesbury.
5 and 124 have no other contents.

4. 34, (147,) 152

These manuscripts all have English associations. 34 (*c*. 1200) was later at Wells Cathedral, Somerset. The binding of 147 is original and attributed to the 'Scales' binder, *c*. 1465. 152 dates from the first half of the fifteenth century. It is unprovenanced but script and contents suggest an English origin.

5. 76, 92, 97

This well-established group appears to have originated in Normandy (76 was catalogued at Le Bec in the 1160s) and subsequently to have migrated to England. Its latest representative, 97 (later fourteenth-century), is unprovenanced, but at some stage a fifteenth-century copy of Philip of Leicester's *Mandata Christi* (in English) was appended to the text.

6. 156, 161, 212

Fourteenth-century inscriptions associate 161 with the Benedictine alien priory of Eye, Suffolk, and 212 with a canon of Southwell Cathedral (see above,

---

[38] Compare Legge, *Anglo-Norman in the Cloisters*, pp. 72–73.
[39] Blum, *La Biblioteca della Badia*, pp. 140 and 168.
[40] On whom see Taylor, 'The Chronicle', pp. 138–39.

pudibundus Brito). There is no indication of the origin or provenance of 156, the earliest of the three manuscripts.

7. 23, 96

The script of both manuscripts indicates an English origin and date of about the third quarter of the twelfth century.

8. 40, 111

A late medieval inscription locates 111 (*c.* 1400) at the church of St Peter's, Cornhill. The provenance of 40 (later fourteenth-century) is disputed but the manuscript has been assigned to Glastonbury as it includes the rare *De excidio Britannie* of Gildas, a work known to have been at that house.[41]

9. 48, 128

These double-dedication manuscripts both date from the second half of the twelfth century. 128 bears the pressmark of the Cistercian abbey of Roche, Yorks. 48 has an Early Modern Welsh inscription and, it has been suggested, may have been in Wales earlier in its history.[42]

10. 71, 181

The striking visual resemblance between the rubrication of 71 and of the Le Bec manuscript, 76, suggests that 71 may also have originated in Normandy. Both date from about the mid-twelfth century. 71 had migrated to Florence (Franciscans) by the fourteenth century and belonged in 1633 to Santa Croce (of the same order). 181 (*c.* 1400) contains material relating to Florence (on 83va–84rb) but its first known home was the Visconti-Sforza library in Milan, where it was listed in 1426.

11. 78, 206

Both these apparently English manuscripts date from the fifteenth century. 78 was in the library of Richard III, king of England (1483–85), and evidently remained in the royal library at least until the seventeenth century as it also bears the signatures of James I, Charles I, and Oliver Cromwell.

12. 104, 194

The script of 194 suggests that it was written in France in the thirteenth century. 104 bears a scribal note stating that it was copied in 1349 by Albertus, *presbiter* of Diest, Brabant.

---

[41] James, Cambridge University Library manuscript notes; compare Watson, *Medieval Libraries*, p. 38.

[42] James, Cambridge University Library manuscript notes.

13. 107, 136

136 was copied in the late twelfth century and was at the Cistercian abbey of Jervaulx (Yorks.) by the thirteenth. 107 dates from *c.* 1200; it is unprovenanced. Both bear the Robert-Waleran dedication.

Medieval Provenances

These then are the networks of association indicated by this survey. In order to place them in context, information about the origins and provenances of extant *Historia*-manuscripts is listed below, together with references from medieval and Early Modern library catalogues (indicated in square brackets).

Institutions

A Augustinian, B Benedictine, Br Brigettine, C Cistercian, Cl Cluniac, D Dominican, P Premonstratensian S Savigniac.

1. Britain

?B Abingdon (*saec.* xiii/xiv) 88
B Battle (*c.* 1300) 108
[?Cl Bermondsey (1310–28)][43]
?D Boston (*saec.* xvi) 110[44]
[?A Bridlington (*saec.* xiii)][45]
A Bridlington (*saec.* xiv *in.*) 30
B Canterbury, St Augustine's (*saec.* xv) 66, 95
F Canterbury (*saec.* xiv) 91
??B Colchester (Early Modern) 92
S (post 1139; C post 1447) Dublin (*saec.* ?) 1
A Duleek (*saec.* xv) 120
Durham abbey (*saec.* ?) 93
B (alien priory) Eye (*saec.* xiv) 161
[?B Faversham (*saec.* xiii *ex.*)][46]
[?B Glastonbury (*c.* 1170)][47]
?B Glastonbury 40, 137
?Gonville & Caius College, Cambridge (*saec.* xv 2) 29

---

43 Denholm-Young, 'Edward', p. 441.
44 Included in a list sometimes erroneously attributed to John Leland: Carley: 'John Leland', p. 356.
45 Omont, 'Anciens Catalogues', p. 204; Ker, *Medieval Libraries*, p. 12. This catalogue has been attributed to a Cistercian library, however: Cheney, 'English Cistercian Libraries', p. 341.
46 Palgrave, *Documents*, p. 92.
47 Williams, *Somerset Mediaeval Libraries*, p. 50.

B Hatfield Peverel (*saec.* xv [in.]) 155
A Hickling (*saec.* xiv) 99
?B Hyde Abbey (*saec.* xiii) 6
C Jervaulx (*saec.* xiii) 136
?C Kirkstall (?s. xiii) 210
[?A Lanthony *secunda* (*saec.* xiv)][48]
A Lanthony *secunda* (*saec.* xv) 120
[A Leicester (*saec.* xv/xvi)][49]
London, church of St Peter's, Cornhill (*saec.* xv) 111
London, Hospital of St Thomas Acon, Cheapside (*saec.* xv) 115
C Margam (*saec.* xv) 112, ?48
[C Meaux (*saec.* xiv/xv)][50]
B Norwich (*saec.* xiv [in.]) 50, 114
[B Peterborough (*saec.* ?)][51]
?B Peterborough (*saec.* xiv) 24
[B Ramsey (*saec.* xiii [ex.])]
[C Rievaulx (*saec.* xiii)][52]
C Roche 128
[B Rochester (1202)][53]
B St Albans (*saec.* xiii) 22, 113; (*saec.* xv) 42, 155
B St Benet's Hulme (*saec.* xiii [ex.]) 99
Br Syon (1504 x 1526) 74
B Tynemouth 162
[P Titchfield (1400)][54]
B Wells (Leland) 34
[B Westminster (1672)][55]
C Whalley (*saec.* xv) 38
C Whitland Abbey (*c.* 1300) 70
[B Worcester (1622–23)][56]
Worcester (1327) 52
B Wymondham (*saec.* xiv) 22, (42,) 65
[A York (1372)][57]

48 Omont, 'Anciens catalogues', p. 222.
49 James, 'Catalogue of the Library of Leicester', p. 361.
50 Bell, 'The Books', pp. 66–67, 78.
51 James, *Lists of Manuscripts*, pp. 39, 63, 77.
52 James, *A Descriptive Catalogue of the Manuscripts in the Library of Jesus College*, p. 49.
53 Rye, 'Catalogue', p. 57.
54 Wilson, 'The Medieval Library', pp. 159, 273.
55 Robinson & James, *The Manuscripts*, p. 33.
56 Atkins & Ker, *Catalogus*, p. 54.
57 James, 'The Catalogue of the Library of the Augustinian Friars', p. 77.

2. Continental

P Amiens, Saint-Jean (*saec.* xv) 167
B Anchin (?) 59
B Arras, Saint-Vaast (1698) 13
[Avignon, Pope Boniface VIII][58]
C Belle-Perche (*saec.* xiii) 151
[P Bonne-Espérance (1641)][59]
Cambrai (Early Modern) 85
C Chaalis (*saec.* xii *ex.*) 188
C Clairvaux (*saec.* xv) 208
[Cl Cluny (1252)][60]
[Corbie (*saec.* xiii *in.*)][61]
[B *Eynhamensis*, ?Eenaeme (1641)][62]
?B Fécamp (*saec.* xii *ex.*) 15
S. Maria, Florence 72
F Florence (*saec.* xiv) 71
B Jumièges (*saec.* xiii *ex.*) 200
B Le Bec (*saec.* xii *med.*) 76
A Leuven, Val Saint-Martin (*saec.* xvi) 132
C Les Dunes (1641) 17
[?Cl Limoges (*saec.* xiii)][63]
C Loos (1644) 79
A Marbach 56
[B Marchiennes (*saec.* xii/xiii)][64]
B Marchiennes (*saec.* xiii *ex.*) 60
B Metz, Saint-Vincent 183
A Mont-Saint-Eloi (Early Modern) 16
[B Oudenburg (1641)][65]
C Pontigny (*saec.* xii) 126
C St Bernardts opt Scheldt (*saec.* xiii *ex.*) 19
?B Saint-Bertin (*saec.* xiv) 202
B Saint-Evroul (*saec.* xii) 12
B Sankt Gallen (*saec.* xv) 205
B Saint-Germain-des-Prés (*saec.* xii) 184
C Salem abbey (*saec.* xiii) 75

---

58 Faucon, *La Librairie*, II.14.
59 Sanderus, *Bibliothecae*, I.310.
60 *Inventaire des manuscrits de la Bibliothèque nationale, fonds de Cluni*, p. 374.
61 Delisle, *Le Cabinet*, II.438.
62 Sanderus, *Bibliothecae*, I.278.
63 Delisle, *Le Cabinet*, II.500.
64 Dehaisnes, *Catalogue général*, VI.767.
65 Sanderus, *Bibliothecae*, I.224.

[C Tournai, BVM de laude (1644)][66]
B Tournai, Saint-Martin (*saec.* xiii [1r]) 21, (1641) 190
C Vauluisant (*saec.* ?) 14
P Vicoigne (Early Modern) 211
[C Viller, BVM (1641)][67]
Würzburg, Schottenkloster (*saec.* xvii [in.])[68]

Private owners

1. Britain

Austell, Thomas, treasurer of Exeter Cathedral (1492–1515), volume given by
　Patrick for circulation among cathedral clergy 32
[Baldock, Ralph de, bishop of London (1313)][69]
[Bartholomeus and de Bratton, B Exeter (1327)][70]
Bernham, W. de (*saec.* xiii [med.]) 133
Blesocv, John (*saec.* xv) 57
Bliclingge, Roger[us] de, monk of Norwich (*saec.* xiv [in.]) 50
Buria, Guillelmus de, friar (*saec.* xv) 134
Cole, Iohannes, bought MS. from *domnus Iohannes Clerk* (*saec.* xv) 137
Couton, Helias de, canon of Southwell (*saec.* xiv) 212
Dalton, *frater* [ ] de, abbot of Furness (1412–1423) 143
[Erghom, John, Augustine friar of York (*saec.* xiv [med.])][71]
London, Iohannes de, gave manuscript to St Augustine's, Canterbury
　(*saec.* xiv) 66
Mablethorpe, John, fellow of Lincoln College, Oxford (*saec.* xv [med.]), scribe
　of 33
More, John, bought MS. from *magister* Thomas Quirk (*saec.* xv) 137
?Neville, George (1470–77) 140
Populton, Robert, Carmelite friar at Hulne (Northumb.), compiler of 164
Richard III, king of England (1483–85) 78
Richardus ap Robert cantarist. sancte Anne infra monesterium (sic) Sheftonie
　(*saec.* xv) 124
Shenley, Edmund, monk of St Albans 42
Smalbergh, Galfrid[us] de, monk of Norwich (*saec.* xiv) 114
Spycer, Henricus, canon of Windsor (*saec.* xv) 115
Strecche, John, canon of cellula of Brooke, Rutland (*saec.* xv [1]), compiler of
　84
?Walmesford, Thomas (*saec.* xv) 118

66 *Ibid.*, II.118.
67 *Ibid.*, I.271.
68 Thurn, *Die Handschriften*, II.136.
69 Cavanaugh, 'A Study', I.64–65.
70 Oliver, *Lives*, p. 305.
71 James, 'The Catalogue of the Library of the Augustinian Friars', p. 35.

Waynflete, Guido de, *frater* (*saec.* xiv) 100
Wherton, Iohannes, de Kirkebythore (*saec.* xv/xvi) 93
Wodecherche, William de, *laicus* of (C) Robertsbridge (*saec.* xiii [2]), scribe of 4
Wolston, Reginald de, canon of Hereford (1396–1411), see 11

2. Continental

Albertus, priest of Diest, *filius Iohannis* (1349), scribe of 104
[Philippe de Harcourt, bishop of Bayeux (*saec.* xii *med.*)][72]
[Henry I, count of Champagne (1127–81, library as extant 1319–20)][73]
Le Bègue, Jean (*saec.* xv *in.*) 163
[Philippe de Lévis, bishop of Mirepoix (1466–1537)][74]
Lyra, Martinus de, *magister* 19
Tritemius, *Ioannes*, *abbas* (of Spanheim, diocese of Mainz) 213[75]
Visconti-Sforza, counts of Milan 181, 182

This list indicates a number of areas of interest. Those outside the jurisidiction of the English king will be considered first.

Low Countries

The largest single concentration of *Historia*-manuscripts anywhere (boosted by catalogue-references)[76] is, surprisingly enough, in the Low Countries. These represent at least four textual varieties. Members of the main subgroup of the 117/188 type mostly cluster around the dioceses of Arras and Tournai, with two outliers in northern France: Amiens and Chaalis (diocese of Senlis). The two localizable Second-Variant γ-manuscripts are Flemish. A nameless-dedication manuscript, 19, belonged to a Cistercian house near Antwerp and another was at Leuven by the sixteenth century. A vulgate manuscript of different type (104) was written in nearby Diest.

Even though the development and relationship of the branches of the *Historia*-text have yet to be established, this concentration of textual varieties can hardly be explained by genealogical connection: several of these groups were evidently better established in other areas at an earlier date. Texts must therefore have been obtained from a number of sources.

Extant manuscripts suggest a context for this process. The Belgian nameless-dedication witness, 19, was donated in the thirteenth century by a University man

---

72 Dumville, 'The Early History', p. 24.
73 Stirnemann, 'Quelques bibliothèques', p. 22.
74 Pellegrin, 'Possesseurs', p. 291.
75 Compare Fletcher, *The Arthurian Material*, p. 239.
76 Bonne-Espérance, Corbie, Eenaeme, Marchiennes, Oudenburg, Tournai, Viller.

(*magister*), perhaps connected with the schools of Liège or Tournai. His name, *de Lyra*, perhaps suggests Norman origin (Lyre).[77]

The earliest associations of the 117/188 type are with histories, concerning remote as well as local subjects, written at certain Benedictine houses in this area in the later twelfth and thirteenth centuries. Two *Historia*-texts are found in early and authoritative manuscripts of local products, those of Hermann of Tournai and Andrew of Marchiennes (and Anchin).[78] Association with the best and oldest copy of Hermann is intriguing in view of Hermann's famous (and possibly fabricated) report in another work concerning pre-Galfridian Arthurian stories in England.[79] A contemporary of Hermann's at the same house (Saint-Martin) has been credited with the composition of *Status imperii Iudaici*,[80] a work particularly associated with Geoffrey's History as we have seen (above, II: *Status*). Such Benedictine histories reached the houses of other orders – the earliest extant manuscript of *Status* is Cistercian[81] – but the version of the *Historia* sometimes accompanying them is associated with other houses only on late evidence.

There are several indications of why Geoffrey's History should have been so popular in the Low Countries. The area, perhaps because of its political import-ance, impinged on Geoffrey's consciousness sufficiently for him to have included in his History the Flemings, in the guise of the *Ruteni*, under their count, Holdinus.[82] Tastes in history in the region were far from provincial as the circulation of a work on so remote a subject as *Status* shows. Arthurian stories seem to have been known before Geoffrey: apart from the material included by Lambert and Hermann, Arthurian names have been found in charters of *c*. 1120.[83] There was prolonged lay interest in British material in vernacular form. Chrétien de Troyes wrote *Le Conte du Graal* for Philip, count of Flanders; Lambert of Ardres in the thirteenth century, using works from his nearby collegiate church, enlivened his history of the Flemish counts with tales of the Holy Land, France, and Britain; in his *Spiegel Historiael*, commissioned *c*. 1284 by Floris V, count of Holland and Zeeland, Jacob van Maerlant used Latin sources to correct British history and inform his account of the princely virtues of Arthur.[84] The *Historia* could have been known to these authors. Jacob drew on it indirectly, making use of the *Auctarium Ursicampinum*, compiled between 1155 and 1200 by a monk of the Cistercian house of Ourscamp (diocese of Noyon), from the Chronicle of Sigebert of Gembloux and Geoffrey among other sources.[85]

---

77 In the late eleventh century, Odo, bishop of Bayeux, was dispatching clerks to Liège to be educated: Bezzola, *Les Origines*, II.405.
78 MSS 21 and 16. Boutemy, 'Note', p. 66; Werner, 'Andreas', p. 406.
79 Chambers, pp. 18, 249; Loomis, *Wales*, p. 180; Faral, *La Légende*, I.225–33.
80 Boutemy, 'Note', p. 69.
81 From Aulne: Boutemy, 'Une Copie nouvelle', p. 196.
82 For example, *Historia*, §172. See Tatlock, *The Legendary History*, pp. 95–96.
83 Derolez, 'King Arthur', p. 245.
84 *Ibid.*, p. 244; Duby, 'The Culture', p. 261; and Gerritsen, 'Jacob', pp. 368 & 379–80.
85 *Ibid.*, p. 379. Herbert of Bosham withdrew to Ourscamp and wrote his biography of Becket there: Hamel, 'Manuscripts', p. 39.

Champagne

Geoffrey's History found an early place in another area famous for secular Arthurian compositions, Champagne – in three Cistercian libraries and that of Count Henry I of Champagne, on whose court the literary movement centred and to whose wife, Marie, Chrétien is known to have dedicated work. Unfortunately Henry's manuscript is untraced and so its text cannot be compared with the others, all of which bear the nameless dedication. It is not inconceivable that there should have been a connection. Boundaries between secular and clerical culture, vernacular and Latin, were far from sharply defined:[86] a monk of Cîteaux has been identified as the author of one vernacular Grail romance.[87]

The count's collection included patristics, Classics, and numerous Latin histories,[88] some doubtless acquired by means of his exceptional scholarly and ecclesiastical connections, particularly with Englishmen. Henry was a correspondent of John of Salisbury and a patron of Herbert of Bosham (from whom he sought books) and of Thomas Becket, who spent two years in exile at Pontigny (1164–66).[89] Pontigny happens to be the other certainly twelfth-century Champenois home of the *Historia*. Late evidence associates other twelfth-century manuscripts with its Cistercian neighbours Vauluisant and Clairvaux.

The presence of the *Historia* in Henry's library is intriguing because of its proximity to romance-writers like Chrétien.[90] Certainly we have little evidence that the courts of Champagne, like those of Flanders, fostered vernacular history.[91] John F. Benton argued that authors spent comparatively little time at court and that 'the importance of direct personal contact was probably slight'. Such men drew on Latin works, such as the Gospel of Nicodemus,[92] but at least one critic has been adamant that Geoffrey was not known to romance-writers: various internal factors made it unlikely that they, 'especially those who were clerics, had been familiar with Geoffrey and Wace'.[93] These arguments, proposed by Loomis, were intended to counter claims made by Tatlock and others that the *Historia* was a significant element in the formulation of Arthur-stories.[94] Tatlock had allowed that Geoffrey was ignored by romancers but considered that ' "he helped give them an audience or vogue" '.[95]

There is something to be said for Tatlock's surmise. It seems anomalous that

---

86 The courtly audience had a clerical element: Benton, 'The Court', p. 590.
87 See Loomis, *The Development*, pp. 101–2. Legge noted that the *Speculum caritatis* of Aelred of Rievaulx, again a Cistercian, influenced the Grail legend: 'Gautier', p. 621.
88 Stirnemann, 'Quelques bibliothèques', p. 22; Williams, 'William', pp. 365–66.
89 Thompson, *The Literacy*, p. 142–43; Mare *et al.*, 'Pietro', p. 223.
90 See Benton, 'The Court'.
91 Tyson, 'Patronage', p. 188.
92 In the Romance of the Grail by Robert de Boron: Bozóky, 'Les Apocryphes', pp. 436–37.
93 Loomis, *Wales*, p. 218.
94 For example, Tatlock, 'The Dates', pp. 357–58; Parry, 'Geoffrey of Monmouth and the Paternity'.
95 Quoted by Loomis, *Wales*, p. 217.

while Chrétien may have used a private library in Flanders[96] he had no contact with that of Henry of Champagne when he wrote for Marie. It is curious that Flemish counts should have commissioned histories in Latin[97] when their southern neighbours, with whom there were many feudal and family links,[98] should have been so indifferent to the past. If this difference between Flemish and Champenois tastes is real, and not produced by uneven evidence, then it deserves investigation. There are signs, however, that it could be modified: Guido de Bazoches, canon of Châlons, wrote a world history and, in his letters, digressed on the ancestry of Count Henry.[99]

Remainder of France

No areas within the jurisdiction of the French king other than Champagne contain a real concentration of evidence. Two extant nameless-dedication manuscripts appear to come from the Midi.[100] There are, besides, thirteenth-century references to manuscripts at Cluny and Limoges but we know, thanks to the testimony of Richard of Poitou,[101] that the text reached Aquitaine in the 1160s, when that region was still part of the Anglo-Norman kingdom.

Germany

Nameless-dedication manuscripts are found in houses of various orders in Western Germany: two in the diocese of Konstanz, one at Marbach (diocese of Basel), another further North at Metz. The only other witness with German associations is the sixteenth-century 117/188 type manuscript owned and used by the historian, Iohannes Tritemius.

Italy

Five manuscripts have Italian associations. 71 was possibly written in Normandy in the twelfth century and migrated to Florence, perhaps in the hands of the friars; 181, its descendant, has Florentine material and belonged to the Visconti-Sforza library, Milan. 182 was listed there too but may have originated in France. 72 has an Early Modern provenance of Florence but at least one English relative. 172 was apparently written in Italy.

---

96   Holmes, 'The Arthurian Tradition', p. 102.
97   For example, Lambert of Ardres wrote 1194–98 for Baldwin of Ardres: *ibid.*, p. 100.
98   Compare Huon d'Oisy, castellan of Cambrai, viscount of Meaux: Benton, 'The Court', p. 577.
99   *Ibid.*, pp. 572–73.
100   MSS 81, 151.
101   Fletcher, *The Arthurian Material*, pp. 171–72. I am grateful to Professor Michael Reeve for drawing my attention to this chronicle.

Normandy

All *Historia*-manuscripts attributed to Normandy date from the first century of transmission, and perhaps before the duchy was lost to the English king in 1204. All are associated with Benedictine houses.[102] Representatives of the Bern group were found at Fécamp and Jumièges, one of the Leiden group was at Le Bec (*c.* 1160), and a *Merlinus iste* manuscript, containing only the second half of the text, belonged to Saint-Evroul. The text of the *Historia Brittonum* has suggested some connection between first the two groups[103] but the Saint-Evroul manuscript seems to be unrelated to them.

Britain

Particular textual types have been found in certain areas: the First Variant in Wales, the Second Variant α in Canterbury and the β-group in the Eastern Midlands, the double dedication in Yorkshire. These observations can now be extended.

It is clear that the vulgate was circulating in the Eastern Midlands at the same time as the Second Variant. 99, whose text is related to a witness later at Whalley, Lancashire, belonged to a Benedictine and later an Augustinian house in Norfolk in the late thirteenth and early fourteenth centuries. It contains the only known copy of a chronicle used by Bartholomew Cotton,[104] who was working at Norwich in the 1290s (and using a Second-Variant *Historia*). At about this time, a different kind of vulgate text was copied at Wymondham, Norfolk (65). Two other unrelated manuscripts were in the area in the fourteenth century: MS. 161 at Eye and 24 at Peterborough (the identification is not certain). This variety of texts suggest that the work was readily available. The four extant copies from St Albans demonstrate this, too. Two contain the *pudibundus Brito* version but there is also a Second-Variant β-witness and a 117/188 type.

The list of Yorkshire Cistercian houses owning early copies of Geoffrey's History may be expanded. The catalogue of Rievaulx includes a *Historia Britonum*; annotations in a single-dedication manuscript indicate Northern interest *c.* 1200, and perhaps association with Kirkstall.[105] The manuscripts from Roche and Jervaulx provide the only provenanced examples of the double dedication. Continental Cistercian houses in the same period are known only to have owned copies bearing the nameless dedication, whose text is not known to be connected to the double-dedication type.

The Yorkshire associations of the Robert-Waleran dedication raise a second issue: the significance of the dedication after presentation. The earliest recorded appearance of the *Historia* in Yorkshire is in the possession of Walter Espec

---

102 But this imbalance perhaps reflects the thoroughness of Nortier's work on these libraries (*Les Bibliothèques*) rather than any historical reality.
103 Dumville, 'An Early Text', pp. 5–6.
104 Dodwell, 'History', p. 46.
105 Levison, 'A Combined Manuscript', pp. 44–49.

(above, n. 2). Another copy was in the hands of Alfred of Beverley not long afterwards.[106] Walter appears to have had a particular interest in the *matière de Bretagne* and possibly passed on Geoffrey's work to David, king of Scotland.[107] Powicke speculated that Espec's interest brought Arthurian material to the attention of Aelred of Rievaulx,[108] via whom it might have reached other Cistercian houses in a manner comparable with the circulation of the nameless dedication among Continental Cistercian houses. The transmission of the *Historia*, however, offers no justification for regarding Espec as the source for a Northern Cistercian text. In the first place, the extant witnesses are not textually homogeneous. Secondly, it seems unlikely that the version obtained by Walter from Robert of Gloucester would have included the dedication to Robert's enemy, Waleran. It seems reasonable to assume that the Waleran-Robert text was obtained from a source other than Espec himself via Rievaulx.

There is a parallel instance where dedications do not conform to expectation: the version of the *Historia* at Le Bec. A copy was bequeathed to that house by Philippe de Harcourt, 'Waleran [of Meulan]'s clerical *protégé*',[109] but our extant manuscript, at that house in the 1160s, is dedicated to Robert alone.[110] One of two deductions can be made: that the dedication was so little regarded that copies circulated among the associates of Robert and Waleran bearing the rival dedication, or, more probably, that the text was sufficiently widely available for extant copies to have been derived from sources other than those known from literary references to have been in the immediate locality.

There is strong evidence for continuing interest in the *Historia* in Northern England. Copies were at the Cistercian houses of Furness, Whalley, and Meaux in the fifteenth century. In the fourteenth, two were at Augustinian houses at York and Bridlington. Two others have associations with the extreme North: Tynemouth and perhaps Hulne (MS. 164). Other concentrations are apparent. Several copies were in the London area in the late Middle Ages (in two churches and at the monasteries of Bermondsey, Syon, and perhaps Westminster). Some belonged to houses in the South and West of Britain: at Winchester, Lanthony *secunda*, Exeter, and, at an early date, Glastonbury. In the Western Midlands, copies were found at Leicester, Southwell, Kenilworth. Extant manuscripts suggest that a variety of texts was available in each of these areas.

Type of ownership

Monasteries constitute the largest single group of owners, as might have been expected given the circumstances of manuscript-survival. Benedictine houses,

---

106 Taylor, *Medieval Historical Writing*, p. 7.
107 From about 1142, David's charters use the Galfridian phrase *castellum puellarum* for Edinburgh: Legge, 'Gautier', p. 621.
108 *The Life*, p. lxxxviii.
109 Crouch, *The Beaumont Twins*, p. 208. See also p. 45.
110 As Dumville observed: 'An Early Text', p. 23.

particularly in England, seem to have been particularly important in the transmission of the work, as one might have anticipated. St Albans, bastion of historical studies in the later Middle Ages, owned four copies at various times. The large number of early Cistercian provenances, notably on the Continent, is more surprising. In explanation one may note the rapidity with which texts were disseminated between Continental Cistercian houses,[111] the connection of certain English intellectual figures with such foundations and the interest of English Cistercians in history.[112] There is little indication that Geoffrey's own order, the Augustinians, were instrumental in the work's diffusion.

Two copies were in private hands on the Continent very early but the evidence thereafter is patchy. The English situation is rather the reverse. Private owners only begin to appear in the early fourteenth century but from then until the early sixteenth century a large number of owners are known. These are predominantly monks or clergy.

There are indications that the *Historia* circulated outside the strictly monastic and aristocratic orbit: a number of manuscripts have scholastic associations, as did Geoffrey himself. Apart from the nameless-dedication manuscript donated by *magister Martinus* and another containing the letters of a Scottish scholar, MS. 182 appears to have been written in a scholastic hand and 180 contains a school-text, William of Ockham's *Summa logica*. Literature certainly found an audience in such circles. The *Alexandreis*, composed by Walter de Châtillon (former clerk at the English royal court) and dedicated to the younger brother of Henry of Champagne, has been described as 'a great favorite in the schools, even supplanting the classics themselves'.[113] Geoffrey's Prophecies attracted the attention of the scholar John of Cornwall, who had studied at Paris under Peter Lombard and Robert de Melun and who wrote a commentary on them for another *magister*, Thierry de Chartres.[114]

Popularity

Manuscript-evidence indicates that interest in the *Historia* was at its height in the twelfth century (fifty-eight witnesses) and remained strong until the beginning of the fifteenth, when it began to decline.[115] Only five manuscripts postdate the appearance of the first edition in 1508.

The provenanced manuscripts produce distinct distribution-patterns. Of those owned by Continental institutions, fifteen are twelfth-century, four from *c.* 1200, seven thirteenth-century and four fourteenth-century. The equivalent sample from England divides differently: only six are twelfth-century, four date from *c.* 1200, four are thirteenth-century but ten are fourteenth-century. If we transfer the

---

111 Leclercq, 'La Diffusion', pp. 22–24.
112 Cheney, 'English Cistercian Libraries', pp. 339–40.
113 Williams, 'William', pp. 374–75; Bezzola, 'Les Origines', II.517.
114 Fleuriot, 'Les fragments', p. 44.
115 *Saec.* xii/xiii, 23 manuscripts; *saec.* xiii, 37; *saec.* xiii/xiv, 15; *saec.* xiv, 40; *saec.* xiv/xv, 9; *saec.* xv, 26.

Norman manuscripts from the Continental list the English figures become eight for the twelfth century (against thirteen on the Continent) and five for *c*. 1200 (three on the Continent).

While the processes of survival make it dangerous to place too much weight on these figures, continuing, apparently even increasing, popularity of the *Historia* in England is evident.

Conclusions

This discussion shows the extensiveness of the *Historia*'s popularity on the Continent, where interest largely concentrated in the region of Flanders with lesser patches in Normandy and Champagne. Two substantial groups of manuscripts, many of them early, have overwhelmingly Continental connections. These are the nameless-dedication manuscripts (with the exception of a subgroup including single-dedication witnesses), and the 117/188 type (again except for one subgroup). The only known provenances of the Stephen-Robert dedication group are Norman. Two pairs of manuscripts have exclusively Continental associations.

Conversely there are several groups which our present evidence suggests to be predominantly English: manuscripts bearing the Robert-Waleran dedication, the *pudibundus Brito* type, the β-version of the Second Variant, besides four smaller groups and four pairs of manuscripts. The First Variant survives in Welsh and Continental manuscripts. Two smaller groups also seem to have mixed Insular/Continental provenances (MSS 72, 133, 89, 160, and 76, 92, 97).

X

RECEPTION

So far this study has largely been concerned with the immediate circumstances in which Geoffrey's History was transmitted, a subject hardly separable from the broader question of how the *Historia* was regarded and used, which will now be addressed. Works associated with the History provide a starting point for such an investigation.

Thanks to the evidence of test-collations, the original list of associated contents presented in Chapter II can now be sorted: material which was evidently transmitted together with the *Historia* can be distinguished from repeated patterns of association not explained by the filiation of Geoffrey's History. The apparently non-inherited or rather repeatedly observed connections suggest the natural affinity of certain subject-areas with Geoffrey's History. This is indisputable when different works of similar nature accompany Geoffrey's History.

Such apparently non-inherited associations are of various kinds (a list may be found in Appendix III). There are numerous histories dealing with Troy, Alexander, the Crusades, the East, Britain, not to mention Universal histories, local and monastic chronicles from England and the Continent, chronologies, genealogies, and origin-stories. Texts concerning the geography (often marvellous) of Britain, the East, and the World as a whole also appear. Legal texts are found in *Historia*-manuscripts. Less obviously apposite texts include well circulated devotional literature (including hagiography) and a significant quantity of apocrypha and apocalyptic. Prophecy and wisdom literature are also associated with the *Historia*.

These associations must be handled with caution. Works could become associated purely by chance. Even when a scribe or compiler deliberately selected the contents of a manuscript, his choice may have been determined not by the works' compatibility but by convenience or availability. On the other hand, association which is repeated without textual explanation is unlikely to be purely accidental; the quantity of material available for Geoffrey permits some degree of confidence. To be made to yield their full results, the associated classes just described must be compared with profiles of the works accompanying other histories, information which is as yet unavailable. A few associations are sufficiently marked, nevertheless, to deserve comment, however one-dimensional.

Many *Historia*-manuscripts (from the twelfth century to the fifteenth) contain serious histories, both Insular and Continental, and sometimes historical collections.[1] Although this association cannot be interpreted as suggesting that the *Historia* was accepted wholeheartedly as historical,[2] it does imply that the work was considered to have some factual foundation and value as a source. We may note that even Geoffrey's critics were sometimes prepared to make limited use of his material.[3]

Stronger indications of Geoffrey's historical credibility may be inferred from the association of the *Historia* with texts relating to the debate about the lordship of Scotland.[4] Walter Ullmann noted twenty-five years ago the indebtedness to Geoffrey of the letter of Edward I to Pope Boniface VIII (1301) in which he laid out his claim to Scotland.[5] This formed the second phase of a royal propaganda campaign: the first had been launched in 1291 when Edward had appealed to religious houses for information relevant to his case.[6] The *Historia* had been conspicuously absent on this occasion perhaps, it has been suggested, because of historical scruples.[7] The inclusion of Edward's letter in two *Historia*-manuscripts, in the original hand in one instance,[8] and of other documents relating to the claim,[9] seems to suggest that, although the propagandists did not cite Geoffrey by name, the work was not generally considered entirely disreputable.

The *Historia* evidently had an affinity with crusading histories. This perhaps reflects audience. One would imagine that crusading material particularly appealed to the laity – many members of noble families, especially in France and Flanders, had taken the Cross. 'An enthusiasm for the crusading exploits of Charlemagne', 'at first restricted to a small group of uneducated knights', has been identified by Ian Short as one element in the success of the *Historia Turpini* in twelfth-century France.[10] Short's discussion focussed on the vernacular Turpin, however. As with Arthurian literature, there were in addition to the vernacular works various Latin texts in circulation which may have attracted an audience of a different sort. Little work seems to have been done on the readership of such literature.[11]

Classical pseudo-histories, especially those of Troy and Alexander, may be found in English and Continental *Historia*-manuscripts, primarily of the fourteenth century or earlier. The degree of historical credence attached to Classical

---

1 See MS. 200.
2 Compare Gerritsen, 'L'Episode', pp. 344–45. It was also the subject of parody by Walter Map (*De Nugis curialium*, ii.17): see Brooke, *apud* James, *Walter Map*, pp. xxxix–xli.
3 Fletcher, *The Arthurian Material*, pp. 179–82 and 185–91. see also Crick, 'Geoffrey'.
4 See Appendix IV.
5 'On the Influence', p. 267.
6 Gransden, *Historical Writing*, I.441–42; Guenée, 'L'Enquête'.
7 Stones & Simpson, *Edward I*, I.138 and 148; Guenée, 'L'Enquête', p. 579.
8 MS. 133; in MS. 24 in a fourteenth-century collection appended to an earlier manuscript.
9 MSS 135 and 150.
10 Short, 'The Pseudo-Turpin', p. 19.
11 Tatlock noted Geoffrey's own interest in the Crusades: 'Certain contemporaneous matters'.

pseudo-histories in the Middle Ages remains an open question[12] but it was probably not inconsiderable. Alexander was a historical figure, after all; the medieval reader had few means of detecting that the legend of Troy was not also based on historical fact.[13]

It is noticeable that *Historia*-manuscripts containing Histories such as those of Bede, Henry of Huntingdon, William of Malmesbury, and Higden rarely include Classical pseudo-histories,[14] but this may reflect their Insular subject-matter rather than their perceived historical authority. French historians had claimed Trojan origins for their nation from the time of Fredegar.[15] The myth was still potent in the fifteenth century, when French propagandists aimed to score political points by claiming that the Britons had forfeited their Trojan lineage and their hegemony when the Saxons invaded.[16] It has even been suggested that French sympathy with Scotland and Ireland was founded not only on a community of interest but on a perceived common descent.[17] Even the descendants of the Scandinavian settlers of Normandy claimed Trojan ancestry.[18] Geoffrey had given the Anglo-Normans a stake in an increasingly important game: legitimation of political power by appeal to the heritage of Antiquity.[19] To avoid suggestions of past subjection to Rome, one appealed directly to the ancestors of the Romans, the Trojans.[20] Lee Patterson has noted the popularity at Henry II's court of vernacular epics on Classical themes.[21] The Trojans feature in genealogies and origin-legends which travel with *Historia*-manuscripts, a genre stoked by the *Historia* itself.[22]

The Alexander-legend was put to a number of uses. Cary's study of the legend concentrated on its moral and didactic value: how, much like certain Roman histories, the subject-matter provided a theatre for the portrayal of moral issues,[23] especially those concerning the exercise of power. It is possible that Geoffrey's History served a similar purpose. It is associated with wisdom literature, including the textbook for kingship, *Secreta Secretorum*; G. R. Owst's study of preaching *exempla* provides two instances of the use of Arthurian material, one quite

---

12 Chronicles and histories hardly feature in the main study of the medieval attitude to Alexander: Cary, *The Medieval Alexander*. See, however, Bunt, 'Alexander'.

13 Compare Crick, 'Geoffrey'.

14 Only in MSS 32, 70, 83, 92, 163. A similar trend emerges when the early circulation of the *Historia* is compared with that of the histories of Henry of Huntingdon and William of Malmesbury.

15 And onwards: see Bossuat, 'Les Origines troyennes'.

16 Curley, 'Fifteenth-century Glosses', pp. 336–37; Bossuat, 'Les Origines troyennes'.

17 Bossuat, *ibid.*, p. 197.

18 Searle, 'Fact', p. 125.

19 Compare the revival of the Roman senate in the twelfth century: Benson, 'Political *Renouatio*', pp. 340–59.

20 On the rationale of such appeals to the Classical and Trojan past see Southern, 'Aspects . . . 3', pp. 189–90.

21 *Negotiating the Past*, pp. 158–59, 202.

22 Compare Matter, *Englische Gründungssagen*, pp. 234–47.

23 Compare Smalley on Sallust: *Historians*, pp. 19–20.

possibly taken from Geoffrey.[24] The text evidently reached appropriate circles: MS. 124 belonged to a priest, and a document concerning the rector of a Scottish parish is copied into MS. 87.

Alexander was more than a figure of historical myth. He presented a supreme model of power and empire, extending even to the eschatological: the Alexander who confines Gog and Magog until the Last Times. We have already seen how Alexander-texts are often accompanied by the Pseudo-Methodian Revelations and stories of Antichrist (above, II). While there is evidently considerable justice in setting side by side the stories of two secular heroes[25] – Geoffrey's Arthur may anyway be modelled on Alexander[26] – it is not impossible that the apocalyptic resonances of Alexander's story extended to Geoffrey's work.[27] Non-Galfridian narratives about Arthur attribute to him a messianic function. Perhaps the presence of Merlin in the *Historia* imparts a similar atmosphere. Whatever the explanation, association with widely maintained eschatological stories suggests that that work was regarded as far from frivolous.

Prophecy, which often carried a comparable apocalyptic message – the Sibylline material, for example[28] –, forms another well represented class of associated material. This is not unexpected. The figure of Merlin was too compelling to be ignored. His mysterious prophecies gain validity within the *Historia* by the ancient technique of masking history as prophecy,[29] but at the same time they remained largely open to interpretation, a challenge undertaken from time to time by commentators, professional and amateur (above, III: Commentaries). This material constituted 'matter of grave concern to serious and practical men', deriving cogency and intellectual respectability from its Biblical roots[30] and from its interpretation by charismatic public figures such as Joachim of Fiore. Prophecy impinged on large and vital issues – the threat of Islam after the fall of Jerusalem in 1187[31] and, later, the Black Death.[32]

Prophetic and apocalyptic texts suggest a certain milieu. According to R. W. Southern, 'The keenest students of Merlin ... were University men with intellectual aspirations'.[33] Similarly, it was the 'well-educated and well-situated clerical

---

24 The depiction of the Virgin on Arthur's shield (compare §147) is mentioned in a vernacular sermon; a Latin work describes the story of Vortigern's tower, beginning 'Lego in gestis Britonum': *Literature and Pulpit*, p. 161 and n. 2. For *Gesta Britonum* as a title for the *Historia*, see above, VI.

25 Nykrog, 'The Rise', pp. 596–97; for later associations see Matthews, *The Tragedy*, pp. 33–39, 66–67. Compare the association with material about Charlemagne (*Historia Turpini*, Einhard).

26 Compare Tatlock, *The Legendary History*, pp. 312–14.

27 On the apocalyptic element in Geoffrey's History itself, see Roberts, 'Geoffrey of Monmouth', p. 40.

28 Southern, 'Aspects ... 3', pp. 166–68.

29 Compare McGinn, *Visions*, p. 7.

30 Southern, 'Aspects ... 3', pp. 168 and 162–77.

31 *Ibid.*, pp. 174–75.

32 Lerner, 'Western European Eschatological Mentalities', p. 78.

33 'Aspects ... 3', p. 168.

intelligentsia' who were able to exploit prophecy and apocalyptic for political and religious purposes:[34] the political commentary which passed as the prophecy of John of Bridlington was composed by an Augustinian canon. Vaticination was a convenient vehicle for political messages. Sibylline prophecies were being exploited in thirteenth-century France to boost the royal prestige of Philip Augustus.[35] The figure of Merlin, which gained widespread acceptance in Europe,[36] acquired an increasingly political importance. The Galfridian Merlin-prophecies appeared on an English dynastic roll *c.* 1250.[37] Merlin became a pawn in the propaganda war between England and France in the fifteenth century. Christine de Pisan claimed that Merlin had predicted the success of Joan of Arc; Jean Brehal turned prophecies found 'in historia Bruti' to a similar purpose.[38]

Alexander-stories have another facet: Alexander's journeys to the East. Tatlock suggested that the marvellous geography of the East supplied by Alexander-texts inspired the *mirabilia* found in Geoffrey.[39] This may be an over-simplification – the *Historia Brittonum* is a more obvious source – but certainly Geoffrey's History was frequently copied with the *Epistola Alexandri* and a variety of other geographies besides, often mythical, particularly concerning the East.

Legal texts constitute a final class of material whose association with the *Historia* suggests that it was regarded seriously. Geoffrey's occasional allusions to law-making, for example the Molmutine code, are entirely spurious historically but, as Tatlock noted, strikingly relevant to early twelfth-century legal issues.[40]

Lee Patterson has recently stressed the instability and uncertain status of material about the remote past of Britain, both Trojan[41] and British: the *Historia* is, in his view, 'a myth of origins that deconstructs the origin', a '*Gründungssage* that undermines the very ground upon which it rests'.[42] Although the evidence presented here cannot be taken to represent the whole reception of the text, there is nothing to imply that this perceived subversiveness and ambiguity was communicated to the work's audience. It certainly did not impede the use of the *Historia* as a historical source and the present discussion indicates that the work was lent sufficient credence for it to be associated with documents and ideologically important material – eschatological and prophetic. This last association displaces any connotations the *Historia* may have of elegant courtly badinage with a different image – the work as carrier of potent prophetic material.

These observations about how and why the *Historia* circulated offer promising

---

34 McGinn, *Visions*, p. 32.
35 Brown, 'La Notion', pp. 78, 89–93.
36 See Zumthor, *Merlin*, pp. 76–78, 85–87, 97–113.
37 Gerould, 'A Text'.
38 Curley, 'Fifteenth-century Glosses', pp. 335–36.
39 *The Legendary History*, p. 319.
40 *Ibid.*, p. 283; compare pp. 278–83. For a different view see Williams, 'Geoffrey of Monmouth'.
41 *Negotiating the Past*, pp. 203–4.
42 *Ibid.*, p. 202.

material to test a contentious statement made recently by Per Nykrog: 'Writing is costly and rare, and it seems that civilizations have to reach a certain level of technology and productivity before downright and avowedly first-hand fiction can be put into writing'.[43] Taking this proposition at face value, where does Geoffrey's work belong on Nykrog's scale of cultural sophistication?

Much of the answer depends on an issue hardly considered here, Geoffrey's use of sources. How much of the *Historia* is his invention? If Geoffrey's narrative was dictated by oral Celtic stories, then his fiction is not first-hand but 'consecrated as truth' by long oral transmission.[44] Published studies provide ample evidence of Geoffrey's creative exploitation of material. Geoffrey took sources perceived as factual – histories, chronologies, and genealogies[45] – and moulded them to his own design. Even viewed from the surface, Geoffrey's work betrays its artificiality: it is free from the unevennesses and parataxis typical of medieval chronicles,[46] it is too elegant, well structured, smoothly crafted. When the *Historia* is set against the poverty of written materials available to its author, the imaginative input is undeniable.

Geoffrey's manipulation of the past in the cause of contemporary concerns has precedents, some related to vernacular, oral literature. Such material had occasionally crossed into Latin. The Latin History of Dudo of Saint-Quentin has been described by Eleanor Searle as deriving inspiration and direction from Norse saga; Dudo's aim was to legitimate the ruling dynasty of Normandy.[47] David Dumville has identified elements of the Celtic synchronising history in the ninth-century *Historia Brittonum*.[48] Indeed, Celtic conceptions of history provide a convincing background for Geoffrey's historical mythologizing, as Patrick Sims-Williams has shown.[49]

Although Geoffrey may have composed rather than compiled, imaginative expression was not his primary motivation, as is especially clear when his work is viewed in the Celtic tradition. Nykrog, pointing out the historical trappings of Geoffrey's work – the use of histories as models, the historical framework –, classified it as a transitional work, belonging to the period before 'avowedly first-hand' written fiction emerged a generation later.[50] Geoffrey was not inventing

---

43 Nykrog, 'The Rise', pp. 593–94.
44 *Ibid.*, p. 594.
45 Compare Wright, 'Geoffrey of Monmouth and Bede', p. 53; Miller, 'Geoffrey's Early Royal Synchronisms', Piggott, 'The Sources', pp. 275–76.
46 Compare Partner, *Serious Entertainments*, pp. 197–200 and 'The New Cornificius', p. 18; Spiegel, 'Genealogy', p. 44; Fleischmann, 'On the Representation', pp. 291–92.
47 'Fact', pp. 121, 137.
48 'The Historical Value', pp. 5–7. Compare Sims-Williams, 'Some Functions', pp. 97–98, 105–6.
49 *Ibid.*, especially pp. 97–98, 114, 117–19. The process is not of course a Celtic preserve: contemporary concerns naturally tend to influence, sometimes benignly, or to motivate the investigation of the past.
50 Nykrog, 'The Rise', pp. 594–96. Compare Olson, *Literature as Recreation*, p. 230; Shepherd, 'The Emancipation', especially p. 50.

freely but picking the spoils from the post-Conquest degeneration of the Celtic epic tradition, a process which Nykrog has called 'secondary, creative re-composition'.[51]

Nykrog's definition of fiction requires that both author and public acknowledge the narrative as the product of creative imagination. If Geoffrey's position in this equation is ambiguous, that of his audience certainly is not. The reception of the *Historia* suggests that, despite the work's potential as an entertaining narrative, it circulated, both in and outside Britain, by virtue of its functional value. Interest often concentrated in regions of historiographical activity. The work served as a historical source, accompanying legal and historical documents. Association with geographical, prophetic, and apocalyptic literature indicates too that it was read primarily for information. This is not to claim that it was not enjoyed by some nor that it was unreservedly approved by others. As, by the thirteenth century, the Galfridian early history of Britain appears to have been consecrated as historical truth (albeit decorated), we cannot take the observation that the work was not regarded as fictional literature as an index of the 'level of technology and productivity' in later generations. But even in the twelfth century, when the work's status was disputed by some, its great popularity apparently depended on its informational rather than a recreational or even edifying value.[52]

If, on both counts, the *Historia* fits better into the realm of history than of literature, should we regard its success as a monument of medieval gullibility and lack of sophistication? I see reason to reject this idea. The opposition between history and literature which it implies is crudely anachronistic. A professional, technical record of the past was provided by annalistic chronicles; but history proper was expected by its patrons 'to arrest the attention and divert the imagination' and was valued for 'information, morality, amusement, and beauty of language'.[53] As a branch of rhetoric,[54] history-writing required considerable imaginative power in order to arrange and embellish the materials available. The result can be paradoxical, as Southern has noted in one case: 'The more successful Einhard is in handling his subject, the less reliable he is as a source for modern historians'.[55] If the aim was to divert and entertain and if the noblest theme available was the destiny of nations,[56] then Geoffrey was an exceptionally accomplished historian. The skeleton of the narrative, admittedly disarticulated and reconstituted by Geoffrey, could be found in genealogies, chronologies, and especially the *Historia Brittonum*. The story Geoffrey tells is of a kingdom unified from the first, but we cannot accuse him of propagandizing. His sources described a succession of kings, not a tribal polity; the models of government available to

51 Nykrog, 'The Rise', p. 595.
52 Compare Olson, *Literature as Recreation*, pp. 229–31.
53 Partner, *Serious Entertainments*, pp. 2–3.
54 Southern, 'Aspects . . . 1', p. 181.
55 *Ibid.*, p. 184.
56 *Ibid.*, p. 188.

him were overwhelmingly monarchic – even Roman consuls are king-like in Geoffrey's portrayal.

Viewed in these terms, the *Historia*'s success does not prove an indictment of the powers of discrimination of Geoffrey's contemporaries. Readers could and did cull information from the book, while acknowledging that the account was embellished. History, as Nancy Partner has shown, tended in any case to imitate the conventions of narrative fiction besides enjoying 'many of the freedoms of fiction; and fiction, in turn, conventionally masqueraded as fact – no serious deception was intended by either'.[57] The peculiarity of the *Historia* lies in its subject matter – a lost, essentially irrecoverable, past. Here Geoffrey's audience could be accused of gullibility: they accepted that, under the imaginatively crafted surface, Geoffrey's material was fundamentally historical. But, apart from the absence of corroborating sources (except for the *Historia Brittonum*, that is) and the initial novelty of the material, Geoffrey's History was no less plausible than others circulating at the time. Other areas of knowledge were accessible through a single work. Criticism of parallel accounts was a luxury available to very few professional historians, let alone their readers.

But no direct connection can be drawn between the success of Geoffrey's work as a history and a presumed paucity of information which impaired the judgement of medieval readers. The historical writing popular even in a sophisticated, highly literate community such as the educated élite of Imperial Rome and the Hellenistic Empire (where histories are known to have been available in public libraries)[58] is likewise often concerned with remote origins; it too deals with the past with unabashed creativity, whether or not sources existed.[59] In fact technical rhetorical training encouraged such authors in their manipulation of the facts.[60] So what were the conditions which should have produced comparable treatments of the past in two such apparently different societies? Propaganda was of course a constant motivation: political circumstances in the fourth and third centuries B.C. made it expedient for Messenia to acquire a (pseudo-) historical past.[61] There was also literary interest: the past provided moral lessons which found expression in the composition of both history and poetry.[62] The potency of the past was such that it could hardly be treated with detachment.

Secondly, in the medieval and Classical periods, history was not a free-standing discipline but an auxiliary one;[63] it was used to grind the axes of men whose concerns were moral, political, theological, and occasionally personal, but rarely those of professional scholarship. Lacking a niche in the academic world,

57 *Serious Entertainments*, p. 195.
58 Momigliano, 'The Historians', p. 68.
59 Wiseman, *Clio's Cosmetics*, especially pp. 9–10, 31–37. Wiseman notes the analogy with Geoffrey: *ibid.*, pp. 21–22.
60 *Ibid.*, pp. 31–37.
61 *Ibid.*, p. 23; Pearson, 'The Pseudo-History', p. 402.
62 Wiseman, *Clio's Cosmetics*, pp. 38, 144–46.
63 Compare Guenée, 'Y-a-t-il une historiographie médiévale?', pp. 264–65; Momigliano, 'The Historians', p. 60.

historians in both periods had to catch their audience in a way that writers of technical literature generally did not. One recent critic has noted how Classical historians

> 'had continuously to repeat the claim that their histories were either instructive or pleasurable or both, because the word "history" did not by itself suggest either instruction or pleasure'.[64]

In such a market content, style, and general appeal to the reader were essential to a work's success.

I should contend that Geoffrey did not perpetrate one of the best hoaxes of the Middle Ages but that he was an exceptional artist fully governing and not governed by his material. His choice of subject was a brilliant success. The remote past of Britain held the attention not only of later inheritors of the island kingdom (to borrow Galfridian sentiments) but of readers outside Britain. Geoffrey portrayed an ordered and rational world beginning not with the Romans or even the coming of Christ but with the first pagan inhabitants of Britain; his heroes were secular figures with whose human rather than Christian virtues the reader could identify.

64 *Ibid.*, p. 61.

Appendix 1

SUMMARY OF RESULTS

This table presents a summary of the groups which have emerged from this study and their characteristics.

1. Nameless-dedication manuscripts

MSS 2, 3, 14, 19, 20, 36, 53, 56, 58, 75, 81, 83, 125, 126, 127, 132, 151, 166, 168, 171, 173, 175, 176, 182, 183, 184, 185, 186, 205, 208
None is divided into books. Several subgroups are apparent.

1. 56, 58, 205

58 and 205 bear the type-i form of nameless dedication; 56 is acephalous. Linked by rubrics.

2. 20, 83, 126, (151,) 166, 173, 175

§§83–84, 173–174, and 184 are abbreviated in all these manuscripts (except the lacunose 83). 20, 126, 166 and 173 bear the type-v nameless dedication. 83 is acephalous. 151 and 175 have the closely-related third type. The type-v manuscripts and 83 are linked by rubrics. Bede's *Historia ecclesiastica* is found in MSS 83, 126, 166.

3. 3, 14, 81, 168, 171, 183, 184, 189

All manuscripts of types vii, viia, and viii nameless dedication and one type-iii (168). Some agreement between rubrics of type-viii and type-vii manuscripts. Poems of Ausonius found in MSS 14 and 183.

4. 36, 53, 127, 196, 208

Includes manuscripts bearing types i, ii, iii, and v of the nameless dedication. The type-ii witnesses, 127 and 208, have clearly related rubrics. Those in 53 and 196 (type-iii) may be compared with the second subgroup above, and bear some textual similarity.

227

5. Single-dedication relatives of the nameless-dedication type

105 (125, 130,) 154, (180, 182,) 214

MSS 130 and 214 (both single-dedication), unlike the nameless-dedication proper, are divided into books. MSS 105 and 214 have a distinctive opening rubric: 125, 154, and 180 lack rubrics. 105, 130, and 214 include the account of the foundation of Britain beginning 'Ab origine mundi'.

2. *117/188 type*

MSS 7, 13, 16, 21, 59, 60, 79, 117, 135, 155, 172, 174, 188, 190, 197, 198, 211, 213

All except the sub-group 172, 174, 187, 198 are divided into books. These four and MSS 79, 135, 155, 169, 190 bear the rubric 'Explicit prologus. Incipit prophetia eiusdem'. 135 and 213 uniquely begin Book VII at 110; their other divisions are comparable to those in 155, 169, 190.

7, 135, 155, and 213 contain the (apparently unique) apocryphal letter of Arthur. Texts recurring in this group include Dares, the prophecy of the Eagle, *Status*, *Gesta Normannorum ducum*, and crusading chronicles.

3. *Tres filios*

MSS 8, 10, 28, 30, 32, 39, 45, 61, 73, 98, 100, 109, 119, 123, 134, 141, 142, 153, 165

This category includes a subgroup (32, 73, 98, 153, 165) evident from scribal verses, an interpolation, rubrics, and book-divisions. Other manuscripts in the group have no rubrics or those that there are are idiosyncratic, or minimal. Many bear *Brutus* rubrics. Book-divisions are similarly scattered throughout the group. The overall capriciousness of rubrics and book-divisions may suggest that the text travelled without rubrication at an early stage.

No particular texts may be associated with this group.

4. *Pudibundus Brito*

MSS 9, 31, 41, 42, 44, 93, 113, 118, 132, 140, 150, 156, 167, 178, 212

Identified on the grounds of a reworking of §§109–110. Six manuscripts omit the opening chapters (9, 41, 132, 140, 143, 178). 19, 143, and 41, and 31 and 113 have sets of unusual rubrics. Twelve lack book-divisions, the exceptions being MSS 9, 140, and 156.

5. *Prologus/editio*

MSS (5,) 26, 51, 90, 103, 112, 137, 162; 149: 63, 120, 203 (18, 74, 87, 154)

Connected by rubrics and book-divisions (a ten- or eleven-book arrangement beginning at §6, with VII at §111 or 118). MSS 90, 112, 137, and 149 contain commentaries on the Prophecies.

6. *Smaller groups*

Manuscripts evidently related but whose wider filiation has not yet been identified.
38, 131; 99, 122 (Seaxburh interpolation, §204)
72, 89, 133, 160
5, 84, 124 (Seaxburh interpolation, §204)
?34, (147,) 152 + 40, 111 etc. (associated contents)
23, 96 (rubrics)
48, 128 (double dedication, truncated at §207)
71, 181 (rubrics)
78, 206
107, 136 (double dedication)

Appendix 2

TEST-COLLATIONS

The following apparatus are designed to make accessible as much as possible of the information recorded by test-collations. Editorial judgement has been suspended temporarily; minor traits or slips such as in word-order and spelling are given for the time being.

The text of each chapter is printed from the Bern manuscript (Wright's edition). All manuscripts witnessing each variant are listed by their numerical sigla. Manuscripts agreeing with the Bern text are recorded for §§1 and 100 only. This reflects partly the experimental nature of the undertaking – the method has evolved with trial and error – and partly the nature of those chapters: the tradition divides more markedly than in §§2 and 208.

§1

Not present in 1, 4, 9, 12, 17, 18, 31, 40, 41, 44, 52, 56, 64, 67, 68, 69, 75, 86, 89, 94, 101, 102, 106, 110, 119, 139, 140, 142, 143, 144, 145, 146, 148, 157, 158, 159, 163, 165, 178, 179, 180, 186, 195, 200, 204. Parts of 37 and 56 illegible. 201 transcript.

Cum[1] [2]mecum multa[2] et[3] de multis [4]sepius animo reuoluens[4] in hystoriam[5] [6]regum

[1]   2, 3, 5, 6, 7, 8, 10, 13, 14, 15, 19, 20, 21, 22, 23, 24, 26, 28, 29, 30, 32, 33, 34, 35, 36, 37, 38, 39, 42, 43, 45, 46, 47, 48, 49, 50, 51, 53, 54, 55, 57, 58, 59, 60, 61, 62, 63, 65, 66, 71, 72, 73, 74, 76, 77, 78, 79, 80, 81, 82, 83, 84, 85, 87, 88, 90, 91, 92, 93, 95, 97, 98, 99, 103, 104, 105, 107, 109, 111, 112, 113, 114, 115, 116, 117, 118, 120, 121, 123, 124, 125, 126, 127, 128, 130, 131, 132, 133, 134, 135, 136, 137, 138, 141, 147, 149, 150, 151, 152, 153, 154, 155, 156, 161, 162, 164, 166, 167, 168, 169, 172, 173, 174, 175, 176, (177,) 181, 182, 183, 184, 185, 187, 188, 189, 190, 192, 195, 197, 198, 199, 202, 203, 205, 206, 207, 208, 209, 210, 211, 212, 213, 214; *[]um*, 11, 27, 70, 122, 170, 171, 193, 196; *Dum*, 16, 25, 96, 100, 108, 129, 160, 191, 194.
2..2   3, 6, 7, 8, 10, 11, 13, 14, 15, 16, 19, 20, 21, 22, 23, 24, 25, 26, 28, 29, 30, 32, 33, 34, 35, 36, 38, 39, 42, 43, 45, 46, 47, 48, 49, 50, 51, 53, 54, 55, 57, 59, 60, 62, 63, 66, 70, 71, 72, 73, 74, 77, 78, 79, 80, 81, 82, 83, 84, 85, 87, 88, 91, 93, 95, 96, 97, 98, 99, 100, 103, 104, 105, 107, 108, 109, 111, 112, 113, 114, 115, 116, 117, 118, 120, 121, 122, 123, 124, 125, 126, 127, 128, 129, 130, 131, 132, 133, 134, 135, 136, 137, 138, 141, 147, 149, 150, 151, 152, 153, 154, 155, 156, 160, 161, 162, 164, 166, 168, 169, 170, 171, 172, 174, 175, 176, 177, 181, 182, 183, 184, 185, 187, 188, 189, 191, 192, 194, 196, 197, 198, 199, 202, 203, 206, 207, 208, 209, 210, 211, 212, 213; *multa* (canc.) *mecum multa*, 214; *multa mecum*, 2, 27, 37, 61, 65, 76, 92, 97, 167, 190; *mecum \multa*, 173; *mecum*, 90; *\mecum\ multa*, 5; *mecum multi*, 193; *multum mecum*, 58, 205; *mecum sepius multa*, 11.

Britannie inciderem,[6] [107]in mirum[7] contuli[8] quod[9] infra mentionem[10] quam[11] [12]de

3 2, 3, 5, 6, 7, 8, 10, 11, 13, 14, 15, 16, 19, 20, 21, 22, 23, 24, 25, 26, 27, 28, 29, 30, 32, 33, 34, 35, 36, 37, 38, 39, 42, 43, 45, 46, 47, 48, 49, 50, 51, 53, 54, 55, 57, 58, 59, 60, 61, 62, 65, 66, 71, 72, 73, 74, 76, 77, 78, 79, 80, 81, 82, 83, 84, 85, 87, 88, 90, 91, 92, 93, 95, 96, 97, 98, 99, 100, 103, 104, 105, 107, 108, 109, 111, 112, 113, 114, 115, 116, 117, 118, 121, 122, 123, 124, 125, 126, 127, 128, 129, 130, 131, 132, 133, 134, 135, 136, 137, 138, 141, 147, 149, 150, 151, 152, 153, 154, 155, 156, 160, 161, 162, 164, 166, 167, 168, 169, 170, 171, 172, 173, 174, 175, 176, 177, 181, 182, 183, 184, 185, 188, 189, 190, 191, 192, 193, 194, 196, 197, 198, 199, 202, 205, 206, 207, 208, 209, 210, 211, 212, 213, 214; om., 63, 70, 120, 187, 203.

4...4 3, 5, 7, 8, 10, 11, 14, 15, 16, 19, 20, 21, 22, 23, 24, 25, 26, 27, 28, 29, 30, 32, 33, 34, 35, 36, 37, 38, 39, 43, 45, 46, 47, 48, 49, 50, 51, 53, 54, 55, 57, 59, 60, 61, 62, 63, 65, 66, 70, 71, 72, 73, 74, 76, 79, 80, 81, 82, 83, 84, 85, 87, 88, 90, 91, 92, 93, 95, 96, 97, 98, 100, 103, 104, 105, 108, 109, 112, 113, 114, 115, 116, 117, 118, 120, 121, 122, 123, 124, 125, 126, 127, 128, 129, 130, 131, 132, 133, 134, 135, 136, 137, 138, 141, 147, 149, 150, 151, 152, 153, 154, 155, 156, 160, 161, 162, 164, 166, 167, 168, 169, 170, 171, 172, 173, 174, 175, 176, 177, 181, 182, 183, 184, 185, 187, 188, 189, 190, 191, 192, 193, 194, 196, 197, 198, 199, 203, 206, 207, 208, 209, 210, 211, 212, 213, 214; *sepius animo reuuoluens*, 99; *animo sepius reuoluens*, 2, 58, 107, 205; *animo reuoluens sepius*, 202; *pius animo reuoluens*, 77; *sepius in animo reuoluens*, 111; *sepius animalia reuoluens*, 13; *animo reuolues*, 42; *sepius animo inuoluens*, 6; *sepius animo te uoluens* (corr. to *reuoluens*), 78.

5 2, 3, 5, 6, 7, 8, 10, 11, 13, 14, 15, 16, 19, 20, 21, 22, 23, 24, 25, 26, 27, 28, 29, 30, 32, 33, 34, 35, 36, 37, 38, 39, 42, 43, 45, 46, 47, 48, 49, 50, 51, 53, 54, 55, 57, 58, 59, 60, 61, 62, 63, 66, 70, 71, 73, 74, 76, 77, 80, 81, 82, 83, 84, 85, 87, 88, 90, 91, 92, 93, 95, 96, 97, 98, 99, 100, 103, 104, 105, 107, 108, 109, 111, 112, 113, 114, 115, 116, 117, 118, 120, 121, 122, 123, 125, 126, 127, 128, 129, 130, 131, 132, 134, 135, 136, 137, 138, 141, 147, 149, 150, 151, 152, 153, 154, 155, 156, 161, 162, 164, 166, 167, 168, 169, 170, 171, 172, 173, 174, 175, 176, 177, 181, 182, 183, 184, 185, 187, 188, 189, 190, 191, 192, 193, 194, 196, 197, 198, 199, 202, 203, 205, 206, 207, 208, 209, 210, 211, 212, 213, 214; *historia*, 65, 160; *hystoria*, 72, 124, 133; *istoria*, 79; *ystoria*, 78.

6...6 2, 3, 5, 7, 8, 10, 14, 15, 16, 19, 20, 21, 22, 23, 24, 25, 26, 27, 28, 29, 30, 32, 33, 34, 35, 36, 37, 38, 39, 42, 43, 45, 46, 47, 48, 49, 50, 51, 53, 54, 55, 57, 58, 59, 60, 61, 62, 65, 66, 71, 73, 74, 76, 77, 78, 79, 80, 81, 82, 83, 84, 86, 87, 90, 91, 92, 93, 95, 96, 97, 99, 100, 103, 104, 105, 107, 108, 109, 111, 112, 113, 114, 115, 117, 118, 120, 121, 122, 123, 124, 125, 126, 127, 128, 129, 130, 131, 132, 134, 135, 136, 137, 138, 141, 147, 149, 150, 151, 152, 153, 154, 155, 161, 162, 164, 166, 167, 168, 169, 170, 171, 172, 173, 174, 175, 176, 177, 181, 182, 183, 184, 185, 187, 188, 189, 190, 191, 192, 193, 194, 196, 197, 198, 199, 202, 203, 205, 206, 207, 208, 209, 210, 213, 214; *Britannie inciderem regum*, 72, 133, 160; \regum/ *Britannie inciderem*, 156, 212; *regum Britannie inciderem et*, 150; *Britannie inciderem*, 88, 116; *regum Britannie inciderim*, 63, 70, 200, 203; *regum Brittannie incidens*, 211, 213; *regum Britannie incideret*, 11; *regum Britannie incidi*, 13; *regum Britannie incidem*, 98; *regum Britannorum inciderem*, 6.

7...7 5, 6, 7, 8, 11, 15, 16, 23, 24, 26, 27, 28, 30, 32, 33, 34, 37, 42, 43, 45, 48, 49, 51, 54, 55, 57, 61, 62, 63, 65, 70, 71, 72, 73, 74, 76, 77, 78, 79, 80, 81, 82, 84, 85, 87, 88, 90, 93, 95, 96, 97, 98, 100, 107, 108, 111, 112, 113, 115, 116, 120, 121, 122, 123, 128, 129, 130, 131, 134, 135, 136, 137, 141, 149, 152, 153, 155, 156, 160, 161, 162, 164, 169, 170, 172, 177, 190, 191, 192, 198, 203, 206, 207, 208, 210, 211, 213; *nimirum*: 2, 3, 10, 14, 19, 20, 21, 22, 25, 29, (35,) 36, (39,) 46, 47, 50, 53, 58, 59, 60, (66,) 83, 91, 99, 103, 104, 105, 109, 114, 117, (118,) 124, 125, 126, 127, 132, 133, 138, 147, 150, 151, 154, 167, 168, 171, 173, 174, 175, 176, 182, 183, 184, 185, 187, 188, 189, 193, (194,) 196, 197, 199, 202, 205, 206, 209, 212, 214; *in unum*, 38, (92); *initurum*, 19; *mirum*, 181; *sed mihi mirum*, 13.

eis Gildas[12] et Beda[13] luculento[14] tractatu[15] fecerant[16] nichil[17] de[18] regibus[19] [20]qui ante[20] [21]incarnationem Christi[21] inhabitauerant,[22] nichil[23] [24]etiam de Arturo[24] cete-

8   5, 6, 7, 8, 10, 11, 15, 16, 21, 22, 23, 24, 25, 26, 27, 28, 29, 30, 32, 33, 34, 35, 37, 38, 39, 42, 43, 45, 46, 47, 48, 49, 50, 51, 54, 55, 57, 59, 60, 61, 62, 63, 65, 66, 70, 71, 72, 73, 74, 76, 77, 78, 80, 82, 84, 85, 87, 88, 90, 91, 92, 93, 95, 96, 97, 98, 99, 100, 103, 104, 107, 108, 109, 111, 112, 113, 114, 115, 116, 117, 118, 120, 121, 122, 123, 124, 128, 129, 130, 131, 133, 134, 135, 136, 137, 138, 141, 147, 149, 150, 152, 153, 155, 156, 160, 161, 162, 164, 167, 169, 170, 172, 174, 175, 177, 181, 185, 188, 190, 191, 192, 194, 197, 198, 199, 202, 203, 206, 207, 209, 210, 211, 212, 213; *attulit*, 13; *contutuli*, 206; om., 2, 3, 14, 19, 20, 36, 53, 58, 79, 81, 83, 105, 125, 126, 127, 132, 151, 154, 166, 168, 171, 173, 176, 182, 183, 184, 187, 189, 193, 196, 205, 208, 214.

9   2, 3, 5, 6, 7, 8, 10, 11, 13, 14, 15, 16, 19, 20, 21, 22, 23, 24, 25, 26, 27, 28, 29, 30, 32, 33, 34, 36, 37, 38, 39, 42, 43, 45, 46, 47, 48, 49, 50, 51, 53, 54, 55, 57, 58, 59, 60, 61, 62, 63, 65, 70, 71, 72, 73, 76, 78, 79, 80, 81, 82, 83, 84, 85, 87, 88, 90, 91, 92, 93, 95, 96, 97, 98, 99, 100, 103, 104, 105, 107, 108, 109, 111, 112, 113, 114, 115, 116, 117, 118, 120, 121, 122, 123, 124, 125, 126, 127, 128, 129, 130, 131, 132, 133, 134, 135, 136, 137, 138, 141, 147, 149, 150, 151, 152, 153, 154, 155, 156, 160, 161, 162, 164, 166, 167, 168, 169, 170, 171, 172, 173, 174, 175, 176, 177, 181, 182, 183, 184, 187, 188, 189, 190, 191, 192, 193, 194, 196, 197, 198, 199, 202, 203, 205, 206, 207, 208, 209, 210, 211, 212, 213, 214; *quia*, 74; *mecum quod*, 35, 66; om., 77, 185.

10...10   Glossed *id est in narracione*, 120; *cum in narracione*, 111.

11   *qui*, 185.

12...12   2, 3, 5, 7, 8, 10, 11, 13, 14, 15, 16, 19, 20, 21, 22, 23, 24, 25, 26, 27, 28, 29, 30, 32, 33, 34, 35, 36, 37, 38, 39, 42, 45, 46, 47, 48, 49, 50, 51, 54, 55, 57, 58, 59, 60, 61, 62, 63, 65, 66, 70, 71, 72, 74, 76, 77, 78, 79, 80, 83, 85, 87, 90, 91, 92, 93, 95, 96, 97, 99, 100, 103, 104, 105, 107, 108, 109, 111, 112, 113, 114, 117, 118, 120, 121, 122, 123, 125, 127, 128, 129, 130, 131, 132, 133, 134, 135, 136, 137, 141, 149, 150, 151, 152, 154, 155, 156, 160, 161, 162, 164, 166, 167, 168, 169, 170, 171, 172, 173, 174, 175, 176, 177, 181, 183, 184, 185, 187, 188, 189, 190, 191, 192, 193, 196, 197, 198, 199, 202, 203, 206, 207, 208, 209, 210, 211, 212, 213, 214; *Gildas de eis*, 6, 84, 115, 124; *de his Gildas*, 205; *deis Gildas*, 53, 182; *donnus Gildas*, 82; *de eis Gyldas*, 43, 81, 126, 194; *de eis Gildes*, 147; *de eis Gillas*, 73, 98, 153; *de eis Suldas*, 138; *de his Gildas sapientissimus historiographus eorum*, 88, 116.

13   *Wereda*, 47.

14   *luculente*, 198; ?*luculenter*, 174; *luculentu*, 35; *loculento*, 123, 141 (but corrected), 147; *liculento*, 27, 51; *et luculento*, 118.

15   *tractu*, 171; *tractu uel tractatu*, 168; *tractatum*, 174, 198; *tractato*, 35.

16   2, 6, 7, 8, 10, 11, 13, 14, 15, 16, 19, 20, 21, 22, 23, 24, 25, 26, 27, 29, 30, 32, 33, 34, 35, 36, 37, 38, 39, 42, 43, 45, 46, 47, 48, 49, 50, 51, 53, 54, 55, 57, 58, 59, 60, 61, 63, 65, 66, 70, 71, 72, 73, 74, 76, 78, 79, 80, 81, 82, 83, 85, 87, 88, 90, 91, 92, 93, 95, 96, 97, 98, 99, 103, 104, 105, 107, 108, 111, 112, 113, 114, 115, 116, 117, 118, 120, 121, 122, 123, 125, 126, 127, 128, 129, 130, 131, 132, 133, 134, 135, 136, 137, 138, 141, 149, 150, 151, 152, 154, 155, 156, 160, 161, 162, 164, 166, 167, 169, 170, 172, 173, 174, 175, 176, 177, 181, 182, 183, 184, 185, 187, 188, 189, 190, 191, 192, 193, 194, 196, 197, 198, 199, 202, 203, 205, 206, 207, 208, 209, 211, 212, 213, 214; *fecerunt*, 3, 5, 84, 124, 168, 171; *fecerent*, 147; *fecerat*, 152; *feceram*, 77; *fecant*, 153; *fecerant et*, 28, 62, 100, 109, 210.

17   *nichil etiam*, 26, 27, 51, 61, 118; *nichil eos dixisse*, 5 (added in different hand), 84, 124; *ubi*, 78.

18   *de eis*, 70; *de*\\, 210; om., 207.

19   *regibus*\\, 210; om., 207.

20...20   *q^a nte*, 27; om., 207.

risque[25] compluribus[26] qui[27] post[28] incarnationem[29] successerunt[30] repperissem,[31]

21...21 *Christi incarnationem*, 167; *incarnationem*, 65; *incarnationem Domini*, 33, 34, 152; om., 207.

22 *Britanniam inhabitauerant*, 5 (added), 84, 87, 115, 192; *Britanniam habitauerant*, 124; *ipsam inhabitauerunt*, 35, 66; *in ea inhabitauerant*, 38; om., 207.

23 After *nichil, de regibus* (cancelled), 210; om., 207.

24...24 2, 5, 6, 7, 8, 10, 11, 13, 14, 15, 16, 19, 20, 21, 22, 23, 24, 25, 26, 27, 28, 30, 33, 36, 37, 42, 43, 45, 47, 48, 49, 51, 53, 54, 55, 57, 58, 59, 60, 61, 63, 66, 71, 72, 73, 74, 76, 77, 78, 79, 80, 82, 83, 85, 90, 91, 92, 95, 96, 97, 98, 99, 100, 103, 105, 107, 108, 109, 112, 117, 118, 120, 121, 122, 123, 125, 126, 127, 128, 129, 130, 131, 132, 133, 134, 135, 136, 138, 141, 147, 155, 160, 162, 164, 166, 167, 168, 169, 170, 171, 172, 173, 174, 176, 177, 181, 182, 183, 184, 185, 187, 188, 189, 190, 191, 192, 193, 194, 196, 197, 198, 199, 203, 206, 207, 208, 209, 211, 213; *etiam de Art\h/uro*, 115, 150; *etiam de Arthuro*, 29, 35, 38, 39, 50, 62, 70, 84, 87, 93, 104, 111, 114, 124, 137, 149, 152, 153, 154, 210, 214; *etiam de Arcturo*, 34, 113, 151, 175, 205; *etiam de Artturo*, 202; *etiam de Artuso*, 81; *etiam de Arturio*, 3; *de Arturo etiam*, 65; *de Arturo*, 70, 156, 161; *de Arthuro*, 212; *de Arcturo*, 46; *etiam de rege Arthuro*, 116; *de rege Arturo*, 88; *etiam de Arthuro rege*, 32.

25 *et ceteris*: 111; *ceteris\quel*, 76; *ceteris*, 3.

26 2, 3, 5, 6, 7, 13, 14, 15, 16, 19, 21, 22, 23, 24, 26, 28, 30, 32, 33, 34, 35, 38, 39, 42, 43, 45, 46, 47, 48, 49, 50, 53, 54, 55, 57, 58, 60, 61, 62, 63, 65, 66, 70, 71, 72, 73, 74, 76, 79, 80, 82, 84, 85, 91, 93, 95, 96, 97, 98, 99, 100, 103, 105, 107, 108, 109, 111, 112, 113, 115, 117, 120, 121, 122, 123, 124, 125, 127, 131, 133, 135, 136, 137, 138, 141, 149, 150, 151, 152, 153, 154, 155, 156, 160, 161, 168, 169, 170, 171, 172, 175, 176, 181, 182, 183, 184, 185, 187, 188, 189, 190, 191, 192, 193, 194, 196, 197, 199, 202, 203, 205, 207, 208, 209, 210, 211, 212, 24; *compliribus*, 92; *cum pluribus*, 8, 36, 59, 77, 81, 167; *quam pluribus*, 10, 11, 20, 25, 27, 29, 33, 37, 51, 78, 83, 87, 88, 90, 104, 114, 116, 118, 126, 128, 129, 130, 132, 134, 147, 162, 164, 166, 173, 174, 177, 198, 206, 213.

27 Om., 78.

28 2, 3, 5, 6, 7, 8, 10, 11, 13, 14, 15, 16, 19, 20, 21, 22, 23, 24, 25, 26, 27, 28, 29, 30, 32, 33, 34, 35, 36, 37, 38, 39, 42, 43, 45, 46, 47, 48, 49, 50, 51, 53, 54, 55, 57, 58, 59, 60, 61, 62, 63, 65, 66, 70, 71, 73, 74, 76, 77, 78, 79, 80, 81, 82, 83, 84, 85, 87, 88, 90, 91, 92, 93, 95, 96, 97, 99, 100, 103, 104, 105, 107, 108, 109, 111, 112, 113, 114, 115, 116, 117, 118, 120, 121, 122, 123, 124, 125, 126, 127, 128, 129, 130, 131, 132, 133, 134, 135, 136, 137, 138, 141, 147, 149, 150, 151, 152, 153, 154, 155, 156, 160, 161, 162, 164, 166, 167, 168, 169, 170, 171, 172, 173, 174, 175, 176, 177, 181, 182, 183, 184, 185, 187, 188, 189, 190, 191, 192, 193, 196, 197, 198, 199, 202, 203, 205, 206, 207, 209, 211, 212, 213, 214; *p^{i}o*, 72; *primo*, 98; *p^a*, 194.

29 2, 3, 5, 6, 7, 8, 10, 11, 13, 14, 15, 16, 19, 20, 21, 22, 23, 24, 25, 26, 27, 28, 29, 30, 32, 33, 34, 35, 36, 37, 38, 39, 42, 43, 45, 46, 47, 48, 49, 50, 51, 53, 54, 55, 57, 58, 59, 60, 61, 62, 63, 65, 66, 70, 71, 72, 73, 74, 76, 77, 78, 79, 80, 81, 82, 83, 84, 85, 87, 88, 90, 91, 92, 95, 96, 97, 98, 99, 100, 103, 105, 107, 108, 109, 111, 112, 113, 114, 115, 116, 117, 120, 121, 122, 123, 124, 125, 126, 128, 129, 130, 131, 132, 133, 134, 135, 136, 137, 138, 141, 147, 149, 150, 151, 152, 153, 154, 155, 156, 160, 161, 162, 164, 166, 167, 168, 169, 170, 171, 172, 173, 174, 175, 176, 177, 181, 182, 183, 184, 185, 187, 188, 189, 190, 191, 192, 193, 194, 196, 197, 198, 199, 202, 203, 205, 206, 209, 211, 212, 213, 214; *glossed Domini*, 127; *Domini incarnationem*, 208; *incarnationem Domini*, 118, 207; *incarnationem dominicam*, 192; *incarnationem Christi*, 93, 104, 210.

30 3, 5, 6, 7, 8, 10, 11, 13, 14, 15, 16, 19, 20, 21, 22, 23, 24, 25, 26, 27, 28, 29, 30, 32, 33, 34, 35, 36, 37, 38, 39, 42, 43, 45, 46, 47, 48, 49, 50, 51, 53, 54, 55, 57, 59, 60, 61, 62, 63, 66, 70, 71, 72, 73, 74, 76, 77, 78, 79, 80, 81, 82, 83, 84, 85, 87, 88, 90, 91, 92, 93, 95, 96, 97, 98, 99, 100, 103, 104, 105, 107, 108, 109, 112, 113, 114, 115, 116, 117, 118, 120, 121, 122,

cum[32] et[33] [34]gesta eorum[34] [35]digna eternitate laudis[35] [36]constarent et[36] [37]a multis

123, 124, 125, 126, 127, 128, 129, 130, 132, 133, 134, 135, 136, 137, 138, 141, 147, 149, 150, 151, 152, 154, 155, 156, 160, 161, 162, 164, 166, 167, 168, 169, 170, 171, 172, 173, 175, 176, 177, 181, 183, 184, 185, 187, 188, 189, 190, 191, 192, 193, 196, 197, 198, 199, 202, 203, 206, 207, 208, 209, 210, 211, 212, 213, 214; *successerant*, 2, 58, 65, 111, 131, 174, 205; *successerint*, 182; om. but entered by corrector, 153; *susceperunt*, 202.

31 *recepissent*, 72, 133.

32 5, 6, 7, 8, 10, 11, 13, 15, 16, 21, 22, 23, 24, 25, 26, 27, 28, 29, 30, 32, 33, 34, 35, 37, 38, 39, 42, 43, 45, 46, 47, 48, 49, 50, 51, 54, 55, 57, 59, 60, 61, 62, 63, 65, 66, 70, 71, 72, 73, 74, 76, 77, 78, 79, 80, 82, 83, 84, 85, 87, 88, 90, 91, 92, 93, 95, 96, 97, 98, 99, 100, 103, 104, 107, 108, 109, 111, 112, 113, 114, 115, 116, 117, 118, 120, 121, 122, 123, 124, 128, 129, 130, 131, 133, 134, 135, 136, 137, 138, 139, 140, 141, 147, 149, 150, 152, 153, 155, 156, 160, 161, 162, 164, 167, 169, 170, 172, 174, 181, 185, 187, 188, 190, 191, 192, 193, 194, 197, 198, 199, 202, 203, 206, 207, 209, 210, 211, 212, 213; om., 2, 3, 14, 19, 20, 30, 36, 53, 58, 81, 83, 105, 125, 126, 127, 132, 151, 154, 166, 168, 171, 173, 175, 176, 182, 183, 184, 189, 196, 205, 208, 214; *cumque*, 177.

33 2, 3, 5, 6, 7, 8, 10, 11, 13, 14, 15, 16, 19, 20, 21, 22, 23, 24, 25, 26, 27, 28, 29, 30, 32, 33, 34, 35, 36, 37, 38, 39, 43, 46, 47, 48, 49, 50, 51, 53, 54, 55, 57, 58, 59, 60, 61, 62, 63, 65, 66, 70, 71, 72, 73, 74, 76, 77, 78, 79, 80, 81, 82, 83, 84, 85, 87, 88, 90, 91, 92, 93, 95, 96, 97, 98, 99, 100, 103, 104, 105, 107, 108, 109, 112, 113, 114, 115, 116, 117, 118, 120, 121, 122, 123, 124, 125, 126, 127, 128, 129, 130, 131, 132, 133, 134, 136, 137, 138, 141, 147, 149, 150, 151, 152, 153, 155, 156, 160, 161, 162, 164, 166, 167, 168, 169, 170, 171, 172, 173, 174, 175, 176, 177, 181, 182, 183, 184, 187, 188, 189, 190, 191, 192, 193, 194, 196, 197, 198, 199, 202, 203, 205, 206, 207, 208, 209, 211, 212, 213, 214; *etiam*, 45, 185; om., 42, 111, 135, 210; *e*, 154.

34...34 *eorum gesta*, 160; *gesta ipsorum*, 174; *gesta*, 113.

35...35 5, 8, 10, 15, 22, 23, 25, 26, 27, 28, 29, 30, 32, 34, 35, 38, 39, 42, 43, 45, 46, 47, 48, 49, 50, 51, 54, 61, 63, 66, 70, 71, 72, 73, 74, 78, 80, 84, 85, 88, 90, 91, 93, 95, 96, 98, 99, 100, 103, 109, 112, 113, 114, 116, 118, 120, 121, 122, 123, 128, 130, 131, 133, 134, 136, 137, 141, 149, 150, 152, 156, 160, 161, 162, 170, 181, 182, 187, 202, 203, 206, 207, 209, 212; *eternitate digna laudis*, 107, 210; *digna laudis eternitate*, 33, 192; *et digna eternitate laudis*, 108, 210; *digna eternitatis laude*: 2, 3, 6, 7, 11, 13, 14, 16, 19, 20, 21, 36, 53, 57, 58, 59, 60, 62, 65, 76, 77, 79, 81, 82, 83, 87, 92, 97, 104, 105, 111, 115, 117, 125, 126, 127, 129, 132, 135, 138, 147, 151, 154, 155, 166, 167, 168, 169, 171, 172, 173, 174, 175, 176, 177, 182, 183, 184, 188, 189, 190, 191, 193, 194, 196, 197, 198, 199, 205, 208, 211, 212, 213, 214; 24 (supply), 153 (corrector), *digna eternita[] laude*, 124; *digna eterne laudis*, 37, 55, 164; *externitate laudis*, 185.

36...36 *constarentque*, 39.

37...37 After *multis*, *pluribus* (cancelled), 77; *in multis populis*, 111, 212.

38...38 2, 3, 5, 7, 8, 10, 11, 13, 14, 15, 16, 19, 21, 22, 23, 24, 25, 27, 28, 30, 32, 33, 34, 35, 36, 38, 42, 43, 45, 46, 48, 49, 50, 51, 53, 54, 55, 57, 58, 60, 61, 62, 65, 66, 70, 71, 72, 73, 74, 76, 77, 78, 79, 80, 81, 82, 84, 85, 88, 90, 91, 92, 93, 95, 96, 97, 98, 99, 100, 103, 104, 105, 107, 108, 109, 111, 112, 113, 114, 115, 116, 117, 118, 120, 121, 122, 123, 124, 125, 127, 130, 131, 132, 133, 134, 135, 136, 137, 138, 139, 141, 149, 150, 152, 153, 154, 155, 156, 160, 161, 162, 164, 167, 168, 169, 170, 171, 172, 174, 181, 182, 183, 184, 185, 187, 188, 189, 190, 191, 192, 193, 194, 196, 197, 198, 199, 202, 203, 205, 206, 207, 208, 212, 213, 214; *quasi inscripta iocunde ac memoriter*, 37, 87; *quasi inscripta iocunde et immemoriter*, 29; *quasi iocunde inscripta et memoriter*, 39; *iocunde et memoriter quasi inscripta*, 59; *quasi inscripta* bracketted, 147; *quasi inscripta iocunde*, 20, 83, 126, 151, 166, 173, 175, 176; *q. inscripta iocunde et memoriter*, 26, 47, 209; *quasi*/ *inscripta iocunde et memoriter*, 210;

234

populis[37] [38]quasi inscripta iocunde et memoriter[38] predicarentur.[39]

quasi inscriptis iocunde et memoriter, 63; *quasi inscripta iocunda et memoriter*, 177; *quasi inscripta iocondo et memoriter*, 129; *quasi inscripta rotunde et memoriter*, 6.

[39] 20, 23, 32, 39, 48, 49, 76, 78, 83, 96, 107, 126 (?over erasure), 128, 134, 136, 166, 170, 173, 188, 205, 206, 208; *predicarentur, ar* cancelled, 71; *predicerentur*, 2, 19, 58, 131, 176; *predicentur*, 3, 5, 6, 7, 8, 10, 11, 13, 14, 16, 21, 22, 25, 26, 27, 28, 29, 30, 33, 34, 35, 36, 37, 38, 42, 43, 45, 46, 47, 50, 51, 53, 54, 55, 57, 59, 60, 61, 62, 63, 65, 66, 70, 72, 73, 74, 77, 79, 80, 81, 82, 84, 85, 87, 88, 90, 91, 92, 93, 95, 97, 98, 99, 100, 103, 104, 105, 108, 109, 111, 112, 113, 114, 115, 116, 117, 118, 120, 121, 122, 123, 124, 125, 127, 129, 130, 132, 133, 135, 137, 138, 141, 147, 149, 150, 151, 152, 153, 154, 155, 156, 160, 161, 162, 164, 167, 168, 169, 171, 172, 174, 175, 177, 181, 182, 183, 184, 185, 187, 189, 190, 191, 192, 193, 194, 196, 197, 198, 199, 202, 207, 209, 210, 211, 212, 213, 214; *predicarent*, 15.

§2

Not found in 4, 9, 12, 17, 18, 31, 40, 41, 44, 52, 56, 64, 69, 75, 86, 89, 94, 101, 102, 110, 119, 139, 140, 142, 143, 144, 145, 146, 148, (154,) 157, 158, 159, 165, 195, 200, (201,) 204; text partly irretrievable in 12, 133; omitting the First-Variant manuscripts 1, 67, 68, 70, 106, 163.

¹Talia michi¹ et ²de talibus multociens cogitanti² optulit³ Walterus⁴ Oxinefordensis⁵ archidiaconus,⁶ uir⁷ ⁸in oratoria arte⁸ atque⁹ in¹⁰ ¹¹exoticis historiis¹¹ eruditus,¹²

1...1 *Talia \nichi/*, 168; *Talia igitur michi*, 53, 62, 99, 122, 196; *Talia igitur*, 39, 88, 116; *Talia uero*, 70.

2...2 *\de/ talibus multociens cogitanti*, 122; *talibus multociens cogitanti*, 35; *multociens cogitanti de talibus*, 37, 55, 164; *de talibus multoties cogitanti*, 205; *de talibus \nultociens/ cogitanti*, 150; *de talibus cogitanti*, 8, 10, 30, 32, 38, 45, 73, 84, 93, 98, 100, 109, 123, 124, 131, 141, 153, 192, 210; *de talibus multociens meditanti*, 196; *de talibus multociens cogitanti de talibus*, 87, *multociens cogitanti*, 111.

3 *obtulit*, 3, 8, 11, 13, 14, 22, 28, 33, 37, 50, 53, 54, 57, 58, 59, 70, 76, 77, 80, 85, 91, 92, 96, 113, 115, 129, 132, 147, 151, 164, 167, 168, 171, 173, 174, 175, 176, 177, 182, 185, 189, 190, 192, 193, 196, 198, 199, 202, 205, 206, 209, 210, 211, 213; *optulit mihi*, 35, 66; *obtuli*, 108; *ottulit*, 130; om., 72, 78, 133.

4 *Galterius*, 2, 58, 88, 132, 173, 182, 205; *Galterus*, 7, 60, 65, 87, 107, 136, 172, 174, 177, 197, 202; *Gualterus*, 28, 35, 47, 66, 91, 100, 131, 198, 209, 210; *Gwal.a.terus*, 138; *Gwalter*, 96; *Ualterius*, 169; *Uualteri*, 149; *uualterius*, 20, 83, 166; *uualterus*, 22, 161; *Walterius*, 8, 11, 13, 33, 53, 71, 79, 81, 82, 108, 116, 118, 126, 128, 151, 168, 171, 175, 176, 181, 183, 184, 189, 193; *Walterrus*, 128, 132; *Waltherus*, 213, *wlat.*, 196; om., 72, 98, 133, 160.

5 *Exenefordensis*, 147; *Exinefordensis*, 13, 167, 188, 194, 196; *Exinesordensis*, 104; *Exonfordensis*, 205; *Exonfordiensis*, 78, 206; *Herefordensis*, 110; *?Momnefordensis*, 174; *Orinefordnesis*, 77; *Oxenefordensis*, 8, 22, 25, 34, 35, 39, 42, 48, 50, 66, 70, 84, 87, 107, 114, 120, 128, 136, 138, 170, 198, 212; *Oxenefordiensis*, 88, 116, 210; *Oxenefordis*, 134; *Oxenfordensis*, 6, 33, 49, 65, 124; *Oxenofordensis*, 186; *Oxenofordiensis*, 209; *Oxienfordiensis*, 32; *Oxinefordemsis*, 176; *Oxinefordenisis*, 151; *Oxinefordiensis*, 30, 45, 93, 98, 100, 109, 129, 131, 150, 153; *Oxinefordinensis*, 73, 123, 141; *Oxineforsdensis*, 36; *Oxinefortensis*, 14, 168, 171, 184; *Oxinofordensis*, 58, 205; *Oxnefordensis*, 62, 63, 122; *Oxnifordensis*, 57; *Oxonefordensis*, 5, 86; *Oxoniefordensis*, 46; *Oxoniensis*, 26, 27, 51.

6 *archideaconus*, 47; *archidianus*, 171.

7 om., 65, 111, 156, 161, 177, 212 (but found in margin); *ubi*, 174; *ut*, 114.

8...8 *in aratoria arte* (corrected to *oratoria*), 134, 168; *in arotoria arte*, 82; *in ortatoria arte* (corrected to *oratoria*), 166; *in oratorie artis*, 138; *in oratorio arte*, 5; *in euitoria arte*, 55; *in oratoria arte eruditus*, 10, 26, 27, 51; *in orotoria arte*, 149; *memoria arte*, 113; *in oratoria*, 65; om., 111, 156, 161, 177, 212.

9 om. 111, 156, 161, 177, 212 (but in margin).

10 om., 62, 65, 111, 156, 161, 177, 212 (but in margin).

11...11 *hystoriis \exoticis/*, 210; glossed *id est extraneis*, 103; glossed *id est diuersis*, 135; glossed *id est peregrinus*, 127; glossed *uel peregrinis*, 208; glossed *id est ueterum*, 120; *exodicis historiis*, 35; *exotecis uel exodicis historiis*, 22; *exotecis historiis*, 105, 214; *exhorticis historiis*, 194; *exorticiis historiis*, 172, 174, 198; *exorticis historiis*, 7, 11, 16, 17, 21, 32, 59, 60, 78, 104, 117, 135, 167, 188, 190, 197, 199, 206, 211, 213; *exortitis historiis*, 155; *exorcistis historiis*, 5, 84, 124; *exosticis historiis*, 20, 126, 166, 173; *exotiis historiis*, 10,

quendam[13] [14]Britannici sermonis librum[14] uetustissimum[15] [16]qui a Bruto[16] [17]primo rege[17] Britonum[18] usque[19] ad[20] Cadualadrum[21] filium Caduallonis[22] actus[23] omnium continue[24] et[25] ex[26] ordine[27] perpulcris[28] orationibus[29] proponebat.[30] Rogatu[31]

109, 124; *euotiicis historiis,* 171; *erotucis hystoriis,* 168; *heroicis historiis,* 28, 50, 62 (*uel exoticis* in margin), 100, 114; *hereticis historiis,* 27; *heroticis historiis,* 26, 51; *rusticis historiis,* 65; om., 111, 156, 161, 177, 212 (but in margin).

12 *usus,* 10; om., 26, 27, 51, 111, 156, 161, 212 (but in margin).

13 *quemdam,* 13, 22, 45, 50, 62, 74, 82, 87, 98, 114, 124, 149, 183, 196, 212; *quendem,* 174; *quondam,* 118.

14...14 *l. B. s.,* 26, 27, 51, 111; *B. l. s.,* 39; *Britonici sermonis librum,* 9, 21, 36, 53, 77, 81, 83, 126, 151, 166, 173, 175, 176, 183, 196; *Brittonici sermonis librum,* 185; *Britonei sermonis librum,* 3, 14, 171, 184, 189; (*Britonei* as alternative reading, 168); *Britannici sermonis,* 109; *Britannici sermonis isorum,* 78.

15 *uerissimum et uetustissimum,* 129; *ues.t.utissimum,* 168; *uetussissimum,* 164; *uetutissimum,* 105; *uetutissimum,* 13, 79, 98, 176, 193; *uetuttissimum,* 161; *uenustissimum,* 191 (altered to *uetustissimum*), 210, *uetussimum,* 5, 77; *uetussimmum,* 35; *uetutissimum,* 36, 73; *uetustim.,* 81.

16...16 *et qui a Bruto,* 184; *qui a Brito,* 72; *qui a Brute,* 174; *q[i]a Bruto,* 49; *quia Bruto,* 113; *qui ab ruto,* 74; *qui arbitro,* 29.

17...17 *p[o] rege,* 29, 190; *rege primo,* 72, 104, 194; *primorum rege,* 55, 164; *rege post,* 32.

18 *Britorum,* 19.

19 om., 190.

20 om., 62.

21 *Cadaualdrum,* 131; *Ca\d/ualadrum,* 49; *Cadual\a/drum,* 121; *Cadauualdadrum,* 109; *Cadauualdrum,* 45; *Caduualarum,* 151; *Cadawaladrum,* 10, 28, 30, 38, 100, 141, 210; *Cadawald\r/um,* 123; *Cadewaladrum,* 6, 73, 98, 150; *Cadualaden.,* 171; *Cadualadum,* 99, 122, 199; *Cadualardum,* 111, 193; *Cadualarum,* 132; *Cadu\a/larum,* 182; *Cadualdrum,* 79, 117; *Cadualladrum,* 5, 36, 81, 83, 91, 125, 126, 138, 160, 166, 173, 177, 183, 198, 208; *Caduallaudrum,* 168; *Caduallanum,* 107, 136; *Caduallaradrum,* 2 (ra canc.), 8; *Caduallarum,* 151, 175, 176; *Caduladrum,* 211; *Caduualadrum,* 34, 152; *Caduualladen.,* 118; *Caduualladrum,* 116; *Cadwaladrum,* 50, 88, 93, 95, 154, 155; *Cadwaldrum,* 32, 147; *Cadwaladrum,* 22, 29, 47, 55, 63, 74, 87, 88, 112, 114, 125, 137, 153, 192, 212; *Cadwalandrum,* 39; *Cadwaldum,* 70; *Cadwalladrum,* 3, 14, 21, 33, 42, 81, 83, 88, 91, 156, 183, 189, 198; *Cadwalradum,* 57; *Calualadrum,* 202, 207; *Caualadrum,* 169; *Caualladrum,* 53, 196; *Cawaladrum,* 214; *Cawalandrum,* 105; *Kaduualadrum,* 164; *Kadwaladrum,* 26, 27, 37, 51.

22 *Cadualonis,* 7, 84, 85, 130, 149, 174, 190, 207; *Cadwalonis,* 63, 87, 212; *Cadewalonis,* 8; *Cadawallonis,* 210; *Cadouallonis,* 131; *Cad\u/allonis,* 125; *Cadua\l/onis,* 115; *Cauallonis,* 111, 193, 196; *Cadwallionis,* 154; *Cat(w)allonis,* 23; *Caduuallonis,* 38, 45, 105, 109, 116, 118, 214; *Cadwallonis,* 10, 22, 28, 29, 30, 32, 33, 34, (39,) 42, 47, 50, 55, 57, 70, 73, 74, 88, 90, 91, 93, 95, 98, 100, 114, 123, 141, 147, 150, 152, 153, 192; *Kadwallonis,* 26, 27, 37, 51; *Kaduualonis,* 164.

23 om., 63.

24 *cotinue,* 42; *cortinue,* 170.

25 om., 33, 103, 147, 152.

26 om., 77.

27 *ordie,* 100.

28 Glossed *scilicet ualde pulcris,* 103; *pulcris,* 10, 30, 32, 37, 38, 45, 55, 88, 100, 109, 116, 118, 123, 131, 141, 164, 192, 210; *\per/pulcris,* 87; *propulcris,* 70, 77, 171; om., 111.

29 *racionibus,* 65; *sermonibus,* 202; om., 111.

[32]itaque illius ductus,[32] tametsi[33] infra[34] [37]alienos[35] ortulos[36] [37] [38]falerata uerba non collegerim,[38] agresti[39] [40]tamen stilo[40] propriisque[41] calamis[42] contentus[43] codicem illum[44] in [45]Latinum sermonem transferre curaui.[45] [46]Nam si[46] ampullosis[47] dictionibus[48] paginam[49] illinissem,[50] [51]tedium legentibus[51] ingererem,[52] dum[53] [54]magis

30 *properabat*, 187; *propoponebat*, 170; *proponet*, 39; *proponebant*, 71, 213.

31 *Rocatu*, 108; *regatu*, 168.

32...32 *illius itaque ductus*, 79, 84, 190; *itaque ductus illius*, 210; *itaque ductus*, 13; *quoque illius ductus*, 113; *que illius ductus*, 7, 114, 124; *itaque/ illius ductus*, 136; *illius ductus*, 129; *igitur/ illius ductus*, 187; *utique illius ductus*, 6, *itaque illius*, 105; *illius itaque ductu*, 78.

33 *tn. etsi*, 68, 87; *tam. si*, 129; *eam etsi*, 26, 27, 51; *tam et*, 43, 124, 130; *tam*, 171; *etsi*, 104, 147, 160, 194; *etiam*, 37; *licet*, 35, 66; *non* (over erasure), 13; after *tametsi, quamuis si* (cancelled), 62, om., 111; *causa etsi*, 78.

34 *inter*, 10, 78; *inita*, 25; om., 111.

35 *alienos/*, 87; *alios*, 78; *alie*, 105, 214.

36 Glossed *s. ornata*, 103; *hortulos*, 59, 60, 129; *ort\ul/os*, 123; *ortos*, 90, 137; *a°rtulos*, 168; *?circulos*, 65; om., 111.

37...37 *o. a.*, 39; om., 111.

38...38 *phalerata non collegerim uerba*, 107; *phalerata uerba non collegerim*, 114, 116, 136, 207; *uerba/ falerata non collegerim*, 95; *falerata uerba non \collegerim/*, 115; *fallerata uerba non colligerim*, 100; *felerata uerba non collegerim*, 152; *falekata uerba non colligerim*, 118; *famulata uerba non collegerim*, 105; *falerata non collegerim*, 37; *non collegerim*, 38, 110, 131; *falerata nisi collegerim*, 147; *falerata uerba collegerim*, 29, 39, 155, 190; *falerata uerba non colligerim*, 26, 36, 37, 47, 51, 168, 196, 209, 214; *falerata uerba non coligerim*, 45; *falerata uerba non collegeram*, 198; *falerata uerba non collegeri*, 13; *fallanus*, 78; glossed *id est humili uel []i*, 103; om., 111.

39 *agresta* (altered to *agresti*), 104; *sed agresti*, 13; om., 78, 111.

40...40 *stilo agresti*, 38 (*tamen* in margin), 202; *tamen/ stilo*, 136; *stilo*, 132; *tamen*, 213; *tantum stilo*, 20, 83, 126, 166, 173; *tn. stilo*, 39; after *stilo, filio* (cancelled), 47; *stilo*, 132; om., 78, 111.

41 *propriis*, 132, 182; *propriis atque*, 7, 155; om., 78, 111.

42 Glossed *scilicet scripta uel ppna.*, 103; *chalamis*, 50; *thalamis*, 45; om., 78, 111.

43 *contem.p.tus*, 126; *contemptus*, 20, 83, 151, 166, 173; om., 111, 187.

44 *istum*, 7.

45...45 *sermonem Latinum transferre curaui*, 132; *sermonem transferre Latinum curaui*, 168; *Latinum sermonem curaui transferre*, 172, 174, 197, 198; *Latinum transferre curaui*, 78; *Latinum sermonem transferre*, 88, 116; *Latinum sermonem transferri curaui*, 99, 122; *Latinum sermonem transferrem curaui*, 134.

46...46 *Nam et si*, 13, 32, 58, 59, 117, 124, 127, 167, 188, 205, 208; *Nam si in*, 55; om., 111.

47 *ampulissimis*, 65; om., 111.

48 *doccionibus*, 152; *uerbis*, 37, 190, 210; om., 111.

49 *paginem*, 15, 81, 97, 100, 150, 210, 211; *peraginam*, 90; om., 111.

50 *illinissem*, altered to *illirassem*, 95; *illirassem*, 35, 47, 66, 91, 138; *illusissem*, 132; *inlinissem*, 2; *illinisse*, 161; *illiuissem*, 121; *inseram*, 39; *dictassem*, 88, 116; *illinissem et*, 184; *inmisissem*, 78; om., 111.

51...51 *te.n.dium legentibus*, 73; *tedium in legentibus*, 83 (*in* cancelled), 176; *tedium \forsitan/ legentibus*, 115; *tedium forsitan legentibus*, 192; om., 111.

52 *ingerere*, 26, 65; om., 111.

53 *ducam*, 97; *duram*, 76; om., 111.

in exponendis uerbis[54] quam in[55] historia[56] intelligenda[57] ipsos[58] commorari[59] oporteret.[60]

54...54 *in exponendis uerbis magis*, 164; *magis exponendis uerbis*, 168; *magis in exponendis*, 46; *magis in \ex/ponendis uerbis*, 34; *magis in exponendis uerbis uerbis*, 169; *magis in componendis uerbis*, 20, 126, 166; *magis in coponendis uerbis*, 83; *magis in exponendis libris*, 156; om., 111.

55 om., 21, 111, 132, 155, 168, 172, 174, 177, 182, 197, 198, 199.

56 *historiam*, 35, 62; om., 111.

57 *intelligendi*, 47; *intelligendam*, 62; *intelligendo*, 87; om., 111.

58 om., 174; *iposos*, 190; om., 111.

59 *commemorari*, 123, 150, 185; *immorari*, 33, 34, 127, 147, ?187, 208; *immorare*, 152; om., 111.

60 *oportet*, 28 (altered to *oporteret*), 48, 85, 128, 134; om., 111.

§100

Not found in 1, 2, 11, 12, 18, (24,) 27, 40, 94, 101, 139, 144, 145, 148, 157, 159, 176, 192, (201). Not including the Variant manuscripts 4, 17, 22, 35, 47, 50, 54, 55, 66, 67, 68, 70, 80, 85, 91, 95, 102, 106, 108, 114, 138, 163, 202, 207, 209.

Interea[1] [3]uero reuersi[2] sunt nuntii[3] ex[4] Germania conduxerantque[5] [6] .x. et .viii.

[1] 3, 5, 6, 7, 8, 9, 10, 13, 14, 15, 16, 19, 20, 21, 23, 25, 26, 28, 29, 30, 31, 32, 33, 34, 36, 37, 38, 39, 41, 42, 43, 44, 45, 46, 48, 49, 51, 52, 53, 56, 57, 58, 59, 60, 61, 62, 63, 64, 65, 69, 71, 72, 73, 74, 75, 76, 77, 78, 79, 81, 82, 83, 84, 86, 87, 88, 89, 90, 92, 93, 96, 97, 98, 99, 100, 103, 104, 105, 107, 109, 110, 111, 112, 113, 115, 116, 117, 118, 119, 120, 121, 122, 123, 124, 125, 126, 127, 128, 129, 130, 131, 132, 133, 134, 135, 136, 137, 140, 141, 142, 143, 146, 147, 149, 150, 151, 152, 153, 154, 155, 156, 158, 160, 161, 162, 164, 165, 166, 167, 169, 170, 171, 172, 173, 174, 175, 177, 178, 179, 180, 181, 182, 183, 184, 185, 187, 188, 189, 190, 191, 193, 194, 195, 196, 197, 198, 199, 200, 203, 204, 205, 206, 208, 210, 211, 212, 213, 214; *In interea,* 186; om., 168.

[2] 3, 5, 6, 7, 8, 9, 10, 13, 14, 15, 16, 19, 20, 21, 23, 25, 26, 28, 29, 30, 31, 32, 33, 34, 36, 37, 38, 39, 41, 42, 43, 44, 45, 46, 48, 49, 51, 52, 53, 56, 57, 58, 59, 60, 61, 62, 63, 64, 65, 69, 71, 72, 73, 74, 75, 76, 77, 78, 79, 81, 82, 83, 84, 86, 87, 88, 89, 90, 92, 93, 96, 97, 98, 99, 100, 103, 104, 105, 107, 109, 110, 111, 112, 113, 115, 116, 117, 118, 119, 120, 121, 122, 123, 124, 125, 126, 127, 128, 129, 130, 131, 132, 133, 134, 135, 136, 137, 140, 141, 142, 143, 146, 147, 149, 150, 151, 152, 153, 154, 155, 156, 160, 161, 162, 164, 165, 166, 167, 168, 169, 170, 171, 172, 173, 174, 175, 177, 178, 179, 180, 181, 182, 183, 184, 185, 186, 187, 188, 189, 190, 191, 193, 194, 195, 196, 197, 198, 199, 200, 203, 204, 205, 206, 208, 210, 211, 212, 213, 214; *reuersi inimici,* 158.

[3...3] 5, 6, 7, 8, 9, 10, 13, 14, 15, 16, 19, 21, 25, 28, 29, 30, 31, 34, 36, 37, 38, 39, 41, 43, 44, 45, 46, 48, 49, 52, 53, 56, 57, 58, 59, 61, 62, 63, 64, 65, 71, 72, 73, 74, 75, 76, 77, 78, 79, 81, 82, 84, 87, 89, 90, 92, 93, 97, 98, 99, 100, 103, 104, 105, 107, 109, 112, 113, 115, 117, 119, 120, 121, 122, 123, 124, 125, 127, 129, 130, 131, 132, 133, 135, 136, 137, 140, 141, 142, 143, 147, 150, 152, 153, 154, 155, 156, 158, 160, 161, 162, 165, 167, 169, 170, 171, 172, 177, 178, 179, 180, 181, 182, 183, 185, 186, 187, 188, 189, 190, 191, 194, 195, 196, 197, 198, 199, 203, 204, 205, 206, 208, 210, 211, 212, 213, 214; *u. n. r. s.,* 26, 51; *n. u. r. s.,* 149; *r. s. n. u.,* 128; *r. s. n.,* 3, 23, 32, 33, 42, 60, 69, 86, 88, 96, 110, 116, 146, 164, 168, 184, 200; *s. r. n.,* 118; *u. r. n.,* 134; *u. r. s.,* 174, 175, 193; *r. s.,* 20, 83, 126, 151, 166, 173; *reuersi sunt legati,* 111.

[4] 3, 5, 6, 7, 8, 9, 10, 13, 14, 15, 16, 19, 20, 21, 23, 26, 28, 29, 30, 31, 32, 33, 34, 36, 37, 38, 39, 41, 42, 43, 44, 45, 46, 48, 49, 51, 52, 53, 56, 57, 58, 59, 60, 61, 62, 63, 64, 65, 69, 71, 72, 73, 74, 75, 76, 77, 78, 79, 81, 82, 83, 84, 86, 87, 88, 89, 90, 92, 93, 96, 97, 98, 99, 100, 103, 104, 105, 107, 109, 110, 111, 112, 113, 115, 116, 117, 118, 119, 120, 121, 122, 123, 124, 125, 126, 127, 128, 129, 130, 131, 132, 133, 134, 135, 136, 137, 140, 141, 142, 143, 146, 147, 149, 150, 151, 152, 153, 154, 155, 156, 158, 160, 161, 162, 164, 165, 166, 167, 168, 169, 170, 171, 172, 173, 174, 175, 177, 178, 179, 180, 181, 182, 183, 184, 185, 186, 187, 188, 189, 190, 191, 193, 194, 195, 196, 197, 198, 199, 200, 203, 204, 205, 206, 208, 210, 211, 212, 213, 214; *de,* 25.

[5] 8, 14, 15, 19, 29, 43, 48, 63, 107, 122, 127, 128, 130, 142, 175, 188, 193, 200; *conduxerunt-que,* 3, 5, 6, 7, 9, 13, 16, 20, 21, 23, 25, 26, 28, 29, 30, 31, 32, 33, 36, 37, 38, 39, 41, 42, 44, 45, 46, 49, 51, 52, 53, 56, 58, 59, 60, 62, 64, 69, 71, 72, 73, 74, 75, 76, 77, 78, 79, 82, 83, 84, 87, 89, 90, 92, 93, 96, 97, 98, 99, 100, 103, 105, 109, 112, 113, 115, 116, 117, 118, 119, 120, 124, 125, 126, 129, 131, 132, 133, 134, 135, 136, 137, 140, 143, 146, 147, 149, 150, 151, 153, 155, 156, 158, 160, 161, 162, 164, 165, 166, 167, 169, 171, 172, 173, 174, 177,

naues[6] [7]electis militibus plenas.[7] [8]Conduxerunt etiam[8] filiam Hengisti[9] [10] uocabulo

178, 179, 180, 181, 182, 183, 184, 185, 186, 187, 189, 190, 191, 194, 195, 196, 197, 198, 199, 203, 204, 205, 206, 208, 210, 211, 212, 213; *conduxerant\que/*, 154; *et conduxerunt*, 57; *\con/duxeruntque*, 24; *duxeruntque*, 111; *conduxerat\que/*, 170; *conduxeratque*, 88; *conduxerunt*, 10, 34, 61, 65, 104, 110, 121, 123, 141, 152, 168, 214; *adduxerantque*, 86; *cum dixerantque*, 81.

[6...6] 15, 37, 48, 56, 57, 58, 63, 104, 109, 128, 133, 136 146, 149, 150, 151, 158, 166, 170, 172, 173, 175, 178, 190, 197, 198, 199, 205, 210; *x.cem et .viii.to naues*, 3, 14, 189; *decem et .viii. naues*, 83; *x.* et octo naues, 120, 132, 147, 168, 171, 174; *decem et octo naues*, 5, 6, 7, 20, 25, 31, 33, 36, 41, 42, 43, 46, 51, 53, 59, 60, 64, 65, 69, 71, 72, 74, 76, 77, 78, 79, 82, 84, 87, 89, 90, 92, 93, 96, 97, 103, 111, 112, 113, 115, 121, 124, 125, 126, 127, 130, 132, 135, 137, 140, 154, 155, 156, 160, 161, 162, 164, 167, 177, 179, 180, 181, 182, 183, 184, 185, 187, 191, 193, 195, 200, 203, 208, 213; *xviii. naues*, 8, 9, 10, 13, 16, 19, 21, 23, (24,) 26, 28, 29, 30, 32, 39, 44, 45, 49, 52, 61, 73, 75, 81, 86, 88, 98, 100, 107, 116, 117, 119, 123, 129, 134, 141, 142, 143, 153, 165, 169, 186, 188, 194, 204, 206, 211, 212; *octo et decem naues*, 34, 152; *x. naues et octo*, 105, 214; *decem et octodecim naues*, 62; *xxxviii. naues*, 110; *ducem et octo naues*, 38, 99, 122, 131, 196.

[7...7] 3, 5, 6, 7, 9, 10, 13, 14, 15, 16, 19, 20, 21, 23, 25, 26, 29, 30, 31, 32, 33, 34, 36, 37, 38, 39, 41, 42, 43, 44, 45, 48, 49, 51, 52, 53, 56, 57, 58, 59, 60, 61, 62, 63, 64, 65, 69, 71, 72, 73, 74, 75, 76, 77, 78, 79, 81, 82, 83, 84, 86, 87, 88, 89, 90, 92, 93, 96, 97, 98, 99, 103, 104, 105, 107, 109, 110, 112, 113, 115, 116, 117, 118, 120, 121, 122, 123, 124, 125, 126, 127, 128, 129, 130, 131, 132, 133, 135, 136, 140, 141, 142, 143, 146, 147, 149, 150, 151, 152, 153, 154, 155, 156, 158, 160, 161, 162, 164, 165, 166, 167, 168, 169, 170, 171, 172, 173, 174, 175, 177, 178, 179, 180, 181, 182, 183, 184, 185, 186, 187, 188, 189, 190, 191, 193, 194, 195, 196, 197, 198, 199, 200, 203, 204, 205, 206, 208, 210, 211, 212, 213, 214; *m. e. p.*, 100, 134; *p. m. e.*, 8; *m. p.*, 28; *electis mili\ti/bus plenas*, 137; *electis militibus plenis*, 119; *elicitis militibus plenas*, 46; *armatis mititibus plenas*, 111.

[8...8] 3, 5, 6, 7, 9, 10, 13, 14, 15, 16, 19, 20, 21, 23, 26, 28, 29, 30, 31, 32, 33, 34, 37, 38, 39, 41, 42, 43, 45, 46, 48, 51, 52, 53, 57, 59, 61, 62, 63, 64, 65, 69, 71, 72, 73, 74, 75, 76, 77, 78, 79, 81, 82, 83, 84, 86, 87, 89, 90, 93, 96, 97, 98, 99, 100, 103, 104, 105, 107, 109, 110, 111, 112, 113, 115, 116, 117, 118, 119, 120, 122, 123, 124, 125, 126, 127, 128, 130, 131, 132, 133, 134, 135, 136, 137, 140, 141, 142, 143, 146, 149, 150, 151, 152, 153, 155, 156, 158, 160, 161, 162, 164, 165, 166, 167, 168, 169, 170, 171, 172, 173, 174, 175, 177, 178, 179, 180, 181, 182. 183, 184, 185, 186, 187, 188, 189, 190, 191, 193, 194, 195, 196, 197, 198, 199, 200, 203, 204, 206, 208, 211, 212, 213, 214; *conduxerant etiam*, 25, 49, 92, 210; *coduxerunt etiam*, 8; *conduxeruntque etiam*, 129; *conduxerunque etiam*, 44; *adduxerunt etiam*, 121; *conduxerunt \etiam/*, 88, 154; *conduxerunt et*, 56, 58, 205; *cuduxerunt et*, 36; *conduxerunt*, 44; *adduxeruntque*, 60; *conduxerunt et' que*, 147.

[9] 3, 5, 6, 7, 8, 9, 10, 13, 14, 15, 16, 19, 20, 21, 23, 25, 26, 28, 30, 31, 32, 33, 34, 36, 37, 38, 39, 41, 42, 43, 44, 45, 46, 49, 51, 52, 53, 56, 57, 58, 59, 60, 61, 62, 63, 64, 65, 69, 71, 72, 73, 74, 75, 77, 78, 79, 81, 82, 83, 84, 86, 87, 88, 89, 90, 92, 93, 96, 97, 98, 100, 103, 104, 105, 107, 109, 110, 111, 112, 113, 115, 116, 117, 118, 119, 120, 121, 122, 123, 124, 125, 126, 127, 128, 129, 130, 131, 132, 133, 134, 135, 136, 137, 140, 141, 142, 143, 146, 147, 149, 150, 151, 152, 153, 154, 155, 156, 158, 160, 161, 162, 164, 165, 166, 167, 168, 169, 170, 171, 172, 173, 174, 175, 177, 178, 179, 180, 181, 182, 183, 184, 185, 186, 187, 188, 189, 190, 191, 193, 194, 195, 196, 197, 198, 199, 200, 203, 204, 205, 206, 208, 210, 211, 212, 213, 214; *Engisti*, 76; *Henguli*, 99 (corrected), 122; *Hensti*, 29.

[10...10] 15, 48, 86, 128, 170, 177, 200; *uocabulo Norguen*, 20, 83, 126, 166; *uocabulo Noruen*, 109; *uocabulo Norwein*, 44; *uocabulo Norwennam*, 161; *uocabulo Redwen*, 69; *uocabulo Renwen*, 49, 107, 136; *uocabulo Ringen*, 110; *uocabulo Rodwen*, 33, 142; *uocabulo Rogen*, 111; *uocabulo Romuem*, 65; *uocabulo Rongem*, 193; *uocabulo Ronguen*, 151, 173, 175;

Renwein[10] cuius[11] pulcritudo[12] nulli[13] [14]secunda uidebatur.[14] Postquam autem[15]

uocabulo Ronixem, 182, 199; *uocabulo Ronrueir,* 197; *uocabulo Ronuen,* 8, 28, 30, 39, 45,
56, 58, 61, 84, 119, 123, 141, 169, 205; *uocabulo Ronuuein,* 24, 38, ?211; *uocabulo
Ronuuem,* 52, 60, 172, ?174, ?198; *uocabulo Ronuuen,* 13, 16, 19, 21, 53, 78, 92, 116, 117,
129, 131, 167, 187, 188, 190, 196; *uocabulo Ronweim,* 154; *uocabulo Ronwein,* 6, 25, 31,
36, 37, 43, 62, 74, 77, 79, 96, 99, 113, 120, 122, 127, 155, 156, 158, 162, 165, 178, 185,
195, 203, 208, 210, 212, 213; *uocabulo Ronwem,* 46, 51, 82, 135, 179, 191; *uocabulo
Ronwe\i/n,* 43; *uocabulo Ronwen,* 5, 23, 26, 29, 32, 34, 41, 42, 57, 59, 64, 71, 73, 76, 88,
90, 93, 97, 98, 103, 104, 112, 115, 121, 124, 130, 132, 137, 146, 147, 149, 150, 153, 164,
180, 183, 194; *uocabulo \Ronwenn/,* 125; *uocabulo Ronwennam,* 133; *uocabulo Ronwen-
niam,* 72; *uocabulo Ronweyn,* 140, 204; *uocabulo Ronwon,* 81; *uocabulo Rouuen,* 75, 211;
uocabulo Rowen, 3, 7, 9, 10, 14, 20, 63, 87, 143, 152, 168, 171, 181, 184, 186, 189; *uocabulo
Rowenne,* 89, 160; *uocabulo dominen?,* 206; *Ro[]uen uocabulo,* 134; *uocabo Ronuen,* 100;
nomine Ronwen, 214; *nomine Rouwen,* 105; *nomine Ronuuen,* 118; *nomine Rogen,* 111.

[11] 3, 5, 7, 8, 9, 10, 13, 14, 15, 16, 19, 20, 21, 23, 25, 26, 28, 29, 30, 31, 32, 33, 34, 36, 37, 38,
39, 42, 43, 44, 45, 46, 48, 49, 51, 52, 53, 56, 57, 58, 59, 60, 61, 62, 63, 64, 65, 71, 72, 73,
74, 75, 76, 77, 78, 79, 81, 82, 83, 86, 87, 88, 89, 90, 92, 93, 96, 97, 98, 99, 100, 103, 104,
105, 107, 109, 110, 112, 113, 115, 116, 117, 118, 119, 120, 121, 122, 123, 125, 126, 127,
128, 129, 130, 131, 132, 133, 134, 135, 136, 137, 140, 141, 142, 143, 146, 147, 149, 150,
151, 152, 153, 154, 155, 156, 158, 160, 161, 162, 164, 165, 166, 167, 168, 169, 170, 171,
172, 173, 174, 175, 177, 178, 179, 180, 181, 182, 183, 184, 185, 186, 187, 188, 189, 190,
191, 193, 194, 195, 196, 197, 198, 199, 200, 203, 204, 205, 206, 208, 210, 211, 212, 213,
214; *cui,* 6, 41, 69, 84, 124; om., 111.

[12] 3, 5, 6, 7, 8, 9, 10, 13, 14, 15, 16, 19, 20, 21, 23, 25, 26, 28, 29, 30, 31, 32, 33, 34, 36, 37,
38, 39, 41. 42, 43, 44, 45, 46, 48, 49, 51, 52, 53, 56, 57, 58, 59, 60, 61, 62, 64, 65, 69, 71,
72, 73, 74, 75, 76, 77, 78, 79, 81, 82, 83, 84, 86, 87, 88, 89, 90, 92, 93, 96, 97, 98, 99, 100,
103, 104, 105, 107, 109, 110, 112, 113, 116, 117, 118, 119, 120, 121, 122, 123, 124, 125,
126, 127, 129, 130, 131, 132, 133, 134, 135, 136, 137, 140, 141, 142, 143, 146, 149, 150,
151, 152, 153, 154, 155, 156, 158, 160, 161, 162, 164, 165, 166, 167, 168, 169, 170, 171,
172, 173, 174, 175, 177, 178, 179, 180, 181, 182, 183, 184, 185, 186, 187, 188, 189, 190,
191, 193, 194, 195, 196, 197, 198, 199, 200, 203, 204, 205, 206, 208, 210, 211, 212, 213,
214; *pulcritudinem,* 128 (corr. to *pulchritudo*); *pulcritudini,* 63, ?147; *in domum suam
pulcritudinem,* 111; *pulctudo,* 115.

[13] 3, 5, 7, 8, 9, 10, 13, 14, 15, 16, 19, 20, 21, 23, 25, 26, 28, 29, 30, 31, 32, 33, 34, 36, 37, 38,
39, 41, 42, 43, 44, 45, 46, 48, 49, 51, 52, 53, 56, 57, 58, 59, 60, 61, 62, 64, 65, 69, 71, 72,
73, 74, 75, 76, 77, 78, 79, 81, 82, 83, 84, 86, 88, 89, 90, 92, 93, 96, 97, 98, 99, 100, 103,
104, 105, 107, 109, 112, 113, 115, 116, 117, 119, 120, 121, 122, 123, 124, 125, 126, 127,
128, 129, 130, 131, 132, 133, 134, 135, 136, 137, 140, 141, 142, 143, 146, 149, 150, 151,
152, 153, 154, 155, 156, 158, 160, 161, 162, 164, 165, 166, 167, 168, 169, 170, 171, 172,
173, 174, 175, 178, 179, 180, 181, 182, 183, 184, 185, 186, 187, 188, 189, 190, 191, 193,
194, 195, 196, 197, 198, 199, 200, 203, 204, 205, 206, 208, 210, 211, 212, 213, 214; om.,
118; *nulla,* 6, 63, 64, 87, 147; *nullo,* 110; *regni* (corr. to *nulli*), 177; *nimis,* 111.

[14...14] 5, 6, 7, 8, 9, 10, 13, 15, 16, 19, 21, 23, 25, 26, 28, 29, 30, 31, 33, 34, 36, 37, 38, 39, 41,
42, 43, 44, 45, 46, 48, 49, 51, 52, 53, 56, 57, 58, 59, 60, 61, 62, 63, 64, 65, 69, 71, 72, 73,
74, 75, 76, 77, 78, 79, 82, 84, 86, 87, 88, 89, 90, 92, 93, 96, 97, 98, 99, 100, 103, 104, 105,
109, 112, 113, 115, 116, 117, 119, 120, 121, 122, 123, 125, 127, 128, 129, 130, 131, 132,
133, 134, 135, 136, 137, 140, 141, 142, 143, 146, 147, 149, 150, 152, 153, 154, 155, 156,
158, 160, 161, 162, 164, 165, 167, 170, 172, 174, 177, 178, 179, 180, 181, 182, 185, 186,
187, 188, 190, 191, 193, 194, 195, 196, 197, 198, 199, 200, 203, 204, 205, 206, 208, 212,
213, 214; *u. s.,* 3, 14, 20, 81, 83, 107, 126, 151, 166, 168, 169, 171, 173, 175, 183, 184, 189;

uenerunt,[16][21] inuitauit[17] Hengistus[18] Uortegirnum[19] regem[20][21] in[22] domum suam

secunda esse uidebatur, 118; *secula uidebatur,* 32, 211; *seccula uidebatur,* 124; *seculo uidebatur,* 110; *prospera uidebatur,* 210; om., 111

[15] 3, 5, 6, 7, 8, 9, 10, 13, 14, 15, 16, 19, 20, 21, 23, 25, 26, 28, 29, 30, 32, 33, 34, 36, 37, 38, 39, 41, 42, 43, 44, 45, 46, 48,49, 51, 52, 53, 56, 57, 58, 59, 60, 61, 62, 63, 65, 69, 71, 72, 73, 74, 75, 76, 77, 78, 79, 81, 82, 83, 86, 87, 88, 90, 92, 93, 96, 97, 98, 99, 100, 103, 104, 105, 107, 109, 110, 111, 112, 115, 116, 117, 118, 119, 120, 121, 122, 123, 124, 125, 126, 127, 128, 130, 131, 132, 133, 134, 135, 136, 137, 140, 141, 142, 143, 146, 147, 149, 150, 151, 152, 153, 155, 156, 158, 161, 162, 164, 165, 166, 167, 168, 169, 170, 171, 172, 173, 174, 175, 177, 178, 179, 180, 181, 182, 183, 184, 185, 186, 187, 188, 189, 190, 191, 193, 194, 195, 196, 197, 198, 199, 200, 203, 204, 205, 206, 208, 210, 211, 212, 213, 214; *uero,* 84; om., 31, 64, 89, 113, 129, 154, 160.

[16] 3, 5, 6, 7, 8, 9, 10, 13, 14, 15, 16, 19, 20, 21, 23, 25, 26, 28, 29, 30, 31, 32, 33, 34, 36, 37, 38, 39, 41, 42, 43, 44, 45, 46, 48, 49, 51, 52, 53, 56, 57, 58, 59, 60, 61, 62, 63, 64, 65, 69, 71, 72, 73, 74, 75, 76, 77, 78, 79, 81, 82, 83, 84, 86, 87, 88, 89, 90, 92, 93, 96, 97, 98, 99, 100, 103, 104, 105, 107, 109, 110, 111, 112, 113, 115, 116, 117, 118, 119, 120, 121, 122, 123, 124, 125, 126, 127, 128, 129, 130, 131, 132, 133, 134, 135, 136, 137, 140, 141, 142, 143, 146, 147, 149, 150, 151, 152, 153, 154, 155, 156, 158, 160, 161, 162, 164, 165, 166, 167, 168, 169, 170, 171, 172, 173, 174, 175, 177, 178, 179, 180, 181, 183, 184, 185, 186, 187, 188, 189, 190, 191, 193, 194, 195, 196, 197, 198, 199, 200, 203, 204, 205, 206, 208, 210, 211, 212, 213, 214; *uenerint,* 182; *inuenerunt,* 24.

[17] 3, 5, 6, 7, 8, 9, 10, 13, 14, 15, 16, 19, 20, 21, 23, 25, 26, 28, 29, 30, 31, 32, 33, 34, 36, 37, 38, 39, 41, 42, 43, 44, 45, 46, 48, 49, 51, 52, 53, 56, 57, 58, 59, 60, 61, 62, 63, 64, 65, 69, 71, 72, 73, 74, 75, 76, 77, 78, 79, 81, 82, 83, 84, 86, 87, 88, 89, 90, 92, 93, 96, 97, 98, 99, 100, 103, 104, 105, 107, 109, 110, 111, 112, 113, 115, 116, 117, 118, 119, 120, 121, 122, 123, 124, 125, 126, 127, 129, 130, 131, 132, 133, 134, 135, 136, 137, 140, 141, 143, 146, 147, 149, 150, 151, 152, 153, 154, 155, 156, 158, 160, 161, 162, 164, 165, 166, 167, 168, 170, 171, 172, 173, 174, 175, 177, 178, 179, 180, 181, 182, 183, 184, 185, 186, 187, 188, 189, 190, 191, 193, 194, 195, 196, 197, 198, 199, 200, 203, 204, 205, 206, 208, 210, 211, 212, 213, 214; *inuictauit,* 142; *inutauit,* 169; *in tempore illo inuitauit,* 128.

[18] 3, 5, 6, 7, 8, 9, 10, 13, 14, 15, 16, 19, 20, 21, 23, 25, 26, 28, 29, 30, 31, 32, 33, 34, 36, 37, 38, 39, 41, 42, 43, 44, 45, 46, 48, 49, 51, 52, 53, 56, 57, 58, 59, 60, 61, 62, 63, 64, 65, 69, 71, 72, 73, 74, 75, 77, 78, 79, 81, 82, 83, 84, 86, 87, 88, 89, 90, 92, 93, 96, 97, 98, 100, 103, 104, 105, 107, 109, 110, 111, 112, 113, 115, 116, 117, 118, 119, 120, 121, 122, 123, 124, 125, 126, 127, 128, 129, 130, 131, 132, 133, 134, 135, 136, 137, 140, 141, 142, 143, 146, 147, 149, 150, 151, 152, 153, 154, 155, 156, 158, 160, 161, 162, 164, 165, 166, 167, 168, 169, 170, 171, 172, 173, 174, 175, 178, 179, 180, 181, 182, 183, 184, 185, 186, 187, 188, 189, 190, 191, 193, 194, 195, 196, 197, 198, 199, 200, 203, 204, 205, 206, 208, 210, 211, 212, 213, 214; *Engistus,* 76; *Henginstus,* 99; *Hengestus* (altered to *Hengistus*), 177.

[19] 5, 8, 10, 13, 15, 16, 19, 20, 21, 25, 26, 28, 30, 32, 33, 36, 37, 39, 43, 45, 46, 48, 49, 52, 53, 57, 58, 59, 61, 64, 65, 69, 71, 72, 73, 74, 76, 77, 79, 82, 83, 84, 87, 88, 89, 90, 92, 93, 98, 99, 100, 103, 104, 107, 109, 111, 112, 113, 116, 118, 119, 120, 121, 122, 123, 124, 125, 126, 127, 130, 133, 134, 135, 136, 141, 143, 146, 147, 149, 150, 151, 152, 153, 154, 155, 158, 161, 162, 165, 169, 170, 173, 175, 179, 180, 181, 185, 186, 188, 191, 193, 194, 195, 196, 197, 200, 203, 205, 208, 211; *Uortigirnum,* 7, 23, 44, 105, 128, 131, 140, 142, 143, 160, 164, 178, 212, 214; *Uortigernum,* 9, 29, 31, 34, 41, 42, 51, 56, 63, 75, 78, 96, 97, 110, 132, 137, 206, 210; *Uortegiruum,* 172; *Uorteguinum,* 86; *Uortegeirgnum,* 174; *Uortigenum,* 187; *Wortegirnum,* 6, 62, 117, 182, 190, 199, 213; *Wortigernum,* 115, 199; *Wort',* 38; *Uoltegirnum,* 81, 183, 184; *Woltegirnum,* 3, 14, 171, 189; *Wotelgirnum,* 168; *Uo\r/tegirnum,* 166; *Uotegirnum,* 156, 167; *Uorthigensi,* 60; *Nortegironum* (altered to *Nortegirnum*), 177; *dux paganorum Uortegirnum* 129.

ut[23] nouum[24] edificium[25] et[26] [27]nouos milites[27] qui applicuerant[28] uideret.[29] Uenit[30]

[20] 3, 5, 6, 7, 8, 9, 10, 13, 14, 15, 16, 19, 20, 21, 23, 25, 26, 28, 29, 30, 31, 32, 33, 34, 36, 37, 38, 39, 41, 42, 43, 44, 45, 46, 48, 49, 51, 52, 53, 56, 57, 58, 59, 60, 61, 62, 63, 64, 65, 69, 71, 72, 73, 74, 75, 76, 77, 78, 79, 81, 82, 83, 84, 86, 87, 88, 89, 90, 92, 93, 96, 97, 98, 99, 100, 103, 104, 105, 107, 109, 110, 111, 112, 113, 115, 116, 117, 118, 119, 120, 121, 122, 123, 124, 125, 126, 127, 128, 130, 131, 132, 133, 134, 135, 136, 137, 140, 141, 142, 143, 146, 147, 149, 150, 151, 152, 153, 154, 155, 156, 158, 160, 161, 162, 164, 165, 166, 167, 168, 169, 170, 171, 172, 173, 174, 175, 177, 178, 179, 180, 181, 182, 183, 184, 185, 186, 187, 188, 189, 190, 191, 193, 194, 195, 196, 197, 198, 199, 200, 203, 204, 205, 206, 208, 210, 211, 212, 213, 214; *regem Britonum,* 129.

[21...21] 5, 6, 7, 9, 15, 16, 19, 20, 21, 23, 25, 26, 31, 33, 34, 36, 37, 38, 41, 42, 43, 48, 49, 51, 52, 53, 56, 57, 59, 61, 62, 63, 65, 69, 71, 72, 74, 75, 76, 77, 78, 79, 81, 82, 83, 84, 86, 87, 88, 89, 92, 93, 96, 97, 99, 103, 104, 105, 107, 111, 112, 113, 115, 116, 118, 120, 124, 125, 126, 127, 128, 129, 130, 131, 132, 133, 135, 136, 140, 142, 143, 146, 147, 149, 150, 151, 152, 154, 155, 156, 158, 160, 161, 162, 164, 166, 167, 169, 170, 172, 173, 174, 175, 177, 178, 179, 180, 181, 182, 183, 186, 187, 190, 191, 193, 194, 195, 196, 197, 198, 199, 200, 203, 204, 206, 208, 210, 211, 212, 213, 214; *H. i. U. r.,* 46; *i. H. r. U.,* 110; *i. U. H. r.,* 60; *i. H. U. \r./,* 122; *i. H. U.,* 3, 13, 14, 29, 44, 90, 137, 168, 171, 184, 189; *i. U. H.,* 117, 188; *i. U. r.,* 185; *i. H. r.,* 8, 10, 28, 30, 32, 39, 45, 58, 64, 73, 98, 100, 109, 119, 123, 134, 141, 153, 165, 205.

[22] 3, 5, 6, 7, 8, 9, 10, 13, 14, 15, 16, 19, 20, 21, 23, 25, 26, 28, 29, 30, 31, 32, 33, 34, 36, 37, 38, 39, 41, 42, 43, 44, 45, 46, 48, 49, 51, 52, 53, 56, 57, 58, 59, 60, 61, 62, 63, 65, 69, 71, 72, 73, 74, 75, 76, 77, 78, 79, 81, 82, 83, 84, 86, 87, 88, 89, 90, 92, 93, 96, 97, 98, 99, 100, 103, 104, 105, 107, 109, 110, 111, 112, 113, 115, 116, 117, 118, 119, 120, 121, 122, 123, 124, 125, 126, 127, 128, 129, 130, 131, 132, 133, 134, 135, 136, 137, 140, 141, 142, 143, 146, 147, 149, 150, 151, 152, 153, 154, 155, 156, 158, 160, 161, 162, 164, 165, 166, 167, 168, 169, 170, 171, 172, 173, 174, 175, 177, 178, 179, 180, 181, 182, 183, 184, 185, 186, 187, 188, 189, 190, 191, 193, 194, 195, 196, 197, 198, 199, 200, 203, 204, 205, 206, 208, 210, 211, 212, 213, 214; om. 64.

[23] 3, 5, 14, 15, 19, 20, 23, 28, 34, 42, 61, 75, 86, 90, 96, 103, 110, 112, 124, 125, 130, 134, 137, 147, 152, 168, 171, 182, 184, 185, 189, 199, 200; *et,* 15, 100; *et ut,* 6, 10, 37, 39, 57, 69, 84, 115, 165, 172, 174, 197, 198, 208; *ut et,* 7, 8, 9, 13, 16, 21, (24,) 25, 26, 29, 30, 31, 32, 33, 36, 38, 41, 43, 44, 45, 46, 48, 49, 51, 52, 53, 56, 58, 59, 60, 62, 63, 64, 65, 71, 72, 73, 74, 76, 77, 78, 79, 81, 82, 83, 87, 88, 89, 92, 93, 97, 98, 99, 104, 105, 107, 109, 111, 113, 116, 117, 118, 119, 120, 121, 122, 123, 126, 127, 128, 129, 131, 132, 133, 135, 136, 140, 141, 142, 143, 146, 149, 150, 151, 153, 154, 155, 156, 158, 160, 162, 164, 166, 167, 169, 170, 173, 175, 177, 178, 179, 180, 181, 183, 187, 188, 190, 191, 193, 194, 195, 196, 203, 204, 205, 206, 210, 211, 212, 213, 214; \ut/ et, 161; *ut etiam,* 186.

[24] 3, 5, 6, 7, 8, 9, 10, 13, 14, 15, 16, 19, 20, 21, 23, 25, 26, 28, 29, 30, 31, 32, 33, 34, 36, 37, 38, 39, 41, 42, 43, 44, 45, 46, 48, 49, 51, 52, 53, 56, 57, 58, 59, 60, 61, 62, 63, 64, 65, 69, 71, 72, 73, 74, 75, 76, 77, 79, 81, 83, 84, 86, 87, 88, 89, 90, 92, 93, 96, 97, 98, 99, 100, 103, 104, 105, 107, 109, 110, 111, 112, 113, 115, 116, 117, 118, 119, 120, 121, 122, 123, 124, 125, 126, 127, 128, 129, 130, 131, 132, 133, 134, 135, 136, 137, 140, 141, 142, 143, 146, 147, 149, 150, 151, 152, 153, 154, 155, 156, 158, 160, 161, 162, 164, 165, 166, 167, 168, 169, 170, 171, 172, 173, 174, 175, 177, 178, 179, 180, 181, 182, 183, 184, 185, 186, 187, 188, 189, 190, 191, 193, 194, 195, 196, 197, 198, 199, 200, 203, 204, 205, 206, 208, 210, 211, 212, 213, 214; *non,* 78; *domum,* 82.

[25] 3, 5, 6, 7, 8, 9, 10, 13, 14, 15, 16, 19, 20, 21, 23, 25, 26, 28, 29, 30, 31, 32, 33, 34, 37, 38, 39, 41, 42, 43, 44, 45, 46, 48, 49, 51, 52, 53, 56, 57, 58, 59, 60, 61, 62, 63, 64, 65, 69, 71, 73, 75, 76, 78, 79, 81, 83, 84, 86, 87, 88, 89, 90, 92, 93, 96, 97, 98, 99, 100, 103, 104, 105, 107, 109, 110, 111, 112, 113, 115, 116, 117, 118, 120, 121, 122, 123, 124, 125, 126, 127,

128, 129, 130, 131, 132, 133, 134, 135, 136, 137, 140, 141, 142, 143, 146, 147, 149, 150, 151, 152, 153, 154, 155, 156, 158, 160, 161, 162, 164, 165, 166, 167, 168, 170, 171, 172, 173, 174, 175, 177, 178, 179, 180, 181, 182, 183, 184, 185, 186, 187, 188, 189, 190, 191, 193, 194, 195, 196, 197, 198, 199, 200, 203, 204, 205, 208, 210, 211, 212, 213, 214; *hedificium*, 169, 206; *hedititium*, 72; *edificatam*, 74; *edificau.*, 77; *edificauit*, 36, 119; *suam*, 82.

26 3, 5, 6, 7, 8, 9, 10, 13, 14, 15, 16, 19, 20, 21, 23, 25, 26, 28, 29, 30, 31, 32, 33, 34, 36, 37, 38, 39, 41, 42, 43, 44, 45, 46, 48, 49, 51, 52, 53, 56, 57, 58, 59, 60, 61, 62, 63, 64, 65, 69, 71, 72, 73, 74, 75, 76, 77, 78, 79, 81, 82, 83, 84, 86, 87, 88, 89, 90, 92, 93, 96, 97, 98, 99, 100, 103, 104, 105, 107, 109, 111, 112, 113, 115, 116, 117, 118, 119, 120, 121, 122, 123, 124, 125, 126, 127, 129, 130, 131, 132, 133, 134, 135, 136, 137, 140, 141, 142, 143, 146, 147, 149, 150, 151, 152, 153, 154, 155, 156, 158, 160, 161, 162, 164, 165, 166, 167, 168, 169, 170, 171, 172, 173, 174, 175, 177, 178, 179, 180, 181, 182, 183, 184, 185, 186, 188, 189, 190, 191, 193, 194, 195, 196, 197, 198, 199, 200, 203, 204, 205, 206, 208, 210, 211, 212, 213, 214; \et/, 128; om., 110; *at*, 187.

27...27 5, 6, 7, 8, 9, 10, 13, 14, 15, 16, 20, 21, 23, 26, 28, 30, 31, 32, 33, 34, 37, 38, 39, 41, 42, 43, 44, 46, 48, 49, 51, 52, 57, 59, 60, 61, 63, 64, 65, 69, 71, 72, 73, 74, 76, 77, 78, 79, 82, 83, 84, 87, 88, 89, 90, 92, 93, 96, 97, 98, 99, 100, 103, 104, 107, 109, 111, 112, 113, 115, 116, 117, 118, 119, 120, 121, 122, 123, 124, 126, 128, 129, 131, 132, 133, 134, 135, 136, 137, 140, 141, 142, 143, 146, 147, 149, 150, 152, 153, 155, 156, 158, 160, 161, 162, 164, 165, 166, 169, 170, 172, 173, 174, 177, 178, 181, 185, 186, 187, 188, 190, 191, 193, 194, 197, 198, 203, 204, 206, 210, 211, 212, 213; *m. n.*, 3, 19, 36, 53, 56, 58, 62, 75, 81, 105, 110, 125, 127, 130, 151, 154, 168, 171, 175, 179, 180, 182, 183, 184, 189, 195, 196, 199, 205, 208. 214; *milites*, 25; *nouos milites inuitatos*, 29; *nouos milites uideret*, 86 (cf. n. 29).

28 3, 5, 6, 7, 9, 10, 14, 15, 16, 19, 20, 21, 23, 26, 30, 31, 32, 33, 34, 36, 37, 41, 42, 44, 45, 46, 48, 49, 51, 52, 53, 56, 57, 58, 59, 60, 61, 62, 63, 64, 69, 71, 73, 74, 75, 76, 77, 79, 81, 82, 83, 84, 86, 87, 88, 89, 90, 92, 93, 96, 97, 98, 99, 100, 103, 104, 105, 107, 109, 110, 111, 112, 113, 115, 116, 117, 120, 121, 122, 123, 124, 125, 126, 127, 128, 129, 130, 131, 132, 133, 134, 135, 136, 137, 140, 141, 142, 143, 146, 149, 150, 151, 152, 153, 154, 155, 156, 158, 161, 162, 164, 165, 166, 167, 168, 169, 170, 171, 172, 173, 174, 175, 177, 179, 180, 181, 182, 183, 184, 185, 186, 187, 189, 190, 191, 193, 194, 195, 196, 197, 198, 199, 200, 203, 204, 205, 206, 208, 210, 211, 212, 213, 214; *amplicuerant*, 43, *amplicuerant [uiderent]* (canc.), 78; *applicuerunt*, 8, 13, 39, 65, 72, 118, 147, 178, 188; *applicunt*, 160; *et applicuerunt*, 29; *nuper applicuerunt*, 25; *uenerant*, 38; *appluerant*, 28; *applucuert*, 119.

29 3, 5, 6, 7, 8, 9, 10, 13, 14, 15, 16, 19, 20, 21, 23, 25, 26, 28, 29, 30, 31, 32, 33, 34, 36, 37, 38, 39, 41, 42, 43, 44, 45, 46, 48, 49, 51, 52, 53, 56, 57, 58, 59, 60, 61, 62, 63, 64, 65, 69, 71, 72, 73, 74, 75, 76, 77, 78, 79, 81, 82, 83, 84, 87, 88, 89, 90, 92, 93, 96, 97, 98, 99, 100, 103, 104, 105, 109, 110, 111, 112, 113, 115, 116, 117, 118, 119, 120, 121, 122, 123, 124, 125, 126, 127, 128, 129, 130, 132, 133, 134, 135, 136, 137, 140, 141, 143, 146, 147, 149, 150, 151, 152, 153, 154, 155, 156, 158, 160, 161, 162, 164, 165, 166, 167, 168, 169, 170, 171, 172, 173, 174, 175, 177, 178, 179, 180, 181, 182, 183, 184, 185, 186, 187, 188, 189, 190, 191, 193, 194, 195, 196, 197, 198, 199, 200, 203, 204, 205, 206, 208, 210, 211, 212, 213, 214; *uiderat*, 131; *uiderent*, 107; *uideret ueniret*, 142; om., 86 (cf. n. 27).

30 3, 5, 6, 7, 8, 9, 10, 13, 14, 15, 16, 19, 20, 21, 23, 25, 26, 28, 29, 30, 31, 32, 33, 34, 36, 37, 38, 39, 41, 42, 43, 44, 45, 46, 48, 49, 51, 52, 53, 56, 57, 58, 59, 60, 61, 62, 63, 64, 65, 69,· 71, 72, 73, 74, 75, 76, 77, 78, 79, 81, 82, 83, 84, 86, 87, 88, 89, 90, 92, 93, 96, 97, 98, 99, 100, 103, 105, 107, 109, 110, 111, 112, 113, 115, 116, 117, 118, 119, 120, 121, 122, 123, 124, 125, 126, 127, 128, 129, 130, 131, 132, 133, 134, 135, 136, 137, 140, 141, 142, 143, 146, 147, 149, 150, 151, 152, 153, 154, 155, 156, 158, 160, 161, 162, 164, 165, 166, 167, 168, 169, 170, 171, 172, 173, 174, 175, 177, 178, 179, 180, 181, 182, 183, 184, 185, 186, 187, 188, 189, 190, 191, 193, 195, 196, 197, 198, 199, 200, 203, 204, 205, 206, 208, 210, 211, 212, 213, 214; *?iuit*, 104; *?fuit*, 194.

ilico[31] rex[32] priuatim[33] et[34] laudauit[35] [36]tam subitum[36] [37]opus et milites[37] [38]inuitatos

[31] 3, 5, 6, 7, 8, 9, 10, 13, 14, 15, 16, 19, 20, 21, 23, 25, 26, 28, 29, 30, 31, 32, 33, 34, 36, 37, 38, 39, 41, 42, 43, 44, 45, 46, 48, 51, 52, 56, 58, 59, 60, 61, 62, 63, 64, 65, 69, 71, 73, 74, 75, 76, 77, 78, 79, 81, 82, 83, 86, 87, 88, 89, 90, 92, 93, 96, 97, 98, 99, 100, 103, 104, 105, 107, 109, 110, 111, 112, 113, 115, 116, 117, 118, 119, 120, 121, 123, 125, 126, 127, 128, 129, 130, 131, 133, 134, 135, 136, 137, 140, 141, 142, 143, 146, 149, 150, 151, 152, 153, 154, 155, 156, 158, 160, 161, 162, 164, 165, 166, 167, 169, 170, 172, 173, 174, 175, 177, 178, 179, 180, 181, 182, 183, 184, 185, 186, 187, 188, 189, 190, 191, 193, 194, 195, 197, 198, 199, 200, 203, 204, 205, 206, 208, 210, 211, 212, 213, 214; *inlico,* 72; *illic,* 168, 171; *illic al. ilico,* 147; *illuc,* 57, *igitur ilico,* 53; *ilico ergo,* 132; *ergo,* 84, 122, 124; *igitur,* 196; om., 49.

[32] 3, 5, 6, 7, 8, 9, 10, 13, 14, 15, 16, 20, 21, 23, 25, 26, 28, 29, 30, 31, 32, 33, 34, 36, 37, 38, 39, 41, 42, 43, 44, 45, 46, 48, 49, 51, 52, 53, 56, 57, 58, 59, 60, 61, 62, 63, 64, 65, 69, 71, 73, 74, 75, 76, 77, 78, 79, 81, 82, 83, 84, 86, 87, 88, 89, 90, 92, 93, 96, 97, 98, 99, 100, 103, 104, 107, 109, 110, 111, 112, 113, 115, 116, 117, 118, 119, 120, 121, 122, 123, 124, 126, 127, 128, 129, 130, 131, 132, 134, 135, 136, 137, 140, 141, 142, 143, 146, 147, 149, 150, 151, 152, 153, 154, 155, 156, 158, 160, 161, 162, 164, 165, 166, 167, 168, 169, 170, 171, 172, 173, 174, 175, 177, 178, 179, 181, 182, 183, 184, 185, 186, 187, 188, 189, 190, 191, 193, 194, 195, 196, 197, 198, 199, 200, 203, 204, 205, 206, 208, 210, 211, 212, 213; om., 19, 72, 105, 125, 133, 180, 214.

[33] 3, 5, 6, 7, 8, 9, 10, 13, 14, 15, 16, 19, 20, 21, 23, 25, 26, 28, 29, 30, 31, 32, 33, 34, 36, 37, 38, 39, 41, 42, 43, 44, 45, 46, 48, 49, 51, 52, 53, 56, 57, 58, 59, 60, 61, 62, 64, 65, 69, 71, 72, 73, 74, 75, 76, 77, 78, 79, 81, 82, 83, 84, 86, 87, 88, 89, 90, 92, 93, 96, 97, 98, 99, 100, 103, 104, 105, 107, 109, 110, 111, 112, 113, 115, 116, 117, 118, 119, 120, 121, 122, 123, 124, 125, 126, 128, 129, 130, 131, 132, 133, 134, 135, 136, 137, 140, 141, 142, 143, 146, 147, 149, 150, 151, 152, 153, 154, 155, 156, 158, 160, 161, 162, 164, 165, 166, 167, 168, 169, 170, 171, 172, 173, 174, 175, 177, 178, 179, 180, 181, 182, 183, 184, 185, 186, 187, 188, 189, 190, 191, 193, 194, 195, 196, 197, 198, 199, 200, 203, 204, 205, 206, 210, 211, 212, 213, 214; om., 63, 127, 208.

[34] 3, 5, 6, 7, 8, 9, 10, 13, 14, 15, 16, 19, 20, 21, 23, 25, 26, 28, 29, 30, 31, 32, 33, 34, 36, 37, 38, 39, 41, 42, 43, 44, 45, 46, 48, 49, 51, 52, 53, 56, 57, 58, 59, 60, 61, 62, 63, 64, 65, 69, 71, 72, 73, 74, 75, 76, 77, 78, 79, 81, 82, 83, 84, 86, 87, 88, 89, 90, 92, 93, 96, 97, 98, 99, 100, 103, 104, 105, 107, 109, 110, 111, 112, 113, 115, 116, 117, 118, 119, 120, 121, 122, 123, 124, 125, 126, 127, 128, 129, 130, 131, 132, 134, 135, 136, 137, 140, 141, 142, 143, 146, 147, 149, 150, 151, 152, 153, 154, 155, 156, 158, 160, 161, 162, 164, 165, 166, 167, 168, 169, 170, 171, 172, 173, 174, 175, 177, 178, 179, 180, 181, 182, 183, 184, 185, 186, 187, 188, 189, 190, 191, 193, 194, 195, 196, 197, 198, 199, 200, 203, 204, 205, 206, 208, 210, 211, 212, 213, 214; om., 133.

[35] 3, 5, 6, 7, 8, 9, 10, 13, 14, 15, 16, 19, 20, 21, 23, 25, 26, 28, 29, 30, 31, 32, 33, 34, 36, 37, 38, 39, 41, 42, 43, 44, 45, 46, 48, 49, 51, 52, 53, 56, 57, 58, 59, 60, 61, 62, 63, 64, 65, 69, 71, 72, 73, 74, 75, 76, 77, 78, 79, 81, 82, 83, 84, 86, 87, 88, 89, 90, 92, 93, 96, 97, 98, 99, 100, 103, 104, 105, 107, 109, 110, 111, 112, 113, 115, 116, 117, 118, 119, 120, 121, 122, 123, 124, 125, 126, 127, 128, 129, 130, 131, 132, 133, 134, 135, 136, 137, 140, 141, 142, 143, 146, 147, 149, 151, 152, 153, 154, 155, 156, 158, 160, 161, 162, 164, 165, 166, 167, 168, 169, 170, 171, 172, 173, 174, 175, 177, 178, 179, 180, 181, 182, 183, 184, 185, 186, 187, 188, 189, 190, 191, 193, 194, 195, 196, 197, 198, 199, 200, 203, 204, 205, 206, 208, 210, 211, 212, 213, 214; *laudabat,* 150.

[36...36] 3, 5, 6, 7, 8, 9, 10, 13, 14, 15, 19, 20, 23, 25, 26, 28, 29, 30, 31, 32, 33, 34, 36, 37, 38, 39, 41, 42, 43, 44, 45, 46, 48, 49, 51, 52, 53, 56, 57, 58, 59, 61, 62, 63, 64, 65, 69, 71, 72, 73, 74, 75, 76, 77, 78, 79, 81, 82, 83, 84, 86, 87, 88, 89, 90, 92, 93, 96, 97, 98, 99, 104, 105, 107, 109, 110, 111, 112, 113, 115, 116, 117, 118, 119, 120, 121, 122, 123, 124, 125, 126,

retinuit.[38] Ut[39] ergo[40] [41]regiis epulis[41] refectus[42] fuit,[43] egressa est[44] puella[45] [46]de

127, 128, 130, 131, 132, 134, 135, 136, 137, 140, 141, 142, 143, 146, 147, 149, 150, 151, 152, 153, 154, 155, 156, 158, 160, 161, 162, 164, 165, 166, 167, 168, 169, 170, 171, 172, 173, 174, 175, 177, 178, 179, 180, 181, 182, 183, 184, 185, 187, 188, 189, 191, 194, 195, 196, 197, 198, 199, 200, 203, 204, 205, 206, 208, 210, 212, 213, 214; *tam subito,* 193; *tantum,* 16, 21, 60, 190, 211; *tam subditum,* 100, 103; *tam,* 129, 186; *subitum,* 133.

[37...37] 3, 5, 6, 8, 9, 10, 13, 14, 15, 16, 19, 20, 21, 23, 25, 26, 28, 29, 30, 31, 32, 33, 34, 36, 37, 38, 39, 41, 42, 43, 44, 45, 46, 48, 49, 51, 52, 53, 56, 57, 58, 59, 60, 61, 62, 63, 64, 65, 69, 71, 72, 73, 74, 75, 76, 77, 78, 79, 81, 82, 83, 84, 86, 87, 88, 89, 90, 92, 93, 96, 97, 98, 99, 100, 103, 105, 107, 109, 110, 111, 112, 113, 115, 116, 117, 118, 120, 121, 122, 123, 124, 125, 126, 127, 128, 130, 131, 132, 133, 134, 135, 136, 137, 140, 141, 143, 146, 147, 149, 150, 151, 152, 153, 154, 155, 156, 158, 160, 161, 162, 164, 165, 166, 167, 168, 169, 170, 171, 172, 173, 174, 175, 178, 179, 180, 181, 182, 183, 184, 185, 187, 188, 189, 190, 191, 193, 194, 195, 196, 197, 198, 199, 200, 203, 204, 205, 206, 208, 210, 211, 212, 213, 214; *opus atque milites,* 142; *opus u.*[e]*t milites,* 177; *milites,* 119; *opus quam milites et,* 129, 186; *opus et milites et,* 104; *opus et militatos* (canc.) *militates,* 7.

[38...38] 3, 5, 6, 7, 8, 9, 10, 13, 14, 15, 16, 19, 20, 21, 23, 25, 26, 28, 29, 30, 31, 32, 33, 34, 36, 37, 38, 39, 41, 42, 43, 44, 45, 46, 48, 49, 51, 52, 53, 57, 59, 60, 61, 62, 63, 64, 65, 69, 71, 72, 73, 74, 76, 77, 79, 81, 82, 83, 84, 86, 87, 88, 89, 90, 92, 93, 96, 97, 98, 99, 100, 103, 104, 105, 107, 109, 110, 111, 112, 113, 115, 116, 117, 118, 120, 121, 122, 123, 124, 125, 126, 127, 128, 129, 130, 131, 132, 133, 134, 135, 136, 137, 140, 141, 142, 143, 146, 147, 149, 150, 151, 153, 154, 155, 156, 158, 160, 161, 162, 164, 165, 166, 167, 168, 169, 170, 171, 172, 173, 174, 175, 177, 178, 179, 180, 181, 182, 183, 184, 186, 187, 188, 189, 190, 191, 193, 194, 195, 196, 197, 198, 199, 200, 203, 204, 206, 208, 210, 211, 212, 213, 214; *r. i.,* 75; *inuitauit retinuit,* 119; *iniuratos retinuit,* 185; *inuitatos,* 205; *inuitatos retenuit,* 152; *inuitatos obtinuit,* 78; *inuitatis retinere,* 56, 58.

[39] 3, 5, 6, 7, 8, 9, 10, 13, 14, 15, 16, 19, 20, 21, 23, 25, 26, 28, 29, 30, 31, 32, 33, 34, 36, 37, 38, 39, 41, 42, 43, 44, 45, 46, 48, 49, 51, 52, 53, 56, 57, 58, 59, 60, 61, 62, 63, 65, 69, 71, 72, 73, 74, 75, 76, 77, 78, 79, 81, 82, 83, 84, 86, 87, 88, 89, 90, 92, 93, 96, 97, 98, 99, 100, 103, 104, 105, 107, 109, 110, 111, 112, 113, 115, 116, 117, 118, 119, 120, 121, 122, 123, 124, 125, 126, 127, 128, 129, 130, 131, 132, 133, 134, 135, 136, 137, 140, 141, 142, 143, 146, 147, 149, 150, 151, 152, 153, 154, 155, 156, 158, 160, 161, 162, 164, 165, 166, 167, 168, 169, 170, 171, 172, 173, 174, 175, 177, 178, 179, 180, 181, 182, 183, 184, 185, 186, 187, 188, 189, 190, 191, 193, 194, 195, 196, 197, 198, 199, 200, 203, 204, 205, 206, 208, 210, 211, 212, 213, 214; *at,* 64.

[40] 3, 5, 8, 9, 10, 14, 15, 16, 21, 26, 28, 30, 31, 32, 34, 38, 39, 41, 42, 44, 45, 48, 49, 52, 56, 58, 59, 60, 61, 62, 72, 73, 74, 86, 90, 92, 93, 98, 99, 100, 103, 107, 109, 110, 112, 113, 115, 118, 119, 122, 123, 128, 129, 130, 131, 132, 134, 136, 137, 140, 141, 142, 143, 147, 150, 152, 153, 156, 164, 165, 168, 170, 171, 177, 182, 184, 186, 189, 199, 200, 205, 212; *igitur,* 51, 57, ?104, 178, 194; *uero,* 6, 7, 13, 19, 20, 23, 25, 29, 33, 36, 37, 43, 46, 53, 63, 64, 65, 69, 71, 75, 76, 77, 78, 79, 81, 82, 83, 84, 87, 88, 89, 96, 97, 105, 111, 116, 117, 120, 121, 124, 125, 126, 127, 133, 135, 146, 149, 151, 154, 155, 158, 160, 161, 162, 166, 167, 169, 172, 173, 174, 175, 179, 180, 181, 183, 185, 187, 188, 190, 191, 193, 195, 196, 197, 198, 203, 204, 206, 208, 210, 211, 213, 214.

[41...41] 3, 5, 6, 7, 8, 9, 10, 13, 14, 15, 16, 19, 20, 21, 23, 25, 26, 28, 29, 30, 31, 32, 33, 34, 36, 37, 38, 39, 41, 42, 43, 44, 45, 48, 49, 51, 52, 53, 56, 57, 58, 60, 61, 62, 63, 64, 65, 69, 71, 72, 73, 74, 75, 76, 77, 78, 79, 81, 82, 83, 84, 86, 87, 88, 89, 90, 92, 93, 96, 97, 98, 99, 100, 103, 104, 105, 107, 109, 110, 111, 112, 113, 115, 116, 117, 118, 120, 121, 122, 123, 124, 125, 126, 127, 128, 129, 130, 131, 132, 133, 134, 135, 136, 137, 140, 141, 143, 146, 147, 149, 150, 151, 152, 153, 154, 155, 156, 158, 160, 161, 162, 164, 165, 166, 167, 168, 170, 171, 172, 173, 174, 175, 177, 178, 179, 180, 181, 182, 183, 184, 185, 186, 187, 188, 189,

thalamo[46] [47]aureum ciphum[47] . [48]plenum uino ferens.[48] Accedens[49] deinde[50] [56]pro-

190, 191, 193, 194, 195, 196, 197, 198, 200, 203, 204, 205, 208, 210, 211, 212, 213, 214; *regi\i/s epulis,* 199; *regis epulis,* 206; *rex regiis epulis,* 169; *rex [ ]epulis,* 46; *ex regiis epulis,* 119, 142; *cibis regiis,* 59.

[42] 5, 6, 7, 8, 9, 10, 13, 15, 16, 21, 23, 25, 26, 28, 29, 30, 31, 32, 34, 36, 37, 38, 39, 41, 42, 43, 44, 45, 46, 48, 49, 51, 52, 57, 59, 60, 61, 62, 63, 64, 65, 69, 71, 72, 73, 74, 76, 79, 81, 82, 84, 86, 87, 88, 89, 90, 92, 93, 96, 97, 98, 99, 100, 103, 104, 105, 107, 109, 110, 111, 112, 113, 115, 116, 117, 118, 119, 120, 121, 122, 123, 124, 125, 128, 129, 130, 131, 132, 133, 134, 135, 136, 137, 140, 141, 142, 143, 146, 149, 150, 152, 153, 154, 155, 156, 158, 160, 161, 162, 164, 165, 167, 168, 169, 170, 171, 172, 174, 177, 178, 179, 180, 181, 182, 183, 185, 186, 187, 188, 190, 191, 193, 194, 195, 197, 198, 199, 200, 203, 204, 210, 211, 212, 213, 214; *refertus,* 3, 14, 184, 189; *repletus,* 20, 33, 52, 56, 58, 75, 83, 126, 127, 151, 166, 173, 175, 196, 205, 208; *effectus,* 77, 147; *infectus,* 19; om., 78, 206.

[43] 3, 5, 7, 8, 9, 10, 13, 14, 15, 16, 19, 20, 21, 23, 25, 28, 29, 30, 31, 32, 33, 34, 36, 37, 38, 39, 41, 42, 43, 44, 45, 46, 48, 49, 52, 53, 56, 57, 58, 59, 60, 61, 62, 63, 64, 65, 69, 71, 72, 73, 74, 75, 76, 77, 78, 79, 81, 82, 83, 84, 86, 87, 88, 89, 90, 92, 93, 96, 97, 98, 99, 100, 103, 104, 105, 107, 109, 110, 111, 112, 113, 116, 117, 118, 119, 120, 121, 122, 123, 124, 125, 126, 127, 128, 129, 130, 131, 132, 133, 134, 135, 136, 137, 140, 141, 142, 143, 146, 147, 149, 150, 151, 152, 153, 154, 155, 156, 158, 160. 161, 162, 164, 165, 166, 167, 168, 169, 170, 171, 172, 173, 174, 175, 177, 178, 179, 180, 181, 182, 183, 184, 185, 186, 187, 188, 189, 190, 191, 193, 194, 195, 196, 197, 198, 199, 200, 203, 204, 205, 206, 208, 210, 21 1, 212, 213, 214; *glossed rex,* 141; *fuisset,* 6, 26, 51, 115.

[44] 3, 5, 6, 7, 8, 9, 10, 13, 14, 15, 16, 19, 20, 21, 25, 26, 28, 29, 30, 32, 33, 34, 36, 37, 38, 39, 42, 45, 48, 49, 51, 53, 56, 57, 58, 59, 60, 61, 62, 64, 65, 69, 73, 75, 76, 77, 78, 79, 81, 82, 83, 84, 86, 87, 88, 90, 92, 93, 97, 98, 99, 100, 103, 104, 105, 107, 109, 110, 111, 112, 115, 116, 117, 119, 121, 122, 123, 124, 125, 126, 127, 128, 129, 130, 131, 133, 134, 135, 137, 140, 141, 142, 143, 146, 147, 149, 150, 151, 152, 153, 154, 155, 162, 164, 165, 166, 167, 168, 169, 171, 172, 173, 174, 175, 179, 180 182, 183, 184, 185, 186, 188, 189, 190, 191, 193, 194, 195, 196, 197, 198, 199, 200, 205, 206, 208, 210, 211, 212, 213, 214; \est/, 63, 136, 177; om., 23, (24,) 31, 41, 43, 44, 46, 52, 71, 72, 74, 89, 96, 113, 118, 120, 132, 156, 158, 160, 161, 170, 178, 181, 187, 203, 204.

[45] 3, 5, 6, 7, 8, 9, 10, 13, 14, 15, 16, 19, 20, 21, 23, 25, 26, 28, 29, 30, 31, 32, 33, 34, 37, 38, 39, 41, 42, 43, 44, 45, 46, 48, 50, 51, 52, 53, 56, 57, 58, 59, 60, 61, 62, 63, 64, 65, 69, 71, 72, 73, 74, 75, 76, 77, 78, 79, 81, 82, 83, 84, 86, 87, 88, 89, 90, 92, 93, 96, 97, 98, 99, 100, 103, 104, 105, 107, 109, 110, 111, 112, 113, 115, 116, 117, 118, 119, 120, 121, 122, 123, 124, 125, 126, 127, 128, 129, 130, 131, 132, 133, 134, 135, 136, 137, 140, 141, 142, 143, 146, 147, 149, 150, 151, 152, 153, 154, 155, 156, 158, 160, 161, 162, 164, 165, 166, 167, 168, 169, 170, 171, 172, 173, 174, 175, 177, 178, 179, 180, 181, 182, 183, 184, 185, 186, 187, 188, 189, 190, 191, 193, 194, 195, 196, 197, 198, 199, 200, 203, 204, 205, 206, 208, 210, 211, 212, 213, 214; om., 36.

[46...46] 3, 5, 6, 7, 9, 10, 13, 14, 15, 16, 19, 20, 21, 23, 25, 26, 28, 29, 30, 31, 32, 33, 34, 36, 37, 38, 39, 41, 42, 43, 44, 45, 46, 48, 49, 51, 52, 53, 59, 60, 61, 62, 63, 65, 69, 71, 72, 73, 74, 75, 76, 78, 79, 81, 82, 83, 84, 86, 88, 89, 90, 92, 93, 96, 97, 98, 99, 100, 103, 104, 105, 107, 109, 110, 111, 112, 113, 115, 116, 117, 118, 119, 120, 121, 122, 123, 124, 125, 126, 127, 128, 129, 130, 133, 134, 135, 136, 137, 140, 141, 142, 143, 146, 147, 149, 150, 151, 152, 153, 154, 155, 156, 158, 160, 161, 162, 164, 165, 166, 167, 168, 169, 170, 171, 173, 174, 175, 177, 178, 179, 180, 181, 182, 183, 184, 185, 186, 187, 188, 189, 190, 191, 193, 194, 195, 196, 197, 198, 199, 200, 203, 204, 205, 206, 208, 210, 211, 212, 213, 214; *de talamo,* 56, 58, 64, 87, 132, 172; *de thalamo suo,* 57, 77; *e thalamo,* 131; om., 8.

[47...47] 3, 5, 6, 7, 8, 9, 10, 13, 14, 15, 16, 19, 20, 21, 23, 26, 28, 29, 30, 31, 32, 33, 34, 36, 37, 38, 39, 41, 42, 43, 44, 45, 46, 48, 49, 51, 52, 57, 59, 60, 61, 62, 63, 64, 65, 69, 71, 72, 73,

248

74, 75, 76, 77, 78, 79, 81, 83, 84, 86, 87, 88, 89, 90, 92, 93, 96, 97, 98, 99, 103, 104, 105, 107, 109, 110, 111, 112, 113, 115, 116, 117, 118, 119, 120, 121, 122, 123, 124, 125, 126, 128, 129, 130, 131, 132, 133, 134, 135, 136, 137, 140, 141, 142, 143, 146, 147, 149, 150, 151, 152, 153, 154, 155, 156, 158, 160, 161, 164, 165, 166, 167, 168, 169, 170, 171, 172, 173, 174, 175, 177, 178, 179, 180, 181, 183, 184, 185, 186, 187, 188, 189, 190, 191, 193, 194, 195, 196, 197, 198, 199, 200, 203, 204, 206, 210, 211, 212, 213, 214; *c. a.*, 25, 56, 58, 182, 205; *aureum sciphum*, 53; *aureum scyphum*, 127, 208; *a\u/reum cifum*, 82, 162; *aur\e/um chiphum*, 100.

48...48 3, 5, 6, 7, 8, 9, 10, 14, 15, 16, 19, 21, 23, 26, 28, 29, 30, 31, 32, 33, 34, 36, 37, 38, 39, 41, 42, 43, 44, 45, 46, 48, 51, 52, 53, 56, 57, 58, 60, 62, 63, 69, 71, 72, 73, 75, 76, 77, 78, 79, 81, 83, 84, 86, 87, 88, 89, 90, 92, 93, 96, 97, 98, 99, 100, 103, 104, 105, 109, 110, 111, 112, 113, 115, 116, 118, 120, 121, 123, 124, 125, 126, 127, 128, 129, 130, 131, 132, 133, 134, 135, 137, 141, 143, 146, 147, 149, 150, 151, 152, 153, 154, 155, 156, 158, 160, 161, 162, 164, 165, 166, 167, 168, 169, 170, 172, 173, 174, 175, 177, 178, 179, 180, 181, 182, 183, 184, 185, 186, 189, 190, 191, 193, 195, 196, 197, 198, 199, 200, 203, 204, 205, 206, 208, 210, 211, 212, 213, 214; *u. p. f.*, 25, 49, 59, 61, 122, 136; *p. f. u.*, 107; *u. f.*, 64; *pleno uino ferens*, 119, 140, 142, 187; *in manu plenum uino ferens*, 117, 188; *plenum uini ferens*, 82; *plenum de* (canc.) *uino ferens*, 171; *plenum uino tenens*, 13, 65, 194; *plenum uino terens*, 20; *plenum uino feretis*, 74.

49 3, 5, 6, 7, 8, 10, 13, 14, 15, 16, 19, 20, 21, 23, 25, 26, 28, 29, 30, 31, 32, 33, 34, 36, 37, 38, 39, 41, 42, 43, 44, 45, 46, 48, 49, 51, 52, 53, 56, 57, 58, 59, 60, 61, 62, 64, 65, 69, 71, 72, 73, 74, 75, 76, 77, 78, 79, 81, 82, 83, 84, 86, 87, 88, 89, 90, 92, 93, 96, 97, 98, 99, 100, 103, 104, 105, 107, 109, 110, 112, 113, 115, 116, 117, 118, 119, 120, 121, 122, 123, 124, 125, 126, 127, 128, 129, 130, 131, 132, 135, 136, 137, 140, 141, 142, 147, 149, 150, 151, 152, 153, 154, 155, 156, 158, 160, 161, 162, 164, 165, 166, 167, 168, 169, 170, 171, 172, 173, 175, 177, 178, 179, 180, 182, 183, 184, 185, 186, 187, 188, 189, 190, 191, 193, 194, 195, 196, 200, 203, 204, 205, 206, 208, 210, 211, 212, 213, 214; *accedens\que/*, 181; *accedensque*, 63, 111, 146; *et accedens*, 9, 143, 174, 198; *accessit*, 199; *accedentes*, 134; *accendens*, 133, 197.

50 3, 5, 6, 7, 8, 10, 13, 14, 15, 16, 19, 20, 21, 23, 25, 26, 29, 30, 32, 33, 34, 36, 37, 38, 39, 41, 42, 43 44, 45, 46, 48, 49, 51, 52, 53, 56, 57, 58, 59, 60, 61, 62, 63, 64, 65, 69, 71, 72, 73, 74, 75, 76, 77, 78, 79, 81, 82, 83, 84, 86 87, 88 89, 90, 92, 96, 97, 98, 99, 103, 104, 105, 107, 109, 112, 115, 116, 117, 118, 119, 120, 121, 122, 123, 124, 125, 126, 127, 128, 129, 130, 131, 133, 135, 136, 137, 141, 142, 146, 147, 149, 151, 152, 153, 154, 155, 156, 158, 161, 162, 164, 165, 166, 167, 168, 169, 170, 172, 173, 174, 175, 177, 179, 180, 181, 182, 183, 185, 186, 187, 188, 190, 191, 193, 194, 195, 196, 197, 198, 199, 200, 203, 204, 205, 206, 208, 210, 211, 212, 213, 214; *dein*, 171, 184, 189; *inde*, 31, ?93, 113, 132, 140, 150, 160, 178; *ergo*, 28, 100, 134; om., 9, 111, 143; *autem eum?*, 110.

51 3, 5, 6, 8, 9, 10, 13, 14, 15, 16, 19, 20, 21, 23, 25, 26, 28, 29, 30, 31, 32, 33, 34, 36, 37, 39, 41, 42, 43, 44, 45, 46, 48, 49, 51, 52, 53, 56, 57, 58, 59, 60, 61, 62, 63, 64, 65, 69, 71, 72, 73, 74, 75, 76, 77, 78, 79, 81, 82, 83, 84, 86, 87, 88, 89, 90, 92, 93, 96, 97, 98, 99, 100, 103, 104, 107, 110, 111, 112, 113, 115, 116, 117, 118, 119, 120, 121, 122, 123, 124, 125, 126, 127, 128, 129, 130, 133, 134, 135, 136, 137, 140, 141, 142, 143, 146, 147, 149, 150, 151, 152, 153, 155, 156, 158, 160, 161, 162, 164, 165, 166, 167, 168, 169, 170, 171, 173, 175, 177, 178, 179, 181, 182, 183, 184, 185, 186, 187, 188, 189, 190, 191, 193, 194, 195, 196, 197, 198, 199, 200, 203, 204, 205, 208, 211, 212, 213, 214; *\propius/*, 154; *proprius* (altered to *propius*), 172; *proprius*, 7, 105, 132, 174; *prius*, 180; *propicius*, 109, 210; *proius*, 206; om., 38, 131.

52 3, 5, 6, 7, 8, 9, 10, 13, 14, 15, 16, 19, 20, 21, 23, 25, 26, 28, 29, 30, 31, 32, 33, 34, 36, 37, 39, 41, 42, 43, 44, 45, 46, 48, 49, 51, 52, 53, 56, 57, 58, 61, 62, 63, 64, 65, 69, 71, 72, 73, 74, 75, 76, 77, 78, 79, 81, 83, 84, 86, 87, 88, 89, 90, 92, 93, 96, 97, 98, 100, 103, 104, 107, 109, 110, 111, 112, 113, 115, 116, 117, 118, 119, 120, 121, 122, 123, 124, 125, 126, 127, 128, 130, 132, 133, 134, 135, 136, 137, 140, 141, 142, 143, 146, 147, 149, 150, 151, 152,

pius[51] regi[52] flexis[53] genibus[54] dixit.[55] [56] [60]'Lauerd[57] king,[58] Waesseil!'[59] [60] [64]At ille,[61]

153, 155, 156, 158, 160, 161, 162, 164, 165, 166, 167, 168, 169, 170, 171, 173, 175, 178, 179, 181, 183, 184, 185, 187, 188, 189, 190, 191, 193, 194, 195, 196, 198, 199, 200, 203, 204, 205, 206, 208, 210, 212, 213, 214; *regi et,* 59, 60; *ad regem,* 38, 131; *regem,* 129, 186; *regis* (altered to *regi*), 172, 177, 197; *regis,* 82, 99, 174, 211; om., 105, 154, 180, 182.

[53] 3, 5, 6, 7, 8, 9, 10, 13, 14, 15, 16, 19, 20, 21, 23, 25, 26, 28, 29, 30, 31, 32, 33, 34, 36, 37, 38, 39, 41, 42, 43, 44, 45, 46, 48, 49, 51, 52, 53, 56, 57, 58, 59, 60, 61, 62, 63, 64, 65, 69, 71, 72, 73, 74, 75, 76, 77, 78, 79, 81, 82, 83, 84, 86, 87, 88, 89, 90, 92, 93, 96, 97, 98, 99, 100, 103, 104, 105, 107, 109, 110, 111, 112, 113, 115, 116, 117, 118, 119, 120, 121, 122, 123, 124, 125, 126, 127, 128, 129, 130, 131, 132, 134, 135, 136, 137, 140, 141, 142, 143, 146, 147, 149, 150, 151, 152, 153, 154, 155, 156, 158, 160, 161, 162, 164, 165, 166, 167, 168, 169, 170, 171, 172, 173, 174, 175, 177, 178, 180, 181, 183, 184, 185, 186, 187, 188, 189, 190, 191, 193, 194, 195, 196, 197, 198, 200, 203, 204, 205, 206, 208, 210, 211, 212, 213, 214; *flexisque,* 179; *et flexis,* 60; *flexibus,* 170; *flexit,* 133, ?182, 199.

[54] 3, 5, 6, 7, 8, 9, 10, 13, 14, 15, 16, 19, 20, 21, 23, 25, 26, 28, 29, 30, 31, 32, 33, 34, 36, 37, 38, 39, 41, 42, 43, 44, 45, 46, 48, 49, 51, 52, 53, 56, 57, 58, 59, 60, 61, 62, 63, 64, 65, 69, 71, 72, 73, 74, 75, 76, 77, 78, 79, 81, 82, 83, 84, 86, 87, 88, 89, 90, 92, 93, 96, 97, 98, 99, 100, 103, 104, 105, 107, 109, 110, 111, 112, 113, 115, 116, 117, 118, 119, 120, 121, 122, 123, 124, 125, 126, 127, 128, 129, 130, 131, 132, 133, 134, 135, 136, 137, 140, 141, 142, 143, 146, 147, 149, 150, 151, 152, 153, 154, 155, 156, 158, 160, 161, 162, 164, 165, 166, 167, 168, 169, 171, 172, 173, 174, 175, 177, 178, 179, 180, 181, 182, 183, 184, 185, 186, 187, 188, 189, 190, 191, 193, 194, 195, 196, 197, 198, 199, 200, 203, 204, 205, 206, 208, 210, 211, 212, 213, 214; om., 170.

[55] 3, 5, 6, 7, 8, 9, 10, 13, 14, 15, 16, 19, 20, 21, 23, 25, 26, 28, 29, 30, 31, 32, 33, 34, 36, 37, 38, 39, 41, 42, 43, 44, 45, 46, 48, 49, 51, 52, 53, 56, 57, 58, 59, 60, 61, 62, 63, 64, 65, 69, 71, 72, 73, 74, 75, 76, 77, 78, 79, 81, 82, 83, 86, 87, 88, 89, 90, 92, 93, 96, 97, 98, 99, 100, 103, 104, 105, 107, 109, 110, 111, 112, 113, 115, 116, 117, 118, 119, 120, 121, 122, 123, 124, 125, 126, 127, 128, 129, 130, 131, 132, 133, 134, 135, 136, 137, 140, 141, 142, 143, 146, 147, 149, 150, 151, 152, 153, 154, 155, 156, 158, 160, 161, 162, 164, 165, 166, 167, 168, 169, 170, 171, 172, 173, 174, 175, 177, 178, 179, 180, 181, 182, 183, 184, 185, 186, 187, 188, 189, 190, 191, 193, 194, 195, 196, 197, 198, 199, 200, 203, 204, 205, 206, 208, 210, 211, 212, 213, 214; *ait,* 84, 104, 194.

[56...56] 3, 5, 6, 7, 8, 9, 10, 13, 14, 15, 16, 19, 20, 21, 23, 25, 26, 28, 29, 30, 31, 32, 33, 34, 36, 37, 38, 39, 41, 42, 43, 44, 45, 46, 48, 49, 51, 52, 55, 56, 57, 58, 59, 60, 61, 62, 63, 64, 65, 69, 71, 72, 73, 74, 75, 77, 78, 79, 81, 82, 83, 84, 86, 87, 88, 89, 90, 93, 96, 98, 99, 100, 103, 105, 107, 109, 111, 112, 113, 115, 116, 117, 118, 119, 120, 121, 122, 123, 124, 125, 126, 127, 128, 130, 131, 132, 133, 134, 135, 136, 137, 140, 141, 142, 143, 146, 147, 149, 150, 151, 152, 153, 154, 155, 156, 158, 160, 161, 162, 164, 165, 166, 167, 168, 169, 170, 171, 172, 173, 174, 175, 177, 178, 179, 180, 181, 182, 183, 184, 185, 187, 188, 189, 190, 191, 193, 195, 196, 197, 198, 200, 203, 204, 205, 206, 208, 210, 211, 212, 213, 214; *r. p. f. g. d.,* 76, 92, 97; *p. f. g. d. r.,* 110, 199; *p. r. g. f. d.,* 129, 186; *p. r. f. g.,* 104, 194.

[57] 3, 5, 6, 8, 10, 13, 14, 15, 16, 20, 21, 23, 28, 29, 30, 31, 32, 33, 34, 37, 38, 39, 41, 42, 43, 44, 45, 46, 48, 49, 50, 51, 52, 59, 60, 61, 65, 69, 71, 73, 76, 77, 78, 82, 83, 84, 86, 89, 90, 92, 93, 96, 97, 98, 99, 100, 105, 107, 109, 110, 111, 112, 113 117, 118, 120, 121, 122, 123, 124, 125, 126, 128, 129, 130, 132, 134, 135, 136 137 140 141, 146, 147, 149, 150 152, 153, 155, 156, 158, 160, 161, 162, 164, 165, 166, 167, 169, 170, 173, 177, 178, 180, 181, 182, 184, 186, 187, 188, 190, 191, 194, 197, 198, 199, 200, 203, 204, 206, 211, 213, 214; *Hlauerd,* (24); *Laured,* 9, 143; *Lauert,* 72, 87; *Laure,* 189; *Lauer,* 19, 36, 53, 62, 79, 81, 127, 151, 171, 175, 179, 183, 184, 193, 195, 196, 208, *Louerd* 25, 26, 63, 64, 88, 103, 104, 115, 131, 154, 212; *Louard,* 142; *Laur,* 168; *Lord,* 7, 116; *Louerdis,* 58; *Lauerding,* 75, *Louerdig,* 56, 205; *Lauerlyng,* 57; *Lauad,* 119; *Lauers,* 172, 174; *Lauerc,* 133; *Lauero,* 185; *Lauard,* 210.

58 3, 5, 6, 7, 8, 9, 10, 14, 15, 16, 19, 20, 21, 23, 25, 26, 28, 29, 30, 31, 32, 33, 34, 37, 38, 39, 41, 43, 44, 45, 46, 48, 49, 51, 52, 58, 59, 60, 61, 62, 63, 64, 65, 69, 71, 72, 73, 74, 76, 77, 78, 79, 81, 82, 84, 86, 87, 88, 89, 90, 92, 93, 96, 97, 98, 99, 100, 103, 104, 105, 109, 110, 111, 112, 113, 115, 116, 118, 119, 120, 121, 122, 123, 126, 128, 129, 130, 131, 132, 133, 134, 135, 137, 140, 141, 142, 143, 146, 147, 149, 150, 152, 153, 155, 156, 158, 160, 161, 162, 164, 165, 166, 167, 168, 169, 170, 171, 172, 174, 175, 177, 178, 179, 181, 183, 184, 185, 187, 189, 191, 194, 195, 197, 198, 200, 203, 204, 206, 210, 211, 212, 213, 214; *Ching,* 107, 125, 136, 154, 180, 182, 199; *Kyng,* 142; *Kynge,* 42; *kinc,* 124; *kinging,* 83; *kind,* (24); *km.,* 190; *hing,* 36, 53, 127, 151, 173, 196, 208; *ring,* 13, 186, 193; *rinc,* 117, 188; om., 56, 57, 58, 75, 205.

59 15, 16, 20, 29, 31, 49, 60, 65, 86, 89, 113, 116, 125, 130, 160, 165, 166, 168, 172, 180, 181; *Gaseil,* 193; *Guesheil,* 126; *Guesseil,* 83, 151, 173; *Uasseil,* 169, 177; *Uesseil,* 131; *Uuashail,* 78; *Uuashan,* 206; *Uuessail,* 56, 58, 175, 205; *Uuesseil,* 187; *Uuasseil,* 197, 198; *Waisseil,* 7; *Waseil,* 46; *Warsseil,* 200; *Washail,* 105, 158, 214; *Wassail,* (24,) 26, 51, 90, 112, 137, 149; *Wassaeil,* 121; *Wasseil,* 21, 25, 41, 43, 52, 57, 59, 61, 63, 64, 76, 77, 79, 82, 92, 97, 99, 104, 120, 122, 135, 140, 147, 155, 156, 162, 167, 170, 174, 178, 185, 194, 203, 204, 211; *Wasseyl,* 28, 111; *Washeil,* 23, 34, 71, 74, 96, 107, 136, 152, 181, 213; *Wasseail,* 49; *Wassehail,* 116; *Wassheil,* 48; *Wassheyl,* 142; *Wesahail,* 165; *Wesail,* 87, 115; *Weseil,* 81, 150, 168; *Weshail,* 6, 33, 84, 153, 161, 188; *Weshal,* 69; *Wesheil,* 28, 32, 42, 73, 84, 88, 117, 132, 134, 146, 164, 210; *Wessail,* 64, 98, 128, 143; *Wessal,* 53, 124, 196; *Wesseheil,* 5; *Wesseil,* 3, 8, 9, 13, 14, 19, 30, 36, 38, 44, 45, 62, 109, 118, 123, 127, 141, 143, 171, 179, 182, 183, 184, 189, 190, 191, 195, 199, 208; *Wessel,* 37, 100, 119; *Wesseyl,* 10, 39, 103, 110; *Wessheil,* 75; *Wosehail,* 154; *Wosheil,* 129, 186, 212; *Wosseil,* 93, 125, 180; *Wsheil,* 160; *Wusheil,* 72, 89, 133.

60...60 3, 5, 6, 7, 8, 9, 10, 13, 14, 15, 16, 19, 21, 23, 25, 26, 28, 29, 30, 31, 32, 33, 34, 36, 37, 38, 39, 41, 42, 43, 44, 45, 46, 48, 49, 51, 52, 53, 56, 57, 58, 59, 61, 62, 63, 64, 65, 69, 71, 72, 73, 74, 75, 76, 77, 78, 79, 81, 82, 84, 86, 87, 88, 89, 90, 92, 93, 96, 97, 98, 99, 100, 103, 105, 107, 109, 110, 111, 112, 113, 115, 116, 117, 118, 119, 120, 121, 122, 123, 124, 125, 126, 127, 128, 129, 130, 131, 132, 133, 134, 135, 136, 137, 140, 141, 142, 143, 146, 147, 149, 150, 151, 152, 153, 154, 155, 156, 158, 160, 161, 162, 164, 165, 167, 168, 169, 170, 171, 172, 173, 174, 175, 177, 178, 179, 180, 181, 182, 183, 184, 185, 186, 187, 188, 189, 190, 191, 193, 195, 196, 197, 198, 199, 200, 203, 204, 205, 206, 208, 210, 211, 212, 213, 214; *L. k. W. ait,* 104, 194; glossed *domine rex uiue sanus,* 83; *domine rex uiue sanus,* 20, 166; *domine rex aue bibe,* 60.

61 3, 6, 7, 8, 9, 10, 13, 14, 15, 16, 19, 20, 21, 23, 25, 26, 28, 29, 31, 33, 34, 36, 37, 38, 39, 41, 42, 43, 44, 45, 46, 48, 49, 51, 52, 53, 56, 57, 58, 59, 60, 61, 62, 63, 64, 65, 69, 71, 72, 73, 76, 77, 78, 79, 81, 82, 83, 84, 86, 87, 88, 89, 90, 92, 93, 96, 97, 98, 99, 100, 103, 105, 107, 109, 110, 111, 112, 113, 115, 116, 117, 118, 120, 121, 122, 123, 124, 125, 126, 127, 128, 129, 130, 131, 132, 133, 134, 135, 136, 137, 140, 141, 142, 143, 146, 147, 149, 150, 151, 152, 153, 154, 155, 156, 158, 160, 161, 164, 165, 166, 167, 168, 169, 170, 171, 172, 173, 174, 175, 177, 178, 179, 180, 181, 183, 184, 185, 186, 187, 188, 189, 190, 191, 193, 194, 195, 196, 197, 198, 199, 200, 203, 204, 205, 206, 208, 211, 212, 213, 214; *illa* (altered to *ille*), 5, 74, 104; *illae,* (24,) 30, 210; *illa,* 32, 75; *illa.,* 119; *ill[],* 162; om., 182.

62 3, 5, 6, 7, 8, 9, 10, 13, 14, 15, 16, 19, 20, 21, 23, 25, 26, 28, 29, 30, 31, 32, 33, 34, 36, 37, 38, 39, 41, 42, 43, 44, 45, 46, 48, 49, 51, 52, 53, 56, 57, 58, 59, 60, 61, 62, 63, 64, 69, 71, 72, 73, 74, 75, 76, 77, 78, 79, 81, 82, 83, 84, 86, 87, 88, 89, 90, 92, 93, 96, 97, 98, 99, 100, 103, 104, 105, 107, 109, 110, 111, 112, 113, 115, 116, 117, 118, 119, 120, 121, 122, 123, 124, 125, 126, 127, 128, 130, 131, 132, 133, 134, 135, 136, 137, 140, 141, 142, 143, 146, 147, 149, 150, 151, 152, 153, 154, 155, 156, 158, 160, 161, 162, 164, 165, 166, 167, 168, 169, 170, 171, 172, 173, 174, 175, 177, 178, 179, 180, 181, 182, 183, 184, 185, 186, 187, 188, 189, 190, 191, 193, 194, 195, 196, 197, 198, 199, 200, 203, 204, 205, 206, 208, 210, 211, 212, 213, 214; *Ronwein* 65; om., 129.

uisa facie[62] puelle,[63] [64] [65]ammiratus est[65] [66]tantum eius decorem[66] [67]et incaluit.[67]

[63] 3, 5, 6, 7, 8, 9, 10, 13, 14, 15, 16, 19, 20, 21, 23, 25, 26, 28, 29, 30, 31, 32, 33, 34, 36, 37, 38, 39, 41, 42, 43, 44, 45, 46, 48, 49, 51, 52, 53, 56, 57, 58, 59, 60, 61, 62, 63, 64, 65, 69, 71, 72, 73, 74, 75, 76, 77, 78, 79, 81, 82, 83, 84, 86, 87, 88, 89, 90, 92, 93, 96, 97, 98, 99, 100, 103, 104, 105, 107, 109, 110, 111, 112, 113, 115, 116, 117, 118, 120, 121, 122, 123, 124, 126, 128, 130, 131, 132, 133, 134, 135, 136, 137, 140, 141, 142, 143, 146, 147, 149, 150, 151, 152, 153, 154, 155, 156, 158, 160, 161, 162, 164, 165, 166, 167, 168, 169, 170, 171, 172, 173, 174, 175, 177, 178, 179, 180, 181, 182, 183, 184, 185, 186, 187, 188, 189, 190, 193, 194, 195, 196, 197, 198, 199, 200, 203, 204, 205, 206, 208, 210, 211, 212, 213, 214; \puelle/, 125; puelle', 119; puellae, 127; puella, 129, 191.

[64...64] 3, 5, 6, 7, 8, 9, 10, 13, 14, 15, 16, 19, 20, 21, 23, 25, 26, 28, 29, 30, 32, 33, 34, 36, 37, 38, 39, 41, 42, 43, 44, 45, 46, 48, 49, 51, 52, 53, 56, 57, 58, 61, 62, 63, 64, 65, 69, 71, 72, 73, 74, 75, 76, 77, 78, 79, 81, 82, 83, 84, 86, 87, 88, 89, 90, 92, 93, 96, 97, 98, 99, 100, 104, 105, 107, 109, 110, 111, 112, 113, 115, 116, 117, 118, 119, 120, 121, 122, 123, 124, 125, 126, 127, 128, 129, 130, 131, 132, 133, 134, 135, 136, 137, 140, 141, 142, 143, 146, 147, 149, 150, 151, 152, 153, 154, 155, 156, 158, 160, 161, 162, 164, 165, 166, 167, 168, 169, 170, 171, 172, 173, 174, 175, 177, 178, 179, 180, 181, 182, 183, 184, 185, 186, 187, 188, 189, 190, 191, 193, 194, 195, 196, 197, 198, 199, 200, 203, 204, 205, 206, 208, 210, 211, 212, 213, 214; a. i. u. p. f., 59; at ille uisa puelle et eius intuita facie, 60; om., 31, 103.

[65...65] 3, 5, 6, 7, 8, 9, 10, 13, 14, 15, 16, 19, 20, 21, 23, 25, 26, 28, 29, 30, 31, 32, 33, 34, 36, 37, 38, 39, 41, 42, 43, 44, 45, 46, 48, 49, 51, 52, 53, 56, 57, 58, 59, 60, 61, 62, 63, 64, 65, 69, 71, 72, 73, 74, 75, 76, 77, 79, 81, 82, 83, 84, 86, 87, 88, 89, 90, 92, 93, 96, 97, 98, 99, 100, 103, 104, 105, 107, 109, 110, 111, 112, 113, 115, 116, 117, 118, 119, 120, 121, 122, 123, 124, 126, 127, 128, 129, 130, 131, 132, 133, 134, 135, 136, 137, 140, 141, 142, 143, 146, 147, 149, 150, 151, 152, 153, 154, 155, 156, 158, 160, 161, 162, 164, 165, 166, 167, 168, 169, 170, 171, 172, 173, 174, 175, 177, 178, 179, 180, 181, 182, 183, 184, 185, 187, 188, 189, 190, 191, 193, 194, 195, 196, 197, 198, 199, 200, 203, 204, 205, 208, 210, 212, 213, 214; ammiratus \est/, 211; ammirans, 78; admirans, 206; admiratum est, 186; om., 125.

[66...66] 3, 5, 7, 8, 9, 10, 13, 14, 15, 16, 19, 20, 21, 23, 25, 26, 28, 29, 30, 31, 32, 33, 36, 37, 41, 42, 43, 44, 45, 46, 48, 49, 51, 52, 53, 56, 58, 59, 60, 61, 62, 63, 65, 69, 71, 72, 73, 74, 75, 76, 77, 78, 79, 81, 83, 84, 86, 87, 90, 92, 93, 96, 97, 98, 99, 100, 104, 105, 107, 109, 110, 112, 113, 117, 119, 120, 121, 123, 124, 126, 127, 128, 129, 130, 131, 133, 135, 136, 137, 140, 141, 142, 143, 146, 149, 150, 151, 153, 154, 155, 156, 158, 161, 162, 165, 166, 167, 168, 169, 170, 171, 172, 173, 175, 177, 178, 179, 180, 181, 182, 183, 184, 185, 186, 187, 188, 189, 190, 191, 193, 194, 195, 196, 197, 199, 200, 203, 204, 205, 206, 208, 210, 211, 212, 213, 214; e. t. d., 115, 174, 198; e. d., 39, 118; eius tantum decore, 6; t. d. e., 38, 64, 89, 111, 122, 160; tantam eius decorem, 103; tamtum eius decorem, 82, 134; tantum illius decorem, 88, 116; tantum esse decorem 132; tantum eius esse decorem, 164; tantam eius speciem, 34, 147, 152; tantum eius pulcritudinem, 118; tantum eius pulcritudinem et decorem, 57; om., 125.

[67...67] 3, 5, 6, 7, 8, 9, 10, 13, 14, 15, 16, 19, 20, 21, 23, 25, 26, 28, 29, 30, 31, 32, 33, 34, 36, 37, 38, 39, 41, 42, 43, 44, 45, 46, 48, 49, 51, 52, 53, 56, 57, 58, 59, 60, 61, 62, 63, 64, 65, 69, 71, 72, 73, 74, 75, 76, 77, 78, 79, 82, 83, 84, 86, 87, 88, 89, 90, 92, 93, 96, 97, 98, 99, 100, 103, 104, 105, 107, 109, 110, 111, 112, 113, 115, 116, 117, 118, 119, 120, 121, 122, 123, 124, 126, 127, 128, 129, 130, 131, 132, 133, 135, 136, 137, 140, 141, 142, 143, 146, 147, 149, 150, 151, 152, 153, 155, 156, 158, 160, 161, 162, 164, 165, 166, 167, 168, 170, 171, 172, 173, 174, 175, 177, 178, 179, 180, 181, 182, 183, 184, 185, 186, 187, 188, 189, 190, 191, 193, 194, 195, 196, 197, 198, 199, 200, 203, 204, 205, 208, 210, 211, 212, 213, 214; et inchaluit, 169; que incaluit, 134; \et/ incaluit, 154; incaluit, 206; imcaluit, 81; om., 125.

[68] 6, 7, 8, 9, 10, 13, 15, 16, 20, 21, 23, 25, 26, 28, 30, 31, 32, 33, 34, 36, 37, 38, 39, 41, 42, 43,

Denique[68] [69]interrogauit [78]interpretem suum[69] quid[70] dixerat[71] puella[72] [76]et quid ei[73]

44, 45, 46, 48, 49, 51, 52, 53, 56, 57, 58, 61, 63, 64, 65, 69, 71, 72, 73, 76, 77, 79, 82, 83, 84, 86, 87, 88, 89, 90, 92, 93, 96, 97, 98, 100, 103, 105, 107, 109, 110, 111, 112, 113, 115, 116, 119, 120, 121, 122, 123, 124, 126, 127, 128, 129, 130, 131, 132, 133, 134, 135, 136, 137, 140, 141, 142, 143, 146, 149, 150, 151, 152, 153, 154, 155, 156, 158, 160, 161, 164, 165, 166, 167, 169, 170, 172, 173, 175, 177, 178, 179, 180, 181, 182, 185, 186, 187, 188, 191, 193, 194, 195, 196, 197, 199, 200, 203, 204, 205, 208, 211, 212, 213, 214; *Deinde,* 3, 5, 14, 19, 29, 59, 60, 62, 75, 78, 81, 99, 104, 117, (? 118,) 147, 162, 168, 171, 174, 183, 184, 189, 190, 198, 206, 210; *denique uocauit rex homines suos et,* 74; om., 125.

[69...69] 5, 8, 9, 10, 15, 24, 26, 29, 30, 31, 32, 34, 37, 38, 39, 41, 42, 43, 44, 45, 46, 48, 49, 51, 52, 60, 61, 62, 63, 64, 65, 71, 72, 73, 74, 86, 89, 90, 93, 96, 98, 99, 100, 103, 105, 107, 109, 112, 113, 118, 119, 120, 121, 122, 123, 128, 131, 132, 133, 134, 136, 137, 141, 142, 143, 146, 147, 149, 150, 152, 153, 154, 156, 158, 160, 161, 162, 164, 165, 170, 177, 178, 180, 182, 183, 185, 187, 194, 200, 203, 204, 210, 212, 214; *interp. s. interr.,* 3, 6, 7, 13, 14, 16, 19, 20, 25, 33, 36, 53, 56, 58, 59, 69, 75, 76, 77, 78, 79, 81, 82, 83, 84, 92, 97, 104, 110, 111, 115, 116, 117, 126, 127, 129, 130, 135, 151, 155, 166, 167, 168, 169, 171, 173, 175, 179, 181, 184, 188, 189, 190, 191, 193, 195, 196, 197, 199, 205, 206, 208, 211, 213; *interp. interr. s.,* 23; *interp. s.,* 88; *interr. interp.,* 57; *s. interp. interr.,* 140; *interr. \interp. s./,* 125; *interp. suum rogauit,* 21; *interrogauit interprete suum,* 87; *interpetrem suum interrogauit,* 124; *interpretem suum uocauit et interrogauit,* 172, 174, 198; *interpretem suum uocat et interrogauit,* 186; *es/ interpretum suum,* 28.

[70] 3, 5, 6, 7, 8, 9, 10, 13, 14, 15, 16, 19, 20, 21, 23, 25, 26, 28, 29, 30, 31, 32, 33, 34, 36, 37, 38, 39, 41, 42, 43, 44, 45, 46, 48, 49, 51, 52, 53, 56, 57, 58, 59, 60, 61, 62, 63, 64, 65, 69, 71, 73, 74, 75, 76, 77, 78, 79, 81, 82, 83, 84, 86, 87, 88, 90, 93, 96, 97, 98, 99, 100, 103, 104, 105, 107, 109, 110, 111, 112, 113, 115, 116, 117, 118, 120, 121, 122, 123, 124, 125, 126, 127, 128, 129, 130, 131, 132, 134, 135, 136, 137, 140, 141, 142, 143, 146, 147, 149, 150, 151, 152, 153, 155, 156, 158, 161, 162, 164, 165, 166, 167, 168, 169, 170, 171, 172, 173, 174, 175, 177, 178, 179, 180, 181, 182, 183, 184, 185, 186, 187, 188, 189, 190, 191, 193, 194, 195, 196, 197, 198, 199, 200, 203, 204, 205, 206, 208, 210, 211, 212, 213, 214; *quid/,* 154; *qui\d/,* 92; *q,* 119; *que,* 72, 89, 133, 160.

[71] 3, 5, 6, 7, 8, 9, 10, 13, 14, 15, 16, 19, 20, 21, 23, 25, 26, 28, 29, 30, 31, 32, 33, 34, 36, 37, 38, 39, 41, 42, 43, 44, 45, 46, 48, 49, 51, 52, 53, 56, 57, 58, 59, 60, 61, 62, 63, 64, 65, 69, 71, 72, 73, 74, 75, 76, 77, 78, 79, 81, 82, 83, 84, 86, 87, 89, 90, 92, 93, 96, 97, 98, 99, 103, 104, 105, 107, 109, 110, 111, 112, 113, 115, 117, 118, 119, 120, 121, 122, 123, 124, 125, 126, 127, 128, 130, 131, 132, 133, 134. 135, 136, 137, 140, 141, 142, 143, 147, 149, 150, 151, 152, 153, 154, 155, 156, 158, 160, 161, 162, 164, 165, 166, 167, 168, 169, 170, 171, 173, 175, 177, 178, 179, 180, 181, 182, 183, 184, 185, 187, 188, 189, 190, 191, 193, 194, 195, 199, 200, 203, 204, 205, 206, 208, 210, 211, 212, 213, 214; *dixerit,* 129, 146, 172, 174, 186, 197, 198; *dixit,* 88; *dixˡ,* 116; *diceret,* 196; *dixit at,* 100.

[72] 3, 5, 6, 7, 8, 9, 10, 13, 14, 15, 16, 19, 20, 21, 23, 25, 26, 28, 29, 30, 31, 32, 33, 34, 36, 37, 38, 39, 41, 42, 43, 44, 45, 46, 48, 49, 51, 52, 53, 56, 57, 58, 59, 60, 61, 62, 63, 64, 65, 69, 71, 72, 73, 74, 75, 76, 77, 78, 79, 81, 82, 83, 84, 87, 88, 89, 90, 92, 93, 96, 97, 98, 99, 103, 104, 105, 107, 109, 110, 111, 112, 113, 115, 116, 117, 118, 119, 120, 121, 122, 123, 124, 125, 126, 127, 128, 129, 130, 131, 132, 133, 134, 135, 136, 137, 140, 141, 142, 143, 146, 147, 149, 150, 151, 152, 153, 154, 155, 156, 158, 160, 161, 162, 164, 165, 166, 167, 168, 169, 170, 171, 172, 173, 174, 175, 177, 178, 179, 180, 182, 183, 184, 185, 186, 187, 188, 189, 190, 191, 193, 194, 195, 196, 197, 198, 199, 200, 203, 204, 205, 206, 208, 210, 211, 212, 213, 214; *puella puella,* 181; om., 86.

[73] 3, 5, 6, 7, 8, 9, 10, 13, 14, 15, 16, 19, 20, 21, 23, 25, 26, 28, 29, 30, 31, 32, 33, 34, 36, 37, 38, 39, 41, 42, 43, 44, 45, 46, 48, 51, 52, 56, 57, 58, 59, 60, 61, 62, 63, 64, 65, 69, 71, 72, 73, 74, 75, 76, 77, 78, 79, 81, 82, 83, 84, 86, 87, 88, 89, 90, 92, 93, 96, 97, 98, 99, 100, 103,

respondere[74] debeat.[75] [76] [77]Cui interpres dixit:[77] [78] [84]'Uocauit[79] te[80] dominum[81]

104, 105, 107, 109, 110, 111, 112, 113, 115, 116, 117, 118, 119, 120, 121, 122, 123, 124, 125, 126, 127, 128, 129, 130, 131, 132, 133, 134, 135, 136, 137, 140, 141, 142, 143, 146, 147, 149, 150, 151, 152, 153, 154, 155, 156, 158, 160, 161, 162, 164, 165, 166, 167, 168, 169, 170, 171, 172, 173, 174, 175, 177, 178, 179, 180, 181, 182, 183, 184, 185, 186, 187, 188, 189, 190, 191, 193, 194, 195, 197, 198, 199, 200, 203, 204, 205, 206, 208, 210, 211, 212, 213, 214; *illi,* 53, 196; om., 49, 156.

[74] 3, 5, 6, 7, 8, 9, 10, 13, 14, 15, 16, 19, 20, 21, 23, 25, 26, 28, 29, 30, 31, 32, 34, 36, 37, 38, 39, 41, 42, 43, 44, 45, 46, 48, 49, 51, 52, 53, 56, 57, 58, 59, 60, 61, 63, 64, 65, 71, 72, 73, 74, 75, 76, 77, 78, 79, 81, 82, 83, 84, 86, 87, 88, 89, 90, 92, 93, 96, 97, 98, 99, 100, 103, 104, 105, 107, 109, 110, 111, 113, 115, 116, 117, 118, 119, 120, 121, 122, 123, 124, 125, 127, 128, 129, 130, 131, 132, 133, 134, 135, 136, 137, 140, 141, 142, 143, 146, 147, 149, 150, 151, 152, 153, 154, 155, 156, 158, 160, 161, 162, 164, 165, 166, 167, 168, 169, 170, 171, 172, 173, 174, 175, 177, 178, 179, 180, 181, 182, 183, 184, 185, 186, 187, 188, 189, 190, 191, 193, 194, 195, 196, 197, 198, 199, 200, 203, 205, 206, 208, 210, 211, 212, 213, 214; *responderet* (corr. to *respondere*), 126; *responderet,* 33, 69, 204; *responderi,* 112; *respondererere,* 62.

[75] 3, 5, 6, 7, 9, 10, 13, 14, 15, 16, 19, 21, 26, 32, 34, 37, 42, 43, 45, 51, 53, 56, 57, 58, 59, 60, 64, 65, 73, 74, 75, 76, 77, 78, 79, 81, 82, 84, 90, 92, 97, 98, 99, 103, 104, 105, 109, 111, 112, 115, 117, 119, 122, 124, 125, 127, 130, 133, 135, 136, 137, 142, 143, 146, 147, 149, 152, 153, 154, 155, 158, 162, 164, 165, 167, 168, 169, 171, 174, 175, 177, 179, 180, 182, 183, 184, 188, 189, 190, 191, 193, 194, 195, 196, 197, 198, 199, 200, 205, 206, 208, 211, 212, 213, 214; *debe\b/at,* 178; *debebat,* 8, 20, (24,) 25, 30, 31, 39, 44, 46, 49, 52, 61, 63, 71, 72, 86, 87, 89, 93, 107, 113, 120, 123, 132, 140, 141, 156, 160, 161, 170, 181, 185, 187, 203; *deberat,* 151; *deberet,* 23, 28, 38, 41, 62, 83 (over erasure), 96, 100, 110, 118, 121, 126, 128, 129, 131, 134, 166, 186, 210; *debere(a)t,* 48; *debeas* (corrected to *debeat*), 150; *debuerat,* 29, 173; *debat,* 172; *debeat inquirit,* 88, 116; om., 33, 69, 204.

[76]...[76] 3, 5, 6, 7, 8, 13, 14, 15, 16, 19, 21, 23, 25, 26, 28, 29, 34, 36, 37, 38, 43, 46, 48, 51, 52, 57, 59, 60, 61, 62, 63, 64, 65, 71, 72, 74, 75, 76, 77, 78, 79, 81, 82, 84, 86, 87, 88, 89, 92, 96, 97, 99, 100, 103, 104, 105, 107, 111, 112, 115, 116, 117, 118, 120, 121, 122, 124, 125, 127, 128, 129, 130, 131, 133, 134, 135, 136, 146, 149, 152, 154, 155, 160, 161, 162, 164, 167, 168, 169, 170, 171, 172, 174, 177, 179, 180, 181, 182, 183, 184, 185, 186, 187, 188, 189, 190, 191, 193, 194, 195, 196, 197, 198, 199, 200, 203, 206, 208, 210, 211, 213, 214; *et q. r. ei d,* 30, 32, 39, 45, 56, 58, 73, 98, 119, 123, 141, 153, 165, 205; *et q. r. d. ei,* 109; *et q. r. d.,* 9, 20, 31, 41, 42, 44, 49, 53, 83, 90, 93, 110, 113, 126, 132, 137, 140, 142, 143, 147, 150, 151, 156, 158, 166, 173, 175, 178, 212; *et q. ei r.,* 33, 69, 204; om., 10.

[77]...[77] 5, 6, 7, 8, 9, 10, 13, 15, 16, 21, 23, 25, 26, 28, 29, 30, 31, 32, 33, 34, 37, 38, 39, 41, 42, 43, 44, 45, 46, 48, 49, 51, 52, 57, 59, 60, 61, 62, 63, 69, 71, 72, 73, 74, 76, 77, 78, 84, 86, 87, 88, 89, 90, 92, 93, 96, 97, 98, 99, 100, 103, 104, 105, 109, 110, 112, 115, 116, 117, 118, 119, 120, 121, 122, 123, 124, 128, 129, 13 1, 132, 133, 134, 135, 136, 140, 141, 142, 143, 146, 147, 149, 150, 152, 153, 154, 155, 156, 158, 160, 161, 162, 164, 165, 167, 169, 170, 172, 174, 177, 178, 180, 181, 185, 186, 187, 188, 190, 191, 194, 197, 198, 199, 200, 203, 204, 206, 210, 211, 212, 213, 214; *C. d. i.,* 107; *C. i. \dJ,* 137; *Cui interpretes* (corr. to *interpres*) *dixit,* 113; *Cui interpretes dixit,* 64, 82; *Cui interpres ait,* 65; *Qui dixit,* 36, 53, 56, 58, 75, 127, 196, 205, 208; *qui ait,* 20, 83, 126, 151, 166, 173, 175; om. but inserted in margin, 130; om., 3, 14, 19, 79, 81, 111, 125, 168, 171, 179, 182, 183, 184, 189, 193, 195.

[78]...[78] 3, 5, 6, 7, 8, 9, 10, 13, 14, 15, 16, 19, 20, 21, 23, 25, 26, 28, 29, 30, 31, 32, 33, 34, 36, 37, 38, 39, 41, 42, 43, 44, 45, 46, 48, 49, 51, 52, 53, 56, 57, 58, 59, 60, 61, 62, 63, 64, 65, 69, 71, 72, 73, 75, 76, 77, 78, 79, 81, 82, 83, 84, 86, 87, 88, 89, 90, 92, 93, 96, 97, 98, 99, 100, 103, 104, 105, 107, 109, 110, 111, 112, 113, 115, 116, 117, 118, 119, 120, 121, 122, 123, 124, 125, 126, 127, 128, 129, 130, 131, 132, 133, 134, 135, 136, 137, 140, 141, 142,

regem et [82]uocabulo salutationis[82] honorauit.[83] [84] Quod[85] autem[86] [87]respondere

143, 146, 147, 149, 150, 151, 152, 153, 154, 155, 156, 158, 160, 161, 162, 164, 165, 166, 167, 168, 169, 170, 171, 172, 173, 174, 175, 177, 178, 179, 180, 151, 182, 183, 184, 185, 186, 187, 188, 189, 190, 191, 193, 194, 195, 196, 197, 198, 199, 200, 203, 204, 205, 206, 208, 210, 211, 212, 213, 214; *illis quid ipsa dederit. Qui responderunt. Denique,* 74.

[79] 5, 6, 7, 9, 10, 13, 15, 16, 21, 23, 25, 26, 28, 29, 30, 31, 32, 33, 34, 37, 38, 39, 41, 42, 43, 44, 45, 46, 48, 49, 51, 52, 57, 59, 60, 61, 62, 63, 64, 65, 69, 71, 72, 74, 76, 77, 78, 82, 84, 86, 87, 88, 89, 90, 92, 93, 96, 97, 98, 99, 100, 103, 104, 105, 107, 109, 110, 112, 113, 115, 116, 117, 118, 119, 120, 121, 122, 123, 124, 129, 131, 132, 133, 134, 135, 136, 137, 140, 141, 142, 143, 146, 147, 149, 150, 152, 154, 156, 158, 160, 161, 162, 164, 165, 167, 168, 169, 170, 171, 172, 174, 177, 178, 180, 181, 185, 186, 187, 188, 190, 191, 194, 197, 198, 199, 200, 203, 204, 206, 210, 211, 212, 213, 214; *uocat,* 73, 153; *uocauitque,* 155; *uocatumque,* 8; *salutauit,* 128; om., 3, 14, 19, 20, 36, 53, 56, 58, 75, 79, 81, 83, 111, 125, 126, 127, 130, 151, 166, 168, 171, 173, 175, 179, 182, 183, 184, 189, 193, 195, 196, 205, 208.

[80] 5, 6, 7, 8, 9, 10, 13, 15, 16, 21, 23, 25, 26, 28, 29, 30, 31, 32, 33, 34, 37, 38, 39, 41, 42, 43, 44, 45, 46, 48, 49, 51, 52, 57, 59, 60, 61, 62, 63, 64, 65, 69, 71, 72, 73, 74, 75, 76, 77, 78, 82, 84, 86, 87, 88, 89, 90, 92, 93, 96, 97, 98, 99, 100, 103, 104, 105, 107, 109, 110, 112, 113, 115, 116, 117, 118, 119, 120, 121, 122, 123, 124, 128, 129, 131, 133, 134, 135, 136, 137, 140, 141, 142, 143, 146, 147, 149, 150, 152, 153, 156, 158, 160, 161, 162, 164, 165, 167, 169, 170, 172, 174, 177, 178, 179, 180, 181, 185, 186, 187, 188, 190, 191, 194, 197, 198, 199, 200, 203, 204, 206, 210, 211, 213, 214; *te*, 154; *te* *que,* 132; *que,* 155; om., 3, 14, 19, 20, 36, 53, 56, 58, 75, 79, 81, 83, 111, 125, 126, 127, 130, 151, 166, 168, 171, 173, 175, 179, 182, 183, 184, 189, 193, 195, 196, 205, 208, 212.

[81] 5, 6, 7, 8, 9, 10, 13, 15, 16, 21, 23, 25, 26, 28, 29, 30, 31, 32, 33, 34, 37, 38, 39, 41, 42, 43, 44, 45, 46, 48, 49, 51, 52, 57, 59, 60, 61, 62, 63, 64, 65, 69, 71, 72, 73, 74, 76, 77, 78, 82, 84, 86, 87, 88, 89, 90, 92, 93, 96, 97, 98, 99, 100, 103, 104, 105, 107, 109, 110, 112, 113, 115, 116, 117, 118, 119, 120, 121, 122, 123, 124, 128, 129, 131, 132, 133, 134, 135, 136, 137, 140, 141, 142, 143, 146, 149, 150, 152, 153, 155, 156, 158, 160, 161, 162, 164, 165, 167, 169, 170, 172, 174, 177, 178, 180, 181, 185, 186, 187, 188, 190, 191, 194, 197, 198, 199, 200, 203, 204, 206, 210, 211, 212, 213, 214; *dominum*, 154; *den.,* 147; om., 3, 14, 19, 20, 36, 53, 56, 58, 75, 79, 81, 83, 111, 125, 126, 127, 130, 151, 166, 168, 171, 173, 175, 179, 182, 183, 184, 189, 193, 195, 196, 205, 208.

[82...82] 5, 6, 7, 8, 9, 10, 13, 15, 16, 21, 23, 25, 26, 28, 29, 30, 31, 32, 33, 34, 37, 38, 39, 42, 43, 44, 45, 46, 48, 49, 51, 52, 57, 59, 60, 61, 62, 63, 64, 65, 69, 71, 72, 73, 74, 76, 77, 78, 82, 84, 86, 87, 88, 89, 90, 92, 93, 96, 97, 98, 100, 103, 104, 105, 107, 109, 110, 112, 113, 115, 116, 117, 118, 119, 120, 121, 122, 123, 124, 129, 131, 133, 134, 135, 136, 137, 140, 141, 142, 143, 146, 147, 149, 150, 152, 153, 155, 156, 158, 160, 161, 162, 164, 165, 167, 169, 170, 172, 174, 177, 178, 180, 181, 185, 186, 187, 188, 190, 191, 194, 197, 198, 199, 200, 203, 204, 206, 210, 211, 212, 213, 214; *s. u.,* 128; *uocabulo salutonis,* 99, 154; *uocabulo salutionis,* 132; *uocabulo salutati omnis,* 41; om., 3, 14, 19, 20, 36, 53, 56, 58, 75, 79, 81, 83, 111, 125, 126, 127, 130, 151, 166, 168, 171, 173, 175, 179, 182, 183, 184, 189, 193, 195, 196, 205, 208.

[83] 5, 6, 7, 8, 9, 10, 13, 15, 16, 21, 23, 25, 26, 28, 29, 30, 31, 32, 33, 34, 37, 38, 39, 41, 42, 43, 44, 45, 46, 48, 49, 51, 52, 57, 59, 60, 61, 62, 63, 64, 65, 69, 71, 72, 73, 74, 76, 77, 78, 82, 84, 86, 87, 88, 89, 90, 92, 96, 97, 98, 99, 100, 103, 104, 105, 107, 109, 110, 112, 113, 115, 116, 117, 118, 119, 120, 121, 122, 123, 124, 128, 129, 131, 132, 133, 134, 135, 136, 137, 140, 141, 142, 143, 146, 147, 149, 150, 152, 153, 154, 155, 156, 158, 160, 161, 162, 164, 165, 167, 169, 170, 172, 174, 177, 178, 180, 181, 185, 187, 188, 190, 191, 194, 197, 198, 199, 200, 203, 204, 206, 210, 211, 212, 213, 214; *honorauit te,* 93; *adhonorauit* (corr. to *honorauit*), 186; om., 3, 14, 19, 20, 36, 53, 56, 58, 75, 79, 81, 83, 111, 125, 126, 127, 130, 151, 166, 168, 171, 173, 175, 179, 182, 183, 184, 189, 193, 195, 196, 205, 208.

debes,[87] est[88] "Drincheil".'[89] [93]Respondens[90] deinde[91] Uortegirnus[92] [93] 'Drin-

[84...84] 5, 6, 7, 8, 9, 10, 13, 15, 16, 21, 23, 25, 26, 28, 29, 30, 31, 32, 33, 34, 37, 38, 39, 41, 42, 43, 44, 45, 46, 48, 49, 51, 52, 57, 59, 60, 61, 62, 63, 64, 65, 69, 71, 72, 73, 74, 76, 77, 78, 82, 84, 86, 87, 88, 89, 90, 92, 93, 96, 97, 98, 99, 100, 103, 104, 105, 107, 109, 110, 112, 113, 115, 116, 117, 118, 119, 120, 121, 122, 123, 124, 128, 129, 131, 132, 133, 134, 135, 136, 137, 140, 141, 142, 143, 146, 147, 149, 150, 152, 153, 154, 155, 156, 158, 160, 161, 162, 164, 165, 167, 169, 170, 172, 174, 177, 178, 180, 181, 185, 186, 187, 188, 190, 191, 194, 197, 198, 199, 200, 203, 204, 206, 210, 211, 212, 213, 214; om. but inserted in margin 125, 130; om., 3, 14, 19, 20, 36, 53, 56, 58, 75, 79, 81, 83, 111, 126, 127, 151, 166, 168, 171, 173, 175, 179, 182, 183, 184, 189, 193, 195, 196, 205, 208.

[85] 3, 5, 6, 7, 9, 10, 13, 14, 15, 16, 19, 20, 21, 23, 25, 26, 29, 31, 33, 34, 36, 37, 38, 41, 42, 43, 44, 45, 46, 49, 51, 52, 53, 56, 57, 58, 59, 60, 61, 62, 63, 64, 65, 69, 71, 72, 75, 76, 77, 78, 79, 81, 82, 83, 84, 86, 87, 88, 89, 92, 93, 96, 97, 99, 103, 104, 107, 110, 111, 112, 113, 115, 116, 117, 118, 120, 121, 122, 125, 126, 127, 128, 129, 130, 131, 132, 133, 134, 135, 136, 137, 140, 143, 146, 147, 149, 150, 151, 152, 153, 155, 156, 158, 160, 161, 162, 164, 166, 167, 168, 169, 170, 171, 172, 173, 174, 175, 177, 178, 181, 182, 183, 184, 185, 186, 187, 188, 189, 190, 191, 193, 194, 195, 196, 197, 198, 199, 200, 203, 204, 205, 206, 208, 210, 211, 212, 213; *Q[],* 48; *quid,* 8, 28, 30, 32, 39, 73, 74, 90, 98, 100, 105, 109, 119, 123, 124, 141, 142, 154, 165, 180, 214; om., 179.

[86] 3, 5, 6, 7, 8, 9, 10, 13, 14, 15, 16, 19, 20, 21, 23, 25, 26, 28, 29, 30, 31, 32, 33, 34, 36, 37, 38, 39, 41, 42, 43, 44, 45, 46, 48, 49, 51, 52, 53, 56, 57, 58, 59, 60, 61, 62, 63, 64, 65, 69, 71, 72, 73, 74, 76, 77, 78, 79, 81, 82, 83, 84, 86, 87, 88, 89, 90, 92, 93, 96, 97, 98, 99, 100, 103, 104, 105, 107, 109, 110, 111, 112, 113, 115, 116, 117, 118, 119, 120, 121, 122, 123, 124, 125, 126, 127, 128, 129, 130, 131, 132, 133, 134, 135, 136, 137, 140, 141, 142, 143, 146, 147, 149, 150, 151, 152, 153, 154, 155, 156, 158, 160, 161, 162, 164, 165, 166, 167, 168, 169, 170, 171, 172, 173, 174, 175, 177, 178, 180, 181, 182, 183, 184, 185, 186, 187, 188, 189, 190, 191, 193, 194, 195, 196, 197, 198, 199, 200, 203, 204, 205, 206, 208, 210, 211, 212, 213, 214; om., 75, 179.

[87...87] 3, 5, 6, 7, 8, 9, 10, 13, 14, 15, 16, 19, 20, 21, 23, 25, 28, 29, 30, 31, 32, 33, 36, 37, 38, 39, 41, 42, 43, 44, 45, 46, 48, 49, 52, 53, 56, 57, 58, 59, 60, 61, 62, 63, 64, 65, 69, 71, 72, 73, 74, 75, 76, 77, 79, 81, 82, 84, 86, 87, 88, 89, 90, 92, 93, 96, 97, 98, 99, 100, 103, 104, 105, 109, 110, 111, 112, 113, 115, 116, 117, 118, 119, 120, 121, 122, 123, 124, 125, 126, 127, 128, 129, 130, 131, 132, 133, 134, 135, 137, 140, 141, 142, 143, 146, 147, 149, 150, 152, 153, 154, 155, 156, 158, 160, 161, 162, 164, 165, 166, 167, 168, 169, 170, 171, 172, 173, 174, 175, 177, 178, 180, 181, 182, 183, 184, 185, 186, 187, 188, 189, 190, 191, 193, 194, 195, 196, 197, 198, 199, 200, 203, 204, 205, 208, 210, 211, 212, 213, 214; *d. r.,* 107, 136; *respondere debeas,* 34, 78, 151, 206; *respondere deberet,* 83, 210; *respondere debere,* 26, 51; om., but in margin, *quod respondere debes,* 179.

[88] 3, 6, 7, 8, 9, 10, 13, 14, 15, 16, 19, 20, 21, 23, 25, 26, 28, 29, 30, 31, 32, 33, 34, 36, 37, 38, 39, 41, 42, 43, 44, 45, 46, 48, 49, 51, 52, 53, 56, 58, 59, 61, 63, 64, 65, 69, 71, 72, 73, 75, 76, 77, 78, 79, 81, 82, 83, 84, 86, 87, 88, 89, 90, 92, 93, 96, 97, 98, 99, 100, 103, 104, 105, 107, 109, 110, 111, 112, 113, 115, 116, 117, 118, 119, 120, 121, 122, 123, 124, 125, 126, 127, 128, 129, 130, 131, 132, 133, 134, 135, 136, 137, 140, 141, 142, 143, 146, 147, 149, 150, 151, 152, 153, 154, 155, 156, 158, 160, 161, 162, 164, 165, 166, 167, 168, 169, 170, 171, 172, 173, 174, 175, 177, 178, 179, 180, 181, 183, 184, 185, 186, 187, 188, 189, 190, 191, 193, 194, 195, 196, 197, 198, 199, 200, 203, 204, 205, 206, 208, 210, 211, 212, 213, 214; *hoc est,* 5, 60; *ee,* 182; om., 57, 62, 74.

[89] 5, 6, 8, 13, 15, 16, 19, 21, 23, 29, 31, 32, 34, 37, 38, 41, 42, 43, 44, 46, 48, 49, 59, 65, 71, 73, 74, 76, 79, 82, 84, 86, 88, 89, 92, 93, 96, 97, 100, 107, 112, 113, 115, 116, 117, 120, 121, 122, 131, 132, 134, 135, 136, 143, 146, 147, 149, 150, 153, 155, 156, 160, 162, 164, 167, 169, 170, 172, 174, 177, 181, 185, 187, 188, 190, 191, 194, 196, 197, 198, 200, 203, 210,

211, 213; *Driachil,* 151; *Drichail,* 189; *Dricheil,* 98, 161, 193; *Driincheil,* 132; *Drincahil,* 53, 196; *Drincail,* 56, 58, 205; *Drinceil,* 63; *Drinchael.* 3, 14; *Drinchahil,* 83, 126; *Drinchail,* 7, 26, 33, 36, 51, 62, 69, 75, 77, 78, 81, 87, 90, 125, 127, 128, 129, 130, 137, 154, 165, 166, 168, 171, 173, 175, 179, 180, 182, 183, 184, 186, 195, 199, 206, 208; *Drinchayl,* 110; *Drincheheil,* 178; *Drinchel,* 99, 124; *Drincheyl,* 45; *Drinckeil,* 30, 109, 123, 141; *Dringheil,* 72, 118, 133; *Dringheyl,* 64; *Drinkehail,* 9; *Drinkeil,* 119; *Drinkeyl,* 10; *Drinkhail,* 105, 152, 214; *Drinkhayl,* 155; *Drinkheil,* 52, 61, 64, 140, 158, 204, 212; *Drinkheyl,* 28, 39, 103, 111; *Drinkkeyl,* 104; *Dryncheil,* 25; *Dryncheyl,* 57; *Drynkheyl,* 142; *bibe sana,* 20 (as a gloss, 126, 166); *bibe tu,* 60.

90 3, 5, 6, 7, 8, 9, 10, 13, 14, 15, 16, 19, 20, 21, 23, 25, 26, 28, 29, 30, 32, 33, 34, 36, 37, 38, 39, 41, 42, 43, 44, 45, 46, 48, 49, 51, 52, 53, 56, 57, 58, 59, 60, 61, 62, 63, 69, 71, 72, 73, 74, 76, 77, 78, 79, 81, 82, 83, 84, 86, 87, 88, 89, 90, 92, 93, 96, 97, 98, 99, 100, 104, 105, 107, 109, 110, 111, 112, 115, 116, 117, 118, 119, 120, 121, 122, 123, 124, 125, 126, 127, 128, 129, 130, 131, 132, 133, 134, 135, 136, 137, 140, 141, 142, 143, 146, 147, 149, 150, 151, 152, 153, 154, 155, 156, 158, 160, 161, 162, 164, 165, 166, 167, 1 68, 169, 170, 171, 172, 173, 174, 175, 177, 178, 179, 180, 181, 182, 183, 185, 186, 188, 189, 190, 191, 193, 194, 195, 196, 197, 198, 199, 200, 203, 204, 205, 206, 208, 210, 211, 212, 213, 214; *Respondit,* 31, 64, 75, 103, 113, 184, 187; *respondens autem,* 65.

91 3, 5, 6, 8, 9, 13, 14, 15, 16, 19, 21, 23, 25, 26, 28, 29, 30, 31, 32, 33, 34, 36, 37, 38, 39, 41, 42, 43, 44, 45, 46, 48, 49, 51, 52, 53, 56, 57, 58, 59, 61, 62, 63, 69, 71, 72, 73, 74, 75, 76, 77, 78, 79, 81, 82, 83, 84, 86, 87, 88, 89, 90, 92, 93, 96, 97, 98, 99, 100, 103, 104, 107, 110, 112, 113, 115, 116, 117, 118, 119, 120, 121, 122, 123, 124, 125, 126, 127, 128, 129, 130, 131, 133, 134, 135, 136, 137, 140, 141, 142, 146, 149, 150, 151, 152, 153, 155, 156, 160, 161, 162, 164, 165, 166, 167, 168, 169, 170, 171, 173, 175, 177, 178, 179, 180, 181, 182, 183, 184, 185, 186, 187, 188, 189, 190, 191, 193, 194, 195, 196, 199, 200, 203, 204, 205, 206, 208, 210, 211, 212, 213; \deinde\, 154; *denique,* 7; *autem,* 20, 65; *igitur,* 105, 111, 214; *itaque,* 60, 147; *inde,* 10; *ei,* 109; om., 64, 132, 143, 158, 172, 174, 197, 198.

92 5, 7, 9, 10, 15, 16, 20, 21, 23, 25, 28, 30, 32, 33, 34, 36, 37, 39, 43, 46, 48, 49, 52, 53, 56, 57, 58, 59, 64, 65, 69, 71, 72, 73, 74, 76, 77, 79, 82, 83, 84, 86, 87, 88, 89, 92, 96, 98, 99, 100, 104, 107, 109, 112, 116, 117, 118, 119, 120, 121, 122, 123, 124, 125, 126, 127, 129, 134, 135, 136, 141, 146, 147, 149, 150, 151, 152, 155, 156, 158, 161, 162, 166, 169, 170, 172, 175, 177, 179, 180, 181, 185, 186, 188, 191, 193, 194, 195, 196, 197, 198, 200, 203, 204, 205, 206, 208, 211, 213; *Uoltegirnus,* 81, 168, 183, 184; *Uorteger,* 153; *Uortegrinus,* 173; *Uorteirgnus,* 174; *Uorthigenus,* 60; *Uortigernus,* 26, 29, 31, 41, 42, 51, 63, 75, 78, 90, 97, 105, 110, 113, 128, 132, 137, 140, 154, 187, 210, 212; *Uortigirnus,* 8, 13, 44, 45, 63, 93, 131, 142, 143, 160, 165, 178, 214; *Uotegirnus,* 19, 133, 167; *Woltegirnus,* 3, 14, 171, 189; *Wortegirnus,* 6, 62, 103, 130, 182, 190; *Wortigernus,* 115, 199; *Wortigirnus,* 38; *Uortegirnus dixit,* 61; *rex,* 111; om., 164; *Uortegirnus deinde,* 65.

93...93 3, 5, 6, 7, 8, 9, 10, 13, 14, 15, 16, 19, 20, 21, 25, 26, 28, 29, 30, 31, 32, 33, 34, 36, 37, 38, 39, 41, 42, 43, 44, 45, 46, 48, 49, 51, 52, 53, 56, 57, 58, 59, 60, 61, 62, 63, 64, 69, 71, 72, 73, 74, 75, 76, 77, 78, 79, 81, 82, 83, 84, 86, 87, 88, 89, 90, 92, 93, 97, 98, 99, 100, 103, 104, 105, 107, 109, 110, 111, 112, 113, 115, 116, 117, 118, 119, 120, 121, 122, 123, 124, 125, 126, 127, 128, 129, 130, 131, 132, 133, 134, 135, 136, 137, 140, 141, 142, 143, 146, 147, 149, 150, 151, 152, 153, 154, 155, 156, 158, 160, 161, 162, 164, 165, 166, 167, 168, 169, 170, 171, 172, 173, 174, 175, 177, 178, 179, 180, 181, 182, 183, 184, 185, 186, 187, 188, 189, 190, 191, 193, 194, 195, 196, 197, 198, 199, 200, 203, 204, 205, 206, 208, 210, 211, 212, 213, 214; *d. r. U.,* 23, 96; *r. U. d.,* 65; om., 37, 57, 121, 177.

94 5, 6, 8, 13, 15, 16, 21, 23, 25, 26, 28, 30, 32, 34, 38, 41, 42, 43, 44, 46, 48, 49, 59, 71, 73, 74, 76, 77, 79, 82, 84, 86, 87, 88, 89, 92, 93, 96, 97, 98, 99, 100, 104, 107, 112, 113, 115, 116, 117, 118, 120, 122, 124, 126, 131, 132, 134, 135, 136, 146, 147, 149, 150, 152, 153, 156, 160, 161, 162, 167, 169, 172, 174, 178, 179, 180, 181, 185, 187, 188, 191, 193, 194, 197, 198, 200, 203, 204, 210, 211, 213; *Dirincheil,* 190; *Dricheil,* 170; *Drincahil,* 53, 196; *Drincail,* 56, 58, 205; *Drinceil,* 63; *Drinchael,* 3, 14; *Drinchail,* 7, 19, 20, 33, 36, 51, 62,

cheil'[94] iussit[95] [96]puellam potare[96] cepitque[97] ciphum[98] [99]de manu[99] i psius[100] et

69, 75, 78, 81, 83, 90, 110, 125, 127, 128, 129, 130, 137, 151, 154, 165, 166, 168, 171, 173, 175, 182, 183, 184, 186, 189, 195, 208; *Drincheyl*, 45; *Drinchil*, 199; *Drinckeil*, 109, 123, 141; *Dringeil*, 119; *Dringheil*, 72, 133; *Dringheyl*, 65, 111; *Drinkeheil*, 143; *Drinkeyl*, 10; *Drinkhail*, 105, 214; *Drinkhayl*, 155; *Drinkheil*, 31, 52, 61, 158, 212; *Drinkheyl*, 103; *Drynkheil*, 140; *Drynkheyl*, 29, 142; *Drinkheil et*, 64; *bibe tu*, 60; om., 9, 37, 39, 57, 121, 177, 206; *Drincheil Uortigirnus*, 164.

[95] 3, 5, 6, 7, 8, 9, 10, 13, 14, 15, 16, 19, 20, 21, 23, 25, 26, 28, 29, 30, 31, 32, 33, 34, 36, 37, 38, 39, 41, 42, 43, 44, 45, 46, 48, 49, 51, 52, 53, 56, 57, 58, 59, 60, 61, 62, 63, 64, 65, 69, 71, 72, 73, 74, 75, 76, 77, 78, 79, 81, 82, 83, 84, 86, 87, 88, 89, 90, 92, 93, 96, 97, 98, 99, 100, 104, 107, 109, 110, 111, 112, 113, 115, 116, 117, 118, 119, 120, 121, 122, 123, 124, 126, 127, 129, 130, 131, 132, 133, 134, 135, 136, 137, 140, 141, 142, 143, 146, 147, 149, 150, 151, 152, 153, 155, 156, 158, 160, 161, 162, 164, 165, 166, 167, 168, 169, 170, 171, 172, 173, 174, 175, 177, 178, 179, 180, 181, 182, 183, 184, 185, 186, 187, 188, 189, 191, 193, 194, 195, 196, 197, 198, 199, 200, 203, 204, 205, 206, 208, 210, 211, 212, 213; *iusit*, 128; *et iussit*, 190; \ac/ *iussit*, 125; *ac iussit*, 105, 154, 214; *iussitque*, 103.

[96...96] 3, 5, 6, 7, 9, 10, 13, 14, 15, 16, 19, 20, 21, 26, 28, 29, 30, 31, 32, 33, 34, 36, 37, 38, 39, 41, 42, 43, 44, 45, 46, 48, 49, 51, 52, 53, 56, 57, 58, 59, 60, 61, 62, 63, 64, 65, 69, 71, 72, 73, 74, 75, 76, 77, 78, 79, 81, 82, 83, 84, 86, 87, 88, 92, 93, 96, 97, 98, 99, 100, 103, 104, 105, 109, 111, 112, 113, 115, 116, 117, 118, 119, 120, 121, 122, 123, 124, 125, 126, 130, 131, 132, 133, 135, 136, 140, 141, 142, 143, 146, 149, 150, 151, 152, 153, 154, 155, 156, 158, 161, 162, 164, 165, 166, 167, 168, 169, 170, 171, 172, 173, 174, 175, 178, 179, 181, 182, 183, 184, 185, 187, 189, 191, 193, 194, 195, 196, 198, 199, 200, 203, 204, 205, 206, 210, 212, 213, 214; *pot. puel.*, 127, 188, 208; *eam potare*, 89, 107, 160; *potare*, 8, 129; *portare*, 134, 186; *puellam po[ ]tare*, 180; *puellam portare*, 23, 25, 90, 110, 128, 137, 147, 177, 197, 211; *puellam a pottare*, 190.

[97] 3, 5, 6, 7, 9, 10, 13, 14, 15, 16, 19, 20, 21, 23, 26, 28, 29, 30, 31, 32, 33, 34, 36, 37, 38, 39, 41, 42, 43, 44, 45, 46, 48, 49, 51, 52, 53, 56, 57, 58, 59, 60, 61, 62, 63, 69, 71, 72, 73, 74, 75, 76, 77, 78, 79, 81, 82, 83, 84, 86, 87, 88, 89, 90, 92, 93, 96, 97, 98, 99, 100, 103, 104, 105, 107, 109, 110, 111, 112, 113, 115, 116, 117, 118, 119, 120, 121, 122, 123, 124, 125, 126, 128, 129, 130, 131, 132, 133, 134, 135, 136, 137, 140, 141, 142, 143, 146, 147, 149, 150, 151, 152, 153, 154, 155, 156, 158, 160, 161, 162, 164, 165, 166, 167, 168, 169, 170, 171, 172, 173, 175, 177, 178, 179, 180, 181, 182, 183, 184, 185, 186, 187, 188, 189, 190, 191, 193, 194, 195, 196, 197, 199, 200, 203, 204, 205, 206, 210, 211, 212, 213, 214; *cepit*, 8, 65, 127, 174, 208; *et cepit*, 25, 198; *accepitque*, 60; *et potauit cepitque*, 64.

[98] 3, 5, 6, 7, 8, 9, 10, 13, 14, 15, 16, 19, 21, 23, 25, 26, 28, 30, 31, 32, 33, 34, 36, 37, 38, 39, 41, 42, 43, 44, 45, 46, 48, 49, 51, 52, 56, 58, 59, 60, 61, 62, 63, 65, 69, 71, 72, 73, 74, 75, 76, 77, 78, 79, 81, 82, 83, 84, 86, 87, 88, 89, 90, 92, 93, 96, 97, 98, 99, 103, 104, 105, 107, 109, 110, 111, 112, 113, 115, 116, 117, 118, 119, 120, 121, 122, 123, 124, 125, 126, 128, 129, 130, 131, 132, 133, 134, 135, 136, 137, 140, 141, 142, 143, 146, 147, 149, 150, 151, 152, 153, 154, 155, 156, 158, 160, 161, 162, 164, 165, 166, 167, 168, 169, 170, 171, 172, 173, 174, 175, 177, 178, 179, 180, 181, 183, 184, 185, 186, 187, 188, 189, 190, 191, 193, 194, 195, 197, 198, 199, 200, 203, 204, 205, 206, 210, 211, 212, 213, 214; *sciphum*, 20, 53, 196; *scyphum* 127, 208; *chiphum*, 100; *ciphum unus*, 64; *ciphum ipsius*, 57; *ciphum aureum*, 182; *?secundum ciphum*, 29.

[99...99] 3, 5, 6, 7, 8, 9, 10, 13, 14, 15, 16, 19, 20, 21, 23, 25, 26, 28, 29, 30, 31, 32, 33, 34, 36, 37, 38, 39, 41, 49, 42, 43, 44, 45, 46, 48, 49, 51, 52, 53, 56, 57, 58, 59, 60, 61, 62, 63, 64, 65, 69, 71, 72, 73, 74, 75, 76, 77, 78, 79, 81, 82, 83, 84, 86, 87, 88, 89, 90, 92, 93, 96, 97, 98, 99, 100, 103, 104, 105, 107, 109, 110, 111, 112, 113, 115, 116, 117, 118, 119, 120, 121, 122, 123, 125, 126, 127, 128, 129, 130, 131, 132, 133, 134, 135, 136, 137, 140, 141, 142, 143, 146, 147, 149, 150, 151, 152, 153, 154, 155, 156, 158, 160, 161, 162, 164, 165, 166,

[101]osculatus est eam[101] et[102] potauit.[103] [104]Ab illo[104] die[105] usque [106]in hodiernum[106]

167, 168, 169, 170, 171, 172, 173, 174, 175, 177, 178, 179, 180, 181, 182, 183, 184, 185, 186, 187, 188, 189, 190, 191, 193, 194, 195, 196, 197, 198, 199, 200, 203, 204, 205, 206, 208, 210, 211, 212, 213, 214; om., 124.

100   3, 5, 6, 7, 8, 10, 14, 15, 16, 19, 20, 21, 25, 26, 28, 30, 32, 34, 36, 37, 39, 43, 44, 45, 46, 48, 49, 51, 52, 53, 56, 57, 58, 59, 60, 61, 62, 63, 65, 69, 71, 72, 73, 74, 76, 77, 78, 79, 81, 82, 83, 84, 86, 87, 88, 89, 90, 92, 97, 98, 103, 104, 105, 107, 109, 110, 111, 112, 115, 116, 117, 119, 120, 121, 123, 124, 125, 126, 127, 128, 129, 130, 133, 135, 136, 137, 141, 142, 146, 147, 149, 152, 153, 154, 155, 156, 158, 161, 162, 166, 167, 168, 169, 170, 171, 172, 173, 174, 177, 179, 180, 181, 182, 183, 184, 185, 186, 187, 188, 189, 190, 191, 193, 194, 195, 196, 197, 198, 199, 200, 203, 204, 205, 206, 208, 210, 211, 212, 213, 214; *eius,* 9, 13, 23, 29, 31, 33, 38, 41, 42, 64, 75, 93, 96, 99, 100, 113, 118, 122, 131, 132, 134, 140, 143, 150, 151, 160, 164, 175, 178; *ipsius puelle,* 165.

101...101   3, 5, 6, 7, 8, 9, 10, 13, 14, 15, 16, 19, 20, 21, 23, 25, 26, 28, 29, 30, 31, 32, 33, 34, 36, 37, 38, 39, 41, 42, 43, 44, 45, 46, 48, 49, 51, 52, 53, 56, 57, 58, 59, 60, 61, 62, 63, 65, 69, 71, 72, 73, 74, 75, 76, 77, 78, 79, 82, 83, 84, 86, 87, 89, 90, 92, 96, 97, 98, 99, 100, 103, 104, 105, 107, 109, 110, 111, 112, 113, 115, 117, 118, 119, 120, 121, 122, 123, 124, 125, 126, 127, 128, 129, 130, 132, 133, 134, 136, 137, 140, 141, 142, 143, 146, 147, 149, 150, 151, 152, 153, 154, 155, 156, 158, 160, 161, 162, 164, 165, 166, 167, 168, 170, 171, 172, 173, 174, 175, 178, 179, 180, 181, 182, 183, 184, 185, 186, 187, 188, 189, 190, 191, 193, 194, 195, 196, 197, 198, 199, 200, 203, 204, 205, 206, 208, 211, 212, 213, 214; *eam o. est,* 88, 116; *o. est,* 210; *eam o.,* 81; *o. eam,* 131; *o. \est/ eam,* 135; *o\s/culatus est eam,* 93; *osclatus est eam,* 169; *osculatus est eum,* 177; *rex osculatus est eam,* 64.

102   3, 5, 6, 7, 8, 9, 10, 13, 14, 15, 16, 19, 20, 21, 23, 25, 26, 28, 29, 30, 31, 32, 33, 34, 36, 37, 38, 39, 41, 49, 42, 43, 44, 45, 46, 48, 49, 51, 52, 53, 56, 57, 58, 59, 60, 61, 62, 63, 64, 65, 69, 71, 72, 73, 74, 75, 76, 77, 78, 79, 81, 82, 83, 84, 86, 87, 88, 89, 90, 92, 93, 96, 97, 98, 99, 100, 103, 104, 105, 107, 109, 111, 112, 113, 115, 116, 117, 118, 119, 120, 121, 122, 123, 124, 125, 126, 127, 128, 129, 130, 131, 132, 133, 134, 135, 136, 137, 140, 141, 142, 143, 146, 147, 149, 150, 151, 152, 153, 154, 155, 156, 158, 160, 161, 162, 164, 165, 166, 167, 168, 169, 170, 171, 172, 173, 174, 175, 177, 178, 179, 180, 181, 182, 183, 184, 185, 186, 187, 188, 189, 190, 191, 193, 194, 195, 196, 197, 198, 199, 200, 203, 204, 205, 206, 208, 210, 211, 212, 213, 214; om., 110.

103   3, 5, 6, 7, 8, 9, 10, 13, 14, 15, 16, 20, 21, 23, 25, 26, 28, 29, 30, 31, 32, 33, 34, 37, 38, 39, 41, 42, 43, 44, 45, 48, 49, 51, 52, 53, 57, 59, 60, 61, 62, 63, 64, 65, 69, 71, 72, 73, 74, 75, 76, 77, 78, 79, 82, 83, 84, 86, 87, 88, 89, 90, 92, 93, 96, 97, 98, 99, 100, 103, 104, 107, 109, 111, 112, 113, 115, 116, 117, 118, 119, 120, 121, 122, 123, 124, 126, 127, 128, 129, 131, 132, 133, 134, 135, 136, 137, 140, 141, 142, 143, 146, 147, 150, 152, 153, 155, 156, 158, 160, 161, 162, 164, 165, 166, 167, 168, 169, 170, 171, 172, 173, 174, 177, 178, 181, 184, 185, 186, 187, 188, 189, 190, 191, 193, 194, 196, 197, 198, 200, 203, 204, 205, 206, 208, 210, 211, 212, 213; *pot[ ]auit,* 149, *patauit,* 46; *optauit* (altered to *potauit*), 56; *optauit,* 19, 36, 58, 81, 151, 175, 179, 183, 195; *adamauit,* 105, 125, 130, 154, 180, 182, 214; *potauit et adamauit,* 110, 199.

104...104   3, 5, 6, 7, 9, 13, 14, 15, 16, 19, 20, 21, 23, 25, 26, 29, 31, 33, 34, 37, 41, 42, 43, 44, 46, 48, 49, 51, 52, 56, 57, 58, 59, 62, 63, 64, 65, 69, 71, 72, 74, 75, 76, 77, 78, 79, 81, 82, 83, 86, 87, 88, 89, 90, 92, 93, 96, 97, 103, 104, 105, 107, 110, 111, 112, 113, 115, 116, 117, 118, 120, 125, 126, 128, 130, 132, 133, 135, 136, 137, 140, 143, 149, 150, 152, 154, 155, 156, 158, 160, 161, 162, 164, 166, 167, 168, 169, 170, 171, 172, 174, 178, 179, 180, 181, 182, 183, 184, 185, 186, 187, 188, 189, 190, 191, 193, 194, 195, 197, 198, 199, 200, 203, 204, 205, 206, 210, 211, 212, 213, 214; *Ab illa,* 36, 38, 53, 99, 122, 127, 131, 151, 173, 175, 196, 208; *Ab ipso,* 177; *Ab illo autem,* 8, 10, 28, 29, 30, 32, 45, 61, 73, 98, 100,

mansit[107] [108]consuetudo illa[108] in[109] Britannia[110] [117]quia[111] [112]in conuiuiis[112] qui

109, 119, 123, 134, 141, ?142, 153, 165; *et ab illo autem,* 39; *ab illo ergo,* 60, 146, 147; *Ab illo igitur,* 84, 124, 129; *Ab illo itaque,* 121.

105   3, 5, 6, 7, 8, 9, 10, 13, 14, 15, 16, 19, 20, 21, 23, 25, 26, 28, 29, 30, 31, 32, 33, 34, 36, 37, 38, 39, 41, 42, 43, 44, 45, 46, 48, 49, 51, 52, 53, 56, 57, 58, 59, 60, 61, 62, 63, 64, 65, 69, 71, 72, 73, 74, 75, 76, 77, 78, 79, 81, 82, 83, 84, 86, 87, 88, 89, 90, 92, 93, 96, 97, 98, 99, 100, 103, 104, 105, 107, 109, 110, 111, 112, 113, 115, 116, 117, 118, 119, 120, 121, 122, 123, 124, 125, 126, 127, 128, 130, 131, 132, 133, 134, 135, 136, 137, 140, 141, 142, 143, 146, 147, 149, 150, 151, 152, 153, 154, 155, 156, 158, 160, 161, 162, 164, 165, 166, 167, 168, 169, 170, 171, 172, 173, 174, 175, 177, 178, 179, 180, 181, 182, 183, 184, 185, 187, 188, 189, 190, 191, 193, 194, 195, 196, 197, 198, 199, 200, 203, 204, 205, 206, 208, 210, 211, 212, 213, 214; *tempore,* 129; *etiam tempore,* 186.

106...106   3, 8, 9, 10, 14, 15, 16, 19, 30, 32, 34, 35, 39, 41, 42, 43, 44, 46, 48, 49, 52, 56, 57, 58, 61, 63, 64, 71, 73, 76, 79, 81, 86, 87, 92, 93, 97, 98, 107, 110, 111, 113, 118, 119, 120, 121, 123, 125, 127, 128, 130, 136, 140, 141, 142, 143, 146, 147, 150, 152, 153, 154, 156, 162, 165, 169, 170, 171, 177, 178, 180, 181, 182, 183, 184, 185, 187, 189, 191, 193, 195, 200, 203, 205, 210, 211; *ad hordiernum* (corr. to *hodiernum*), 36; *ad in hodiernum,* 208; *in hodiernum diem,* 5, 6, 7, 13, 20, 21, 23, (24,) 25, 26, 28, 29, 31, 33, 37, 38, 45, 51, 53, 59, 60, 62, 65, 69, 72, 74, 75, 77, 78, 82, 83, 84, 88, 89, 90, 99, 100, 103, 104, 105, 109, 112, 115, 116, 117, 122, 124, 126, 129, 131, 132, 133, 134, 135, 137, 149, 151, 155, 158, 160, 161, 164, 166, 167, 168, 172, 173, 174, 175, 179, 186, 188, 190, 194, 196, 197, 198, 199, 204, 206, 211, 212, 213, 214; *in hodiernum dierum,* 96.

107   3, 5, 6, 7, 8, 9, 10,13 14, 15, 16, 19, 20, 21, 23, 25, 26, 28, 29, 30, 31, 32, 33, 34, 36, 37, 38, 39, 41, 42, 43, 44, 46, 48, 49, 51, 52, 53, 56, 57, 58, 59, 60, 61, 62, 63, 64, 65, 69, 71, 72, 73, 74, 75, 76, 77, 78, 79, 81, 82, 83, 84, 86, 87, 88, 89, 90, 92, 93, 96, 97, 98, 99, 100, 103, 104, 105, 107, 109, 110, 111, 112, 113, 115, 116, 117, 118, 120, 121, 122, 123, 124, 125, 126, 127, 128, 129, 130, 131, 132, 133, 134, 135, 136, 137, 140, 141, 142, 143, 146, 147, 149, 150, 151, 152, 153, 154, 155, 156, 158, 160, 161, 162, 164, 165, 166, 167, 168, 169, 170, 171, 172, 173, 174, 175, 177, 178, 179, 180, 181, 182, 183, 184, 185, 186, 187, 188, 189, 190, 191, 193, 194, 195, 196, 197, 198, 199, 200, 203, 204, 205, 206, 208, 210, 211, 212, 213, 214; over erasure, 119; om., 45.

108...108   3, 6, 7, 8, 9, 13, 14, 15, 16, 19, 20, 21, 23, 25, 26, 28, 29, 30, 31, 32, 33, 34, 36, 37, 38, 39, 41, 42, 43, 44, 45, 46, 48, 49, 51, 52, 53, 56, 57, 58, 59, 60, 61, 62, 63, 64, 65, 69, 71, 72, 73, 74, 75, 76, 77, 78, 79, 81, 82, 83, 84, 86, 87, 88, 89, 90, 92, 93, 96, 97, 98, 99, 100, 103, 104, 105, 107, 109, 110, 111, 112, 113, 115, 116, 117, 118, 119, 120, 121, 122, 123, 124, 125, 126, 127, 129, 130, 131, 132, 133, 134, 135, 136, 137, 140, 141, 142, 143, 146, 147, 149, 150, 151, 152, 153, 154, 155, 156, 158, 160, 161, 162, 164, 165, 166, 167, 168, 169, 170, 171, 172, 173, 174, 175, 177, 178, 179, 180, 181, 182, 183, 184, 185, 186, 187, 188, 189, 191, 193, 194, 195, 196, 197, 198, 199, 200, 203, 204, 205, 206, 208, 210, 212, 213, 214; *i. c.,* 10, 128; *c.* \i./, 211; *c.,* 5, 190.

109   3, 5, 6, 7, 8, 9, 10, 13, 14, 15, 16, 19, 20, 21, 23, 25, 26, 28, 29, 30, 31, 32, 33, 34, 36, 37, 38, 39, 41, 42, 43, 44, 45, 46, 48, 49, 51, 52, 53, 56, 57, 58, 59, 60, 61, 62, 63, 64, 65, 69, 71, 72, 73, 74, 75, 76, 77, 78, 79, 81, 82, 83, 84, 86, 87, 88, 89, 90, 92, 93, 96, 97, 98, 99, 100, 103, 104, 105, 107, 109, 110, 111, 112, 113, 115, 116, 117, 118, 119, 120, 121, 122, 123, 124, 125, 126, 127, 128, 129, 130, 131, 132, 133, 134, 135, 136, 137, 140, 141, 142, 143, 146, 147, 149, 150, 151, 152, 153, 154, 155, 156, 158, 160, 161, 162, 164, 165, 166, 167, 168, 169, 170, 171, 172, 173, 174, 175, 177, 178, 179, 180, 181, 182, 183, 184, 185, 186, 187, 188, 189, 190, 191, 193, 194, 195, 196, 198, 199, 200, 203, 205, 206, 208, 210, 211, 212, 213, 214; om., 197, 204.

110   3, 5, 6, 7, 8, 9, 10, 13, 14, 15, 16, 19, 20, 21, 23, 25, 26, 28, 29, 30, 31, 32, 33, 34, 36, 37, 38, 39, 41, 42, 43, 44, 45, 46, 48, 49, 51, 52, 53, 56, 57, 58, 59, 60, 61, 62, 63, 64, 65, 69,

potat[113] [114]ad alium[114] dicit[115] 'Waesseil'.[116] [117] [118]Qui uero[118] [122]post illum[119] recipit[120]

71, 72, 73, 76, 77, 79, 81, 82, 84, 86, 87, 88, 89, 90, 92, 93, 96, 97, 98, 99, 100, 103, 104, 105, 107, 109, 110, 111, 112, 113, 115, 116, 117, 118, 119, 120, 121, 122, 123, 124, 125, 126, 127, 128, 129, 130, 131, 132, 133, 134, 135, 136, 137, 140, 141, 142, 143, 147, 149, 150, 151, 152, 153, 154, 155, 156, 158, 161, 162, 164, 165, 166, 167, 168, 170, 171, 172, 173, 174, 175, 177, 178, 179, 180, 181, 182, 183, 184, 185, 186, 187, 188, 189, 190, 191, 193, 194, 195, 196, 197, 198, 199, 200, 203, 205, 208, 210, 211, 212, 213, 214; *Britania*, 169; *Britanniam* (altered to *Britannia*), 83; *Britanniam*, 74, 75, 78, 146; *Britanica*, 206; om., 160, 204.

[111] 3, 5, 6, 7, 8, 9, 10, 13, 14, 15, 16, 19, 20, 21, 23, 26, 28, 29, 30, 31, 32, 33, 34, 36, 37, 38, 39, 41, 42, 43, 44, 45, 46, 48, 49, 51, 53, 56, 57, 58, 59, 60, 61, 62, 63, 64, 65, 69, 71, 72, 73, 74, 75, 76, 77, 78, 79, 81, 82, 83, 84, 86, 87, 88, 89, 90, 92, 93, 96, 97, 98, 99, 100, 103, 104, 105, 107, 109, 110, 112, 113, 115, 116, 117, 118, 120, 121, 122, 123, 124, 125, 126, 127, 128, 129, 130, 131, 132, 133, 134, 135, 136, 137, 140, 141, 142, 143, 146, 147, 149, 150, 151, 152, 153, 154, 155, 156, 158, 161, 162, 164, 166, 167, 168, 169, 170, 171, 172, 173, 174, 175, 177, 178, 179, 180, 181, 182, 183, 184, 185, 186, 187, 188, 189, 190, 191, 193, 194, 196, 197, 198, 199, 200, 203, 204, 205, 206, 208, 210, 211, 213, 214; *q*, 52, 119, 212; *qm.*, 25; *qe*, 195; om., 111, 160, 165.

[112]...[112] 3, 5, 6, 7, 8, 9, 10, 13, 14, 15, 16, 19, 20, 21, 23, 25, 26, 28, 29, 30, 31, 32, 33, 34, 36, 37, 38, 39, 41, 42, 43, 44, 45, 46, 48, 49, 51, 52, 53, 56, 57, 58, 59, 60, 61, 62, 63, 64, 65, 69, 71, 72, 73, 74, 75, 76, 77, 78, 79, 81, 83, 84, 86, 87, 89, 90, 92, 93, 96, 98, 99, 100, 103, 104, 105, 107, 109, 110, 112, 115, 117, 118, 119, 120, 121, 122, 123, 124, 125, 126, 127, 128, 129, 130, 131, 132, 133, 134, 135, 137, 140, 141, 142, 143, 146, 147, 149, 150, 151, 152, 153, 154, 155, 158, 162, 164, 166, 167, 168, 169, 170, 171, 173, 174, 175, 178, 179, 180, 181, 182, 183, 184, 185, 186, 187, 188, 189, 190, 191, 193, 194, 195, 197, 198, 199, 200, 203, 204, 205, 206, 208, 210, 212, 213, 214; *in conuiuis*, 82; *in conuiis*, 97, 161, 172; *in couiuis*, 156; *conuiuiis*, 160, 211; *in conuiisiis*, 177; *in B'ta conuiuiis*, 136; *in coniug^aiis*, 113; *in diuis*, 196; *ut*, 111, 165; om., 88, 116.

[113] 3, 5, 6, 8, 9, 10, 13, 14, 15, 16, 19, 20, 21, 23, 25, 26, 28, 29, 30, 31, 32, 33, 34, 36, 37, 38, 39, 41, 42, 43, 44, 45, 46, 48, 49, 51, 52, 53, 56, 57, 58, 59, 60, 61, 62, 63, 64, 65, 69, 72, 73, 74, 75, 76, 77, 78, 79, 81, 82, 83, 84, 86, 87, 88, 90, 92, 93, 96, 97, 98, 99, 100, 103, 104, 105, 107, 109, 110, 111, 112, 113, 115, 116, 117, 118, 120, 121, 123, 124, 125, 126, 127, 128, 129, 130, 131, 132, 134, 135, 136, 137, 140, 141, 142, 143, 146, 147, 149, 150, 151, 152, 153, 154, 156, 158, 161, 162, 164, 165, 166, 167, 168, 169, 170, 171, 172, 173, 174, 175, 177, 178, 179, 181, 182, 183, 184, 185, 186, 187, 188, 189, 190, 191, 193, 194, 196, 197, 198, 199, 200, 203, 204, 205, 206, 208, 210, 211, 212, 213, 214; *po[]tat*, 71, 180, 195; *portat*, 7, 155; *potet*, 89, 133, 160; *potat.*, 119; *tat*, 122.

[114]...[114] 3, 5, 6, 7, 8, 9, 10, 13, 14, 15, 16, 19, 20, 21, 23, 25, 26, 28, 29, 30, 31, 32, 33, 34, 36, 37, 38, 39, 41, 42, 43, 44, 45, 46, 48, 49, 51, 52, 53, 56, 57, 58, 59, 60, 61, 62, 63, 64, 65, 69, 71, 72, 73, 74, 75, 76, 77, 78, 79, 81, 82, 83, 84, 86, 87, 88, 89, 90, 92, 93, 96, 97, 98, 99, 100, 103, 104, 105, 107, 109, 110, 111, 112, 113, 115, 116, 117, 118, 119, 120, 121, 122, 123, 124, 125, 126, 127, 128, 129, 130, 131, 132, 133, 134, 135, 136, 137, 140, 141, 142, 143, 146, 147, 149, 150, 151, 152, 153, 154, 155, 156, 158, 160, 161, 162, 164, 165, 166, 167, 168, 169, 170, 171, 172, 173, 174, 175, 177, 178, 179, 181, 182, 183, 184, 185, 186, 187, 188, 189, 190, 191, 193, 194, 195, 197, 198, 199, 200, 203, 204, 205, 206, 208, 210, 211, 212, 213, 214; *ad [] alium*, 195; *alium*, 180; *ad illum*, 7, 155; *ad altum*, 196; *dicit ad alium* 20.

[115] 3, 5, 6, 7, 8, 10, 13, 14, 15, 16, 19, 21, 23, 25, 26, 28, 29, 30, 31, 32, 33, 34, 36, 37, 38, 39, 41, 42, 43, 44, 45, 46, 48, 49, 51, 52, 56, 57, 58, 59, 60, 61, 62, 63, 64, 65, 69, 71, 72, 73, 74, 75, 76, 77, 78, 79, 81, 82, 83, 84, 86, 87, 88, 89, 90, 92, 93, 96, 97, 98, 99, 100, 103, 104, 105, 107, 109, 110, 111, 112, 113, 115, 116, 117, 118, 119, 120, 121, 122, 123,

potum,[121] [122] respondet[123] 'Drincheil'.[124] Uortegirnus[125] autem[126] diuerso genere[127]

124, 125, 126, 127, 128, 129, 130, 131, 132, 133, 134, 135, 136, 137, 140, 141, 142, 143, 146, 147, 149, 150, 151, 152, 153, 154, 155, 156, 158, 161, 162, 164, 165, 166, 167, 168, 169, 170, 171, 173, 175, 177, 178, 179, 180, 181, 182, 183, 184, 185, 186, 187, 188, 189, 190, 191, 193, 194, 195, 196, 198, 199, 200, 203, 204, 205, 208, 210, 211, 212, 213, 214; *dixit*, 53, 206; *dicat*, 160, 172, 174, 197; *dicit ad alium*, 9; om., 20.

[116] 15, 16, 39, 73, 83, 86, 93, 111, 130, 162, 194, 200; *Euasail*, 206; *Gaisseil* (altered to *Gaseil*), 193; *Guesheil*, 126; *Guesseil*, 20, 147, 151, 166, 173; *Uasseil*, 169; *Ueshail*, 33; *Uesseil*, 131; *Uuasheil*, 213; *Uuasseil*, 172, 187, 197; *Uuasseill*, 198; *Uuessail*, 56, 58; *Uuesseil*, 175; *Uuissail*, 205; *Waesheil*, 23, 190; *Waiseil*, 7; *Waseil*, 21, 167; *Washail*, 105, 214; *Washeil*, 34, 48, 107, 136, 212; *Wassail*, (24,) 26, 31, 49, 90, 113, 149, 154; *Wassehail*, 116; *Wasseil*, 13, 25, 37, 41, 43, 44, 57, 59, 61, 76, 77, 79, 82, 92, 97, 104, 112, 120, 121, 135, 137, 140, 155, 156, 167, 170, 174, 177, 178, 185, 191, 203, 204, 211; *Wasseyl*, 103, 110; *Wassheil*, 30, 74; *Weiheil*, 72; *Weisseil*, 118; *Wesail*, 87, 115; *Wesayl*, 65; *Weseheil*, 165; *Weseil*, 150, 168; *Weshail*, 6, 69, 71, 75, 78, 84, 158; *Wesheil*, 5, 10, 28, 32, 42, 88, 96, 100, 117, 128, 132, 133, 134, 146, 152, 153, 161, 164, 181, 186, 188, 210; *Wessail*, 46, 51, 64, 98, 124; *Wesseil*, 3, 8, 9, 14, 19, 36, 38, 52, 53, 62, 63, 81, 92, 109, 119, 122, 123, 127, 141, 143, 171, 182, 183, 189, 195, 196, 199, 208; *Wesseyl*, 29, 45, 110, 142; *Wessheil*, 74; *Wisseil*, 179; *Wosheil*, 129; *Wosseil*, 99, 125, 180; *Wosshail*, 184; *Wusheil*, 89; *uis bibere*, 60; om., 160.

[117...117] 3, 5, 6, 7, 8, 9, 10, 13, 14, 15, 16, 19, 20, 21, 23, 25, 26, 28, 29, 30, 31, 32, 33, 34, 36, 37, 38, 41, 42, 43, 44, 45, 46, 48, 49, 51, 52, 53, 56, 57, 58, 59, 60, 61, 62, 63, 64, 65, 69, 71, 72, 73, 74, 75, 76, 77, 78, 79, 81, 82, 83, 84, 86, 87, 88, 89, 90, 92, 93, 96, 97, 98, 99, 100, 103, 104, 105, 107, 109, 110, 111, 112, 113, 115, 116, 117, 118, 119, 120, 121, 122, 123, 124, 125, 126, 127, 128, 129, 130, 131, 132, 133, 134, 135, 136, 137, 140, 141, 142, 143, 146, 147, 149, 150, 151, 152, 153, 154, 155, 156, 158, 160, 161, 162, 166, 167, 168, 169, 170, 171, 172, 173, 174, 175, 177, 178, 179, 180, 181, 182, 183, 184, 185, 186, 187, 188, 189, 190, 191, 193, 194, 195, 196, 197, 198, 199, 200, 203, 204, 205, 206, 208, 210, 211, 212, 213, 214; *quia qui p. i. c. ad a. d. W.*, 164, 165; om., 39.

[118...118] 3, 5, 6, 7, 8, 9, 10, 13, 14, 15, 16, 19, 20, 21, 23, 25, 26, 28, 29, 30, 31, 32, 33, 34, 36, 37, 38, 39, 41, 42, 43, 44, 45, 46, 48, 49, 51, 52, 53, 57, 59, 60, 61, 62, 63, 64, 65, 69, 71, 72, 73, 74, 75, 76, 77, 78, 79, 81, 82, 83, 84, 86, 87, 88, 89, 90, 92, 93, 96, 97, 98, 99, 100, 103, 104, 105, 107, 109, 110, 111, 112, 113, 115, 116. 117, 118, 119, 120, 121, 122, 123, 124, 125, 126, 127, 128, 129, 130, 131, 132, 133, 134, 135, 136, 137, 140, 141, 142, 143, 146, 147, 149, 150, 151, 152, 153, 154, 155, 156, 158, 161, 162, 164, 165, 166, 167, 169, 170, 171, 172, 173, 174, 175, 177, 178, 179, 180, 181, 182, 183, 184, 185, 186, 187, 188, 189, 190, 191, 193, 194, 195, 196, 197, 198, 199, 200, 203, 204, 205, 206, 208, 210, 211, 212, 213, 214; *Qui uerum*, 168; *Qui*, 56, 58, 205; om., 160.

[119] 3, 5, 6, 7, 8, 9, 10, 13, 14, 15, 16, 19, 20, 21, 23, 25, 26, 28, 29, 30, 31, 32, 33, 36, 37, 38, 39, 41, 42, 43, 44, 45, 46, 48, 49, 51, 52, 53, 56, 57, 58, 59, 60, 61, 62, 63, 64, 65, 69, 71, 72, 73, 74, 75, 76, 77, 78, 79, 81, 82, 83, 84, 86, 87, 88, 89, 90, 92, 93, 96, 97, 98, 99, 100, 103, 104, 105, 107, 109, 110, 112, 113, 115, 116, 117, 118, 119, 120, 121, 122, 123, 124, 125, 126, 127, 128, 130, 131, 132, 133, 134, 135, 136, 137, 140, 141, 142, 143, 146, 147, 149, 150, 151, 153, 154, 155, 156, 158, 160, 161, 162, 164, 165, 166, 167, 168, 169, 170, 171, 172, 173, 174, 175, 177, 178, 179, 180, 181, 182, 183, 184, 185, 186, 187, 188, 189, 190, 191, 193, 194, 195, 197, 198, 199, 200, 203, 204, 205, 208, 210, 211, 212, 213, 214; *ipsum*, 34, 152; *alium*, 111, 196; om., 129, 206.

[120] 3, 5, 6, 7, 8, 9, 10, 13, 14, 15, 16, 19, 20, 21, 23, 25, 26, 28, 29, 30, 31, 32, 33, 34, 36, 38, 39, 41, 42, 43, 44, 45, 46, 48, 49, 51, 52, 53, 56, 57, 58, 59, 60, 61, 62, 63, 65, 69, 71, 72, 73, 75, 76, 77, 79, 81, 82, 83, 84, 86, 87, 88, 89, 90, 92, 93, 96, 97, 99, 104, 105, 107, 109, 110, 111, 112, 113, 115, 116, 117, 118, 120, 121, 122, 123, 124, 125, 126, 127, 128, 129,

130, 131, 132, 133, 134, 135, 136, 137, 140, 141, 142, 143, 146, 147, 149, 150, 151, 152, 153, 154, 155, 156, 158, 160, 161, 162, 164, 166, 167, 169, 170, 171, 172, 173, 174, 175, 177, 178, 179, 181, 182, 183, 184, 186, 188, 189, 190, 191, 193, 194, 196, 200, 203, 204, 205, 208, 210, 211, 212, 213, 214; *recepit* (altered to *recipit*), 195; *recepit,* 37, 64, 74, 78, 98, 100, 103, 119, 168, 180, 185, 187, 197, 198, 199, 206; *accipit,* 165.

121 3, 5, 6, 8, 9, 10, 14, 15, 16, 19, 20, 21, 23, 25, 26, 28, 29, 30, 31, 32, 33, 34, 36, 37, 38, 39, 41, 42 43, 44, 45, 46, 48, 49, 51, 52, 53, 56, 57, 58, 60, 61, 62, 63, 64, 65, 69, 71, 72, 73, 74, 75, 76, 77, 78, 79, 81, 82, 83, 86, 87, 88, 89, 90, 92, 93, 96, 97, 98, 99, 100, 103, 104, 105, 107, 109, 110, 112, 113 116, 118, 119, 120, 121, 122, 123, 124, 125, 126, 127, 128, 129, 130, 131, 132, 133, 134, 135, 136, 137, 140, 141, 142, 143, 146, 147, 149, 150, 151, 152, 153, 154, 155, 156, 158, 160, 161, 162, 164, 166, 168, 169, 170, 171, 172, 173, 174, 175, 177, 178, 179, 180, 181, 182, 183, 184, 185, 186, 187 189, 190, 191, 193, 194, 195, 196, 197, 198, 199, 200, 203, 204, 205, 206, 208, 210, 211, 212, 213, 214; *ciphum,* 13, 59, 84, 117, 167, 188; *calicem,* 25; *dicit,* 7; *ciphum/,* 115, om., 111, 165.

122...122 3, 5, 6, 7, 9, 10, 13, 14, 5, 15, 16, 19, 21, 23, 25, 28, 29, 30, 31, 32, 33, 34, 36, 37, 41, 42, 43, 44, 45, 46, 48, 49, 51, 52, 53, 56, 57, 58, 59, 60, 61, 62, 63, 64, 69, 71, 72, 73, 74, 75, 76, 77, 78, 79, 81, 82 83, 84, 86, 87, 89, 90, 92, 93, 96, 97, 98, 100, 103, 104, 105, 109, 110, 111, 112, 113, 119, 120, 121 123, 124, 125, 126, 127, 128, 130, 132, 133, 134, 135, 136, 137, 140, 141, 142, 143, 146, 147, 149 150, 151, 152, 153, 154, 155, 156, 158, 161, 162, 164, 165, 166, 167, 168, 169, 170, 171, 172, 173 174, 175, 177, 178, 179, 180, 181, 182, 183, 184, 185, 186, 187, 189, 190, 191, 193, 194, 195, 196, 197, 198, 199, 200, 203, 204, 205, 208, 210, 211, 212, 213, 214; *r. pot. post i.* 20; *r. post i. pot.,* 25, 26, 38, 39, 99, 122, 131; *post i. post i. r. pot.,* 118; *post i. pot. r.,* 8, 107, 117, 188; *post i. r. \pot./,* 115; *post r. pot.,* 129, 206; *r. pot.,* 65, 88, 116; om., 160.

123 5, 6, 8, 13, 15, 16, 19, 20, 23, 25, 26, 28, 30, 31, 34, 36, 37, 38, 39, 41, 42, 43, 45, 46, 48, 49, 52, 53, 56, 57, 58, 59, 60, 61, 62, 63, 65, 69, 72, 76, 77, 78, 79, 81, 82, 83, 86, 87, 88, 89, 90, 96, 98, 99, 100, 103, 104, 110, 112, 113, 115, 116, 117, 121, 126, 127, 128, 129, 130, 131, 132, 133, 134, 135, 136, 137, 141, 143, 146, 150, 151, 155, 156, 161, 162, 165, 166, 167, 170, 171, 173, 174, 175, 177, 179, 180, 183, 184, 185, 186, 188, 189, 190, 191, 193, 194, 195, 196, 198, 199, 200, 204, 205, 208, 210, 212, 213; *respond ᵗ,* 142; *respondit,* 3, 6, 14, 21, 29, 32, 33, 44, 51, 64, 71, 73, 74, 75, 92, 93, 97, 105, 118, 119, 120, 122, 123, 125, 140, 147, 149, 152, 153, 154, 158, 164, 168, 169, 172, 181, 182, 187, 197, 203, 211, 214; *rnt,* 46; *respondeat,* 84, 124; *dicit,* 107, 178; *d ᵗ,* 29, 111; om., 160, 206

124 5, 6, 7, 8, 13, 15, 16, 21, 23, 25, 28, 30, 31, 32, 33, 37, 38, 41, 42, 44, 46, 48, 49, 52, 59, 62, 65, 71, 73, 74, 76, 77, 79, 82, 86, 87, 88, 89, 92, 93, 96, 97, 99, 100, 104, 107, 109, 112, 113, 115, 116, 117, 119, 120, 121, 122, 124, 126, 128, 131, 132, 135, 136, 137, 146, 147, 149, 152, 153, (156,) 157, 160, 161, 162, 164, 167, 169, 170, 172, 174, 175, 177, 181, 185, 187, 188, 191, 193, 194, 196, 197, 198, 200, 203, 204, 210, 211, 213; *Drincahil,* 33; *Drincail,* 36, 56, 58, 205; *Drinceil,* 43; *Drinchaeil,* 134; *Drinchael,* 3, 14; *Drinchail,* 19, 20, 26, 34, 51, 69, 75, 78, 81, 83, 84, 90, 98, 125, 127, 129, 130, 151, 154, 165, 166, 168, 171, 173, 179, 180, 182, 183, 184, 186, 189, 195, 199, 206, 208; *Drinchayl,* 110; *Drincheheil* (altered to *Drinheheil),* 178; *Drincheyl,* 45; *Drinckeil,* 123, 141; *Dringheil,* 72, 118, 133, 190; *Dringheyl,* 111; *Drinkeil,* 63; *Drinkeyl,* 10; *Drinkhail,* 105, 214; *Drinkheil,* 9, 39, 61, 64, 140, 143, 150, 155, 158, 212; *Drinkheyl,* 103; *Dryncheil,* 57; *Drynkheyl,* 29, 142; *bibe tu et da mihi,* 60

125 5, 6, 7, 10, 13, 15, 16, 20, 21, 25, 28, 30, 31, 32, 33, 36, 39, 43, 46, 48, 49, 52, 53, 56, 57, 58, 61, 65, 69, 71, 72, 73, 74, 76, 77, 79, 82, 83, 84, 87, 88, 89, 92, 93, 98, 99, 100, 104, 107, 110, 112, 116, 117, 120, 121, 122, 123, 124, 125, 126, 127, 129, 133, 134, 135, 136, 141, 146, 147, 149, 150, 151, 152, 153, 155, 156, 158, 161, 162, 165, 166, 167, 169, 170, 173, 175, 177, 179, 180, 181, 185, 186, 188, 191, 193, 194, 195, 196, 197, 198, 200, 203, 204, 205, 208, 210, 211; *Uoltegirnus,* 81, 183, 184, 189; *Uortegirguus,* 172; *Uorteirgnus,* 174; *Uorteguinus,* 86; *Uorthegirnus,* 59; *Uorthigernus,* 60; *Uortigernus,* 9, 26, 29, 34, 41, 42, 51, 64, 78, 90, 96, 97, 109, 111, 113, 132, 137, 142, 164, 187; *Uortigirnus,* 8, 23, 37,

potus[128] inhebriatus[129] [130]intrante Sathana[130] in [131]corde suo[131] amauit[132] puellam et

44, 45, 63, 75, 105, 118, 128, 131, 140, 143, 154, 178, 206, 212, 214; *Uotegirnus,* 19;
Uotigirnus, 160; *Wltegernus,* 168; *Woltegirnus,* 3, 14, 171; *Wortagirnus,* 199; *Wortegirnus,*
62, 103, 119, 130, 182, 190, 213; *Wortigernus,* 115; *Wortigirnus,* 38; *respondens deinde*
Uortegirnus Drincheil iussit puellam potare cepitque ciphum de manu ipsius et osculatus
est eam et potauit. Ab illo die usque in hodiernum mansit consuetudo illa in Britannia quia
in conuiuiis qui potat ad alium dicit Waesseil. Qui uero post illum, recipit potum, respondet
Drincheil. U, .

126 3, 5, 7, 9, 10, 13, 14, 15, 16, 20, 21, 23, 25, 26, 28, 29, 30, 31, 32, 33, 34, 36, 37, 38, 39,
41, 43, 44, 46, 48, 49, 51, 52, 53, 56, 57, 58, 59, 60, 61, 62, 63, 64, 65, 69, 71, 72, 73, 74,
75, 76, 77, 78, 79, 81, 82, 83, 84, 86, 87, 88, 89, 92, 93, 96, 97, 98, 99, 100, 103, 104, 105,
107, 109, 111, 112, 113, 116, 117, 118, 119, 120, 121, 122, 123, 124, 125, 126, 127, 128,
130, 131, 132, 133, 134, 135, 136, 137, 140, 141, 142, 143, 146, 147, 149, 150, 151, 152,
153, 154, 155, 156, 158, 160, 161, 162, 165, 166, 167, 168, 169, 170, 171, 172, 173, 174,
175, 177, 178, 179, 180, 181, 182, 183, 184, 185, 188, 189, 190, 191, 193, 194, 195, 196,
197, 198, 199, 200, 203, 204, 206, 208, 210, 211, 212, 213, 214; *autem post,* 45; *ergo,*
164; *etiam,* (24); *igitur,* 8, 187; *itaque,* 6, 115, 129, 186; *uero,* 19, 42, 110; om., 90, 205.

127 3, 5, 6, 7, 8, 9, 10, 13, 14, 15, 16, 19, 20, 21, 23, 25, 26, 28, 30, 31, 32, 33, 34, 36, 37, 38,
39, 41, 42, 43, 44, 45, 46, 48, 49, 51, 52, 53, 56, 57, 58, 59, 60, 61, 62, 63, 64, 65, 69, 71,
72, 73, 74, 75, 76, 77, 78, 79, 81, 82, 83, 84, 86, 87, 88, 89, 90, 92, 93, 96, 97, 98, 99, 100,
103, 104, 105, 107, 109, 110, 111, 112, 113, 115, 116, 117, 118, 119, 120, 121, 122, 123,
124, 125, 126, 127, 128, 129, 130, 131, 132, 133, 134, 135, 136, 137, 140, 141, 142, 143,
146, 147, 149, 150, 151, 152, 153, 154, 155, 156, 158, 160, 161, 162, 164, 165, 166, 167,
168, 169, 170, 171, 172, 173, 174, 175, 177, 178, 179, 180, 181, 182, 183, 184, 185, 186,
187, 188, 189, 190, 191, 193, 194, 195, 196, 197, 198, 199, 200, 203, 204, 205, 206, 208,
210, 211, 212, 213, 214; om., 29.

128 3, 5, 6, 7, 8, 9, 10, 13, 14, 15, 16, 19, 20, 21, 23, 25, 26, 28, 29, 30, 31, 32, 33, 34, 36, 37,
38, 39, 41, 42, 43, 44, 46, 48, 49, 51, 52, 53, 56, 57, 58, 59, 60, 61, 62, 63, 64, 65, 69, 71,
72, 73, 74, 75, 76, 77, 78, 79, 81, 82, 83, 84, 86, 87, 88, 89, 90, 92, 93, 96, 97, 98, 99, 100,
103, 104, 105, 107, 109, 110, 111, 112, 113, 115, 116, 117, 118, 119, 120, 121, 122, 123,
124, 125, 126, 127, 128, 129, 130, 131, 132, 133, 135, 136, 137, 140, 141, 142, 143, 146,
147, 149, 150, 151, 152, 153, 154, 155, 156, 158, 160, 161, 162, 164, 165, 166, 167, 168,
169, 170, 171, 172, 173, 174, 175, 177, 178, 180, 181, 182, 183, 184, 185, 186, 187, 188,
189, 190, 191, 193, 194, 195, 196, 197, 198, 199, 200, 203, 204, 205, 206, 208, 210, 212,
213, 214; \potus/, 179; *potu,* 29; om., 45, 134, 211.

129 15, 16, 43, 81, 93, 120; *inebriatus,* 3, 5, 6, 7, 8, 9, 10, 13, 14, 19, 20, 21, 23, (24,) 25, 26,
28, 29, 30, 31, 32, 33, 34, 36, 37, 38, 39, 41, 42, 44, 45, 46, 48, 49, 51, 52, 53, 56, 57, 58,
59, 60, 61, 62, 63, 64, 65, 69, 71, 72, 73, 74, 75, 76, 77, 78, 79, 82, 83, 84, 86, 87, 88, 89,
90, 92, 96, 97, 98, 99, 100, 103, 104, 105, 107, 109, 111, 112, 113, 115, 116, 117, 118,
119, 121, 122, 123, 124, 125, 126, 127, 128, 129, 130, 131, 132, 133, 134, 135, 136, 137,
140, 141, 142, 143, 146, 147, 149, 150, 151, 152, 153, 154, 155, 156, 158, 160, 161, 162,
164, 165, 166, 167, 168, 169, 170, 171, 172, 173, 174, 175, 177, 178, 179, 180, 181, 182,
183, 184, 185, 186, 187, 188, 189, 190, 191, 193, 194, 195, 196, 197, 198, 199, 200, 203,
204, 205, 206, 208, 210, 211, 212, 213, 214; *absortus,* 110

130...130 3, 5, 6, 7, 8, 9, 10, 13, 14, 15, 16, 19, 20, 21, 23, 25, 28, 29, 30, 31, 32, 33, 34, 36, 37,
38, 39, 41, 42, 43, 44, 45, 46, 48, 49, 51, 52, 53, 56, 57, 58, 59, 60, 61, 62, 63, 64, 65, 69,
71, 72, 73, 75, 76, 77, 78, 79, 81, 82, 83, 84, 86, 87, 88, 89, 90, 92, 93, 96, 97, 98, 99, 103,
104, 107, 109, 110, 111, 112, 113, 115, 116, 117, 118, 119, 120, 121, 122, 123, 124, 126,
127, 128, 129, 130, 132, 133, 135, 136, 137, 140, 141, 142, 143, 146, 147, 149, 150, 151,
152, 153, 155, 156, 158, 160, 162, 165, 166, 167, 168, 169, 170, 171, 172, 173, 174, 175,
177, 178, 179, 181, 183, 184, 185, 186, 187, 188, 189, 190, 191, 193, 194, 195, 196, 197,

postulauit[133] eam[134] [135]a patre[135] suo.[136] Intrauerat,[137] inquam,[138] [142]Sathanas[139] in

198, 199, 200, 203, 204, 205, 206, 208, 210, 211, 212; *intrante Sathan,* 131; *intrante Sathane,* 74, 213; *intrante Sathanam,* 164; *intrante autem Sathana,* 100; *intrante autem Sathanas,* 134; *est* (canc.) *intrante Sathan,* 125; *est intrante Sathana,* 214; *est intrante Sathan,* 105, 154, 180; *et intrantem Sathana,* 182; *intrauit Sathanas,* 161; *uirtute Sathane,* 26.

131...131   3, 5, 6, 7, 8, 9, 10, 13, 14, 15, 16, 19, 20, 21, 23, 25, 26, 28, 29, 30, 31, 32, 33, 34, 36, 37, 38, 39, 41, 42, 43, 44, 45, 46, 48, 49, 51, 52, 53, 56, 57, 58, 59, 60, 61, 62, 63, 64, 65, 69, 71, 72, 73, 74, 75, 76, 77, 78, 79, 81, 82, 83, 84, 87, 88, 89, 90, 92, 93, 96, 97, 98, 99, 103, 104, 105, 109, 110, 111, 112, 113, 115, 116, 117, 118, 119, 120, 121, 122, 123, 124, 125, 126, 128, 129, 130, 131, 132, 133, 134, 135, 136, 137, 140, 141, 142, 143, 146, 149, 150, 151, 153, 155, 156, 158, 160, 161, 162, 165, 166, 167, 168, 169, 170, 171, 172, 173, 174, 177, 178, 179, 180, 181, 182, 183, 184, 185, 186, 187, 188, 189, 190, 191, 193, 194, 195, 196, 197, 198, 199, 200, 203, 204, 205, 206, 210, 211, 212, 213, 214; *s. c. [ ],* 154; *s. c.,* 127, 208; *c.,* 147; *corde ipsius,* 100, 152; *cor suum,* 86, 107, 164.

132   3, 5, 6, 7, 8, 9, 10, 14, 15, 16, 19, 21, 23, 25, 26, 28, 29, 30, 31, 32, 33, 34, 36, 37, 38, 39, 41, 42, 43, 44, 45, 46, 48, 49, 51, 52, 53, 56, 57, 58, 60, 61, 62, 63, 65, 69, 71, 72, 73, 74, 76, 77, 78, 79, 84, 86, 88, 89, 90, 92, 93, 96, 97, 98, 99, 100, 103, 104, 105, 107, 109, 110, 111, 112, 113, 115, 116, 118, 119, 120, 121, 122, 123, 124, 125, 127, 128, 129, 130, 131, 132, 133, 134, 135, 136, 137, 140, 141, 142, 143, 146, 147, 149, 150, 151, 152, 153, 154, 155, 156, 160, 161, 162, 164, 165, 168, 169, 170, 171, 172, 174, 175, 177, 178, 180, 181, 182, 183, 184, 185, 186, 187, 189, 190, 191, 193, 194, 195, 196, 197, 198, 199, 200, 203, 204, 205, 206, 208, 210, 211, 212, 213, 214; *amauit eam,* 179; *et amauit,* 158; *adamauit,* 13, 20, 59, 64, 75, 81, 83, 87, 117, 126, 166, 167, 173, 188; *quia cum Christianus esset amauit,* 82.

133   3, 5, 6, 7, 9, 10, 13, 14, 15, 16, 19, 20, 21, 23, 25, 26, 28, 29, 30, 31, 32, 33, 34, 36, 37, 38, 39, 41, 42, 43, 44, 45, 46, 48, 49, 51, 52, 53, 56, 57, 58, 59, 60, 61, 62, 63, 64, 65, 69, 71, 72, 74, 75, 76, 77, 78, 79, 81, 82, 83, 84, 86, 87, 88, 89, 90, 92, 93, 96, 97, 98, 99, 100, 103, 104, 105, 107, 109, 110, 111, 112, 113, 115, 116, 117, 118, 119, 120, 121, 122, 123, 124, 125, 126, 127, 128, 129, 130, 131, 132, 133, 134, 135, 136, 137, 140, 141, 142, 143, 146, 147, 149, 150, 151, 152, 153, 154, 155, 156, 158, 160, 162, 164, 165, 166, 167, 168, 169, 170, 171, 173, 174, 175, 177, 178, 179, 180, 181, 182, 183, 184, 185, 186, 187, 188, 189, 190, 191, 193, 194, 195, 196, 197, 198, 199, 200, 203, 204, 205, 206, 208, 210, 211, 212, 213, 214; *post* (canc.) *postulauit,* 172; *postulauit.,* 73; *postulauit a.,* 161; om., 8.

134   3, 5, 6, 7, 8, 9, 10, 13, 14, 15, 16, 19, 20, 21, 23, 28, 29, 30, 31, 32, 33, 34, 37, 38, 39, 41, 42, 43, 44, 45, 46, 48, 49, 52, 56, 57, 58, 59, 60, 61, 62, 63, 65, 69, 71, 72, 73, 74, 75, 76, 77, 78, 79, 81, 82, 83, 84, 86, 87, 88, 89, 90, 92, 93, 96, 97, 98, 99, 100, 103, 104, 105, 107, 109, 110, 111, 112, 113, 115, 116, 117, 119, 120, 121, 122, 123, 124, 125, 126, 128, 129, 130, 131, 132, 133, 134, 135, 136, 137, 140, 141, 142, 143, 146, 147, 149, 150, 151, 152, 153, 154, 155, 156, 158, 160, 161, 162, 164, 165, 166, 167, 168, 169, 170, 171, 172, 173, 174, 175, 177, 178, 179, 180, 181, 182, 183, 184, 185, 186, 187, 188, 189, 190, 191, 193, 194, 195, 197, 198, 199, 200, 203, 204, 205, 206, 210, 211, 212, 213, 214; *illam,* 25, 26, 51, 118; *puellam,* 64; om., 36, 53, 127, 196, 208.

135...135   3, 5, 7, 8, 9, 10, 13, 14, 15, 16, 19, 20, 21, 23, 25, 26, 28, 29, 30, 31, 32, 33, 34, 36, 37, 38, 39, 41, 42, 43, 44, 45, 46, 48, 49, 51, 52, 53, 56, 57, 58, 59, 60, 61, 62, 63, 64, 65, 69, 71, 72, 73, 74, 75, 76, 77, 78, 79, 81, 82, 83, 84, 86, 87, 88, 89, 90, 92, 93, 96, 97, 98, 99, 100, 103, 105, 107, 109, 110, 111, 112, 113, 115, 116, 117, 118, 119, 120, 121, 122, 123, 124, 125, 126, 127, 128, 129, 130, 131, 132, 133, 134, 135, 136, 137, 140, 141, 142, 143, 146, 147, 149, 150, 151, 152, 153, 154, 155, 156, 158, 160, 161, 162, 164, 165, 166, 167, 168, 169, 170, 171, 172, 173, 174, 175, 177, 178, 179, 180, 181, 183, 184, 185, 186,

corde[140] suo[141] [142] quia,[143] [149]cum[144] Christianus[145] esset,[146] cum[147] pagana[148] [149]

187, 188, 189, 190, 191, 193, 195, 196, 197, 198, 199, 200, 203, 204, 205, 206, 208, 210, 211, 212, 213, 214; *patri*, 104, 194; *a pre*, 6; *a parte*, 182.

136 3, 5, 6, 7, 9, 10, 13, 14, 15, 16, 19, 20, 21, 23, 25, 26, 28, 29, 30, 31, 32, 33, 36, 37, 38, 39, 41, 42, 43, 44, 45, 46, 48, 49, 51, 52, 53, 56, 57, 58, 59, 60, 61, 62, 63, 64, 65, 69, 71, 72, 73, 74, 75, 76, 77, 78, 79, 81, 82, 83, 84, 86, 87, 88, 89, 90, 92, 93, 96, 97, 98, 99, 103, 104, 105, 107, 109, 110, 111, 112, 113, 115, 116, 117, 118, 119, 120, 121, 122, 123, 124, 125, 126, 127, 128, 129, 130, 131, 132, 133, 134, 135, 136, 137, 140, 141, 142, 143, 146, 147, 149, 150, 151, 152, 153, 154, 155, 156, 158, 160, 161, 162, 164, 165, 166, 167, 168, 169, 170, 171, 172, 173, 174, 175, 177, 178, 179, 180, 181, 182, 183, 184, 185, 186, 187, 188, 189, 190, 191, 193, 194, 195, 196, 197, 198, 199, 200, 203, 204, 205, 206, 208, 210, 211, 212, 213, 214; *suo quia*, 100; *suo peciit*, 8; *eius*, 34.

137 3, 5, 6, 7, 9, 13, 14, 15, 16, 20, 21, 25, 26, 29, 31, 33, 34, 36, 37, 41, 42, 43, 44, 48, 49, 51, 52, 53, 56, 57, 58, 59, 60, 62, 63, 69, 71, 72, 74, 75, 76, 77, 79, 81, 82, 83, 84, 86, 87, 88, 90, 92, 93, 97, 99, 103, 104, 105, 107, 110, 112, 113, 115, 116, 117, 118, 120, 121, 124, 125, 126, 127, 128, 129, 131, 132, 133, 135, 136, 137, 140, 143, 146, 149, 150, 151, 152, 154, 155, 156, 162, 164, 166, 167, 168, 169, 170, 171, 172, 173, 174, 175, 177, 178, 179, 180, 181, 183, 184, 185, 186, 187, 188, 189, 190, 191, 193, 194, 195, 196, 197, 198, 199, 200, 203, 204, 205, 208, 210, 211, 213, 214; *Intrauerit*, 122; *intrau[t]*, 119; *intrauit*, 8, 10, 23, 28, 30, 32, 38, 39, 45, 46, 61, 64, 65, 73, 78, 89, 96, 98, 100, 109, 123, 130, 134, 141, 142, 147, 153, 158, 160, 161, 165, 182, 206, 212; *intrauitque*, 111; om., 19.

138 3, 5, 6, 7, 8, 10, 13, 14, 15, 16, 21, 23, 25, 26, 28, 29, 30, 31, 32, 33, 34, 36, 37, 39, 41, 43, 44, 45, 46, 48, 49, 51, 52, 53, 56, 58, 59, 60, 61, 62, 63, 65, 69, 71, 72, 73, 74, 75, 76, 77, 79, 81, 82, 84, 86, 87, 88, 89, 90, 92, 93, 96, 97, 98, 99, 100, 104, 105, 107, 109, 111, 112, 113, 115, 116, 119, 120, 121, 122, 123, 124, 125, 126, 127, 128, 129, 130, 132, 133, 135, 136, 137, 140, 141, 142, 143, 146, 149, 151, 152, 153, 154, 155, 156, 158, 160, 161, 162, 164, 165, 167, 168, 170, 171, 172, 173, 174, 175, 178, 179, 180, 181, 182, 183, 184, 185, 187, 188, 189, 190, 191, 193, 194, 195, 196, 197, 198, 199, 200, 203, 204, 205, 208, 210, 211, 213, 214; *inquam/*, 103; *itaque*, 118; *inquam in eum*, 20, 126, 166; *in eum* (over erasure), 83; *enim*, 186; *autem*, 64, 78, 134, 169, 206; *namque*, 9, 38, 42, 131, 147, 150; *quoque*, 110; *ea* (canc.) *a patre suo adamauit*, 117; om., 19, 57, 177, 212.

139 3, 5, 6, 7, 8, 9, 10, 13, 14 15, 16, 20, 21, 23, 25, 26, 28, 29, 30, 31, 32, 33, 34, 37, 38, 39, 41, 42, 43, 44, 46, 48, 49, 51, 52, 53, 56, 57, 58, 59, 60, 61, 62, 63, 64, 65, 69, 71, 72, 73, 74, 75, 76, 78, 79, 81, 82, 83, 84, 86, 87, 89, 90, 92, 93, 96, 97, 98, 99, 100, 103, 104, 107, 109, 110, 111, 112, 113, 115, 116, 117, 118, 119, 120, 121, 122, 123, 124, 127, 128, 129, 130, 131, 132, 133, 134, 135, 136, 137,140, 142, 143, 146, 147, 149, 150, 151, 152, 153, 154, 155, 156, 158, 160, 161, 162, 164, 165, 166, 167, 168, 169, 170, 171, 172, 173, 174, 175, 177, 178, 179, 180, 181, 182, 183, 184, 185, 186, 187, 188, 189, 190, 191, 193, 194, 195, 196, 197, 198, 199, 200, 203, 204, 205, 206, 208, 210, 211, 212, 213, 214; *Sathan*, 105; *Satan*, 88; *Sathanam* (altered to *Sathanas*), 77; *Satha\nas/*, 141; *\Sathanas/*, 125; *Saxonas* (altered to *Sathanas*), 36; om., 19, 45.

140 3, 5, 6, 7, 8, 9, 10, 13, 14, 15, 16, 19, 20, 21, 23, 25, 26, 29, 29, 30, 31, 32, 33, 34, 36, 37, 38, 39, 41, 42, 43, 44, 45, 46, 48, 49, 51, 52, 53, 56, 57, 58, 59, 60, 61, 62, 63, 64, 65, 69, 71, 72, 73, 74, 75, 76, 77, 78, 79, 81, 82, 83, 84, 87, 88, 89, 90, 92, 93, 96, 97, 98, 99, 100, 103, 104, 105, 109, 110, 111, 112, 113, 115, 116, 117, 118, 119, 120, 121, 122, 123, 124, 125, 126, 127, 128, 129, 130, 131, 132, 133, 134, 135, 136, 137, 140, 141, 142, 143, 146, 147, 149, 150, 152, 153, 154, 155, 156, 158, 160, 161, 162, 164, 165, 166, 167, 168, 169, 170, 171, 172, 173, 174, 175, 177, 178, 179, 180, 181, 182, 183, 184, 185, 186, 187, 188, 189, 190, 191, 193, 194, 195, 196, 197, 198, 199, 200, 203, 204, 205, 206, 208, 210, 211, 212, 213, 214; *cor*, 86, 107; *eum*, 151.

141 3, 5, 6, 7, 8, 9, 10, 13, 14, 15, 16, 19, 20, 21, 23, 25, 26, 28, 29, 30, 31, 32, 33, 34, 36, 37,

38, 39, 41, 42, 43, 44, 45, 46, 48, 49, 51, 52, 53, 56, 57, 58, 59, 60, 61, 62, 63, 64, 65, 69, 71, 72, 73, 74, 75, 76, 77, 78, 79, 81, 82, 83, 84, 87, 88, 89, 90, 92, 93, 96, 97, 98, 99, 100, 103, 104, 105, 109, 110, 111,112, 113, 115, 116, 117, 118, 119, 120, 121, 122, 123, 124, 125, 126, 127, 128, 129, 130, 131, 132, 133, 134, 135, 136, 137, 140, 141, 142, 143, 146, 147, 149, 150, 152, 153, 154, 155, 156, 158, 160, 161, 162, 164, 165, 166, 167, 168, 169, 170, 171, 172, 173, 174, 175, 177, 178, 179, 180, 181, 182, 183, 184, 185, 186, 187, 188, 189, 190, 191, 193, 194, 195, 196, 197, 198, 199, 200, 203, 204, 205, 206, 208, 210, 211, 212, 213, 214; *suum,* 86, 107; om., 151.

142...142   3, 5, 6, 7, 8, 9, 10, 13, 14, 15, 16, 21, 23, 25, 26, 28, 29, 30, 31, 32, 33, 34, 36, 38, 39, 41, 42, 43, 44, 46, 48, 49, 51, 52, 53, 56, 57, 58, 59, 60, 61, 62, 63, 64, 65, 69, 71, 72, 73, 74, 75, 76, 77, 78, 79, 81, 82, 84, 86, 87, 88, 89, 90, 92, 93, 96, 97, 98, 99, 100, 103, 104, 107, 109, 110, 111, 112, 113, 115, 116, 117, 118, 119, 120, 121, 122, 123, 124, 125, 127, 128, 129, 130, 131, 132, 133, 134, 135, 136, 137, 140, 141, 142, 143, 146, 147, 149, 150, 151, 152, 153, 154, 155, 156, 158, 160, 161, 162, 164, 165, 167, 168, 169, 170, 171, 172, 174, 175, 177, 178, 179, 180, 181, 182, 183, 184, 185, 186, 187, 188, 189, 190, 191, 193, 194, 195, 196, 197, 198, 199, 200, 203, 204, 205, 206, 208, 210, 211, 212, 213, 214; *i. c. s. S.,* 45; *S.,* 20, 37, 83, 126, 166, 173; *i. c. s.,* 19; *i. c. s. S. amauit puella . . . Sathan in corde suo,* 105.

143   3, 5, 6, 7, 8, 9, 10, 13, 14, 15, 16, 19, 20, 21, 23, 25, 26, 28, 29, 30, 31, 32, 33, 34, 36, 37, 38, 39, 41, 42, 43, 44, 45, 46, 48, 49, 51, 52, 53, 56, 58, 59, 61, 62, 63, 64, 65, 69, 71, 72, 73, 74, 75, 76, 77, 78, 79, 81, 82, 83, 84, 86, 87, 88, 89, 90, 92, 93, 96, 97, 98, 99, 103, 104, 105, 107, 109, 110, 111, 112, 113, 115, 116, 117, 118, 120, 121, 122, 123, 124, 125, 126, 127, 128, 130, 131, 132, 133, 134, 135, 136, 137, 140, 141, 142, 143, 146, 147, 149, 150, 151, 152, 153, 154, 155, 156, 158, 160, 161, 162, 164, 165, 166, 167, 168, 169, 170, 171, 172, 173, 174, 175, 177, 178, 179, 180, 181, 182, 183, 184, 185, 186, 187, 188, 189, 190, 191, 193, 194, 196, 197, 198, 199, 203, 204, 205, 206, 208, 210, 211, 212, 213, 214; *qui,* 57, 100, 129, 200; *et qui,* 60; *que,* 119; *qe,* 195.

144   3, 5, 6, 7, 8, 9, 10, 13, 14, 15, 16, 19, 20, 21, 23, 25, 26, 28, 29, 30, 31, 32, 33, 34, 36, 37, 38, 39, 41, 42, 43, 44, 45, 46, 48, 49, 51, 52, 53, 56, 57, 58, 59, 60, 61, 62, 63, 64, 65, 69, 71, 72, 73, 74, 75, 76, 77, 78, 79, 81, 82, 83, 84, 86, 87, 88, 89, 90, 92, 93, 96, 97, 98, 99, 100, 103, 104, 105, 107, 109, 110, 111, 112, 113, 115, 116, 117, 118, 119, 120, 121, 122, 123, 124, 125, 126, 127, 128, 129, 130, 131, 132, 133, 134, 135, 136, 137, 140, 141, 142, 143, 146, 147, 149, 150, 151, 152, 153, 154, 155, 156, 158, 160, 161, 162, 164, 165, 166, 168, 169, 170, 171, 172, 173, 174, 175, 177, 178, 179, 180, 181, 182, 183, 184, 185, 186, 187, 188, 189, 190, 191, 193, 194, 195, 196, 197, 198, 199, 200, 203, 204, 205, 206, 208, 210, 211, 212, 213, 214; om., 167.

145   3, 5, 6, 7, 8, 9, 10, 13, 14, 15, 16, 19, 20, 21, 23, 25, 26, 28, 29, 30, 31, 32, 33, 34, 36, 37, 38, 39, 41, 42, 43, 44, 45, 46, 48, 49, 51, 52, 53, 56, 57, 58, 59, 60, 61, 62, 63, 64, 65, 69, 71, 73, 74, 75, 76, 77, 78, 79, 81, 82, 83, 81, 86, 87, 88, 89, 90, 92, 93, 96, 97, 98, 99, 100, 103, 101, 105, 107, 109, 110, 111, 112, 113, 115, 116, 117, 118, 119, 120, 121, 122, 123, 124, 125, 126, 127, 128, 129, 130, 131, 132, 133, 134, 135, 136, 137, 140, 141, 142, 143, 146, 147, 149, 150, 151, 152, 153, 154, 155, 156, 158, 160, 161, 162, 164, 165, 166, 167, 168, 169, 170, 171, 172, 173, 174, 175, 177, 178, 179, 180, 181, 182, 183, 184, 185, 186, 187, 188, 189, 190, 191, 193, 194, 195, 196, 197, 198, 199, 200, 203, 204, 205, 206, 208, 210, 211, 212, 213, 214; *Christianis,* 72.

146   3, 5, 6, 7, 8, 9, 10, 13, 14, 15, 16, 19, 20, 21, 23, 25, 26, 28, 29, 30, 31, 32, 33, 34, 36, 37, 38, 39, 41, 42, 43, 44, 45, 46, 48, 49, 51, 52, 53, 56, 57, 58, 59, 60, 61, 62, 63, 64, 65, 69, 71, 72, 73, 74, 75, 76, 77, 78, 79, 81, 82, 83, 84, 86, 87, 88, 89, 90, 92, 93, 96, 97, 98, 99, 100, 103, 104, 105, 107, 109, 110, 111, 112, 113, 115, 116, 117, 118, 119, 120, 121, 122, 123, 124, 125, 126, 127, 128, 130, 131, 132, 133, 134, 135, 136, 137, 140, 141, 142, 143, 146, 147, 149, 150, 151, 152, 153, 154, 155, 156, 158, 160, 161, 162, 164, 165, 166, 167, 168, 169, 170, 171, 172, 173, 174, 175, 177, 178, 179, 180, 181, 182, 183, 184, 185, 186,

[152]coire[150] desiderabat.[151] [152] Hengistus ilico,[153] ut erat[154] prudens, comperta[155]

187, 188, 189, 190, 191, 193, 194, 196, 197, 198, 199, 200, 203, 204, 205, 206, 208, 210, 211, 213, 214; *cum esset,* 129; om. but inserted in margin, 195; om., 212.

[147] 3, 5, 6, 7, 8, 9, 10, 13, 14, 15, 16, 19, 20, 21, 23, 25, 26, 28, 29, 30, 31, 32, 33, 34, 36, 37, 38, 39, 41, 42, 43, 44, 45, 46, 48, 49, 51, 52, 53, 56, 57, 58, 59, 60, 61, 62, 63, 64, 65, 69, 71, 72, 73, 74, 75, 76, 77, 78, 79, 81, 82, 83, 84, 86, 87, 89, 90, 92, 93, 96, 97, 98, 99, 100, 103, 104, 105, 107, 109, 110, 111, 112, 113, 115, 117, 118, 119, 120, 121, 122, 123, 124, 125, 126, 127, 128, 129, 130, 131, 132, 133, 134, 135, 136, 137, 140, 141, 142, 143, 146, 147, 149, 150, 151, 152, 153, 154, 155, 156, 158, 160, 161, 162, 164, 165, 166, 167, 168, 169, 170, 171, 172, 173, 174, 175, 177, 178, 179, 180, 181, 182, 183, 184, 185, 186, 187, 188, 189, 190, 191, 193, 194, 195, 196, 197, 198, 199, 200, 203, 204, 205, 206, 208, 210, 211, 212, 213, 214; om., 88, 116.

[148] 3, 5, 6, 7, 8, 9, 10, 13, 14, 15, 16, 20, 21, 23, 25, 26, 28, 29, 30, 31, 32, 33, 34, 36, 37, 38, 39, 41, 42, 43, 44, 45, 46, 48, 49, 51, 52, 53, 56, 57, 58, 59, 60, 61, 62, 63, 65, 69, 71, 72, 73, 74, 75, 76, 77, 78, 79, 81, 82, 83, 84, 86, 87, 88, 89, 90, 92, 93, 96, 97, 98, 99, 100, 103, 104, 105, 107, 109, 110, 111, 112, 113, 115, 116, 117, 118, 119, 120, 121, 122, 123, 124, 125, 126, 127, 128, 129, 130, 131, 132, 133, 134, 135, 136, 137, 140, 141, 142, 143, 146, 147, 149, 150, 151, 152, 153, 154, 155, 156, 158, 160, 161, 162, 164, 165, 166, 167, 168, 169, 170, 171, 172, 173, 174, 175, 177, 178, 179, 180, 181, 182, 183, 184, 185, 186, 187, 188, 189, 190, 191, 193, 194, 195, 196, 197, 198, 199, 200, 203, 204, 205, 206, 208, 210, 211, 212, 213, 214; *paganis,* 64; *illa,* 19.

[149...149] 3, 5, 6, 7, 8, 9, 10, 13, 14, 15, 16, 20, 21, 23, 26, 28, 29, 30, 31, 32, 33, 34, 36, 38, 39, 41, 42, 43, 44, 45, 46, 49, 51, 52, 53, 56, 57, 58, 59, 60, 61, 62, 64, 65, 69, 71, 72, 73, 74, 75, 76, 77, 78, 79, 81, 82, 83, 84, 86, 87, 88, 89, 90, 92, 93, 96, 97, 98, 99, 100, 103, 104, 105, 107, 109, 110, 111, 112, 113, 115, 116, 117, 118, 119, 120, 121, 122, 123, 124, 125, 126, 127, 129, 130, 131, 132, 133, 134, 135, 136, 137, 140, 141, 142, 143, 146, 147, 149, 150, 151, 152, 153, 154, 155, 156, 158, 160, 161, 162, 164, 165, 166, 167, 168, 169, 170, 171, 172, 173, 174, 175, 177, 178, 179, 180, 181, 182, 183, 184, 185, 187, 188, 189, 190, 191, 193, 194, 196, 197, 198, 199, 200, 203, 201, 205, 206, 208, 210, 211, 212, 213, 214; *C. c. p. e. c. illa,* 19; \c./ *C. e. c. p.,* 25, 63; *c. e. C. c. p.,* 37; *C. c. e. c. p.,* 48, 128, 186; *c. C.* \e./ *c. p.,* 195.

[150] 3, 5, 6, 7, 8, 9, 10, 13, 14, 15, 16, 19, 20, 21, 23, 25, 26, 28, 29, 30, 31, 32, 33, 34, 36, 37, 38, 39, 41, 42, 43, 44, 45, 46, 48, 49, 51, 52, 53, 56, 57, 58, 59, 60, 61, 62, 63, 64, 65, 69, 71, 72, 73, 74, 75, 76, 77, 78, 79, 81, 82, 83, 84, 86, 87, 88, 89, 90, 92, 93, 96, 97, 98, 99, 100, 103, 104, 105, 107, 109, 111, 112, 113, 115, 116, 117, 118, 119, 120, 121, 122, 123, 124, 125, 126, 127, 128, 129, 130, 131, 132, 133, 134, 135, 136, 137, 140, 141, 142, 143, 146, 149, 150, 151, 152, 153, 154, 155, 156, 158, 160, 161, 162, 164, 165, 166, 167, 168, 169, 170, 171, 172, 173, 174, 175, 177, 178, 179, 180, 181, 182, 183, 184, 185, 186, 187, 188, 189, 190, 191, 193, 194, 195, 196, 197, 198, 199, 200, 203, 204, 205, 206, 208, 210, 211, 212, 213, 214; *corde* (corr. to *coire*), 110; *edire,* 147.

[151] 3, 5, 6, 7, 8, 9, 10, 13, 14, 15, 16, 19, 20, 21, 23, 25, 26, 28, 29, 30, 31, 32, 33, 34, 36, 37, 39, 41, 42, 43, 44, 45, 46, 48, 49, 51, 52, 53, 56, 57, 58, 59, 60, 61, 63, 64, 65, 69, 71, 72, 73, 74, 75, 76, 77, 78, 79, 81, 82, 83, 84, 86, 87, 88, 89, 90, 92, 93, 96, 97, 98, 99, 100, 103, 104, 105, 107, 109, 110, 111, 112, 113, 115, 116, 118, 119, 120, 121, 122, 123, 124, 125, 126, 127, 128, 129, 130, 132, 133, 134, 135, 136, 137, 140, 141, 142, 143, 146, 147, 149, 150, 151, 152, 153, 154, 155, 156, 158, 160, 161, 162, 164, 165, 166, 167, 168, 169, 170, 171, 172, 173, 174, 175, 177, 178, 179, 180, 181, 182, 183, 184, 185, 186, 1 87, 189, 190, 191, 193, 194, 195, 196, 197, 198, 199, 200, 203, 204, 205, 206, 208, 210, 211, 212, 213, 214; *desiderauit,* 117, 188; *desiderasset,* 62; *uellet,* 38, 131.

[152...152] 3, 5, 6, 7, 8, 9, 10, 13, 14, 15, 16, 19, 20, 21, 23, 25, 26, 28, 29, 30, 31, 32, 33, 34, 36, 37, 38, 39, 41, 42, 43, 44, 45, 46, 48, 49, 51, 52, 53, 56, 57, 58, 59, 60, 61, 62, 63, 64, 69,

[156]leuitate animi[156] regis[157] [160]consuluit[158] fratrem suum Horsum[159] [160] ceterosque[161]

71, 72, 73, 74, 76, 77, 78, 79, 81, 82, 83, 84, 86, 87, 88, 89, 90, 92, 93, 96, 97, 98, 99, 100, 103, 104, 105, 107, 109, 110, 111, 112, 113, 115, 116, 117, 118, 119, 120, 121, 122, 123, 124, 125, 126, 127, 128, 129, 130, 131, 132, 133, 134, 135, 136, 137, 140, 141, 142, 143, 146, 147, 149, 150, 151, 152, 153, 154, 155, 156, 158, 160, 161, 162, 164, 165, 166, 167, 168, 169, 170, 171, 172, 173, 174, 175, 177, 178, 179, 180, 181, 182, 183, 184, 185, 186, 187, 188, 189, 190, 191, 193, 194, 195, 196, 197, 198, 199, 200, 203, 204, 205, 206, 208, 210, 211, 212, 213, 214; *d. c.*, 65, 75.

153 5, 6, 7, 8, 9, 10, 13, 15, 16, 19, 20, 21, 23, 28, 30, 31, 32, 33, 34, 36, 37, 38, 39, 42, 43, 44, 45, 46, 48, 49, 51, 52, 53, 56, 57, 58, 59, 60, 61, 62, 63, 64, 65, 69, 71, 72, 73, 74, 75, 76, 77, 78, 79, 81, 82, 83, 84, 86, 87, 89, 90, 92, 96, 97, 98, 99, 100, 103, 104, 105, 107, 109, 110, 111, 112, 113, 115, 116, 117, 118, 119, 120, 121, 122, 123, 124, 125, 126, 127, 128, 129, 130, 131, 132, 133, 134, 135, 136, 137, 141, 143, 146, 147, 149, 150, 151, 152, 153, 154, 155, 156, 158, 161, 162, 164, 165, 166, 167, 169, 170, 172, 173, 174, 175, 177, 179, 180, 181, 182, 183, 184, 185, 186, 187, 188, 189, 190, 191, 193, 194, 195, 196, 197, 198, 199, 200, 203, 204, 205, 206, 208, 210, 211, 212, 213, 214; *illic\o/*, 168; *illic*, 171; *uero illico*, 93; *uero*, 26, 41, 89, 160; *ergo*, 29, 140, 178; *igitur*, 3, 14; *statim*, 25; om. but inserted in margin, 142.

154 3, 5, 6, 7, 8, 9, 10, 13, 14, 15, 16, 19, 20, 21, 23, 25, 26, 28, 29, 30, 31, 32, 33, 34, 36, 37, 38, 39, 41, 42, 43, 44, 46, 51, 52, 53, 56, 57, 58, 59, 60, 61, 62, 63, 64, 65, 69, 71, 72, 73, 74, 75, 76, 77, 78, 79, 81, 82, 83, 84, 86, 87, 88, 89, 90, 92, 93, 96, 97, 98, 99, 100, 103, 104, 105, 107, 109, 110, 111, 112, 113, 115, 116, 117, 119, 120, 121, 122, 123, 124, 125, 126, 127, 128, 129, 130, 131, 132, 133, 134, 135, 136, 137, 140, 141, 142, 143, 146, 147, 149, 150, 151, 152, 153, 154, 155, 156, 158, 160, 161, 162, 164, 165, 166, 167, 168, 169, 170, 171, 172, 173, 174, 175, 177, 178, 179, 180, 181, 182, 183, 184, 185, 186, 187, 188, 189, 190, 191, 193, 194, 195, 197, 198, 199, 200, 203, 204, 205, 206, 208, 210, 211, 212, 213, 214; *\erat/*, 48; *erat uir*, 49, 118, 196; om., 45.

155 3, 5, 6, 7, 8, 9, 10, 13, 14, 15, 16, 19, 20, 21, 23, 25, 28, 29, 30, 31, 32, 33, 34, 36, 37, 38, 39, 41, 42, 43, 44, 45, 46, 48, 49, 51, 52, 53, 56, 57, 58, 59, 60, 61, 62, 63, 64, 65, 69, 71, 72, 73, 74, 75, 76, 77, 79, 81, 82, 83, 84, 86, 87, 88, 89, 90, 92, 93, 96, 97, 98, 99, 100, 103, 104, 105, 107, 109, 110, 111, 112, 113, 115, 116, 117, 118, 119, 120, 121, 122, 123, 124, 125, 126, 127, 128, 129, 130, 131, 132, 133, 134, 135, 136, 137, 140, 141, 142, 143, 146, 147, 149, 150, 151, 152, 153, 154, 155, 156, 160, 161, 162, 164, 165, 166, 167, 168, 169, 170, 171, 172, 173, 174, 175, 177, 178, 179, 180, 181, 182, 183, 184, 185, 186, 187, 188, 189, 190, 191, 193, 194, 195, 196, 197, 198, 199, 200, 203, 204, 205, 206, 208, 210, 211, 212, 213, 214; over erasure, 158; *comperte*, 26; om., 78.

156...156 3, 5, 7, 8, 9, 10, 13, 14, 15, 16, 19, 20, 21, 23, 25, 26, 28, 29, 30, 31, 32, 33, 34, 36, 37, 38, 39, 41, 42, 43, 44, 45, 46, 48, 49, 51, 52, 53, 56, 57, 58, 59, 60, 61, 62, 63, 64, 65, 69, 71, 72, 73, 74, 76, 77, 79, 81, 82, 83, 84, 86, 87, 88, 89, 90, 92, 93, 96, 97, 98, 99, 100, 103, 105, 107, 109, 111, 112, 113, 116, 117, 118, 119, 120, 121, 122, 123, 124, 125, 126, 127, 128, 129, 130, 131, 132, 133, 134, 135, 136, 137, 140, 142, 143, 146, 147, 149, 150, 151, 152, 153, 154, 155, 156, 158, 160, 161, 162, 164, 165, 166, 167, 168, 170, 171, 173, 175, 177, 178, 179, 180, 181, 182, 183, 184, 185, 186, 187, 188, 189, 190, 191, 193, 194, 195, 196, 199, 200, 203, 204, 205, 206, 208, 210, 211, 212, 213, 214; *a. l.*, 172, 174, 197, 198; *lenitate animi*, 104; *leuita\te/ animi*, 169; *leuitate \animi/*, 115; *leuitate*, 6, 75, 110; *leuitate anima*, 141; om., 78.

157 3, 5, 7, 8, 10, 13, 14, 15, 16, 19, 20, 21, 23, 25, 26, 28, 29, 30, 31, 32, 33, 34, 36, 37, 38, 39, 41, 42, 43, 44, 45, 46, 48, 49, 51, 52, 53, 56, 57, 58, 59, 60, 61, 62, 63, 64, 65, 69, 71, 72, 73, 74, 75, 76, 77, 79, 81, 82, 83, 84, 86, 87, 88, 89, 92, 93, 96, 97, 98, 99, 100, 103, 104, 105, 107, 109, 110, 111, 112, 113, 115, 116, 117, 118, 119, 120, 121, 122, 123, 124, 125, 126, 127, 128, 129, 130, 131, 132, 133, 134, 135, 136, 137, 140, 141, 142, 146, 147,

maiores[162] natu[163] [166]qui secum[164] aderant[165] [166] [167]quid de[167] peticione[168] regis[169]

149, 150, 151, 152, 153, 154, 155, 156, 158, 160, 161, 162, 164, 165, 166, 167, 168, 169, 170, 171, 172, 173, 174, 175, 177, 178, 179, 180, 181, 182, 183, 184, 185, 186, 187, 188, 189, 190, 191, 193, 194, 195, 196, 197, 198, 199, 200, 203, 204, 205, 206, 208, 210, 211, 212, 213, 214; *?unus regis,* 90; *eius,* 9, 143; *legis,* 6; om., 78.

158 3, 6, 7, 8, 9, 10, 13, 14, 15, 16, 19, 20, 21, 23, 25, 26, 28, 29, 30, 31, 32, 33, 34, 36, 37, 38, 41, 42, 43, 46, 48, 49, 51, 52, 53, 57, 58, 59, 60, 62, 63, 65, 69, 71, 72, 73, 74, 75, 76, 77, 79, 81, 82, 83, 84, 86, 87, 88, 89, 90, 92, 93, 96, 97, 99, 100, 103, 104, 105, 107, 110, 111, 112, 113, 115, 116, 118, 120, 121, 122, 124, 125, 126, 127, 128, 129, 130, 132, 133, 134, 135, 136, 137, 140, 143, 146, 147, 149, 150, 151, 152, 154, 155, 156, 158, 160, 161, 162, 164, 166, 167, 168, 169, 170, 171, 172, 173, 174, 175, 177, 178, 179, 180, 181, 182, 183, 184, 185, 186, 187, 188, 189, 190, 191, 193, 194, 195, 196, 197, 198, 199, 200, 203, 204, 205, 206, 208, 210, 211, 212, 213, 214; *consulit,* 39, 45, 61, 64, 98, 109, 119, 123, 141, 142, 153, 165; *consuliuit,* 117; *consuliit,* 5, 56; *consiluit,* 44; *consueuit,* 131; om., 77, 78.

159 3, 5, 6, 7, 8, 9, 10, 13, 14, 15, 16, 19, 20, 21, 23, 25, 26, 28, 29, 30, 31, 32, 33, 34, 36, 37, 38, 39, 41, 42, 43, 44, 45, 46, 48, 51, 52, 53, 56, 57, 58, 59, 60, 61, 62, 63, 64, 65, 69, 71, 72, 73, 74, 75, 76, 77, 98, 79, 81, 82, 83, 84, 86, 87, 88, 89, 90, 92, 93, 96, 97, 98, 99, 100, 103, 104, 105, 107, 109, 110, 111, 112, 113, 115, 116, 117, 118, 119, 120, 121, 122, 123, 124, 125, 126, 127, 128, 129, 130, 131, 132, 133, 134, 135, 136, 137, 140, 141, 142, 143, 146, 147, 149, 150, 151, 152, 153, 155, 156, 158, 160, 161, 162, 164, 165, 166, 167, 168, 170, 171, 172, 173, 174, 175, 177, 178, 179, 180, 181, 182, 183, 184, 185, 186, 187, 188, 189, 190, 191, 194, 195, 196, 197, 198, 199, 200, 203, 204, 205, 206, 208, 210, 211, 212, 213, 214; *Horsum*, 154; *Horosum,* 193; *Orsium,* 169; om., 49.

160...160 3, 5, 6, 7, 9, 13, 14, 15, 16, 19, 20, 21, 23, 25, 26, 29, 31, 33, 34, 36, 37, 38, 41, 42, 43, 44, 46, 48, 51, 52, 53, 56, 57, 58, 59, 60, 62, 63, 64, 65, 69, 71, 74, 75, 76, 79, 81, 82, 83, 84, 86, 87, 88, 89, 90, 92, 93, 96, 97, 99, 103, 104, 105, 107, 110, 112, 113, 115, 116, 117, 118, 120, 121, 122, 124, 125, 126, 127, 128, 129, 130, 131, 132, 133, 135, 136, 137, 140, 143, 146, 147, 149, 150, 151, 152, 154, 155, 156, 158, 160, 161, 162, 164, 166, 167, 168, 169, 170, 171, 172, 173, 174, 175, 177, 178, 179, 180, 181, 182, 183, 184, 185, 186, 187, 188, 189, 190, 191, 193, 194, 195, 196, 197, 198, 199, 200, 203, 204, 205, 206, 208, 210, 211, 212, 213, 214; *f. s. H. c.,* 111; *c. H. f. s.,* 8, 10, 28, 30, 32, 39, 45, 61, 72, 73, 98, 100, 109, 119, 123, 134, 141, 142, 153, 165; *c. f. s.,* 49; *c. f. f. s. H.,* 92; *H.,* 78; om., 77.

161 3, 5, 6, 7, 8, 9, 10, 13, 14, 15, 16, 19, 20, 21, 23, 25, 26, 28, 29, 30, 31, 32, 33, 34, 36, 37, 38, 39, 41, 42, 43, 44, 45, 46, 48, 49, 51, 52, 53, 56, 57, 58, 59, 60, 61, 62, 63, 65, 69, 71, 72, 73, 74, 75, 76, 78, 79, 81, 82, 83, 84, 86, 87, 88, 89, 90, 92, 93, 96, 97, 98, 99, 103, 104, 105, 107, 109, 110, 111, 112, 113, 115, 116, 117, 118, 119, 120, 121, 122, 123, 124, 125, 126, 127, 128, 129, 130, 131, 132, 133, 135, 136, 137, 141, 142, 143, 146, 149, 150, 151, 152, 153, 154, 155, 156, 158, 160, 161, 162, 164, 165, 166, 167, 168, 169, 170, 171, 172, 173, 174, 175, 177, 178, 179, 180, 181, 182, 183, 185, 186, 187, 188, 189, 190, 191, 193, 194, 195, 196, 197, 198, 199, 200, 203, 204, 205, 206, 208, 210, 211, 212, 213, 214; *et ceteros,* 134, 147; *ceteros,* 64, 100; *ceterosque que,* 140; *ceterosque amicos,* 184; om., 77.

162 3, 5, 6, 7, 8, 9, 10, 13, 14, 15, 16, 19, 20, 21, 23, 25, 26, 28, 29, 30, 31, 32, 33, 34, 36, 37, 38, 39, 41, 42, 43, 44, 45, 46, 48, 49, 51, 52, 53, 56, 57, 58, 59, 61, 62, 63, 64, 65, 69, 71, 72, 73, 74, 75, 76, 78, 79, 81, 82, 83, 84, 86, 87, 88, 89, 90, 92, 93, 96, 97, 98, 99, 100, 103, 104, 105, 107, 109, 110, 111, 112, 113, 115, 116, 117, 118, 119, 120, 121, 122, 123, 124, 125, 126, 127, 128, 129, 130, 131, 132, 133, 134, 135, 136, 137, 140, 141, 142, 143, 146, 147, 149, 150, 151, 152, 153, 154, 155, 156, 158, 160, 161, 162, 164, 165, 166, 167, 168, 169, 170, 171, 172, 173, 174, 175, 177, 178, 179, 180, 181, 182, 183, 184, 185, 186,

187, 188, 189, 190, 191, 193, 194, 195, 196, 197, 198, 199, 200, 203, 204, 205, 206, 208, 210, 211, 212, 213, 214; *maioresque,* 60; om., 77.

163   3, 5, 6, 7, 8, 9, 10, 13, 14, 15, 16, 19, 20, 21, 23, 25, 26, 28, 29, 30, 31, 32, 33, 34, 36, 37, 38, 39, 41, 42, 43, 44, 45, 46, 48, 49, 51, 52, 53, 56, 57, 58, 59, 60, 61, 62, 63, 64, 65, 69, 71, 72, 73, 74, 75, 76, 78, 79, 81, 82, 83, 84, 86, 87, 88, 89, 90, 92, 93, 96, 97, 98, 99, 100, 103, 104, 105, 107, 109, 110, 111, 112, 113, 115, 116, 117, 118, 119, 120, 121, 122, 123, 124, 125, 126, 127, 128, 129, 130, 131, 132, 133, 134, 135, 136, 137, 140, 141, 142, 143, 146, 147, 149, 150, 151, 152, 153, 154, 155, 156, 158, 160, 161, 162, 164, 165, 166, 167, 168, 169, 170, 171, 172, 173, 174, 175, 177, 178, 179, 180, 181, 182, 183, 184, 185, 186, 187, 188, 189, 190, 191, 193, 194, 195, 196, 197, 198, 199, 200, 203, 204, 205, 206, 208, 210, 211, 212, 213, 214; om., 77.

164   3, 5, 6, 7, 8, 9, 10, 13, 14, 15, 16, 19, 20, 21, 23, 25, 26, 28, 29, 30, 31, 32, 33, 34, 36, 37, 38, 39, 41, 42, 43, 44, 45, 46, 48, 49, 51, 52, 53, 56, 57, 58, 59, 60, 61, 62, 63, 64, 65, 69, 71, 72, 73, 74, 75, 76, 77, 78, 79, 81, 83, 84, 86, 87, 88, 89, 90, 92, 93, 96, 97, 98, 99, 100, 103, 104, 105, 107, 109, 110, 111, 112, 113, 115, 116, 117, 118, 119, 120, 121, 122, 123, 124, 125, 126, 127, 128, 129, 130, 131, 132, 133, 134, 135, 136, 137, 140, 141, 142, 143, 146, 147, 149, 150, 151, 152, 153, 154, 155, 156, 158, 160, 161, 162, 164, 165, 166, 167, 168, 169, 170, 171, 172, 173, 174, 175, 177, 178, 179, 180, 181, 182, 183, 184, 185, 186, 187, 188, 189, 190, 191, 193, 194, 195, 196, 197, 198, 199, 200, 203, 204, 205, 206, 208, 210, 211, 212, 213, 214; *scdm.,* 82.

165   3, 5, 6, 7, 8, 9, 10, 13, 14, 15, 16, 19, 20, 21, 23, 25, 26, 28, 29, 30, 31, 32, 33, 34, 36, 37, 38, 39, 41, 42, 43, 44, 45, 46, 48, 49, 51, 52, 53, 56, 57, 58, 59, 60, 61, 62, 63, 64, 65, 69, 71, 72, 73, 74, 75, 76, 77, 78, 79, 81, 82, 83, 84, 86, 87, 88, 89, 90, 92, 93, 96, 97, 98, 99, 100, 103, 104, 105, 107, 109, 110, 111, 112, 113, 115, 116, 117, 118, 119, 120, 121, 122, 123, 124, 125, 126, 127, 128, 129, 130, 131, 132, 133, 134, 135, 136, 137, 141, 142, 143, 146, 147, 149, 151, 152, 153, 154, 155, 156, 158, 160, 161, 162, 164, 165, 166, 167, 168, 169, 170, 171, 172, 173, 174, 175, 177, 178, 179, 180, 181, 182, 183, 184, 185, 186, 187, 188, 189, 190, 191, 193, 194, 195, 196, 197, 198, 199, 200, 203, 204, 206, 208, 210, 211, 212, 214; *adherant,* 140, 150; *erant,* 205, 213; *aderant secum,* 104.

166...166   3, 5, 6, 7, 9, 10, 13, 14, 15, 16, 19, 20, 21, 23, 25, 26, 28, 29, 30, 31, 32, 33, 34, 36, 37, 38, 39, 41, 43, 44, 45, 46, 48, 49, 51, 52, 53, 56, 57, 58, 59, 60, 61, 62, 63, 64, 69, 71, 72, 73, 74, 76, 78, 79, 81, 82, 83, 84, 87, 88, 89, 90, 92, 93, 96, 97, 98, 99, 100, 103, 105, 107, 109, 110, 111, 112, 113, 115, 116, 117, 118, 119, 120, 121, 122, 123, 124, 125, 126, 127, 128, 129, 130, 131, 132, 133, 134, 135, 136, 137, 140, 141, 142, 143, 146, 147, 149, 150, 151, 152, 153, 154, 155, 156, 158, 160, 161, 162, 164, 165, 166, 167, 168, 169, 170, 171, 172, 173, 174, 175, 177, 178, 179, 180, 181, 182, 183, 184, 185, 186, 187, 188, 189, 190, 191, 193, 195, 196, 197, 198, 199, 200, 203, 204, 205, 206, 208, 210, 211, 212, 213, 214; *q. a. s.,* 65, 104, 194; *q. a.,* 8, 42, 75; om., 77, 86.

167...167   3, 5, 6, 7, 8, 9, 10, 13, 14, 15, 16, 19, 20, 21, 23, 25, 26, 28, 29, 30, 31, 32, 33, 34, 36, 37, 38, 39, 41, 42, 43, 45, 46, 48, 49, 51, 52, 53, 56, 57, 58, 59, 60, 61, 62, 63, 64, 65, 69, 71, 72, 73, 74, 75, 76, 78, 79, 82, 83, 84, 86, 87, 88, 89, 90, 92, 93, 96, 97, 98, 99, 100, 103, 101, 105, 107, 109, 111, 112, 113, 115, 116, 117, 118, 119, 120, 121, 122, 123, 124, 125, 126, 127, 128, 129, 130, 131, 132, 133, 134, 135, 136, 137, 140, 141, 142, 143, 146, 147, 149, 150, 151, 152, 153, 154, 155, 156, 158, 160, 161, 162, 164, 165, 166, 167, 168, 170, 171, 172, 173, 174, 175, 177, 178, 179, 180, 181, 182, 183, 184, 185, 186, 187, 188, 189, 190, 191, 193, 194, 196, 197, 198, 199, 200, 203, 204, 205, 206, 208, 210, 211, 212, 213, 214; *qu\id/ de,* 195; *qui de.,* 44, 81; *quid,* 110, 169; *quod,* 110; om., 77.

168   3, 5, 6, 7, 8, 9, 10, 13, 14, 15, 16, 19, 20, 21, 23, 25, 26, 28, 29, 30, 31, 32, 33, 34, 36, 37, 38, 39, 41, 42, 43, 44, 45, 46, 49, 51, 52, 53, 56, 57, 58, 59, 60, 61, 62, 63, 64, 65, 69, 71, 72, 73, 74, 75, 76, 78, 79, 81, 82, 83, 84, 86, 87, 88, 89, 90, 92, 93, 96, 97, 98, 99, 100, 103, 104, 105, 107, 109, 110, 111, 112, 113, 115, 116, 117, 118, 119, 120, 121, 122, 123, 124, 125, 126, 127, 128, 129, 130, 131, 132, 133, 134, 135, 136, 137, 140, 141, 142, 143, 146, 147, 149, 150, 151, 152, 153, 155, 156, 158, 160, 161, 162, 164, 165, 166, 167, 168,

facerent. [170] Sed[171] [175]omnibus[172] unum[173] consilium fuit[174] [175] ut[176] [178]puella regi

170, 171, 172, 173, 174, 175, 177, 178, 179, 180, 181, 182, 183, 184, 185, 186, 188, 189, 190, 191, 193, 194, 195, 196, 197, 198, 199, 200, 203, 204, 205, 206, 208, 210, 211, 212, 213, 214; *petone,* 154; *petione,* 187; *petitionis regi,* 169; om., 77.

[169] 3, 5, 6, 7, 8, 9, 10, 13, 14, 15, 16, 19, 20, 21, 23, 25, 26, 28, 29, 30, 31, 32, 33, 34, 36, 37, 38, 39, 41, 42, 43, 44, 45, 46, 48, 49, 51, 52, 53, 56, 57, 58, 59, 60, 61, 62, 63, 64, 65, 69, 71, 72, 73, 74, 75, 76, 78, 79, 81, 82, 83, 84, 86, 87, 88, 89, 90, 92, 93, 96, 97, 98, 99, 100, 103, 104, 105, 107, 109, 110, 111, 112, 113, 116, 117, 118, 119, 120, 121, 122, 123, 124, 125, 126, 127, 128, 129, 130, 131, 132, 133, 134, 135, 136, 137, 140, 141, 142, 143, 146, 147, 149, 150, 151, 152, 153, 154, 155, 156, 158, 160, 161, 162, 164, 165, 166, 167, 168, 169, 170, 171, 172, 173, 174, 175, 178, 179, 180, 181, 182, 183, 184, 185, 186, 187, 188, 189, 190, 191, 193, 194, 195, 196, 197, 198, 199, 200, 203, 204, 205, 206, 208, 210, 211, 212, 213, 214; *rgis,* 115; *regis quid de peticioni regis* (canc.), 177; om., 77.

[170] 3, 5, 6, 7, 8, 9, 14, 15, 20, 23, 28, 29, 30, 34, 37, 39, 43, 45, 46, 49, 51, 52, 53, 57, 58, 59, 63, 64, 71, 73, 74, 75, 76, 77, 79, 81, 82, 83, 86, 87, 92, 96, 97, 100, 103, 107, 109, 119, 120, 121, 123, 124, 126, 127, 134, 135, 136, 141, 142, 149, 152, 155, 158, 162, 164, 166, 167, 168, 169, 170, 171, 173, 174, 175, 179, 180, 181, 183, 184, 185, 187, 188, 189, 190, 191, 193, 194, 195, 197, 200, 203, 204, 208, 210; *facerent* (altered to *faceret*), 172; *facet.,* 129; *faceret,* 10, 13, 16, 19, 21, 25, 26, 31, 32, 33, 36, 41, 42, 44, 48, 56, 58, 60, 61, 62, 65, 69, 78, 84, 88, 89, 90, 93, 98, 99, 104, 105, 111, 112, 113, 115, 116, 117, 118, 122, 125, 128, 130, 131, 132, 133, 137, 140, 143, 146, 147, 150, 151, 153, 154, 156, 160, 161, 165, 177, 178, 182, 186, 196, 198, 199, 205, 206, 211, 212, 213, 214; *facerat,* 72; *responderet,* 110.

[171] 3, 5, 6, 7, 8, 9, 10, 13 14, 15, 16, 19, 20, 21, 23, 25, 26, 28, 29, 30, 31, 32, 33, 34, 36, 37, 38, 39, 41, 42, 43, 44, 45, 46, 49, 51, 52, 53, 56, 57, 58, 59, 60, 61, 62, 63, 64, 65, 69, 71, 72, 73, 74, 75, 76, 77, 78, 79, 81, 82, 83, 84, 86, 87, 88, 89, 90, 92, 93, 96, 97, 98, 99, 100, 103, 104, 105, 107, 109, 110, 111, 112, 113, 115, 116, 117, 118, 119, 120, 121, 122, 123, 124, 125, 126, 127, 130, 131, 132, 133, 134, 135, 136, 137, 140, 141, 142, 143, 146, 147, 149, 150, 151, 152, 153, 154, 155, 156, 158, 160, 161, 162, 164, 165, 166, 167, 168, 169, 170, 171, 172, 173, 174, 175, 178, 179, 180, 181, 182, 183, 184, 185, 187, 188, 189, 190, 191, 193, 194, 195, 196, 197, 198, 199, 200, 203, 204, 205, 206, 208, 210, 211, 212, 213, 214; *Sed et,* 177; *Qui,* 129, 186; om., 48, 128.

[172] 3, 5, 7, 8, 9, 10, 13, 14, 15, 16, 19, 20, 21, 23, 25, 26, 28, 29, 30, 31, 32, 33, 36, 37, 38, 39, 41, 42, 43, 44, 46, 48, 49, 51, 52, 53, 56, 57, 58, 59, 60, 61, 62, 63, 64, 65, 69, 71, 72, 73, 74, 75, 76, 77, 78, 79, 81, 82, 83, 84, 86, 87, 88, 89, 90, 92, 93, 96, 97, 98, 99, 100, 103, 104, 105, 107, 109, 110, 111, 112, 113, 115, 116, 117, 118, 119, 120, 121, 122, 123, 124, 125, 126, 127, 128, 130, 131, 132, 133, 134, 135, 136, 137, 140, 141, 142, 143, 146, 147, 149, 150, 151, 152, 153, 154, 155, 156, 158, 160, 161, 162, 164, 165, 166, 167, 168, 169, 170, 171, 172, 173, 174, 175, 177, 178, 179, 180, 181, 182, 183, 184, 185, 186, 187, 188, 189, 190, 191, 193, 194, 195, 196, 197, 198, 199, 200, 203, 204, 205, 206, 208, 210, 211, 212, 213, 214; *in omnibus,* 45; *omnes,* 129; om., 6, 34.

[173] Compare n. 175. 3, 5, 6, 8, 9, 10, 13, 14, 15, 16, 19, 20, 21, 23, 25, 26, 28, 29, 30, 31, 32, 33, 34, 36, 37, 38, 39, 41, 42, 43, 44, 45, 46, 49, 51, 52, 53, 56, 57, 58, 59, 60, 61, 62, 63, 64, 65, 69, 71, 72, 73, 74, 75, 76, 77, 78, 79, 81, 82, 83, 84, 86, 87, 88, 89, 90, 92, 96, 97, 98, 99, 100, 103, 104, 105, 107, 109, 110, 111, 112, 113, 115, 116, 117, 118, 119, 120, 121, 122, 123, 124, 125, 126, 127, 129, 130, 131, 132, 133, 134, 135, 136, 137, 140, 141, 142, 143, 146, 147, 149, 150, 151, 152, 153, 154, 156, 158, 160, 161, 162, 164, 165, 166, 167, 168, 169, 170, 171, 172, 173, 174, 175, 177, 178, 179, 180, 181, 182, 183, 184, 185, 186, 187, 188, 189, 190, 191, 193, 194, 195, 196, 197, 198, 199, 200, 203, 204, 205, 206, 208, 210, 211, 212, 213, 214; *in unum,* 7, 155; *itaque unum,* 48, 128; *unum fuit (fuit* canc.), 93.

174 3, 7, 8, 9, 10, 14, 15, 16, 19, 20, 21, 23, 25, 26, 28, 30, 31, 32, 34, 36, 38, 39, 41, 42, 43, 44, 45, 46, 48, 49, 51, 52, 53, 56, 57, 58, 59, 60, 61, 62, 63, 64, 71, 72, 73, 74, 75, 78, 81, 83, 84, 86, 87, 88, 89, 93, 96, 98, 100, 104, 105, 107, 109, 110, 111, 113, 116, 117, 118, 119, 120, 121, 123, 124, 125, 126, 127, 128, 130, 132, 133, 134, 135, 136, 140, 141, 142, 143, 146, 147, 149, 150, 151, 152, 153, 154, 155, 156, 158, 160, 161, 164, 165, 166, 167, 168, 170, 171, 172, 173, 174, 175, 177, 178, 180, 181, 182, 183, 184, 187, 188, 189, 193, 194, 195, 196, 197, 198, 199, 200, 203, 204, 205, 206, 208, 210, 211, 212, 214; \fuit/, 115; *erat,* 33; *placuit,* 5, 90, 112, 137, 213; *dederunt,* 129, 186; om., 6, 13, 29, 37, 65, 69, 76, 77, 79, 82, 92, 97, 99, 103, 122, 131, 162, 169, 179, 185, 190, 191.

175...175 3, 5, 7, 9, 10, 14, 15, 16, 19, 21, 23, 26, 28, 30, 31, 32, 38, 39, 41, 42, 43, 44, 45, 46, 48, 49, 51, 52, 61, 62, 64, 65, 69, 71, 72, 74, 76, 77, 78, 79, 81, 82, 84, 86, 87, 88, 89, 90, 92, 93, 96, 97, 99, 100, 103, 104, 105, 107, 109, 111, 112, 113, 115, 116, 118, 119, 120, 121, 122, 123, 124, 125, 128, 129, 130, 131, 132, 133, 134, 136, 137, 140, 141, 142, 143, 146, 149, 150, 154, 155, 156, 158, 160, 161, 162, 164, 168, 169, 170, 171, 177, 178, 179, 180, 181, 182, 183, 185, 186, 187, 189, 190, 191, 193, 194, 195, 199, 200, 203, 204, 206, 210, 211, 212, 214; *o.* \u./ *c, f.,* 184; *u. o. c. f.,* 20, 36, 53, 56, 58, 75, 83, 127, 151, 166, 173, 196, 205, 208; *o. u. f. c.,* 57, 60, 135, 147; *o. c. u. f.,* 8, 34, 63, 73, 98, 110, 152, 153, 165; *o. f. u. c.,* 13, 117, 188; *o.* \f./ *u. c.,* 167; *u. f. o. c.,* 59; *u. c. o. f,* 25, 126; *o. pl. c.* \u./, 213; *o. u. pl. erat c.,* 33; *o. uisum est c.,* 172, 174, 198; *o, uisum est,* 197; *uisum o. c. f.,* 175; *o. u. c.,* 6, 29, 37, 82.

176 3, 5, 6, 7, 8, 9, 10, 13, 14, 15, 16, 19, 20, 21, 23, 25, 26, 28, 29, 30, 31, 32, 33, 34, 36, 37, 38, 39, 41, 42, 43, 44, 45, 46, 48, 49, 51, 52, 53, 56, 57, 58, 59, 60, 61, 62, 63, 64, 65, 69, 71, 72, 73, 74, 75, 76, 77, 78, 79, 81, 83, 84, 86, 87, 88, 89, 90, 92, 93, 96, 97, 98, 99, 100, 103, 104, 105, 107 109, 110, 111, 112, 113, 115, 116, 117, 118, 119, 120, 121, 122, 123, 124, 125, 126, 127, 128, 129, 130, 131, 132, 133, 134, 135, 136, 137, 140, 141, 142, 143, 146, 147, 149, 150, 151, 152, 153, 154, 155, 156, 158, 160, 161, 162, 164, 165, 166, 167, 168, 169, 170, 171, 172, 173, 174, 175, 177, 178, 179, 180, 181, 182, 183, 184, 185, 186, 187, 188, 189, 190, 191, 193, 194, 195, 196, 197, 198, 199, 200, 203, 204, 205, 206, 208, 210, 211, 212, 213, 214; *dederunt uidelicet quod,* 82.

177 3, 5, 6, 7, 8, 9, 10, 13, 14, 15, 16, 19, 20, 21, 23, 25, 26, 28, 29, 30, 31, 32, 33, 34, 36, 37, 38, 39, 41, 42, 43, 44, 45, 46, 48, 49, 51, 52, 53, 56, 57, 58, 59, 60, 61, 62, 63, 64, 65, 69, 71, 73, 75, 76, 77, 78, 79, 81, 82, 83, 84, 86, 87, 88, 89, 90, 92, 93, 96, 97, 98, 99, 100, 103, 104, 105, 107, 109, 110, 111, 112, 113, 115, 116, 117, 118, 119, 120, 121, 122, 123, 124, 125, 126, 127, 128, 129, 130, 131, 132, 134, 135, 136, 137, 140, 141, 142, 143, 146, 147, 149, 150, 151, 152, 153, 154, 155, 156, 158, 160, 161, 162, 164, 165, 166, 167, 168, 169, 170, 171, 172, 173, 174, 175, 177, 178, 179, 180, 181, 182, 183, 184, 185, 186, 187, 188, 189, 190, 191, 193, 194, 195, 196, 197, 198, 199, 200, 203, 204, 205, 206, 208, 210, 211, 212, 213, 214; *donaretur,* 72, 133; *darent,* 74.

178...178 9, 15, 23, 25, 31, 41, 42, 43, 44, 46, 48, 49, 52, 63, 64, 65, 71, 72, 74, 86, 87, 88, 89, 93, 96, 107, 113, 116, 118, 120, 128, 132, 133, 136, 140, 143, 146, 149, 150, 156, 158, 160, 161, 164, 170, 174, 177, 178, 181, 187, 200, 203, 204, 210, 212; *r. p. d.,* 8; *p. d. r.,* 3, 5, 6, 7, 10, 13, 14, 16, 19, 20, 21, 26, 28, 29, 30, 32, 33, 34, 37, 38, 39, 45, 51, 53, 56, 57, 58, 59, 60, 61, 62, 69, 73, 75, 76, 77, 78, 79, 81, 82, 83, 84, 90, 92, 97, 98, 99, 100, 103, 104, 105, 109, 110, 111, 112, 115, 117, 119, 121, 122, 123, 124, 125, 126, 127, 129, 130, 131, 134, 135, 137, 141, 142, 147, 151, 152, 153, 154, 155, 162, 165, 166, 167, 168, 169, 171, 172, 173, 175, 179, 180, 182, 183, 184, 185, 186, 188, 189, 190, 191, 193, 194, 195, 196, 197, 198, 199, 205, 206, 208, 211, 213, 214; *p. d.,* 36.

179...179 3, 5, 6, 7, 8, 9, 10, 13, 14, 15, 16, 20, 21, 23, 25, 26, 28, 29, 30, 31, 32, 33, 34, 37, 38, 39, 41, 42, 43, 44, 45, 46, 48, 49, 51, 52, 53, 56, 57, 58, 60, 61, 62, 63, 64, 65, 69, 71, 72, 73, 74, 75, 76, 77, 78, 79, 81, 82, 83, 86, 87, 88, 89, 90, 92, 93, 96, 97, 98, 99, 100, 103, 104, 105, 107, 109, 110, 111, 112, 113, 115, 116, 117, 118, 119, 120, 121, 122, 123, 125, 126, 127, 128, 130, 131, 132, 133, 134, 135, 136, 137, 140, 141, 142, 143, 146, 147, 149,

daretur[177] [178] [179]et ut[179] peterent[180] [186]pro[181] ea[182] prouinciam[183] Cantie ab[184] illo.[185] [186]

150, 151, 152, 153, 154, 155, 156, 158, 160, 161, 162, 164, 165, 166, 167, 168, 169, 170, 171, 172, 173, 174, 175, 177, 178, 179, 180, 181, 182, 183, 184, 185, 186, 187, 188, 189, 190, 191, 193, 194, 195, 196, 197, 198, 199, 200, 203, 204, 205, 206, 208, 210, 211, 212, 213, 214; *u. e.,* 129; *et,* 19, 84, 124; om., 36, 59.

180 3, 5, 6, 9, 10, 13, 14, 15, 16, 19, 20, 21, 23, 28, 29, 30, 31, 37, 39, 41, 43, 44, 45, 46, 48, 51, 52, 53, 56, 57, 58, 62, 63, 64, 71, 72, 73, 74, 75, 76, 77, 78, 79, 81, 82, 83, 84, 86, 87, 88, 90, 92, 93, 96, 97, 100, 104, 105, 107, 109, 112, 113, 115, 116, 117, 118, 119, 120, 121, 123, 124, 126, 127, 128, 130, 133, 134, 136, 137, 140, 141, 142, 146, 149, 150, 151, 155, 156, 158, 161, 162, 164, 165, 166, 167, 168, 169, 170, 171, 172, 173, 174, 175, 177, 178, 179, 180, 181, 182, 183, 184, 185, 187, 188, 189, 190, 191, 193, 194, 195, 196, 197, 198, 199, 200, 203, 204, 205, 208, 211, 212, 213, 214; *petere\n\t,* 154; *peteret,* 7, 25, 26, 32, 33, 38, 42, 59, 60, 61, 65, 69, 78, 89, 98, 99, 110, 111, 122, 129, 132, 135, 153, 154, 160, 186, 206, 210; *peteretur,* 8, 34, 49, 103, 143, 147, 152; *petet,* 131; *peterent*, 125; om., 8, 36.

181 3, 5, 6, 7, 8, 9, 10, 13, 14, 15, 16, 19, 20, 21, 23, 25, 26, 28, 29, 30, 31, 32, 33, 34, 36, 37, 38, 39, 41, 42, 43, 44, 46, 48, 49, 51, 52, 56, 57, 58, 59, 60, 61, 62, 63, 64, 65, 69, 71, 73, 74, 75, 76, 77, 78, 79, 81, 82, 83, 84, 86, 87, 90, 92, 93, 96, 97, 98, 99, 100, 103, 104, 105, 107, 109, 110, 111, 112, 113, 115, 117, 118, 119, 120, 121, 122, 123, 124, 125, 126, 127, 128, 129, 130, 131, 132, 134, 135, 136, 137, 140, 141, 142, 143, 146, 147, 149, 150, 151, 152, 153, 154, 155, 156, 158, 161, 162, 164, 165, 166, 167, 168, 169, 170, 171, 172, 173, 174, 175, 177, 178, 179, 180, 181, 182, 183, 184, 185, 186, 187, 188, 189, 190, 191, 193, 194, 195, 196, 197, 198, 199, 200, 203, 204, 205, 206, 208, 210, 211, 212, 213, 214; *pro*, 53; *ab,* 88, 116; om., 45, 72, 89, 133, 160, 199.

182 3, 5, 6, 7, 8, 9, 10, 13, 14, 15, 16, 19, 20, 21, 23, 25, 26, 28, 29, 30, 31, 32, 33, 34, 36, 37, 38, 39, 41, 42, 43, 44, 46, 48, 49, 51, 52, 56, 57, 59, 60, 61, 62, 63, 64, 65, 69, 71, 73, 74, 75, 76, 77, 78, 79, 81, 82, 83, 84, 86, 87, 90, 92, 93, 96, 97, 98, 99, 100, 103, 104, 105, 107, 109, 110, 111, 112, 113, 115, 117, 118, 119, 120, 121, 122, 123, 124, 125, 126, 127, 128, 129, 130, 131, 132, 134, 135, 136, 137, 140, 141, 142, 143, 146, 147, 149, 150, 151, 152, 153, 154, 155, 156, 158, 161, 162, 165, 166, 167, 168, 169, 170, 171, 172, 173, 174, 175, 177, 178, 179, 180, 181, 182, 183, 184, 185, 186, 187, 188, 189, 190, 191, 193, 194, 195, 196, 197, 198, 199, 200, 203, 204, 205, 206, 208, 210, 211, 212, 213, 214; *illa,* 164; *eo,* 88, 116, *ea*, 53; *doctrina,* 72; om., 45, 89, 133, 160, 199.

183 3, 5, 6, 7, 8, 10, 13, 14, 15, 16, 19, 20, 21, 23, 25, 26, 28, 29, 30, 31, 32, 33, 36, 37, 38, 39, 41, 42, 43, 44, 45, 46, 48, 51, 52, 53, 56, 57, 58, 59, 60, 61, 62, 63, 64, 65, 69, 71, 73, 74, 75, 76, 77, 78, 79, 81, 82, 83, 84, 86, 87, 88, 89, 90, 92, 93, 96, 97, 98, 99, 100, 104, 105, 107, 109, 110, 111, 112, 113, 115, 116, 117, 118, 119, 120, 121, 122, 123, 124, 125, 126, 127, 128, 129, 130, 131, 132, 133, 134, 135, 136, 137, 140, 141, 142, 146, 149, 150, 151, 153, 154, 155, 156, 158, 160, 162, 164, 165, 166, 167, 168, 169, 170, 171, 172, 173, 174, 175, 177, 178, 179, 180, 181, 182, 183, 184, 185, 186, 187, 190, 191, 193, 194, 195, 196, 197, 198, 199, 200, 203, 204, 205, 206, 208, 210, 211, 212, 213, 214; *prouintia,* 9, 34, 49, 72, 103, 143, 147, 152, 161, 188, 189.

184 3, 5, 6, 7, 8, 9, 10, 13, 14, 15, 16, 19, 20, 21, 23, 25, 26, 28, 29, 30, 31, 32, 33, 34, 36, 37, 38, 39, 41, 42, 43, 44, 45, 46, 48, 49, 51, 52, 53, 56, 57, 58, 59, 60, 61, 62, 63, 64, 65, 69, 71, 72, 73, 74, 75, 76, 77, 78, 79, 81, 82, 83, 84, 86, 87, 89, 90, 92, 93, 96, 97, 98, 99, 100, 103, 104, 105, 107, 109, 110, 111, 112, 113, 115, 117, 118, 119, 120, 121, 122, 123, 125, 126, 127, 128, 129, 130, 131, 132, 133, 134, 135, 136, 137, 140, 141, 142, 143, 146, 147, 149, 150, 151, 152, 153, 154, 155, 156, 158, 160, 161, 162, 164, 165, 166, 167, 168, 169, 170, 171, 172, 173, 174, 175, 177, 178, 179, 180, 181, 182, 183, 184, 185, 186, 187, 188, 189, 190, 191, 193, 194, 195, 196, 197, 198, 200, 203, 204, 205, 206, 208, 210, 211, 212, 213, 214; *pro,* 88, 116, 199; om., 124.

[187]Nec mora[187] [188]data fuit[188] puella[189] Uortegirno[190] et[191] prouincia[192] Cantie[193]

[185] 3, 4, 6, 7, 8, 9, 10, 13, 14, 15, 16, 19, 20, 21, 23, 25, 26, 28, 29, 30, 31, 32, 33, 34, 36, 37,
38, 39, 41, 42, 43, 44, 45, 46, 48, 49, 51, 52, 53, 56, 57, 58, 59, 60, 61, 62, 63, 64, 65, 69,
71, 72, 73, 74, 75, 76, 77, 78, 79, 81, 82, 83, 84, 86, 87, 89, 90, 92, 93, 96, 97, 98, 99, 100,
103, 104, 105, 107, 109, 110, 111, 112, 113, 115, 117, 118, 119, 120, 121, 122, 123, 125,
126, 127, 128, 129, 130, 131, 132, 133, 134, 135, 136, 137, 140, 141, 142, 143, 146, 147,
149, 150, 151, 152, 153, 154, 155, 156, 158, 160, 161, 162, 164, 165, 166, 167, 168, 169,
170, 171, 172, 173, 174, 175, 177, 178, 179, 180, 181, 182, 183, 184, 185, 186, 187, 188,
189, 190, 191, 193, 194, 195, 196, 197, 198, 200, 203, 204, 205, 206, 208, 210, 211, 212,
213, 214; *illa,* 88, 116; *ea,* 199; om., 124.

[186...186] 5, 6, 9, 10, 13, 15, 16, 19, 21, 25, 26, 28, 29, 30, 31, 32, 33, 34, 37, 38, 39, 41, 42, 43,
44, 46, 48, 49, 51, 52, 56, 57, 58, 59, 60, 61, 62, 63, 64, 65, 69, 71, 72, 73, 74, 75, 76, 77,
78, 79, 81, 82, 83, 84, 86, 87, 88, 90, 92, 93, 97, 98, 99, 100, 103, 104, 105, 107, 109, 110,
111, 112, 113, 115, 116, 117, 118, 119, 120, 121, 122, 123, 126, 127, 128, 129, 130, 131,
132, 134, 135, 136, 137, 140, 141, 142, 143, 146, 149, 150, 151, 152, 153, 154, 155, 156,
158, 161, 162, 164, 165, 166, 167, 170, 172, 173, 175, 177, 178, 179, 180, 181, 182, 183,
185, 186, 187, 188, 190, 191, 193, 194, 195, 196, 197, 198, 200, 203, 204, 205, 206, 208,
210, 211, 213, 214; *prou. C. pro e. a. i.,* 3, 14, 147, 168, 171, 184, 189; *prou. C. pro e.,*
199; *prou. C. a. i. pro e.,* 20, 212; *Pro ea/ prou. C. a. i.,* 53, 125, 174; *prou. C. a. i.,* 45,
89, 133, 160; *pro e. a. i. prou. C. peteretur,* 8; *pro e. prou. C.,* 7, 124, 169; *pro e. prou. C.
sibi a. i.,* 96; *pro e. prou. C. sibi,* 23; om., 36.

[187...187] 3, 5, 6, 8, 9, 10, 13, 14, 15, 16, 19, 20, 21, 23, 25, 26, 28, 29, 30, 31, 32, 33, 34, 37,
38, 39, 41, 42, 43, 44, 45, 46, 48, 49, 51, 52, 53, 56, 57, 58, 59, 60, 61, 62, 63, 64, 65, 69,
71, 72, 73, 74, 75, 76, 77, 78, 79, 81, 82, 83, 84, 86, 87, 88, 89, 90, 92, 93, 96, 97, 98, 99,
100, 103, 104, 105, 107, 109, 110, 111, 112, 113, 115, 116, 117, 118, 119, 120, 121, 122,
123, 125, 126, 127, 128, 129, 130, 131, 132, 133, 134, 135, 136, 137, 140, 141, 142, 143,
146, 147, 149, 150, 151, 152, 153, 154, 155, 156, 158, 160, 161, 162, 164, 165, 166, 167,
168, 170, 171, 172, 173, 174, 175, 177, 178, 179, 180, 181, 182, 183, 184, 185, 186, 187,
188, 189, 190, 191, 193, 194, 195, 196, 197, 198, 199, 200, 203, 204, 205, 206, 208, 210,
211, 212, 213, 214; om., 7, 36, 124, 169.

[188...188] 3, 5, 6, 8, 9, 10, 13, 14, 15, 16, 19, 20, 21, 23, 25, 26, 28, 29, 30, 31, 32, 33, 34, 37,
38, 39, 41, 42, 43, 44, 45, 46, 49, 51, 52, 53, 56, 57, 58, 59, 60, 61, 62, 63, 64, 69, 71, 73,
74, 75, 76, 77, 78, 79, 81, 82, 83, 86, 87, 88, 90, 92, 93, 96, 97, 98, 99, 100, 103, 104, 105,
107, 109, 110, 111, 112, 113, 115, 116, 117, 118, 119, 120, 121, 122, 123, 125, 126, 127,
129, 130, 131, 132, 134, 135, 136, 137, 140, 141, 142, 143, 146, 147, 149, 150, 151, 152,
153, 154, 155, 156, 158, 161, 162, 164, 165, 166, 167, 168, 170, 172, 173, 174, 175, 177,
178, 179, 180, 181, 182, 183, 184, 185, 186, 187, 188, 189, 190, 191, 193, 194, 195, 196,
197, 198, 199, 200, 203, 204, 205, 206, 208, 210, 211, 212, 213, 214; *f. d.,* 72, 89, 133;
data est, 48, 65, 84, 128; *data,* 160, 171; om., 7, 36, 124, 169.

[189] 3, 5, 6, 8, 9, 10, 13, 14, 15, 16, 19, 20, 21, 23, 25, 26, 28, 29, 30, 31, 32, 33, 34, 37, 38,
39, 41, 43, 44, 45, 46, 48, 49, 51, 52, 53, 56, 57, 58, 59, 60, 61, 62, 63, 64, 69, 71, 72, 73,
74, 75, 76, 77, 78, 79, 81, 82, 83, 84, 86, 87, 88, 89, 90, 92, 93, 96, 97, 98, 99, 100, 103,
104, 105, 107, 109, 110, 111, 112, 113, 115, 116, 117, 118, 119, 120, 121, 122, 123, 125,
126, 127, 128, 129, 130, 131, 132, 133, 134, 135, 136, 137, 140, 141, 142, 143, 146, 149,
150, 151, 152, 153, 155, 156, 158, 160, 161, 162, 164, 165, 166, 167, 168, 170, 171, 172,
173, 174, 175, 177, 178, 179, 180, 181, 182, 183, 184, 185, 186, 187, 188, 189, 190, 191,
193, 194, 195, 196, 197, 198, 199, 200, 203, 204, 205, 206, 208, 210, 211, 212, 213, 214;
Ronwein puella, 65; *puella regi,* 105, 147, 154, 214; om., 7, 36, 42, 124, 169.

[190] 5, 10, 13, 15, 16, 19, 20, 21, 25, 28, 29, 30, 32, 33, 34, 36, 37, 39, 43, 46, 48, 49, 52, 53,
56, 57, 58, 59, 61, 62, 69, 71, 72, 73, 74, 76, 77, 79, 82, 83, 86, 87, 88, 89, 92, 93, 98, 99,
100, 103, 104, 107, 109, 116, 117, 119, 120, 121, 122, 123, 126, 127, 128, 129, 133, 134,

Hengisto[194] nesciente [197]Gorangono[195] comite[196] [197] qui in[198] eadem[199] regnabat.[200]

135, 136, 140, 141, 142, 146, 147, 149, 150, 151, 152, 153, 155, 156, 158, 161, 162, 167, 170, 172, 173, 175, 177, 179, 180, 181, 184, 185, 186, 188, 189, 191, 193, 194, 195, 196, 197, 198, 200, 203, 204, 205, 208, 210, 211, 212; *Uoltegirno,* 81, 183; *Uorteirgno,* 174; *Uortigeno,* 42, 187; *Uortigerno,* 9, 31, 41, 51, 60, 63, 75, 78, 84, 90, 96, 97, 110, 111, 113, 125, 132, 137, 165; *Uortigero,* 164; *Uortigirno,* 8, 23, 26, 44, 45, 64, 112, 118, 131, 143, 160, 178, 206; *Uotegirno* (altered to *Uortegirno*), 166; *Woltegirno,* 3, 14, 168, 171; *Wortegirmis* (altered to *Wortegiro*), 182; *Wortegirno,* 6, 65, 130, 190, 213; *Wortigerno,* 115; *Wortigirgno,* 199; *Wortigirno,* 38; *\Wortigirno\,* 154; om., 7, 105, 124, 169, 214.

191   3, 5, 6, 8, 9, 10, 13, 14, 15, 16, 19, 20, 21, 23, 25, 26, 28, 29, 30, 31, 32, 33, 34, 36, 37, 38, 39, 41, 42, 43, 44, 45, 46, 48, 49, 51, 52, 53, 56, 57, 58, 59, 60, 61, 62, 63, 64, 65, 69, 71, 72, 73, 74, 75, 76, 77, 79, 81, 82, 83, 84, 86, 87, 88, 89, 90, 92, 93, 96, 97, 98, 99, 100, 103, 104, 105, 107, 109, 110, 111, 112, 113, 115, 116, 117, 118, 119, 120, 121, 122, 123, 125, 126, 127, 128, 129, 130, 131, 132, 133, 134, 135, 136, 137, 140, 141, 142, 143, 146, 147, 149, 150, 151, 152, 153, 154, 155, 156, 158, 160, 161, 162, 164, 165, 166, 167, 168, 170, 171, 172, 173, 174, 175, 177, 178, 179, 180, 181, 182, 183, 184, 185, 186, 187, 188, 189, 190, 191, 193, 194, 195, 196, 197, 198, 199, 200, 203, 204, 205, 208, 210, 211, 212, 213, 214; *pro,* 78, 206; om., 7, 124, 169.

192   3, 5, 6, 8, 9, 10, 13, 14, 15, 16, 19, 20, 21, 23, 25, 26, 28, 29, 30, 31, 32, 33, 34, 36, 37, 38, 39, 41, 42, 43, 44, 45, 46, 48, 49, 51, 52, 53, 57, 59, 60, 61, 62, 63, 64, 65, 69, 71, 72, 73, 74, 75, 76, 77, 78, 79, 81, 82, 83, 84, 86, 87, 88, 89, 90, 92, 93, 96, 97, 98, 99, 100, 103, 104, 105, 107, 109, 110, 111, 112, 113, 115, 116, 117, 118, 119, 120, 121, 122, 123, 125, 126, 127, 128, 129, 130, 131, 132, 133, 134, 135, 136, 137, 140, 141, 142, 143, 146, 147, 149, 150, 151, 152, 153, 154, 155, 156, 158, 160, 161, 162, 164, 165, 166, 167, 168, 170, 171, 172, 173, 174, 175, 177, 178, 179, 180, 181, 182, 183, 184, 185, 186, 187, 188, 189, 190, 191, 193, 194, 195, 196, 197, 198, 199, 200, 203, 204, 206, 208, 210, 211, 212, 213, 214; *pro ea prouincia,* 56, 58, 205; *prouinci,* 100; om., 7, 124, 169.

193   3, 5, 6, 8, 9, 10, 13, 14, 15, 16, 19, 20, 21, 23, 25, 26, 28, 29, 30, 31, 32, 33, 34, 36, 37, 38, 39, 41, 42, 43, 44, 45, 46, 48, Q, 51, 52, 53, 56, 57, 58, 59, 60, 61, 62, 63, 64, 65, 69, 71, 72, 73, 74, 75, 76, 77, 78, 79, 81, 82, 83, 84, 86, 87, 88, 89, 90, 92, 96, 97, 98, 99, 100, 103, 104, 105, 107, 109, 110, 111, 112, 113, 115, 116, 117, 118, 119, 120, 121, 122, 123, 125, 126, 127, 128, 129, 130, 131, 132, 133, 134, 135, 136, 137, 140, 141, 142, 143, 146, 147, 149, 150, 151, 152, 153, 154, 155, 156, 158, 160, 161, 162, 164, 165, 166, 167, 168, 170, 171, 172, 173, 174, 175, 177, 178, 179, 180, 181, 182, 183, 184, 185, 186, 187, 188, 189, 190, 191, 193, 194, 195, 196, 197, 198, 199, 200, 203, 204, 205, 206, 208, 210, 211, 212, 213, 214; om., 7, 93, 124, 169.

194   3, 5, 6, 7, 8, 9, 10, 13, 14, 15, 16, 19, 20, 21, 23, 25, 26, 28, 29, 30, 31, 32, 33, 34, 36, 37, 38, 39, 41, 42, 43, 45, 46, 48, 49, 51, 52, 53, 56, 57, 58, 59, 60, 61, 62, 63, 64, 65, 69, 71, 72, 73, 74, 75, 77, 78, 79, 81, 82, 83, 84, 86, 87, 88, 89, 90, 92, 93, 96, 97, 98, 99, 100, 103, 104, 105, 107, 109, 110, 111, 112, 113, 115, 116, 117, 118, 119, 120, 121, 122, 123, 124, 125, 126, 127, 128, 129, 130, 131, 132, 133, 134, 135, 136, 137, 140, 141, 142, 143, 146, 147, 149, 150, 151, 152, 153, 154, 155, 158, 160, 161, 162, 164, 165, 166, 167, 168, 169, 170, 171, 172, 174, 175, 177, 178, 179, 180, 181, 182, 183, 184, 185, 186, 187, 188, 189, 190, 191, 193, 194, 195, 196, 197, 198, 199, 200, 203, 204, 205, 206, 208, 210, 211, 212, 213, 214; *Hestingo,* 44, 156; *Engisto,* 66, 76, 173.

195   3, 5, 6, 8, 9, 10, 13, 14, 15, 16, 19, 20, 21, 23, 25, 28, 29, 30, 31, 32, 33, 34, 36, 38, 39, 41, 42, 43, 44, 46, 48, 49, 51, 53, 56, 59, 60, 63, 64, 65, 69, 71, 72, 73, 75, 76, 77, 78, 79, 81, 82, 83, 86, 88, 89, 90, 92, 93, 96, 97, 98, 99, 100, 103, 104, 107, 109, 112, 113, 115, 116, 117, 119, 120, 122, 123, 124, 126, 127, 128, 129, 131, 132, 133, 134, 135, 136, 137, 140, 141, 142, 146, 147, 149, 150, 151, 152, 156, 158, 160, 161, 162, 164, 165, 166, 167, 168, 169, 170, 171, 173, 175, 177, 179, 181, 183, 184, 185, 187, 188, 189, 190, 191, 193,

194, 195, 198, 200, 203, 204, 205, 206, 208, 210, 211, 212, 213; *Garangono,* 61; *Gonargono,* 45; *Gonragono,* 58; *Goragono,* 52, 62, 87, 143; *Gorangan,* 26; *Gorangano,* 155, 178, 196; *Gorangno,* 37; *Gorangonao,* 7; *Gorangone,* 118; *Gorangonio,* 121; *Gorangoro,* 186; *Goranngono,* 111; *Gorano,* 172, 174, 197; *Gorganno,* 182; *Goroganno,* 105, 125, 130, 199, 214; *Gorogano,* 153, 154; *Goromantia,* 110; *Goroneu,* 180; *Gorongano,* 84; *Gorongono,* 57, 74.

196 3, 5, 6, 7, 8, 9, 10, 13, 14, 15, 16, 19, 20, 21, 23, 25, 26, 29, 30, 31, 32, 33, 34, 36, 37, 38, 39, 41, 42, 43, 44, 45, 46, 48, 49, 51, 52, 53, 56, 57, 58, 59, 60, 61, 62, 63, 64, 65, 69, 71, 72, 73, 74, 75, 76, 77, 78, 79, 81, 82, 83, 84, 86, 87, 88, 89, 90, 92, 93, 96, 97, 98, 99, 100, 103, 104, 105, 109, 112, 113, 115, 116, 117, 118, 119, 120, 121, 122, 123, 124, 125, 126, 127, 128, 129, 130, 131, 132, 133, 134, 135, 137, 140, 141, 142, 143, 146, 147, 149, 150, 151, 152, 153, 154, 155, 156, 158, 160, 161, 162, 164, 165, 166, 167, 168, 169, 170, 171, 172, 173, 174, 175, 177, 178, 179, 180, 181, 182, 183, 184, 185, 186, 187, 188, 189, 190, 191, 193, 194, 195, 196, 197, 198, 199, 200, 203, 204, 205, 206, 208, 210, 211, 212, 213, 214; *comitem,* 110; om., 28, 107, 111, 136.

197...197 3, 5, 6, 7, 8, 9, 10, 13, 14, 15, 16, 19, 20, 21, 23, 25, 26, 28, 29, 30, 31, 32, 33, 34, 36, 37, 38, 39, 41, 42, 43, 44, 45, 46, 48, 49, 51, 52, 53, 56, 57, 58, 59, 60, 61, 62, 63, 64, 65, 69, 71, 72, 73, 74, 75, 76, 77, 78, 79, 81, 82, 83, 84, 86, 87, 88, 89, 90, 92, 93, 96, 97, 98, 99, 100, 103, 104, 105, 107, 109, 110, 111, 112, 113, 115, 116, 117, 118, 119, 120, 121, 122, 123, 124, 125, 126, 127, 128, 129, 130, 131, 132, 133, 134, 135, 136, 137, 140, 141, 142, 143, 146, 147, 149, 150, 151, 152, 153, 154, 155, 156, 158, 160, 161, 162, 165, 166, 167, 168, 169, 170, 171, 172, 173, 174, 175, 177, 178, 179, 180, 181, 182, 183, 184, 185, 186, 187, 188, 189, 190, 191, 193, 194, 195, 196, 197, 198, 199, 200, 203, 204, 205, 206, 208, 210, 211, 212, 213, 214; *c. G.,* 164.

198 3, 5, 6, 7, 8, 9, 10, 13, 14, 15, 16, 19, 20, 21, 23, 25, 26, 28, 29, 30, 31, 32, 33, 34, 36, 37, 42, 43, 44, 45, 46, 48, 49, 51, 52, 53, 56, 57, 58, 59, 60, 61, 62, 63, 64, 65, 69, 71, 72, 73, 74, 75, 76, 78, 79, 81, 82, 83, 84, 86, 87, 88, 89, 90, 92, 93, 96, 97, 98, 99, 100, 103, 104, 105, 107, 109, 110, 111, 112, 113, 115, 116, 117, 118, 119, 120, 121, 122, 123, 124, 125, 126, 127, 128, 129, 130, 131, 132, 133, 134, 135, 136, 137, 140, 141, 142, 143, 146, 147, 149, 150, 151, 152, 153, 154, 155, 156, 158, 160, 161, 162, 164, 165, 166, 167, 168, 169, 170, 171, 172, 173, 174, 175, 177, 178, 179, 180, 181, 182, 183, 184, 185, 186, 187, 188, 189, 190, 191, 193, 194, 195, 196, 197, 198, 199, 200, 203, 204, 205, 206, 208, 210, 211, 212, 213, 214; om., 77.

199 5, 6, 7, 8, 9, 10, 13, 15, 16, 19, 20, 21, 23, 25, 26, 28, 29, 30, 31, 32, 33, 36, 37, 39, 41, 42, 43, 44, 45, 46, 48, 49, 51, 52, 53, 56, 57, 58, 59, 60, 61, 62, 63, 64, 65, 69, 71, 72, 73, 74, 75, 76, 77, 78, 79, 82, 83, 84, 86, 87, 88, 89, 90, 92, 93, 96, 97, 98, 100, 103, 104, 105, 109, 110, 111, 112, 113, 115, 116, 117, 119, 120, 121, 123, 124, 125, 126, 127, 128, 130, 132, 133, 135, 136, 137, 140, 141, 142, 143, 146, 147, 149, 150, 151, 152, 154, 155, 156, 158, 160, 161, 162, 164, 165, 166, 167, 169, 170, 172, 173, 174, 175, 177, 178, 179, 180, 181, 185, 186, 187, 188, 190, 191, 193, 194, 195, 196, 197, 198, 199, 200, 203, 204, 205, 206, 208, 210, 211, 212, 213, 214; *eandem* (altered to *eadem*), 34; *e\a*/*dem,* 134, 182; *illa,* 107; *ea.,* 99, 122; *ea,* 3, 14, 38, 81, 118, 129, 131, 153, 168, 171, 183, 184, 189.

200 3, 5, 6, 7, 8, 9, 10, 13, 14, 15, 16, 19, 20, 21, 23, 25, 26, 28, 29, 30, 31, 32, 33, 34, 37, 38, 39, 41, 42, 43, 44, 45, 46, 48, 49, 51, 52, 53, 56, 57, 58, 59, 60, 61, 62, 63, 64, 65, 69, 71, 72, 73, 74, 75, 76, 77, 78, 79, 81, 82, 84, 86, 87, 88, 89, 90, 92, 93, 96, 97, 98, 99, 100, 103, 104, 107, 109, 110, 111, 112, 113, 115, 116, 117, 118, 119, 120, 121, 122, 123, 124, 125, 126, 127, 128, 129, 130, 131, 132, 133, 134, 135, 137, 140, 141, 142, 143, 146, 147, 149, 150, 151, 152, 153, 154, 155, 156, 158, 160, 161, 162, 164, 165, 166, 167, 168, 169, 170, 171, 172, 174, 175, 177, 178, 179, 180, 181, 182, 183, 184, 185, 186, 187, 188, 189, 190, 191, 193, 194, 195, 196, 197, 198, 199, 200, 203, 204, 205, 206, 208, 210, 211, 212, 213; *manebat,* (corr. to *regnabat*), 136; *reppunabat,* 36; *regna habitabat,* 173, (corr. to *regnabat*), 83; *dominabatur,* 105, 214.

Nupsit itaque[201] rex[202] [205]eadem[203] nocte[204] [205] pagane[206] que[207] [212]ultra[208] modum[209]

[201] 3, 5, 6, 7, 8, 9, 10, 13, 14, 15, 16, 19, 20, 21, 23, 25, 26, 28, 29, 30, 31, 32, 33, 34, 36, 37, 38, 39, 41, 42, 43, 44, 45, 46, 48, 49, 51, 52, 53, 56, 57, 58, 59, 60, 61, 62, 63, 64, 65, 69, 71, 72, 73, 74, 75, 76, 77, 78, 79, 81, 82, 83, 84, 86, 87, 89, 90, 92, 93, 96, 97, 98, 99, 100, 103, 104, 105, 107, 109, 112, 113, 115, 117, 118, 119, 120, 121, 122, 123, 124, 125, 126, 127, 128, 129, 130, 131, 132, 133, 134, 135, 136, 137, 140, 141, 142, 143, 146, 147, 149, 150, 151, 152, 153, 154, 155, 156, 158, 160, 161, 162, 164, 165, 166, 167, 168, 169, 170, 171, 172, 173, 174, 175, 177, 178, 179, 180, 181, 182, 183, 184, 185, 186, 187, 188, 189, 190, 191, 194, 195, 196, 197, 198, 199, 200, 203, 204, 205, 206, 208, 210, 211, 212, 213, 214; *ergo,* 110, 111, 193; *autem,* 88, 116.

[202] 3, 5, 6, 7, 8, 9, 10, 13, 14, 15, 16, 19, 21, 23, 25, 26, 28, 29, 30, 31, 32, 33, 34, 37, 39, 41, 42, 43, 44, 45, 46, 48, 49, 51, 52, 57, 59, 60, 61, 62, 63, 64, 65, 69, 71, 72, 73, 74, 76, 77, 78, 79, 81, 82, 84, 86, 87, 88, 89, 90, 92, 93, 96, 97, 98, 99, 100, 103, 104, 105, 109, 110, 111, 112, 113, 115, 116, 117, 119, 120, 121, 122, 123, 124, 125, 128, 129, 130, 132, 133, 134, 135, 137, 140, 141, 142, 143, 146, 147, 149, 150, 152, 153, 154, 155, 156, 158, 160, 161, 162, 164, 165, 167, 168, 169, 170, 171, 172, 174, 177, 178, 179, 180, 181, 182, 183, 184, 185, 186, 187, 188, 189, 190, 191, 193, 194, 195, 197, 198, 199, 200, 203, 204, 206, 210, 211, 213, 214; *puella regi,* 38, 131; *pagana regi,* 118; *regi,* 107, 136; *pagane,* 75; *ei/ rex,* 212; om., 20, 36, 53, 56, 58, 83, 110, 126, 127, 136, 151, 166, 173, 175, 196, 205, 208.

[203] 9, 15, 23, 31, 41, 42, 43, 44, 46, 48, 49, 52, 63, 64, 71, 72, 74, 75, 78, 86, 87, 88, 89, 93, 96, 107, 113, 116, 120, 128, 130, 133, 136, 140, 143, 146, 149, 150, 156, 158, 160, 161, 164, 166, 170, 177, 178, 181, 187, 200, 203, 204, 210, 212; *in eadem* (*in* cancelled), 115; *in eadem,* 3, 5, 6, 7, 8, 10, 13, 14, 16, 19, 21, 25, 26, 28, 29, 30, 32, 33, 34, 36, 37, 38, 39, 45, 51, 53, 56, 57, 58, 59, 60, 61, 62, 65, 69, 73, 76, 77, 79, 81, 82, 83, 84, 90, 92, 97, 98, 99, 100, 103, 104, 105, 109, 110, 111, 112, 117, 118, 119, 121, 122, 123, 124, 125, 126, 127, 129, 131, 132, 134, 135, 137, 141, 142, 147, 151, 152, 153, 154, 155, 162, 165, 167, 168, 169, 171, 172, 173, 174, 175, 179, 180, 182, 183, 184, 185, 186, 188, 189, 190, 191, 193, 194, 195, 196, 197, 198, 199, 205, 206, 208, 211, 213, 214; *in illa,* 20.

[204] 3, 5, 6, 7, 8, 9, 10, 13, 14, 15, 16, 19, 20, 21, 23, 25, 26, 28, 29, 30, 31, 32, 33, 34, 36, 37, 38, 39, 41, 42, 43, 44, 45, 46, 48, 49, 51, 52, 53, 56, 57, 58, 59, 60, 61, 62, 63, 64, 65, 69, 71, 72, 73, 74, 75, 76, 77, 78, 79, 81, 82, 83, 84, 86, 87, 88, 89, 90, 92, 93, 96, 97, 98, 99, 100, 103, 104, 107, 109, 111, 112, 113, 115, 116, 117, 118, 119, 120, 121, 122, 123, 124, 125, 126, 127, 128, 129, 130, 131, 132, 133, 134, 135, 136, 137, 140, 141, 142, 143, 146, 147, 149, 150, 151, 152, 153, 154, 155, 156, 158, 160, 161, 162, 164, 165, 166, 167, 168, 169, 170, 171, 172, 173, 174, 175, 177, 178, 179, 180, 181, 182, 183, 184, 185, 186, 187, 188, 189, 190, 191, 193, 194, 195, 196, 197, 198, 199, 200, 203, 204, 205, 206, 208, 210, 211, 212, 213, 214; om., 105.

[205...205] 3, 5, 6, 7, 8, 9, 10, 13, 14, 15, 16, 19, 20, 21, 23, 25, 26, 28, 29, 30, 31, 32, 33, 34, 36, 37, 38, 39, 41, 42, 43, 44, 45, 46, 48, 49, 51, 52, 53, 56, 57, 58, 59, 60, 61, 62, 63, 64, 65, 69, 71, 72, 73, 74, 75, 76, 77, 78, 79, 81, 82, 83, 84, 86, 87, 88, 89, 90, 92, 93, 96, 97, 98, 99, 100, 103, 104, 105, 107, 109, 111, 112, 113, 115, 116, 117, 118, 119, 120, 121, 122, 123, 124, 125, 126, 127, 128, 129, 130, 131, 132, 133, 134, 135, 136, 137, 140, 141, 142, 143, 146, 147, 149, 150, 151, 152, 153, 154, 155, 156, 158, 160, 161, 162, 164, 165, 166, 167, 168, 169, 170, 171, 172, 173, 174, 175, 177, 178, 179, 180, 181, 182, 183, 184, 185, 186, 187, 188, 189, 190, 191, 193, 194, 195, 196, 197, 198, 199, 200, 203, 204, 205, 206, 208, 210, 211, 212, 213, 214; *n. e.,* 110.

[206] 3, 6, 7, 8, 9, 10, 13, 14, 15, 16, 19, 20, 21, 23, 25, 26, 28, 29, 30, 31, 32, 33, 34, 36, 37, 39, 42, 43, 45, 46, 48, 49, 51, 52, 53, 56, 57, 58, 59, 60, 61, 62, 63, 65, 69, 71, 72, 73, 74, 76, 77, 78, 79, 81, 82, 83, 84, 86, 87, 88, 89, 90, 92, 96, 97, 98, 99, 100, 103, 104, 105, 109, 110, 111, 112, 113, 115, 116, 117, 119, 120, 121, 122, 123, 124, 125, 126, 127, 128,

129, 130, 134, 135, 137, 141, 142, 143, 146, 147, 149, 151, 152, 153, 154, 155, 158, 160, 161, 162, 164, 165, 166, 167, 168, 169, 170, 171, 172, 173, 174, 175, 177, 179, 180, 181, 182, 183, 184, 185, 186, 187, 188, 189, 190, 191, 193, 194, 195, 196, 197, 198, 199, 200, 203, 204, 205, 206, 208, 210, 211, 213, 214; *paganem,* 5; *paganam,* 64; *pagana,* 107, 136; *pagane puelle,* 133; *paganel,* 150; om., 38, 41, 44, 75, 93, 118, 131, 132, 140, 156, 178, 212; *rex pagane,* 110.

207   3, 5, 6, 7, 8, 9, 10, 13, 14, 15, 16, 19, 20, 21, 23, 25, 26, 28, 29, 30, 31, 32, 33, 34, 36, 37, 38, 39, 41, 42, 43, 44, 45, 46, 48, 49, 51, 52, 53, 56, 57, 58, 59, 60, 61, 62, 63, 64, 65, 69, 71, 73, 75, 76, 77, 78, 79, 81, 82, 83, 84, 86, 87, 88, 89, 90, 92, 93, 96, 97, 98, 99, 100, 103, 104, 105, 107, 109, 110, 111, 112, 113, 115, 116, 117, 118, 119, 120, 121, 122, 123, 124, 126, 127, 128, 129, 130, 131, 132, 133, 134, 135, 136, 137, 140, 141, 142, 143, 146, 147, 149, 150, 151, 152, 153, 154, 155, 156, 158, 160, 161, 162, 164, 165, 166, 167, 168, 169, 170, 171, 172, 173, 174, 175, 177, 178, 179, 180, 181, 182, 183, 184, 185, 186, 187, 188, 189, 190, 191, 193, 194, 195, 196, 197, 198, 199, 200, 203, 204, 205, 206, 208, 210, 211, 212, 213, 214; *qui,* 72; *quel,* 125; om., 74.

208   3, 5, 6, 7, 8, 9, 10, 13, 14, 15, 16, 19, 20, 21, 23, 26, 28, 29, 30, 31, 32, 33, 34, 36, 37, 38, 39, 41, 42, 43, 44, 45, 46, 48, 49, 51, 52, 53, 56, 57, 58, 59, 60, 61, 62, 63, 64, 65, 69, 71, 72, 73, 74, 75, 76, 77, 78, 79, 81, 82, 83, 84, 86, 87, 88, 89, 90, 92, 93, 96, 97, 98, 99, 100, 103, 104, 105, 107, 109, 110, 111, 112, 113, 115, 116, 117, 118, 119, 120, 121, 122, 123, 124, 125, 126, 127, 128, 129, 130, 131, 132, 133, 134, 135, 136, 137, 140, 141, 142, 143, 146, 147, 149, 150, 151, 152, 153, 154, 155, 156, 158, 160, 161, 162, 164, 165, 166, 167, 168, 169, 170, 171, 172, 173, 174, 175, 177, 178, 179, 180, 181, 182, 183, 184, 185, 186, 187, 188, 189, 190, 191, 193, 194, 195, 196, 197, 198, 199, 200, 203, 204, 205, 206, 208, 210, 211, 212, 213, 214; *supra,* 25.

209   3, 5, 6, 7, 8, 9, 10, 13, 14, 15, 16, 19, 20, 21, 23, 25, 26, 29, 30, 31, 32, 33, 34, 36, 37, 38, 39, 41, 42, 43, 44, 45, 46, 48, 49, 51, 52, 53, 56, 57, 58, 59, 60, 61, 62, 63, 64, 65, 69, 71, 72, 73, 74, 75, 76, 77, 78, 79, 81, 82, 83, 84, 86, 87, 88, 89, 90, 92, 93, 96, 97, 98, 99, 100, 103, 104, 105, 107, 109, 110, 111, 112, 113, 115, 116, 117, 118, 119, 120, 121, 122, 123, 124, 125, 126, 127, 128, 129, 130, 131, 132, 133, 134, 135, 136, 137, 140, 141, 142, 143, 146, 147, 149, 150, 151, 152, 153, 154, 155, 156, 158, 160, 161, 162, 164, 165, 166, 167, 168, 169, 170, 171, 172, 173, 174, 175, 177, 178, 179, 180, 181, 182, 183, 184, 185, 186, 187, 188, 189, 190, 191, 193, 194, 195, 196, 197, 198, 199, 200, 203, 204, 205, 206, 208, 210, 211, 212, 213, 214; om., 28.

210   3, 5, 6, 7, 8, 9, 10, 13, 14, 15, 16, 19, 20, 21, 23, 25, 26, 28, 29, 30, 31, 32, 33, 34, 36, 37, 38, 39, 41, 42, 43, 44, 45, 46, 48, 49, 51, 52, 53, 56, 57, 58, 59, 60, 61, 62, 63, 64, 65, 69, 71, 72, 73, 74, 75, 76, 77, 78, 79, 81, 82, 83, 84, 86, 87, 88, 89, 90, 92, 93, 96, 97, 98, 99, 100, 103, 104, 105, 107, 110, 111, 112, 113, 115, 116, 117, 118, 119, 120, 121, 122, 123, 124, 125, 126, 127, 128, 129, 130, 131, 132, 133, 134, 135, 136, 137, 140, 141, 142, 143, 146, 147, 149, 150, 151, 152, 153, 154, 155, 156, 158, 160, 161, 162, 164, 165, 166, 167, 168, 169, 170, 171, 172, 173, 174, 175, 177, 178, 179, 180, 181, 183, 184, 185, 186, 187, 188, 189, 190, 191, 193, 194, 195, 196, 197, 198, 199, 200, 203, 204, 205, 206, 208, 210, 211, 212, 213, 214; *placuiit* (corr. to *placuit*), 109; *pacuit,* 182.

211   3, 5, 6, 7, 8, 9, 10, 13, 14, 15, 16, 19, 20, 21, 23, 25, 26, 28, 29, 30, 31, 32, 33, 34, 36, 37, 38, 39, 41, 42, 43, 44, 45, 46, 48, 49, 51, 52, 53, 56, 57, 58, 59, 60, 61, 62, 63, 64, 65, 69, 71, 72, 73, 74, 75, 76, 77, 78, 79, 81, 82, 83, 84, 86, 87, 88, 89, 90, 92, 93, 96, 97, 98, 99, 100, 103, 104, 105, 107, 109, 111, 112, 113, 115, 116, 117, 118, 119, 120, 121, 122, 123, 124, 125, 126, 127, 128, 129, 130, 131, 132, 133, 134, 135, 136, 137, 140, 141, 142, 143, 146, 147, 149, 150, 151, 152, 153, 154, 156, 158, 160, 161, 162, 164, 165, 166, 167, 168, 169, 170, 171, 172, 173, 174, 175, 177, 178, 179, 180, 181, 182, 183, 184, 185, 186, 187, 188, 189, 190, 191, 193, 194, 195, 196, 197, 198, 199, 200, 203, 204, 205, 206, 208, 210, 211, 212, 213, 214; *sibi,* 110; *eum,* 155.

placuit[210] ei[211] [212] unde[213] inimicitiam[214] [218]procerum[215] et[216] filiorum suorum[217] [218]

[212..212] 3, 5, 6, 7, 10, 13, 14, 15, 16, 19, 20, 21, 23, 26, 28, 29, 30, 31, 32, 33, 34, 36, 37, 38, 39, 41, 42, 43, 44, 45, 46, 48, 49, 51, 52, 53, 57, 59, 60, 61, 62, 63, 64, 65, 69, 71, 72, 73, 74, 75, 76, 77, 78, 79, 81, 82, 83, 84, 86, 87, 88, 89, 90, 92, 93, 96, 97, 98, 99, 100, 103, 104, 105, 107, 109, 111, 112, 113, 115, 116, 117, 118, 119, 120, 121, 122, 123, 124, 125, 126, 127, 128, 129, 130, 131, 132, 133, 134, 135, 136, 137, 140, 141, 142, 143, 146, 147, 149, 150, 151, 152, 153, 154, 155, 156, 158, 160, 161, 162, 164, 165, 166, 167, 168, 169, 170, 171, 172, 173, 174, 175, 177, 178, 179, 180, 181, 182, 183, 184, 185, 186, 187, 188, 189, 190, 191, 193, 194, 195, 196, 197, 198, 199, 200, 203, 204, 206, 208, 210, 211, 212, 213, 214; *u. m. e. p.,* 8, 25, 110; *e. u. m. p.,* 56, 58, 205; *u. m. p.,* 9.

[213] 3, 5, 6, 8, 9, 10, 13, 14, 15, 16, 19, 20, 21, 23, 25, 26, 28, 29, 30, 31, 32, 33, 34, 36, 37, 38, 39, 41, 42, 43, 44, 45, 46, 48, 49, 51, 52, 53, 56, 57, 58, 59, 60, 61, 62, 63, 64, 65, 69, 71, 72, 73, 75, 76, 77, 78, 79, 81, 82, 83, 84, 86, 87, 88, 89, 90, 92, 93, 96, 97, 98, 99, 103, 104, 105, 107, 109, 110, 111, 112, 113, 115, 116, 117, 118, 119, 120, 121, 122, 123, 124, 125, 126, 127, 128, 129, 130, 131, 132, 133, 135, 136, 137, 140, 141, 142, 143, 146, 147, 149, 150, 151, 152, 153, 154, 156, 158, 160, 161, 162, 164, 165, 166, 167, 169, 170, 171, 172, 173, 174, 175, 177, 178, 179, 180, 181, 182, 183, 184, 185, 186, 187, 188, 189, 190, 191, 193, 194, 195, 196, 197, 198, 199, 200, 203, 204, 205, 206, 208, 210, 211, 212, 213, 214; *unde*/, 168; *et,* 7, 155; om., 74, 100, 134.

[214] 3, 5, 8, 10, 13, 14, 15, 16, 20, 30, 36, 37, 38, 39, 42, 43, 44, 45, 48, 49, 53, 56, 59, 61, 64, 69, 72, 75, 76, 77, 78, 79, 81, 83, 84, 87, 89, 92, 97, 99, 103, 105, 109, 110, 118, 119, 121, 122, 126, 127, 128, 130, 131, 132, 137, 141, 142, 151, 154, 160, 161, 167, 168, 169, 170, 171, 179, 180, 181, 183, 184, 185, 187, 188, 189, 190, 193, 196, 197, 199, 200, 204, 205, 208, 211, 212; *inimicicia,* 65; *inimi\ci/tiam,* 21; *imicitiam,* 166; *inimiciam,* 32, 123, 133, 165; *in inimiciam,* 62, 73, 210; *in/ inimicitiam,* 6, 93, 164, 177, 214; *in inimicitiam,* 7, 9, 19, 23, 25, 26, 28, 29, 31, 33, 34, 41, 46, 51, 52, 57, 58, 60, 63, 71, 74, 82, 86, 90, 96, 98, 104, 107, 111, 112, 113, 115, 117, 120, 124, 125, 129, 135, 136, 140, 143, 146, 147, 149, 150, 152, 153, 155, 156, 158, 162, 172, 173, 174, 175, 178, 182, 186, 191, 194, 195, 198, 203, 206, 212; *inimicicias,* 88, 116, 213; om., 100, 134.

[215] 3, 5, 6, 7, 8, 9, 10, 13, 14, 15, 16, 19, 20, 21, 23, 25, 26, 28, 29, 30, 31, 32, 33, 34, 36, 31, 38, 39, 41, 42, 43, 44, 46, 48, 49, 52, 53, 56, 57, 58, 59, 60, 61, 62, 63, 64, 65, 69, 71, 72, 73, 74, 75, 76, 77, 78, 79, 81, 82, 83, 84, 86, 87, 88, 89, 90, 92, 93, 96, 97, 98, 99, 103, 104, 105, 107, 109, 110, 111, 112, 113, 115, 116, 117, 118, 119, 120, 121, 122, 123, 124, 125, 126, 127, 128, 129, 130, 132, 133, 135, 136, 137, 140, 141, 142, 143, 146, 147, 149, 150, 151, 152, 153, 154, 155, 156, 158, 160, 161, 162, 164, 165, 166, 167, 168, 169, 170, 171, 172, 173, 174, 175, 177, 178, 179, 180, 181, 182, 183, 184, 185, 186, 187, 188, 189, 190, 191, 193, 194, 195, 196, 197, 198, 199, 200, 203, 204, 205, 206, 208, 210, 211, 212, 213, 214; *procerum suorum,* 45; *procerum suarum,* 131; *procerorum* 51; om., 100, 134.

[216] 3, 5, 7, 8, 10, 13, 14, 15, 16, 19, 20, 21, 23, 25, 26, 28, 29, 30, 31, 32, 33, 34, 36, 37, 38, 39, 41, 42, 43, 44, 45, 46, 48, 49, 51, 52, 53, 56, 57, 58, 59, 60, 61, 62, 63, 64, 65, 69, 71, 72, 73, 74, 75, 76, 77, 78, 79, 81, 82, 83, 84, 86, 87, 88, 89, 90, 92, 93, 96, 97, 98, 99, 103, 104, 105, 107, 111, 112, 113, 116, 117, 118, 119, 120, 121, 122, 123, 124, 125, 126, 127, 128, 129, 130, 131, 132, 133, 135, 136, 137, 140, 141, 142, 143, 146, 147, 149, 150, 151, 152, 153, 154, 155, 156, 155, 160, 161, 162, 164, 165, 166, 167, 168, 169, 170, 171, 172, 173, 174, 175, 177, 178, 179, 180, 181, 182, 183, 184, 185, 186, 187, 188, 189, 190, 191, 193, 194, 195, 196, 197, 198, 199, 200, 203, 204, 205, 206, 208, 210, 211, 212, 213, 214; om., 6, 9, 100, 109, 110, 115, 134.

[217] 3, 5, 6, 7, 8, 9, 10, 13, 14, 15, 16, 19, 20, 21, 23, 25, 26, 28, 29, 30, 31, 32, 33, 34, 36, 37, 38, 39, 41, 42, 43, 44, 45, 46, 48, 49, 51, 52, 53, 56, 57, 58, 59, 60, 61, 62, 63, 64, 65, 69, 71, 72, 73, 74, 75, 76, 77, 78, 79, 81, 82, 83, 84, 86, 87, 88, 89, 90, 92, 93, 96, 97, 98, 99, 103, 104, 105, 107, 109, 110, 111, 112, 113, 116, 117, 118, 119, 120, 121, 122, 123, 124,

[221]citissime[219] incidit.[220] [221] Generauerat[222] nanque[223] [228]filios[224] primitus[225] quibus[226]

125, 126, 127, 129, 130, 131, 132, 133, 135, 136, 137, 140, 141, 142, 143, 146, 147, 149, 150, 151, 152, 153, 154, 155, 156, 158, 160, 161, 162, 164, 165, 166, 167, 168, 169, 170, 171, 172, 173, 174, 175, 177, 178, 179, 180, 181, 182, 183, 184, 185, 186, 187, 188, 189, 190, 191, 193, 194, 195, 196, 197, 198, 199, 200, 203, 204, 205, 206, 208, 210, 211, 212, 213, 214; *suorumque,* 115; *suuorum,* 128; om., 100, 134, 156.

[218...218] 3, 5, 7, 10, 13, 14, 15, 16, 19, 20, 21, 23, 25, 26, 28, 30, 32, 33, 34, 36, 37, 38, 39, 43, 45, 48, 49, 51, 52, 56, 57, 58, 59, 60, 61, 63, 64, 65, 69, 71, 72, 73, 74, 75, 76, 77, 78, 79, 81, 82, 83, 84, 86, 87, 88, 89, 90, 92, 96, 97, 98, 99, 103, 104, 105, 107, 109, 111, 112, 115, 116, 117, 119, 120, 121, 122, 123, 124, 125, 126, 127, 128, 129, 130, 131, 133, 135, 136, 137, 141, 142, 146, 147, 149, 151, 152, 153, 154, 158, 160, 162, 164, 165, 166, 167, 168, 169, 170, 171, 172, 173, 174, 175, 177, 179, 180, 181, 182, 183, 184, 185, 186, 187, 188, 189, 190, 191, 193, 194, 195, 197, 198, 199, 200, 203, 204, 205, 206, 208, 210, 211, 213, 214; *p. s. et f.,* 53, 62, 143, 196; *f. et p. s.,* 29; *p. f. s. et,* 9; *p. et f.,* 8, 31, 41, 42, 44, 46, 93, 113, 118, 132, 140, 150, 156, 161, 178, 212; *p. et s. f.,* 155; *p. suorum filiorumque,* 6; *p. suorum,* 110; om., 100, 134.

[219] 3, 5, 6, 7, 9, 10, 13, 14, 15, 16, 19, 20, 21, 23, 26, 28, 30, 31, 32, 33, 34, 36, 37, 39, 41, 42, 43, 44, 45, 46, 48, 51, 52, 53, 56, 57, 58, 59, 60, 61, 62, 63, 64, 65, 69, 71, 72, 73, 74, 75, 76, 77, 78, 79, 82, 83, 84, 86, 87, 88, 90, 92, 96, 97, 98, 99, 103, 104, 105, 107, 109, 110, 111, 112, 113, 115, 116, 117, 118, 119, 120, 121, 122, 124, 125, 126, 127, 128, 129, 130, 131, 132, 133, 135, 136, 137, 140, 141, 142, 143, 146, 147, 149, 150, 151, 152, 153, 154, 155, 156, 158, 161, 162, 164, 165, 166, 167, 168, 169, 170, 171, 172, 173, 174, 175, 177, 178, 179, 180, 181, 182, 183, 184, 185, 186, 187, 188, 189, 190, 191, 193, 194, 195, 196, 197, 198, 199, 200, 203, 204, 205, 206, 208, 210, 211, 212, 213, 214; *certissime,* 89, 93, 123, 160; *ortissime,* 81; *festinanter,* 25; om., 8, 29, 38, 49, 100, 134.

[220] 3, 5, 6, 7, 9, 10, 13, 14, 15, 16, 19, 20, 21, 23, 25, 26, 28, 29, 30, 31, 32, 33, 34, 36, 37, 39, 41, 42, 43, 44, 45, 46, 48, 51, 52, 53, 56, 57, 58, 59, 60, 61, 62, 63, 64, 65, 69, 71, 72, 73, 74, 75, 76, 77, 78, 79, 81, 82, 83, 84, 86, 87, 88, 89, 90, 92, 93, 96, 97, 98, 99, 103, 104, 105, 107, 109, 110, 111, 112, 113, 115, 116, 117, 118, 119, 120, 121, 122, 123, 124, 125, 126, 127, 128, 129, 130, 132, 133, 135, 136, 137, 140, 141, 142, 143, 146, 147, 149, 150, 151, 152, 153, 154, 155, 156, 158, 160, 161, 162, 164, 165, 166, 167, 168, 169, 170, 171, 172, 173, 174, 175, 177, 178, 179, 180, 181, 182 183, 184, 185, 186, 187, 188, 189, 190, 191, 194, 195, 196, 197, 198, 199, 200, 203, 204, 205, 206, 208, 210, 211, 212, 213, 214; *incurrit,* 8, 38, 49; *incurrit uel incidit,* 131; *inuidit,* 193; om., 100, 134.

[221...221] 3, 5, 6, 7, 8, 9, 10, 13, 14, 15, 16, 19, 20, 21, 23, 25, 26, 28, 29, 30, 31, 32, 33, 34, 36, 37, 38, 39, 41, 42, 43, 44, 45, 46, 48, 49, 51, 52, 53, 56, 57, 58, 59, 60, 61, 62, 63, 64, 65, 69, 71, 72, 73, 74, 75, 76, 77, 78, 79, 81, 82, 83, 84, 86, 87, 88, 89, 90, 92, 93, 96, 97, 98, 99, 103, 104, 105, 107, 109, 110, 111, 112, 113, 115, 116, 117, 118, 119, 120, 121, 122, 123, 124, 125, 126, 127, 128, 129, 130, 131, 133, 135, 136, 137, 140, 141, 142, 143, 146, 147, 149, 150, 151, 152, 153, 154, 155, 156, 158, 160, 161, 162, 164, 165, 166, 167, 168, 169, 170, 171, 172, 173, 174, 175, 177, 178, 179, 180, 181, 182, 183, 184, 185, 186, 187, 188, 189, 190, 191, 193, 194, 195, 196, 197, 198, 199, 200, 203, 204, 205, 206, 208, 210, 211, 212, 213, 214; *i. c.,* 132; om. 100, 134.

[222] 5, 6, 7, 9, 10, 13, 15, 16, 19, 21, 23, 25, 26, 28, 29, 30, 31, 33, 34, 36, 37, 39, 42, 43, 44, 45, 46, 48, 51, 52, 53, 56, 57, 58, 59, 60, 61, 62, 63, 64, 69, 71, 72, 73, 74, 75, 76, 77, 78, 79, 81, 82, 83, 84, 86, 87, 88, 89, 90, 92, 93, 96, 97, 98, 100, 103, 104, 105, 107, 109, 111, 112, 113, 115, 116, 117, 118, 119, 120, 121, 123, 124, 125, 126, 127, 128, 130, 132, 133, 135, 136, 137, 140, 141, 142, 143, 146, 147, 149, 150, 151, 153, 154, 156, 158, 160, 161, 162, 164, 165, 166, 167, 168, 170, 171, 173, 174, 175, 177, 178, 179, 180, 181, 182, 183, 184, 185, 187, 188, 189, 190, 191, 193, 194, 195, 196, 198, 199, 200, 203, 204, 205, 206, 208, 210, 211, 212, 213, 214; *generauͭ,* 122; *generauit,* 8, 38, 41, 65, 99, 131, 134, 169;

erant[227] nomina[228] Uortimer,[229] [232]Katigernus,[230] Paschent.[231] [232] In[233] [234]tempore

gen.uerat, 110; *genuerat*, 3, 14, 20, 32, 152, 155; *generat*, 172, 197; *generaueuerat*, 186; *geneuit* (altered to *genauit*), 110; om., 129.

223 3, 5, 6, 8, 9, 10, 13, 14, 15, 16, 19, 20, 21, 23, 25, 26, 28, 29, 30, 31, 32, 33, 34, 36, 37, 38, 39, 41, 42, 43, 44, 45, 46, 48, 49, 51, 52, 53, 56, 57, 58, 59, 60, 61, 62, 63, 64, 65, 69, 71, 72, 73, 74, 76, 77, 78, 79, 81, 82, 83, 84, 86, 87, 89, 90, 92, 93, 96, 97, 98, 99, 100, 103, 104, 105, 107, 109, 110, 112, 113, 115, 117, 118, 119, 120, 121, 122, 123, 124, 125, 126, 127, 128, 130, 131, 132 133, 134, 136, 137, 140, 141, 142, 143, 146, 147, 149, 150, 151, 152, 153, 154, 156, 158, 160, 161, 162, 164, 165, 166, 167, 168, 169, 170, 171, 172, 173, 174, 175, 177, 178, 179, 180, 181, 182, 183, 184, 185, 186, 187, 188, 189, 190, 191, 193, 194, 195, 196, 197, 198, 199, 200, 203, 204, 205, 206, 208, 210, 211, 212, 213, 214; *autem*, 88, 116; *?enim*, 75, 111; om., 7, 129, 135, 155.

224 3, 5, 6, 7, 9, 13, 14, 15, 16, 19, 20, 21, 23, 25, 26, 29, 31, 33, 34, 36, 37, 38, 41, 42, 43, 44, 46, 48, 51, 52, 53, 56, 57, 58, 59, 60, 62, 63, 64, 65, 69, 71, 72, 73, 74, 75, 76, 77, 78, 79, 81, 82, 83, 84, 86, 87, 89, 90, 92, 93, 96, 97, 99, 103, 104, 105, 107, 110, 111, 112, 113, 115, 117, 118, 120, 121, 122, 124, 125, 126, 127, 128, 130, 131, 132, 135, 136, 137, 140, 143, 146, 147, 149, 150, 151, 152, 154, 155, 156, 158, 160, 161, 162, 164, 166, 167, 168, 169, 170, 171, 172, 173, 174, 175, 177, 178, 179, 180, 181, 182, 183, 184, 185, 186, 187, 188, 189, 190, 191, 193, 194, 195, 196, 197, 199, 200, 203, 204, 205, 206, 208, 210, 211, 212, 213, 214; *.iii. filios*, 8, 32, 39, 49, 109, 119, 165; *tres filios*, 10, 28, 30, 45, 61, 88, 98, 100, 116, 123, 133, 134, 141, 142, 153; *ex pelice tres filios*, 198; om., 129.

225 3, 5, 6, 7, 8, 9, 10, 13, 14, 15, 16, 19, 20, 21, 23, 25, 26, 28, 29, 30, 31, 32, 33, 34, 36, 37, 38, 39, 41, 42, 43, 44, 45, 46, 48, 49, 51, 52, 53, 56, 57, 58, 59, 60, 61, 62, 63, 65, 69, 71, 72, 73, 74, 75, 76, 77, 78, 79, 81, 82, 83, 84, 86, 87, 89, 90, 92, 93, 96, 97, 98, 99, 100, 103, 104, 105, 107, 109, 110, 112, 113, 115, 117, 118, 119, 120, 121, 122, 123, 124, 125, 126, 127, 128, 130, 131, 132, 133, 134, 135, 136, 137, 140, 141, 142, 143, 146, 147, 149, 150, 151, 152, 153, 154, 155, 156, 158, 160, 161, 162, 164, 165, 166, 167, 168, 169, 170, 171, 172, 173, 175, 177, 178, 179, 180, 181, 182, 183, 184, 185, 186, 187, 188, 189, 190, 191, 193, 194, 195, 196, 197, 198, 199, 200, 203, 204, 205, 206, 208, 210, 211, 212, 213, 214; *primitus \ex pelice tres*, 174; *prius*, 111; om., 64, 88, 116, 129.

226 3, 5, 6, 7, 8, 9, 10, 13, 14, 15, 16, 19, 20, 21, 23, 25, 26, 28, 29, 30, 31, 32, 33, 34, 36, 37, 38, 39, 41, 42, 43, 44, 45, 46, 48, 49, 51, 52, 53, 57, 59, 61, 63, 64, 65, 69, 71, 72, 73, 74, 75, 76, 77, 78, 79, 82, 83, 84, 86, 87, 88, 89, 90, 92, 93, 96, 97, 98, 99, 100, 103, 104, 105, 107, 109, 110, 111, 112, 113, 115, 116, 117, 118, 119, 120, 121, 122, 123, 124, 125, 126, 127, 128, 130, 131, 132, 133, 134, 135, 136, 137, 140, 141, 143, 146, 147, 149, 150, 151, 152, 153, 154, 155, 156, 158, 160, 161, 162, 164, 165, 166, 167, 168, 169, 170, 171, 172, 173, 174, 175, 177, 178, 179, 180, 181, 182, 183, 184, 185, 186, 187, 188, 189, 190, 191, 193, 194, 195, 196, 197, 198, 199, 200, 203, 204, 206, 208, 210, 211, 212, 213, 214; *quorum*, 56, 58, 205; *qui*, 81; *filios quibus*, 60; *ex alia coniuge quibus*, 142; *ex alia coniuge iam defuncta quibus*, 62; om., 129.

227 3, 5, 6, 7, 8, 9, 10, 13, 14, 15, 16, 19, 20, 21, 23, 25, 26, 28, 29, 30, 31, 32, 33, 34, 36, 37, 38, 39, 41, 42, 43, 44, 45, 46, 48, 49, 51, 52, 53, 57, 60, 61, 62, 63, 65, 69, 71, 72, 73, 74, 75, 76, 77, 78, 79, 81, 82, 83, 84, 86, 88, 89, 90, 92, 93, 96, 97, 98, 99, 100, 103, 104, 105, 107, 110, 111, 112, 113, 115, 116, 117, 118, 119, 120, 121, 122, 123, 124, 125, 126, 127, 128, 130, 131, 132, 133, 134, 135, 136, 137, 140, 141, 142, 143, 146, 147, 149, 150, 151, 152, 153, 154, 155, 156, 158, 160, 161, 162, 164, 165, 166, 167, 168, 169, 170, 171, 172, 173, 174, 175, 177, 178, 179, 180, 181, 182, 183, 184, 185, 186, 187, 188, 189, 190, 191, 193, 194, 195, 196, 197, 198, 199, 200, 203, 204, 206, 208, 210, 211, 212, 213, 214; *hec erant*, 59, 64, 87; *erat*, 109; om., 56, 58, 129, 205.

228...228 3, 5, 6, 7, 8, 9, 10, 13, 14, 15, 16, 19, 20, 21, 23, 25, 26, 28, 29, 30, 31, 32, 33, 34, 36, 37, 38, 39, 41, 42, 43, 44, 45, 46, 48, 49, 51, 52, 53, 56, 57, 58, 59, 61, 62, 63, 64, 65, 69,

71, 72, 73, 74, 75, 76, 77, 78, 79, 81, 82, 83, 84, 86, 88, 89, 90, 92, 93, 96, 97, 98, 99, 100, 103, 104, 107, 109, 110, 111, 112, 113, 115, 116, 117, 118, 119, 120, 121, 122, 123, 124, 125, 126, 127, 128, 130, 131, 132, 133, 134, 135, 136, 137, 140, 141, 142, 143, 146, 147, 149, 150, 151, 152, 153, 154, 155, 156, 158, 160, 161, 162, 164, 165, 166, 167, 168, 169, 170, 171, 172, 173, 174, 175, 177, 178, 179, 180, 181, 182, 183, 184, 185, 187, 188, 189, 190, 191, 193, 194, 195, 197, 198, 199, 200, 203, 204, 205, 206, 208, 210, 211, 212; *p. f. q. e. n.*, 60, 87, 186, 196; *p. f. e. n. q.*, 105, 213, 214; *p. f. q. e.* \n./, 33; om., 129.

229   5, 8, 9, 10, 13, 15, 16, 19, 21, 23, 25, 26, 29, 30, 31, 32, 33, 34, 37, 38, 39, 41, 42, 43, 45, 46, 48, 49, 52, 53, 56, 57, 58, 60, 61, 63, 64, 65, 69, 71, 73, 74, 76, 77, 79, 82, 84, 86, 87, 89, 90, 92, 93, 96, 97, 103, 111, 112, 113, 115, 118, 119, 120, 121, 122, 123, 124, 125, 127, 128, 130, 131, 132, 136, 137, 140, 141, 143, 146, 149, 150, 152; *Ueltimerius*, 171; *Uolcimer*, 183; *Uoltimer*, 81; *Uoltimerius*, 184, 189; *Uorcimer*, 36, 83, 151, 173; *Uortauer.*, 172; *Uortiger*, 98; *Uortigerimus*, 110; *Uortimer.*, 51, 78, 133, 214; *Uortimerius*, 20, 28, 72, 75, 100, 104, 109, 126, 134, 135, 142, 147, 166, 205, 206, 213; *Uortimerus*, 7, 88, 105, 116, 161; *Uortimor*, 107; *Uortiner*, 99; *Uortumer*, 117; *Uortymer*, 59; *Uotimer*, 199, 211; *Wltimerius*, 168; *Woltimerius*, 3, 14; *Worcimer*, 182; *Woremer*, 180; *Wortimer*, 6, 62, 181, 210; *uidelicet U.*, 142; om., 129.

230   9, 15, 29, 39, 42, 48, 77, 79, 81, 86, 89, 105, 107, 120, 128, 136, 147, 152, 160, 165, 170, 199, 200, 203, 204, 214; *Cantigern*, 45; *Carigern*, 74; *Carthgernus*, 7; *Cartigern*, 99; *Castigern*, 21; *Castigernus*, 16, 109, 211; *Catigern*, 8, 30, 61, 123, 141; *Catigernus*, 28, 100, 134; *Catingernus*, 10; *Kaertigern*, 168; *Kaetigern*, 182; *Kangern*, 150; *Kantegern*, 93; *Kantiger*, 64; *Kantigern*, 143; *Karcartigernus*, 13, 117, 167; *Karkartigem*, 190; *Karkartigern*, 33, 69, 76, 82, 97, 104, 115, 124, 172, 191, 195, 197; *Karkartigern* (altered to *Kartigern*), 92; *Karkartinger*, 84; *Karkatigen*, 186; *Karkatigern*, 169, 194; *Karkatigernus*, 213; *Karkertigern*, 6; *Kartartigernus*, 188; *Kartigem*, 174; *Kartigen*, 53, 130, 137, 175, 193; *Kartigerii*, 56, 205; *Kartigerin* 37; *Kartigern*, 26, 28, 38, 51, 57, 58, 62, 65, 121, 122, 131, 162, 179, 184, 189, 198, 208, 212; *Kartigernus*, 3, 14, 75, 88, 110, 116, 135, 155; *Kartirgen*, 20, 83, 126, 151, 173; *Kartirgern*, 36; *Karugen*, 196; *Kategern*, 46; *Katergerus*, 187; *Kathigernus*, 78; *Katigebus*, 133; *Katigen*, 5, 34, 90, 112, 118, 137, 152; *Katigern*, 19, 23, (24,) 25, 31, 32, 41, 43, 44, 49, 52, 63, 71, 72, 73, 87, 96, 98, 103, 113, 125, 127, 132, 140, 146, 149, 153, 154, 156, 158, 161, 164, 171, 177, 178, 181, 183, 185; *Katigren*, 210; *Rartirgen*, 166; *Ratigen*, 111; , *Ratigernus*, 206; *Gaugern*, 119; *Gaugernus*, 142; *Iabin*, 60; *Iabyn* 59; *Worthigrin*, 180; om., 129.

231   6, 7, 8, 9, 10, 19, 25, 29, 30, 31, 32, 33, 36, 41, 43, 44, 45, 46, 48, 49, 52, 53, 57, 61, 62, 64, 65, 69, 72, 73, 74, 76, 77, 78, 79, 82, 84, 86, 87, 88, 92, 93, 98, 99, 107, 111, 113, 115, 116, 119, 120, 121, 123, 124, 125, 127, 130, 135, 136, 140, 141, 143, 149, 150, 153, 154, 155, 156, 161, 162, 164, 165, 167, 168, 169, 170, 171, 172, 173, 174, 177, 178, 180, 182, 183, 184, 185, 187, 189, 190, 191, 193, 194, 195, 197, 198, 200, 203, 205, 206, 208, 210, 212; *Paaschet.*, 37; *Pacencius*/, 128; *Pacetius*, 186; *Pachent*, 26, 196; *Parcentius*, 75; *Pascent*, 63, 81; *Pascentius*, 20, 42, 71, 83, 89, 104, ?166; *Paschen.*, 99; *Paschen*, 5, 23, 24, 34, 38, 56, 58, 90, 96, 103, 112, 118, 122, 131, 137, 146, 151, 152, 175; *Paschencius*, 28, 100, 105, 133, 204; *Paschencus*, 214; *Pasc\h/ent*, 15, 179; *Paschentius*, 110, 117, 126, 134, 147, 158, 181, 188, 213; *Paschentus*, 3, 14; *Pashentius*, 109; *Paschet*, 199; *Poschen*, 132; *et/ Pascentsius*, 51; *et Paschencius*, 142, 160; *et Paschent*, 97; *et Paschentius*, 13; *et Goman* 59, 60; *Paschent uel*, 39; om., 16, 21, 129, 211.

232...232   3, 5, 6, 7, 8, 9, 10, 13, 14, 15, 16, 19, 20, 21, 23, 25, 26, 28, 29, 30, 31, 32, 33, 34, 36, 37, 38, 39, 41, 42, 43, 44, 45, 46, 48, 49, 51, 52, 53, 57, 59, 60, 61, 62, 63, 64, 65, 69, 71, 72, 73, 74, 75, 76, 77, 78, 79, 81, 82, 83, 84, 86, 87, 88, 89, 90, 92, 93, 96, 97, 98, 99, 100, 103, 104, 105, 107, 109, 110, 111, 112, 113, 115, 116, 117, 118, 119, 120, 121, 122, 123, 124, 125, 126, 127, 128, 129, 130, 131, 132, 133, 134, 135, 136, 137, 140, 141, 142, 143, 146, 147, 149, 150, 151, 152, 153, 154, 155, 156, 158, 160, 161, 162, 164, 165, 166, 167, 168, 169, 170, 171, 172, 173, 174, 175, 177, 178, 179, 180, 181, 182, 183, 184, 185, 186,

illo[234] [238]uenit[235] sanctus[236] Germanus[237] [238] [240]Altissiodorensis[239] episcopus[240] et[241]

187, 188, 189, 190, 191, 193, 194, 195, 196, 197, 198, 199, 200, 203, 204, 206, 208, 210, 211, 212, 213, 214; *P. K.*, 56, 58, 205.

233   3, 5, 6, 7, 8, 9, 10, 13, 14, 15, 16, 19, 20, 21, 23, 25, 26, 28, 29, 30, 31, 32, 33, 34, 36, 37, 38, 39, 41, 42, 43, 44, 45, 46, 48, 49, 51, 52, 53, 56, 57, 58, 59, 60, 62, 63, 64, 65, 69, 71, 72, 73, 74, 75, 76, 77, 78, 79, 81, 82, 83, 84, 86, 87, 88, 89, 90, 92, 93, 96, 97, 98, 99, 100, 103, 104, 105, 107, 109, 110, 111, 112, 113, 115, 116, 117, 118, 119, 120, 121, 122, 123, 124, 125, 126, 127, 128, 129, 130, 131, 132, 133, 134, 135, 136, 137, 140, 141, 142, 143, 146, 147, 149, 150, 151, 152, 153, 154, 155, 156, 158, 160, 161, 162, 164, 165, 166, 167, 168, 169, 170, 171, 172, 173, 174, 175, 177, 178, 179, 180, 181, 182, 183, 184, 185, 186, 187, 188, 189, 190, 191, 193, 194, 195, 196, 197, 198, 199, 200, 203, 204, 205, 206, 208, 210, 211, 212, 213, 214; om., 61.

234...234   3, 5, 6, 7, 9, 10, 13, 14, 15, 16, 19, 23, 25, 30, 31, 32, 33, 34, 36, 37, 38, 41, 43, 44, 45, 46, 48, 49, 52, 53, 57, 59, 60, 61, 62, 63, 64, 65, 69, 71, 72, 73, 74, 75, 76, 77, 78, 79, 81, 82, 83, 86, 87, 88, 89, 90, 92, 93, 96, 97, 98, 99, 103, 104, 105, 107, 109, 110, 111, 112, 113, 115, 117, 118, 119, 120, 121, 122, 123, 125, 126, 127, 128, 129, 130, 131, 132, 133, 135, 136, 137, 140, 141, 142, 143, 146, 147, 149, 150, 151, 152, 154, 155, 156, 158, 160, 161, 162, 164, 165, 166, 167, 168, 170, 171, 172, 173, 174, 175, 177, 178, 179, 180, 181, 182, 183, 184, 186, 187, 188, 189, 190, 191, 193, 195, 197, 198, 200, 203, 204, 206, 208, 210, 211, 212, 213, 214; *i. t.,* 8, 20, 21, 26, 28, 29, 39, 42, 51, 56, 58, 84, 100, 116, 124, 134, 153, 185, 194, 196, 199, 205; *t. autem* (canc.) *illo,* 169.

235   3, 5, 6, 7, 8, 9, 10, 13, 14, 15, 16, 19, 20, 21, 23, 25, 26, 28, 29, 30, 31, 32, 33, 34, 36, 37, 38, 39, 41, 42, 43, 44, 45, 46, 48, 49, 51, 52, 53, 56, 57, 58, 59, 60, 61, 62, 63, 64, 65, 69, 71, 72, 73, 74, 75, 76, 77, 79, 81, 82, 83, 84, 86, 87, 88, 89, 90, 92, 93, 96, 97, 98, 99, 100, 103, 105, 107, 109, 110, 111, 112, 113, 115, 116, 117, 118, 120, 121, 122, 123, 124, 125, 126, 127, 128, 129, 130, 131, 132, 133, 134, 135, 136, 137, 140, 141, 142, 143, 146, 147, 149, 150, 151, 152, 153, 154, 155, 156, 158, 160, 161, 162, 164, 165, 166, 167, 168, 169, 170, 171, 172, 173, 174, 175, 177, 178, 179, 180, 181, 182, 183, 184, 185, 186, 187, 188, 189, 190, 191, 193, 194, 195, 196, 197, 198, 199, 200, 203, 204, 205, 206, 208, 210, 211, 212, 213, 214; *uero ut,* 119; *fuit et uenit,* 78, 104.

236   3, 5, 6, 7, 8, 9, 10, 13, 14, 15, 16, 19, 20, 21, 23, 25, 26, 28, 29, 30, 31, 32, 33, 34, 36, 37, 38, 39, 41, 42, 43, 44, 45, 46, 48, 49, 51, 52, 53, 56, 57, 58, 59, 60, 61, 62, 63, 65, 69, 71, 72, 73, 74, 75, 76, 77, 78, 79, 81, 82, 83, 84, 86, 87, 88, 89, 90, 92, 93, 96, 97, 98, 99, 100, 103, 104, 105, 107, 109, 110, 111, 112, 113, 115, 116, 117, 118, 119, 120, 121, 122, 123, 124, 125, 126, 127, 129, 130, 131, 132, 133, 134, 135, 136, 137, 140, 141, 142, 143, 146, 147, 149, 150, 151, 152, 153, 154, 155, 156, 158, 160, 161, 162, 164, 165, 166, 167, 168, 169, 170, 171, 172, 173, 174, 175, 177, 178, 179, 180, 181, 182, 183, 184, 185, 186, 187, 188, 189, 190, 191, 193, 194, 195, 196, 197, 198, 199, 200, 203, 204, 205, 206, 208, 210, 211, 212, 213, 214; om., 64, 128.

237   3, 5, 6, 7, 8, 9, 10, 13, 14, 15, 16, 19, 20, 21, 23, 25, 26, 28, 29, 30, 31, 32, 33, 34, 36, 37, 38, 39, 41, 42, 43, 44, 45, 46, 48, 49, 51, 52, 53, 56, 57, 58, 59, 60, 61, 62, 63, 64, 65, 69, 71, 72, 73, 74, 75, 76, 77, 78, 79, 82, 83, 84, 86, 87, 88, 89, 90, 92, 93, 96, 97, 98, 99, 100, 103, 104, 105, 107, 109, 111, 112, 113, 115, 116, 117, 118, 119, 120, 121, 122, 123, 124, 125, 126, 127, 128, 129, 130, 131, 132, 133, 134, 135, 136, 137, 140, 141, 142, 143, 146, 147, 149, 150, 151, 152, 153, 154, 155, 156, 158, 160, 161, 162, 164, 165, 166, 167, 168, 169, 170, 171, 172, 173, 174, 175, 177, 178, 179, 180, 181, 182, 183, 184, 185, 186, 187, 188, 189, 190, 191, 193, 194, 195, 196, 197, 198, 199, 200, 203, 204, 205, 206, 208, 210, 211, 212, 213, 214; *Jermanus,* 81; *Iermannus,* 110.

238...238   3, 5, 6, 7, 8, 9, 10, 13, 14, 15, 16, 19, 20, 21, 23, 25, 26, 28, 29, 30, 31, 32, 33, 34, 36, 37, 38, 39, 41, 42, 43, 44, 45, 46, 48, 49, 51, 52, 53, 56, 57, 58, 59, 60, 61, 62, 63, 64, 65, 69, 71, 72, 73, 74, 75, 76, 77, 78, 79, 81, 82, 83, 84, 86, 87, 88, 89, 90, 92, 93, 96, 97, 98,

Lupus[242] Trecacensis[243] ut uerbum Dei[244] [246]Britonibus predicarent.[245] [246] Corrupta

99, 103, 104, 105, 107, 109, 110, 111, 112, 113, 115, 116, 117, 118, 119, 120, 121, 122, 123, 124, 125, 126, 127, 128, 129, 130, 131, 132, 133, 135, 136, 137, 140, 141, 142, 143, 146, 147, 149, 150, 151, 152, 153, 154, 155, 156, 158, 160, 161, 162, 164, 165, 166, 167, 168, 169, 170, 171, 172, 173, 174, 175, 177, 178, 179, 180, 181, 182, 183, 184, 185, 186, 187, 188, 189, 190, 191, 193, 194, 195, 196, 197, 198, 199, 200, 203, 204, 205, 206, 208, 210, 211, 212, 213, 214; *s. G. u.*, 100, 134.

[239] 5, 7, 8, 10, 15, 16, 19, 26, 29, 33, 37, 43, 44, 46, 51, 52, 60, 63, 65, 71, 77, 89, 98, 99, 103, 109, 110, 115, 120, 130, 135, 136, 142, 146, 155, 156, 161, 170, 174, 179, 180, 181, 185, 195, 196, 199, 203, 204, 210, 212; *Alti\diosi/ensis,* 36; *Altiodorensis,* 74; *Altisiodorensi,* 206; *Altisiodorensis,* 6, 28, 30, 45, 48, 49, 53, 57, 61, 64, 73, 78, 79, 82, 92, 97, 105, 107, 111, 119, 122, 123, 125, 141, 151, 158, 160, 162, 165, 169, 172, 173, 175, 191, 197, 198, 211, 214; *Altisiodornensis,* 100; *Altisiodronensis,* 32; *Anthisiodorensis,* 13, 171; (corr. to *Authisiodorensis),* 182; *Antisiodorensis,* 153, 190; *Antisodorensis,* 3, 41, 72, 76, 132, 133, 134; *Astissiodorensis,* 177; *Authisiodorensis,* 167; *Autidiodorensis* (altered to *Autisiodorensis),* 178; *Autisidiorensis,* 87; *Autisiodorensis,* 9, 14, 20, 21, 23, 25, 31, 34, 38, 39, 56, 58, 59, 62, 69, 75, 81, 84, 88, 90, 93, 112, 113, 116, 117, 118, 121, 124, 126, 127, 128, 129, 131, 137, 140, 143, 147, 149, 150, 152, 154, 164, 166, 168, 183, 184, 186, 187, 188, 189, 193, 194, 200, 205, 208, 213; *Autisidorensis,* 87; *Autisiodoriensis,* 96; *Autissiodorensis,* 42, 83, 86, 104; *Dorensis,* 78.

[240...240] 3, 5, 6, 7, 8, 9, 10, 14, 15, 16, 19, 20, 21, 23, 25, 26, 28, 29, 30, 31, 32, 33, 34, 36, 37, 38, 39, 41, 42, 43, 44, 45, 46, 48, 49, 51, 52, 53, 56, 57, 58, 59, 60, 61, 62, 63, 64, 65, 69, 71, 72, 73, 74, 75, 76, 77, 79, 81, 82, 83, 84, 86, 87, 88, 89, 90, 92, 93, 96, 97, 98, 99, 100, 103, 104, 105, 107, 109, 110, 111, 112, 113, 115, 116, 118, 119, 120, 121, 122, 123, 124, 125, 126, 127, 128, 130, 131, 132, 133, 134, 135, 136, 137, 140, 141, 142, 143, 146, 147, 149, 150, 151, 152, 153, 154, 155, 156, 158, 160, 161, 162, 164, 165, 166, 168, 169, 170, 171, 172, 173, 174, 175, 177, 178, 179, 180, 181, 182, 183, 184, 185, 186, 187, 189, 190, 191, 193, 194, 195, 196, 197, 198, 199, 200, 203, 204, 205, 206, 208, 210, 211, 212, 213, 214; *e. A.,* 78, 117, 188, 199; *A.,* 13, 129, 167.

[241] 3, 5, 6, 7, 8, 9, 10, 13, 14, 15, 16, 19, 20, 21, 23, 25, 26, 28, 29, 30, 31, 32, 33, 34, 36, 37, 38, 39, 41, 42, 43, 44, 45, 46, 48, 49, 51, 52, 53, 56, 57, 58, 59, 60, 61, 62, 63, 64, 65, 69, 71, 72, 73, 74, 75, 76, 77, 78, 79, 81, 82, 83, 84, 86, 87, 88, 89, 90, 92, 93, 96, 97, 98, 99, 100, 103, 104, 105, 107, 109, 110, 111, 112, 113, 116, 117, 118, 119, 120, 121, 122, 123, 124, 125, 126, 127, 128, 129, 130, 131, 132, 133, 134, 135, 136, 137, 140, 141, 142, 143, 146, 147, 149, 150, 151, 152, 153, 154, 155, 156, 158, 160, 161, 162, 164, 165, 166, 167, 168, 169, 170, 171, 172, 173, 174, 175, 177, 178, 179, 180, 181, 182, 183, 184, 185, 186, 187, 188, 189, 190, 191, 193, 194, 195, 196, 197, 198, 199, 200, 203, 204, 205, 206, 208, 210, 211, 212, 213, 214; \et/, 115.

[242] 3, 5, 6, 7, 8, 9, 10, 13, 14, 15, 16, 19, 20, 23, 25, 26, 28, 29, 30, 31, 32, 33, 34, 36, 37, 39, 41, 42, 43, 44, 45, 46, 48, 49, 51, 52, 53, 56, 57, 58, 59, 60, 61, 62, 63, 64, 65, 69, 71, 72, 73, 75, 76, 77, 78, 79, 81, 82, 83, 84, 86, 88, 89, 90, 92, 93, 96, 97, 98, 99, 100, 103, 104, 105, 107, 109, 110, 111, 112, 113, 115, 116, 117, 118, 119, 120, 121, 122, 123, 124, 125, 126, 127, 128, 129, 130, 131, 132, 133, 134, 135, 136, 137, 140, 141, 142, 143, 146, 147, 149, 150, 151, 152, 153, 154, 155, 156, 158, 160, 161, 162, 164, 165, 166, 167, 168, 169, 170, 171, 172, 173, 175, 177, 178, 179, 180, 181, 182, 183 184 185, 186, 187, 188, 189, 190, 191, 193, 194, 195, 196, 197, 198, 199, 200, 203, 204, 205, 206, 208, 210, 211, 212, 213, 214; \Lu/pus, 74; *sanctus Lupus,* 21, 38, 87; om., 174.

[243] 5, 6, 7, 8, 15, 16, 19, 21, 26, 28, 29, 30, 31, 32, 33, 34, 37, 38, 39, 43, 44, 46, 48, 49, 51, 57, 59, 60, 61, 62, 63, 65, 71, 73, 75, 76, 77, 78, 81, 86, 86, 89, 90, 92, 93, 97, 98, 99, 100, 103, 105, 109, 111, 112, 113, 115, 117, 120, 121, 122, 123, 125, 126, 128, 130, 131, 132, 134, 135, 137, 140, 141, 142, 146, 149, 150, 152, 154, 155, 156, 160, 161, 162, 164, 165,

[249]namque fuerat[247] christianitas eorum[248] [249] tum[250] propter[251] paganos[252] tum[253]

167, 168, 170, 171, 172, 174, 177, 178, 179, 180, 181, 182, 183, 184, 185, 186, 187, 188, 189, 190, 191, 193, 194, 197, 198, 199, 200, 203, 206, 210, 211, 212, 213, 214; *Crecacensis*, 119; *Cretacensis*, 45, 84, 118; *Tecracanensis*, 10; *Tercasesis*, 41; *Terracensis*, ?107, 136; *Tetracensis*, 69, 195; *Thecasensis*, 204; *Tracacensis*, 53, 104, 116, 169; *Tracensis*, 196; *Treacensis*, 36, 151, 173; *Treacensis* (altered to *Treccensis*), 175; *Treacensis* (altered to *Trecensis*), 83; *Tre\c\acensis*, 79; *Trecacencis*, 74; *Trecarensis*, 82; *Trecascensis*, 9, 143; *Trecasensis*, 13, 42, 64, 87, 158, *Trecassensis*, 52; *Trecassinus*, 129; *Trecatensis*, 124; *Trecensis*, 20, 23, 56, 58, 96, 127, 166, 205, 208; *Treracensis*, 153; *Tretasensis*, 147; *Trecasensis episcopus*, 25; *Trecatensis episcopus*, 72; *Trecensis episcopus*, 110; *Trechacensis episcopus*, 3, 14; *Treu'ensis episcopus*, 133.

[244] 3, 5, 6, 7, 8, 9, 10, 13, 14, 15, 16, 19, 20, 21, 23, 25, 26, 28, 29, 30, 31, 32, 33, 34, 36, 37, 38, 39, 41, 42, 43, 44, 45, 46, 48, 49, 51, 52, 53, 56, 57, 58, 59, 60, 61, 62, 63, 64, 65, 69, 71, 72, 73, 74, 75, 76, 77, 78, 79, 81, 82, 83, 84, 86, 87, 88, 89, 90, 92, 93, 96, 97, 98, 99, 100, 103, 104, 105, 107, 109, 110, 111, 112, 113, 115, 116, 117, 118, 120, 121, 122, 123, 124, 125, 126, 127, 128, 129, 130, 131, 132, 133, 134, 135, 136, 137, 140, 141, 142, 143, 146, 147, 149, 150, 151, 152, 153, 154, 155, 156, 158, 160, 161, 162, 164, 165, 166, 167, 168, 169, 170, 171, 172, 173, 174, 175, 177, 178, 179, 180, 181, 182, 183, 184, 185, 186, 187, 188, 189, 190, 191, 193, 194, 195, 196, 197, 198, 199, 200, 203, 204, 205, 206, 208, 210, 211, 212, 213, 214; *dicitur Dei*, 119.

[245] 3, 5, 6, 7, 8, 9, 10, 13, 14, 15, 16, 19, 20, 21, 23, 25, 26, 29, 30, 31, 32, 33, 34, 36, 37, 38, 39, 41, 42, 43, 44, 45, 46, 48, 49, 51, 52, 53, 56, 57, 58, 59, 60, 61, 62, 63, 64, 65, 69, 71, 72, 73, 74, 75, 76, 77, 78, 79, 81, 82, 83, 84, 86, 87, 88, 89, 90, 92, 93, 96, 97, 98, 99, 100, 103, 104, 105, 107, 109, 110, 111, 112, 113, 115, 116, 117, 118, 119, 120, 121, 122, 123, 124, 126, 127, 128, 129, 130, 131, 132, 133, 134, 135, 136, 137, 140, 141, 142, 143, 146, 147, 149, 150, 151, 152, 153, 154, 156, 158, 160, 161, 162, 164, 165, 166, 167, 168, 170, 171, 172, 173, 174, 175, 177, 178, 179, 181, 182, 183, 184, 185, 186, 187, 188, 189, 190, 191, 193, 194, 195, 196, 197, 198, 199, 200, 203, 204, 205, 206, 208, 210, 211, 212, 213, 214; *predicaret*, 125, 155, 180; *predirent*, 28; *nuntiarent* (glossed *predicarent*), 169.

[246...246] 3, 5, 6, 7, 8, 9, 10, 13, 14, 15, 16, 19, 20, 21, 23, 25, 26, 28, 29, 30, 31, 33, 34, 36, 38, 39, 41, 42, 43, 44, 45, 46, 48, 49, 51, 52, 53, 56, 58, 59, 60, 62, 63, 64, 69, 71, 72, 73, 74, 75, 76, 77, 78, 79, 81, 82, 83, 84, 86, 87, 88, 89, 90, 92, 93, 96, 97, 98, 99, 100, 103, 104, 105, 107, 109, 110, 111, 112, 113, 115, 116, 117, 118, 119, 120, 121, 122, 123, 124, 125, 126, 127, 128, 129, 130, 131, 132, 133, 134, 135, 136, 137, 140, 141, 142, 143, 146, 147, 149, 150, 151, 152, 153, 154, 155, 156, 158, 160, 161, 162, 164, 165, 166, 167, 168, 169, 170, 171, 172, 173, 174, 175, 177, 178, 179, 180, 181, 182, 183, 184, 185, 186, 187, 188, 189, 190, 191, 193, 194, 195, 196, 197, 198, 199, 200, 203, 204, 205, 206, 208, 210, 211, 212, 213, 214; *p. B.*, 32, 37, 57, 61, 65.

[247] 3, 5, 6, 7, 9, 10, 13, 14, 15, 16, 19, 20, 23, 25, 26, 28, 29, 30, 31, 32, 33, 34, 37, 38, 39, 41, 42, 43, 44, 46, 48, 49, 51, 52, 53, 57, 59, 60, 61, 62, 63, 65, 69, 71, 72, 73, 74, 76, 77, 78, 81, 82, 83, 84, 86, 87, 88, 89, 92, 93, 96, 97, 98, 99, 100, 103, 104, 107, 109, 111, 112, 113, 115, 116, 117, 118, 119, 120, 121, 123, 124, 125, 126, 127, 128, 129, 130, 131, 132, 133, 134, 135, 136, 137, 140, 141, 142, 143, 146, 147, 149, 150, 151, 152, 153, 154, 155, 156, 158, 160, 161, 162, 164, 165, 166, 167, 168, 169, 170, 171, 172, 173, 174, 175, 177, 178, 179, 180, 181, 182, 183, 184, 185, 186, 187, 188, 189, 190, 191, 193, 194, 195, 197, 198, 199, 200, 203, 204, 206, 208, 210, 211, 212, 213; *fu.*, 8, 110; *fuit*, 21, 45, 56, 58, 64, 105, 122, 205, 214; *fierat*, 36; *erat*, 75, 196; *fuerat/, 79; om., 90.

[248] 3, 5, 6, 7, 8, 9, 10, 13, 14, 15, 16, 19, 20, 21, 23, 25, 26, 28, 30, 31, 32, 33, 34, 37, 38, 39, 41, 42, 43, 44, 45, 46, 48, 49, 51, 52, 53, 56, 57, 58, 59, 60, 61, 62, 63, 64, 65, 69, 71, 72, 73, 74, 75, 76, 77, 78, 79, 81, 82, 83, 84, 86, 87, 88, 89, 90, 92, 93, 96, 97, 98, 99, 100, 103, 104, 105, 107, 109, 110, 111, 112, 113, 115, 116, 117, 118, 119, 120, 121, 122, 123,

124, 125, 126, 127, 128, 129, 130, 131, 132, 133, 134, 135, 136, 137, 140, 141, 142, 143, 146, 149, 150, 151, 152, 153, 154, 155, 156, 158, 160, 161, 162, 164, 165, 166, 167, 168, 169, 170, 171, 172, 173, 174, 175, 177, 178, 179, 180, 181, 182, 183, 184, 185, 186, 187, 188, 189, 191, 193, 194, 195, 196, 197, 198, 199, 200, 203, 204, 205, 206, 208, 210, 211, 212, 213, 214; *ipsorum,* 29, 36, 190; om., 147, 173.

249...249   3, 5, 6, 7, 8, 9, 13, 14, 15, 16, 19, 20, 21, 23, 25, 26, 28, 29, 30, 31, 32, 33, 34, 36, 37, 38, 39, 41, 42, 43, 44, 45, 46, 48, 49, 51, 52, 53, 56, 57, 58, 59, 60, 61, 62, 63, 65, 69, 71, 72, 73, 74, 75, J6, 77, 78, 79, 81, 82, 83, 84, 86, 87, 88, 89, 90, 92, 93, 96, 97, 98, 99, 100, 103, 104, 105, 107, 109, 110, 111,112, 113, 115, 116, 117, 118, 119, 120, 121, 122, 123, 124, 125, 126, 127, 128, 129, 130, 131, 132, 133, 134, 135, 136, 137, 140, 141, 142, 143, 146, 147, 149, 150, 151, 152, 153, 154, 155, 156, 158, 160, 161, 162, 164, 165, 166, 167, 168, 169, 170, 171, 172, 173, 174, 175, 177, 178, 179, 180, 181, 182, 183, 184, 185, 186, 187, 188, 189, 191, 193, 194, 195, 196, 197, 198, 199, 200, 203, 204, 205, 206, 208, 210, 211, 212, 213, 214; *n. C. e. f.,* 10; *F. n. C. e.,* 64, 190.

250   6, 7, 8, 9, 10, 13, 15, 16, 19, 21, 23, 25, 26, 28, 29, 30, 31, 32, 33, 34, 36, 37, 38, 39, 42, 43, 44, 46, 48, 49, 51, 52, 53, 56, 57, 58, 59, 60, 61, 62, 63, 64, 65, 69, 71, 72, 73, 74, 75, 76, 78, 79, 82, 83, 84, 86, 87, 88, 89, 90, 92, 93, 96, 97, 98, 99, 100, 103, 104, 105, 107, 109, 110, 111, 112, 113, 115, 117, 118, 120, 121, 122, 123, 124, 125, 126, 127, 128, 129, 131, 132, 133, 134, 135, 136, 137, 140, 141, 142, 143, 146, 147, 150, 152, 153, 154, 155, 156, 158, 160, 161, 162, 164, 165, 166, 167, 169, 170, 171, 172, 173, 174, 175, 177, 178, 179, 180, 181, 182, 185, 186, 187, 188, 190, 191, 193, 194, 195, 196, 197, 198, 200, 203, 204, 208, 210, 21 1, 212, 213, 214; *cum,* 41, 116; *dum,* 205; *tunc,* 5, 20, 199; *tam,* 45, 77, 130, 149; *tamen,* 206; *tu,* 119; om., 3, 14, 81, 151, 168, 171, 183, 184, 189.

251   5, 6, 7, 8, 9, 10, 13, 15, 16, 19, 20, 21, 23, 25, 26, 28, 29, 30, 31, 32, 33, 34, 36, 37, 38, 39, 41, 42, 43, 44, 45, 46, 48, 49, 51, 52, 53, 56, 57, 58, 59, 60, 61, 62, 63, 64, 65, 69, 71, 72, 73, 74, 75, 76, 77, 78, 79, 82, 83, 84, 86, 87, 88, 89, 90, 92, 93, 96, 97, 98, 99, 100, 103, 104, 105, 107, 109, 110, 111, 112, 113, 115, 116, 117, 118, 119, 120, 121, 122, 123, 124, 125, 126, 127, 128, 129, 130, 131, 132, 133, 134, 135, 136, 137, 140, 141, 142, 143, 146, 147, 149, 150, 151, 152, 153, 154, 155, 156, 158, 160, 161, 162, 164, 165, 166, 167, 169, 170, 172, 173, 175, 178, 179, 180, 181, 182, 185, 186, 187, 188, 190, 191, 193, 194, 195, 196, 197, 198, 199, 200, 203, 204, 205, 206, 208, 210, 211, 212, 213, 214; *propter Pelagianam (Pelagianam* canc.), 177; *propter Pellaginam heresim (p. h.* canc.), 174; om., 3, 14, 81, 168, 171, 183, 184, 189.

252   15, 16, 48, 86, 107, 119, 120, 128, 136, 152, 168, 170, 188, 200; *paganos Hengistum et Horsum quos rex Uortegirnus in societatem eorum posuerat,* 69; *paganos quos rex in societatem adduxerat,* 111; *paganos quos rex in societatem eorum posuerat,* 5, 6, 7, 8, 9, 10, 13, 19, 20, 21, 23, (24,) 25, 26, 28, 29, 30, 31, 32, 33, 34, 36, 37, 38, 39, 41, 42, 43, 44, 45, 46, 49, 51, 52, 53, 56, 57, 58, 59, 60, 61, 62, 63, 64, 65, 71, 72, 73, 74, 75, 76, 77, 78, 79, 82, 83, 84, 87, 89, 90, 92, 93, 96, 97, 98, 99, 100, 103, 104, 105, 109, 110, 112, 115, 116, 117, 118, 121, 122, 123, 124, 125, 126, 127, 129, 130, 131, 132, 133, 134, 135, 137, 140, 141, 143, 146, 147, 149, 150, 151, 154, 155, 156, 158, 160, 161, 162, 164, 165, 166, 167, 169, 172, 173, 174, 175, 177, 178, 179, 180, 181, 182, 185, 187, 188, 190, 191, 193, 194, 195, 196, 197, 198, 199, 203, 204, 205, 206, 208, 210, 211, 212, 213, 214; *paganos quos rex posuerat in societatem eorum,* 186; *paganos quos rex in societatem eorum proposuerat,* 113; *paganos quos rex in societatem eorum posuisset,* 153; *paganos quos rex in societatem illorum posuerat,* 88; *paganos quos rex Uortigernus in suum regnum inuitauerat sicut predr.,* 142; om., 3, 14, 81, 168, 171, 183, 184, 189.

253   3, 6, 7, 8, 9, 10, 13, 14, 15, 16, 19, 21, 25, 26, 28, 29, 30, 31, 32, 33, 34, 36, 37, 38, 39, 42, 43, 44, 46, 48, 49, 51, 52, 53, 56, 57, 58, 59, 60, 61, 62, 63, 64, 65, 69, 71, 72, 73, 75, 76, 78, 79, 81, 82, 83, 84, 86, 87, 88, 89, 90, 92, 93, 97, 98, 99, 100, 103, 104, 105, 107, 109, 110, 111, 112, 113, 115, 117, 120, 121, 122, 123, 124, 125, 126, 127, 128, 129, 130, 131, 132, 134, 135, 136, 137, 140, 141, 143, 146, 147, 149, 150, 151, 152, 153, 154, 155, 156, 158, 160, 161, 162, 164, 165, 166, 167, 168, 169, 170, 171, 172, 173, 174, 175, 177,

propter[254] Pelagianam[255] heresim[256] cuius[257] uenenum[258] [261]ipsos[259] multis[260] die-

178, 179, 180, 181, 182, 183, 184, 185, 186, 187, 188, 189, 190, 191, 193, 194, 195, 196, 197, 198, 200, 203, 204, 205, 206, 208, 211, 212, 213, 214; *cum*, 41, 116, 133, 210; *tunc*, 5, 20, ?74, 199; *tam*, 23, 45, 77, 96, 149; *tum etiam*, 142; om., 118, 119.

254   3, 5, 6, 7, 8, 9, 10, 12, 14, 15, 16, 19, 20, 21, 23, 25, 26, 29, 30, 31, 32, 33, 34, 36, 37, 38, 39, 41, 42, 43, 44, 45, 46, 48, 49, 51, 52, 53, 56, 57, 58, 59, 60, 61, 62, 63, 64, 65, 69, 71, 72, 73, 74, 75, 76, 77, 78, 79, 81, 82, 83, 84, 86, 87, 88, 89, 90, 92, 93, 96, 97, 98, 99, 103, 104, 105, 107, 109, 110, 111, 112, 113, 115, 116, 117, 118, 120, 121, 122, 123, 124, 125, 126, 127, 128, 129, 130, 131, 132, 134, 135, 136, 137, 140, 141, 142, 143, 146, 147, 149, 150, 151, 152, 153, 154, 155, 156, 158, 160, 161, 162, 164, 165, 166, 167, 168, 169, 170, 171, 172, 173, 174, 175, 177, 178, 179, 180, 181, 182, 183, 184, 185, 186, 187, 188, 189, 190, 191, 193, 194, 195, 196, 197, 198, 199, 200, 203, 204, 205, 206, 208, 210, 211, 212, 213, 214; om., 28, 100, 119, 133.

255   3, 5, 6, 7, 9, 10, 13, 14, 15, 16, 19, 20, 21, 23, 25, 26, 28, 29, 30, 31, 33, 34, 36, 37, 38, 39, 41, 42, 43, 44, 45, 46, 48, 49, 51, 52, 53, 57, 58, 59, 60, 61, 62, 63, 65, 69, 71, 72, 73, 74, 75, 76, 77, 78, 79, 81, 82, 83, 84, 86, 87, 88, 89, 90, 93, 96, 97, 99, 100, 103, 104, 105, 107, 109, 110, 111, 112, 113, 115, 116, 118, 119, 120, 121, 122, 123, 125, 126, 127, 128, 129, 130, 131, 132, 133, 135, 136, 137, 141, 142, 143, 146, 147, 149, 150, 151, 152, 154, 155, 156, 158, 160, 161, 162, 164, 165, 166, 167, 168, 170, 171, 172, 173, 174, 175, 177, 179, 180, 181, 182, 183, 184, 185, 186, 187, 188, 189, 190, 191, 193, 194, 195, 196, 197, 198, 199, 200, 203, 204, 205, 206, 210, 211, 212, 213; *Peligianam*, 140, 178; *pelagianiam* (corr. to *pelagianam*), 117; *pelagi\a\nam*, 214; *pelaginam*, 208; *pelagiam*, 8, 32, 64, 92, 98, 124, 134, 153, 169; *pelaianam*, 56.

256   3, 5, 6, 7, 8, 9, 10, 13, 14, 15, 16, 19, 20, 21, 23, 25, 26, 28, 29, 30, 31, 32, 33, 34, 36, 37, 38, 39, 41, 42, 43, 44, 45, 46, 48, 49, 51, 52, 53, 56, 57, 58, 59, 60, 61, 62, 63, 64, 65, 69, 71, 72, 73, 74, 75, 76, 77, 78, 79, 81, 82, 83, 84, 86, 87, 88, 89, 90, 92, 93, 96, 97, 98, 99, 100, 103, 104, 105, 107, 109, 110, 111, 112, 113, 115, 116, 117, 118, 120, 121, 122, 123, 124, 125, 126, 127, 128, 129, 130, 131, 132, 133, 134, 135, 136, 137, 140, 141, 142, 143, 146, 147, 149, 150, 151, 152, 153, 154, 155, 156, 158, 160, 161, 162, 164, 165, 166, 167, 168, 169, 170, 171, 172, 173, 174, 175, 177, 178, 179, 180, 181, 182, 183, 184, 185, 186, 187, 188, 189, 190, 191, 193, 194, 195, 196, 197, 198, 199, 200, 203, 204, 205, 206, 208, 210, 211, 212, 213, 214; *heresum*, 119.

257   3, 5, 6, 7, 8, 9, 10, 13, 14, 15, 16, 19, 20, 21, 23, 25, 26, 28, 29, 30, 31, 32, 33, 34, 36, 37, 38, 39, 41, 42, 43, 45, 46, 48, 49, 51, 52, 53, 56, 57, 58, 59, 60, 61, 62, 63, 64, 65, 69, 71, 72, 73, 74, 75, 76, 77, 78, 79, 81, 82, 83, 84, 86, 87, 88, 89, 90, 92, 93, 96, 97, 98, 99, 100, 103, 104, 105, 107, 109, 110, 111, 112, 113, 115, 116, 117, 118, 119, 120, 121, 122, 123, 124, 125, 126, 127, 128, 129, 130, 131. 132, 133, 134, 135, 136, 137, 140, 141, 142, 143, 146, 147, 149, 150, 151, 152, 153, 154, 155, 156, 158, 160, 161, 162, 164, 165, 166, 167, 168, 169, 170, 171, 172, 173, 174, 175, 177, 178, 179, 180, 181, 182, 183, 184, 185, 186, 187, 188, 189, 190, 191, 193, 194, 195, 196, 197, 198, 199, 200, 203, 204, 205, 206, 208, 210, 211, 212, 213, 214; om., 44.

258   3, 5, 6, 7, 9, 10, 13, 14, 15, 16, 19, 20, 21, 23, 25, 26, 28, 29, 30, 31, 32, 33, 34, 36, 37, 38, 39, 41, 42, 43, 44, 45, 46, 48, 49, 51, 52, 53, 56, 57, 58, 59, 60, 61, 62, 63, 64, 65, 69, 71, 72, 73, 74, 75, 76, 77, 78, 79, 81, 82, 83, 84, 86, 87, 88, 89, 90, 92, 93, 96, 97, 98, 99, 100, 103, 104, 105, 107, 109, 110, 111, 112, 113, 115, 116, 117, 118, 119, 120, 121, 122, 123, 124, 125, 126, 127, 128, 129, 130, 131, 132, 134, 135, 136, 137, 140, 141, 142, 143, 146, 147, 149, 150, 151, 153, 154, 155, 156, 158, 160, 161, 162, 164, 165, 166, 167, 168, 169, 170, 171, 172, 173, 174, 175, 177, 178, 179, 180, 181, 182, 183, 184, 185, 186, 187, 188, 189, 190, 191, 193, 194, 195, 196, 197, 198, 199, 200, 203, 204, 205, 206, 208, 210, 211, 212, 213, 214; *ueneno*, 133; *uenemini?*, 152; *uentum*, 8.

259   3, 5, 6, 7, 8, 9, 10, 13, 14, 15, 16, 19, 20, 21, 23, 25, 26, 28, 29, 30, 31, 32, 33, 34, 36, 37,

288

bus[261] affecerat.[262] Beatorum[263] igitur[264] [268]uirorum[265] predicatione[266] restituta[267]

38, 39, 41, 42, 43, 44, 45, 46, 48, 49, 52, 53, 57, 59, 60, 61, 62, 63, 64, 69, 71, 72, 73, 74, 75, 76, 77, 78, 79, 81, 82, 83, 84, 86, 87, 88, 89, 90, 92, 93, 96, 97, 98, 99, 100, 103, 104, 105, 107, 109, 110, 111, 112, 113, 115, 116, 117, 118, 119, 120, 121, 122, 123, 124, 125, 126, 127, 128. 129, 130, 131, 132, 133, 134, 135, 136, 137, 140, 141, 142, 143, 146, 149, 150, 151, 152, 153, 154, 155, 156, 158, 160, 161, 162, 164, 165, 166, 167, 168, 169, 170, 171, 172, 173, 174, 175, 177, 178, 179, 180, 181, 182, 183, 184, 185, 186, 187, 188, 189, 190, 191, 193, 194, 195, 196, 197, 198, 199, 200, 203, 204, 205, 206, 208, 210, 211, 212, 213, 214; *ipsis,* 65; *illos,* 51, 56, 58; om., 147.

260   3, 5, 6, 7, 8, 9, 10, 13, 14, 15, 16, 19, 20, 21, 23, 25, 26, 28, 29, 30, 31, 32, 33, 34, 36, 37, 38, 39, 41, 42, 43, 44, 45, 46, 48, 49, 51, 52, 53, 56, 57, 58, 59, 60, 61, 62, 63, 64, 69, 71, 72, 73, 74, 75, 76, 77, 78, 79, 81, 82, 83, 84, 86, 87, 88, 89, 90, 92, 93, 96, 97, 98, 99, 100, 103, 104, 105, 1o7, 109, 110, 111, 112, 113, 115, 116, 117, 118, 119, 120, 121, 122, 123, 124, 125, 126, 127, 128, 129, 130, 131, 132, 133, 134, 135, 136, 137, 140, 141, 142, 143, 146, 147, 149, 150, 151, 152, 153, 154, 155, 156, 158, 160, 161, 162, 164, 165, 166, 167, 168, 169, 170, 171, 172, 173, 174, 175, 177, 178, 179, 180, 181, 182, 183, 184, 185, 186, 187, 188, 189, 190, 191, 193, 194, 195, 196, 197, 198, 199, 200, 203, 204, 205, 206, 208, 210, 211, 212, 213, 214; *multos,* 65.

261...261   3, 5, 6, 7, 8, 9, 10, 13, 14, 15, 16, 19, 20, 21, 23, 25, 26, 28, 29, 30, 31, 32, 33, 34, 36, 37, 38, 39, 41, 42, 43, 44, 45, 46, 48, 49, 51, 52, 53, 56, 57, 58, 59, 60, 61, 62, 63, 64, 69, 71, 72, 73, 74, 75, 76, 77, 78, 79, 81, 82, 83, 84, 86, 87, 88, 89, 90, 92, 93, 96, 97, 98, 99, 100, 103, 104, 105, 109, 110, 111, 112, 113, 115, 116, 117, 118, 119, 120, 121, 122, 123, 124, 125, 126, 127, 128, 129, 130, 131, 132, 133, 134, 135, 136, 137, 140, 141, 142, 143, 146, 147, 149, 150, 151, 152, 153, 154, 155, 156, 158, 160, 161, 162, 164, 165, 166, 167, 168, 169, 170, 171, 172, 173, 174, 175, 177, 178, 179, 180, 181, 182, 183, 184, 185, 186, 187, 188, 189, 190, 191, 193, 194, 195, 196, 197, 198, 199, 200, 203, 204, 205, 206, 208, 210, 211, 212, 213, 214; *m. d. i.,* 107; *i. d. m.,* 65.

262   5, 6, 7, 8, 9, 10, 13, 15, 16, 19, 20, 21, 23, 25, 26, 29, 30, 31, 33, 34, 36, 37, 38, 39, 41, 42, 43, 44, 46, 48, 49, 51, 52, 53, 56, 57, 58, 59, 60, 61, 62, 63, 64, 65, 69, 71, 73, 74, 75, 76, 77, 78, 79, 82, 83, 84, 86, 87, 88, 89, 90, 92, 93, 96, 97, 98, 103, 104, 105, 107, 109, 110, 111, 112, 113, 115, 116, 117, 120, 123, 124, 125, 126, 127, 128, 130, 131, 132, 135, 136, 137, 140, 141, 142, 143, 146, 149, 150, 151, 152, 153, 154, 155, 156, 158, 160, 161, 161, 164, 165, 166, 167, 169, 170, 172, 173, 174, 175, 177, 178, 179, 180, 181, 182, 185, 186, 187, 188, 190, 191, 193, 194, 195, 196, 197, 198, 199, 200, 203, 204, 205, 206, 208, 210, 211, 212, 213, 214; *afecerat,* 118; *affeceret,* 99, 122; *afficerat,* 45; *affecit,* 147; *effecerat,* 32; *infecerat,* 28, 72, 100, 121, 129, 134; *inffecerat,* 119; *inferunt,* 133; *affecerat tum propter paganos quos rex in societatem eorum posuerat,* 3, 14, 81, 168, 171, 183, 184, 189.

263   3, 5, 6, 7, 8, 9, 10, 13, 14, 15, 16, 19, 20, 21, 23, 25, 26, 28, 29, 30, 31, 32, 33, 34, 36, 37, 38, 39, 41, 42, 43, 44, 45, 46, 48, 49, 51, 52, 53, 56, 57, 58, 59, 60, 61, 62, 63, 64, 65, 69, 71, 72, 73, 75, 76, 77, 78, 79, 81, 82, 83, 84, 86, 87, 88, 89, 90, 92, 93, 96, 97, 98, 99, 100, 103, 104, 105, 107, 109, 110, 111, 112, 113, 115, 116, 117, 118, 119, 120, 121, 122, 123, 124, 125, 126, 127, 128, 129, 130, 131, 132, 133, 134, 135, 136, 137, 140, 141, 142, 143, 146, 147, 149, 150, 152, 153, 154, 155, 156, 158, 160, 161, 162, 164, 165, 166, 167, 168, 169, 170, 171, 172, 173, 174, 175, 177, 178, 179, 180, 181, 183, 184, 185, 186, 187, 188, 189, 190, 191, 193, 194, 195, 196, 197, 198, 199, 200, 203, 204, 205, 208, 210, 211, 212, 213, 214; *beatus* (*us* canc.), 182; *batorum,* 151; *bonorum,* 206; om. but inserted by scribe in margin, 74.

264   3, 5, 6, 7, 8, 9, 10, 13, 14, 15, 16, 19, 20, 21, 23, 25, 26, 28, 29, 30, 31, 32, 33, 34, 36, 37, 38, 39, 41, 42, 43, 44, 45, 46, 48, 49, 51, 52, 53, 56, 57, 58, 59, 60, 61, 62, 63, 64, 65, 71, 72, 73, 75, 77, 78, 79, 81, 82, 83, 84, 86, 87, 88, 89, 93, 96, 97, 98, 99, 100, 103, 104, 105,

289

est[268 269] inter eos[269 270]uere fidei[270] religio[271] quia[272] multis[273 277]miraculis[274] cotidie[275]

107, 109, 111, 113, 115, 116, 117, 118, 119, 120, 121, 122, 123, 124, 125, 126, 127, 128, 129, 130, 131, 132, 133, 134, 135, 136, 140, 141, 142, 143, 146, 147, 149, 150, 151, 152, 153, 154, 155, 156, 158, 160, 161, 162, 164, 165, 166, 167, 168, 169, 170, 171, 172, 173, 175, 177, 178, 179, 180, 181, 182, 183, 184, 185, 186, 187, 188, 189, 190, 191, 193, 194, 195, 196, 197, 199, 200, 203, 204, 205, 206, 208, 210, 211, 212, 214; *ergo,* 69, 76, 90, 92, 97, 112, 137; *que,* 174, 198; om. but inserted in margin, 74; om., 110, 213.

265 3, 5, 6, 7, 8, 9, 10, 13, 14, 15, 16, 19, 20, 21, 23, 25, 26, 28, 29, 30, 31, 32, 33, 34, 36, 37, 38, 39, 41, 42, 43, 44, 45, 46, 48, 49, 51, 52, 53, 56, 57, 58, 59, 60, 61, 62, 63, 64, 65, 69, 71, 72, 73, 74, 75, 76, 77, 78, 79, 81, 82, 83, 84, 86, 87, 88, 89, 90, 92, 93, 96, 97, 98, 99, 100, 103, 104, 105, 107, 109, 110, 111, 112, 113, 115, 116, 117, 118, 119, 120, 121, 122, 123, 124, 125, 126, 127, 128, 129, 130, 131, 132, 133, 134, 135, 136, 137, 140, 141, 142, 143, 146, 147, 149, 150, 151, 153, 154, 155, 156, 158, 160, 161, 162, 164, 165, 166, 167, 168, 169, 170, 171, 172, 173, 174, 175, 177, 178, 179, 180, 181, 182, 183, 184, 185, 186, 187, 188, 190, 191, 193, 194, 195, 196, 197, 198, 199, 200, 203, 204, 205, 206, 208, 210, 211, 212, 213, 214; *ub'orum* (over erasure), 152; *eorum,* 189.

266 3, 5, 6, 7, 8, 9, 10, 13, 14, 15, 16, 19, 20, 21, 23, 25, 26, 28, 29, 30, 31, 32, 33, 34, 36, 37, 38, 39, 41, 42, 43, 44, 45, 46, 48, 49, 51, 52, 53, 56, 57, 58, 59, 60, 61, 62, 63, 64, 65, 69, 71, 72, 73, 74, 75, 76, 77, 78, 79, 81, 82, 83, 84, 86, 87, 88, 89, 90, 92, 93, 96, 97, 98, 99, 100, 103, 104, 105, 107, 109, 110, 111, 112, 113, 115, 116, 117, 118, 119, 120, 121, 122, 123, 124, 125, 126, 127, 128, 129, 130, 131, 132, 133, 134, 135, 136, 137, 140, 141, 143, 146, 147, 149, 150, 151, 152, 153, 154, 155, 156, 158, 160, 161, 162, 164, 165, 166, 167, 168, 170, 171, 172, 173, 174, 175, 177, 178, 179, 180, 181, 183, 184, 185, 186, 187, 188, 189, 190, 191, 193, 194, 195, 196, 197, 198, 199, 200, 203, 204, 205, 206, 208, 210, 211, 212, 213, 214; *preditione,* 169; *officio,* 182; *cum Germani et Lupi predicatione,* 142.

267 3, 5, 6, 7, 8, 9, 10, 13, 14, 15, 16, 19, 20, 21, 23, 26, 28, 29, 30, 31, 32, 33, 34, 36, 37, 38, 39, 41, 42, 43, 44, 45, 46, 48, 49, 51, 52, 53, 56, 57, 58, 59, 60, 61, 62, 63, 64, 65, 69, 71, 72, 73, 74, 75, 76, 77, 78, 79, 81, 82, 83, 84, 86, 87, 88, 89, 90, 92, 93, 96, 97, 98, 99, 100, 103, 104, 105, 107, 109, 110, 111, 112, 113, 115, 116, 117, 118, 119, 120, 121, 122, 123, 124, 125, 126, 127, 128, 129, 130, 131, 132, 133, 134, 135, 136, 137, 140, 141, 146, 147, 149, 150, 151, 152, 153, 154, 156, 158, 160, 161, 162, 164, 165, 166, 167, 168, 169, 170, 171, 172, 173, 174, 175, 177, 178, 179, 180, 181, 182, 183, 184, 185, 186, 187, 188, 189, 190, 191, 193, 194, 195, 196, 197, 198, 199, 200, 203, 204, 205, 206, 208, 210, 211, 212, 213, 214; *restitututa,* 155; *restaurata,* 25; *instituta,* 143; *et miraculis extne. sunt hereses iste et restituta,* 142.

268...268 3, 5, 6, 7, 8, 9, 10, 13, 14, 15, 16, 19, 20, 21, 23, 25, 26, 28, 29, 30, 31, 32, 33, 34, 36, 37, 38, 39, 41, 42, 43, 44, 46, 48, 49, 51, 52, 53, 56, 57, 58, 59, 60, 61, 62, 63, 65, 69, 71, 72, 73, 75, 76, 77, 78, 79, 81, 82, 83, 84, 86, 87, 88, 89, 90, 92, 96, 97, 98, 99, 100, 103, 104, 105, 107, 109, 110, 111, 112, 113, 115, 116, 117, 118, 119, 120, 121, 122, 123, 124, 125, 126, 127, 128, 129, 130, 131, 132, 133, 134, 135, 136, 137, 140, 141, 142, 143, 146, 147, 149, 150, 151, 152, 153, 154, 155, 156, 158, 160, 161, 162, 164, 165, 166, 167, 168, 169, 170, 171, 172, 173, 174, 175, 177, 178, 179, 180, 181, 182, 183, 184, 185, 186, 187, 188, 189, 190, 191, 193, 194, 195, 196, 197, 198, 199, 200, 203, 204, 205, 206, 208, 210, 211, 212, 214; *u. r. e. p.,* 45; *p. u. r. e.,* 93; *u. p. r.,* 64, 213; om. but inserted in margin, 74.

269...269 3, 5, 6, 7, 8, 9, 10, 13, 14, 15, 16, 19, 20, 21, 23, 25, 26, 28, 29, 30, 31, 32, 33, 34, 36, 37, 38, 39, 41, 42, 43, 44, 45, 46, 48, 49, 51, 52, 53, 56, 57, 58, 59, 60, 61, 62, 64, 65, 69, 71, 72, 73, 75, 76, 77, 78, 79, 81, 82, 83, 84, 86, 87, 88, 89, 90, 92, 93, 96, 97, 98, 99, 100, 103, 104, 105, 107, 109, 110, 111, 112, 113, 116, 117, 118, 119, 120, 121, 122, 123, 124, 125, 126, 127, 128, 129, 130, 131, 132, 133, 134, 135, 136, 137, 140, 141, 143, 146, 147, 149, 150, 151, 152, 153, 154, 155, 156, 158, 160, 161, 162, 164, 165, 166, 167, 168, 169, 170, 171, 172, 173, 174, 175, 177, 178, 179, 180, 181, 182, 183, 184, 185, 186, 187, 188,

189, 190, 191, 193, 194, 195, 196, 197, 198, 199, 200, 203, 204, 205, 206, 208, 210, 211, 212, 213, 214; *inter Britones,* 142; om. but inserted in margin, 74; om., 63, 115.

270...270 3, 5, 6, 7, 8, 9, 10, 13, 14, 15, 16, 19, 20, 21, 23, 25, 26, 28, 29, 30, 31, 32, 33, 36, 37, 38, 39, 41, 42, 43, 44, 45, 46, 48, 49, 51, 52, 53, 56, 57, 58, 59, 60, 61, 62, 63, 64, 65, 69, 71, 72, 73, 75, 76, 77, 78, 79, 81, 82, 83, 84, 86, 87, 88, 89, 90, 92, 93, 96, 97, 98, 99, 100, 103, 104, 105, 107, 109, 110, 111, 112, 113, 115, 116, 117, 118, 119, 120, 121, 122, 123, 124, 126, 127, 128, 129, 130, 131, 132, 133, 134, 135, 136, 137, 140, 141, 142, 143, 146, 147, 149, 150, 151, 152, 153, 154, 155, 156, 158, 160, 161, 162, 164, 165, 166, 167, 168, 169, 170, 171, 172, 173, 175, 177, 179, 180, 181, 182, 184, 185, 187, 188, 189, 190, 191, 193, 194, 195, 196, 197, 198, 199, 200, 203, 204, 205, 206, 208, 210, 211, 212, 213, 214; *f. u.,* 125; *uerae fidei,* 34; *uera fidei,* 174; *uere fidi,* 183; *uere,* 174; *fidei,* 140, 178, 186; om., but inserted in margin, 74.

271 3, 5, 6, 7, 8, 9, 10, 14, 15, 16, 19, 20, 21, 23, 25, 26, 29, 30, 31, 32, 33, 34, 36, 37, 38, 39, 41, 42, 43, 44, 45, 46, 48, 49, 51, 52, 53, 56, 57, 58, 59, 60, 61, 62, 63, 64, 65, 69, 71, 72, 73, 75, 76, 77, 78, 79, 51, 82, 83, 84, 86, 87, 88, 89, 90, 92, 93, 96, 97, 98, 99, 100, 103, 104, 105, 107, 109, 110, 111, 112, 113, 115, 116, 117, 118, 119, 120, 121, 122, 123, 124, 125, 126, 127, 128, 129, 130, 131, 132, 133, 134, 135, 136, 137, 140, 141, 143, 146, 147, 149, 150, 151, 152, 153, 154, 155, 156, 158, 160, 161, 162, 164, 165, 166, 167, 168, 169, 170, 171, 172, 173, 174, 175, 177, 178, 179, 180, 181, 182, 183, 184, 185, 186, 187, 188, 189, 190, 191, 193, 194, 195, 196, 197, 198, 199, 200, 203, 204, 205, 206, 208, 210, 211, 212, 213, 214; *religios[],* 13; *regligilio* (altered to *regligio*), 28; om. but inserted in margin, 74; *religio circa annum domini 449,* 142.

272 3, 5, 6, 7, 8, 9, 10, 13, 14, 15, 16, 19, 20, 21, 23, 25, 26, 28, 29, 30, 31, 32, 33, 34, 36, 37, 38, 39, 41, 42, 43, 44, 45, 46, 48, 49, 51, 52, 53, 56, 57, 58, 59, 60, 61, 62, 63, 64, 65, 69, 71, 72, 73, 75, 76, 77, 78, 79, 81, 82, 83, 84, 86, 87, 88, 89, 90, 92, 93, 96, 97, 98, 99, 100, 103, 104, 105, 107, 109, 110, 111, 112, 113, 115, 116, 117, 118, 119, 120, 121, 122, 123, 124, 125, 126, 127, 128, 129, 130, 132, 133, 134, 135, 136, 137, 140, 141, 142, 143, 146, 147, 149, 150, 151, 152, 153, 154, 156, 158, 160, 161, 162, 164, 165, 166, 167, 168, 169, 170, 171, 172, 173, 174, 175, 177, 178, 179, 180, 181, 182, 183, 184, 185, 186, 187, 188, 189, 190, 191, 193, 194, 195, 196, 197, 198, 199, 200, 203, 204, 205, 206, 208, 210, 211, 212, 213, 214; *que,* 131; *multis diebus,* 155; om. but inserted in margin, 74.

273 3, 5, 6, 7, 8, 9, 10, 13, 14, 15, 16, 19, 20, 21, 23, 25, 26, 28, 29, 30, 31, 32, 33, 34, 36, 37, 38, 39, 41, 42, 43, 44, 45, 46, 48, 49, 51, 52, 53, 56, 57, 58, 59, 60, 61, 62, 63, 64, 65, 69, 71, 72, 73, 75, 76, 77, 78, 79, 81, 82, 83, 84, 86, 87, 88, 89, 90, 92, 93, 96, 97, 98, 99, 100, 103, 104, 105, 107, 109, 110, 111, 112, 113, 115, 116, 117, 118, 119, 120, 121, 122, 123, 124, 125, 126, 127, 128, 129, 130, 131, 132, 133, 134, 135, 136, 137, 140, 141, 142, 143, 146, 147, 149, 150, 151, 152, 153, 154, 155, 156, 158, 160, 161, 162, 164, 165, 166, 167, 168, 169, 170, 171, 172, 173, 174, 175, 177, 178, 179, 180, 181, 182, 183, 184, 185, 186, 187, 188, 189, 190, 191, 193, 194, 195, 196, 197, 198, 199, 200, 203, 204, 205, 206, 208, 210, 211, 212, 213, 214; om., but inserted in margin by scribe, 74.

274 3, 5, 6, 7, 8, 9, 10, 13, 14, 15, 16, 19, 20, 21, 23, 25, 26, 28, 29, 30, 31, 32, 33, 34, 36, 37, 38, 39, 41, 42, 43, 44, 45, 46, 48, 49, 51, 52, 53, 56, 57, 58, 59, 60, 61, 62, 63, 64, 65, 69, 71, 72, 73, 74, 75, 76, 77, 78, 79, 81, 82, 83, 84, 86, 87, 88, 89, 90, 92, 93, 96, 97, 98, 99, 100, 103, 104, 105, 107, 109, 110, 111, 112, 113, 115, 116, 117, 118, 119, 120, 121, 122, 123, 124, 125, 126, 127, 128, 129, 130, 131, 132, 133, 134, 135, 136, 137, 140, 141, 142, 143 146, 147, 149, 150, 151, 152, 153, 154, 155, 156, 158, 160, 161, 162, 164, 165, 166, 167, 168, 169, 170, 171, 172, 173, 174, 175, 177, 178, 179, 180, 181, 182, 183, 184, 185, 187, 188, 189, 190, 191, 193, 194, 195, 196, 197, 198, 199, 200, 203, 204, 205, 206, 208, 210, 211, 212, 213, 214; *miraculi,* 186.

275 3, 5, 6, 7, 8, 9, 10, 13, 14, 15, 16, 19, 21, 23, 25, 26, 28, 29, 30, 31, 32, 33, 34, 36, 37, 38, 39, 42, 43, 44, 45, 46, 48, 49, 51, 52, 53, 56, 57, 59, 60, 61, 62, 63, 64, 65, 69, 71, 72, 73, 74, 76, 77, 78, 79, 81, 82, 83, 84, 86, 87, 88, 89, 90, 92, 93, 96, 97, 98, 99, 100, 103, 104, 105, 107, 109, 110, 111, 112, 113, 115, 116, 117, 118, 119, 120, 121, 122, 123, 124, 125,

preclarebant.[276] [277] Multa[278] [282]per eos miracula[279] ostendebat[280] Deus[281] [282] que[283]

126, 127, 128, 129, 130, 131, 132, 133, 134, 135, 136, 137, 140, 141, 142, 143, 146, 147, 149, 150, 151, 152, 153, 154, 155, 156, 158, 160, 161, 162, 164, 165, 166, 167, 168, 169, 170, 171, 172, 173, 174, 175, 177, 178, 179, 180, 181, 182, 183, 184, 185, 186, 188, 189, 190, 191, 193, 194, 195, 196, 197, 198, 199, 200, 203, 204, 205, 208, 210, 211, 212, 213, 214; *cottidie*, 20, 75; *quotidie*, 187, 206; *coitidie*, 58; om., 41.

[276] 3, 6, 8, 9, 10, 13, 14, 15, 16, 20, 21, 23, 25, 26, 28, 29, 30, 32, 33, 34, 36, 37, 38, 39, 41, 42, 43, 44, 46, 48, 49, 51, 52, 56, 57, 59, 60, 61, 62, 63, 64, 65, 69, 71, 73, 74, 75, 76, 77, 78, 79, 81, 82, 83, 84, 86, 87, 88, 89, 90, 92, 93, 96, 97, 98, 99, 103, 104, 105, 107, 109, 110, 112, 113, 115, 116, 117, 118, 119, 120, 121, 122, 123, 124, 125, 126, 127, 128, 130, 131, 132, 135, 136, 137, 140, 141, 143, 146, 147, 149, 150, 151, 152, 153, 154, 155, 156, 158, 160, 162, 164, 165, 166, 167, 169, 170, 171, 173, 174, 175, 177, 178, 179, 180, 181, 182, 183, 184, 185, 186, 187, 188, 189, 190, 191, 193, 194, 195, 196, 198, 199, 200, 203, 204, 206, 210, 211, 212, 214; *preclarabant* (altered to *preclarebant*), 53, 168, 197, 208; *preclarabant,* 7, 19, 58, 100, 134, 161, 172, 205; *clarebant,* 5, 129, 133; *precalebant,* 31; *declarebant,* 72; *corruscabant,* 111; *coruscabant,* 54; *preclarebat,* 213; *clarebat,* 186; *preclarebant beatissimi uiri predicti,* 142.

[277...277] 3, 5, 6, 7, 8, 9, 10, 13, 14, 15, 16, 19, 21, 23, 25, 26, 28, 29, 30, 31, 32, 33, 34, 36, 37, 38, 39, 41, 42, 43, 44, 45, 46, 48, 49, 51, 52, 53, 56, 57, 58, 59, 60, 61, 62, 63, 64, 65, 69, 71, 72, 73, 75, 76, 77, 78, 79, 81, 82, 84, 86, 87, 88, 89, 90, 92, 93, 96, 97, 98, 99, 100, 103, 104, 105, 109, 110, 111, 112, 113, 115, 116, 117, 118, 119, 120, 121, 122, 123, 124, 125, 127, 128, 129, 130, 131, 132, 133, 134, 135, 136, 137, 140, 141, 142, 143, 146, 149, 150, 151, 152, 153, 154, 155, 156, 158, 160, 161, 162, 164, 165, 167, 168, 169, 170, 171, 172, 174, 175, 177, 178, 179, 180, 181, 182, 183, 184, 185, 187, 188, 189, 190, 191, 193, 194, 195, 196, 197, 198, 199, 200, 203, 204, 205, 206, 208, 210, 212, 213, 214; *c. m. p.,* 20, 83, 107, 126, 166, 173; *m. p. c.,* 147; *m. p.,* 186; *miraculis (c. p.* om. but inserted in margin), 74, 211.

[278] 3, 5, 6, 7, 8, 9, 10, 13, 14, 15, 16, 19, 20, 21, 23, 25, 26, 28, 29, 30, 31, 32, 33, 34, 36, 37, 38, 39, 41, 42, 43, 44, 45, 46, 48, 49, 51, 52, 53, 56, 57, 58, 59, 60, 61, 62, 63, 64, 65, 69, 71, 72, 73, 74, 75, 76, 77, 78, 79, 81, 82, 83, 84, 86, 87, 88, 89, 90, 92, 93, 96, 97, 98, 99, 100, 103, 104, 105, 107, 109, 110, 112, 113, 115, 116, 117, 118, 119, 120, 121, 122, 123, 124, 125, 126, 127, 128, 129, 130, 131, 132, 133, 134, 135, 136, 137, 140, 141, 143, 146, 147, 149, 150, 151, 152, 153, 154, 155, 156, 158, 160, 161, 162, 164, 165, 166, 167, 168, 169, 170, 171, 172, 173, 174, 175, 177, 178, 179, 180, 181, 182, 183, 184, 185, 186, 187, 188, 189, 190, 191, 193, 194, 195, 196, 197, 198, 199, 200, 203, 204, 205, 206, 208, 210, 212, 213, 214; *Multa quidem,* 142; om., but inserted in margin, 211; om., 111.

[279] 3, 5, 6, 7, 8, 9, 10, 13, 14, 15, 16, 19, 20, 21, 23, 25, 26, 28, 29, 30, 31, 32, 33, 34, 36, 37, 39, 41, 43, 44, 45, 46, 48, 49, 51, 52, 53, 56, 57, 58, 59, 60, 61, 62, 63, 64, 65, 69, 71, 72, 73, 74, 75, 76, 77, 78, 79, 81, 82, 83, 84, 86, 87, 88, 89, 90, 92, 93, 96, 97, 98, 100, 103, 104, 105, 107, 109, 111, 112, 113, 115, 116, 117, 118, 119, 120, 121, 123, 124, 125, 126, 127, 128, 129, 130, 131, 132, 133, 134, 135, 136, 137, 140, 141, 142, 143, 146, 147, 149, 150, 151, 152, 153, 154, 155, 156, 158, 160, 161, 162, 164, 165, 166, 167, 168, 169, 170, 171, 172, 173, 174, 175, 177, 178, 179, 180, 181, 182, 183, 184, 185, 186, 187, 188, 189, 190, 191, 193, 194, 195, 196, 197, 198, 199, 200, 203, 204, 205, 206, 208, 210, 211, 212, 213, 214; *miracla,* 42; *.ii. miracula,* 110; om., 38, 99, 122.

[280] 3, 5, 6, 7, 8, 9, 10, 13, 14, 15, 16, 19, 20, 21, 25, 26, 28, 29, 30, 31, 32, 33, 34, 36, 37, 38, 39, 41, 42, 43, 44, 45, 46, 48, 49, 51, 52, 53, 56, 58, 59, 60, 61, 62, 63, 64, 65, 69, 71, 72, 73, 74, 75, 76, 77, 78, 79, 81, 83, 84, 86, 87, 88, 89, 90, 92, 93, 97, 98, 99, 100, 103, 104, 105, 107, 109, 111, 112, 113, 116, 117, 118, 119, 120, 121, 122, 123, 124, 125, 126, 127, 128, 129, 130, 132, 133, 134, 135, 136, 137, 140, 141, 142, 143, 146, 147, 149, 150, 151, 152, 153, 154, 155, 156, 158, 160, 161, 162, 164, 166, 167, 168, 169, 170, 171, 172, 173,

174, 175, 177, 178, 179, 180, 181, 182, 183, 184, 185, 186, 187, 188, 189, 190, 191, 193, 194, 195, 196, 197, 198, 199, 200, 203, 204, 205, 206, 208, 210, 212, 213, 214; *hostendebat*, 131; *ostndebat*, 165, *ostendit*, 23, 57, 96, 115; *osidit.*, 110; *suo*\ *ostendebat*, 211; *ostendit eis*, 82.

281 3, 5, 6, 7, 8, 9, 10, 13, 14, 15, 16, 19, 20, 21, 23, 25, 26, 28, 29, 30, 31, 32, 33, 34, 36, 37, 38, 39, 41, 42, 43, 44, 45, 46, 48, 49, 51, 52, 53, 56, 57, 58, 59, 60, 61, 62, 63, 64, 65, 69, 71, 72, 73, 74, 76, 77, 78, 79, 81, 82, 83, 84, 86, 87, 88, 89, 90, 92, 93, 96, 97, 98, 99, 100, 103, 104, 105, 107, 109, 110, 111, 112, 113, 115, 116, 117, 118, 119, 120, 121, 122, 123, 124, 125, 126, 127, 128, 129, 130, 131, 132, 133, 134, 135, 136, 137, 140, 141, 142, 143, 146, 147, 149, 150, 151, 152, 153, 154, 155, 156, 158, 160, 161, 162, 164, 165, 166, 167, 168, 169, 170, 171, 172, 173, 174, 175, 177, 178, 179, 180, 181, 182, 183, 184, 185, 186, 187, 188, 189, 190, 191, 193, 194, 195, 196, 197, 198, 199, 203, 204, 206, 208, 210, 211, 212, 213, 214; *Deus*\, 200; om., 75, 205.

282...282 3, 5, 6, 7, 8, 9, 13, 14, 15, 16, 19, 20, 21, 23, 25, 26, 29, 30, 31, 32, 33, 34, 36, 37, 38, 39, 41, 43, 44, 45, 46, 48, 49, 51, 52, 53, 56, 58, 59, 60, 61, 62, 63, 64, 65, 69, 71, 73, 74, 75, 76, 77, 78, 79, 81, 82, 83, 84, 86, 87, 89, 90, 92, 93, 96, 97, 98, 99, 103, 104, 105, 109, 113, 115, 117, 118, 119, 120, 121, 122, 123, 124, 125, 126, 127, 128, 129, 130, 131, 132, 135, 137, 140, 141, 142, 143, 146, 147, 149, 150, 151, 152, 153, 154, 155, 156, 158, 160, 161, 162, 164, 165, 166, 167, 168, 170, 171, 172, 173, 174, 175, 177, 178, 179, 180, 181, 183, 184, 185, 187, 188, 189, 190, 191, 193, 195, 196, 197, 199, 200, 203, 204, 206, 208, 212, 213, 214; *p. e. D. m. o.*, 42, 205; *m. p. e. o. D.*, 10, 28, 57, 72, 88, 100, 107, 110, 112, 116, 133, 134, 136, 169, 182, 194; *p. e. D. o. m.*, 210; *p. e. m. D. o.*, 174, 186, 198; *p. e. m.*, inserted in margin by scribe, 211; om., 111.

283 3, 5, 6, 7, 8, 9, 10, 13, 14, 15, 16, 19, 20, 21, 23, 25, 26, 28, 29, 30, 31, 32, 33, 34, 36, 37, 38, 39, 41, 42, 43, 44, 45, 46, 48, 49, 51, 52, 53, 56, 57, 58, 59, 60, 61, 62, 63, 64, 65, 69, 71, 72, 73, 74, 75, 76, 77, 78, 79, 81, 82, 83, 84, 86, 87, 88, 89, 90, 92, 93, 96, 97, 98, 100, 103, 104, 105, 107, 109, 110, 112, 113, 115, 116, 117, 118, 119, 120, 123, 124, 125, 126, 127, 128, 129, 130, 132, 133, 134, 135, 136, 137, 140, 141, 142, 143, 146, 147, 149, 150, 151, 152, 153, 154, 155, 156, 158, 160, 161, 162, 164, 165, 166, 167, 168, 169, 170, 171, 172, 173, 174, 175, 177, 178, 179, 180, 181, 182, 183, 184, 185, 186, 187, 188, 189, 190, 191, 193, 194, 195, 196, 197, 198, 199, 200, 203, 204, 205, 206, 208, 210, 211, 212, 213, 214; *qui*, 99, 122, 131; *quem* 121; om., 49, 111.

284 15, 200; *Gildas*, 3, 5, 6, 7, 8, 9, 10, 13, 14, 19, 20, 21, 23, (24,) 25, 26, 28, 29, 30, 31, 32, 33, 34, 36, 37, 38, 39, 41, 42, 43, 44, 45, 46, 48, 49, 51, 52, 53, 56, 57, 58, 59, 60, 61, 62, 63, 64, 65, 71, 72, 74, 75, 76, 77, 78, 79, 81, 82, 83, 84, 86, 87, 88, 89, 90, 92, 93, 96, 97, 98, 99, 100, 103, 105, 109, 110, 112, 113, 115, 116, 117, 118, 119, 120, 121, 122, 123, 124, 125, 126, 127, 128, 129, 130, 131, 132, 133, 134, 135, 136, 137, 140, 141, 142, 143, 146, 147, 149, 150, 151, 152, 153, 154, 155, 156, 158, 160, 161, 162, 164, 165, 166, 167, 168, 169, 170, 171, 172, 173, 174, 175, 177, 178, 179, 180, 181, 182, 183, 184, 185, 186, 187, 188, 189, 190, 191, 193, 195, 196, 197, 198, 199, 203, 204, 205, 206, 208, 210, 211, 212, 213, 214; *Gilda.s*, 107; *Gillas*, 73, *Gu.das*, 104; *Gyldas*, 194; *prout Gildas*, 111.

285 3, 5, 6, 7, 8, 9, 10, 13, 14, 15, 16, 19, 20, 21, 23, 25, 26, 28, 29, 30, 31, 32, 33, 34, 36, 37, 38, 39, 41, 42, 43, 44, 45, 46, 48, 49, 51, 52, 53, 56, 57, 58, 59, 60, 61, 62, 63, 64, 65, 69, 71, 72, 73, 74, 75, 76, 77, 78, 79, 81, 82, 83, 84, 86, 87, 88, 89, 90, 92, 93, 96, 97, 98, 99, 100, 103, 104, 105, 107, 109, 110, 111, 112, 113, 115, 116, 118, 120, 121, 122, 123, 124, 125, 126, 127, 128, 129, 130, 131, 132, 133, 134, 135, 136, 137, 140 141, 142, 143, 146, 147, 149, 150, 151, 152, 153, 154, 155, 156, 158, 160, 161, 162, 164, 165, 166, 167, 168, 169, 170, 171, 172, 173, 174, 175, 177, 178, 179, 180, 181, 182, 183, 184, 185, 186, 187, 189, 190, 191, 193, 194, 195, 196, 197, 198, 199, 200, 203, 204, 205, 206, 208, 210, 211, 212, 213, 214; om., 117, 119, 188.

286 3, 5, 6, 7, 9, 13, 14, 15, 16, 19, 20, 21, 23, 25, 26, 28, 29, 32, 33, 34, 36, 37, 38, 39, 41, 42, 43, 44, 45, 46, 48, 49, 51, 52, 53, 57, 58, 59, 60, 61, 62, 63, 64, 65, 69, 71, 72, 73, 74, 75, 76, 77, 78, 81, 82 83, 84, 86, 87, 89, 90, 92, 93, 96, 97, 99, 100, 103, 105, 107, 109,

293

110, 111, 112, 115, 118, 121, 122, 124, 125, 126, 127, 128, 129, 130, 131, 132, 133, 134, 135, 136, 137, 140, 142, 143, 146, 147, 149, 150, 151, 152, 154, 158, 160, 161, 162, 164, 165, 167, 170, 171, 172, 173, 175, 177, 178, 179, 180, 181, 182, 183, 184, 185, 187, 189, 191, 193, 194, 195, 196, 197, 198, 200, 203, 204, 205, 206, 208, 210, 211, 212, 213, 214; *tractati*, 120; *tract\a/tu*, 169; *tractu*, 10, 31, 79, 98, 113, 123, 141, 155, 156, 166, 174, 190; *t^actu*, 8, 30, 56, 104, 153; *tra\c/tatu*, 199; *tratatu*, 186; *libro*, 88, 116; *intrante*, 9; om., 117, 188.

287 3, 5, 6, 7, 8, 9, 10, 14, 15, 19, 20, 23, 25, 26, 28, 29, 30, 31, 32, 33, 34, 37, 38, 39, 41, 42, 43, 44, 45, 46, 48, 49, 51, 52, 53, 56, 57, 58, 60, 61, 62, 63, 64, 65, 69, 71, 72, 73, 74, 75, 76, 77, 78, 79, 81, 82, 83, 84, 86, 87, 88, 89, 90, 92, 93, 96, 97, 98, 99, 100, 103, 104, 105, 107, 109, 110, 111, 112, 113, 115, 116, 118, 119, 120, 121, 122, 123, 124, 125, 126, 127, 128, 130, 131, 132, 133, 134, 135, 136, 137, 140, 141, 142, 143, 146, 147, 149, 150, 151, 152, 153, 154, 155, 156, 158, 160, 161, 162, 164, 165, 166, 168, 169, 170, 171, 172, 173, 174, 175, 177, 178, 179, 180, 181, 182, 183, 184, 185, 187, 189, 191, 193, 194, 195, 196, 197, 198, 199, 200, 203, 204, 205, 208, 210, 212, 213, 214; *tuo* (corr.), 36; om., 13, 16, 21, (24,) 59, 78, 117, 129, 167, 186, 188, 190, 206, 211.

288 3, 5, 6, 7, 8, 9, 13, 14, 15, 16, 19, 20, 21, 23, 25, 26, 28, 29, 30, 31, 32, 33, 34, 36, 37, 38, 39, 41, 42, 43, 44, 45, 46, 48, 49, 51, 52, 53, 56, 57, 58, 59, 60, 61, 62, 63, 65, 69, 71, 72, 73, 74, 75, 76, 77, 78, 79, 81, 82, 83, 84, 86, 87, 89, 90, 92, 93, 96, 97, 98, 99, 100, 103, 104, 105, 107, 109, 110, 111, 112, 113, 115, 117, 118, 119, 120, 121, 122, 123, 124, 125, 126, 127, 128, 129, 130, 131, 132, 133, 134, 135, 136, 137, 140, 141, 142, 143, 146, 149, 150, 151, 152, 153, 154, 155, 156, 158, 160, 161, 162, 164, 165, 166, 167, 168, 169, 170, 171, 172, 173, 175, 177, 178, 179, 180, 181, 182, 183, 184, 185, 186, 187, 188, 189, 190, 191, 193, 194, 195, 196, 197, 198, 199, 200, 203, 204, 205, 206, 208, 210, 211, 212, 213, 214; *leculento*, 41; *liculento*, 64; *loculento*, 10, 147, 174; *luculentu*, 152; om., 88, 116.

289 3, 5, 6, 8, 9, 10, 13, 14, 15, 16, 19, 21, 23, 25, 26, 28, 29, 30, 31, 32, 33, 34, 36, 37, 38, 39, 41, 42, 43, 44, 45, 46, 48, 49, 51, 52, 53, 56, 57, 58, 59, 66, 61, 62, 63, 64, 65, 69, 71, 73, 74, 76, 77, 78, 79, 81, 82, 84, 86, 87, 89, 90, 92, 93, 96, 97, 98, 99, 100, 103, 104, 105, 107, 109, 110, 112, 113, 115, 117, 118, 119, 120, 121, 122, 123, 124, 125, 127, 128, 129, 130, 131, 132, 133, 135, 136, 137, 140, 141, 142, 143, 146, 147, 149, 150, 152, 153, 154, 155, 156, 158, 160, 161, 162, 164, 165, 168, 169, 170, 171, 172, 174, 177, 178, 179, 181, 182, 183, 184, 185, 186, 187, 188, 189, 191, 193, 194, 195, 196, 197, 198, 199, 200, 203, 204, 205, 206, 208, 210, 211, 212, 213, 214; *ditamine*, 72, 134, 167, 180; *sermone*, 20, 75, 83, 111, 126, 151, 166, 173, 175, 190; om., 7, 88, 116.

290 3, 5, 8, 10, 15, 16, 30, 32, 36, 37, 39, 40, 53, 58, 63, 64, 69, 74, 75, 77, 78, 79, 81, 84, 86, 92, 99, 103, 105, 107, 109, 118, 119, 122, 129, 130, 132, 133, 134, 136, 141, 151, 155, 161, 165, 168, 169, 170, 171, 172, 175, 177, 181, 183, 185, 186, 190, 195, 196, 200, 204, 206, 211, 213, 214; *annotauit*, 48, 128; *descripsit*, 38; *p.a\ra/uit*, 197; *p\ar/rauit*, 25; *p.ar\ra/uit*, 182; *parauerat*, 57; *parauerit*, 65; *p.arauit*, 6, 9, 13, 14, 19, 23, 26, 28, 31, 33, 34, 41, 42, 43, 44, 46, 49, 51, 56, 59, 60, 61, 62, 65, 71, 72, 73, 76, 82, 87, 90, 93, 96, 97, 100, 112, 113, 115, 117, 120, 121, 123, 124, 125, 127, 135, 137, 142, 143, 146, 149, 150, 152, 153, 154, 156, 162, 164, 167, 174, 178, 179, 180, 184, 187, 189, 191, 193, 198, 199, 203, 205, 208, 210; 212; *p.a\ra/uit*, 197; *peragrauit*, 140; *perarauit*, 21; *perauit*, 98; *perorauit*, 20, 29, 45, 52, 83, 110, 126, 147, 158, 160, 166, 173; *p.errauit*, 89; *preparauit*, 104, 194; *reparauit*, 131; *scribit*, 88; *scripsit*, 116; *tractauit*, 111; om., 7, 188.

291...291 3, 5, 6, 7, 8, 9, 10, 14, 15, 16, 19, 20, 21, 23, 25, 26, 28, 29, 30, 31, 32, 33, 34, 36, 37, 38, 39, 41, 42, 43, 44, 45, 46, 48, 49, 51, 52, 53, 56, 57, 58, 59, 60, 61, 62, 63, 64, 65, 69, 71, 72, 73, 74, 75, 76, 77, 78, 79, 81, 82, 83, 84, 86, 87, 88, 89, 90, 92, 93, 96, 97, 98, 99, 100, 103, 104, 105, 109, 110, 111, 112, 113, 115, 116, 118, 119, 120, 121, 122, 123, 124, 125, 126, 127, 128, 129, 130, 131, 132, 133, 134, 135, 136, 137, 140, 141, 142, 143, 146, 147, 149, 150, 151, 152, 153, 154, 155, 156, 158, 160, 161, 162, 164, 165, 166, 168, 169,

Gilotas[284] [291]in[285] tractatu[286] suo[287] luculento[288] dictamine[289] parauit.[290] [291]

170, 171, 172, 173, 174, 175, 177, 178, 179, 180, 181, 182, 183, 184, 185, 186, 187, 189, 190, 191, 193, 194, 195, 196, 197, 198, 199, 200, 203, 204, 205, 206, 208, 210, 211, 212, 213, 214; *l. d. i. t. p.*, 13, 167; *i. t. s. l. p. d.*, 107; *i. t. s. l.*, 7; *l. d.*, 117, 188.

§208

Not present in 11, 20, 27, 28, 31, 35, 38, 44, 48, 58, 63, 69, 73, 79, 81, 83, 86, 88, 89, 91, 98, 101, 102, 110, 123, 128, 132, 139, 143, 144, 145, 146, 148, 149, 156, 167, 176, 180, 181, 192, 193; text lacunose in 12, 133, 157; omitting First-Variant manuscripts 67, 68, 70, 106, 163.

[20]Reges autem[1] eorum[2] qui[3] ab illo[4] tempore[5] [9]in[6] Gualiis[7] successerunt[8] [9] Karadoco[10] [14]Lancarbanensi[11] contemporaneo[12] meo[13] [14] [18]in[15] materia[16] scribendi[17] [18]

1   *enim*, 97, (canc.) 214.
2   *illorum*, 40, 53, 111, 118, 129, 134, 178, 186, 187, 196, 207; om., 3, 14, 168, 171, 183, 184, 189, 214.
3   *qui*/, 118.
4   *ipso*, 202; *eo*, 207; *alban. est* (canc.) *illo*, 206.
5   *tempora*, 109.
6   om., 74, 105, 126, 142, 166, 214.
7   *Galiis*, 3, 14, 74, 77, (82,) 151, 173, 175, 182, 183, 200; *Galliis*, 36, 194; *Gauliis*, 208; *Gualais*, 29; *Gualliis*, 22, 34, 39, 41, 42, 45, 47, 50, 52, 57, 62, 64, 65, 66, 67, 75, 78, 84, 90, 103, 114, 115, 118, 131, 137, 140, 152, 153, (154,) 155, 157, 160, 165, 178, 185, 186, 187, 202, 210; *Guualiis*, 213; *Guualliis*, 133; *Gwaliis*, 33, 46, 59, 60, 96; *Gwalliis*, 109, 138, 158; *Waliis*, 9; *Walliis*, 26, 40, 51, 55, 104, 105, 111, 116, 214; *Gaulia*, 177; *Gualia*, 198, 206; om., 126, 142, 166.
8   *successerant*, 2; *successere*, 17, 66, 85, 95, 139, 142, 207, 209; *successer.*, 110; *successere.*, 108; *successeret*, 202; *sucsesserunt*, 109; *sucserunt*, 157; *successerunt et*, 131; *suscepit*, 78, 206; *regnabant*, 61; om., 214.
9...9   *s. i. G.*, 25, 38.
10 *Caradoc*, 48; *Caradoco*, 7, 9, 37, 60, 66, 95, 133, 152, 158, 173, 202; *Carodoco*, 157; *Karadaco*, 5, 131; *Karadoca*, 74; *Karadocc*, 141; *Karadocho*, 24, 194; *Karadocon*, 90; *Karaloco*, 169; *Kardaco*, 29; *Karodoco*, 2, 13, 18, 47, 56, 75, 77, 97, 109, 117, 119, 168, 172, 191; *Kradoco*, 197; *Raradoco*, 54, 161; om., 96.
11 *doarbariensi*, 205; *docarbariensi*, 2, 56; *Lambarbanensi*, 165; *Lamcarbanensi*, 22, 27, 30, 45, 50, 113, 119, 141, 153, (154,) 186, 200; *Lamkarbanensi*, 142; *Lanc. albanensi*, 206; *Lancabanensi*, 41; *Lancabarnensi*, 8, 59, 60, 64, 90, 93, 166; *Lancabernensi*, 126, 150; *Lancabrenissis*, 131; *Lancanrbanensi* (altered to *Lancarbanensi*), 161; *Lancaranensi*, 134; *Lancarbainensi*, 130; *Lancarbanesi*, 151; *Lancarbarnensi*, 157; *Lancarbensi*, 147; *Lancarbrenensi*, 99; *Lancarbrenensis*, 122; *Lancardanensi*, 7, 194; *Lanc'banensi*, 78; *Lancorbanensi*, 37; *Lanicarbanensi*, 32; *Lankarbanensi*, 39, 158; *Langabarnensi*, 23; *Langarbanensi*, 5; *Langarbarnensi*, 196; *Lankarbanessi*, 42; *Lankarbrensi*, 25, 38; *Larcabanensi*, 41; *Larcarbanensi*, 212; *Lencarbanensi*, 17, 85, 95; *Llangaruanensi*, 55; *Loncarbanensi*, 47, 65, 66, 77, (82,) 121, 191, 202, 207, 209; *Longarbanensi*, 138; *Lonkarbanensi*, 51; om., 40, 111.
12 *contempecaneo*, 134; *comtemporaneo*, 16; *conporaneo*, 199; *contemperaneo*, 151; *contemporanee*, 115; *contemporanio*, 51, 138; *contemporano*, 206; *contempraneo*, 140; *contomporane*, 5; *co temporaneo*, 117; *cum tempaneo*(?), 131; *cum temporaneo*, 13, 19, 22, 36, (82), (*cum* canc.) 188; *e. tempraneo*, 56.
13 *mea*, 47; *nostro*, 74; *omo.*, 5; om., 12, 57.
14...14 *c. m. L.*, 182, 207.
15 om., 4, 40, 64, 87, 111, 134.
16 *materiam*, 32, 55, 64, 71, 85, 87, 96, 119, 134, 158, 164; *materio*, 152; *mea*, 47; om., 40, 111.

permitto,[19] [20] reges[21] uero[22] Saxonum[23] Willelmo[24] Malmesberiensi[25] et[26] [29]Henrico[27] Huntendonensi;[28] [29] quos[30] de[31] regibus[32] [66]Britonum[33] tacere[34] iubeo[35] [36] cum[37]

[17] *scribende*, 74; *scribendo*, 19, 34, 36, 105, 151, 152, 173, 182, 183, 195, 214; *scribere*, 40, 111; *scribendos*, 127, 208.

[18...18] *s. i. m.*, 6, 33, 84, 100, 115, 124; *s. materiam*, 64, 87, 134.

[19] *permitte*, 78; *promitto*, 84; *perempto*, 33; *perito*, 206; om., 90.

[20...20] om., 10.

[21] *rex* (but *reges* in margin), 169; om., 90.

[22] *autem*, 74, 104, 194; om., 8, 90, 93, 150.

[23] *Saxnum*, 189; *Saxones*, 100, 134; *Carorum*, 169; om., 90.

[24] *Guilelmo*, 66; *Guillelmo*, 7, 34, 36, 108, 118, 125, 126, 127, 151, 152, 173, 175, 177; *Guillermo*, 198, 208; *Gwilelmo*, 33; *Gwillelmo*, 138; *Uillelmo*, 205; *Uuilelmo*, 82; *Uuillelmo*, 17, 72, 74, 131, 206; *Uuillermo*, 213; *Wilelmo*, 2, 49; *Willehelmo*, 56; *Willelmo*, *Willemmo*, 170; *Willermo*, 92, 117, 186, 187, 190; *Willhelmo*, 207; *Witlelmo*, 49; *Vl'mo*, 169; *Wmo*, 172; *Willelmus*, 87; om., 3, 14, 90, 168, 171, 183, 184, 189.

[25] *i. almesberiensi*, 197; *Malberiensi*, 3, 5, 22, 54, 80, 126, 166, 168, 171, 173, 184, 189; *Malbmesburiensi*, 7; *Malbusberiensi*, 78; *Malesberiensi*, 77; *Malesbiriensi*, 32; *Malmeberiensi*, 10, 59, 60, 117, 188; *Malme\s/beriensi*, 82; *Malmeberniensi*, 114; *Malmelberiensi*, 36, ?95, 175; *Malmesbenensi*, 41; *Malmesberiendi* (altered to *Malmesberiensi*), 150; *Malmesbiensi*, 130; *Malmesbiriensi*, 9, 24, 26, 38, 45, 52, 107, 129, 136, 142, 153, 158, 160, 164, 165; *Malmesbiriensi Salesbiriensi*, 40; *Malmesbirmensi*, 50; *Malmesbriensi*, 56; *Malmesbrigensi*, 109; *Malmesburiensi*, 37, 39, 51, 55, 64, 65, 87, 99, 103, 104, 105, 116, 122, 131, 138, 157, 161; *Malmesburiensi Salesburiensi*, 111; *Malmesbyriensi*, 25; *Malmesonensi*, 151; *Malmisburiensi*, 214; *Malnieberiensi*, 13; *Malniesberiensi*, 18; *Malnsburiensi*, 206; *Mamesberiensi*, 169; *Manesbiriensi*, 186; *Masmesberiensi*, 72; *Masmesbiriensi*, 199; *Ualmesberoensi*, 205; *Walmesbiriensi*, 8; om., 90.

[26] *et et*, 174; om., 78, 84, 104, 206.

[27] *Heinrico*, 129, 205; *Henrrico*, 194; *Hurrico*, 38.

[28] *bontondonensi*, 194; *Contendonensi*, 78, 206; *Hentedonensi*, 131; *Hontedonensi*, 164, 185; *Hontendonensi*, 7, 9, 24, 26, 32, 49, 52, 57, 76, 92, 97, 99, 103, 112, 113, 118, 120, 121, 122, 135, 136, 137, 140, 150, 162, 169, 170, 172, 174, 177, 178, 187, 197, 198, 203, 210, 213; *Hontendunensi*, 202; *Honthondoniensi*, 186; *Hontenensi*, 212; *Hontendoniensi*, ?5, ?12, 18, 93, 142, 155, 161; *Hontodonensi*, 117; *Hontodonesi*, 13, 34, 59, 60, 199; *Hontondonensi*, 188; *Hontondoniensi*, 129; *Hontonensi*, 211; *Hotendonensi*, 49; *Humtendonensi*, 3; *Humtendonensis*, 208; *Hundodenensi*, 74; *Hundonensi*, 152; *Huntedonensi*, 2, 40, (82,) 111, 126, 205; *Huntedoniensi*, 153; *Huntendenensi*, 147; *Huntendonensi*, 10, 22, 30, 50, 54, 61, 80, 114, 141, (154,) 165, 204; *Huntendunensi*, 17, 47, 64, 66, 85, 95, 96, 100, 108, 134, 184, 207, 209; *Huntenduniensi*, 23, 37, 45, 87, 158, 160; *Hunteodonensi*, 196; *Huntidoniensi*, 41; *Huntindonensi*, 65; *Huntingtoniensi*, 33; *Huntodonensi*, 25, 38, 56, 77; *Huntondoniensi*, 29, 119; *Huntundonensi*, 6; *Huntyngdoniensi*, 51; *Hutendonensi*, 107; *Ontendonensi*, 16, 21, 190, 211; *doutenensi* (canc.) *Hontendonensi*; om., 157.

[29...29] *Hu. He.*, 75; om., 104.

[30] *quo*, 29, 182, 206; *quam*, 10; om., 187.

[31] om., 187, 200.

[32] *rege*, 160; *t'bus*, 199; om., 187, 190.

[33] om., 24, 117, 187, 188.

[34] om., 7, 187.

[35] *iubeo ut*, 122.

[36] *t. i. B.*, 10; om., 187.

[37] om., 160, 187.

non[38] habeant[39] [41]librum istum[40] [41] Britannici[42] sermonis[43] quem[44] Gualterus[45] Oxenefordensis[46] archidiaconus[47] [51]ex[48] Britannia[49] aduexit,[50] [51] quem de[52] hystoria

[38] *ut*, 99; om., 122, 160, 187.

[39] *habebant*, 66, 152, 189; *habent*, 38, 131; om., 160, 187.

[40] *illum*, 2, 3, 5, 6, 7, 8, 9, 10, 12, 13, 14, 16, 17, 18, 19, 21, 22, 23, 24, 25, 26, 29, 30, 32, 33, 34, 36, 37, 39, 40, 41, 42, 43, 45, 46, 47, 50. 51. 52. 53. 54, 55, 56, 57, 59, 60, 61, 62, 64, 65, 66, 71, 72, 74, 76, 77, 78, 80, (82,) 84, 87, 90, 92, 93, 95, 96, 97, 99, 100, 103, 104, 105, 108, 111, 112, 113, 114, 115, 116, 117, 118, 119, 120, 121, 122, 124, 125, 126, 127, 130, 131, 133, 134, 135, 137, 138, 140, 141, 142, 147, 150, 151, 152, 153, (154,) 155, 157, 158, 161, 162, 165, 164, 165, 166, 168, 171, 173, 175, 178, 179, 182, 183, 184, 185, 186, 188, 189, 190, 191, 194, 195, 196, 202, 203, 204, 205, 206, 207, 208, 209, 210, 211, 212, 213, 214; om., 75, 85, 109, 129, 169, 186.

[41...41] *i. l.*, 43, 71, 158, 165, 204; om., 160, 187.

[42] *Britanci*, 50; *Britannice*, 152, (altered to *Britannici*), 3; *Britonici*, 171; om., 160, 187.

[43] *semonis*, 3; om., 134, 160, 187.

[44] *quam*, 131.

[45] *Galci.*, 173; *Galterius*, 17, 40, 111, 151, 182, 197; *Galterus*, 12, 49, 107, 126, 147, 177, 199, 202, 207; *Gauterius*, 196; *Gualterius*, 53, 66, 108, 152, 166, 172, 174, 175; *Guauterius*, 36; *Gwalterus*, 45, 138; *Ualterius*, 56, 206; *Ualterus*, 77; *U\u/alterus*, 169; *Uualterus*, 43, (82,), 131, 213; *Walterius*, 2, 3, 16, 18, 33, 117, 168, 183, 184, 189, 195, 211; *Walterus*, 5, 6, 7, 8, 9, 10, 13, 14, 18, 21, 22, 23, 24, 25, 26, 29, 30, 32, 37, 39, 41, 42, 46, 47, 50, 51, 52, 54, 57, 59, 60, 61, 62, 64, 65, 74, 75, 76, 78, 80, 84, 85, 90, 92, 93, 95, 96, 97, 99, 100, 103, 104, 105, 109, 112, 113, 114, 115, 116, 118, 119, 120, 121, 122, 124, 127, 130, 133, 134, 135, 139, 140, 141, 142, 150, 153, (154,) 155, 157, 158, 160, 161, 162, 164, 178, 179, 185, 186, 187, 188, 190, 191, 194, 203, 204, 208, 210, 212, 214; *Waltherius*, 205; *Wolterius*, 171.

[46] *Exefordis*, 196; *Exenefordensis*, 17, 194; *Exenefrodensis*, 174; *Exenfordensis*, 64; *Exinesordensis*, 104; *Exnefordensis*, 209; *Exonefordiensis*, 75, 206; *Exonfordiensis*, 206; *H.fordensis*, 40, 111; *Hoxenefordensis*, 157, 169; *?Menefordensis*, 72; *Orenefordensis*, 151, 175; *Osenefordensis*, 134; *Oxdenefordensis*, 47; *Oxefordis* 53; *Oxenefordesis*, 74; *Oxeneford\i/ensis*, 80; *Oxenefordiensis*, 54, 62, 78, 161, 211; *Oxenefordis*, 19, 36, 127, 182, 195, 208; *Oxenfordensi*, 116; *Oxenfordensis*, 5, 9, 25, 32, 33, 43, 52, 90, 99, 105, 109, 122, 133, 140, 150, (154,) 168, 171, 178, 214; *Oxenofordensis*, 59, 60, 77, 117, 188, 191; *Oxenfordis*, 34; *Oxifordensis*, 38, 131; *Oxinefordensis*, 3, 10, 14, 92, 158, 164, 166, 173, 177, 199; *Oxin\e/fordensis*, 126; *Oxinofordensis*, 13; *Oxnefordensis*, 18, 84, 103, 115, 165; *Oxnefordiensis*, 93, 153; *Oxonefordensis*, 2, 26, 37; *Oxonfordensis*, 204; *Oxonofordis*, 152; *Oxoniensis*, 61.

[47] *adchidiaconus*, 92; *archiadiaconus*, 45; *archidaconus*, 199; *archideaconus*, 41, 64, 74; *archidiachonus*, 6, 22, 171; *archidia\co/nus*, 36; *archidyaconus*, 134; *archidiconus*, 57, 131.

[48] *de*, 17, 42, 66, 71, 84, 95, 108, 138, 142, 158, 202, 207, 209.

[49] *Britannia.*, 147; *Britannia Armoricana*, 61.

[50] *adux^1*, 7; om., 77.

[51...51] *a. e. B.*, 99, 122.

[52] *etiam de*, 25; om., 36, 208.

eorum[53] ueraciter[54] editum[55] in honore[56] [59]predictorum[57] principum[58] [59] hoc[60] modo[61] in [65]Latinum[62] sermonem[63] transferre[64] [65]

[53] *istorum*, 78, 133, 206; om., 147.
[54] *uerasciter*, 100.
[55] *edictum*, 64, 77, 134, 168, 171, 184, 189; *aditum*, 96; om., 56.
[56] *honorem*, 126, 133, 166, 190; *honor\e/*, 209.
[57] (bis), 157; om., 78, 206.
[58] *principium*, 50, 121, 171.
[59...59] *prin. pred.*, 18, 95, 120, 185, 187, 203.
[60] *hunc*, 61; *ho.c*, (altered to *huc*), 119.
[61] *ordine*, 16; om., 61, 119.
[62] *Latino*, 138.
[63] om., 5, 22, 50, 114; lacking, 179.
[64] *tran\s/ferre*, 96; *trasferre*, 203; *transferri*, 133; canc., 107; lacking, 179.
[65...65] *s. L. t.*, 40, 111; *L. t. s.*, 207.
[66...66] *curauit*, 99, 122, 131, 205; *curaui ualete*, 39, 40, 111; *curauit Deo gracias etc. etc.*, 174; *curaui Deo gracias refl.it*, 198; *curaui ?katarticum magnum imperiale*, 100; canc., 107; lacking, 179.

Appendix III

MAPS

The following relate to the discussion in Chapter IX of
the circulation of groups of manuscripts.

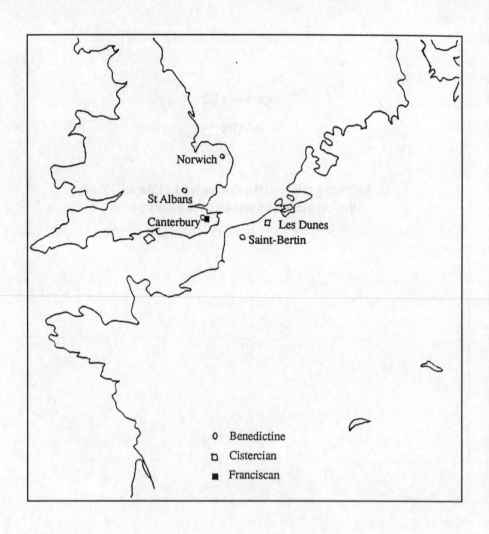

1. The Second Variant

Jervaulx

Roche

Fécamp
Jumièges

○ Benedictine
□ Cistercian

2. The Double Dedication

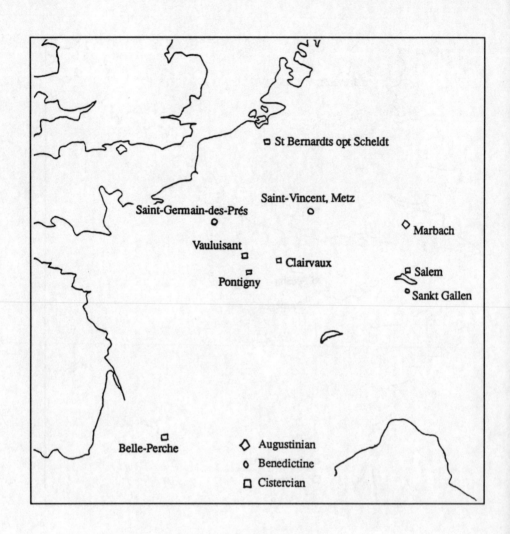

St Bernardts opt Scheldt

Saint-Vincent, Metz

Saint-Germain-des-Prés

Marbach

Vauluisant

Clairvaux

Pontigny

Salem

Sankt Gallen

Belle-Perche

◇ Augustinian

○ Benedictine

□ Cistercian

3. The Nameless Dedication

Hatfield Peverel

Les Dunes

Mont-Saint-Eloi   Tournai
Arras   Marchiennes
Amiens   Anchin   • Würzburg

Chaalis

◇ Augustinian

○ Benedictine

□ Cistercian

. Premonstratensian

4. 117/188 type

5. Pudibundus Brito Type

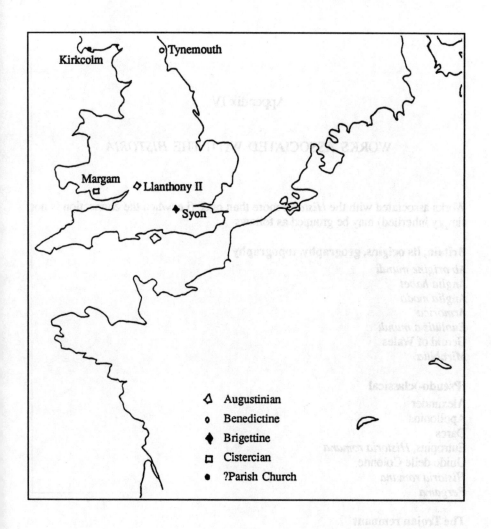

6. Prologus/editio Type

Appendix IV

WORKS ASSOCIATED WITH THE *HISTORIA*

Works associated with the *Historia* more than once (i.e. when the connection is not simply inherited) may be grouped as follows

Britain, its origins, geography, topography

Ab origine mundi
Anglia habet
Anglia modo
Armorica
Euolutis a mundi
Gerald of Wales
Mirabilia

(Pseudo-)classical

Alexander
Apollonius
Dares
Eutropius, *Historia romana*
Guido delle Colonne
Historia romana
Pergama

The Trojan remnant

Antenor
Superius autem excidio

The East

Crusading chronicles (Baudri de Bourgueil, Fulcher of Chartres, Peter Tudebode, Robert of Reims)
Crusade letters
Descriptions of Holy Land (Bede, *De locis sanctis*, Fretellus, Ludulphus de Sudheim, anon. works)
Texts on Islam and Mohammed (Embricon of Augsburg)
Jacques de Vitry, *Historia orientalis*
Marco Polo

Universal history
Robert Abilaut
Ages of the World
Freculph
Higden, *Polichronicon*
Martinus Polonus
Edmond de Pontigny, *Speculum de tempore mundi*

Geography, other
Cosmographia
Liber prouincialis
Mappa mundi
Epistola Alexandri
Prester John
Solinus

Continental history
Local histories (sees of Cologne, Trier)
Einhard, *Uita Karoli*
French histories (Andreas Syluius, *Cum animaduerterem*)
Historia Gothorum, Wandalorum, Sueuorum
Historia Turpini
Robert de Torigni
Ximenes, *Chronica Hispanie*

Insular history
Alfred of Beverley
Bede, *Historia ecclesiastica*
Gildas, *De excidio*
Henry of Huntingdon
Historia Brittonum
Peter Langtoft
Nicholas Trivett
William of Malmesbury
Monastic chronicles
Material relating to the Scottish question

Chronology

Genealogy

Law
Articles of Munster
Magna carta
Quadripartitus
Book of Briefs
?Richard FitzRalph

Devotional texts
Hagiography
Meditationes
Innocent III, *De mysteriis misse*
Hugh of Saint-Victor
Biblical commentaries
Vision literature

Apocalyptic
De Antichristo
Methodius, *Reuelationes*
Sibylline prophecies

Apocryphal
Finding of the True Cross
Gesta Saluatoris
Gospel of Nicodemus
Infancy gospels
Testamenta xii patriarcharum
Uita Ade et Eue

Prophecy

Wisdom literature
Petrus Alphonsus
Secreta Secretorum

BIBLIOGRAPHY

Anderson, A. O., M. O. Anderson, W. C. Dickinson, facs. ed., *The Chronicle of Melrose from the Cottonian Manuscript, Faustina B.ix, in the British Museum* (London, 1936)

Ardenne, S. R. T. O. d', 'The Cistercian Origin of MS Liège University Library 369 C', *Studies in Language and Literature in Honour of Margaret Schlauch*, edited by I. Dobrzycka *et al.* (Warsaw, 1966), pp. 31–35

Ardenne, S. R. T. O. d', 'Un Extrait peu connu de l'*Historia Brittonum* de Nennius MS. Liège 369 C', in *Mélanges offerts a Rita Lejeune*, 2 vols (Gembloux, 1969), I.1–4

Ardenne, S. R. T. O. d', 'A Neglected Manuscript of British History, MS. Liège Univ. Lib. 369 C', in *English and Medieval Studies Presented to J. R. R. Tolkien*, edited by N. Davis and C. L. Wrenn (London, 1962), pp. 84–93

Arnold, Thomas, ed., *Henrici archidiaconi Huntendunensis Historia Anglorum* (London, 1879)

Atkins, Ivor, and Neil R. Ker, edd., *Catalogus librorum manuscriptorum bibliothecae Wigorniensis made in 1622–1623 by Patrick Young, librarian to King James I* (Cambridge, 1944)

Auerbach, Erich, *Literary Language and its Public in Late Latin Antiquity and in the Middle Ages*, translated by Ralph Manheim (New York, 1965)

Avril, F., 'Notes sur quelques manuscrits bénédictins normands du xie et du xiie siècle', *Mélanges d'archéologie et d'histoire (École française de Rome)*, 76 (1964), 491–525; 77 (1965), 209–48

Baker, D., 'Legend and Reality: the Case of Waldef of Melrose', *Studies in Church History*, 12 (1975), 59–82

Baker, Derek, 'Patronage in the Early Twelfth-Century Church: Walter Espec, Kirkham and Rievaulx', in *Traditio – Krisis – Renovatio aus theologischer Sicht: Festschrift W. Keller zum 65. Geburtstag*, edited by Bernd Jaspert and Rudolf Mohr (Marburg, 1976), pp. 92–100

Barlow, Frank, *The English Church 1066–1154* (London, 1979)

Bartlett, Robert, *Gerald of Wales 1146–1223* (Oxford, 1982)

Becker, Gustav, ed., *Catalogi bibliothecarum antiqui* (Bonn, 1885)

Beddie, James Stuart, 'Libraries in the Twelfth Century: their Catalogues and Contents', in *Anniversary Essays in Mediaeval History by Students of Charles Homer Haskins*, edited by C. H. Taylor (Boston, Mass., 1929), pp. 1–23

Bédier, J., *Les Légendes épiques. Recherches sur la formation des chansons de geste*, 3 vols (Paris, 1912)

Bell, David N., 'The Books of Meaux Abbey', *Analecta Cisterciensia*, 40 (1984), 25–83

Benson, C. David, *The History of Troy in Middle English Literature: Guido delle Colonne's Historia destructionis Troiae in Medieval England* (Woodbridge, 1980)

Benson, Robert L., 'Political *Renovatio*: Two Models from Roman Antiquity', in *Renaissance and Renewal in the Twelfth Century*, edited by R. L. Benson and Giles Constable (Oxford, 1982), pp. 339–86

Benton, John F., 'The Court of Champagne as a Literary Center', *Speculum*, 36 (1961), 551–91

Berger, Elie, 'Richard le Poitevin, moine de Cluny, historien et poète', *Bibliothèque des Écoles françaises d'Athènes et de Rome*, 6 (1879), 45–138

Bévenot, Maurice, *The Tradition of Manuscripts: a Study in the Transmission of St. Cyprian's Treatises* (London, 1961)

Beverley Smith, J., 'The "Cronica de Wallia" and the Dynasty of Dinefwr: a Textual and Historical study', *Bulletin of the Board of Celtic Studies*, 20 (1962–64), 261–82

Bezzola, Reta R., *Les Origines et la formation de la littérature courtoise en occident (500–1200)*, 3 vols (Paris, 1944–60)

Bischoff, B., G. I. Lieftinck, and G. Battelli, *Nomenclature des écritures livresques du ixe au xvie siècle* (Paris, 1954)

Blum, Rudolf, *La Biblioteca della Badia fiorentina e i codici di Antonio Cortinelli* (Vatican City, 1951)

Boitani, Piero, and Anna Torti, edd., *Intellectuals and Writers in Fourteenth-Century Europe* (Cambridge, 1986)

Bongars, J., ed., *Gesta Dei per Francos sive orientalium expeditionum et regni Francorum hierosolimitani historia*, 3 vols in 2 (Hanover, 1611)

Bossuat, A., 'Les Origines troyennes: leur rôle dans la littérature historique au xve siècle', *Annales de Normandie*, 8 (1958), 187–97

Boussard, J., 'Influences insulaires dans la formation de l'écriture gothique', *Scriptorium*, 5 (1951), 238–64

Boutarie, E., 'Vincent de Beauvais et la connaissance de l'Antiquité classique au treizième siècle', *Revue des questions historiques*, 17 (1895), 5–57

Boutemy, A., 'Une Copie nouvelle du *Status Imperii Iudaici* conservée dans un manuscrit d'Aulne', *Hommages à Léon Herrmann* [Collection Latomus 44] (Bruxelles, 1960), pp. 194–204

Boutemy, A., 'Note sur l'origine et la date du *Status Imperii Iudaici*', *Scriptorium*, 1 (1946/7), 66–69

Boutemy, A., 'Le Poème *Pergama flere uolo* . . . et ses imitateurs de xiie siècle', *Latomus*, 5 (1946), 233–44

Boutemy, A., 'Le Recueil poétique du manuscrit lat. 5129 de la Bibliothèque nationale de Paris', *Scriptorium*, 2 (1948), 47–55

Bozoy, E., 'Les Apocryphes bibliques', in *Le Moyen Age et la Bible*, edited by P. Riché and Guy Lobrichon (Paris, 1984), pp. 429–48

Brandt, William J., *The Shape of Medieval History: Studies in Modes of Perception* (New Haven, Conn., 1966)

Brett, Martin, 'John of Worcester and his Contemporaries', in *The Writing of History in the Middle Ages: Essays Presented to Richard William Southern*, edited by R. H. C. Davis, J. M. Wallace-Hadrill *et al.* (Oxford, 1981), pp. 101–26

Brewer, J. S., *et al.*, ed., *Giraldi Cambrensis Opera*, 8 vols (London 1861–91)

Brincken, Anna-Dorothea von den, 'Studien zur Überlieferung der Chronik des Martin von Troppau (Erfahrungen mit einem massenhaft überlieferten historischen Text)', *Deutsches Archiv für Erforschung des Mittelalters*, 41 (1985), 460–531

Bromwich, Rachel, *Trioedd Ynys Prydein: the Welsh Triads*, second edition (Cardiff, 1978)

Brooke, Christopher N. L., *The Church and the Welsh Border in the Central Middle Ages* (Woodbridge, 1986)

Brooke, Christopher N. L., 'Historical Writing in England between 850 and 1150', *Settimane di studio del Centro italiano di studi sull' alto medioevo*, 17 (1969), 223–47

Brown, E. A. R., 'La Notion de la légitimité et la prophétie à la cour de Philippe Auguste', *La France de Philippe Auguste: le temps des mutations*, edited by Robert-Henri Bautier (Paris, 1982), pp. 77–110

Brugger, E., 'Zu Galfrid von Monmouth's *Historia Regum Britanniae*', *Zeitschrift für französische Sprache und Literatur*, 57 (1933), 257–312

Bruns, G. L., 'The Originality of Texts in a Manuscript Culture', *Comparative Literature*, 32 (1980), 113–29

Bunt, G. H. V., 'Alexander and the Universal Chronicle: Scholars and Translators', in *The Medieval Alexander Legend and Romance Epic: Essays in Honour of David J. A. Ross*, edited by P. Noble, L. Polak, and C. Isoz (New York, 1982), pp. 1–10

Burrow, J. A., *Medieval Writers and their Work: Middle English Literature and its Background 1100-1500* (Oxford, 1982)

Burton, Janet, 'The Foundation of the British Cistercian Houses', in *Cistercian Art and Architecture in the British Isles*, edited by C. Norton and D. Park (Cambridge, 1986), pp. 24–39

Butler, H. E., transl., *The Autobiography of Giraldus Cambrensis* (London, 1937)

Buttenweiser, Hilda, 'Popular Authors of the Middle Ages: the Testimony of the Manuscripts', *Speculum*, 17 (1942), 50–55

Cahen, Claude, *La Syrie du Nord à l' époque des croisades et la principauté franque d'Antioche* (Paris, 1940)

Caldwell, R. A., 'The Use of Sources in the Variant and Vulgate Versions of the *Historia Regum Britannie* and the Question of the Order of the Versions', *Bulletin bibliographique de la Société internationale arthurienne*, 9 (1957), 123–24

Caldwell, R. A., 'Wace's *Roman de Brut* and the *Variant Version* of Geoffrey of Monmouth's *Historia Regum Britanniae*', *Speculum*, 31 (1956), 675–82

Callus, D. A., 'Robert Grosseteste as Scholar', in *Robert Grosseteste as Scholar and Bishop: Essays in Commemoration of the Seventh Centenary of his Death*, edited by D. A. Callus (Oxford, 1955), pp. 1–69

Campbell, James, 'Some Twelfth-Century Views of the Anglo-Saxon Past', *Peritia*, 3 (1984), 131–50, reprinted in his *Essays in Anglo-Saxon History* (London, 1986), pp. 209–28

Cantor, Norman F. 'The Interpretation of Medieval History', in *Essays on the Reconstruction of Medieval History*, edited by Vaclav Mudroch and Gordon S. Couse (Montreal, 1974), pp. 1–18

Carley, James P., 'John Leland and the Contents of English Pre-Dissolution Libraries: Lincolnshire', *Transactions of the Cambridge Bibliographical Society* 9 (1986–), 330–57

Cary, George, *The Medieval Alexander*, edited by David J. A. Ross (Cambridge, 1956)

Castellani, Arrigo, *Bédier avait-il raison? La méthode de Lachmann dans les éditions de textes du moyen âge* (Fribourg-en-Suisse, 1957)

Cavanaugh, Susan H., 'A Study of Books Privately Owned in England: 1300–1450' (unpublished Ph.D dissertation, University of Pennsylvania, 1980)

Chambers, E. K., *Arthur of Britain* (London, 1927)

Chambers, E. K., 'The Date of Geoffrey of Monmouth's History', *Review of English Studies*, 1 (1925), 431–36

Chédeville, André, and Noël-Yves Tonnerre, *La Bretagne féodale xie–xiie siècle* (Rennes, 1987)

Cheney, C. R., 'English Cistercian Libraries: the First Century', in *Medieval Texts and Studies* (Oxford, 1973), pp. 328–45

Cheney, C. R., *English Bishops' Chanceries* (Manchester, 1950)

Chevreux, P., and J. Vernier, *Les Archives de Normandie et de la Seine-Inférieure* (Rouen, 1911)

Chibnall, Marjorie, *The World of Orderic Vitalis* (Oxford, 1984)

Christianson, C. Paul, 'A Century of the Manuscript-Book Trade in Late Medieval London', *Medievalia et humanistica*, NS, 12 (1984), 143–65

Clarke, Basil, ed. & transl., *Life of Merlin: Geoffrey of Monmouth, Vita Merlini* (Cardiff, 1973)

Colgrave, Bertram, and R. A. B. Mynors, edd. & transl., *Bede's Ecclesiastical History of the English People* (Oxford, 1969)

Colophons de manuscrits occidentaux des origines au xvie siècle, 6 vols (Fribourg-en-Suisse, 1965–82)

Contamine, Philippe, 'Une Interpolation de la "Chronique Martinienne": le "Brevis tractatus" d'Etienne de Conty, official de Corbie (ob. 1413)', *Annales de Bretagne et des Pays de l'Ouest*, 87 (1980), 367–86

Coss, P. R., 'Aspects of Cultural Diffusion in Medieval England: the Early Romances, Local Society and Robin Hood', *Past and Present*, 108 (1985), 35–79

Crick, J. C., 'Geoffrey of Monmouth and Early Insular History',

Crick, J. C., 'Manuscripts of Geoffrey of Monmouth's *Historia regum Britannie*', *Arthurian Literature*, 7 (1987), 158–62

Crick, J. C., 'The Manuscripts of the Works of Geoffrey of Monmouth: a New Supplement', *Arthurian Literature*, 6 (1986), 157–62

Crick, Julia C., *The Historia regum Britannie of Geoffrey of Monmouth, III: a Summary Catalogue of the Manuscripts* (Cambridge, 1989)

Crouch, David, *The Beaumont Twins: the Roots and Branches of Power in the Twelfth Century* (Cambridge, 1985)

Crouch, D., 'Robert, Earl of Gloucester, and the Daughter of Zelophehad', *Journal of Medieval History*, 11 (1985), 227–43

Croydon, F. E., 'Abbot Laurence of Westminster and Hugh of St. Victor', *Mediaeval and Renaissance Studies*, 2 (1950), 169–71

Curley, Michael J., 'Fifteenth-century Glosses on the *Prophecy of John of Bridlington*: a Text, its Meaning and its Purpose', *Mediaeval Studies*, 46 (1984), 321–39

Daly, Saralyn R., 'Peter Comestor: Master of Histories', *Speculum*, 32 (1957), 62–73

Dekkers, D. E., and J. Fraipont, edd., *Sancti Aurelii Augustini Enarrationes in Psalmos I–L* (Turnhout, 1956)

Delhaye, Philippe, 'L'Organization scolaire au xiie siècle', *Traditio*, 5 (1947), 211–68

Delisle, Léopold, *Le Cabinet des manuscrits de la Bibliothèque impériale: étude sur la formation de ce dépôt comprenant les éléments d'une histoire de la calligraphie, de la miniature, de la reliure, et du commerce des livres à Paris avant l'invention de l'imprimerie*, 3 vols (Paris, 1868–81)

Delisle, Léopold, ed., *Chronique de Robert de Torigni, abbé du Mont-Saint-Michel, suivie de divers opuscules historiques de cet auteur et de plusieurs réligieux de la même abbaye,* 2 vols (Rouen, 1872/3)

Delisle, L., *Inventaire des manuscrits de la Bibliothèque nationale, fonds de Cluni* (Paris, 1884)

Delisle, Léopold, ed., 'Matériaux pour l'édition de Guillaume de Jumièges préparée par Jules Lair', *Bibliothèque de l'École des chartes,* 71 (1910), 481–526

Denholm-Young, N., 'Edward of Windsor and Bermondsey Priory', *English Historical Review,* 48 (1933), 431–43

Dept, Gaston G., *Les Influences anglaise et française dans le comté de Flandre au début du xiiie siècle* (Gent, 1928)

Derolez, A., *Les Catalogues de bibliothèques* (Turnhout, 1979)

Derolez, R., 'An Epitome of the Anglo-Saxon Chronicle in Lambert of Saint-Omer's "Liber floridus" ', *English Studies,* 48 (1967), 226–31

Derolez, R., 'King Arthur in Flanders', in *Festschrift Rudolf Stamm zu seinem sechzigsten Geburtstag am 12. April 1969,* edited by E. Kolb and Jörg Hasler (Bern-Munich, 1969), pp. 239–47

Destrez, Jean, and G. Fink-Errera, 'Des Manuscrits apparemment datés', *Scriptorium,* 12 (1958), 56–93

Dickinson, J. C., 'English Regular Canons and the Continent in the Twelfth Century', *Transactions of the Royal Historical Society,* 5th ser., 1 (1951), 71–89

Dodwell, Barbara, 'History and the Monks of Norwich Cathedral Priory', *Reading Medieval Studies,* 5 (1979), 38–56

Draak, Maartje, 'Virgil of Salzburg versus "Aethicus Ister" ', in *Dancwerc opstellen aangeboden aan Prof. Dr. D. Th. Enklaar* (Groningen, 1959), pp. 33–42

Dronke, P., 'Peter of Blois and Poetry at the Court of Henry II', *Mediaeval Studies,* 38 (1976), 185–235

Duby, Georges, 'The Culture of the Knightly Class: Audience and Patronage', in *Renaissance and Renewal in the Twelfth Century,* edited by Robert L. Benson and Giles Constable (Oxford, 1982), pp. 248–62

Duby, G., 'Problèmes et méthodes en histoire culturelle', in *Objet et méthodes de l'histoire de la culture,* edited by Jacques Le Goff and Bela Kopeczi (Paris, 1982), pp. 13–17

Duggan, Anne, *Thomas Becket: a Textual History of his Letters* (Oxford, 1980)

Dumville, D. N., 'Anecdota from Manuscripts of Geoffrey of Monmouth', *Arthurian Literature* (forthcoming)

Dumville, David N., 'Celtic-Latin Texts in Northern England, c. 1150 – c. 1250', *Celtica,* 12 (1977), 19–49, reprinted in his *Histories and Pseudo-Histories,* XI

Dumville, D. N., 'An Early Text of Geoffrey of Monmouth's *Historia regum Britanniae* and the Circulation of some Latin Histories in Twelfth-Century Normandy', *Arthurian Literature,* 4 (1985), 1–36, reprinted in his *Histories and Pseudo-Histories,* XIV

Dumville, David N., ed., *The Historia Brittonum,* 10 vols (Cambridge, 1985–)

Dumville, David N., 'The Historical Value of the *Historia Brittonum*', *Arthurian Literature,* 6 (1986), 1–26, reprinted in his *Histories and Pseudo-Histories,* VII

Dumville, David N., *Histories and Pseudo-histories of the Insular Middle Ages* (Aldershot, 1990)

Dumville, David N., 'The *Liber floridus* of Lambert of Saint-Omer and the *Historia Brittonum*', *Bulletin of the Board of Celtic Studies*, 26 (1974–76), 103–22, reprinted in his *Histories and Pseudo-Histories*, XII

Dumville, David N., 'The Manuscripts of Geoffrey of Monmouth's *Historia regum Britanniae*', *Arthurian Literature*, 3 (1983), 113–28

Dumville, David N., 'The Manuscripts of Geoffrey of Monmouth's *Historia regum Britanniae*: Addenda, Corrigenda, and an Alphabetical List', *Arthurian Literature*, 4 (1985), 164–71

Dumville, D. N., 'The Origin of the C-text of the Variant Version of the *Historia Regum Britannie*', *Bulletin of the Board of Celtic Studies*, 26 (1974-76), 315-22

Dumville, D. N., 'A Paraphrase of the *Historia Brittonum*: Two Fragments', *Bulletin of the Board of Celtic Studies*, 25 (1972–74), 101–05, reprinted in his *Histories and Pseudo-Histories*, XIII

Dumville, David, and Michael Lapidge, edd., *The Annals of St Neots with Vita Prima Sancti Neoti* (Cambridge, 1985)

Dyson, A. G., 'The Monastic Patronage of Bishop Alexander of Lincoln', *Journal of Ecclesiastical History*, 26 (1975), 1–24

East, W. G., 'De Contemptu Britonum: A History of Prejudice', *Dissertation Abstracts International*, A 36 (1975), 270

Eckhardt, C. D., 'The Date of the 'Prophetia Merlini' Commentary in MSS Cotton Claudius B.VII and Bibliothèque nationale fonds latin 6233', *Notes and Queries*, 221 [NS, 23] (1976), 146–47

Eckhardt, Caroline D., ed., *The Prophetia Merlini of Geoffrey of Monmouth: a Fifteenth-Century English Commentary* (Cambridge, Mass., 1982)

Eckhardt, C. D., 'The *Prophetia Merlini* of Geoffrey of Monmouth: Latin Manuscript Copies', *Manuscripta*, 26 (1982), 167–76

Edwards, A. S. G., 'The Influence and Audience of the *Polychronicon*: Some Observations', *Proceedings of the Leeds Philosophical and Literary Society (literary and historical section)*, 17 (1978–81), 113–19

Eliade, Mircea, *The Myth of the Eternal Return or Cosmos in History* (New York, 1954)

Emanuel, Hywel D., 'Geoffrey of Monmouth's *Historia Regum Britannie*: a Second Variant Version', *Medium Ævum*, 35 (1966), 103–10

Evans, J. Gwenogvryn, ed., *The Poetry in the Red Book of Hergest* (Llanbedrog, 1911)

Faral, E., 'Geoffroy de Monmouth: les faits et les dates de sa biographie', *Romania*, 53 (1927), 1–42

Faral, Edmond, 'L'*Historia regum Britanniae* de Geoffroy de Monmouth à propos d'une édition récente', *Romania*, 55 (1929), 482–527

Faral, Edmond, ed., *La Légende arthurienne: études et documents. Les plus anciens textes*, 3 vols (Paris, 1929)

Faral, E., 'Le Manuscrit 511 du "Hunterian Museum" de Glasgow', *Studi medievali*, NS, 9 (1936), 18–121

Faucon, M., *La Librairie des papes d'Avignon: sa formation, sa composition, ses catalogues (1316–1420)*, 2 vols (Paris, 1886/7)

Fauroux, M., 'Deux autographes de Dudon de Saint-Quentin (1011, 1015)', *Bibliothèque de l'École des chartes*, 111 (1953), 229–34

Fleischmann, Suzanne, 'On the Representation of History and Fiction in the Middle Ages', *History and Theory*, 22 (1983), 278–310

Fletcher, Robert Huntington, *The Arthurian Material in the Chronicles, especially those of Great Britain and France* (Boston, Mass., 1906)

Fletcher, R. H., 'Two Notes on the *Historia regum Britanniae* of Geoffrey of Monmouth', *Publications of the Modern Language Association of America*, NS, 9 (1901), 461–74

Fleuriot, L., 'Les Fragments du texte brittonique de la "Prophetia Merlini" ', *Etudes celtiques* 14 (1974/5), 43–56

Flint, Valerie I. J., 'The *Historia Regum Britanniae* of Geoffrey of Monmouth: Parody and its Purpose. A Suggestion', *Speculum*, 54 (1979), 447–68

Flint, Valerie, 'World History in the Early Twelfth Century; the "Imago mundi" of Honorius Augustodunensis', in *The Writing of History in the Middle Ages: Studies Presented to Richard William Southern*, edited by R. H. C. Davis, J. M. Wallace-Hadrill *et al.* (Oxford, 1981), pp. 211–38

Flower, Robin, *The Irish Tradition* (Oxford, 1947)

Foreville, R., 'Robert de Torigni et "Clio" ', in *Millénaire monastique du Mont Saint-Michel*, 4 vols (Paris, 1966–71), II.141–53

Fotheringham, John Knight, ed., *The Bodleian Manuscript of Jerome's Version of the Chronicle of Eusebius* (Oxford, 1905)

Fotheringham, John Knight, ed., *Eusebii Pamphili Chronici Canones* (London, 1923)

Fox, James J., 'A Rotinese Dynastic Genealogy: Structure and Event', in *The Translation of Culture: Essays to E. E. Evans-Pritchard* edited by T. O. Beidelman (Tavistock, 1971), pp. 37–77

France, John, 'Note sur le manuscrit 6041A du fonds latin de la Bibliothèque nationale: un nouveau fragment d'un manuscrit de l'*Historia Belli Sacri*', *Bibliothèque de l'École des chartes*, 126 (1968), 413–16

Frappier, Jean, [review of Hammer, *Geoffrey of Monmouth 'Historia Regum Britanniae', A Variant Version Edited from Manuscripts* (Cambridge, Mass., 1951),] *Romania*, 74 (1953), 125–28

Gaiffier d'Hestroy, B. de, 'L'Hagiographe et son public au xie siècle', in *Miscellanea historica in honorem Leonis van der Essen*, 2 vols (Bruxelles, 1947), I.135–66

Galbraith, V. H., *Historical Research in Medieval England* (London, 1951), reprinted in his *Kings and Chroniclers: Essays in English Medieval History* (London, 1982), XI

Galbraith, V. H., 'The Literacy of the Medieval English Kings', *Proceedings of the British Academy*, 21 (1935), 201–38, reprinted in his *Kings and Chroniclers: Essays in English Medieval History* (London, 1982), I

Gallais, P., 'La *Variant Version* de l'*Historia Regum Britanniae* et le *Brut* de Wace', *Romania*, 87 (1966), 1–32

Garand, M.-C., 'Auteurs latins et autographes des xie et xiie siècles', *Scrittura e civiltà*, 5 (1981), 77–104

Garand, Monique-Cécile, 'Le Scriptorium de Guibert de Nogent', *Scriptorium*, 31 (1977), 3–29

Genet, Jean-Philippe, 'Essai de bibliométrie médiévale: l'histoire dans les bibliothèques anglaises', *Revue française d'histoire du livre*, NS, 16 (1977), 531–68

Gerould, G. H., 'King Arthur and Politics', *Speculum*, 2 (1927), 33–51

Gerould, G. H., 'A Text of Merlin's Prophecies', *Speculum*, 23 (1948), 102–3

Gerritsen, W. P., 'L'Episode de la guerre contre les Romains dans *La mort artu* neérlandaise', in *Mélanges de langue et de littérature du moyen âge et de la renaissance offerts à Jean Frappier, Professeur à la Sorbonne par ses élèves et ses amis*, 2 vols (Geneva, 1970), I.337–49

Gerritsen, William P., 'Jacob van Maerlant and Geoffrey of Monmouth', in *An Arthurian Tapestry: Essays in Memory of Lewis Thorpe*, edited by Kenneth Varty (Glasgow, 1981), pp. 368–88

Ghellinck, J. de, *L'Essor de la littérature latine au xii*^{e} *siècle*, 2 vols in 1 (Brussels, 1946)

Gibson, M., 'History at Bec in the Twelfth Century', in *The Writing of History in the Middle Ages: Essays Presented to Richard William Southern*, edited by R. H. C. Davis, J. M. Wallace-Hadrill *et al.* (Oxford, 1981), pp. 167–86

Giles, Phyllis M., 'A Handlist of the Bradfer-Lawrence Manuscripts Deposited on Loan at the Fitzwilliam Museum', *Transactions of the Cambridge Bibliographical Society*, 6 (1972–76), 86–99

Gilissen, Léon, 'La Composition des cahiers: le pliage du parchemin et l'imposition', *Scriptorium*, 26 (1972), 3-33

Goddu, A. A., and R. H. Rouse, 'Gerald of Wales and the *Florilegium Angelicum*', *Speculum*, 52 (1977), 488–521

Gotoff, Harold. C., *The Transmission of the Text of Lucan in the Ninth Century* (Cambridge, Mass., 1971)

Goy, Rudolf, *Die Überlieferung der Werke Hugos von St. Viktor: ein Beitrag zur Kommunikationsgeschichte des Mittelalters* (Stuttgart, 1976)

Gransden, Antonia, 'The Continuations of the *Flores historiarum* from 1265 to 1327', *Mediaeval Studies*, 36 (1974), 472–92

Gransden, Antonia, 'The Growth of the Glastonbury Traditions and Legends in the Twelfth Century', *Journal of Ecclesiastical History*, 27 (1976), 337–58

Gransden, Antonia, *Historical Writing in England, c. 550 to c. 1307* (London, 1974)

Gransden, Antonia, *Historical Writing in England ii: c. 1307 to the Early Sixteenth Century* (London, 1982)

Gransden, Antonia, 'Propaganda in English Medieval Historiography', *Journal of Medieval History*, 1 (1975), 363–81

Gransden, A., 'Realistic Observation in Twelfth-century England', *Speculum*, 47 (1972), 29–51

Greenway, Diana, 'Henry of Huntingdon and the Manuscripts of his *Historia Anglorum*', *Anglo-Norman Studies*, 9 (1986), 103–21

Greenway, Diana E., ed., *John Le Neve. Fasti Ecclesiae Anglicanae 1066–1300*, 12 vols (London, 1968–)

Grierson, Philip, 'La Bibliothèque de St-Vaast d'Arras au xiie siècle', *Revue Bénédictine*, 52 (1940), 117–40

Grierson, Philip, 'Les Livres de l'abbé Seiwold de Bath', *Revue Bénédictine*, 52 (1940), 96–116

Griscom, A., 'The Date of Composition of Geoffrey of Monmouth's *Historia*: New Manuscript Evidence', *Speculum*, 1 (1926), 129–56

Griscom, Acton, and Robert E. Jones, edd. & transl., *The Historia Regum Britanniæ of Geoffrey of Monmouth with Contributions to the Study of its Place in Early British History* (New York, 1929)

Guenée, B., 'La Culture historique des nobles: le succès des *Fait des romains* (xiiie–xve siècles)', in *La Noblesse au moyen âge, xie–xve siècles. Essais à la mémoire de Robert Boutruche*, edited by Philippe Contamine (Paris, 1976), pp. 261–88, reprinted in his *Politique et histoire au moyen-âge: recueil d'articles* *sur l' histoire politique et l' historiographie médiévale (1956–1981)* (Paris, 1981), pp. 299–326

Guenée, Bernard, 'L'Enquête historique ordonée par Édouard 1er, roi d'Angleterre, en 1291', *Comptes rendus des séances de l' Académie des inscriptions et belles-lettres* (1975), 572–84, reprinted in his *Politique et histoire au moyen-âge: recueil d' articles sur l' histoire politique et l' historiographie médiévale (1956–1981)* (Paris, 1981), pp. 239–51

Guenée, Bernard, *Histoire et culture historique dans l' Occident médiéval* (Paris, 1980)

Guenée, B., 'L'Histoire entre l'éloquence et la science. Quelques remarques sur le prologue de Guillaume de Malmesbury à ses *Gesta regum Anglorum*', *Comptes rendus des séances de l'Académie des inscriptions et belles-lettres* (1982), 357–70

Guenée, B., 'Y a-t-il une historiographie médiévale?', *Revue historique*, 258 (1977), 261–75, reprinted in his *Politique et histoire au moyen-âge: recueil d' articles sur l' histoire politique et l' historiographie médiévale (1956–1981)* (Paris, 1981), pp. 205–19

Hagenmeyer, Heinrich, ed., *Fulcherii Carnotensis Historia hierosolimitana* (Heidelberg 1913)

Hagenmeyer, Heinrich, ed., *Die Kreuzzugsbriefe aus den Jahren 1088–1100* (Innsbruck, 1901)

Hahn, Thomas, 'Notes on Ross's Check-list of Alexander Texts', *Scriptorium*, 34 (1980), 275–78

Hallaire, E., 'Quelques manuscrits de Jean le Bègue', *Scriptorium*, 8 (1954), 291–92

Hamel, Christopher de, *Glossed Books of the Bible and the Origins of the Paris Book Trade* (Woodbridge, 1984)

Hamel, C. F. R. de, 'Manuscripts of Herbert of Bosham', in *Manuscripts at Oxford: an Exhibition in Memory of Richard William Hunt (1908–1979)*, edited by A. C. de la Mare & B. C. Barker-Benfield (Oxford, 1980), pp. 38–41

Hamilton, Bernard, 'Prester John and the Three Kings of Cologne', in *Studies in Medieval History presented to R. H. C. Davis*, edited by Henry Mayr-Harting and R. I. Moore (London, 1985), pp. 177–91

Hamilton, George L., 'Quelques notes sur l'histoire de la légende d'Alexandre le grand en Angleterre au Moyen Age', in *Mélanges de philologie et d' histoire offerts à M. Antoine Thomas par ses élèves et ses amis* (Paris, 1927), pp. 195–202

Hammer, J., ed., 'Bref Commentaire de la Prophetia Merlini du ms 3514 de la bibliothèque de la cathédrale d'Exeter', in *Hommages à Joseph Bidez et à Franz Cumont*, edited by Jacob Hammer (Brussels, 1949), pp. 111–19

Hammer, J., ed., 'A Commentary on the *Prophetiae Merlini* (Geoffrey of Monmouth's *Historia Regum Britanniae*, Book VII)', *Speculum*, 10 (1935), 3–30; 15 (1940), 409–31

Hammer, J., ed., 'Another Commentary on the *Prophetia Merlini* (Geoffrey of Monmouth's *Historia Regum Britanniae*, Book VII)', *Bulletin of the Polish Institute of Arts and Sciences in America*, 1 (1942/3), 589–601

Hammer, Jacob, ed., *Geoffrey of Monmouth 'Historia Regum Britanniae', A Variant Version Edited from Manuscripts* (Cambridge, Mass., 1951)

Hammer, J., 'Note on Geoffrey of Monmouth's *Historia Regum Britanniae* VI.12 and VI.15', *Modern Language Notes*, 49 (1934), 94–95

Hammer, J., 'Note on a Manuscript of Geoffrey of Monmouth's *Historia Regum Britanniae*', *Philological Quarterly*, 12 (1933), 225–34

Hammer, J., ed., 'The Poetry of Johannes Beverus with Extracts from his *Tractatus de Bruto abbreviato*', *Modern Philology*, 34 (1936/7), 119–32

Hammer, J., 'Remarks on the Sources and Textual History of Geoffrey of Monmouth's *Historia Regum Britanniae*, with an Excursus on the *Chronica Polonorum* of Wincenty Kadłubek (Magister Vincentius)', *Bulletin of the Polish Institute of Arts and Sciences in America*, 2 (1943/4), 501–64

Hammer, J., 'Some Additional Manuscripts of Geoffrey of Monmouth's *Historia Regum Britanniae*', *Modern Language Quarterly*, 3 (1942), 235–42

Hammer, J., ed., 'Some Leonine Summaries of Geoffrey of Monmouth's *Historia Regum Britanniae* and Other Poems', *Speculum*, 6 (1931), 114–23

Hammer, J., ed., 'An Unedited Commentary on the *Prophetia Merlini* in Dublin, Trinity College MS 496 E.6.2 (Geoffrey of Monmouth's *Historia Regum Britanniae*, Book VII)', in *Charisteria Thaddaeo Sinko: quinquaginta abhinc annos amplissimis in philosophia honoribus ornato ab amicis collegis discipulis oblata* (Warsaw, 1951), pp. 81–89

Hammer, J., 'An Unrecorded *Epitaphium Ceadwallae*', *Speculum*, 6 (1931), 607–08

Hammer, J., and H. Friedmann, '*Status imperii iudaici*. Part One', *Scriptorium*, 1 (1946/7), 50–65

Hanning, Robert W., *The Vision of History in Early Britain from Gildas to Geoffrey of Monmouth* (London, 1966)

Hardy, T. D., *Descriptive Catalogue of Materials Relating to the History of Great Britain and Ireland to the End of the Reign of Henry VII*, 3 vols in 4 (London, 1862–71)

Haskins, C. H., 'The Spread of Ideas in the Middle Ages', *Speculum*, 1 (1926), 19–30

Hauréau, Barthélemy, *Initia operum scriptorum latinorum medii potissimum aevi ...*, 8 vols (Turnhout, 1973/4)

Hay, D., 'History and Historians in France and England during the Fifteenth Century', *Bulletin of the Institute of Historical Research*, 35 (1962), 111–27

Hermanns, J. M. M., and E. M. C. Van Houts, 'The History of a membrum disiectum of the Gesta Normannorum Ducum, now Vatican, Reg. lat. 733 fol. 51*', *Mededelingen van het Nederlands Instituut te Rome*, 44–45 [NS, 9–10] (1982/3), 79–94

[Herold, B. J., ed.,] *Pantheon sive universitatis libri, qui chronici appellantur, XX, omnes omnium seculorum et gentium, tam sacras quam prophanas historias complectentes ...* (Basel 1559)

Hilka, A., 'Studien zur Alexandersage', *Romanische Forschungen*, 29 (1911), 1–71

Hilka, Alfons, and Werner Solderhjelm, edd., *Die Disciplina clericalis des Petrus Alfonsi, das älteste Novellenbuch des Mittelalters* (Heidelberg, 1911)

Hill, B., '*Epitaphia Alexandri* in English Medieval Manuscripts', *Leeds Studies in English*, 8 (1975), 96–104

Hill, B., 'The Fifteenth-century Prose *Legend of the Cross before Christ*', *Medium Ævum*, 34 (1965), 203–22

Hillion, Yannick, 'La Bretagne et la rivalité capétiens-plantagenets: un exemple: la duchesse Constance (1186–1202)', *Annales de Bretagne et des Pays de l'Ouest*, 92 (1985), 111–14

Hinde, Hodgson, ed., *Symeonis Dunelmensis opera* (Durham, 1868)

Hinnebusch, John F., ed., *The 'Historia occidentalis' of Jacques de Vitry* (Fribourg-en-Suisse, 1972)

Hirsch, Eric D., *The Aims of Interpretation* (Chicago, 1976)

Hoiling, Norbert, ' "Die Trierer Stilübungen": ein Denkmal der Frühzeit Kaiser Friedrich Barbarossa', *Archiv für Diplomatik*, 1 (1955), 257–329

Holder-Egger, O., ed., 'Italienische Prophetieen des 13. Jahrhunderts', *Neues Archiv der Gesellschaft für ältere deutsche Geschichtskunde*, 33 (1907/8), 97–187

Holdsworth, C. J., 'John of Ford and English Cistercian Writing, 1167–1214', *Transactions of the Royal Historical Society*, 5th ser. 11 (1961), 117–36

Holmes, Urban T., 'The Arthurian Tradition in Lambert d'Ardres', *Speculum*, 25 (1950), 100–3

Holzknecht, Karl Julius, *Literary Patronage in the Middle Ages* (Philadelphia, Pa., 1923)

Houck, Margaret, *Sources of the Roman de Brut of Wace* (Berkeley, Cal., 1941)

Housman, A. E., ed., *M. Annaei Lucani Belli civilis libri decem* (Oxford, 1926)

Howlett, R., ed., *Chronicles of the Reigns of Stephen, Henry II, and Richard I*, 4 vols (London, 1884–89)

Huisman, Gerda C., 'Notes on the Manuscript Tradition of Dudo of St-Quentin's *Gesta Normannorum*', *Anglo-Norman Studies*, 6 (1983), 122–35

Hunt, R. W., 'The "Lost" Preface to the *Liber derivationum* of Osbern of Gloucester', *Medium Ævum*, 4 (1958), 267–82

Hunt, R. W., et al., *A Summary Catalogue of Western Manuscripts in the Bodleian Library at Oxford*, 6 vols + index (Oxford 1922–53, reprinted Munich, 1980)

Hunter Blair, Peter, with R. A. B. Mynors, facs. ed., *The Moore Bede: Cambridge, University Library, MS Kk.5.16* (Copenhagen, 1959)

Huws, D., and B. F. Roberts, 'Another Manuscript of the Variant Version of the "Historia regum Britanniae" ', *Bulletin bibliographique de la Société internationale arthurienne*, 25 (1973), 147–52

Huygens, R. B. C., ed., *Lettres de Jacques de Vitry (1160/1170–1240), évêque de Saint-Jean d'Acre* (Leiden, 1960)

Isaac, Marie-Thérèse, *Les Livres manuscrits de l'abbaye des Dunes* (Aubel, 1984)

Jackson, Kenneth, *Language and History in Early Britain: a Chronological Survey of the Brittonic Languages, First to Twelfth Century A.D.* (Edinburgh, 1953)

Jacqueline, Bernard, 'Écoles et culture dans l'Avranchin, le Mortainais et le Cotentin au temps de Saint Anselme', in *Les Mutations socio-culturelles au tournant des xie–xiie siècles*, edited by R. Foreville (Paris, 1984), pp. 203–12

James, M. R., ed., *The Ancient Libraries of Canterbury and Dover* (Cambridge, 1903)

James, M. R., Cambridge University Library Manuscript Notes, unpublished

James, M. R., ed., 'The Catalogue of the Library of the Augustinian Friars at York now First Edited from the Manuscript at Trinity College, Dublin', in *Fasciculus Ioanni Willis Clark dicatus* (Cambridge, 1909), pp. 2–96

James, Montague Rhodes, ed., 'Catalogue of the Library of Leicester Abbey', *Transactions of the Leicester Archaeological Society*, 19 (1936/7), 118–61, 378–440; 21 (1940/1), 1–88

James, M. R., *A Descriptive Catalogue of the Manuscripts in the Library of Gonville and Caius College*, 2 vols (Cambridge, 1907/8)

James, M. R., *A Descriptive Catalogue of the Manuscripts in the Library of Jesus College, Cambridge* (London, 1895)

James, Montague R., *A Descriptive Catalogue of the Western Manuscripts in the Library of Clare College, Cambridge* (Cambridge, 1905)

James, M. R., ed., *Lists of Manuscripts formerly in Peterborough Abbey Library* (Oxford, 1926)

James, M. R., *et al.*, edd. and transl., *Walter Map. De Nugis Curialium. Courtiers' Trifles*, revised edition (Oxford, 1983)

Jarman, A. O. H., 'The Welsh Myrddin Poems', in *Arthurian Literature in the Middle Ages: a Collaborative History*, edited by Roger Sherman Loomis (Oxford, 1959), pp. 20–30

Jauss, Hans-Robert, 'Literary History as a Challenge to Literary Theory', *New Literary History*, 2 (1970), 7–37

Johanek, Peter, 'König Arthur und die Plantagenets: über den Zusammenhang von Historiographie und höfischer Epik in mittelalterlicher Propaganda', *Frühmittel-alterliche Studien*, 21 (1987), 346–89

Johnston, James P., *Place-names of Scotland*, 3rd edition (London, 1934)

Jonge, Marinus de, *The Testaments of the Twelve Patriarchs: a study of their Text, Composition and Origin* (Assen, 1953)

Jones, W. Lewis, 'Geoffrey of Monmouth', *Transactions of the Honourable Society of Cymmrodorion* (1898/9), 52–95

Jones, W. L., 'Geoffrey of Monmouth and the Legend of Arthur', *Quarterly Review*, 205 (1906), 54–78

Joranson, Einar, 'The Problem of the Spurious Letter of Emperor Alexius to the Count of Flanders', *American Historical Review*, 55 (1949/50), 811–32

Keeler, L., 'The *Historia Regum Britanniae* and Four Mediaeval Chroniclers', *Speculum*, 21 (1946), 24–37

Kendrick, T. D., *British Antiquity* (London, 1950)

Ker, N. R., *Medieval Libraries of Great Britain: a list of surviving books*, 2nd edition (London, 1964)

Ker, N. L., and W. A. Pantin, edd., 'Letters of a Scottish Student at Paris and Oxford c. 1250', *Formularies which bear on the History of Oxford c. 1204–1420*, edited by H. E. Salter, W. A. Pantin, and H. G. Richardson, 2 vols (Oxford, 1942), II.472–91

Kim, Hack C., ed., *The Gospel of Nicodemus. Gesta Saluatoris edited from the Codex Einsidlensis, Einsiedeln Stiftsbibliothek, MS 326* (Toronto, 1973)

King, E., 'Waleran, Count of Meulan, Earl of Worcester (1104–1166)', *Tradition and Change: Essays in Honour of Marjorie Chibnall*, edited by Diana Greenway *et al.* (Cambridge, 1985), pp. 165–81

Kirchner, J., *Scriptura gothica libraria* (Munich, 1966)

Kortekaas, G. A. A., ed., *Historia Apollonii regis Tyri: Prolegomena, Text Edition of the Two Principal Latin Recensions, Bibliography, Indices and Appendices* (Groningen 1984)

Kuebler, Bernhard, ed., *Iuli Valeri Alexandri Polemi Res Gestae Alexandri Macedonis* (Leipzig, 1888)

Lapidge, Michael, 'An Edition of the *Uera historia de morte Arthuri*', *Arthurian Literature*, 1 (1981), 79–93

Lawrence, A., 'English Cistercian Manuscripts of the Twelfth Century', in *Cistercian Art and Architecture in the British Isles*, edited by C. Norton and D. Park (Cambridge, 1986), pp. 24–39

Le Goff, Jacques, 'Contacts et non-contacts dans l'Occident médiéval', in *Culture et travail intellectuel dans l'Occident médiéval*, edited by R. P. Hubert *et al.* (Paris, 1981), pp. 61–79

Leckie, R. William Jr, *The Passage of Dominion: Geoffrey of Monmouth and the Periodization of Insular History in the Twelfth Century* (Toronto, 1981)

Leclercq, J., 'L'Archétype clarévallien des traités de Saint Bernard', *Scriptorium*, 10 (1956), 229–32

Leclercq, J., 'Une Bibliothèque vivant', in *Millénaire monastique du Mont Saint-Michel*, 4 vols (Paris, 1966–71), II.247–55

Leclercq, Jean, 'La Diffusion des manuscrits bernardins dans les régions de langue allemande', *Storia e letteratura*, 104 (1966), 19–33

Leclercq, J., 'Les Manuscrits de l'abbaye d'Hautmont', *Scriptorium*, 7 (1953), 59–67

Leclercq, J., 'Les Manuscrits de l'abbaye de Liessies', *Scriptorium*, 6 (1952), 51–62

Leclercq, J., 'Saint-Bernard à Jumièges', *Storia e letteratura*, 104 (1966), 41–48

Legge, Mary Dominica, *Anglo-Norman in the Cloisters: the Influence of the Orders upon Anglo-Norman Literature* (Edinburgh, 1950)

Legge, Mary Dominica, 'Anglo-Norman Hagiography and the Romances', *Medievalia et humanistica*, NS, 6 (1975), 41–49

Legge, Mary-Dominica, 'Gautier Espec, Ailred de Rievaulx et la matière de Bretagne', in *Mélanges de langue et de littérature du moyen âge et de la renaissance offerts à Jean Frappier*, 2 vols (Geneva, 1970), II.619–23

Legge, M. D., 'L'Influence littéraire de la cour d'Henri Beauclerc', in *Mélanges offerts à Rita Lejeune, Professeur à l'Université de Liège*, 2 vols (Gembloux, 1969), I.679–87

Legge, M. Dominica, 'A List of Langtoft Manuscripts, with Notes on MS. Laud misc. 637', *Medium Ævum*, 4 (1935), 20–24

Legge, M. D., 'Master Geoffrey Arthur', in *An Arthurian Tapestry: Essays in Memory of Lewis Thorpe*, edited by Kenneth Varty (Glasgow, 1981), pp. 22-27

Leitzmann, A., 'Bemerkungen zu Galfred von Monmouth', *Archiv für das Studium der neueren Sprachen und Literatur*, 134 (1916), 373–78

Lerner, Robert E., 'The Black Death and Western European Eschatological Mentalities', in *The Black Death: the Impact of the Fourteenth-century Plague*, edited by Daniel Williman (New York, 1982), pp. 77–105

Levison, W., 'A Combined Manuscript of Geoffrey of Monmouth and Henry of Huntingdon', *English Historical Review*, 58 (1943), 41–51

Liebermann, F., *Die Gesetze der Angelsachsen*, 3 vols (Halle a. S., 1898–1916)

Liebmann, Charles J., 'Art and Letters in the Reign of Philip II Augustus of France: the Political Background', in *The Year 1200: a Centennial Exhibition at the Metropolitan Museum of Art*, edited by Konrad Hoffmann and Florens Deuchler, 2 vols (New York, 1970), II.1–6

Lieftinck, G. I., *Manuscrits datés conservés dans les Pays-Bas: catalogue paléographique des manuscrits en écriture latine portant des indications de date*, 2 vols in 4 (Amsterdam, 1964–88)

Lieftinck, G. I., 'De Librijen en scriptoria der Westvlaamse Cisterciënser-abdijen Ter Duinen en Ter Doest in de 12e en 13e eeuw . . .', *Mededelingen van de koninklijke vlaamse Academie voor wetenschappen, letteren en schone kunsten van België*, 15.2 (1953), 3–89

Lloyd, John Edward, 'Geoffrey of Monmouth', *English Historical Review*, 57 (1942), 460–68

Loomis, Roger Sherman, *The Development of Arthurian Romance* (London 1963)

Loomis, Roger Sherman, 'Edward I, Arthurian Enthusiast', *Speculum*, 28 (1953), 114–27

Loomis, Roger Sherman, *Wales and the Arthurian Legend* (Cardiff, 1956)

Lot, F., 'Nouvelles études sur la provenance du cycle arthurien', *Romania*, 28 (1899), 321–47

Louis, R., 'Aimery Picaud, *alias* Olivier d'Asquins, compilateur du *Liber Sancti Iacobi*', *Bulletin de la Société nationale des antiquaires de France* (1948/9), 80–97

Löwe, Heinz, 'Ein literarischer Widersacher des Bonifatius: Virgil von Salzburg und die Kosmographie des Aethicus Ister', *Abhandlungen der Akademie der Wissenschaften und der Literatur in Mainz, geistes- und sozialwissenschaftliche Klasse*, 11 (1959), 899–988

Loyn, H. R., *The "Matter of Britain" : a Historian's Perspective* (London, 1989)

Luard, Henry Richards, ed., *Matthæi Parisiensis, monachi Sancti Albani, Chronica majora*, 7 vols (London, 1872–83)

Luscombe, D. E., *The School of Peter Abelard: the Influence of Abelard's Thought in the Early Scholastic Period* (Cambridge, 1969)

Maas, Paul, *Textual Criticism* (Oxford, 1958)

Macray, W. Dunn, ed., *Chronica abbatiae Rameseiensis, a saec. x usque ad an. circiter 1200* (London, 1886)

Madden, F., 'The Historia Britonum of Geoffrey of Monmouth', *Archaeological Journal*, 15 (1858), 299–312

Major-Poetzl, Pamela, *Michel Foucault's Archaeology of Western Culture: toward a New Science of History* (Brighton, 1983)

Mandach, André de, *Naissance et développement de la chanson de geste en Europe: 1 La geste de Charlemagne et de Roland* (Paris, 1961)

Manitius, Max, *Geschichte der lateinischen Literatur des Mittelalters*, 3 vols (Munich, 1911–31)

Mare, A. C. de la, P. K. Marshall, and R. H. Rouse, 'Pietro da Montagnana and the Text of Aulus Gellius in Paris B.N. lat. 13038', *Scriptorium*, 30 (1976), 219–25

Marshall, P. K., J. Martin, and R. H. Rouse, 'Clare College MS. 26 and the Circulation of Aulus Gellius 1–7 in Medieval England and France', *Mediaeval Studies*, 42 (1980), 353–94

Martin, Janet, 'John of Salisbury as Classical Scholar', in *The World of John of Salisbury*, edited by Michael Wilks (Oxford, 1984), pp. 179–201

Martin, Janet, 'The Uses of Tradition: Gellius, Petronius and John of Salisbury', *Viator*, 10 (1979), 57–76

Maslowski, T., and R. H. Rouse, 'Twelfth-Century Extracts from Cicero's *Pro Archia* and *Pro Cluentio* in Paris B.N. MS lat. 18104', *Italia medioevale e umanistica*, 22 (1979), 97–122

Masai, F., 'De la condition des enlumineurs et d'enluminure à l'époque romane', *Bulletino dell'Archivio paleografico italiano*, NS, 2–3 (1956/7), 135–44

Mathieu, M., 'Le Manuscrit 162 d'Avranches et l'édition princeps des Gesta Roberti Wiscardi de Guillaume d'Apulie', *Byzantion*, 24 (1954), 111–30

Mathieu, M., 'Le MS 162 d'Avranches ou Robert de Torigni et Robert Guiscard', *Sacris erudiri*, 17 (1966), 66–70

Matter, Hans, *Englische Gründungssagen von Geoffrey of Monmouth bis zur Renaissance* (Heidelberg, 1922)

Matthews, William, 'Egyptians in Scotland: the Political History of a Myth', *Viator*, 1 (1970), 289–306

Matthews, William, *The Tragedy of Arthur: a Study of the Alliterative "Morte Arthure"* (Berkeley, Cal., 1960)

McGinn, Bernard, *Visions of the End: Apocalyptic Traditions in the Middle Ages* (New York, 1979)

McLaughlan, E. P., 'The Scriptorium of Bury St. Edmunds in the Third and Fourth Decades of the Twelfth Century: Books in Three Related Hands and Their Decoration', *Mediaeval Studies*, 40 (1978), 328–48

Medcalf, Stephen, 'On Reading Books from a Half-Alien Culture', in *The Context of English Literature: the Later Middle Ages*, edited by S. Medcalf (London, 1981), pp. 1–55

Meehan, B., 'Geoffrey of Monmouth, *Prophecies of Merlin*: New Manuscript Evidence', *Bulletin of the Board of Celtic Studies*, 28 (1978–80), 37–46

Meek, Mary Elizabeth, transl., *Historia destructionis Troiae. Guido delle Colonne* (Bloomington, Ind., 1974)

[Mellot, A.,] *Catalogus codicum manuscriptorum Bibliothecae Regiae*, 4 vols (Paris, 1739–44)

Meredith-Jones, Cyril, ed., *Historia Karoli Magni et Rotholandi ou Chronique du pseudo-Turpin, textes revus et publiés d' après 49 manuscrits* (Paris, 1939)

Meyer, W., ed., 'Vita Adae et Evae', *Abhandlungen der philosophisch-philologischen Classe der königlich Bayerischen Akademie der Wissenschaften*, 14.3 (1878), 186–250

Meyvaert, Paul, 'John Erghome and the *Vaticinium Roberti Bridlington*', *Speculum*, 41 (1966), 656–64

MGH, AA *Monumenta Germaniae Historica, Auctores antiquissimi*, 15 vols in 13 (Berlin/Leipzig, 1877–1919)

MGH, SS *Monumenta Germaniae Historica, Scriptores*, 32 vols in 34 (Hanover, 1826–1934)

Migne, J-. P., ed., *Patrologiae cursus completus sive bibliotheca universalis, integra, uniformis, commoda, oeconomica omnium SS. patrum, doctorum scriptorumque ecclesiasticarum qui ab aevo apostolico ad usque Innocentii III tempora floruerunt . . .*, Ser. latina, vols 1–79, 80–217 (Paris 1844–55)

Miller, M., 'Geoffrey's Early Royal Synchronisms', *Bulletin of the Board of Celtic Studies*, 28 (1978–80), 373–89

Millor, W. G., and S. J. and H. E. Butler, edd., revised by C. N. L. Brooke, *The Letters of John of Salisbury*, 2 vols, (Edinburgh, 1955; Oxford, 1979)

Miraeus, Aubertus, ed., *Notitia episcopatuum orbis Christiani* (Antwerp, 1613)

Molinier, Auguste, *et al.*, edd., *Les Sources de l' histoire de France depuis les origines jusqu' en 1815*, 18 vols (Paris, 1901–35)

Momigliano, Arnaldo, 'The Historians of the Classical World and their Audiences: Some Suggestions', *Annali della Scuola normale superiore di Pisa (Classe di lettere e filosofia)*, 8.1 (1978), 59–75

Mommsen, Theodor, ed., *C. Iulii Solini Collectanea rerum memorabilium* (Berlin, 1854)

Moore, Samuel, 'General Aspects of Literary Patronage in the Latin Middle Ages', *The Library*, 3rd ser., 4 (1913), 369–92

Morey, Adrian, and C. N. L. Brooke, *Gilbert Foliot and his Letters* (Cambridge, 1965)

Morgan, Nigel, *Early Gothic Manuscripts [1] 1190–1250* (London, 1982)

Morgan, N., 'Matthew Paris, St Albans, London, and the Leaves of the "Life of St Thomas Becket" ', *Burlington Magazine*, 130 (February 1988), 85–96

Morris, Rosemary, 'Uther and Igerne: a Study in Uncourtly Love', *Arthurian Literature*, 4 (1985), 70–92

Mozley, J. H., ed., 'A New Text of the Story of the Cross', *Journal of Theological Studies*, 31 (1930), 113–27

Mozley, J. H., ed., 'The "Vita Adae" ', *Journal of Theological Studies*, 30 (1928/9), 121–49

Musset, Lucien, 'Un Aspect de l'esprit médiéval: la "cacogéographie" des Normands et de la Normandie', *Revue du moyen âge latin*, 2 (1946), 129-43

Mynors, R. A. B., *Durham Cathedral Manuscripts to the End of the Twelfth Century* (Oxford, 1939)

Natunewicz, Chester F., 'Freculphus of Lisieux, his Chronicle and a Mont-Saint-Michel Manuscript', *Sacris Erudiri* 17 (1966), 90–134

Nelis, Hubert, 'De l'influence de la minuscule romaine sur l'écriture, au xiie et xiiie siècle en Belgique', *Bulletin de l'Institut historique belge de Rome*, 3 (1924), 5–30

Newhauser, Richard, 'Towards a History of Human Curiosity: a Prolegomenon to its Medieval Phase', *Deutsches Vierteljahrsschrift für Literaturwissenschaft und Geistesgeschichte*, 56 (1982), 559–75

Nortier, G., *Les Bibliothèques médiévales des abbayes bénédictines de Normandie* (Paris, 1971)

Nykrog, Per, 'The Rise of Literary Fiction', in *Renaissance and Renewal in the Twelfth Century*, edited by Robert L. Benson and Giles Constable (Oxford, 1982), pp. 593–612

O'Meara, John J., ed., 'Giraldus Cambrensis in Topographia Hibernie: Text of the First Recension', *Proceedings of the Royal Irish Academy*, 52 C (1948–50), 113–78

Offler, H. S., *Medieval Historians of Durham* (Durham, 1958)

Oliver, G., *Lives of the Bishops of Exeter and a History of the Cathedral* (Exeter, 1861)

Olschki, Leonardo, *Marco Polo's Asia. An Introduction to his "Description of the World" called "Il milione"* (Berkeley, Cal., 1960)

Olson, Glending, *Literature as Recreation in the Later Middle Ages* (Ithaca, N.Y., 1982)

Omont, H., ed., 'Anciens catalogues de bibliothèques anglaises (xiie–xive siècle)', *Centralblatt für Bibliothekswesen*, 9 (1892), 201–22

Owst, G. R., *Literature and Pulpit in Medieval England: a Neglected Chapter in the History of English Letters and of the English People* (Cambridge, 1933)

Padel, O. J., 'Geoffrey of Monmouth and Cornwall', *Cambridge Medieval Celtic Studies*, 8 (1984), 1–27

Palgrave, Francis, ed., *Documents and Records Illustrating the History of Scotland and the Transactions between the Crowns of Scotland and England Preserved in the Treasury of her Majesty's Exchequer* (London, 1837)

Parkes, M. B., *English Cursive Book Hands 1250–1500* (Oxford, 1969; revised impression, London, 1979)

Parry, John Jay, ed. and transl., *Brut y Brenhinedd: Cotton Cleopatra Version* (Cambridge, Mass., 1937)

Parry, J. J., 'Celtic Tradition and the Vita Merlini', *Philological Quarterly*, 4 (1925), 193–207

Parry, J. J., 'The Chronology of Geoffrey of Monmouth's *Historia*, Books I and II', *Speculum*, 4 (1929), 316–22

Parry, J.J., 'Geoffrey of Monmouth and the Paternity of Arthur', *Speculum*, 13 (1938), 271–77

Parry, J. J., 'The Welsh Texts of Geoffrey of Monmouth's *Historia*', *Speculum*, 5 (1930), 424–31

Parry, John J., and Robert A. Caldwell, 'Geoffrey of Monmouth', in *Arthurian Literature in the Middle Ages: a Collaborative History*, edited by Roger Sherman Loomis (Oxford, 1959), pp. 72–93

Partner, Nancy F., 'The New Cornificius: Medieval History and the Artifice of Words', in *Classical Rhetoric and Medieval Historiography*, edited by Ernst Breisach (Kalamazoo, Mich., 1985), pp. 5–59

Partner, Nancy F., *Serious Entertainments: the Writing of History in Twelfth-Century England* (London, 1977)

Patterson, Lee, *Negotiating the Past: the Historical Understanding of Medieval Literature* (Madison, Wisc., 1987)

Patterson, Robert B., 'William of Malmesbury's Robert of Gloucester: a Re-evaluation of the *Historia Novella*', *American Historical Review*, 70 (1965), 983–97

Pearsall, Derek, 'The Origins of the Alliterative Revival', in *The Alliterative Tradition in the Fourteenth Century*, edited by B. E. Levy and P. E. Szarmach (Kent, Ohio, 1981), pp. 1–24

Pearson, Lionel, 'The Pseudo-History of Messenia and its Authors', *Historia*, 11 (1962), 397–426

Pellegrin, E., *La Bibliothèque des Visconti et des Sforza, ducs de Milan, au xv*e *siècle* (Paris, 1955)

Pellegrin, E., 'Manuscrits de l'abbaye de Saint-Victor et d'anciens collèges de Paris à la Bibliothèque municipale de Berne, à la Bibliothèque Vaticane et à Paris', *Bibliothèque de l'École des chartes*, 103 (1942), 69–98

Pellegrin, Élisabeth, 'Possesseurs français et italiens de manuscrits latins du fonds de la Reine à la Bibliothèque Vaticane', *Revue d'histoire des textes*, 3 (1973), 271–97

Penzer, Norman M., *The Most Noble and Famous Travels of Marco Polo together with the Travels of Nicolo de' Conti* (London, 1937)

Piggott, Stuart, 'The Sources of Geoffrey of Monmouth: 1. The "Pre-Roman" King-List', *Antiquity*, 15 (1941), 269–86

Plummer, Charles, ed., *Uenerabilis Baedae opera historica*, 2 vols (Oxford, 1896)

Pollard, Graham, 'The University and the Book Trade in Mediaeval Oxford', *Miscellanea mediaevalia*, 3 (1964), 336–44

Potter, K. R., ed. & transl., *The Historia Novella by William of Malmesbury* (Edinburgh, 1955)

Potthast, A., *Regesta pontificum Romanorum inde ab a. post Christum natum mcxcviii ad a. mccciv*, 2 vols (Berlin, 1874/5)

Powicke, Frederick M., *The Life of Ailred of Rievaulx by Walter Daniel* (Edinburgh, 1950)

Prevenier, W., 'La Chancellerie des comtes de Flandre dans le cadre européen à la fin du xiie siècle', *Bibliothèque de l'École des chartes*, 125 (1967), 34–93

Prinz, Otto, 'Untersuchungen zur Überlieferung und zur Orthographie der Kosmographie des Aethicus', *Deutsches Archiv für Erforschung des Mittelalters*, 37 (1981), 474–510

Prou, M., *Nouveau recueil des fac-similés d'écritures du xii*e *au xvii*e *siècle* (Paris, 1896)

Quinn, Kenneth, *Texts and Contexts: the Roman Writers and their Audience* (London, 1979)

Ray, Roger, 'Rhetorical Scepticism and Verisimilar Narrative in John of Salisbury's

327

Historia pontificalis', in *Classical Rhetoric and Medieval Historiography*, edited by Ernst Breisach (Kalamazoo, Mich., 1985), pp. 61–102

Reeves, Marjorie, *The Influence of Prophecy in the Later Middle Ages: a Study in Joachimism* (Oxford, 1969)

Reeves, M. E., 'History and Prophecy in Medieval Thought', *Medievalia et humanistica*, NS, 5 (1974), 51–75

Reiss, E., 'The Welsh Versions of Geoffrey of Monmouth's *Historia*', *Welsh History Review*, 4 (1968/9), 97–127

Remley, Paul, 'Geoffrey of Monmouth: in his Own Words?', *Peritia*, 5 (1986), 452–61

Richter, Michael, ed., *Canterbury Professions* ([London], 1973)

Richter, Michael, *Giraldus Cambrensis: the Growth of the Welsh Nation*, 2nd edn (Aberystwyth, 1976)

Riese, Alexander, ed., *Geographi latini minores* (Heilbronn, 1878)

Roberts, Brinley F., 'Geoffrey of Monmouth and Welsh Historical Tradition', *Nottingham Mediaeval Studies*, 20 (1976), 29–40

Robertson, James C., and J. Brigstoke Sheppard, edd., *Materials for the History of Thomas Becket, Archbishop of Canterbury*, 7 vols (London, 1875–85)

Robinson, J. Armitage, and Montague Rhodes James, *The Manuscripts of Westminster Abbey* (Cambridge, 1908)

Rosenhaus, M. J., 'Britain between Myth and Reality: the Literary-Historical Vision of Geoffrey of Monmouth's *Historia Regum Britanniae*', *Dissertation Abstracts International*, A 44 (1983), 748

Ross, David J. A., *Alexander Historiatus: a Guide to Medieval Illustrated Alexander Literature* (London, 1963)

Ross, D. J. A., 'A Check-List of Manuscripts of Three Alexander Texts: the Julius Valerius *Epitome*, the *Epistola ad Aristotelem* and the *Collatio cum Dindimo*', *Scriptorium*, 10 (1956), 127–32

Ross, D. J. A., '*Parva Recapitulacio*: an English Collection of Texts Relating to Alexander the Great', *Classica et mediaevalia*, 33 (1981/2), 191–203

Ross, E. Denison, 'Marco Polo and his Book', *Proceedings of the British Academy*, 20 (1934), 181–205

Rouse, R. H., 'Florilegia and Latin Classical Authors in Twelfth- and Thirteenth-century Orléans', *Viator*, 10 (1979), 131–60

Rouse, R. H., 'Manuscripts Belonging to Richard de Fournival', *Revue d'histoire des textes*, 3 (1973), 253–69

Rye, W. B., ed., 'Catalogue of the Library of the Priory of St. Andrew, Rochester, A.D. 1202', *Archaeologia Cantiana*, 3 (1860), 47–64

Sackur, Ernst, ed., *Sibyllinische Texte und Forschungen. Pseudomethodius, Adso und die Tiburtinische Sibylle* (Halle, 1898)

Salter, Herbert E., ed., *Eynsham Cartulary*, 2 vols (Oxford, 1907/8)

Salter, H. E., 'Geoffrey of Monmouth and Oxford', *English Historical Review*, 34 (1919), 382–85

Samaran, Charles, and Robert Marichal, *Catalogue des manuscrits en écriture latine portant des indications de date, de lieu ou de copiste*, 7 vols in 14 (Paris, 1959–84)

Sanderus, A., ed., *Bibliotheca belgica manuscripta*, 2 vols (Lille, 1641–44)

Sandford, E. M., 'The Study of Ancient History in the Middle Ages', *Journal of the History of Ideas*, 5 (1944), 21–43

Schirmer, Walter F., and Ulrich Broich, *Studien zum literarischen Patronat im England des 12. Jahrhunderts* (Cologne, 1962)

Schneider, Ambrosius, 'Skriptorium und Bibliothek der Cistercienserabtei Himmerod im Rheinland: zur Geschichte klösterlichen Bibliothekswesens im Mittelalter', *Bulletin of the John Rylands Library*, 35 (1952/3), 155–205

Schnith, Karl, 'Von Symeon von Durham zu Wilhelm von Newburgh. Wege der englischen "Volksgeschichte" im 12. Jahrhundert', in *Speculum Historiale: Geschichte im Spiegel von Geschichtsschreibung und Geschichtsdeutung*, edited by Clemens Bauer *et al.* (Freiburg i. B., 1965), pp. 242–56

Schulz, Albert, ed., *Gottfried von Monmouth, Historia regum Britanniae, mit literarhistorischer Einleitung und ausführlichen Anmerkungen, und Brut Tysilio, altwälsche Chronik in deutscher Uebersetzung* (Halle a. S., 1854)

Scott, A. B. and F. X. Martin, edd. & transl., *Expugnatio hibernica: the Conquest of Ireland by Giraldus Cambrensis* (Dublin, 1978)

Searle, Eleanor, ed. & transl., *The Chronicle of Battle Abbey* (Oxford, 1980)

Searle, Eleanor, 'Fact and Pattern in Heroic History: Dudo of Saint-Quentin', *Viator*, 15 (1984), 119–37

Segre, Cesare, 'The Problem of Contamination in Prose Texts', in *Medieval Manuscripts and Textual Criticism*, edited by Christopher Kleinhenz (Chapel Hill, N. C., 1976), pp. 117–22

Shepherd, G. T., 'The Emancipation of Story in the Twelfth Century', in *Medieval Narrative: a Symposium*, edited by H. Bekker-Nielsen *et al.* (Odense, 1979), pp. 44–57

Short, Ian, 'The Pseudo-Turpin Chronicle: Some Unnoticed Versions and their Sources', *Medium Ævum*, 38 (1969), 1–22

Sims-Williams, P. P., 'Some Functions of Origin Stories in Early Medieval Wales', *History and Heroic Tale: a Symposium*, edited by Tore Nyberg *et al.* (Odense, 1985), pp. 97–131

Smalley, Beryl, 'Ecclesiastical Attitudes to Novelty c. 1100 – c. 1250', in *Studies in Medieval Thought and Learning* (London, 1981), pp. 97–115

Smalley, Beryl, *Historians in the Middle Ages* (London, 1974)

Smith, D. M., 'The Episcopate of Richard, Bishop of St. Asaph: a Problem of Twelfth-Century Chronology', *Journal of the Historical Society of the Church in Wales*, 24 (1974), 9–12

Smyser, Hamilton M., ed., *The Pseudo-Turpin Edited from Bibliothèque nationale, Fonds Latin, MS. 17656 with an Annotated Synopsis* (Cambridge, Mass., 1937)

Southern, R. W., 'Aspects of the European Tradition of Historical Writing: 1. The Classical Tradition from Einhard to Geoffrey of Monmouth', *Transactions of the Royal Historical Society*, 5th ser., 20 (1970), 173–96

Southern, R. W., 'Aspects of the European Tradition of Historical Writing: 2. Hugh of St Victor and the Idea of Historical Development', *Transactions of the Royal Historical Society*, 5th ser., 21 (1971), 159–79

Southern, R. W., 'Aspects of the European Tradition of Historical Writing: 3. History as Prophecy', *Transactions of the Royal Historical Society*, 5th ser., 22 (1972), 159–80

Southern, R. W., 'Aspects of the European Tradition of Historical Writing: 4. The Sense of the Past', *Transactions of the Royal Historical Society*, 5th ser., 23 (1973), 243–63

Southern, R. W., 'Master Vacarius and the Beginning of an English Academic Tradition', in *Medieval Learning and Literature: Essays Presented to Richard*

William Hunt, edited by J. J. G. Alexander and M. T. Gibson (Oxford, 1976), pp. 257–86

Southern, R. W., *Medieval Humanism and Other Studies* (Oxford, 1970)

Southern, R. W., 'The Place of England in the Twelfth-Century Renaissance', *History*, NS, 45 (1960), 201–16

Southern, Richard W., *St Anselm and his Biographer: a Study of Monastic Life and Thought 1059–c. 1130* (Cambridge, 1963)

Southern, R. W., 'From Schools to University', *The History of the University of Oxford: 1, The Early Oxford Schools*, edited by J. I. Catto (Oxford, 1984), pp. 1–36

Spiegel, Gabrielle M., 'Genealogy: Form and Function in Medieval Historical Narrative', *History and Theory*, 22 (1983), 43–53

Sprandel, Rolf, *Gesellschaft und Literatur im Mittelalter* (Paderborn, 1982)

Starkey, David, 'The Age of the Household: Politics, Society and the Arts c. 1350 – c. 1550', in *The Context of English Literature: the Later Middle Ages*, edited by S. Medcalf (London, 1981), pp. 225–90

Stepsis, Robert, 'Pierre de Langtoft's Chronicle: an Essay in Medieval Historiography', *Medievalia et humanistica*, NS, 3 (1972), 51–73

Sterckx, Claude, ' "Princeps militiae" dans l'Historia Regum Britanniae de Geoffrey de Monmouth', *Annales de Bretagne et des Pays de l'Ouest*, 76 (1969), 725–30

Stiennon, J., with G. Hasenohr, *Paléographie du moyen âge* (Paris, 1973)

Stirnemann, P. Danz, 'Quelques bibliothèques princières et la production hors scriptorium au xiie siècle', *Bulletin archéologique du comité des travaux historiques et scientifiques*, NS, 17–18 (1981/2), 7–38

Stock, Brian, 'Medieval Literacy, Linguistic Theory, and Social Organization', *New Literary History*, 16 (1984/5), 13–29

Stones, E. L. G., and Grant G. Simpson, edd., *Edward I and the Throne of Scotland, 1290–1296: an Edition of the Record Sources for the Great Cause*, 2 vols (Oxford, 1978)

Strayer, J. R., 'The Laicization of French and English Society in the Thirteenth Century', *Speculum*, 15 (1940), 76–86

Strongman, Sheila, ed., 'John Parker's Manuscripts: an Edition of the Lists in Lambeth Palace MS 737', *Transactions of the Cambridge Bibliographical Society*, 7 (1977–80), 1–27

Stubbs, W., 'Learning and Literature at the Court of Henry II', in *Lectures in Medieval and Modern History* (Oxford, 1886), pp. 136–55

Stubbs, W., ed., *Willelmi Malmesbiriensis monachi de gestis regum Anglorum*, 2 vols (London, 1887–89)

Suleiman, Susan R., and Inge Crosman, *The Reader in the Text: Essays on Audience and Interpretation* (Princeton, N. J., 1980)

Sutton, Anne F., and Livia Visser-Fuchs, 'Richard III's books: VII Guido delle Colonne's *Historia destructionis Troiae*. VIII Geoffrey of Monmouth's *Historia Regum Britanniae*, with *The Prophecy of the Eagle* and Commentary', *The Ricardian*, 8 (1988–90), 136–48, 351–62, 403–13

Talbot, C. H., 'Notes on the Library of Pontigny', *Analecta sacri ordinis Cisterciensis*, 10 (1954), 106–68

Tatlock, J. S. P., 'Certain Contemporaneous Matters in Geoffrey of Monmouth', *Speculum*, 6 (1931), 206–24

Tatlock, J. S. P., 'The Date of Henry I's Charter to London', *Speculum*, 11 (1936), 461–69

Tatlock, J. S. P., 'The Dates of the Arthurian Saints' Legends', *Speculum*, 14 (1939), 345–65

Tatlock, J. S. P., 'Geoffrey and King Arthur in *Normannicus Draco*', *Modern Philology*, 31 (1933/4), 1–18; 113–25

Tatlock, J. S. P., 'Geoffrey of Monmouth's Motives for Writing his *Historia*', *Proceedings of the American Philosophical Society*, 79 (1938), 693–703

Tatlock, J. S. P., 'Geoffrey of Monmouth's *Vita Merlini*', *Speculum*, 18 (1943), 265–87

Tatlock, J. S. P., *The Legendary History of Britain: Geoffrey of Monmouth's Historia Regum Britanniae and its Early Vernacular Versions* (Berkeley, Cal., 1950)

Tatlock, J. S. P., 'The Origin of Geoffrey of Monmouth's Estrildis', *Speculum*, 11 (1936), 121–24

Taylor, Frank, 'The Chronicle of John Strecche for the Reign of Henry V (1414–1422)', *Bulletin of the John Rylands Library*, 16 (1932), 137–87

Taylor, John, *English Historical Literature in the Fourteenth Century* (Oxford, 1987)

Taylor, John, ed., *The Kirkstall Abbey Chronicles* (Leeds, 1952)

Taylor, J., *Medieval Historical Writing in Yorkshire* (York, 1961)

Taylor, John, *The Universal Chronicle of Ranulf Higden* (Oxford, 1966)

Taylor, Rupert, *The Political Prophecy in England* (New York, 1911)

Thompson, James Westfall, *The Literacy of the Laity in the Middle Ages* (New York, 1960)

Thompson, James Westfall, *The Mediaeval Library* (Chicago, 1939; revised impression, New York, 1957)

Thomson, R. M., ed. & transl., *The Chronicle of the Election of Hugh Abbot of Bury St. Edmunds and later Bishop of Ely* (Oxford, 1974)

Thomson, R. M., 'John of Salisbury and William of Malmesbury: Currents in Twelfth-Century Humanism', in *The World of John of Salisbury*, edited by Michael Wilks (Oxford, 1984), pp. 117–25

Thomson, R. M., *Manuscripts from St Albans Abbey 1066–1235*, 2 vols (Woodbridge, 1982)

Thomson, R. M., 'The "Scriptorium" of William of Malmesbury', *Medieval Scribes, Manuscripts and Libraries: Essays presented to N. R. Ker*, edited by Malcolm B. Parkes and Andrew G. Watson (London, 1978), pp. 117–42

Thomson, R. M., 'William of Malmesbury as Historian and Man of Letters', *Journal of Ecclesiastical History*, 29 (1978), 387–413

Thomson, S. Harrison, *Latin Bookhands of the Later Middle Ages, 1100–1500* (Cambridge, 1969)

Thomson, S. Harrison, *The Writings of Robert Grosseteste, Bishop of Lincoln, 1235–1253* (Cambridge, 1940)

Thorpe, Lewis, transl., *Geoffrey of Monmouth: The History of the Kings of Britain* (Harmondsworth, 1966)

Thorpe, L., 'The Last Years of Geoffrey of Monmouth', in *Mélanges de langue et littérature françaises du moyen-âge offerts à Pierre Jonin* (Aix-en-Provence, 1979), pp. 663–72

Thorpe, Lewis, 'Le Mont Saint-Michel et Geoffroi de Monmouth', in *Millénaire monastique du Mont Saint-Michel*, 4 vols (Paris, 1966–71), II.377–82

Thorpe, Lewis, 'Orderic Vitalis and the *Prophetiae Merlini* of Geoffrey of Monmouth', *Bulletin bibliographique de la Société internationale arthurienne*, 29 (1977), 190–208

Thurn, H., *Die Handschriften der Universitätsbibliothek Würzburg*, 2 vols (Wiesbaden, 1970–73)

Turner, Ralph V. 'The *Miles literatus* in Twelfth- and Thirteenth-Century England: How Rare a Phenomenon?', *American Historical Review*, 83 (1978), 928–45

Tyson, Diana B., 'Patronage of French Vernacular History Writers in the Twelfth and Thirteenth Centuries', *Romania*, 100 (1979), 180–222

Ullmann, W., 'On the Influence of Geoffrey of Monmouth in English History', in *Speculum Historiale: Geschichte im Spiegel von Geschichtsschreibung und Geschichtsdeutung*, edited by Clemens Bauer *et al.* (Freiburg i. B., 1965), pp. 257–76

Vaillant, André, *L'Evangile de Nicodème: texte slave et texte latin* (Geneva, 1968)

Van Houts, E. M. C., 'The *Gesta Normannorum Ducum*: a History without an End', *Anglo-Norman Studies*, 3 (1980), 106–18

Van Houts, Elisabeth M. C., *Gesta Normannorum Ducum: een studie over de hand-schriften, de tekst, het geschiedwerk en het genre* (Groningen, 1982)

Vance, Eugene, 'The Modernity of the Middle Ages in the Future: Remarks on a Recent Book', *Romanic Review*, 64 (1973), 140–51

Vaughan, Richard, ed., *The Chronicle Attributed to John of Wallingford* (London, 1958)

Verhelst, D., ed., *Adso Dervensis De ortu et tempore Antichristi necnon et tractatus qui ab eo dependunt* (Turnhout, 1976)

Vinaver, Eugène, 'Principles of Textual Emendation', in *Medieval Manuscripts and Textual Criticism*, edited by Christopher Kleinhenz (Chapel Hill, 1976), pp. 139–66

Voorbij, J. B., 'Additions to Ross's Check-List of Alexander Texts', *Scriptorium*, 38 (1984), 116–20

Wailly, Natalis de, 'Examen de quelques questions relatives à l'origine des chroniques de Saint-Denys', *Mémoires de l'Institut royal de France. Académie des inscriptions et belles-lettres*, 17.1 (1847), 379–407

Waitz, G., 'Ueber die sogenannte *Abbreviatio Gestorum regum Franciae*', *Neues Archiv der Gesellschaft für ältere deutsche Geschichtskunde*, 7 (1881/2), 385–90

Walther, Hans, *Initia carminum ac versuum medii aevi posterioris Latinorum*, 1 vol. + supplement (Göttingen, 1959–69)

Walther, Hans, *Proverbia sententiaeque latinitatis medii aevi*, 5 vols + supplement (Göttingen, 1963–69)

Walther Boer, W., ed., *Epistola Alexandri ad Aristotilem ad codicum fidem edita et commentario critico instructa* (The Hague, 1953)

Ward, H. L. D., and Herbert, J. A., *Catalogue of Romances in the Department of Manuscripts in the British Museum*, 3 vols (London, 1883–1910)

Ward, John O., 'Some Principles of Rhetorical Historiography in the Twelfth Century', in *Classical Rhetoric and Medieval Historiography*, edited by Ernst Breisach (Kalamazoo, Mich., 1985), pp. 103–65

Watson, Andrew G., *Medieval Libraries of Great Britain. A List of Surviving Books: Supplement to the Second Edition* (London, 1987)

Watson, Colin, *Snobbery with Violence: English Crime Stories and their Audience* (London, 1979)

Webb, C. C. J., 'Note on Books Bequeathed by John of Salisbury to the Cathedral Library of Chartres', *Mediaeval and Renaissance Studies*, 1 (1941–43), 128–29

Werner, Karl Ferdinand, 'Andreas von Marchiennes und die Geschichtsschreibung von Anchin und Marchiennes in der zweiten Hälfte des 12. Jahrhunderts', *Deutsches Archiv für Erforschung des Mittelalters*, 9 (1952), 402–63

White, Geoffrey H., 'The Career of Waleran, Count of Meulan and Earl of Worcester 1104–66', *Transactions of the Royal Historical Society*, 4th ser., 17 (1934), 19–48

Whitelock, Dorothy, transl., *English Historical Documents c. 500–1042*, 2nd edition (London, 1979)

Williams, John R., 'William of the White Hands and Men of Letters', in *Anniversary Essays in Mediaeval History by Students of Charles Homer Haskins*, edited by C. H. Taylor (Boston, Mass., 1929), pp. 365–87

Williams, Schafer, 'Geoffrey of Monmouth and the Canon Law', *Speculum*, 27 (1952), 184–90

Williams, Thomas Webb, ed., *Somerset Mediæval Libraries and Miscellaneous Notices of Books in Somerset Prior to the Dissolution of the Monasteries* (Bristol, 1897)

Wilson, R. M., ed., 'The Medieval Library of Titchfield Abbey', *Proceedings of the Leeds Philosophical and Literary Society (Literary and Historical Section)*, 5 (1938–43), 150–77; 252–76

Wiseman, T. P., *Clio's Cosmetics: Three Studies in Greco-Roman Literature* (Leicester, 1979)

Wright, C. E., *The British Museum: Catalogue of Additions to the Manuscripts, 1936–1945*, 2 vols (London, 1970)

Wright, John Kirtland, *The Geographical Lore at the Time of the Crusades: a Study in the History of Medieval Science and Tradition in Western Europe* (New York, 1925)

Wright, N., 'Geoffrey of Monmouth and Bede', *Arthurian Literature*, 6 (1986), 27–59

Wright, N., 'Geoffrey of Monmouth and Gildas', *Arthurian Literature*, 2 (1982), 1–40

Wright, Neil, ed., *The Historia Regum Britannie of Geoffrey of Monmouth, I: Bern, Burgerbibliothek, MS. 568* (Cambridge, 1985)

Wright, Neil, ed., *The Historia Regum Britannie of Geoffrey of Monmouth, II: The First Variant Version* (Cambridge, 1988)

Wuttke, Heinrich, ed., *Die Kosmographie des Istrier Aithikos* (Leipzig, 1853)

Zacher, J., *Pseudocallisthenes: Forschungen zur Kritik und Geschichte der ältesten Aufzeichnung der Alexandersage* (Halle a. S., 1867)

Zumthor, P., *Histoire littéraire de la France médiévale (vi^e–xive siècles)* (Paris, 1954)

Zumthor, Paul, *Merlin le prophète: un thème de la littérature polémique, de l'histo-riographie, et des romans* (Lausanne, 1943)

Zumthor, Paul, 'Le Texte médiéval et l'histoire: propositions méthodologiques', *Romanic Review*, 64 (1973), 5–15

GENERAL INDEX

'Ab Adam usque ad diluuium ann.
.ii.cc.xlii. . . .' 20, 33–34
Ab origine mundi circa annos tria milia 20,
22, 56, 175, 228, 308
Abel 50, 71
Abelard, works of 196
Abilaut, Robert 309
Abingdon 206
Abraham 50, 77
Adam 42, 45, 71–72
Adam, (?sub-)prior of Evesham 71
Adrian IV, pope 40
Adso, *De Antichristo* 20, 31
Aelred, abbot of Rievaulx 6, 212 n. 87, 215
Vita Edwardi 20, 22
Æneas 3, 6, 70, 95, 182
Æthicus Ister, *Cosmographia* 20, 35–36
Ages of the World 62, 309
Aimery Picaud 53
Alain de Lille 86
Albanactus, son of Brutus 7
Albania 7
Albéric, abbot of Vézelay, cardinal-bishop
of Ostia 53
Albertus, *filius Iohannis, presbiter de Dyst*
140, 205, 210
Albina, daughter of king of Greece 22
Albuin(us), *De Antichristo* 20, 31, 47, 59
Alexander the Great 22, 28, 32, 219–221
confines Gog and Magog 47, 58, 221
correspondence with Dindymus, *see*
Collatio Alexandri
letter to Aristotle, *see Epistola Alexandri*
visits Jerusalem 27
events after his death 27, 46
texts concerning 55, 61, 69, 183, 218,
222, 308 (*see also* Iulius Ualerius,
Principium hystorie)
Alexander, bishop of Lincoln 5, 7, 17, 98,
102, 111, 113, 115, 138
Alexander III, pope 41, 62
Alexander de Pundsoneby 203

Alfred of Beverley 2 n. 7, 114, 215, 309
Alphonse, count of Poitou 36
Amiens, Saint-Jean 202, 208, 210
Anchin 202, 208, 211
Andrew of Marchiennes (Andreas
Syluuius) 69, 211, 309
'Anglia habet in longitudine . . .' 20,
29–30, 74
'Anglia modo dicta olim Albion dicebatur
. . .' 20, 30, 35, 308
'Anglia transmittet leopardum . . .' 21, 63,
75
Anglo-Saxon Chronicle 3
Anglo-Saxon Heptarchy, account of 37
'Anna et Emeria . . .' 34
Annals 37
'Anno ab incarnacione Domini .d.ccc.lxxui.
Rollo . . .' 54
'Anno Cephas Cocadrille . . .' 21, 63, 68,
75
Anselm 11
(ps-)Anselm, *De Antichristo* 20, 31, 34, 59
'Antenor et alii profugi . . .' 20, 24, 30, 75,
187, 308
Antichrist 31–32, 67, 221, 310
Antioch 41
church at Antioch, founded by Peter
156
king of 32
Antwerp 210
Apocrypha 45, 70, 218
Apollonius of Tyre 20, 26, 32, 69 n. 240,
75, 177, 308
Aquitaine 213
Arab philosophers 61
Arabic 28
'Arbor fertilis . . .' 63, 65–66
see also Eagle of Shaftesbury
Aristotle 28
Armorica 3
'Armorica siue Latauia . . .' 78, 89, 175,
190, 194–195, 308

335

INDEX OF SCHOLARS MENTIONED IN THE TEXT

INDEX OF MANUSCRIPTS